CREDO

Economic beliefs in a world in crisis

Brian Davey

Published by: FEASTA Limited

The Foundation for the Economics of Sustainability

Registration Number: 319430

Charity Number: CHY13052

Administrative Office
1 Ard na gCapaill
Cloughjordan
Co. Tipperary
Ireland

Tel: +353 (0)86 364 2728
General information: *info@feasta.org*
Website: *website@feasta.org*

Website for this book with updates and further information *www.credoeconomics.com*

CRO registered office
C/o Hayden Brown Accountants
Grafton Buildings
34 Grafton St
Dublin 2

Book design:

Book cover design: Brian Davey with assistance from UK Book Publishing

Printed and bound by CPI Group (UK) Ltd, Croydon, CR0 4YY

Credo: Economic Beliefs in a World in Crisis

By Brian Davey

ISBN 978-0-9540510-3-7

Cover photos:

'Rig Explosion' – *https://commons.wikimedia.org/wiki/Category:Deepwater_Horizon_drilling_rig_explosion#/media/File:Deepwater_Horizon_fire_2010-04-21.jpg*
'The Conjurer' – *http://commons.wikimedia.org/wiki/File:Conjurer_Bosch.jpg#/media/File:Der-gaukler-hieronymus-bosch_1-480x400.jpg*
'The Tower of Babel' – *http://commons.wikimedia.org/wiki/File:Pieter_Bruegel_the_Elder_-_The_Tower_of_Babel_%28Vienna%29_-_Google_Art_Project_-_edited.jpg*

Contents

How this book came about.

This book opens with an explanation of the term "faiths" used in the book and goes on to discuss the inertia of established ideas. It describes economics as an orientation system for a market society and argues that bad economics has become a source of disorientation which serves the elite well.

This chapter connects economic theory to the role that economists play in society and the kind of people that they are likely to be given their social role as part of the elite. It explores themes such as elite psychopathology, the way that observation changes that which is observed while that which is observed changes the observer.

The chapter covers the early history of economic thought as slave owning classes reflected upon "self-actualisation" and on the management of their households and estates. Medieval economics was a branch of moral philosophy taught by monks and yet the subject subsequently evolved to justify robbery and enslavement in service to the rising merchant class. Economics became, in effect, a quasi-religion. The new original sin was "scarcity" while the new chief virtue has become "efficiency".

Nineteenth century economics is described in this chapter as a subject used to train a psychopathic imperial elite – this is illustrated by the policies recommended by economists to manage famines in Ireland and India. The poor had only themselves to blame for their desperate state.

What Schumpeter called the "Ricardian Vice" was a mode of reasoning in which the required conclusions are buried in the assumptions of an argument. The free trade argument of David Ricardo are described in these terms and unpicked. The ideas of the German-American economist Frederich List challenged Ricardo's view.

Micro-economics has a philosophical foundation – preference utilitarianism. Jeremy Bentham's clunky one dimensional understanding of human beings and human society still underpins the thinking of economists. (TEXT BOX: Jeremy Bentham's Rational Punishment)

Mainstream micro-economics works from a model where consumers are imagined choosing between just two commodities. The theory is unworkable in a multi-product world. The "prospect theory" of Daniel Kahneman and Amos Tversky is contrasted to utilitarian thinking. People are loss averse in an uncertain world. Kahneman's and Tversky's ideas open a can of worms for mainstream micro-economics.

Some of the ridiculous assumptions on which much of mainstream economics is constructed are explored in this chapter – for example the methodology that stresses individual decision-making, the assumption that decision-makers have the information that they need, the assumption of honesty, the default assumption of competition. (TEXT BOX Labour market competition as an alternative to corporal punishment according to Hayek).

This chapter explores the assumptions about human nature on which mainstream economics is based. The description of "rational economic man" ignores most psychological and psychotherapy understandings of people.

This chapter about the power elite on display and the economics of Thorsten Veblen covers topics like conspicuous consumption and the consumer society, branding and the manufacture of wants. The role of advertisers is explored as well as the way that attention grabbing has become an economic sector that affects the quality of life radically and for the worse.

The chapter draws on the ideas of Erich Fromm and, more recently, Oliver James, to describe the problem of Affluenza. It critiques the recent enthusiasm of some economists like Richard Layard for a theory of "happiness" and "positive psychology".

Information is lost as well as gained during the processes of economic development and change. There is a great deal of difference between direct knowledge and knowledge that is taken in through a variety of media. Much of what we take for granted is actually better understood as "consensus trance". To orientate to the world properly we need to have a proper feel for the huge amount of what we don't know – and there are multiple categories of unknowing.

Chapter 13: Inequality, epidemiology and economics

Public health is an alternative indicator of well-being and is strongly correlated to levels of equality or inequality. Greater equality means greater well-being for everyone and a smaller need for the state - yet inequality has been increasing dramatically.

Chapter 14: The centrality of externalities

What economists call "externalities" are not unusual or a special case, they are ubiquitous. They are rooted in private property and the relationships of market society. The way in which non market societies protect bio-diversity through totem arrangements is described.

Chapter 15: Ethical disconnections and re-connections – corporations and NGOs

Externalities involve ethical choices. The mechanisms that allow corporate actors to distance themselves from responsibility from their anti-social and anti-environmental choices are described – for example the role of corporate personhood and evasions of regulation, taxation and control. NGOs and Civil Society Organisations have evolved to counter unethical corporate choices. Unfortunately they are often co-opted and neutralised.

Part Two – Economics, Land and Nature

Chapter 16: Indigenous Economics

Mainstream economics regards environmental protection as a matter of finding the "right price" for environmental preferences. This is not how indigenous people think about environmental issues. The chapter contrasts the mentalities of people that belong to places vs the mind-set of the population when places belong to people. There are differing epistemes in different societies and "traditional environmental knowledge" is a totally different way of knowing to that taken for granted by economists.

Chapter 17: Colonialist economics - the contrast with indigenous land care principles

Many, though by no means all, indigenous peoples practiced sustainable land care and used concepts that contrast strongly with modern economics thinking. Much economic thinking is intrinsically ecologically destructive.

Chapter 18: Concepts for a fenced off world

Private property in land means enclosure and exclusion. Economists typically assume that economic choices involve inevitable trade-offs. However, it is not true that alternatives must always be forgone. There is often a potential for sharing and mutual accommodation that is being ignored. Not all choices are rivalrous.

Chapter 19: Commoning

This chapter explores the features of sustainable commons and the extent of commons today. It describes the practice of commoning as a possible response to the ecological crisis.

Part Three – Households and Lifestyles

Chapter 28: Household economics

Do households exist to service the economy or vice versa? The composition of different kinds of households will depend on demographic structures which have profound political and economic consequences. Household arrangements can become out of balance and re-creating efficient habitats can be seen as a legitimate economic goal. The time spent in households versus the time spent in paid work time is a central feature of any pattern of economic arrangements.

Chapter 29: Demographics

As John Maynard Keynes put it: "In the long run we are all dead". Economics has to include consideration of the long run trends of births, deaths, migration and of the age composition of societies. As we reach the limits to economic growth the death rate may start to rise. Globalisation may make the spread of diseases very rapid. Preventing novel diseases like Ebola may prove expensive and the health and well being of the population at large may become dependent on some of the most exploited and devalued people in our society – cleaners, carers and grave diggers.

Chapter 30: Allocating time

Temporal inequality is a little noticed feature of our society. Poor people wait for things – the well-off are waited on. Temporal inequality is crucial to understanding people's time choices.

Chapter 31: Life Management, stability and life transitions

Lifestyles and routines can be considered as "packages" of elements which must be held in balance one with another like income, habitat, relationships and activities. Lifestyle transitions involve moving from one "package" to another. There are different kinds of transitions including downshifting and upshifting. Downshifters can sometimes be part of a pioneering minority in a society that is facing the limits to economic growth.

Part Four – Production in the Paid Work Sector

Chapter 32: Energy in the Economic System

The production economy is embedded in the physical world and thus, subject to the laws of physics. Concepts like "entropy", "sources" and "sinks", are useful to help us understand the embedded and embodied character of economic activity. Energy is converted through our bodies and through technical devices. The idea that economic development has meant a movement from an "empty world" to a "full world" is useful – but we must take care to acknowledge that we label the earlier state of an "empty world" which was often a sustainable low impact way of living by an indigenous society.

Chapter 38: Employment in Theory and in Real Life

The economic theory of the labour market bears little resemblance to what really happens in the labour market. Workers don't just make material products, they arrange things and attend to people. As society has evolved and become more complex, the office has becomes the more common workplace and work is largely conceptual and intangible. Mainstream economic theory has little to say about intangible work in bureaucratic empires. As the economy becomes more unstable, paid work becomes a nightmare for many people and the temptation to work longer hours for little extra return is great.

In the religion of economics, the entrepreneur is a hero engaged in a narrative of destructive creation. Entrepreneurs are tragically noble figures on a treadmill of competition – but who is really making the sacrifices? Often it is the entrepreneur's family or other "stakeholders" who are carrying the costs and risks. What motivates entrepreneurs and what are "animal spirits" anyway? As their organisations develop, the role of the entrepreneur changes and, at their most powerful, they seek to co-opt officials and politicians for their agendas. Management can be exercised through over centralised control freakery or via distributed decision-making systems. Many entrepreneurs and managers are psychopaths, and criminals are entrepreneurs too. In the modern world, control fraud i.e. looting your own company is not uncommon. The City of London as tax haven and secrecy jurisdiction is one of a number of places to hide out.

Co-operatives have been described as freshwater fish in a saltwater environment. In the 1930s, the co-operative sector in many countries was very powerful but it was destroyed by fascist and communist regimes. What was it that the authoritarians found so threatening in co-operation? Alternative economic models like co-operatives and social enterprises are explored, together with the arrangements that can help sustain them, like co-operative federations and support networks. However, there are no panaceas – co-ops and social enterprises fail too.

The history of the financial sector goes back a long way. Usury was long regarded as ethically unacceptable but both Calvin and Adam Smith tried to justify it with arguments that are still suspect. The finance sector played a role in financing wars and it evolved, strongly linked to the real estate market. This chapter looks at the functions of money and how bank credit creation creates debt money. It explores risk management and the tendency of the finance sector to turn into a casino.

When collective confidence goes too far, prudent lending standards go out of the window, and there is a great deal of criminal activity. In the modern world the financial sector is on a collision course with ecological reality. (TEXT BOX – Discounting – Financial Logic misapplied to sustainability)

Mental health problems and debt finance are strongly linked. People in debt have a higher incidence of psychiatric problems, and there is a higher rate of psychiatric symptoms among the people working in the finance sector too. During a bubble, egos are pumped up with asset values – and, when the bubble bursts, reputational collapse occurs with corresponding psychological effects.

Money experiments took place during the financial crises of the 1930s. Although these were repressed by central banks, the need to control the finance sector during and after the world war was recognised so that the 1940s and 1950s was an era of "tamed banks". It would be possible to write off debts and clip the wings of the banks without collapsing the financial system in today's world too. In the absence of a political will to do this, other reforms and DIY financial initiatives are possible. Community finance needs to be part of a solidarity economy

Vested interests who wish to deny the climate crisis have created a dishonest PR sector fostering delusion about a huge threat to humanity. This chapter presents a thumbnail sketch of climate science and then explores issues of civic epistemology – how to handle public debate about a complex controversial issue where most people lack the expertise to assess the facts. The chapter explores why climate science upsets the market faithful and whether a production and finance system collapse would be terrible but might actually save humanity from an even worse climate catastrophe.

Mainstream economics frames the climate crisis in a particular way but this approach is not at all helpful. There have been a variety of controversies which show clearly how economists think – like the "price of a life" controversy. The findings of the Stern Review were widely quoted but how were they calculated? Much of the controversy about the Stern Review among economists was about the discount rate to be applied to future projections. These issues are explained.

A major issue in climate economics is whether it is possible to halt the growth in carbon emissions and to achieve, instead, a rapid reduction. It concludes that carbon emissions will never fall at a sufficient rate in a growth economy. Unfortunately, the EU operates a climate policy framework, the EU Emissions Trading System, that was designed by BP and it doesn't work. Policies that might work were the political will there are described. However, the fossil fuel industry still has a stranglehold on policy.

Land use and land use change are also major contributors to greenhouse gas emissions. There are climate threats from emissions that arise as a result of corporate forestry and large scale agribusiness. A technology like biochar, which could be used to sequester carbon in soils, is not likely to be helpful if applied by giant corporations – only if developed by small local actors.

Most economics textbooks include a little homily about the difference between facts and value. Economics is supposed to describe the world as it is, rather than as economists think it should be. This homily is deconstructed. Power asymmetries in the political process mean that there is no clear separation between politics and economics and there never has been. Powerful economic actors have always had a predominant influence in the political institutions. In current conditions - of crisis at the limits to economic growth – dystopian politics are on the rise.

The chapter draws together themes for an alternative narrative for the future of society many of which have already been explored through the book. The chief focus is on household and local level community arrangements managed through distributed and federated arrangements that are democratic. Linked themes like what to do about land and human resources; the need for debt cancellation, money and tax reform are explained. If sufficient change can be brought about it will also be necessary to drive decarbonisation with an upstream cap on carbon emissions.

Without sufficient action a time may come when we have to admit that it is too late to prevent runaway climate change and/or that other forms of collapse has become inevitable, indeed that we are in the middle of a collapse. Then what?

FOR STUDENTS OF ECONOMICS

Stop seeing what you are taught to believe. Believe what you see.

Acknowledgements

This book is the result of many people who have influenced me going back many years. Going back the furthest Craig Newnes encouraged and supported my thinking and writing on psychological and psychotherapy theory which is a reoccurring theme through this book – and he used a part of the chapter on household economics in the Journal of Critical Psychology, Counselling and Psychotherapy. In more recent years the support and encouragement of friends and colleagues in the mainly Irish organisation, Feasta, has helped me develop other ideas that will be found here in many enjoyable and relaxed discussions at Rossbeigh in Kerry and in Cloughjordan in Co. Tipperary. The late Richard Douthwaite and John Jopling particularly stand out as having been a source of stimulation and support. John's summer seminars by the sea were a wonderful opportunity to take in new ideas from all sorts of people and it was Richard who, when he was terminally ill, suggested that I take over the teaching of an economics module on an MA course in Religion and Ecology at Dublin City University. This book then arose out of the preparation for that course. If I had not taught it, the book would not have been written. Thanks are also due, therefore, to the leader of that MA course, Dr Cathrionna Russell and the students themselves.

Colleagues in Germany and the US have influenced my thinking about degrowth and the commons – particularly Silke Helfrich, Heike Loeschmann and David Bollier at some stimulating and inspiring events made possible on a low income not only by subsidy by the Heinrich Boell Foundation but also because my friend Doris Buhss, her father and his partner have put me up time and again. Thanks are due to colleagues in Croatia for giving me the opportunity to draw my thoughts on degrowth together – Mladen Domazet, Danijela Dolenec, Igor Matutinovic and to Lidija Zivcic in Slovenia.

I owe especial thanks to Dr Nick Bardsley for many helpful comments and a very close reading of a late draft. Caroline Whyte, editor of the Feasta website made suggestions to change the chapter on services and office employment which improved what I wrote a lot. Caroline was also helpful and encouraging by publishing some of the draft chapters as articles on the Feasta blog. Justin Kenrick has been a particular influence and inspiration as regards the situation of people in the global south and other indigenous peoples who do not share the mind set of western economics. In most cases I have responded to their criticism by altering the text and, very often, used suggested alternative formulations. Laurence Matthews also made helpful suggestions re editing.

Harminder Singh and his partner Cathy Kirk have been really central to bringing this book to completion. They helped with proof reading and editorial work, and constructive criticism about the title and cover. At an earlier stage Harminder also helped me focus on some of the technological issues in teaching that we did together at Warwick University.

Finally, all the following deserve a thanks too – Justin Cast at the Christian Duplicating Service in Nottingham, Oliver James, the staff at Bromley House Library in Nottingham where I did a lot of the writing. Paul Mobbs for his engineering and scientific expertise. Members of the Cap and Share campaign. Jon Walker and Angela Espinosa for their help in understanding the ideas of Stafford Beer. Phillip Jackson for his encouragement and support through reading a draft. Sarah Gretton of Leicester University for giving me a chance to teach on a multi-disciplinary sustainability module and thus another opportunity to use some of this material. Trent Schroyer who supplied the idea for the comment in the dedication.

As the saying goes, the errors remain my responsibility...

Preface

How this book came about

The experience of life can be paradoxical. Probably the most important thing that ever happened to me was to have a succession of psychiatric breakdowns in my early adult years that shattered my belief in myself and left me struggling to start all over again. It was frequently terrifying and utterly confusing but it led me into a struggle to understand my mind and emotions. In order to make sense of my experience I was forced to study psychotherapy theory and it led to me evolving my own theory of what caused breakdowns. As I was fortunate enough to get employment on the margins of the mental health service I was able to work on my own problems as part of my job and eventually, in the 1990s, to lecture and write material that even appeared in professional and academic journals and books about clinical psychology.

Along the way I could not help reflecting that what I was discovering was very different from what I had been led to believe in my training as an economist. When you go to a therapist the first thing on the agenda is not whether your income is high enough or the utility that you are (not) getting from your purchases. The therapy concepts of mental wellbeing could not be more different from the economist's concept of 'welfare'. This book explores the consequences of these contrasts and is the result of following a career and a life path very different from the one that most economists tread. If you read this book in depth you will notice that I feel no loyalty to economics as a subject, or to a professional peer group. Being an outsider seems to be a problem but it is one of those paradoxes again – it gives me tremendous freedom that I don't have to worry about who I upset.

One of my favourite quotes, which I originally picked up in a book of clinical psychology by therapist Dorothy Rowe, is often attributed to the Talmud though it seems it may have come from a novel by Anaïs Nin. It goes: "We do not see things as they are, we see things as we are" (Weiss, 2011). In this respect I think I should say that I do not feel as if I am an economist. It does not feel as if it is part of my identity. I have never really practiced as one in a conventional sense. However, I think that I know the subject well enough. I have two degrees in it.

What originally interested me in economics as a teenager in the late 1960s was that it might provide the tools by which I thought that I could understand what, at that time, I conceived of as "underdevelopment". The Vietnam War led to me questioning contemporary political and economic issues and I became very left wing. As I embarked on a study of economics at university I was sceptical – from a left wing and Marxist standpoint.

However, as said already, I never really practiced economics but instead got involved in local community development. I struggled to make the transition to adulthood in a state of mental and emotional turmoil, with no emotional understanding or skills. A small political sect provided a purpose to my life, a belief system and a social network. Leaving it was traumatic in the sense of leaving me lost and disorientated. That eventually led me into my long detour through the mental health system and the study of psychotherapy understandings of people. This partly helps to explain a lot of what I have written in this book. It also helps explain my loyalties – a deep scepticism of official viewpoints in favour of that of victims and "losers".

Working in community development I became interested in local economic development and that eventually led me back into a sort of economics as I re-stabilised my life on the fringes – finding myself working with people who were and are sceptical of economic growth and "development" because of its destructive social and environmental effects.

This book subsequently arose out of a short series of 6 lectures on economics, environment and ethics for non-economists at Dublin City University who were studying for an MA in *Religion and Ecology*. A friend and colleague who had been teaching on the course before me, Richard Douthwaite, became seriously ill and recommended that I take over. I was interviewed and got half the module. The challenge in preparing the lectures was to present core concepts without assuming any prior knowledge so that a lay person could understand, with maximal brevity – and yet not **over**simplify.

While preparing the course I came across a book by an American economist called Robert Nelson who argues very cogently that economics is a religion. (Nelson R. H. 2001). I do not want to get into a deep discussion here defining what religion is because there have been many different attempts to do this and there is much disagreement. Obviously economics is not about a relationship to a supernatural being whose will, like that of a parent in the sky, decides what happens in the world of its children. Nor does economics have a story that explains the beginning of the universe. Economists leave the explanation of the origins of the universe and how it works to natural scientists.

This also explains the title of the book. A **Credo** is a statement of religious belief made, in the Roman church, in a statement which starts with the Latin word "Credo". Credo means "I believe". One of the exercises for the students towards the end of the Dublin course module was to write a Credo to express the core beliefs of economists, as in " I believe in the Free Market, in market competition, and economic growth..."

The idea that economists are akin to a priesthood is not new and nor are critiques of mainstream economics. Some excellent demolitions of mainstream concepts have been published in recent years by heretical economists or critics from outside of the economics profession – the most thorough that I have read is Steve Keen's "The Naked Emperor Dethroned", now in its second expanded edition. (Keen, 2011) It is a sort of anti-textbook. After Keen there is not much left that is credible in mainstream economics teaching materials. There are other critical texts too – some of them more focused on ecological and bio-physical realities.

So economics is a subject field and a profession entering a period of deep change – a variety, a heterodoxy of approaches is emerging that is critiquing the mainstream from many different angles –

post Keynesian economics, ecological economics, social-ecological economics, bio-physical economics, feminist economics, Marxist economics.

This fragmentation is bad news for those who would prefer economics to present a unified and simple message of "how things are". Many people have speculated as to why the economics mainstream manages to persist despite so much good critique. Perhaps it is that orthodoxy presents a simple message – if you want answers to things you go to experts who give you a definite answer. What you don't want are experts who answer your questions by telling you that there are several points of view and that the issues are very much in dispute. How could you hang onto that?

Preparing the Dublin lectures was a learning experience not just for the students but for me. It forced me to go back to the foundational ideas of economics in order to re-examine them. This review helped me to make sense of current ecological, economic and social difficulties. It seemed to me that the way economists think about issues is, in large part, a root cause of what is wrong.

A final point: I think the best way to learn about this subject is rather like learning a language as a small child. No child learns its first language by memorising lists of words together with the rules of grammar and then bringing them together. It struggles to make sense of the topical stream of sounds made by adults in the world as it finds it. The stream of sounds becomes a stream of meaning in which the infant learns to participate. In my view the best way to understand economics is to struggle to understand what has actually happened and what is going on here and now. Economics should be learned through economic history and through current affairs and always relates to a time in the historical process. When we do this we will notice that critics are shoved out to the margins – they are not given much of a place to participate because economics is a language of and for the elite and if you are not playing the elite game and using their ideas then you must get used to being on the margin. In addition when economics is largely derived and presented from topical events it is inevitably going to be out of date quite soon. The *best before date* on this book is not that far in the future. That is part of the reason why there is a website for this book.

www.credoeconomics.com. On the website I will try to stay up to date on new developments from time to time and, who knows, respond to critique.

1st January 2015

PART ONE

The Evolution of the "theory"

Chapter 1

Personal Introduction – On faiths, keeping them and losing them...

This book opens with an explanation of the term "faiths" used in the book and goes on to discuss the inertia of established ideas. It describes economics as an orientation system for a market society and argues that bad economics has become a source of disorientation. In fact important ideas are delusionary.

Although we may not think that we do, we all live with faiths – ideas that we take for granted that appear so obvious that we do not feel a need to re-examine them – ideas that we do not usually want to re-examine. At points in life we make up our minds about things that we decide that we believe in and these beliefs have consequences perhaps for what we do, for who becomes our friends and colleagues, for how we earn a living or perhaps even for how we die. These faiths may be, but are not necessarily, about the ideas espoused by religions. They may be political ideas, about science, or they may be ideas about economics. If we stop for a minute to think what the consequences would be of abandoning our faiths, we typically find the prospect unappealing. For one thing, if and when we were to abandon our faiths, we would have to unlearn and rethink a lot of what we thought that we knew and know. The people with whom we have relationships based on similar beliefs may be dismayed, horrified and then perhaps hostile or sarcastic. Worse still, because our faith's structure – not just beliefs but our purposes; the things that we do; the direction of our lives; the structure of our days and weeks the loss of our faiths could leave us with the frightening prospect of being without a life altogether – losing relationships, purposes and day to day structure. Loss of faith in some circumstances would mean being alive in the sense of still being able to breath, still being able to eat – and yet all the important relationships and activities that we had would evaporate. Unless we could in some way step from one belief system into another, at the same time step into another pattern of meaningful and purposeful relationships, perhaps also into another way of earning a living, we would find ourselves living in an empty life, in a limbo.

How do I know this? Because early in my adult life I lost my faith in my Marxist belief system and therefore drifted out of a political sect that I was in, lost the purposes of my life as well as the activities that underpinned my relationships, and ended up under the care of the psychiatric system. The emotional turmoil, the disorientation and the feeling at times of being lost, lasted almost two decades. From being an economist my life went on a long detour. This taught me a lot that I have brought into this book – including these ideas about faith. As time has gone on it has occurred to me that what I went through says something not just about the psychology of being in small Marxist political sects – it tells us about the psychology of belonging to groups and institutions in general. Thus, while it is obvious to everyone that faith underpins institutions like the Roman Catholic church, it is also true that a variety of faiths underpin many social institutions... and necessarily so.

I do not mean to say therefore that faiths are ipso facto always wrong. The faiths that we believe may be absolutely right. I am not against all faiths - that would be absurd. The point I am making is different. It is that we have to have them, and when we do, there are powerful reasons not to go back and re-examine them continually. For example, as an ecological economist it is one of my faiths that climate change is a serious threat to humanity. In my professional role I have, from time to time, read peer reviewed studies by climate scientists and I think that I understand the basics of the science. However, I am not a climate scientist and, beyond a certain point, I take the peer reviewed literature on trust, or on faith, without feeling the need to examine every point, as long as the scientific procedures like peer review have been kept to in producing it. What I notice is that most so called sceptics, more accurately called climate change deniers, do not play the game by those rules...

Even so there is an element of faith in my approach – and there has to be in everyone's life because we cannot study all issues that confront us in huge depth with a level of professional expertise. Nor, once we make up our minds on things, can we repeatedly revisit the foundations of our belief systems. Our lives would become unstable and unliveable if we did this.

The inertia of established ideas

That is also why even science established theories have inertia. They are often sticky and difficult to change. The famous physicist Max Planck said that in science people rarely change their ideas radically in the way that Saul changed his ideas on the road to Damascus and became the apostle Paul. Rather, what does happen is that radical new ideas circulate among young scientists and only become the new way of thinking when the older scientists retire and die. I suppose that we should not be surprised by this because one of the things about faith is that, the older you get, the more investment of time you are likely to have put into pursuing the ideas and purposes associated with a belief system. It may be associated with what a person sees as the narrative of their life, what was worked for, promoted and lived for decades. Then to acknowledge, at the end of one's life, that it was all based on a mistake, an illusion, the wrong paradigm, or that there is a very different way of seeing things might be terrifying. It would almost be as if one had never existed.

It should not surprise that it is the young who are open to new ideas – and that it becomes more difficult as we get older to relinquish the ideas that we adopt.

The economist John Maynard Keynes said it in a slightly different way. The problem, he wrote, is not in the creation of new ideas but in escaping old ones.

There is an argument that escaping old ideas in economics is particularly difficult because there are so many powerful interests at stake. For this reason I have no illusions that this book will pull economics off its pedestal no matter how cogent my arguments are. Mainstream economists have a devastating weapon against their opponents – they ignore them. That's how most of us cope most of the time with critics whose ideas produce cognitive dissonance for us and economists are no different. What's more, they can get away with it, for now at least. Because they are sponsored by corporations and institutions with money, power and media attention and because they are the people still setting the academic courses, they do not need to pay much attention to their critics and they don't. If you are getting the attention and not your critics, you do not need to devote attention to the critics either. You only need to devote attention to critics when they are getting more and more attention because that is when, in the world of ideas, power is slipping away from you. In that sense faith is not just an individual choice, there is a social dynamic to it. Faith is easier to sustain when many others believe the same things and the experts with the faith are the ones that attract all the attention. When well-resourced social institutions exist to uphold a faith it can persist a long time.

Nevertheless, I believe that in ten years economics will be in serious difficulties and in twenty, mainstream economics will look nothing like it does today – if indeed there still is such an academic subject. This will not be mainly because of how eloquent I have been, or the other critics, although hopefully we will play some role. Rather it will be because the next two decades will see catastrophic effects because the economic system has overshot the limits to economic growth and crashed - given the limited and limiting capacity of the ecological system.

Economics as an orientation system

To return to the discourse about faiths – the point about them is that, when they are right it matters because they help us make sense of our worlds, and when our faiths are wrong we are liable to end up profoundly disorientated. Political economy should be a pattern of ideas that enables us to make sense of the world. It may not provide us with a detailed understanding of all that is going on but it should give us a general sense of world affairs. It ought to help us fit together otherwise apparently unrelated events into a bigger pattern – a bigger story of what is happening and what is likely to happen. If it doesn't do that it is failing badly.

In order to illustrate what I mean by this I will mention events that are occurring at the time that I am writing this book. The civil war in Syria is presented to us every day in the mass media, particularly as regards human rights violations, religious extremism and the horror of the conflict. What is not mentioned, or rarely, are the backgrounds to the conflict which would relate Syria to a bigger world picture. In the year before the conflict broke out, food prices in Syria doubled against the backdrop of a worsening of the agricultural crisis in that country. There had been many years of severe drought which seem related to climate change and growing water shortage in many countries in the globe. At the same time oil production in Syria had fallen to a half of its level in 1996 when Syria was at the peak of its production. This produced rising fuel prices, which are a problem in agriculture, as well as a crisis in state finances. Furthermore, during the years of oil boom there had been a rapid growth of population. A young population eats more food as it approaches adult years. Many of the Sunni Muslim population migrated from the countryside to towns dominated by the Alawite sect which is the power base of the Assad regime. This is a large part of what drove the rise in tensions. These tensions were then exploited by political forces who have been sponsored with money, weapons and food to try to destabilise the Assad regime not only because it is not friendly to Israel, but because the outside forces have their own agenda for Syria which is not that of the Syrian government and its allies. These include pipeline routes through Syria to take natural gas from Qatar through Syria to Turkey and Europe. This would then be competition for Russia whose current political power is heavily dependent on its gas supply to Europe. (Ahmed, 2013)

Seen thus, the conflict in Syria is a reflection of global energy politics in an era of increasingly expensive fossil fuel supplies and in an era of climate change. The bigger story of which it is a part is the crisis for the world at the limits of economic growth. Of course, the Syrian crisis is not only this. It is also a religious conflict. It is a story about armaments, about human rights, about refugees. It has multiple dimensions. But that it is part of the limits to growth crisis is without doubt.

Also at the time of writing, multiple political conflicts have broken out in the UK about technologies that involve fracturing underground geological formations in order to recover shale gas and oil. Similar conflicts have occurred in the USA and other countries, particularly Australia. Just as in Syria oil production has fallen since 1996, in the British sectors of the North Sea oil and gas fields are now in rapid decline. "Conventional natural gas production" has been in decline too in the USA. Alternative arrangements for energy must be made but these alternative arrangements, in the form of the plans and technologies of the fossil fuel industry, carry huge risks and costs for communities, as well as for the climate. These costs and problems will be explored later on, suffice it here to make the point that what we are witnessing are problems arising at the limits to economic growth. Although we cannot and should not reduce fracking to being solely a limits to growth issue, that it is this, is again without doubt.

Nor can there be any doubt that the financial crisis is connected to the energy crisis and the limits to economic growth and again it is connected through the energy system. Once again, I am not claiming that the global financial crisis is solely a result of rising energy and other costs. The financial crisis is far more complicated than that. Later in this book, I will look at some of these other influences – the too big to fail financial institutions; the way that financial institutions have been able to make money making loans to people who could not afford to service their debts and then have been able to pass the risk of these loans to other institutions; reckless credit creation to fund speculation on the asset markets; the inability to adjust for changing international competitiveness between nations in artificial currency constructions like the euro. All these have been causes of the monetary and financial sector turmoil. At root though the finance sector creates credit, lends or otherwise advances money on the expectation of repayment PLUS interest payments or other forms of financial return. Paying the interest and repaying the principle is possible if there is growth in the economy because the increased income provides the wherewithal for that payment. But as we will see, if the economy cannot grow, because the additional energy, the additional water, the additional raw materials are not there without an unacceptable amount of harm being done to extract them... or because climate change leads to falling harvests, then the financial system is bound to get into trouble.

There is no need to go into more depth on this point in the first part of the book. My point here is a general one. The economy is embodied and embedded in the physical world and in the ecological system. It sources energy and materials from the world and puts wastes and pollution back into land, water and atmospheric sinks. Beyond a certain scale the depletion of sources and the destructive effects on sinks floods back into the economy in such a way that the costs are greater than the benefits. What is happening in Syria, the conflicts over fracking and the growing instability of the financial sector, are all in one way or another connected.

That bigger picture that helps to make sense of the multitude of apparently disconnected events is what I call "orientation". With orientation we can see the direction that events are going and we can see how they can get a whole lot worse – even though we may not have any idea what the detailed course of events will be. With orientation we can clarify what we ought to be doing.

I am using the word 'orientation' here in a particular way. In its more limited meaning it is the ability of people to recognise time, place and immediately surrounding physical objects. It is about coping. A somewhat expanded meaning might encompasses the ability to cope in the personal contexts and circumstances in which our lives are situated - an ability to cope in our homes and domestic arrangements, with our income and expenditure, in our jobs and in our personal and work relationships. Beyond this though there is a wider sense which I term 'civic orientation'. This is necessary if one is to participate in the economic, social and political life of a community and have some impact on the life of the broader society and indeed of the world. Aristotle regarded political participation as vital to be able to flourish as a full person - however to be able to participate in our society one must understand the world as the elite itself understands it (and have all those resources and connections that the elite do).

Bad economics as a source of disorientation

To have a wider "civic orientation" requires a good education – whether formal or self taught – which a large number of people never get. What they get instead is a continual exposure to television, radio, newspapers and internet media where those who do play the political-economic game opine using a framework of ideas that are taken for granted among politicians, journalists, business and other interest groups. While differing over details almost all of these "public figures" share assumptions about how the world is which in what has been called the "elite consensus". It represents their common orientation to the world. It is sometimes claimed that the market economy works in an apparently co-ordinated way despite no one controlling behind the scenes because of Adam Smith's "invisible hand". This quasi religious idea of an "invisible hand" is supposed to explain the coherence of self organising markets. The invisible hand works, according to the faithful, because people are pursuing their self interest. In reality the coherence of a market economy (to the extent that it has coherence) is not explained in self interest as such but the fact that a large enough number of participants in the economy share the same purpose – which in the case of a market economy is calculating and pursuing their self interest. Sharing the same motivations and rules of the self interest game created a common orientation and thus a common operating system for economic actors to participate in.

At the beginning of this chapter I described as faiths those ideas and systems of belief that one would be reluctant to give up – but this pre-supposes that one is aware that one is holding what others, who do not agree with you, regard as a belief. The deepest and most firmly anchored faiths are however those held without people even being aware that they hold them – ideas used automatically in the interpretation of events. The deepest faiths are in the words and in implicit concept frameworks that one is not aware that one is using. Many of the ideas and the words used by economics have become like that.

John Maynard Keynes was saying much the same thing when he wrote:

> The ideas of economists and political philosophers, both when they are right and when they are wrong, are more powerful than is commonly understood. Indeed the world is ruled by little else. Practical men, who believe themselves to be quite exempt from any intellectual influence, are usually the slaves of some defunct economist.

So can we break free of these intellectual influences which we are not aware that we have absorbed? How do we break free of the taken for granted assumptions that we do not notice framing our thinking?

In one of his poems Rudyard Kipling wrote "What do they know of England, who only England know."

It is by comparison with other places, other ideas, and other things that one notices what would otherwise be taken for granted. Taken-for-granted situations become visible when seen in contrast. By leaping above the surface a fish become aware of the water in which it is living.

That is why repeatedly through this book I compare how economists think about the world with the way that earlier societies thought. It is why I am interested in contrasts with how indigenous societies think. This throws into view the fact that "economics think" is not a natural or inevitable way of understanding things. It is the particular way of understanding peculiar to our society. It is our society's system of belief.

For example, implicit in the economists' belief system is the taken for granted assumption that the natural world is the property of human beings. It is for humans to do with it, to make from it, as they wish. After a money purchase large parts of the world can be fenced off and arrangements made for access and use rights that exclude other people. With the aid of pesticides other species can be excluded too.

But let us compare these taken for granted assumptions of the economic world view with how indigenous societies see things. In indigenous societies people belong to places rather than places belonging to the people. The difference is profound. Belonging to a community which belongs to a place translates into a set of obligations and responsibilities which are not to be found in the economic religion. When people belong to places then individuals take different things for granted. They accept as a matter of course that they must look after the community, they must look after the place and often that they must look after the other species in the place (totem responsibilities). This is a responsibility that extends to future generations but it also extends as obligations to ancestors who came before and who have now died.

The *Ubuntu* philosophy of the Bantu speaking peoples of Africa is a triad comprised of the living, the living dead (ancestors) and the yet to be born. The living community answers to the living dead who ensure that the living can provide for the yet to be born. But to provide for the yet to be born the environment must be regarded as the fourth dimension of the community and it too must be cared for. (Ramose, Mogobe B. 2014)

It will be noted here that the Bantu people's belief system is orientated in time and space. The past, the future and the place are all included in it as well as a set of duties, a code of ethics.

In the economics religion no such rootedness applies because the economic faith emerged in a different kind of society. When William the Conqueror invaded England in 1066 he awarded all the land in the country to himself and parcelled it out to his military commanders. Colonial invaders do not belong to places – they intrude into the places occupied by others with an assumption of superiority. The natives are perceived as inferiors. In later centuries the descendants of William's gangster aristocracy took it on themselves to launch further wars of conquest in alliance with merchants. Traders were another group who, by operating between places, did not belong anywhere – rather they aspired to take over the places that they operated in so that those places belonged to them.

In this mind-set it is taken for granted that those people (and corporations) who own parcelled up parts of the planet can do with it as they wish. Ethical obligations of care and maintenance are no longer primary. Indeed the colonialists usually assumed that the people who were in the places that they invaded belonged to them too – as serfs or as slaves they were not different from wildlife that could be tamed, turned into work animals, transported and traded as property. "Economics" therefore evolved as a way of thinking about wealth production in dis-located and dis-placed societies, for people who were invaders and traders, people who had little understanding of the places, the species and people that they were taking over. Their exclusive focus was on making themselves richer and more powerful.

In brief, economics emerged as an orientation system for colonial gangsters. Of course the PR of economics made it look a lot better that this. Economics supposed to be a theory about what philosophers call "Hurrah words" like prosperity, progress and well being. However, because it was justifying practices that dislocated the multi-generational relationships where people looked after each other and places it sowed destruction, oppression and chaos. It got the name the "dismal science" for good reasons.

Faiths are attractive when they help us to make sense, help us to find meaning and orientation – and thus, to know what it makes sense for us as individuals and groups to do, given the bigger picture. Faiths are thus not only a way of making sense of what we read in the papers and hear on the news broadcasts. Faiths help us choose our purposes – they help frame our imagination of what way we might live out our personal and collective story. They contextualise what we decide will be the projects, the agendas, the games or the careers to which we devote ourselves. However, there is a problem when we just absorb the destructive frames of reference of the power elite without even noticing that we are doing this. In the language of a variety of French thinkers we have allowed our "imaginaries" to be "colonised". (Latouche 2014)

The use of the adjective "imaginary" as a noun, as "the imaginary" has a long intellectual tradition in France. Novelists like Gide, philosophers like Sartre and Castoriadis and psychoanalysts like Lacan all used "L'Imaginaire" in different contexts. The idea is that the words and symbols used in human communication, as well as in our thinking, do not necessarily match or correspond to the realities they represent. The words and symbols that we use may have an invented component that corresponds to nothing 'out there' in the world. In fact imagination is necessary to thought. Our ability to shape patterns of words, images and symbols in creative writing or painting is not merely a capacity to create fictitious realities. The mind *has to have* this capacity to imagine if it is to be able to think at all. How else can a scientist theorise except by imagining what might be the explanatory causes for some phenomena? The imagination can later be tested against evidence and found to be true or false but the initial act of making a hypothesis is an ability to construct what might be, to imagine. (Castoriadis C. 1987)

Furthermore it is through our ability to imagine the way in which things might be otherwise arranged that our freedom to act in the world lies. Our imagination can create visions of how future technological, social, economic and political realities might be constructed differently. This is why, according to the Greek-French philosopher Cornelius Castoriadis, history cannot be analysed in a determinist way. A significant role in the historical process must be acknowledged to be the creative imagination of people in societies. Once we give way to the idea that "there is no alternative" (e.g. to neo-liberal economics) we have not only got a failure of the imagination but have allowed our freedom to disappear. We have given up our *autonomy* – in the sense of not exercising our ability to give rules and laws to ourselves independently and consciously in co-operation with others. (Deriu, M 2014 (a))

Hence the case made by Serge Latouche in for the need to "decolonise" our "imaginaries" from the ideas of market economics. (Latouche 2014)

While true this is true within limits. I can imagine that I can raise a bag of ten apples one metre into the air with one joule of energy but that is an 'imaginary' that I cannot make happen "in real life". (An average weighted apple takes one joule to raise one metre). While some imaginaries can be made to fly, some imaginaries are too off-the-wall and crash to the ground. Some imaginaries are nice to look at in a surrealist painting but non functional. Some imaginaries are not only crazy but criminally insane and plain dangerous. As a matter of fact "perpetual economic growth" is a political imaginary that is collectively suicidal. Imaginaries have to have some connection to practical possibilities and actual developments in material reality and current mainstream 'economic imaginaries' of growth are problems because they are imaginary in another sense of that word in the English language - as in where "imaginary" means "existing *only* in imagination" (Oxford English Dictionary 1964). Where there is strong belief in something that only exists in the imagination then this belief is delusionary. Where acting on the delusion has consequences that are dangerous then it is akin to a form of insanity.

However, collective insanities are not recognised as psychiatric symptoms because to qualify as evidence of insanity a delusional belief must be held by only one person. A man who is eating fish and chips with a cup of tea and believes that he is eating the body and blood of Jesus might be judged to be insane by a psychiatrist – but not if he is eating and drinking communion wafers and wine together with others.

Unfortunately, with mainstream growth economics firmly embedded inside the organisations of the state and inside companies the failure to question this faith is going to leads to a lot of people becoming bewildered, confused and unable to make out what is actually a very clearly emerging big picture in the decades ahead. Economics as it is will fail them, and fail them very badly.

From all that I have written thus, far I do not mean to imply only that economics needs to take on board the embeddedness of the economy in the ecological system, as well as the limits to growth. That is only a part, albeit a crucial part, of the story. If we are going to survive the turmoil of the years ahead, we are going to need a deeper understanding of ourselves and what makes for our emotional well-being. I believe that we will need ideas which are very different from the current concepts of "economic man" and "welfare".

Chapter 2

Economics and economists...

This chapter connects economic theory to the role that economists play in society and the kind of people that they are likely to be given their social role as part of the elite. It explores themes such as elite psychopathology, the way that observation changes that which is observed while that which is observed changes the observer.

To repeat again the saying: "We do not see things as they are, we see things as we are". The truth in this statement applies to economics too – economics tells us about economists. It tells us how they understand the world and therefore it tells us something about what economists are like.

What we are **able** to notice in the world and what we **choose** to notice, what we focus upon, how we frame concepts to explain our objects of focus, how we describe things and/or how we frame hypotheses about reality – all these crucially reflect the kind of people we have been, we are and that we aspire to become.

It follows from this that if many, perhaps most, economists start their analysis with an assumption of how "rational economic men" are motivated, then it might say something about them and the jobs that they typically do. The starting points of much economic thinking are **axioms** – things about how people behave and act which are held to be self-evident. These axioms of economics tell us a lot about the internal mental and emotional life of mainstream economists.

They are self-interested calculating machines who assume that other people are like themselves. Indeed, if others are not self-interested calculating machines then economists are rude about them – these others are held not to be "rational".

There is plenty of evidence for this. For example, a study of economic and non-economics students in 1993 by Frank, Gilovich and Regan found that most people learn to be more co-operative as they get older – but that learning economics slows this process of social maturity. (Saka, 2011)

> "On the one hand, cooperative tendencies increase over time, with age. This is true for everyone, economist or not. Children are much more selfish than adults, for instance. Among university students, upper class men exhibit more pro-social behaviour than lower class men. Controlling for this, though, authors show that the pattern of falling defection rates, or increasing cooperation rates, "holds more strongly for non-economics majors than for economics majors." This means, while students in other disciplines learn to be cooperative over college years, students majoring in economics learn the same fact much more slowly."

Further to that they found that micro-economics teaching over 4 months had a noticeable effect:

"They picked three classes at Cornell University. Two of these were introduction to microeconomics. The third was introduction to astronomy. In the first microeconomics class (class A), the professor was a game theorist with interests in mainstream economics, and he focused on prisoner's dilemma and how cooperation might hinder survival. In the second microeconomics class (class B), the professor's interests were in development economics and he was a specialist in Maoist China.

"To the students in all these introductory classes, the authors posed simple ethical dilemmas, including questions such as "If you found an envelope with $100 with the owner's address written on it, would you return it?" The questions were asked twice, first in September, in the beginning of the fall semester and once again during the final week of classes in December, not even a full four months apart.

"Comparing results against the astronomy control group, students in economics class A became much more cynical and gave less ethical responses at the end of the semester. Students in class B grew to be more unethical, yet not by so much compared to students in class A. The results clearly show that no matter what their initial ethical tendencies were, students who were exposed to a mere four months of "rational" reasoning became less cooperative. " (Saka, 2011)

Observation changes the observed and the observed changes the observer

Although the Anaïs Nin quote contains an important truth, it nevertheless simplifies if just taken on its own. The act of observation establishes a connection between observers and the objects of observation. Through this connection the objects of observation are changed – by measuring things they come to be changed. To describe an object, to theorise it and then to communicate the theory, will change the object. So to speak, it pulls the observed object out of Tao, the vast interflowing flux of nameless and unnoticed processes, and makes it a named thing, now a focus of human attention, an object of interest - and perhaps of concern for attempts at understanding in order to facilitate intervention and control. (LaoTzu)

When economists observe and describe economic reality, their observations, descriptions and measurements are influences shaping that reality. There is a loop here – neoclassical economics is claimed to be a description of reality and it shapes the reality that is described. If economists claim that people act as self-interested calculating machines and deduce models of economic life and markets based on this axiom, then they help to shape a reality in which more people tend to become self-interested calculating machines.

And first and foremost this helps to bring this kind of reality about in the world in which they themselves work. As we have just written, observer and observed are actually always tied into an interacting system.

It is also true that when we focus our attention on certain things and frame our understanding of these things in particular ways, we are also choosing NOT to focus our attention on other things. If we neglect to theorise co-operative and social behaviour in the economy, focusing only on self-interest, this too has an effect in our economic life. What we do not think about remains out of sight. We do not attempt to measure it, for example, or rate its importance. It does not count. The history of economic thought is full of things that do not count, that do not make it into the theory. We will observe that over and again in the accounts that follows. We will observe also how some things that were in economic theory at one point in time disappear from consideration later. Quite often these topics disappear because it is the interest of a group of people that they disappear. The theory of land and rent is a case in point. At the point in history where common lands are being taken from communities, for example, there is a theory of land, labour and property developed by John Locke to justify the process. At the end of the 19ᵗʰ century the owners of landed property perceived a threat to their interests in the idea, derived from Adam Smith and Ricardo by Henry George, that land rents were the ideal source of taxation in his campaign for a land value tax. It was the university departments that theorised land as just another kind of capital input, and disappeared such ideas, that got the generous endowments.

That this happened is at least consistent with the theory – if the market supplies what those with purchasing power want, then in the market of ideas, university departments of economics will have their theories for sale – and indeed they did and still do. At the end of the 1960s and early 1970s, the leading economic thinkers disappeared the history of economic thought from the curriculum altogether.

Economists notice self-interested calculating behaviour in the worlds that they typically inhabit and intuit that behaviour as being typical everywhere else. So what kind of worlds do they inhabit, when they have left academe after their training? What are they being trained for typically?

Economists are a part of the elite

I will look at this in greater detail later, but for now let me note the simple fact that, in Britain, a year after graduation in economics, of those who are in employment, about 50% have become business, finance sector and associated professionals, with a further 12% becoming commercial, industrial and public sector managers. In contrast only about 1% are to be found in the arts, design, culture and sport, another 1% in education and slightly less than 1% in social and welfare jobs. (Howie, 2013)

These are not the only ways that we can describe the world of economists. Economists, like everyone else, typically live in a world that is familiar to them, that they take for granted – and there is a paradox in taken for granted realities. The paradox is that what we take for granted is typically unnoticed. In a strange way it is hidden to us. The development theorist Robert Chambers showed this very eloquently many years ago when he contrasted the world lived in by the typical development professional and the lived reality of those people in so-called "developing countries" who the professionals are employed "to help". His aim was to show why development professionals were so often out of touch with the realities of the poor and so often made recommendations which were inappropriate and did not work. Chambers described the development professionals using a term from the New Testament. They are the "first" – whereas the people who they are supposedly advising are "the last". (Chambers, 1983)

Settings within which theory has been conceived contrasted to settings where it is applied

Indoors	Outdoors
Office	Village, homestead, field, forest
Accessible	Remote
High status/powerful	Low status/powerless
Educated	Illiterate/vernacular knowledge
Urban	Rural
Industrial	Agricultural/pastoral
High cost	Low cost
Capital using	Labour using
Mechanical	Labour using
Inorganic	Organic
Large scale	Small scale

These kinds of contrasts apply not only to development professionals and people in poor countries. They apply to economists and the rest of society too. Economists are largely part of the elite. They are part of that group that Chambers calls "the first" – as opposed to "the last". They live comfortable lives, are powerful and influential. Their direct contact with the natural world is very limited – as they will live and work in financial and political centres. The comfortable neighbourhoods that they live in cut off "the first" from poorer communities. Their theories and their policy suggestions reflect the separations. Indeed among the "first", among the elite, there is a general assumption that their education, their experience of well-being, their power, qualify them with the skills and access to the knowledge that best equips a person to be an important decision-maker – and to decide for and on behalf of others. All these things in life means that the theories that one spins are more likely to be plausible or correct and that this gives one important rights over others, the rights to leadership and authority. It not only qualifies one to theorise, it entitles one to theorise too – and it is then a small step to belief that one's theorisations are better than those of other people and justify one's right to power.

In her book "Econned" Yves Smith draws out the consequences when she describes the resulting mentality:

> ... they assume that only they are qualified to opine about matters economic. That in turn produces two considerable biases. First, if an argument about economics comes from a non-economist and does not happen to fall in line with the orthodoxy, it must be wrong. It will be rejected even if it contains useful information. Secondly, the scientific mantle gives economists the trump card in policy discussions, even though, as we have seen (elsewhere in her book – BD) those aspirations are not born out in practice.

> "When an elite succeeds in monopolising discussion on a given topic, an additional danger is that members of the privileged caste can become overconfident. The economics discipline has had, in fact, attacks of hubris. (Smith, 2010)

Elite psychopathology and its opposite

A number of studies that tell us about the motivations and culture of those people who participate in the exclusive club of financial and economic power. A study by the University of St. Gallen asked 28 professional traders in financial instruments and a group of psychopaths in a Swiss gaol to undertake a computer simulation to test how much each group was prepared to co-operate, how egotistical they were and what kind of risks they were prepared to take. The result exceeded the expectation of Thomas Noll, a Forensic Scientist and Director of a Swiss gaol near Zurich. "Naturally we cannot describe the traders as mentally ill, but they behave in a more egotistical way and take greater risks than a group of psychopaths that took the same test."

The traders did not actually make more profit than the comparison group – but what Noll found particularly shocking was that instead of working methodically and soberly in order to make the highest profit "the thing that mattered above all else to the traders was to get more than those who they were playing against and they used a lot of energy to damage these others". Noll described this with a comparison in which someone who is very status conscious discovers that a neighbour has the same kind of prestige car and resolves the rivalry using a baseball bat. (my translation) (Börsenturbulenzen: Aktienhändler riskieren mehr als Psychopathen, 2011) in *Der Spiegel*.

Similar studies confirm the same finding. As related by George Monbiot another example was a test of 39 senior managers and chief executives from leading British businesses who are compared with patients at a hospital for the criminally insane. The study was by Belinda Board and Katarina Fritzon, in the Journal "Psychology, Crime and Law".

They compared the results to the same tests on patients at Broadmoor special hospital, where people who have been convicted of serious crimes are incarcerated. On certain indicators of psychopathology, the bosses' scores either matched or exceeded those of the patients. In fact on these criteria they beat even the subset of patients who had been diagnosed with psychopathic personality disorders. (Monbiot, 2011)

As many economists live inside and theorise this kind of culture it is not surprising that it appears axiomatic to them that economic decisions are explainable solely by calculations of individual self-interest. For those of us that don't live close to this world and observe people sacrificing their interests for others, looking after each other, co-operating, dedicating themselves to causes, caring, acting out of empathy, compassion and love for others, are we not entitled to ask whether these motivations also constitute "rational human behaviour"? Is it not important to explain these too when we try to explain how people make decisions and allocate resources?

Reproduced with the permission of Ad Busters.

A cynical, but a not unjustified answer, is that these kind of behaviours are what make people more exploitable to those with the self-interested mind set. Harvesting the benefits of these kind of behaviours and motivations in the interest of the financial elite was the idea behind the "Big Society" policy from our betters in Britain. A public spirit, and caring, are the kind of thing that can enable the political economic elite to cut local authority, health and welfare expenditure so as to release the resources which then enables them to reduce taxation on the bonuses to the bankers. If people are so stupid as to be altruistic in a self-interested society then they are suckers that deserve to be ripped off. The more we give to the "Big Society" – the more our betters can take for themselves – a situation which paradoxically "dis-incentivizes" giving because one feels oneself ripped off, not by the poor, but actually by the rich.

The household economy and the paid work economy

These ideas are not new and original. As I have said, theory is developed and applied to phenomena that have been noticed and considered worthy of attention. When women started to consider what a feminist economics would look like, the focus of attention and interest was applied to activities and "resource use" in the household which had hitherto been scarcely considered worth a mention in a theory almost entirely developed by men.

Yet the truth is that most people spend most of their lives outside of paid employment. A benchmark figure suggested by 3 biophysical economists, Giampietro, Mayumi and Sorman, is that in a "developed economy" each person will spend 7,900 hours per year in "household activities" (outside paid employment). As there are 8,760 hours in a year that means that only 10% of time is spent by most people in employment. We are not in paid employment as children. When we are old enough, we are not in paid employment most of the time because we need to rest, sleep and "re-create" plus, sometimes, we are unemployed, sick and out of work. Finally, as elderly people, we are again not in employment. (Giampietro, Mayumi, & Sorman, 2011)

Despite this, the management and arrangement of this part of our lives; the motivations and kinds of relationships that apply here; the technologies that we can bring to bear at home; all these remain an unexplored continent to most economists. They are only interested when, as people struggle to hold their lives in balance and cope with the problems on this unknown continent, it registers in the consciousness of the managing elite that there are strains in the health, welfare and local authority budgets. For example, in recent years there has been the dawning realisation that an ageing population of "baby boomers", born after world war two, will be a significant claim on health and social care resources in the years ahead.

In reality, there are multiple ways in which, without taking into account the specific features of the "non- paid" sector and how it is changing, we cannot hope to understand what really motivates people and, crucially, for this is the point of the exercise, how their well-being is constituted. Economist, Robert Nelson, is aware of some of these issues and refers to another economist, Jennifer Roback Morse, whose thinking changed when she had a child:

> As a lifetime libertarian, she finds that having a child, among other things, altered her perspective. Perhaps there is an essential truth to the feeling of many ordinary mothers, as they commonly express it themselves, that a child is not supposed to be an economic asset paying a return on investment but an outlet for love – an "opportunity to give" that is deliberately sought for this very

purpose of giving of oneself. It is a maternal sentiment that is very much at odds with the standard framework of economic thinking. (Nelson, 2001)

Most of our lives are spent outside what has become called "the economy" and yet, there appears to be an assumption among the economically orthodox that this part of our lives has very little relevance to understanding how "the economy" works. Indeed, if we are to believe economic theorists like Gary Becker or Richard Posner, we apply calculations of individual self-interest in all our human relationships and activities just the same as we do in our consumption and our business decisions.

It can be said that Mi (Man i) loves Fj (Female j) if her welfare enters his utility function, and perhaps also if Mi values emotional and physical contact with Fj. Clearly, Mi can benefit from a match from Fj, because he can then have a more favourable effect on her welfare – and thereby his own utility – and because the commodities measuring "contact" with Fj can be produced more cheaply when they are matched than when Mi has to seek an "illicit" relationship with Fj. Gary Becker. (Quoted in Nelson, 2001 op. cit)

In describing prostitution as a substitute for marriage in a society that has a surplus of bachelors, I may seem to be overlooking a fundamental difference: the "mercenary" character of the prostitute's relationship with her customer. The difference is not fundamental. In a long-term relationship such as marriage, the participants can compensate each other for services performed by performing reciprocal services, so they need not bother with pricing each service, keeping books of account, and so forth. But in a spot-market relationship such as a transaction with a prostitute, arranging for reciprocal services is difficult. It is more efficient for the customer to pay in a medium [of money] that the prostitute can use to purchase services from others. Richard Posner (quoted in Nelson, 2001)

With Becker and Posner we witness a kind of conceptual imperialism. Becker imagines that the economic mentality conceived by neoclassical economists applies to all human life. Behind all human actions is an individual making calculations aimed at maximisation. The mentality of market, management and shopping is all there is.

Chapter 3

Early economic thought from Aristotle to the "invisible hand"

The chapter covers the early history of economic thought as slave owning classes reflected upon "self-actualisation" and on the management of their households and estates. Medieval economics was a branch of moral philosophy taught by monks and yet the subject subsequently evolved to justify robbery and enslavement in service to the rising merchant class. Economics became, in effect, a quasi-religion. The new original sin was "scarcity" while the new chief virtue has become "efficiency".

Slave owners reflect on self-actualisation and household management

It was not always thus,. The original meaning of the word "economics" is derived from the Greek *"oikomomia"*, and meant the art of managing a household. To the philosopher Aristotle there were two kinds of exchange and trade – those which provided for the genuine provisioning needs of a household, and those activities focused on the accumulation of money and possessions for their own sake – which he described as "chrematistics". What we call the economy today can be seen as a vast expansion of what Aristotle would have called "chrematistics". This vast expansion still takes up the minority of our individual lives – but its management, its mind set, its priorities has come to completely dominate all aspects of social life and all aspects of our environment. The theorists of present day chrematistics, economists, have become a quasi-priesthood whose way of thinking and suggestions for how to prioritise what we do dominates power and political discourses. (Aristotle, 350 BC)

It is unlikely that Aristotle would have approved. For him the end of all human activity is sometimes translated as "happiness". However, this can be misleading to a modern understanding of that word because what Aristotle meant by happiness was a very specific idea of living a virtuous life in accordance with reason. The virtues included personal characteristics like integrity, honour, loyalty, courage and forthrightness. Ideally life meant developing oneself and flourishing in and through ones dealings - and particularly through participation in the life and management of the community.

This did involve some need for provisions, and if fortune was on your side, your women and your slaves could take care of your needs in this respect, but Aristotle did not think that happiness involved accumulating lots of possessions. The amount of property needed for a good life was limited. That's why he saw there being two kinds of exchange and trade – exchange in order to satisfy a genuine need – and exchange to accumulate beyond this. The latter Aristotle thought of as unnatural, as he did usury, because it involved money growing without limits which violated the laws of nature where everything in nature has limits.

This unnatural process has subsequently become the whole purpose of economic activity and, arguably, that is where things have gone wrong. In this connection it is important to note that, integral to contemporary criticism of a growth economy, is a re-consideration of the ultimate aim of human life and thus, of economic activity. There has been a revival of the idea of "flourishing" and happiness through personal growth that arises through the development of one's powers and through participation in a community.

The difference from Aristotle's time is that, nowadays, some people think that women and slaves are entitled to flourish too – although by no means does everyone share this viewpoint. According to the International Labour Organisation, there are an estimated 20.9 million men, women and children in the modern world in slavery – either as bonded labourers trapped by debt; as child slaves; people forced by violence or its threat to work; women forced or tricked into marriages, domestic servitude or sex industries; people who are trafficked and people born into slave classes. Then there are many who are nominally "employees" who are really little better than slaves employed by multinational suppliers operating in so called "free trade zones" in China, Sri Lanka, Bangladesh, El Salvador and elsewhere. In such places there are no minimum wages, 12 hour shifts are the norm, health and safety arrangements abused, child labour common and trade unions are banned. (War on Want, 2013)

Working a 12 hour day for low wages does not allow one to flourish – it merely allows one to provide for the most basic needs.

The psychologist Maslow formulated a way of thinking about this with his well-known concept of a "hierarchy of needs". Peoples' physiological needs must be provided for first, otherwise they simply cannot stay alive. Then they need to feel safe and have some security. After that their needs encompass the means to feel that they belong (in a self-determining way). If they are able to satisfy these it may become possible to move up to higher needs – being able to feel self-esteem, being able to self-actualise (to flourish) and transcendence. (Maslow, 2013)

Maslow's ideas are useful but are not necessarily to be thought of in a rigid way. Men or women who might be thought of as being poor in a material sense, who wished to "self-actualise" and even to seek "transcendence", have often been able to do so in a limited way by doing without the expenses of a sexual and family life by joining a religious order. This gave them some basic economic security which allowed them the time to pray, study and meditate after their fashion.

This reminds us that wealth can be measured not just in possessions but also in leisure time – which you can have a lot of when slaves are working for you. The maverick economist, Thorsten Veblen, explained laconically what might, perhaps, have been Aristotle's attitude:

From the days of the Greek philosophers to the present, a degree of leisure and of exemption from contact with such industrial processes as serve the immediate everyday purposes of human life has ever been recognised by thoughtful men as a prerequisite to a worthy or beautiful, or even a blameless, human life. In itself and in its consequences the life of leisure is beautiful and ennobling in all civilised men's eyes.

This direct, subjective value of leisure and of other evidences of wealth is no doubt in great part secondary and derivative. It is in part a reflex of the utility of leisure as a means of gaining the respect of others, and in part it is the result of a mental substitution. The performance of labour has been accepted as a conventional evidence of inferior force; therefore it comes itself, by a mental short-cut, to be regarded as intrinsically base. (Veblen, 1899)

Medieval economics as a branch of moral philosophy

But let us return from the theorists to the theories. It will be noticed that the early thinking on economics was framed in philosophical and ethical discourses about what it means to be human. For centuries economics was taught as a branch of moral philosophy. Thus, if we fast forward to early medieval Europe, and the founding of the universities, economics was a topic of concern to monks like St Augustine and St Thomas Aquinas. (Mueller, 2006)

Just as Aristotle was unconcerned with slavery and women, Augustine and Aquinas both turned a blind eye to the power structures of the feudal society in which they lived. However, as monks who had taken vows of poverty, they presumably thought the reason for living was firstly, as it says in the Ten Commandments, to love God and also to love your neighbour. Life involved transcending yourself and, as already noted, their vow of poverty in material possessions no doubt "purchased" them the time to study and think about such things.

Augustine and Aquinas did not automatically assume that production was for the benefit of the producer. They assumed that you gave to, and provided for, the people that you loved, and that you exchanged with strangers. Obviously if you exchanged with strangers, this was, at the next stage, to have the things needed for the people that you love and for oneself.

To Augustine every person has a choice - to provide his or her goods for himself or to provide them for other people. This depends on the love people have for themselves compared to the love they have for other people. Thus, distribution at the local and personal level, as economists call it, involves a moral choice. What is being described here is what is going on inside families and households – it is a description of a provisioning economy. With Aristotle this was extended a little further in that there was also an idea that you shared wealth with a wider community, which in his case was the polis, the political community. (This was the men who were not slaves).

For the scholastic economists, even when we exchange with people who we do not love we still have ethical obligations. For Aquinas exchange involved a "just price". This was the price that emerged through haggling which then clears the market. However, and this is crucial, a just price is not imposed or experienced by some parties under conditions of duress. To charge someone high prices during times of famine was most definitely not charging the just price.

So the context prevailing in the market was important. Indeed, the scholastics appear to have made moral judgements similar to those of modern economists in their condemnation of monopoly control of the market and its abuse. That said, the structure of the economy was very different so we should beware of taking comparisons too far. In particular for many centuries the ethical ideas about how markets should work were reflective of actual practices that made sure that prices were "just". This was something that was organised by deliberate market intervention and regulation at a local level.

Marvin T Brown quotes Mark Overton to give an example of the civic rules for a market from Wiltshire in England in 1564. The rules included the following:

1. Before the market sellers of grain agreed with local justices what the price should be.
2. When the market opened purchases should be for the customers own use and be limited to 2 bushels of grain (between 9am and 11am)
3. After 11am grain could be purchased by those who resold it (bakers, brewers, badgers etc.)
4. Those buying grain to resell had to be licensed by a Justice of the Peace
5. Grain could only be purchased on market day
6. No person could buy grain in the market if she has sufficient of her own.

A market like this is embedded in a local community and makes sure that the local community is not ripped off. It is a market in which people are trading with each other directly and merchants are not the dominant actors – indeed they play a minor role, if any at all. (Brown, 2010)

The early medieval period was characterised by power structures somewhat akin to protection rackets where militarised hierarchical gangs effectively imposed themselves on ordinary people and extracted labour and products, claiming that they had their authority and rights from God, but in effect having their power from their ability and preparedness to act as ruthless gangsters operating out of heavily fortified castles. (Nelson L. H., 2001)

The church was no doubt complicit in all of this but it also acted as a form of social welfare agency in difficult times because the aged, sick and poor could turn to the monasteries. In addition, in England, the ordinary people had certain rights to use the forests, the wastes and commons lands for their own maintenance that were protected, in England, in the "Charter of the Forests" which was adopted in 1217. This was a statement of rights, extracted from the monarch, adopted at the same time as the Magna Charta. (Rothwell, 1975)

This was a time, therefore, when households were located in the immediate natural environment from which they got the bulk of their sustenance. From this it follows that people would need a detailed vernacular knowledge of this environment and what it could yield in order to get by. Economy and ecology were, in this sense, still closely integrated at the practical level. The households of more powerful people were their estates and these provided for most needs of the rulers too.

Things were changing However, and what Aristotle would have termed "chrematistics" were on the rise. Towns were growing and were places both to escape feudal servitude to the landed aristocracy as well as locations to find new economic opportunities. The new opportunities included craft production, participation in a growing amount of long distance trade and, in money lending, in banking and financial services.

Wanted: an economics to justify robbery and enslavement – the rise of the merchant class

The rise of the merchant class and of commercial society in towns, and along trade routes outside the power of the military elite, changed the conditions in which economics was theorised. Aquinas had recognised and acknowledged a positive role for merchants who fulfilled the useful function of bringing goods from where they were abundant to where they were scarce. However, that's not all that merchants did. Over several centuries in Europe they created economic conditions where it paid the elite to take the common land from the commoners to enrich themselves by using that land for the production of commodities for trade, for example, putting sheep on the land and then selling the wool). Land that had been taken away from the people also became available for sale from time to time. As a land market developed it also became a source of money for the monarch, who was strapped for cash to pay for wars. At the time of the Reformation in England, Henry VIII dissolved the monasteries and sold them to his courtiers, and in the process, dismantled the welfare provision role of resort to the church by ordinary people. (EnglishHeritage)

Merchants make their money by buying cheap and selling dear and it was a small step in a lawless era plagued by wars, to acquire goods very cheaply indeed by taking them by force in privateering – piracy legitimised by one's own state. Trade was also developed – in slaves or in the goods from slave plantations or from products that the population of colonies were forced to sell, extracted by taxes or other forms of forced labour.

Thus, more and more wealth was accumulated in a few hands under conditions that the earlier scholastic economists would probably have described as "under duress". While colonial economies and slavery were developed abroad, at home the commons lands were enclosed, so that ordinary people using the commons lost their rights to sustenance. These processes meant they had to work for the emerging capitalist class as wage labourers or pay rent to the landowners on onerous terms. The price of labour and the price of land was the result of an institutionalised form of duress in that the ordinary people had no other options but to work on terms set by employers and landowners.

Elite theorisation of economics turned a blind eye to the institutionalised violence in these processes. Instead, the philosophers and early economists provided both philosophical justification for the robbery of ordinary people at home and abroad and ideas to facilitate the processes at the technical level. Alternatively, they turned a blind eye to what was going on, appearing not to notice it at all.

Take, for example, John Locke. As well as being a philosopher, Locke was an investor in the Royal Africa Company which traded in slaves. From 1673 to 1675, Locke was the Secretary of the Council of Trade and Plantations. Here was a man whose ideas were a beacon for future generations - upholding the right to "life, liberty and the pursuit of happiness" and yet he put his money in the slave trade. In his "Second Treatise on Government" Locke appears to justify the taking of slaves "who being captives taken in a just war, are by the right of nature subjected to the absolute dominion and arbitrary power of their masters."

As Marvin T Brown comments "surely the large scale assaults on African communities to kidnap millions of men and women could hardly be described as a 'just war'." (Brown, 2010, p. 242)

At the same time Locke was ready with the arguments as to why Europeans had the right to settle the "vacant places of America" without the current inhabitants having reason to complain:

> God gave the World to Men in Common but... it cannot be supposed He meant it should always remain common and uncultivated. He gave it to the use of the Industrious and the Rational (and *Labour* is to be *his Title* to it). (John Locke, *"Two Treatises on Government"*) (O'Neill, 2007, pp. 118-119)

So what's the reason that land was taken away from indigenous peoples abroad and people back in England? It was obvious, God intended the industrious and rational to improve the land and these were peoples that were not industrious or rational enough. The truth was that the commons had been developed and looked after by the ordinary people in England for centuries. And the truth abroad was that, what appeared to be uncultivated land was actually also commons lands and had been shaped by the management practices of the indigenous peoples.

If we move on in time to Adam Smith's theorisations of "The Wealth of Nations" we find that, once again, slavery and colonial pillage only played a small part in the theorisation of why the European nations and their colonies had become wealthier. However, if we dig into the text we can find the reason.

To be fair to Adam Smith he was not in favour of slavery and he did mention it. In his famous text he described slavery as an inefficient way of organising productive labour.

> The experience of all ages and nations, I believe, demonstrates that the work done by slaves, though it appears to cost only their maintenance is in the end the dearest of any. A person who can acquire no property, can have no other interest but to eat as much, and to labour as little as possible. (Smith A. , 1776, p. 212)

Why then did it flourish in the colonies?

Smith didn't go into this in depth but, in part of his book he explained how there was plenty of land available in the colonies but to "improve it" would require much labour. This implied the question of where colonial "improvers" would get their labour from but he did not address that issue explicitly. However, you can sense that he is aware of the question and knows the answer:

> Waste lands of the greatest natural fertility are to be had for a trifle. The increase of revenue which the proprietor, who is always the undertaker, expects from their improvement, constitutes his profit which in these circumstances is commonly very great. But this great profit cannot be made without employing the labour of other people in clearing and cultivating the land; and the disproportion between the great extent of the land and the small number of the people, which commonly takes place in new colonies, makes it difficult for him to get this labour. (Smith A 1776)

Trying to get other Europeans to work as employees would have been problematic. Why would they work for someone else if they could find land and work for themselves? The "would be employers" had little power to get other Europeans to work for them. No matter how "high born" the colonial landed proprietor might be, and how "inferior" his fellow countryman was, the existence of land to be taken by these "inferiors" meant that, in the colonies, a gentleman businessman did not have the power that the enclosures had given at home to impose service on his "inferiors"... and he was certainly not going to beg for anyone to work for him.

In these circumstances the answer was slavery.

> The pride of man makes him love to domineer, and nothing mortifies him so much as to be obliged to condescend to persuade his inferiors. Wherever the law allows it, and the nature of the work can afford it, therefore, he will generally prefer the service of slaves to that of freemen. The planting of sugar and tobacco can afford the expense of slave-cultivation. The raising of corn, it seems, in the present times, cannot. In the English colonies, of which the principal produce is corn, the far greater part of the work is done by freemen. The late resolution of the Quakers in Pennsylvania to set at liberty all their Negro slaves may satisfy us that their number cannot be very great. Had they made any considerable part of their property, such a resolution could never have been agreed to. In our sugar colonies, on the contrary, the whole work is done by slaves, and in our tobacco colonies a very great part of it. The profits of a sugar-plantation in any of our West Indian colonies are generally much greater than those of any other cultivation that is known either in Europe or America; and the profits of a tobacco plantation, though inferior to those of sugar, are superior to those of corn, as has already been observed. Both can afford the expense of slave-cultivation, but sugar can afford it still better than tobacco. The number of negroes accordingly is much greater, in proportion to that of whites, in our sugar than in our tobacco colonies. (Smith, 1776)

So here we have it. The colonialists could not get other Europeans to work for them – so they resorted to slavery.

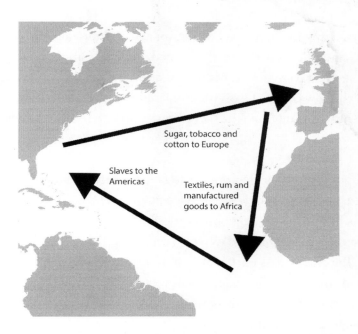

The Triangular Trade of the late 16ᵗʰ to the early 19ᵗʰ century

http://commons.wikimedia.org/wiki/Category:Triangular_trade#mediaviewer/File:Triangle_trade2.png

Slavery was therefore central to the international economy at that time. Yet Smith did not dwell on it as an ethical issue. The professor of moral philosophy was more interested in writing page after detailed page about the relative merits of trade and governance policies imposed by different colonial powers. And when it came to describing the "improvement" that the "Age of Commerce" was bringing about he gave his readers the famous little homily about the butcher, baker and brewer as if source of the wealth of nations was principally to be found in the work done on the high streets of small market towns.

Creating "primitives" – improvement and progress

The Chinese philosopher Lao Tzu would have seen what the idea of progress and improvement was going to lead to:

When people see some things as beautiful,

Other things become ugly.

When people see some things as good,

Other things become bad

Tao Te Ching from Verse 2

When people see some things as improved then other things become left behind. When people see themselves as embodying progress, other people become primitives.

29

Smith regarded himself as living in a new kind of age, an age of improvement. The commercial society had changed the game as far as economics was concerned. He wrote about how more "primitive societies" might be more equalitarian but, in his own society, the labouring classes had their needs met and the more important thing was that the division of labour and specialisation was making possible a continuous improvement in production. Thus, everyone could be regarded as better off, even if unequally so.

Was this really true though? Or did his view appear to be true only because the slaves and the colonised had no voice when the learned texts were written. If we put them back in then their losses would have to be set against the gains in Europe in the global accounts. It would have meant recognising that the wealth of rich nations was based on stealing from other nations that, largely as a result, became poor. Had these things been acknowledged as part of the analysis it would have made "improvement" look distinctly less positive. But this is not what happens in writings of learned men serving the elite as a matter of course. It still doesn't today. "Progress" is measured by its beneficiaries. Its victims are usually too busy trying to survive to get a hearing.

For the victims of progress there has usually been scant consideration as their point of view is automatically discounted because of their "primitive status". This primitive status was the conceptual consequence of the view of historical evolution that Adam Smith and his contemporaries adopted. History was a story of successive stages: hunter gatherers were succeeded by pastoralists, then by agriculturists and now by an "Age of Commerce". It followed that the best thing that could happen to "primitive people" would be for them to get pulled into the age of commerce as quickly as possible. Their way of understanding their world, their life arrangements and economic activities were, and still are, to be regarded as archaic. The charitable thing to do is to help them catch up – rather like children who are helped to help them grow up. From this point of view, it was a short step to colonialism and enslavement.

As Kenrick, following Brantlinger, argues: "the myth of progress can only be maintained by reference to a category of those who are backward, and by denying the savage way in which those deemed backwards are treated in the ongoing colonial project". Margaret Thatcher in her 1988 Bruges speech is quoted as saying that: "The story of how Europeans explored and colonised and – yes, without apology – civilised much of the world is an extraordinary tale of talent, skill and courage". This is a discourse of the superiority and inevitability of European civilisation which depends on the inferiority and inevitable extinction of the "primitive races" of the world. It was used to justify inadequate action by the British government in the face of the Irish potato famine and assumes the inevitability of "progress" for those following the iron laws of liberal political economy and the inevitable demise of the inferior backward other. The supposedly inevitable triumph of colonisation and progress only makes sense in contrast to this inevitable vanishing of primitive peoples. (Kenrick, 2011)

The attitude is not very different today. "Development" is the word now used to describe the "vanishing of the inferior backward other". Thus, poor countries are described as "developing", that is to say that are going to become like "developed" countries. They have suffered the misfortune of being "left behind" in the global drama of development and their peoples should therefore be grateful if multinational companies want to move in, bringing their technologies and bank loans to "help" (in return for the corporations' commandeering land and resources).

As is well known, Prime Minister Margaret Thatcher, was a grocer's daughter. To quote again, Anaïs Nin, "we do not see things as they are, we see things as we are". To a grocer's daughter it no doubt appeared obvious that spreading the civilisation of the commercial society would be a noble act. "Are they one of us?" was one of her famous phrases. If they were not "one of us" then making them become so must have seemed heroic and noble. Civilising the natives was, as Kipling expressed it "The White Man's Burden". Surprisingly, they were not always grateful:

> Upon their arrival, they justified their deeds by saying that they came to civilise us. I wonder what did they mean by "civilisation"? In our understanding and experience, civilisation means the dispossession of our lands, the demise of our culture and the attempt to make White people out of us. We had our stories, our knowledge and our ways of organising, our ways of praying and our ways of mapping our territories. But none of this was important to the Whites. They made their written words and their maps the only valid ones. Thus, we lost our territories, and the younger generation were turned away from the ways of our ancestors... from the beginning our relations with the Whites has been based on mistaken ideas and lack of knowledge of Indigenous people's realities. (Barras, 2004, p. 47)

Given the mind-set of the land grabbers, the colonialists and later corporate barbarians, the sheer destructiveness of their project to other peoples and to natural systems has always been largely invisible to the perpetrators themselves. The "civilisers of commerce" had no ability and no reason to acknowledge the knowledge, the abilities and the sophistication of the peoples they sought to dominate – that would have undermined the very rationale that justified colonialism and "development".

Nothing much has changed since "de-colonisation". In recent times the processes of land grabbing to promote development, has been supplemented by the theft of the knowledge from indigenous peoples – so called "bio-piracy".

> ... companies are being granted patents for products and technologies that make use of the genetic materials, plants and other biological resources that have long been identified, developed and used by farmers and indigenous peoples, mainly in countries of the South. Whilst the corporations stand to make huge revenues from this process, the local communities are unrewarded and in fact face the threat in future of having to buy the products of these companies at high prices. The transnational corporations are racing one another to manufacture pharmaceutical and agricultural products, the main ingredients of which are the genetic materials of the medicinal plants and food crops of these local communities. The firms are also collecting other living things, ranging from soil microorganisms to animals and the genes of indigenous people, which they use for research and making new products.

(Khor, 1995)

It is important to dwell on these issues, and they are covered in much greater length in the second part of this book, because "modern economics" as a way theorising the marketised way of life in the countries of the west, was evolved at the time that European societies were involved in a process of land enclosure at home and colonial take-over across continents. Economics was, and always has been, a handy pattern of ideas to justify and celebrate the "civilising" agendas of kleptocratic elites who could see themselves as "improving" the places that they took over.

It is, on the other hand, possible to switch the perspective and take a look at "economics" from another viewpoint – that of the people who had to endure having their lives "improved". A number of crucial issues for these people were neglected when economics became about "efficiency" and "improvement" conceived as "production growth". These are the issues of risk, vulnerability and resilience.

People living in human communities situated in specific biological communities (eco-systems) may come, over time, to recognise that the eco-system in which they live has a "balance level" of health. This is not the same as what economists understand by equilibrium but a dynamic negotiation between the different elements beyond which "tipping points" occur and the system flips into a different state altogether. The sense of responsibility for the maintenance of a place and the way of life embodies and embeds a recognition of the need to stay back from these ecological tipping points. This is based on a keen appreciation of the needs of the whole human community, as well as the need to maintain balance in the community of species of which it is a part (the eco-system).

This holistic vision of the "Great Spirit", as some indigenous societies envisage the cosmic life process, recognises the centrality of balance rather than continual production growth. Growth is only possible within narrow limits before it becomes destructive. Beyond the limits, beyond the zone of resilience, systems flip and make "state-changes" from which there is no going back. It is this realisation – regarding risks and vulnerability – about which tribal and indigenous peoples have a wisdom that most economists lack. (See the description of the significance of the knowledge of villagers in New Caledonia mentioned above).

The New Original Sin – Scarcity; the new chief virtue – Efficiency; the new religion - Economics

A critical evaluation of the ideas of Adam Smith's praise of the Commercial Society has to take these other issues on board. The monkish idea of progress as moral progress had changed into an idea of improvement as technical progress which was presented as the source of more wealth. Scarcity was the chief problem facing humanity and overcoming scarcity was the chief task to be achieved by the new virtue: "efficiency". This meant "resources" were to be used as efficiently as possible and technological progress brought about by industriousness and rationality then applied to increasing the division of labour and specialisation in the production process. These were ideas created by gentlemen who lived mainly in towns and who did not live as part of commons. They were separated from direct and immediate dependence on the land and had no deep appreciation of, or respect for, the experience of those who were in that dependent relationship. They assumed that they knew better, oblivious to their own ignorance.

In religious terms it was as if "scarcity" had become the original sin of a new economic religion and efficiency and technological progress became the new means of salvation – with economists functioning rather like a new priesthood, a role that they still enjoy. For the contemporaries of Smith, the production and use of this greater wealth would bring about better people because the commercial society had its own virtues and rewarded hard work, discipline, thrift, delayed gratification etc.

Within the framework of this new "quasi religion" it was still realised that human and social relationships were not always just, and that the ends that people pursued were less than perfect. However, it was increasingly assumed that these problems too required economic and technological progress. It would be when people were all much better off that humanity would be able to get to grips with these problems.

This is what the philosopher David Hume, a contemporary of Smith argued:

> Let us suppose that nature has bestowed on the human race such profuse abundance of all external conveniences, that... every individual finds himself fully provided with whatever his most voracious appetite can want, or luxurious imagination wish or desire. (David Hulme...)

If this state of affairs should ever be reached, Hume suggested "it seems evident that, in such a happy state, every other social virtue would flourish, and receive tenfold increase" (Nelson R. H., 2001, p. 26).

The same notion has been shared by many subsequent thinkers. Karl Marx thought that the "highest phases of communism" would be prepared by the ability of capitalism to lay the foundations for the further development of an economy of abundance. Social and class conflict would then "wither away". Without believing in the need for revolution Keynes also thought that, in the distant future, humanity would overcome its scarcity problem and the accompanying psychology of self-interestedness. (In his essay, *"The Economic Possibilities for our Grandchildren"* published *in Essays in Persuasion*).

The problems for humanity were no longer problems between people and God (or between people and Nature) or between people – they were problems of inadequately developed technology.

Even more important was Smith's abandonment of the ideas of Augustine and Aquinas, about loving your neighbour in economic activity. For him a properly working market delivered socially beneficial results even though people were pursuing their self-interest - or perhaps I should write, *because* people were pursuing their self-interest.

This is the famous quote from Adam Smith:

It is not from the benevolence of the butcher, the brewer, or the baker, that we expect our dinner, but from their regard to their own self-interest. We address ourselves, not to their humanity but to their self-love, and never talk to them of our own necessities but of their advantages. (Smith A. , 1776)

Having abandoned considerations of distribution which were rooted in ethical considerations of love for one's neighbour and one's obligations to a wider community, the new economics asserted that by pursuing private advantages - and self-love - the market would in any case organise a social outcome in the interest of everyone.

People got what they wanted through the "invisible hand" of the market because, if they decided they wanted more beer and less bread, then this would be reflected by changes in their market demand. The price of bread would fall and that of beer would rise. Some bakers would switch to brewing and some farmers would switch from wheat for flour to hops and barley for brewing... Prices would act as signals that resources needed to be re-directed. As long as there were no restraints to resources flowing from one use to another there was no need for the state to intervene. The price signals of the market did the re-allocation automatically as if there were an "invisible hand".

This was not a revolutionary new idea. The notion that market activities motivated by self-interest, delivered what people wanted, was being said over a hundred years before Adam Smith. Moreover, we should try to understand the ideas as contemporaries would have understood it. Humanity had fallen – we are sinners. And yet God had a providential plan for the world and he realised his plan through the self-love of people operating through the "laws of the market".

A major intellectual influence at this time was Isaac Newton. He had shown that things did not happen because of continual divine intervention. God did not micro-manage. He set up the basic design of the universe and then it ran itself. In a similar way, the market and the "social physics" of the economy worked through the predictable self-interested behaviour of people expressed in economic laws. As the poet Pope put it:

"Thus, God and Nature formed the general frame,

And bade self-love and social be the same."

Chapter 4

Economics in Darwinist mode – the competitive struggle for existence

Nineteenth century economics is described in this chapter as a subject used to train a psychopathic imperial elite – this is illustrated by the policies recommended by economists to manage famines in Ireland and India. The poor had only themselves to blame for their desperate state.

God died in economic thinking sometime in the 19th century, for most theorists anyway. Instead, economics would be contextualised in popular thinking by a philosophical standpoint derived from Darwin. Darwin in turn had been influenced by economist Thomas Malthus, who lectured in economics to at the East India Company training college. The theories developed reflect again the truth of the phrase from Anaïs Nin - "we do not see things as they are, but as we are" and Victorian industrial society was ruthless. As Andreas Weber explains:

> Malthus, was obsessed by the idea of scarcity as explanation of social change – there would never be enough resources to feed a population that steadily multiplies. Charles Darwin, the biologist, adapted that piece of theory which had clearly been derived from the observation of Victorian industrial society and applied it to a comprehensive theory of natural change and development. In its wake such concepts as "struggle for existence", "competition", "growth" and "optimisation" tacitly became centrepieces of our self-understanding: biological, technological and social progress is brought forth by the sum of individual egoisms. In perennial competition, fit species (powerful corporations) exploit niches (markets) and multiply their survival rates (return margins), whereas weaker (less efficient) ones go extinct (bankrupt). The resulting metaphysics of economy and nature, however, are less an objective picture of the world than society's opinion about its own premises. (Weber, 2012)

The claim that the self-organising character of the competitive market would optimise resource allocation in the face of scarcity became the centrepiece of a general ideology. An emerging belief system, which seemed self-evident to powerful men - that the strong were fitter and more competitive. The weak could assume no automatic entitlement to support because that was not nature's way, it was not efficient. This ideology had expelled considerations of social justice from the economic concept system. "Survival of the fittest" meant those best able to win in a struggle with others – rather than "the survival of those best able to adapt to their immediate environment" which might, alternatively, have meant things like "best able to co-operate for mutual benefit with others and thus, get looked after".

This was not how the elite of Victorian society operated and the implicit philosophy that prevailed was elaborated by people like Nietzsche:

> To speak of just or unjust in itself is quite senseless; in itself, of course, no injury, assault, exploitation, destruction can be "unjust," since life operates essentially, that is in its basic functions, through injury, assault, exploitation, destruction and simply cannot be thought of at all without this character. One must indeed grant something even more unpalatable: that, from the highest biological standpoint, legal conditions can never be other than exceptional conditions, since they constitute a partial restriction of the will of life, which is bent upon power, and are subordinate to its total goal as a single means: namely, as a means of creating greater units of power. A legal order thought of as sovereign and universal, not as a means in the struggle between power complexes but as a means of preventing all struggle in general perhaps after the communistic cliché of Dühring, that every will must consider every other will its equal—would be a principle hostile to life, an agent of the dissolution and destruction of man, an attempt to assassinate the future of man, a sign of weariness, a secret path to nothingness. (Nietzsche, 2009)

Training for psychopaths – economics and famine management

In case this seems an over the top and an extreme quote, chosen for rhetorical effect, then one has only to examine the political economic policies adopted during the Irish famine of the 1840s and the Indian famines of the mid-1870s. In both cases, a sociopathic political elite held rigidly to policies after crop failure that made the situation infinitely worse than they need to have been. Elite thinking was within the framework taught by teachers like Thomas Malthus, at the East India Company's Staff training College at Hailsbury, on Hertford Heath.

In Ireland, and then in India, the extreme vulnerability of the population before the famines had been already been created by previous policy. In the case of Ireland, the parasitism of the Anglo-Irish landlord class sucked away resources from agriculture to their high life in London that might have been otherwise used to raise the abilities and conditions of the cultivators. Simultaneously, alternative industries and employment could make no headway against English competition when protective tariffs were removed after a brief period of prosperity at the time of the Napoleonic and American wars.

In India, the famines were prepared by the disintegration of community relationships and obligations under the impact of the market. As Davis states:

> The worsening depression in world trade had been spreading misery and igniting discontent throughout cotton-exporting districts of the Deccan, where in any case forest enclosures and the displacement of *gram* by cotton had greatly reduced local food security. The traditional system of household and village grain reserves regulated by complex networks of patrimonial obligation had been largely supplanted since the Mutiny by merchant inventories and the cash nexus. Although rice and wheat production in the rest of India (which now included bonanzas of coarse rice from

the recently conquered Irrawaddy delta) had been above average... much of the surplus had been exported to England. (Davis, 2002, p. 26)

According to the free trade evangelists, rising prices in a time of dearth would attract imports of grain and people would consume less. Problem solved.

But the problem was not solved – because of price speculation. What actually happened in the 1870s was described by one of the few members of the elite who was not a free market fundamentalist, Richard Grenville, the Duke of Buckingham and Chandos. The refusal to intervene in the market to bring down the price (by selling grain from places of relative abundance) encouraged an orgy of price speculation as people with wealth bought up grain to profit from the rising prices and made the situation worse. Commented Grenville:

> The rise [of prices] was so extraordinary, and the available supply, as compared with well-known requirements, so scanty that merchants and dealers, hopeful of enormous future gains, appeared determined to hold their stocks for some indefinite time and not to part with the article which was becoming of such unwonted value. It was apparent to the Government that facilities for moving grain by the rail were rapidly raising prices everywhere, and that the activity of apparent importation and railway transit, did not indicate any addition to the food stocks of the Presidency... retail trade up-country was almost at standstill. Either prices were asked which were beyond the means of the multitude to pay, or shops remained entirely closed. (Davis, 2002, p. 27)

In both Ireland and India, any idea of intervening in the market to hold down prices was rejected since markets were self-correcting. It would involve the state in needless expense that could be better spent on other things. In the case of India, these greater priorities were the preparation for a military adventure in Afghanistan for the glory of the Viceroy, opium addict Lord Lytton. Then there was a week-long feast for 68,000 VIPs during Queen Victoria's visit to India – during which time an estimated 100,000 people starved to death in Madras and Mysore.

In both Ireland and India, food was exported out of the country in bulk during the famine. As the population fell by 2 million in Ireland, exports of food from Cork in a single day in November 1848 were 147 bales of bacon, 255 barrels of pork, 5 casks of hams, 3,000 sacks and barrels of oats, 300 bags of flour, 300 head of cattle, 239 sheep, 542 boxes of eggs, 9,300 firkins [about one-fourth of a barrel] of butter, and 150 casks of miscellaneous foodstuffs. (Gallagher, 1995)

In both Ireland and India there was utter terror of supporting the poor during times of hardship. It would create a precedent! It would interfere in the market for labour. It would create dependency. The iron laws of political economy forbad it. Public works as a source of relief might favour some business interests rather than others so they were not to be supported either. At the height of the Irish Famine in 1846, Treasury Head, Sir Charles Trevelyan wrote:

The only way to prevent people from becoming habitually dependent on government, is to bring [relief] operations to a close. The uncertainty about the new crop only makes it more necessary... These things should be stopped now, or you run the risk of paralyzing all private enterprise and having this country on you for an indefinite number of years. (Gallagher, 1995)

The poor have only themselves to blame

In both cases the elite convinced themselves, using the ideas of Malthus, that the deaths were Nature's way of dealing with overpopulation by the poor who were incapable of exercising self-control, and who were therefore bringing down the holocaust upon themselves. "[E]very benevolent attempt made to mitigate the effects of famine and defective sanitation serves but to enhance the evils resulting from overpopulation."

In the same vein, an 1881 report concluded that:

80% of the famine mortality were drawn from the poorest 20% of the population, and if such deaths were prevented this stratum of the population would still be unable to adopt prudential restraint. Thus, if the government spent more of its revenue on famine relief, an even larger proportion of the population would become penurious." As in Ireland thirty years before, those with the power to relieve famine convinced themselves that overly heroic exertions against implacable natural laws, whether of market prices or population growth, were worse than no effort at all. (Davis, 2002, p. 32)

Having thus, degraded fellow human beings as low as they could go through applying "economic principles", the sociopathic gentlemen then witnessed the resulting wretches and failed to recognise their own handiwork. Accompanying Queen Victoria in Ireland, historian Charles Kingsley commented:

I am daunted by the human chimpanzees I saw along that 100 miles of horrible country. I don't believe they are our fault. I believe that there are not only many more of them than of old, but that they are happier, better and more comfortably fed and lodged under our rule than they ever were. But to see white chimpanzees is dreadful; if they were black, one would not feel it so much. (Gallagher, 1995)

What is called "political economy" then was a set of doctrines that suited a gentleman elite of genocidal sociopaths. The statement is not written to be read as indignant rhetoric, but as strictly factual. I seek to describe the world as it was then, not as I would have liked it to have been. There is plenty of evidence. The art and journalism of the time shows how these men regarded themselves.

The ego size of sociopaths - how the imperialists saw themselves. Cecil Rhodes announces plans for telegraph between Cairo and Cape Town. Cartoon in Punch 1892. Creative Commons Licence

The invisible hand of the market was ideal (and remains ideal) for a sociopathic elite to deny their responsibility to their fellow human beings because it claims to be a way of automatically reconciling self-interested behaviour with optimal economic outcomes. As Kingsley said: "I don't believe they are our fault".

It was, and it still is, an argument tailor-made to allow the elite to avoid asking whether appalling suffering and disaster was in any way due to their actions taken in their self-interest. If people starved it was nothing to do with their rental extraction and systems of land tenure that had destroyed the communal arrangements that preceded them. It was nothing to do with their market arrangements. It was nothing to do with their speculation driving prices up further. It was nothing to do with their policies which wanted to use tax revenues for status displays or for war adventures to their greater glory. No, one had to obey the invisible hand – and if the inferior people, the little people, the chimpanzees, white or black, starved – then they had called it down on themselves and Nature was now taking them away, as it was bound to. Economics, once a branch of moral philosophy, had become the new theology for money power.

As I have said, economists had constructed a set of arguments that took attention away from the propertied elite. Many economists would have been well aware that prices and the allocation of resources depends on the prior allocation of rights to the different factors of production – but so what? This insight could be consigned to the small print of economics, not the up-front centre of attention. By a process of enclosure, a land market and a labour market were created simultaneously, since people who could no longer draw from the resources of the commons to support themselves had to sell their ability to work on a labour market. But the duress involved in the enclosures, of being forced to work on the terms of the employers, was not something to theorise about. To give deep consideration to issues of justice and duress would have been to stand in the way of improvement and progress. It would be, in the words of Nietzsche, to embark on a path to nothingness. By attacking the poor law for the support of destitute people, and by the expropriation involved in enclosures, the elite ensured that the poor worked on terms that could be dictated by their employers. The path to improvement on the improved lands and through increasing specialisation in the industrial factories was held open. As land and labour became market commodities this could only be regarded as "progress", because it was a process of completing the creation of a market society which professors of moral philosophy sanctified.

However, neither land nor labour are originally "produced" with the explicit purpose of becoming commodities. There is no sense in which they are "natural commodities" as Polanyi, who documented these processes, pointed out. Land is part of the living natural system of the biosphere and "labour" is the lives of people who have been forced to work on terms dictated by the people who own the land and other resources.

In the ideology of the market, the important idea was that the market produces according to the wishes of the society – but it is true only when those wishes are backed with purchasing power. Here is a theory of what gets produced with available resources – a theory of allocation. The issue of how purchasing power came to be distributed, reflecting the power relationships in the economic and property system, is different by the end of the 19th century. The economists produced more apologetic ideas on this theme when their rich patrons came under political pressure. It is not, however, a theme to which most economists pay any deep attention. Distribution has been a question that could be mostly ignored because, eventually, with technical progress, everyone would be rich. As we have seen, the original roots of the property system, globally and nationally, lie in power, violence and theft. But a theft justified by the chrematistic religion of economics as "improvement" from which everyone would benefit from... eventually... if they survived.

Chapter 5

Specialisation and trade – David Ricardo versus Frederich List

What Schumpeter called the "Ricardian Vice" was a mode of reasoning in which the required conclusions are buried in the assumptions of an argument. The free trade argument of David Ricardo are described in these terms and unpicked. The ideas of the German-American economist Frederich List challenged Ricardo's view.

Initially technical improvement was seen as being rooted in increased specialisation. The famous example from Adam Smith was that of a pin factory. The production process was broken down into a succession of clearly defined modular steps: the wire was cut, the ends were sharpened, the head stamped, the head was soldered onto the pin.

Later economists like David Ricardo took the idea of specialisation and refined it into a theory of why free trade would supposedly improve everyone's welfare because it led to specialisation between countries.

Economics was now more than a theory about the local butcher, baker and brewer. Economics was advancing a market agenda for international economic relationships. The idea of the division of labour, the specialisation of people's work, is carried over into a specialisation of countries, of places.

The implications of spatial specialisation are considered later, for now let us notice that the Ricardian agenda favoured holding open the market for British manufactures, to be sold in exchange for cheaper imports, particularly grain imports, so as to keep down the price of food. Thus, it was also about making possible a cheaper price of labour. Naturally this was going to be in everyone's interest...

> Under a system of perfectly free commerce, each country naturally devotes its capital and labour to such employments as are most beneficial to each. This pursuit of individual advantage is admirably connected with the universal good of the whole. By stimulating industry, by regarding ingenuity, and by using most efficaciously the peculiar powers bestowed by nature, it distributes labour most effectively and most economically: while, by increasing the general mass of productions, it diffuses general benefit, and binds together by one common tie of interest and intercourse, the universal society of nations throughout the civilized world. It is this principle which determines that wine shall be made in France and Portugal, that corn shall be grown in America and Poland, and that hardware and other goods shall be manufactured in England.
> (Ricardo, 1819)

Ricardo gives a hypothetical example of England and Portugal who start out both producing cloth and wine. A situation in which Portugal's costs in labour inputs are lower for the production of both products compared to the situation in England, but most favourable in the production of wine. He then deduces that they would both gain from specialisation – England in cloth production, Portugal in wine production, followed by trade. Later, in a footnote to his text, he gives another, much shorter, example to make the same point, though not from foreign trade:

> Two men can both make shoes and hats, and one is superior to the other in both employments; but in making hats, he can only exceed his competitor by one-fifth or 20 per cent, and in making shoes he can excel him by one-third or 33 per cent;—will it not be for the interest of both, that the superior man should employ himself exclusively in making shoes, and the inferior man in making hats?

To this day most US and British economists are still enthusiasts for Ricardo's argument of "comparative advantage". As Paul Krugman put it in 1987: "If there were an economists' creed it would surely contain the affirmations 'I believe in the Principle of Comparative Advantage' and 'I believe in Free Trade'".

Yet not all economists have been true believers and with good reason. From as early as 1790 Andrew Hamilton in the United States counterpoised the "infant industry" argument which pointed out that newly developing industries have higher costs until they gain "economies of scale" and thus, need protection. Indeed from 1816 to 1945 the tariffs protecting US industry were some of the highest in the world – and then the US saw the light. (Chang, 2002)

The argument was picked up by others including a German born economist who migrated to America, Frederich List. For List, the calls for free trade from Britain were insincere, as indeed they were, and as US and European trade policy are today:

> Any nation which by means of protective duties and restrictions on navigation has raised her manufacturing power and her navigation to such a degree of development that no other nation can sustain free competition with her, can do nothing wiser than to throw away these ladders of her greatness, to preach to other nations the benefits of free trade, and to declare in penitent tones that she has hitherto wandered in the paths of error, and has now for the first time succeeded in discovering the truth. Quoted in (Wikipedia, Frederich List, 2013)

The Ricardian Vice - constructing arguments with required conclusions already buried in the premises

The method used by Ricardo is also interesting, for it is used repeatedly in a particular style of economics and was termed, by another economist, Joseph Schumpeter, as "the Ricardian vice". A set of isolated assumptions is made that give the required deduced results. The conclusions are already contained in the assumptions. More on this practice is discussed in chapter eight. For now, let me quote two ecological economists, Daly and Farley who write that "Within the world of its assumptions the logic of comparative advantage is unassailable." (Daly & Farley, 2004, p. 312)

However, let us now follow Daly and Farley in examining those assumptions to see what is left out of the picture – and add a few more points into the bargain.

Firstly, as already pointed out, it is an exercise in comparative statics. The infant industry argument is a dynamic one in which industries develop the capacity to look after themselves later in their development, rather as children do.

Secondly, Ricardo only mentions labour costs. The theory can be adapted to capital and labour costs but very typically "natural capital costs" are not taken into account. All production involves an energy input and, since the industrial revolution, has typically involved a fossil fuel input, with increasing greenhouse gas emissions. Where are the depletion costs for fuel or the cost of climate change in the model?

Thirdly, there are transport costs. To be fair to Ricardo, he did acknowledge these but in the case of heavy and bulk goods they could be considerable. To this, from a modern perspective we must add the emissions and the environmental costs from increasing transport.

Fourthly, in order for Portugal to specialise in wine and England in cloth, it not only meant an international "division of labour" it meant an international "division of land" – specialised land use. But specialised land use involves total transformation of eco-systems, radical reduction of bio-diversity and the destruction of natural processes. This is obvious when it comes to the creation of urban industrial landscapes that displace the countryside, for example, centres for cloth production. But wine making and viniculture is a monoculture too. Left to itself, nature evolves into diverse plant and animal communities, guilds of species appropriate to places. Nature is multi-functional and diverse when it is healthy. In and of itself the loss of the experience of living in conditions of biodiversity represents a reduction in the quality of life and experience. That's why towns have parks, gardens and other green spaces. It is why rental values are higher when there are trees in a street and why property values are higher in New York around Central Park. Above and beyond the welfare dimensions of biophilia, there are more fundamental issues of specialised land use (Monocultures). There are limits for the pushing of the international division of labour because, beyond a certain point, the generalised reduction in biodiversity threatens to destabilise the entire planet. No doubt Ricardo could not have foreseen so far into the future but at the beginning of the 21st century the issues look different. Scientists are warning that, on a global scale, there is a danger of an ecological tipping point when biodiversity loss goes so far as to produce a change of phase state.

Fifthly, Ricardo ignored the costs of transition to the more specialised economy. Economists typically celebrate specialisation by comparative static models but ignore the costs, inconveniences and disruptions to the lives of people as they adjust - in this case, from being cloth makers to wine makers or vice versa. What is missing here is the idea that, even if the more specialised state with trade is superior in some way to the less specialised state, the costs of the transition from one state to the other might exceed the gains once in that new state.

Sixthly, once an economy has developed a specialisation, it is costly and difficult to reverse this situation. Specialisation renders some countries vulnerable if the terms under which they export their specialised products in exchange for their imports moves against them. Further, as Daly and Farley point out, countries are likely to be especially vulnerable if they import essentials in exchange for exporting less essential goods. Their bargaining power will be less, particularly if they only export one or just a few products. The more that they are specialised the less bargaining power they have. It should also be pointed out that Ricardo wrote in a period of expanding colonialism which was hardly conducive to favourable terms of trade for the subordinated countries.

Seventhly, Ricardo explicitly assumed that, while goods are mobile and can be traded between countries, capital and labour does not move between countries. This is what Ricardo said:

> Experience, however, shews, that the fancied or real insecurity of capital, when not under the immediate control of its owner, together with the natural disinclination which every man has to quit the country of his birth and connexions, and intrust himself with all his habits fixed, to a strange government and new laws, check the emigration of capital. These feelings, which I should be sorry to see weakened, induce most men of property to be satisfied with a low rate of profits in their own country, rather than seek a more advantageous employment for their wealth in foreign nations.

Writing at the end of the Napoleonic Wars towards the beginning of the 19th century, this made sense as a description of the state of affairs given the relations between many countries. Although the capital and labour flight from Ireland to England when tariffs were brought down in Ireland in the early 19th century was a very real phenomenon.

Times change – capital immobility is a ridiculous assumption in the modern world

Nowadays however, a capital immobility assumption does not make any sense since capital can move around the world at the speed of light. The implications are considerable. In the cloth and wine example, if capital can move then, if there are conditions where costs are lower (and profits higher) for **both** products in one country, capital will move to that country and invest in both sectors. It will abandon the country with the higher costs as a production location altogether. (Daly & Farley, 2004, p. 316)

To sum up, Ricardo was claiming that free trade linked to "the principle of comparative advantage" was another example where the "pursuit of individual advantage is admirably connected with the universal good of the whole". It was put forward as a universal truth of trade theory – another example of what specialisation could achieve.

Yet the argument was deployed in a highly particular set of circumstances and served the interests of the emerging industrial employing class. It was aimed at opening up markets for them and aimed to facilitate cheaper wages (because of cheaper food costs for their workers if food was imported from cheaper sources abroad). Behind the discussion about cloth and wine, or shoes and hats, the real idea was that Britain should produce and export manufactures from their factories to countries who were supposed to specialise in producing and returning cheaper foodstuffs and raw materials in a system of "imperial preference".

To pursue that agenda, the protection of agriculture by import tariffs, the so-called Corn Laws, had to go. Less than 20 years after the publication of Ricardo's book the industrial employers had won their argument and the Corn Laws were repealed. Food prices fell and so did land rents. The industrial employers were able to develop industry under cheaper conditions at the expense of owners of rural land.

Different theories for different times and different places

In other countries, in other conditions, the issues looked different. The argument for tariffs prevailed in the USA. The argument for tariffs was also won in European countries like newly united Germany, as well as in Japan. In these places economic theories guided an elite who were configured differently. For example, in Germany and Japan there were different kinds of relationship between the landowning and military elite and the state. The elite sponsored top-down industrialisation processes, hastened on in order to ensure that their countries kept their independence in the face of what was perceived as the threat of the newly industrialising power of Britain and its empire. In these countries political economy looked different.

For example, Frederich List insisted on the special requirements of each nation according to its circumstances and what he took to be its degree of development. He counterposed a "national system of political economy" to the individualistic notions of Adam Smith. Whereas Smith saw the market bringing about best outcomes from individual actors pursuing their individual interests while the state stayed out of things as far as possible, List saw the role of the state as promoting the welfare of its citizens. To be sure, over-regulation would harm, but there were occasions where pursuing the interests of the individual did not correspond to general well-being and the state had a duty to step in.

As the state played such a crucial role for List, it is not surprising that he thought that statesmen should take a long term view. Statesmen had two responsibilities – one to current generations and the other to future generations. Towards the end of the 20th century, there was an idea that politicians should formulate policies that take into account the needs of future generations. This is described with the word "sustainability" and it has become, in the PR spin at least, a theme of policy. It was already there in Frederich List over a hundred years earlier. That being said, the sustainability idea has been around for a long time. Even List did not invent it. Many indigenous peoples all over the world have a view for land care that takes into account effects up to 7 generations ahead.

The writings of List were eventually published in English translation but the theory went in a more individualistic direction. The rational individual pursuing self-love and self-interest was used to explain how people made their choices in the market and life in general. The explanatory framework that evolved was partly derived from the utilitarian philosophy espoused by Jeremy Bentham.

Chapter 6

The Calculation of Pleasure and Pain

Micro-economics has a philosophical foundation – preference utilitarianism. Jeremy Bentham's clunky one dimensional understanding of human beings and human society still underpins the thinking of economists. (TEXT BOX: Jeremy Bentham's Rational Punishment)

Whereas Aristotle had an ethics based on developing one's virtues as a person, and the church an ethics based on explicit and written codes of principles and duties, the utilitarians had an ethics based on consequences. This **consequentialist** view is grounded in the idea that what matters are outcomes – and in "utilitarian consequentialism" the outcomes are subjective states of pleasure or pain (utility or disutility) that arise as a result of actions.

The idea of "utility" was used in scholastic and early economics but to the earlier thinkers the utility of an object, its use value, meant its fitness for its intended purpose. Now utility was given a different meaning - the ability of an object or service to create a sense of subjective happiness or satisfaction (or in regard to disutility, to dissatisfaction). If people adopt this criteria for their actions then an optimal decision is that which gives rise to the greatest happiness for the greatest number of people. Jeremy Bentham tried to develop this idea as far as he could. He wrote about the "dimensions" and rankings of utility according to its intensity, duration and certainty. He coined new words like "maximize" and "minimize" for pleasure and pain. (Orrell & VanLoon, 2011, pp. 67-69) (Backhouse, 2002, p. 136)

This way of thinking about how humans act has come to provide the underpinnings for economic theorising. For example, students will be told about utility theory supposedly to enable them to understand how people will decide when it comes to allocating their consumption expenditure. The idea is that consumers will choose that combination of goods and services whose purchase gives them the maximum utility or satisfaction for a given amount of available purchasing power.

This is a little bit of a simplification because, in many circumstances, people make choices in advance of outcomes without complete certainty about what will happen. When you buy a house, for example, you cannot exactly know what it will be like to live there. You may discover too late that your neighbours are noisy and aggressive. Decisions are taken on the basis of **expected** utilities. Theorising these decisions entailed building in a calculation of the probability that one's expectations will be fulfilled.

At first however, there appeared to be a major weakness in the Bentham approach. He did not have an answer to the question "how is it possible to measure utility or disutility?" This was thought necessary to make possible aggregations when many people were involved, and comparisons between people. The whole approach assumed that "rational decisions" involved **calculating** outcomes or consequences. It was a numerical approach and thus, "objective". Sure the human feeling was a part of the picture –

the utility or disutility, the pleasure or pain – was what it was based upon. But what mattered was the measurable amount of pleasure or pain. The greatest happiness for the greatest number implied some way of measuring and Bentham didn't have an answer as to how this was to be done.

Preference utilitarianism

Eventually, other economists came up with what appeared to them to be a solution. They argued that there were no absolute measures of utility but this did not matter because what people are prepared to pay is a proxy measure of the additional utility for the last unit of any good that they purchase. When they chose to purchase particular quantities of different goods, at different prices, people demonstrated in practice what their comparative utilities were as between those different goods. By "voting" with their money across a range of goods people "revealed their preferences". Thus, was born the key concepts of what is called "preference utilitarianism". A German economist called H.H. Gossen got to these ideas first, but was closely followed by William Stanley Jevons, Carl Menger and Leon Walras. A new orthodoxy was born.

The key assumption that people act to maximise their total utility was extrapolated from the Benthamite starting point. Money spent provided the numbers. To maximise utility, people make a mental calculation as to whether paying the price for an additional unit of each commodity will give them more or less additional utility than the marginal utility that they will get by spending that same amount of money on other goods.

Nearly two centuries later neoclassical economics is still based on preference utilitarianism. To economists, money spent appears to give a common measuring rod that can be used for all sorts of situations, including policy decisions about issues that do not normally appear in an ordinary market at all, for example, environmental decision-making.

Bentham's utilitarianism is also thought of as laying the foundations for what later became the economics of the consumer, and so-called "welfare economics". By giving a view of what motivated consumers when they decided how they allocated their purchasing power, to purchase some goods and services rather than others, Bentham helped developed the foundations for micro-economic theory still in the textbooks. (And still wrong).

Money payment as a proxy measure for well-being is also thought of as a convenient idea because many situations can involve losers as well as winners. When there are mixed winner–loser situations what does one do? How does one *calculate* the best course of action? What people are prepared to pay, or accept in payment, can be seen as providing a means of solving the dilemma. A mixed winner-loser situation can supposedly be solved by cash compensation.

A compensation test where you might not get compensated

If an action involves increased welfare for one person while decreasing welfare for someone else, it still might involve greater happiness overall. One can tell that is so if the gainer can compensate the loser with cash and still be better off. This is the so-called Kaldor-Hicks principle named after the two economists who dreamed it up. Take note here that to Kaldor and Hicks the winner does not actually have to compensate the loser, they merely have to be able to do so in theory. The point is that the increase in utility of the winner is greater than the decrease in the utility for the loser. So, from the point of view of aggregate utility, "society is better off". That's how a typical economist thinks about the situation anyway. Losses and gains can simply be put together to find out best outcomes for society as a whole – and tough if you're a loser. (Wkipedia, 2013)

Text Box: Jeremy Bentham's "Rationale Punishment"

Bentham was interested in developing conceptual tools, not just for economic life, but for the criminal justice system and the exercise of social control. Deviance was to be deterred by applying "rationally calculated punishment" in state institutions of various kinds such as large centralised prisons, schools, lunatic asylums and poor houses. Bentham advocated prison designs that made prisoners aware that they were under constant observation by unseen observers. The idea was that they would internalise self-control to do what the authorities wanted of them.

Parallel ideas were perceived as useful for the administration of labour discipline and the changing support arrangements for elderly and infirm people. In earlier societies, people living as part of communities and participating in the use and management of the commons had a precarious alternative means of supporting themselves. In their old age and infirmity they could also turn to the church for support. But the church was expropriated by the monarch in Britain, the monasteries sold to his courtiers, to fund the expenses of war. The land enclosures denied the poor access to the commons forcing them to do paid labour. This, in turn, gave rise to different dynamics of labour discipline. Then there was the question of how to support those people too ill or infirm to work, as well as what to do in times of dearth and famine. The elite agonised about not setting precedents for supporting people. They still do.

Many of Bentham's ideas were taken up in this context by the employers and state. They are still part of the mentality of those who govern us. At the time of writing, the "reform of welfare rights" in Britain focuses on punishing claimants into work, no matter how ill or disabled they are. One has only to think of the number of disabled people in Britain who have killed themselves after dealing with the government's sponsored agency ATOS, which purports to assess their fitness for work (Crampton, 2012). The assumption is that people do not want to work. A partially self-fulfilling prophecy given work's oppressive nature for the underclass.

Another Benthamite idea currently in use, in a digital and electronic form, is that of self-control and conformity imposed by the threat, or reality of being continually observed. In the UK and elsewhere there is a pervasive use of CCTV in public and work places. Then there is the use of electronic monitoring to keep employees in line, such as, monitoring computer use, emails and mobile tracking techniques. Above and beyond the aspiration of our betters to have total internet surveillance which may also be intended, not only to identify potential terrorist plotters, but to intimidate absolutely everyone with the idea that everything they do that passes through the internet is being processed by algorithmic analysis for what out betters think is suspicious.

Today, Bentham's influence is still felt in common understandings, transmitted in neoclassical economic theory, which involves conceptually framing what "rationality" consists of. When their power is anchored in the very way we order our thinking it is all the more powerful – even if Bentham and his followers may never have intended any such thing. The tacit acceptance of what "rationality" means is crucial to the power of ruling groups. "What is defined is the rationality of the advantaged, rich and powerful – the rationality of the disadvantaged poor and powerless is either denied or classified as deviant."(Pfohl, 1994, p. 96)

It goes without saying that Bentham would not have thought of it like that. He was another one of those 18th and 19th century men dedicated to "improvement". His social reform proposals were intended to move towards a "rationally organised society". But, as often happens, new ideas intended as "reforming improvement" get taken up and used by the ruling elite and in the process become a new and innovative way of beating up vulnerable people. This was clearly visible a few decades later as the elite wrestled with what support arrangements, if any, to make available during famines in Ireland and India.

This episode has already been described in an earlier chapter but it is worth mentioning that Bentham's ideas were influential when the imperial masters formulated their policy.

For example, in India in 1877 on the instructions of the Viceroy, Lord Lytton, the lieutenant governor of Bengal, Sir William Temple, was given the job of reducing the costs of famine relief. He did so with what he called a "Benthamite experiment".

Temple's brief from the Council of India was described thus,:

"The task of saving life irrespective of cost, is one which is beyond our power to undertake. The embarrassment of debt and weight of taxation consequent on the expense thereby involved would soon become more fatal than the famine itself."

With the idea that greater taxation and state debt is more fatal than starved Indians, Temple set out on his mission to cut the costs of relief work, which fed people in exchange for public works.

In a self-proclaimed Benthamite "experiment" that eerily prefigured later Nazi research on minimal human subsistence diets in concentration camps, Temple cut rations for male coolies, whom he compared to a "school full of refractory children", down to one pound of rice per diem despite medical testimony that the ryots – once "strapping fine fellows" – were now "little more than animate skeletons... utterly unfit for any work"... In the event, the "temple wage", as it became known, provided less sustenance for hard labour than the diet inside the infamous Buchenwald concentration camp and less than half the modern caloric standard recommended for adult males by the Indian government. (Davis, 2002, pp. 37-38)

Jeremy Bentham bequeathed his body to posterity and it is still on display in a glass case at the University College London.

Public Domain Image - http://commons.wikimedia.org/wiki/File:Jeremy_Bentham_Auto-Icon.jpg

Chapter 7

Isn't it time to bury Jeremy Bentham?
– Utilitarian theory deconstructed

Mainstream micro-economics works from a model where consumers are imagined choosing between just two commodities. The theory is unworkable in a multi-product world. The "prospect theory" of Daniel Kahneman and Amos Tversky is contrasted to utilitarian thinking. People are loss averse in an uncertain world. Kahneman's and Tversky's ideas open a can of worms for mainstream micro-economics.

One the oddest and most grotesque parts of London University is the glass case in which the preserved body of Jeremy Bentham is on display. It used to have a poorly mummified head at his feet but there were too many student pranks with that so it was removed. Perhaps it is time to bury it now. It is certainly time to bury his theories which provided the foundation for a lot of misleading economic and social thinking.

His nineteenth century theory of utility and marginal utility is still what is presented in the textbooks for each generation of new economic students. It is still used to explain how people allocate their purchasing power between different consumer goods and services. Psychology and psychotherapy theory to explain human actions has moved on a lot since the 19th century but a lot of economists are still struggling to get into the 20th century, let alone the 21st.

For starters, all the textbook presentations of consumer theory simplify by assuming a world where a single consumer is choosing between two goods. There is nothing wrong with simplifying per se but you have to be careful that, if you drop the simplification, the theory will remain intact.

A theory that collapses in a multiple product world

Unfortunately, moving from a model based on choices in a two commodity world to a model based on choices in a multiple commodity world leaves the theory in distress. Most economics teachers, and most of their students, don't realise this because they don't think through the implications.

Steve Keen explains the problem in his anti-textbook *"Debunking Economics"*. Let us say, for example, that there are 8 quantities that can be purchased for 8 different goods. Thus, one might buy one item of one good and no other items of any other goods at all, two items of the same good and no others at all and so on up to 8 items of the same good and none at all of any other good. Applying the same logic to each of the 8 different kinds of goods would mean that there are 64 shopping trolleys with varying amounts of one good. Then a consumer might choose to have one item of one kind of good and one or another good and no others. And so on with all the different types of possible combinations. Eventually this would make for the number of potential shopping trolley combinations which is 8^8 different combinations. (8 x 8 x 8 x 8 x 8 x 8 x 8 x 8 combinations) (Keen, 2011, p. 71)

Or again, if we think of a supermarket as having just one hundred different product groups and we limit a decision to whether to buy one item from each group or not then there are 2^{100} options – over 1,000 million trillion trillion shopping trolleys. Clearly no one calculates their choice for maximum utility – life is too short.

Keen points out what most people do in real life:

> ... use a range of commonplace heuristics to reduce the overwhelming array of choices you face to something manageable that you can complete in less than an hour. You partition your choices into a few basic groups, rather than looking at every separate product, and within each group you use habit to guide your purchases... Truly rational behaviour is therefore not choosing the best option, but reducing the number of options you consider so that you can make a satisfactory decision in finite time. (Keen, 2011, p. 72)

Leaving aside that there are plenty of situations in life where it is quite impossible to calculate the probability of expected outcomes, there are other important problems with the marginal utility theory. More criticisms will be explored later, for now, let me explain the alternative ideas of Daniel Kahneman and Amos Tversky called "prospect theory". (Kahneman, 2011, pp. 269-374)

Prospect Theory – loss averse decisions in an uncertain world

Kahneman and Tversky explained that utility theory focuses on static situations, rather than on changes. But decision-making is about change. In the orthodox account we have preferences of different strengths for different quantities of specific goods and the more of a specific good that we possess the less the additional satisfaction another unit will bring us (Declining marginal utility). In the mainstream account, if we get an extra unit, there will be extra satisfaction. However, if we lose that extra unit, the same amount of satisfaction will be forfeited so that we would return to the previous level of total satisfaction.

Let's imagine we could measure utility in units called "utils" just to get the point over. A made up illustration of the orthodox account might go something like this. We have 10 tasty widgets and they give us a total of 20 utils satisfaction. Now let us assume that we get another widget so we have 11 and this situation now gives us a total of 21 utils satisfaction. The marginal utility of the last unit is 1 util – in more ordinary language the additional satisfaction from the last widget is one extra util. In the orthodox account, if we were now to lose that last widget, and went back to 10 widgets, then we would go back to 20 utils total satisfaction, losing one util.

That's the theory anyway – but Kahneman and Tversky showed that it is not true. We don't return to the same level of satisfaction because losses weigh more than gains.

So, to use our example, it is as if, when the change upwards was from 10 to 11 widgets, we went up from 20 to 21 utils. But when we change down, from 11 to 10 utils, we might go down to 19 utils.

Empirical research shows that most people are loss averse. Our losses are evaluated against psychological reference points. To lose what we have gained is painful in its own right. Gains are evaluated against reference points – but differently. When evaluating a choice which involves an uncertain future outcome, an outcome that which might involve either a loss or a gain, losses loom larger than gains.

The implication is that people tend to behave in loss-averse ways. However, Kahneman and Tversky showed that in circumstances where all future outcomes look as if they are likely to turn out badly, people become prepared to take risks. Where all future outcomes look potentially bad, there is a tendency to make gambles in which the gambler might conceivably reduce the scale of losses. As Kahneman says, this risk seeking behaviour "... is often observed in entrepreneurs and in generals when all their options are bad". (Kahneman, 2011, p. 276)

It can be observed in the very poor too, which is probably why betting shops are common in poor districts and people risk what little they have against the chance that they might just be a winner. (Or take other risks like turning to crime or what others, like social workers and psychiatrists, see as erratic and reckless behaviour).

There is a reason for the behaviour pattern. According to Kahneman, "Organisms that treat threats as more urgent that opportunities have a better chance to survive and reproduce." (Kahneman, 2011, p. 282)

*(Footnote) Prospect theory has its weaknesses too – as Kahneman acknowledges in his book "Thinking Fast and Slow". For example, it fails to account for emotions like disappointment and regret which may also motivate us in different ways. For example say you are offered a 90% chance of winning £1million or are offered £150,000 with certainty. Now assume that you do not win the £1million and so you don't pocket the £150,000 either. There would be the subjective experience of disappointment at not winning the £1 million **and** regret at not having chosen the £150,000 option. Is there not a possibility therefore that decisions will be taken on the basis of anticipation of possibly experiencing these emotions?*

The point about these theories is that they bring us closer to real life than marginal utility theory. They describe a world where decisions have uncertain, and possibly adverse outcomes. In prospect theory "the reference point" is important because it is what enables us humans to find our balance through adaptation to changes. This reference point is an "adaptation level". As Kahneman argues:

> You can easily set up a compelling demonstration of this principle. Place three bowls of water in front of you. Put ice water into the left hand bowl and warm water into the right hand bowl. The

water in the middle bowl should be at room temperature. Immerse your hands in the cold and the warm water for about a minute, then dip both in the middle bowl. You will experience the same temperature as heat in one hand and as cold in the other. For financial outcomes, the usual reference point is the status quo, but it can also be the outcome that you expect, or perhaps the outcome to which you feel entitled, for example, the raise or bonus that your colleagues receive. Outcomes that are better than the reference point are gains. Below the reference point are losses. (Kahneman, 2011, p. 282)

For all its superiority to the mainstream theory, Prospect Theory is not what is taught in many of the introductory textbooks as Kahneman notes in his book, *Thinking, Fast and Slow*. However, he ingratiates himself to the mainstream by conceding:

> There are good reasons for keeping prospect theory out of introductory texts. The basic concepts of economics are essentially intellectual tools, which are not easy to grasp even with simplified and unrealistic assumptions about the nature of economic agents who interact in markets. Raising questions about these assumptions even as they are introduced would be confusing and perhaps demoralising. It is reasonable to put priority to helping students acquire the basic tools of the discipline. Furthermore, the failure of rationality that is built into prospect theory is often irrelevant to the predictions of economic theory, which work with great precision in some situations and provide good approximations in many others. (Kahneman, 2011, pp. 286-287)

Kahneman cops out on his own theory

This is an extraordinary cop out. The idea is that students of economics might be demoralised to find that what they are being taught is inaccurate is just not true. Other students might find that what is otherwise a deadly dull subject is suddenly much more interesting. The way that I see it, if they are NOT taught the challenges to the neoclassical mainstream, when these challenges are coherent and credible, students have every right to feel cheated and to be angry. That, after all, is why I have gone to the trouble of writing this book.

In fact, *only* being taught mainstream neoclassical approaches when there are challenges to the orthodoxy out there has been the cause of student petitions and walk outs. In Paris in 2000, economics students of the Ecole Normal Superieure (ENS) launched a Post Autistic Economics through a petition signed by hundreds of students demanding reform within the teaching of economics. Students at Cambridge University and then at Oxford followed suit. More recently, at the time of the Occupy Movement against the corruption of Wall Street some economics students in Harvard in the USA walked out of a lecture by textbook writer Gregory Mankiw. More recently there have been other protests at Manchester University at the limited nature of the economics curriculum. The protests are because students are **not** being taught a range of perspectives.

In this connection, prospect theory is no more complicated or difficult to understand than marginal utility theory. Kahneman's book *Thinking Fast and Slow*, is easier to read than mainstream textbooks that many suspect have been deliberately mathematised in order to take economics beyond the reach of a general readership.

To describe the predictions of economic theory as working with "great precision" or as "reasonable approximations" is also extraordinary. Many studies have shown that economic forecasts are next to useless. The failure of the bulk of the economics profession to predict the crash of 2007 is exactly what one would expect. Worse, Kahneman appears to imply that prospect theory shows people failing to act rationally. He cedes the definition of rationality to the mainstream economics definition that he has demolished.

Kahneman's book *Thinking Fast and Slow* is a tremendous compendium of the way in which peoples' thinking can be in error. Yet the loss averse behaviours that underpin prospect theory (or the risk seeking behaviour in adversity) have a clear logic to them. So why are they judged to be "failures of rationality"? I have already quoted the point in the text where Kahneman himself argues that "Organisms that treat threats as more urgent that opportunities have a better chance to survive and reproduce". Is this not an implicit claim to a kind of rationality? It is very much the kind of rationality that humanity needs to cope with a variety of pressing environmental problems...

A can of worms for neoclassical economic theory

What is certainly true is that if we adopt a theory that focuses on how changes affect people then many of the claims made in economic theory about welfare collapse. This is because we would start to look at the cost and benefits not only from the point of view of two compared static states but, instead, as the costs and benefits, gains and losses, in the transition from one state to another.

If we start to acknowledge the greater weight that people give to losses, the negative changes forced on people, more than the gains, where would that end? For example, that romantic and exciting idea of "creative destruction" from economist Joseph Schumpeter sounds reassuringly Darwinian - tough but fair. However, once you let in an idea that losses weigh more heavily than gains then that creative destruction looks different. It becomes creative DESTRUCTION and the logic of the market starts to look cruel.

In his book *Economics as a Religion* Robert Nelson remarks on transitional costs thus,:

> For example, in considering the economic burdens of transitions from one state of economic equilibrium to another, a valid cost of dynamic adjustment for a current economist would include such things as the expense of hiring moving vans for furniture and other household items. The process of economic transition means that some workers have to move their place of residence from one city to another to find a new job. These represent real commitments of social resources. An invalid cost – or at least a cost that economists of Samuelson's time, or of today, almost never incorporate into their economic thinking – would be "psychic pain" experienced by that same worker in the process of making the move. The worker might feel deep grief in

having to leave a familiar community behind; in having to move away from family and friends; or in having to leave a home where he or she has grown up. Or the worker may simply feel a deep anxiety in facing the uncertain prospects of a brand new job and other surroundings. Economics automatically exclude these and many other types of costs from their analyses. (Nelson R. H., 2001, p. 66)

If economists were to champion Prospect Theory they would be opening up a can of worms. Feelings arising in situations of loss, as situations change, that economists had previously not recognised as costs, would now have to be considered as valid costs after all.

It is this situation that would have to change if prospect theory is taken seriously:

> … the normal exclusion by economists of feelings of psychic transitional loss or gain – and many other such 'soft" considerations – thus, really represents a fundamental value choice made by members of the economics profession. It reflects a belief, not that these costs do not exist, or do not affect the perceptions of well-being of many people (economists are not that unaware), but that these particular costs should not be – do not deserve to be – counted. In deciding to incorporate some costs into their thinking while excluding others, economists have quietly and with little explicit recognition introduced a powerful set of value distinctions. (Nelson R. H., 2001, p. 69)

Reference points and comfort zones

As Maslow suggested, people strive for security as one of their primary motivations. In order to achieve security they have to hold their lives in balance – income, habitat arrangements, relationships, work and health must match each other. They must strive to prevent these arrangements slipping into unmanageability – unaffordable habitat arrangements, relationships that cannot be synchronised with work times and so on. People are not solely motivated by a desire to have more, they are also motivated to varying degrees by a desire for security.

A way of thinking about "reference points" is that they help in the management of risk taking when dealing with life practicalities. They are used in multiple dimensions of existence in order to make life non-chaotic. Reference points mark the edge of "comfort zones" and people venture beyond them with reluctance. In order to be secure, people need to establish and then maintain familiar and therefore manageable patterns. Patterns involving emotional and work relationships; a daily routine in a habitat to which they are accustomed; a set of work and other routines; tasks within their abilities and help from others where necessary tasks are beyond their ability and available time. In a world full of uncertainties it makes sense to seek a stable pattern in one's movements and activities around familiar places and spaces. In this respect, the "creative destruction" of capitalism in its creative dimension may certainly open up possibilities for new opportunities and gains. However, in its destructive dimension, like the loss of jobs, it is constantly generating psychic insecurity and oftentimes loss, as people lose access to familiar arrangements and resources with which they have learned to cope.

Chapter 8

Economists as priesthood – a religion based on assumptions

Some of the ridiculous assumptions on which much of mainstream economics is constructed are explored in this chapter – for example the methodology that stresses individual decision-making, the assumption that decision-makers have the information that they need, the assumption of honesty, the default assumption of competition. (TEXT BOX Labour market competition as an alternative to corporal punishment according to Hayek).

Today's leading economic textbook writer, Greg Mankiw, has compared non-economists to "mere Muggles", the ordinary people without magical powers described in the Harry Potter novels. His implication is that economists are "wizards". (Mankiw, 2008)

Perhaps they are. However, people with magical abilities are not always to be trusted.

The Conjuror - school of Hieronymous Bosch c1550 Public Domain Image Wikimedia commons

The ideas of the economists are important because they frame the way we understand the world, sometimes distracting us from understanding and living in the world in other ways. The economists claim that they describe the world as it is, rather than describing it as it should be, but there is an entire value system implicit in economics. It is implicit in their definition of what it is to be "rational". Implicitly, economists are making a truth claim about how human beings are, what makes them tick.

Unaware of the criticism of their model of rationality (or ignoring the criticism) it seems reasonable to economists to theorise human beings as if they act in a predictable way. Calculating their individual self-interest to maximise their utility and then acting accordingly. This makes possible a deterministic view of human action that allows economists to model markets as fundamentally positive social institutions which can solve virtually all problems.

In actual fact, economists are there as advocates for a particular kind of value system. They are not unlike priests whose job it is to argue that their beliefs should be guiding principles for life.

Some economists are well aware of this. Robert Nelson describes debates about economics as having a "theological character". He worked as an economist in the US Department of the Interior with responsibility for the upkeep of national parks and landscapes in the USA:

> If economists had any influence—which they sometimes did, if rarely decisive—it was seldom as literal "problem solvers". Rather, the greatest influence of economists came through their defence of a set of values. Much of my own and other efforts of Interior (Ministry) economists were really to persuade others in the department to act in accordance with the economic value system, as compared with other competing priorities and sets of values also represented within the ranks of the department. (Nelson R. H., 2001, p. xiv)

Ridiculous assumptions

In other sciences ideas evolve by testing hypotheses against the facts. In economics what mostly happens is that simple models are created which have this kind of form:

Assuming human beings behave in a particular kind of way e.g. as consumers seeking to maximise their level of satisfaction through purchasing.

And assuming their behaviour takes place in a particular set of conditions e.g. they are fully aware of all their consumption options available with their purchasing power

Then faced with a particular change in conditions it is possible to state how they will adapt, as well as to quantify this adaptation e.g. faced with a price change they will change how much that they buy by so much

This appears to be an exercise in logic rather like this - All men are mortal, Socrates is a man, therefore Socrates is mortal. The premises of this argument are things asserted to be true which in this case are that "all men are mortal" and that "Socrates is a man". The conclusion that follows automatically is that Socrates is mortal. This conclusion does not really add any new information to the premises that have been proposed, it only draws out the consequence. In a sense, the conclusion is already contained in the premises.

In an apparently similar way the conclusions of economics follow from the starting points of their modelling analyses. However, the starting points of economic models are not premises asserted to be true but assumptions. These assumptions do not have a truth value status based on evidence but, on first impressions, appear to be plausible. (Bardsley, Cubitt, Loomes, Moffat, Starmer, & Sugden, 2010, p. Chtp5)

If many people do not realise that this is a fraud, it is partly because the mathematics, the symbols and the diagrams with which the models are expressed enable economists to distance themselves from ordinary people. Rather in the manner that speaking Latin enabled priests to put themselves above the common people.

Consider this proposition:

If Socrates is assumed to be a woman, and if all women are assumed to live forever, then it can be assumed that Socrates will be immortal.

It is obvious what is wrong with this proposition. Nevertheless, the falsity of economic propositions are not always so obvious. This is partly because some the assumptions have a superficial plausibility and sometimes because the assumptions remain implicit, unstated and unexamined. The most important point here, however, is that there is no evidence for these assumptions. Read any economic textbook and you will find it rich in numerical examples that were made up by the author. They are neither taken from real life nor based on evidence. This is an ideal basis for a self-serving ideology in which this kind of "logic" can prove anything that is wanted according to the starting assumptions. Economics like this is not falsifiable because evidence is implicitly deemed to be unnecessary in the first place.

If you assume no problems at the start of the theory you will conclude that the economic world works without problems. For example, if, as was the case for many years, you assume that there are no problems in getting the information that you need to take economic decisions, then all the uncertainties, the dishonesty, the misinterpretation and the errors that take place in the real world disappear from the theory. The conclusions of models that do not draw on real world evidence are only as accurate as the assumptions they start with - no more and no less. A good deal of textbook economics is a description of what economists assume the world is like.

Even worse, the construction of models based on assumptions enables the imagination of a world akin to the one that Dr Pangloss believes he lives in. He is the character in Voltaire's satire, Candide, who at every misfortune reassures everyone that all is for the best in the best of all possible worlds. Nothing will go wrong in the world of the mainstream economists because growth, technology, innovation, markets and entrepreneurial zeal together have the mechanisms for fixing all problems for ever. The message is perpetually upbeat and reassuring - which it can be when you construct a model of the world with assumptions that don't include the problems.

Thus, markets are "efficient" and welfare outcomes are "optimal" when the starting assumptions contain none of the real life issues that would make them otherwise. In order to arrive at these optimal and efficient outcomes what is needed above all is "competition". This is another very handy conclusion. It enables neoclassical economists to convince themselves and successive generations of students that, as long as the state minimises its involvement in markets, we live in this best of all possible worlds.

Competition is an idea which has many useful ideological functions. Instead of being a place of shambolic chaos, a competitive market is portrayed as having its own kind of order without a single big player – state or monopoly - needing to take all the decisions for overall coherence. With a set of assumptions that portrays this competitive market order as "optimal", here is an argument that can be used as a default presumption against co-operation; against state regulations; against taxation; against trade union combination in the labour market. Competition is an idea that stands for general "freedom" from interference for powerful economic actors, against any limitation on their rights to act – and therefore for a general understanding of what "freedom" means for everyone else in society too. It can be used by those who are the strongest to prevent support for weakest, and generally in a self-celebratory way praising "success" as the result of "efficiency".

But let's look at some of the most common assumptions that underpin the key idea.

Methodological Individualism

To take the first issue - in the textbooks, markets are places where there are lots of actors and, to get a collective picture of what happens, you simply add up the actions of all the separate individuals. Of course, this does not rule out the idea that the separate individuals have previously influenced each other, but that is not what is explored. This is a version of what is called "methodological individualism" and there is no place in it for applying the insights of group psycho-dynamics. This is not because methodological individualists necessarily deny that the "preferences" that form people's choices can be formed by social, interpersonal or community processes – it is rather because they take the "preferences" that give rise to choices as givens. They see themselves as modelling rational behaviour about what people will do with a pattern of preferences, a certain amount of purchasing power when faced with a set of prices. As economists, they are not concerned to delve further. In that sense, methodological individualism is a choice to ignore why people prefer and choose what they do. It is a choice to ignore and thus a choice to remain ignor-ant.

It is no wonder that, when criticising their teachers a few years ago, French economics students described neoclassical economics as "autistic". Autism is a psychiatric disorder where a person is unable to recognise other people as people, as acting subjects. The autistic person is thus, unable to form meaningful reciprocal relationships. Of course, in their private lives even neoclassical economists recognise that people act in groups in which they interact and have a reciprocal influence on each other – in families, in clubs, in associations, in societies, in crowds. A lot of what happens in markets is driven by crowd psychology. What is "fashion" if not a form of collective psychology? Arrangements made by producers try to influence and steer fashion processes which are only partly under their control.

When I go into supermarkets or department stores at the weekend it is full of families who are taking group decisions about purchasing. At other times, there are mothers who are taking decisions for partners and children. But that is not what most of the theories assume.

Ignoring ignorance – the myth of perfect information vs the thinking of the herd

Let's look at another assumption. It is only in the last few decades that a new approach of "information economics" has evolved out of the recognition that access to information is crucial to decisions and market outcomes. Many of the textbooks from which today's elite were taught assumed that markets had all the information that market actors needed. Indeed, some of the more elaborate models that "proved" the superiority of markets to allocate resources assumed that market actors had god like powers because they could make accurate assessments of the future too.

In fact the market is *almost always* shot through with a lack of information and/or information asymmetry. Perhaps in the world of Adam Smith's small town butcher, baker and brewer, people could pick up gossip about their suppliers and even know them personally. But how does information work in a global market? How does it work with products made out of hundreds of components made out of hundreds of materials supplied by global supply chains? How does this work with meat products in the freezers of supermarkets? People buy what they think are beef products and are dependent on public health authorities to discover that they have been eating horse meat.

A very powerful reason why people have so much influence on each other lies in the absence of information and the uncertainty in which many economic decisions are taken. When you don't know, you ask and/or you take your cues from other people.

Margaret Thatcher once famously said that "there is no such thing as society" which is one of those monumentally stupid things that powerful people can say and get away with because they are surrounded by sycophants. A very powerful person like Thatcher could doubt the existence of society because she had little need for the ideas and influence of other people as she would have known that she was always right. By contrast mere mortals are influenced by others because we live in a world of uncertainty and inadequate information. Allowing ourselves to be influenced by what others are doing and saying is a rough and ready way of coping with the information that we lack. Thus, we come to be influenced and swayed by social trends.

One cannot possibly understand the mentality of what are called "bubbles" in asset markets and speculation, except through collective psychology. Whether and how much of a commodity, or an asset, is purchased depends powerfully not just on current prices but on what people expect will happen to prices in the future. When they try to figure out what is likely to happen to future market valuations, perhaps the most powerful influence of all is what other people are saying and thinking. Anyone who reads a newspaper like the *Financial Times* will be struck by the way it is full of reports which convey to the readers what the "market sentiment" is, that is, what others think will happen.

Up to a point, movements in market sentiment are exercises in self-fulfilling prophecy. If a rise in price is taken to be indicative of an ongoing trend, which will lead to even higher prices later, then many traders will follow each other and be tempted to buy more now, before prices go higher. Possibly also to make money in the "rising market". Perhaps speculators imagine that they can sell what they buy now on a rising price for an even higher price later. We have already seen how speculation drove up rising grain prices in the famines of India, taking food out of the mouths of the poor even in areas of good harvests.

Honesty and Dishonesty

Other, sharper, market actors seek to play these movements in a devious fashion. This brings us to the third of our assumptions about why competitive markets deliver wonderful outcomes. It assumes that market players are honest when a lot are not. If people are only motivated by individualistically calculated self-interest why should they not resort to fraud and opportunism, to secrecy and misleading accounts of product quality?

This kind of duplicity affects what happens during speculative manias. For example, if you know that the shares of a company are going to lose value because you have insider information that a company or an industry is heading towards a big loss, if you have no commitment to the company or the industry, and if you no scruples, you will want to sell the shares at a high price before the truth gets out. So you might launch a PR campaign to hype the company or industry that you know is heading for a loss. That way you seek to create a rising market in order to offload your otherwise worthless shares on the people who get taken in. The game being played is to let other suckers take the losses.

That happened at the end of the subprime boom where bank traders sold what they referred to privately as "toxic waste" to unsuspecting customers as if these assets were of real value. A similar thing is happening at the time of writing in the gas fracking industry. All over the world, articles are appearing about the incredible potential for gas fracking. Meanwhile, industry insiders are pointing out the rapid depletion of the wells, the number of wells that come up dry and the high cost of drilling. If you believe the former narrative you put up money to enter the industry – and allow the insiders in the know to get out.

So here you have it. If we assume that most actors do not know what it going on and are able to influence each other, along with insiders who do have the best information acting as crooks trying to mislead and defraud other people, this gives us a far better fit for understanding what actually happens in markets. Instead, we have models which assume the reverse and this is what is taught to students.

Perfect competition

To be fair, neoclassical economists do get rather cross when businesses seek to accumulate monopoly power. This is paradoxical because competitive success leads to the weaker companies being driven out and/or taken over by the stronger ones thereby accumulating more monopoly power. Without competition the bracing Darwinist struggle between businesses does not deliver the benefits advertised in the textbooks, such as, cheaper products for all of us. For that reason some capitalist countries have "competition" policies and police against secret agreements between companies that "restrain trade" in favour of higher prices at the consumer's expense. However, a closer examination of some of these policies often reveals that the intended result is the opposite of the stated one. As already mentioned, the ideology of competition through free trade is intended to clear the field for those companies in those countries that are already in the globally dominant position. It is about preventing competition emerging in the first place and consolidating global dominance. Throughout economic history the ideology of competition has been used to open up markets to the strongest market players and enable them to accumulate further market power. These are the players who will be most influential in political lobbying in the corridors of power. These are the very private sector players who will be influential in university departments of economics.

Text Box– Labour Market Competition as an alternative to Corporal Punishment according to Hayek

Where neoclassical economists can be expected to get indignant if competition is limited is in the labour market. If workers form trade unions to create for themselves a countervailing power over and against their employer then economists are rarely sympathetic and almost always take the side of employers. Not many infants are born because their parents decided to do their bit to supply the future labour market. However, that does not excuse these infants, when they grow up, from their duty to compete in the labour market for work and take the going price. When there is full employment, this gives employees far too much "market power" for "optimality". As Hayek puts it in his book "The Road to Serfdom", without unemployment, managers lose their ability to discipline workers and take on or lay off workers according to their plans.

"... there should be a place from which workers can be drawn, and when a worker is fired he should vanish from the job and from the payroll. In the absence of a free reservoir discipline cannot be maintained without corporal punishment, as with slave labour." Quoted in (Smith & Max-Neef, 2011, p. 35)

Note the verb "should"... at the beginning of most textbooks there are usually little homilies that say economists describe the world as it is and not as it should be – but that's not for Hayek. The labour market needs an alternative for corporal punishment if the workers is to be managed as an input to be used and disposed of as required. Workers are a means to the ends of employers.

At the risk of going off on a tangent, I cannot help but wonder what Hayek would have said about this famous principle from the philosopher Kant:

> "Act in such a way that you treat humanity, whether in your own person or in the person of any other, never merely as a means to an end, but always at the same time as an end." (Kant & (Tr.)Ellington, 1993, p. 30)

I've already claimed that human relationships are not the strong point of economists – neoclassical or Austrian. Hayek's requirement for some kind of discipline derives as a self-fulfilling imperative from the mind-set of employers who use people merely as means, for example, as "factory hands". If you treat and regard people only as means to your end is it surprising that their commitment to those ends is less than enThus,iastic? Why should they feel committed? People do not take well to being used without consideration. It has a cost to their self-esteem, although, if one has no choice, if one is "disciplined" by unemployment, one may have to do it.

When you look at the world using economic concepts you are looking at the world as "snakes in suits" see it. They don't get this idea that "human resources" are actually people with feelings and emotions. They don't get the idea that most people are happy to co-operate with each other if they are treated with respect and their feelings acknowledged. This why they need alternatives to corporal punishment to maintain discipline and so they opt for unemployment to "create competition". (In Britain the snakes are then disconcerted when they get a group of people who become long term unemployed. Rather than resort to corporal punishment for this group they intend to resort to psychological torture – making this group do completely futile time wasting things for their benefits, like looking for employment when there is none).

Garbage hidden in mathematical formulas

I digress from the topic of unrealistic assumptions made by neoclassical and Austrian economists... If you assume away the real world in your model then the model will deliver a picture of ideal allocation outcomes – on the blackboard. Because the conclusions are arrived at in very sophisticated mathematics "mere Muggles" don't understand the fraud that the wizards have perpetrated.

What "the mere Muggles" understand... or think they do... is a simplified version of the ideas of the wizards, or parts of these ideas. If the economists are akin to a priesthood who are trained in the theological details, then the mass of the general public are like a congregation who stitch together a vaguer and partial patchwork quilt of ideas from what they read in the newspapers, hear on the news, or perhaps pick up in books or even in introductory courses in economics.

The more general "congregation" does not know all the fine details but knows bits that they adapt to their lives and local circumstances. This is what Richard B. Norgaard calls "economism":

> The mix of popular, political and policy mythology as well as practical beliefs that help us understand and rationalise the economy and how we live in it. People share some of those beliefs globally; other beliefs people adapt to fit particular national and regional situation; while yet others serve particular groups, including economists. (Norgaard, 2009, p. 80)

As Norgaard expresses it – a half of the global population is deeply immersed in the global economic system and like fish trying to grasp the nature of water, each of these individuals, playing their specialised roles, seeks to some degree or other to understand the bigger system of which they are a part. As the economy has become the window on which they see the world they use economism as "a set of beliefs constituting a secular religion guiding the remnants of our modern hopes for human progress: material, moral and scientific." (Norgaard, 2009, p. 79)

John Maynard Keynes was, I believe, saying much the same thing when he wrote that:

> The ideas of economists and political philosophers, both when they are right and when they are wrong are more powerful than is commonly understood. Indeed, the world is ruled by little else. Practical men, who believe themselves to be quite exempt from any intellectual influences, are usually slaves of some defunct economist. (Keynes 1936, p. XX)

What I am not saying here is that the priesthoods are supposed to have the correct version while the congregation more often have it wrong because of their simplifications and misunderstandings. It is more complicated than that. The mainstream theory always was "defunct" even in the form that is written out in difficult looking equations. You don't need to understand the equations to understand that. You just need to examine the foundations of the subject. That said, the priesthood are a little more aware of the nuances in their theories.

Chapter 9

Mismodelling human beings – "rational economic men" in love, politics and everyday life

This chapter explores the assumptions about human nature on which mainstream economics is based. The description of "rational economic man" ignores most psychological and psychotherapy understandings of people.

Key to the conceptual confidence trick are assumptions about what people in general are like. It is all based on an implicit modelling of human beings. Certain types of behaviour (the type that allows economists to model people and markets) are called "rational". Now, you might think that this description of people is meant by economists to be applicable only to economic and market activities. Certainly this was the point of view of one of the founders of the famous Chicago school of economics, Frank Knight. Although committed to the alleged virtues of the market, Knight was not naive about how far you could take economic analysis. In his book *Risk, Uncertainty and Profit* he concluded that economics only applied to the satisfaction of wants, and that this business of satisfying wants by no means accounted for all of human activity. Indeed Knight questioned how far one could go with a "scientific treatment" of human activity and wrote of his own views:

> In his views on this subject the writer is very much an irrationalist. In his view the whole interpretation of life as activity directed towards securing anything considered as really wanted, is highly artificial and unreal. (Backhouse, 2002, p. 204)

Some contemporary economists of the Chicago school don't see it this way. If people are calculating their individual self interest in their economic dealings why should one assume that they do not do the same thing in their political, their social and their interpersonal dealings? Should we not also assume that government officials are calculating their interests too? At the very least, why should contact between business and government not lead to a cosy relationship, particularly if people can leave government posts and get lucrative jobs with industry? What about bribes and kickbacks from business for special favours?

As I argued earlier, we can take the idea from the Anaïs Nin that we do not see things as they are – we see things as we are. There is likely to be a loop in which a theory which describes how people are assumed to be, when powerfully propagated in textbooks as "social science", will have an influence on how people behave. With economics we have a theory which argues that if people just look after their own interest that's OK because "an invisible hand" described by wizard intellectuals delivers an approximation to an optimal allocation of resources. Under the influence of a view like this, concern about what is in a wider interest is not likely to blossom. It is unlikely to figure as a motivation or concern. As individualists people will look no further than themselves. They do not need to look further than themselves because the "invisible hand" will do the rest.

It is quite logical to believe that if people are actually like this then their attitude to the community and to the state will be framed in the same terms. Such people, customers of the state, rather than citizens and members of communities, will then have an interest in getting the best deal from the state to pursue their own individual agendas.

The context of Keynesian economics

When I studied economics at the end of the 1960s, the textbooks, for example by Paul A Samuelson, pictured a world where the state was essentially benevolent and independent from business. A democratic process determined what policies the state would adopt and economists were the technical advisers making clear what the policy options were. There was an implied idea that governments, politicians and public officials would regulate markets without being contaminated by the self-interest motivation of those markets. The idea that the state could be captured by business interests while the majority of the people were effectively excluded from real influence was not expressed in the textbooks.

At that time, at the end of the 1960s, experience of the depression and then of the war had left an effect on public consciousness, including the consciousness of the elite itself – and it left its mark on economics. Fighting the war had been a massive common project which was collectively transforming. The values of British people shifted as a result of the equalising effect of the Second World War – rationing, conscription, the abolition of first class carriages in trains, evacuation and sharing bomb shelters. Military outlays as a per cent of national income in the UK went from 15% of national income in 1939 to 44% in 1940 to 53% in 1941 and as high as 55% in 1943. (Harrison (ed), 1998) After the war, the sense of what could be done when people worked together and decided what was a priority was quite different and there was a collective rejection of the idea of returning to the politics and economics of the 1930s. (Addison, 1975)

This was the context in which the welfare state and Keynesian economics was adopted. The allocation of resources mobilised for, and by, the state was something that a majority of ordinary people believed in. The mood was little different in the United States too, albeit that the US, having won the war, went straight into the cold war, involvement in Korea and the anti-communist hysteria of McCarthyism. Nevertheless there was a different context for textbooks like that of Paul Samuelson.

But by the late 1960s things were beginning to change again. Young people like myself took the welfare state for granted and chafed under the authoritarian paternalism of the elite. These conditions created the basis for a valid questioning of the disinterestedness of the state and its officials. This idea evolved into "the new left" but also towards the political right. A very different analysis to that of Samuelson in regard to the relationship between business and the state took hold in economics.

The rise of the Chicago School

The idea that the state could be, and was captured by interest groups was valid. The hostility to the communist planned economy, the personal libertarianism born in cynicism about the paternalism and corruption of officials, as well as by backlashes against politicians, officials and the state, led to the growth of fervent market fundamentalism spearheaded by economists at Chicago University. Their ideal was to go all the way and for the state to be driven out of market activity to the maximum extent possible.

Milton Friedman and Arnold Harberger welcome the boys to class at The Chicago School of Economics.
https://www.flickr.com/photos/donkeyhotey/4396155916/ https://creativecommons.org/licenses/by-sa/2.0/

To a new generation of Chicago economists, the rational utility calculating individual was a description that could be applied to the understanding of all human behaviour, not just that in the market place.

For example, to Gary Becker at Chicago, racism is a preference choice of who you want to live near and who an employer might want to employ. Note, Becker did not see himself as endorsing or condemning - he merely saw himself explaining and drawing out the consequences.

The model of "rational economic behaviour" was used by Becker and another theorist, Richard Posner, to explain "love", marriage and prostitution in a utilitarian framework. Marriage is a relationship involving "reciprocal service provision" which saves on the transaction costs like pricing each "service" that a couple provide for each other, as in removing the need to keep accounts for these services. In this way of thinking prostitution is, by contrast, thought of as a "spot" sexual transaction where it is "more efficient" to pay for the service in money.

The same approach is used by Becker to explain crime. Most people don't steal because it would not be profitable but in the life circumstances of criminals, the rational maximisation of costs and benefits of crime does make it pay. This is another form of the redistribution of income in the same broad category as government welfare programmes. (Nelson R. H., 2001, pp. 166-189)

The trouble with this view is that it is at best tautologically true in a sense that is banal. People do things because they want to and thus, they must get satisfaction or utility from doing and deciding what they do. However, it makes little sense of the many actions taken by people where they are conflicted; where they act in ways that involve self-sacrifice for moral reasons; where there is genuine anguish about their difficult decisions and where they do things because they think they ought to, not because it gives them any satisfaction at all. They act altruistically, get depressed, act out of compassion, and do crazy things. None of these fit into the model.

A faulty view of humanity

As Kalle Lasn puts it, in the book *Meme Wars: The Creative Destruction of Neoclassical Economics* "Neoclassical economics has achieved its coherence as a science by amputating most of human nature." (Lasn, 2012)

This amputation is done on the assumption that unless some internal measure of happiness or freedom from pain – utility – acts as a common yardstick, it is not possible for human beings to evaluate between options and make their choices. However, as philosopher Alan Holland points out:

> Happiness is not a homogenous item, but a mosaic of heterogeneous elements. There is just no common substance – no utility – by which to compare, for example, the suffering experienced by an experimental animal with the understanding gained by the experiment. Nor is this a point about moral reasons only but about reasons generally. The determined egoist, confronting a chocolate bar that will ruin his or her waistline, will soon find that he or she has to decide between vanity and greed, and will just as surely fail to find an appropriate value in terms of which to compare the alternatives. Self-interest is not such a value as it is as heterogeneous an objective as happiness. (Holland, 2002, p. 27)

As the example of Britain after World War II shows, values shift according to social, economic and political conditions. This alone makes nonsense of the idea that people are driven by personal utility calculations in the manner described by neoclassical economists.

Rather, psychologists have looked at what motivates people all around the world in different cultures and have come up with a more complex picture. Decades of research and hundreds of cross-cultural studies have identified consistently occurring human values which can be grouped into ten broad categories: universalism, benevolence, tradition, conformity, security, power, achievement, hedonism, stimulation and self-direction. (PIRC, 2011, pp. 12-20)

Each of us is motivated by all 10 of the value categories, albeit to varying degrees – and the ten groups of values can be divided along two major axes:

1. Self-enhancement (based on the pursuit of personal status and success) as opposed to self-transcendence (generally concerned with the well-being of others)
2. Openness to change (centred on independence and readiness for change) as opposed to conservation values (not referring to environmental or nature conservation, but to "order, self-restriction, preservation of the past and resistance to change") (PIRC, 2011, p. 17)

Mainstream economists have identified a part of what motivates people but mislead because they have too narrow a view. The values that economists describe as motivating people are best described as "extrinsic". Values that are centred on external approval and rewards e.g. wealth, material success, concern about image, social status, prestige, social power and authority. However, people are motivated by intrinsic motivations too. One of the themes of this book is to show that we get a clearer picture of reality when we describe actions and economic consequences arising from different starting motivations – some of which are anti-social and some of which are pro-social.

Chapter 10

Consumerism, Collective Psychopathology, Waste

This chapter about the power elite on display and the economics of Thorsten Veblen covers topics like conspicuous consumption and the consumer society, branding and the manufacture of wants. The role of advertisers is explored as well as the way that attention grabbing has become an economic sector that affects the quality of life radically and for the worse.

The Power Elite on Display – the economics of Thorsten Veblen

In 1899 the maverick economist Thorsten Veblen portrayed the power elite of his day in *The Theory of the Leisure Class*. What he described were extrinsic motivations at work. Success for the business elite was demonstrated through conspicuous consumption, by which he meant display to achieve social status, power and authority:

> This growth of punctilious discrimination as to qualitative excellence in eating, drinking, etc. presently affects not only the manner of life, but also the training and intellectual activity of the gentleman of leisure. He is no longer simply the successful, aggressive male — the man of strength, resource, and intrepidity. In order to avoid stultification he must also cultivate his tastes, for it now becomes incumbent on him to discriminate with some nicety between the noble and the ignoble in consumable goods. He becomes a connoisseur in creditable viands of various degrees of merit, in manly beverages and trinkets, in seemly apparel and architecture, in weapons, games, dancers, and the narcotics.

> This cultivation of aesthetic faculty requires time and application, and the demands made upon the gentleman in this direction therefore tend to change his life of leisure into a more or less arduous application to the business of learning how to live a life of ostensible leisure in a becoming way. Closely related to the requirement that the gentleman must consume freely and of the right kind of goods, there is the requirement that he must know how to consume them in a seemly manner. His life of leisure must be conducted in due form. Hence arise good manners in the way pointed out in an earlier chapter. High-bred manners and ways of living are items of conformity to the norm of conspicuous leisure and conspicuous consumption.

> (Veblen, 1899)

Plus ca change... Contemporary narcissism of this type is visible in the "How to Spend it" weekend supplements of the London *Financial Times*. Students of narcissism will find the column "Diary of a Somebody" particularly educational. This celebrates people with the message that you will not be a nobody if you have lots of money to spend and are thus able to hang out with other wealthy (and therefore beautiful) people:

If we are to believe economic theory, these "somebodies" are "maximising their utility". However the word "utility" is an empty concept – it is not information rich in the sense that it does not explain why people of this sort get utility by showing off and profiling themselves in front of all the nobodies. This was a point that Thorsten Veblen made in an essay written in 1909. The idea of marginal utility simply does not tell you very much that can help us understand people like this. (Veblen, The Limitations of Marginal Utility, 1909)

In his essay, Veblen argued that marginal utility theory did have an element of truth in its explanation of people's actions but that "It deals with this conduct only in so far as it may be construed in rationalistic, teleological terms of calculation and choice." In their analysis the marginal utility theorists took the institutional framework in which people's calculations and choices for granted, when it was the very emergence and evolution of the institutional framework, the context, that was the interesting thing. Marginal utility theorists like J. B. Clark were shutting down their exploration and theorisation at the very point at which it scientific inquiry should begin.

> It shuts off the inquiry at the point where the modern scientific interest sets in. The institutions in question are no doubt good for their purpose as institutions, but they are not good as premises for a scientific inquiry into the nature, origin, growth, and effects of these institutions and of the mutations which they undergo and which they bring to pass in the community's scheme of life. (Veblen, 1909)

Marginal utility theory is no help at all if we want to understand where the institutions and practices of a consumer society have come from, how and why they have come into existence and what their consequences are. On the other hand, Veblen's ideas are helpful, at least as a starting point. This is because he had resources that most economists, in his own time and subsequently, did not and still do not have. Firstly, he was an outsider and no sycophant so was able to view the behaviour of rich and powerful people (and of the poor when they were emulating them) from a standpoint that was uncompromised. Secondly, he had read sufficiently in other social scientific fields. He resorted to sociology, anthropology and psychology without artificially hiving off the subject matter of "economics". That made him able to recognise that although a market society had its own features that shaped the form in which various social practices took place, many of the features of that society were not fundamentally different from what occurred in supposedly "more primitive" societies. Thus,:

> Presents and feasts had probably another origin than that of naïve ostentation, but they acquired their utility for this purpose very early, and they have retained that character to the present; so that their utility in this respect has now long been the substantial ground on which these usages rest. Costly entertainments, such as the potlatch or the ball, are peculiarly adapted to serve this end. The competitor with whom the entertainer wishes to institute a comparison is, by this method, made to serve as a means to the end. He consumes vicariously for his host at the same

time that he is a witness to the consumption of that excess of good things which his host is unable to dispose of singlehanded, and he is also made to witness his host's facility in etiquette. (Veblen, The Theory of the Leisure Class, 1899)

Conspicuous Consumption and the Consumer Society

Thus, it is that Veblen's theory of "conspicuous leisure" and of "conspicuous consumption", whose purpose is to make a status display, provide us with a possible starting point for our understanding. It gives us ideas with which we can start to make sense of the motivations and behaviours apparently underpinning a lot of the actions in a "consumer society". In a consumer society not only the rich but other strata of society are using consumption goods to profile and project themselves. As in the diary of a somebody, jewels, hair, make-up, i Pad, purple couture dresses and the names in one's impressive choice of stylists or the beautiful people in one's guest collection are all a means to an extrinsic end.

To a large extent the end in question is to make a status display – status conscious people are pursuing the acquisition of what are called "positional goods". These goods signal one's position in society and depend on relative income. It is the fact that the rich can afford them and others cannot that is on display. If and when poorer people were able to afford a Ferrari then a Ferrari would loses its value for the rich people who first bought them. In that case rich people would pursue another status display. (Kallis G 2014)

In his article Kallis argues that "..positional consumption is not a personal vice. It is a structural social phenomena to which individuals conform to remain part of the mainstream....." For Kallis there are risks for those who try to exit the rat race especially if they are from less privileged backgrounds in which case there will be loss of respectability and economic insecurity. What's more "the system" can co-opt its dissidents, even back to the land and "eco-life style choices" by privileged educated and artistical groups can become types of new positional goods.

Perhaps - but is this too "either-or"? Explaining peoples' actions through 'structures' can be revealing but after a point too much emphasis on the structures within which people act implies this explanation for people's actions: "The system made me do it". It removes the idea that individuals make choices. It can tend to the view that regards people as automatons without freedom. As Erich Fromm pointed out, and other psychologists have since confirmed, a market society creates particular personality types, marketing personalities – people who put great store on marketing themselves. However, individuals can come to recognise the features of their own habitual responses – that's a point of therapy after all. Individuals can and do change and not only in the context of broader "system changes" – one of the tasks at hand is to identify when and under what conditions.

The Helbig Society

It must be admitted however that things have moved on from Veblen's day to make marketing far more prominent – particularly the all-pervasive presence of "brands" which work together with advertising to create what I describe as a "Helbig Society". That is, a society of technicolour appearance and empty narratives designed to manipulate.

To explain: the term "Potemkin Village" is sometimes used to describe a manufactured appearance, designed to impress, which is a deceptive facade. The phrase refers to a tour of the Crimea and the Ukraine in 1787 by Catherine II of Russia in which it was alleged that her former lover, Prince Grigory Aleksandrovich Potemkin, created pasteboard villages along the bank of the Dnieper River which the monarch was travelling down, with the aim of making an illusory show of prosperity. Recent historical research has shown that this story was largely a slander created by the Saxon envoy to Catherine's court, Georg von Helbig. The villages therefore ought, with more justice, to be called Helbig Villages.

If the Potemkin Villages of 1787 were a slander, Helbig Villages have existed at other times in history. A number of places designed to deceive are mentioned in the Wikipedia description of "Potemkin Villages". For example, the Nazi Theresienstadt concentration camp called "the Paradise Ghetto" in World War II was designed as a concentration camp that could be shown to the Red Cross. Apparently attractive, but deceptive and ultimately lethal, with high death rates from malnutrition and contagious diseases, it ultimately served as a way-station to Auschwitz. As is well known, people who arrived at Concentration Camps were sometimes greeted by orchestras playing classical music. An analogous management tool is used today in slaughterhouses. Animals are calmed after a stressful journey before they are put through a process that stimulates their curiosity about what is going to happen just before they are sedated and then slaughtered. If they got upset, the stress hormones would spoil the meat. Or, to put it the other way around - the meat tastes nice to the customers because the animals have been deceived.

Less gruesome, and more like the Helbig Village example, was the PR job done on the town of Enniskillen in Northern Ireland for the G8 Summit in June 2013. Large photographs were put up in the windows of closed shops in the town so as to give the appearance of thriving businesses for visitors driving past them. This has now become a common practice for property companies to cover messy re-development or dereliction. (Wikipedia, Potemkin Village, 2013)

Branding

Deception is ubiquitous in a modern market economy. We might even call a consumer society a Helbig Society. To get a proper sense of the gulf between the illusion and the reality in this kind of economic system we have to delve into the evolution of advertising and of "brands". In her book *No Logo* Naomi Klein shows how the economy has moved a long way from when it was about people selling products to other people in markets that were regulated to ensure that prices were fair. By the end of the 19th century and the early 20th century, adverts were about selling innovations. New kinds of products like cars, telephones and electric lights which producers needed to convince people to use. The advertisements were, as Klein explains, rather like product news bulletins. This was to change as a process began of building an image around a particular brand name. Generic goods like sugar, flour, soap and cereal had hitherto been scooped out of barrels by local shopkeepers. These now had names bestowed on them, particularly with a view to evoking a feeling of folksiness and familiarity. Henceforth it was the product brand names - artificial images of imagined personalities - that interfaced between consumer and producer rather than the shopkeeper - Uncle Ben, Dr Brown, the Quaker Oats man...

> There were those in the industry who understood that advertising wasn't just scientific; it was also spiritual. Brands could conjure a feeling - think of Aunt Jemima's comforting presence - but not only that, entire corporations could themselves embody a meaning of their own. In the early twenties legendary adman Bruce Barton turned General Motors into a metaphor for the American family, "something, personal, warm and human", while GE was not so much the name of the faceless General Electric Company as, in Barton's words, "the initials of a friend". In 1923 Barton said the role of advertising was to help corporations find their soul. The son of a preacher, he drew on his religious upbringing for uplifting messages: "I like to think of advertising as something big, something splendid, something which goes deep down into an institution and gets hold of the soul of it... Institutions have souls, just as men and nations have souls." he told GM president Pierre du Pont. General Motors ads began to tell stories about the people who drove its cars - the preacher, the pharmacist or the country doctor who, thanks to his trusty GM, arrived "at the bedside of a dying child" just in time "to bring it back to life". (Klein, 2000, pp. 6-7)

As advertisers evolved their techniques of psychological manipulation, they delved into psychology, anthropology and culture while coming to see themselves as the "philosopher kings" of "commercial culture. It took a while for people managing companies to finally get it. They were not in business to produce stuff, they were in business to sell brands. This meant continuous and increasingly intrusive advertising - the problem being, as one senior ad executive explained, that consumers "are like roaches - you spray them and they get immune after a while". (Klein, 2000, p. 9)

The manufacture of wants – the role of advertisers

One of the few economists to take this on board was John Kenneth Galbraith, whose book *The Affluent Society*, first published in 1958, argued that, for much of the modern economy, production preceded wants rather than, as economic theory assumes, the other way round.

> The even more direct link between production and wants is provided by the institution of modern advertising and salesmanship. These cannot be reconciled with the notion of independently determined desires, for their central function is to create desires – to bring into being wants that previously did not exist. A broad empirical relationship exists between what is spent on the production of consumer goods and what is spent on synthesizing the desires for it. (Galbraith, 2001, p. 34)

Perhaps economists rarely venture into these fields because we can see that advertising, marketing and public relations employ methodologies which are all about shaping preferences and the "methodological individualists" are not interested in how preferences are formed. They are content to assume that people have given preferences and then act rationally on the basis of these preferences in the face of prices and a certain amount of purchasing power. To find out what happens in aggregate the economists simply add together the individual market behaviours.

Such an approach obviously devotes no attention to the way that people influence each other. The very existence of a fashion industry shows that, as well as the efforts that marketing departments work to create collective consumption trends. These marketing approaches actively foster disutility because they "work" by creating dissatisfaction. They seek to put in people's minds the idea that their intended purchasers cannot live without some new product. They are also intended to be disruptive of relationships because they are based on fostering rival status display.

Sales departments, advertisers and public relations companies do not take people's preferences as given. They are a big part of the economy and mostly, economists ignore them. The sales departments and the marketers do not use ideas from "utility theory". They take ideas from group psychological dynamics, crowd psychology and approaches from psychotherapy theory which explores the interplay between human emotion and cognition. We need to do this too in order to understand advertising and PR on its own terms – and hence its usefulness to the people who pay for it, and its ability to influence the political process.

Well-being and marketing

Money is made when people "have to have" products and stay on the treadmill of work, spending and debt. Society functions by advertisers ensuring that people feel uncomfortable, inadequate and bereft unless they have the latest product designed for their peer group which is also an identifiable market segment. That said, if buying a product were to make you satisfied for too long you would not keep on buying it...

So how do the advertisers do this? Often it is by an astute manipulation which forms motivations through the use of stories, rituals, ceremonies and culture. The moral of the stories told by the advertisers is that the audience is lacking in something that possession of the brand will give them. For example, to be attractive, to be in tune with the American grand narrative of rugged individualism, personified by the cowboy, one needs to buy Marlboro cigarettes and participate in the social ritual of smoking them. In contrast with identity in an indigenous society, where people have totem identification with a creature, or a plant, based on deep knowledge and loyalty to part of the natural world, individuals in the consumer society define themselves partly through brand loyalty. The consumer "totems" are the designer labels that fashionistas wear – a sign of their discrimination, knowledge and affluence as consumers.

The implications for psychological well-being are profound. The message of the advertising stories is to convey how products will make us a better and more desirable person – mother, father and lover – which means that we are not good enough as we are now. The insights of Sigmund Freud that people think in emotionally associative ways (cf his therapeutic technique of free association) is hijacked to design the advertising message. Metaphorical allusion portrayed in vivid colour in high definition and on the biggest possible screens attempt to create emotional links between brands and desirable episodes or scenes in personal life stories. Fizzy drinks with sugar in them, are associated with adolescent sexuality in blue jeans. Getting the boy, getting the girl, getting the job, your forthcoming celebrity status, the perfect mum, dependable dad, the happy family - all are associated with a product - perfume or gravy granules... Messages of this type bombard us all with attention-grabbing messages from street billboards, newspapers, magazines, television and cinema commercials, on the internet, on the radio. Over and over again, visual and narrative connections are made between sex, glamour, wealth, power, speed, desirability, happy families, and shiny new products magnified and flashing in front of our eyes, dynamically displayed with clever graphical effects.

Attention Grabbing as Economic sector

Correspondingly a large part of the economy - its institutions, its technical infrastructure - exists solely for the purpose of grabbing our attention. When we are awake we can only focus on so much during a 24 hour day, a third of which we are asleep and a lot of which we are drilled to attend to employment tasks. At other times advertising agencies, market research companies, public relations companies, publishing companies, theatres, cinemas, television companies, newspapers, internet organisations are all trying to ensure that at every available opportunity, every available surface, every available screen, every available shop window, every available stage, and every broadcast, carries something about their product and/or their message. This is not to mention 9 out of every 10 phone calls on telephone landlines when a complete stranger assumes that they have the right to interrupt whatever you are doing with what they call a "courtesy call" – despite "a service" run by the marketing industry which is supposed to prevent this happening if you don't want it. (Franck, 1998)

Naturally the more power specific people and specific institutions have, the more this "economy of attention" is skewed in their favour. Rather as the passage of light is bent by powerful gravitational fields, so the "information space" used by a society is buckled to massively magnify the concerns and priorities of the super-rich elite and their hangers on. At the same time rendering virtually invisible and unintelligible the suffering, concerns and needs of the large part of the world's population. In the information space these people are driven to the edges and almost literally do become "nobodies".

The nobodies are then only noticed in the crowded messages being transmitted in the information space when they get in the way of elite agendas and/or require expenditure and management because they have become a problem. (For example, because "attention seeking" turns into what is characterised as a mental health issue - mania and depression being opposite emotional reactions to experiencing oneself to be a nobody and being unable to cope with that – excitement at the idea that one is about to become a star as a result of one's brilliant work and thus, attain celebrity status oscillating with depression as one remains in the wilderness).

These are all properly a subject for economics because there are multiple senses in which the attention seeking assault from the marketing sector impacts negatively on well-being now and in the future. We have already mentioned the way that this vast pantomime is about making its audience feel inadequate. But more than this – there is another economic consequence that Veblen realised over a hundred years ago. A part of his argument was that what the Leisure Class consumed as status displays – and also the way in which many members of the poor tried to emulate them – led to a waste of resources. It is stuff that never needed to be produced and is a waste of the time of the producers, a waste of material and natural resources and a waste of energy. And what Veblen could not have known is that the huge pile of garbage which is still being produced today drains depleting fossil fuel and material resources while exhausting carbon and other kinds of sinks. For no good cause other than the need of the "celebrity class" to be noticed, the planet appears to be locked on the road to destruction.

The Facade

Another way of expressing this is to describe "the economy" as operating with a vast deceptive facade. I have used the example of Potemkin/Helbig Villages to describe the resulting culture that we live in – a way in which mass psychology is manipulated by a culture of appearances that hide an underlying reality that is much more shoddy. We look at a mass of separate products on the supermarket shelves and see a bright dazzling multi-colour array of images and styles - on the boxes and tins. Yet when it comes down to it, most of them are produced by just ten different business groups. The variety is an illusion - at least when it comes to who owns and produces them. The conservative reassuring man on the Quaker oats packet is owned by Pepsico. Yves Sant Laurent, Diesel (that celebration of fossil fuel) and Giorgio Armani are owned by Nestle, Uncle Ben's Rice is owned by Mars. (See attached graphic) (Bradford, 2012)

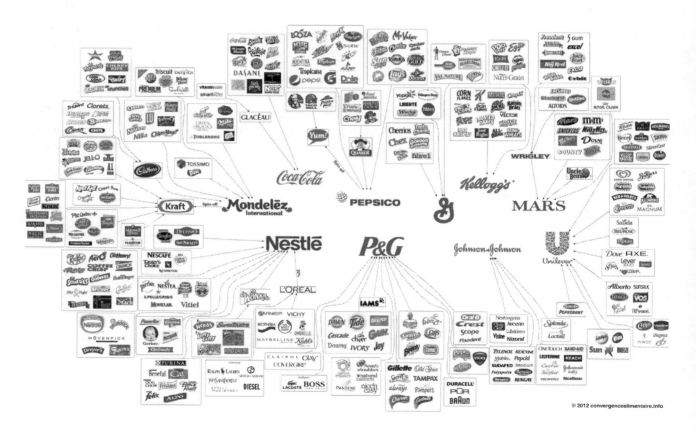

(Convergence Alimentaire, 2012) with permission

There are many other things hidden by the facade. Why else is such a high proportion of world trade and world finance routed through tax havens and secrecy jurisdiction? Behind the gloss, the cute sentimental products on sale at your local supermarket, there are factories producing the stuff staffed by child and slave labour in unsafe conditions; there are oil spills and air and water contamination; there are greenhouse gas emissions; there is military intimidation of workers and there are mountains and mountains of toxic throw away trash.

In her book Klein describes how the American NBC network aired an investigation into Mattell and Disney just days before Christmas 1996. "With the help of hidden cameras, the reporter showed that children in Indonesia and China were working in virtual slavery "so that children in America can put frilly dresses on America's favourite doll". (Klein, 2000, p. 326)

Many other examples can be given between the appearance and the brutal reality. However, if you mock and take on these cuddly friendly folksy corporations you see what they are really like. Like the MacDonald Corporation who tried to ruin activists who took them on with critical leaflets which led to a long running court action in the UK.

Although there is nothing at all glossy and high definition about economics, although it is often tedious and dull, economics is a part of this facade. Too often the descriptions of what is happening stay on the surface. The descriptions of markets are about products not about brands. The fact that branding and advertising are about creating product differentiation makes nonsense of the default assumption in the textbooks that most production is from competitive firms producing homogenous products. Textbooks are still describing a world in which shopkeepers scoop flour, sugar and cereals out of a barrel. Into this barrel the shopkeepers have put the identical products of a large number of producers all of whom were obliged to sell at a going market price. But of course if you go to buy some kind of computer, or a car, or an appliance of some kind there are a bewildering variety of non-comparable products and a barrage of adverts as to the advantages of each. While price plays a role in the choice of a product it is often a minor one.

As regards the huge growth and economic importance of marketing, the textbook writers have little to say. Certainly they do not appear to recognise that the rise and rise of the marketing industry demonstrates that the chief constraints on what companies supply are not production conditions, leading to rising internal costs as companies try to expand. Rather the constraints on firms are external market limits if they try to sell more of their brand beyond their market niche. Pierro Sraffa understood this from as early as the 1920s and wrote a paper to explain his alternative viewpoint. This will be described later. Suffice it to say here, that although Sraffa, and a few others, like Joan Robinson, tried to keep up to date, most economists did not. You don't update the Holy Scriptures – scriptures are true for all time.

Chapter 11

Happiness or authenticity?

The chapter draws on the ideas of Erich Fromm and, more recently, Oliver James, to describe the problem of Affluenza. It critiques the recent enthusiasm of some economists like Richard Layard for a theory of "happiness" and "positive psychology".

A further consequence of the rise and rise of the advertising and marketing industry is its effects on the culture of society and on general psychological well-being. There is a mental health implication of spending a huge amount of money to try to grab people's attention in order to manipulate them in the ways described.

In so far as the marketing industry has drawn upon the insights of Sigmund Freud and later psychologists to relentlessly seek to manipulate the general population, the effect has been massively psychologically toxic. Given their utilitarian worldview, most of the economic profession are barely able to understand this. However, there are some therapists who have and their viewpoint represents a deep critique of the market economy. What they have written and said points to the way in which economic relationships and market imperatives have penetrated the core psychological makeup of people. In place of the banal tautology of 19th century utilitarianism we need a deep study of the relationship between economic activity and mental health because this marketing assault, this religion of consumerism, has many aspects that do not appear to be doing us any good.

Here is necessary to note that mental health is not the same as the "happiness" of the utilitarians. It is not the same as the "happiness" research which some "radical" economists have used to criticise GDP measures in recent years. This "happiness" literature is merely a modernisation of utilitarian thinking and contains all its flaws. (Layard, 2006)

I am not writing here about happiness as a goal for economic activity, I am writing about mental health. I am writing about "authenticity" which finds expressions in emotions that are appropriate to the conditions in which one finds oneself in life.

If you are involved in a futile activity and getting nowhere, the demoralisation and depression that so drains you of the mental energy and willpower to continue, that makes you give up your futile purposes, can create the space to try a different direction in life. In this sense, depression can be very useful. Nor is the misery and grief of losing a loved one some kind of irrational feeling to be wished away. The grief is appropriate to the love and the loss. It is also sometimes the case that the greatest achievements can only be made by ignoring how unhappy one is feeling and ploughing ahead despite that unhappiness, because that way lies self-respect and actions consistent with your values, although not bringing any immediate joy.

When organisations like the New Economics Foundation, who otherwise do some great work, promote "happiness" as a goal of economic activity, I wonder how that is really compatible with addressing the issues like climate change, peak oil, the brutality embodied and embedded in economic policy, the stupidity of the actions of the finance sector. I do not feel "happiness" when I address myself to these issues. I feel fear, rage, and frustration. How is it possible to be "happy" when one lives in a world characterised by ecological destruction, extreme inequality and injustice? It is impossible to feel happy having to listen day after day to celebrities, marketing characters, politicians and officials justifying sociopathic policies and decisions in an information sphere where these small minded fools get a huge amount of attention for the drivel that they talk.

The alternative, as formulated by therapists like Oliver James is to strive to be "authentic" rather than "happy". For me that means living my life by going as far as I can, without overloading myself emotionally, trying to engage with the problems that I see all around me. Writing this book is my best shot at this stage in my life – but writing it is not making me "happy". Having spent many years of my life in a state of emotional and psychiatric turmoil, going through periods that have sometimes been like hell, I know myself enough to know what my limits are, engaging with various causes but staying back from that level of engagement that would be emotionally reckless because psychiatrically self-destructive.

This is why I do not support the activities and proposals of economists like Lord Richard Layard, an economist who started taking an interest in why so many people were unhappy despite economic growth and who has been very influential for the promotion of therapeutic approaches to deal with unhappiness. It is Layard who is credited with the promotion of the widespread availability of cognitive behavioural therapy as a solution for mass unhappiness in the UK.

Having been a "customer" of the mental health services, and having then worked on the edges of that service for almost two decades – and seen what is helpful and what is not helpful up close - I am deeply sceptical of Layard's ideas and his solutions. As Oliver James expresses it:

> Underpinning Cognitive Behavioural Therapy is a "call black white" positive psychology... An American invention, it fits with the conviction that it is healthy to live in a rose-tinted bubble of positive illusions, in which you believe bad things are less likely to happen to you than is actuarially true, or that you are more popular with friends and colleagues than is the case. In this schema, people who make honest, truthful and realistic appraisals are characterised as suffering from "depressive realism". Indeed, some scientists have maintained that the bubble of positive illusions is our natural state, reflecting evolution. This is a classic instance of the American intellectual and cultural imperialism which underlies evolutionary ideology. The truth is that many societies, especially those in east or south-east Asia, do not live in the bubble and start, if anything, from its opposite: a harshly realistic view is valued. (James, 2010) (James, David Cameron should measure mental health, not happiness, 2010)

There seems to me to be something very predictable about cognitive behavioural therapy (CBT) being promoted by an economist as the treatment of choice for people who are unhappy in a market society. If you are miserable or desperate and go for help you get either a pill or CBT. This is fully consistent with the view of the economists in which society is an aggregation of individuals. CBT locates "problems" inside the individuals who are having the problems because they are not thinking correctly about their difficulties and need to train themselves to think more optimistically.

A therapy for the masses would be like this wouldn't it? Not just economics but a lot of psychology takes the form that it does because the therapists, like the economists, are part of the club of winners and think that they are qualified to advise losers how to improve their lives.

In so doing they often do not notice or understand what it is like for people who are struggling to survive under greater constraints than they themselves have ever had to endure - fewer resources of available time, often less skill and most certainly less money, less connections, being in the wrong places, at the wrong times.

Positive psychology is more likely "to work" as "self-fulfilling optimism" for people who are starting out with a better hand of cards in life whereas an optimism that is not anchored in adequate starting resources is more likely to lead to disappointment and failure, to bitter disillusion, to the sorts of losses that Kahneman writes that people fear and which can risk destabilising what little one already has.

It is not surprising then that repeated failure by people who have less going for them leads to "learned helplessness", apathy and passivity. One cannot always pull oneself up by one's bootstraps and there will be conditions in life when enthusiasm for CBT is likely to wither in the harsh reality because the therapy is not complemented by sufficiently altered circumstances.

That is not to deny that CBT sometimes succeeds – or might appear to anyway. Perhaps, however, that will be because for some lucky people the circumstances of their lives, circumstances that they do not fully control, move on anyway. That certainly happened to me after some of my worst times. Things happen which are not expected. Perhaps the best of all is if one finds oneself doing new things, in new places with new people, becoming a new person and starting again.

Sadly, there are a great many people who become "career psychiatric patients". Their lives have been frozen by the institutions, the drugs, the places, the "professionals" that are supposed to be there to help them.

Above all else, if one is to be able to move on, to start a new life, after an old life has fallen to bits, it is important to get one's motivations right. One must be careful about what one is trying to achieve. Having "fallen" once, a "loser" is well advised not to try again by pursuing "extrinsic motivations". If you want to set yourself up for falling again then go for money, go for fame, go for power. If, however, you want to be on firmer ground in regard to psychological well-being then pursue things that are not about wealth and a futile search trying to get others to think well of you, trying to show off – it will not do you any good.

To have or to be

The psychoanalyst and social critic Erich Fromm drew attention to the very different things that might motivate us when he described people who live to "be" and people who live to "have". He described the people who live to "have" as "marketing personalities". This way of putting it is very similar to the ideas of Oliver James, who has written about "Affluenza" as a kind of psychological virus that has done a lot of damage to emotional well-being in market societies through the promotion of extrinsic values. (James, Affluenza, 2007)

Seeking after spiritual, community and environmental goals serves a higher purpose that transcends or goes beyond the self. Activities of this sort are rooted in the quality of one's "being" rather than in "having". People with these motivations are not trying to become "somebodies". They are not trying to be noticed. What they do is not about being admired; accumulating an audience; being envied; winning prizes; getting medals, titles or celebrity status; having some dignitary telling you how well you are doing; some newspaper article congratulating you; lots of paparazzi flashing cameras at you; the Financial Times quoting you as a stock market oracle or getting a huge bonus so that you can feel that you actually exist. "Intrinsic motivations" entail a "life game" in the sense meant by anti-psychiatrist, Thomas Tzsas, i.e. purposes which give meaning, direction and structure to people's lives. These are not purposes that require "incentivisation" because pursuing them brings their own psychological rewards. (Davey, University of the North Pole. Life., 2001) (Davey, BA (Hons) in life, 2001)

A lot of the people pursuing intrinsic motivations, it should be admitted, probably *are* nobodies. They are not trying to climb into the public gaze in order to pursue their interests and have no particular concern for celebrity status or wealth because that is not what drives them. Empirical research suggests that people with intrinsic motivations tend to lead the more satisfying lives (in the sense of authenticity). In contrast it is the people who are pursuing "extrinsic values" such as wealth, or preservation of public image who tend to find that they are never satisfied and whose personal well-being is very fragile. Extrinsic motivations do not encourage "flourishing". If we pursue these things in the way that the textbooks assume that you do, you will more likely end up unhappy.

Thus, to return to the theme of this chapter, mainstream economists, in their clunky banal approach to understanding human psychology and behaviour, which they suppose to be driven by calculations of individual "utility", have no way of making sense of why the market economy not only fails as a producer of goods and services, but also why it is a source of misery and mental health problems - including for those who are "successful" in material terms.

This is a way of understanding that is incompatible with the normal assumptions of economics. In fact it makes nonsense of the economic approach to welfare and well-being. The market economy in its present form undermines psychological well-being. (Saunders & Munro, 2000)

The characteristics of the market form and mould the characters of market actors – or at least those who engage most closely with it and economics is a subject that helps this process. Australian research has shown that if you take a group of students, the business students are far more likely than the arts students to be "marketing characters".

In his book *Affluenza* Oliver James, repeats the findings of Saunders, "Marketing characters experience themselves as commodities whose value and meaning are externally determined." Such characters have the following traits:

> ... eager to consume; wasteful of goods, disposing and replacing them frequently; having conventional tastes and views; uncritical of themselves or society, un-insightful; agreeing with the statement "having makes me more"; a tendency to publicise and promote themselves; experiencing themselves as a commodity whose value is determined by possessions and the opinions of others; and with values portrayed in television advertisements. (James, 2007)

Studies show people like this are more likely to be "materialistic, conformist, unconcerned about ecology, expressive of anger, anxious and depressive." A subsequent study by Saunders, again cited by James, explains how marketing characters:

> ... place little value on beauty, freedoms or inner harmony. Their main pursuits are social recognition, comfort, and having an exciting life. They are extremely individualistic in their social values and do not regard social equality as desirable. They compare themselves obsessively and enviously with others, always having to have more and better things than others, believing inequality to be man's natural state. (James, Affluenza, 2007, p. 66)

Such people are never contented even when they have lots of money. In an article about what matters to the super rich, columnist George Monbiot describes Saudi Prince Alwaleed. His self-esteem appears to depend on where he is placed on the Forbes global rich list. It seems that the Prince was disturbed when he was listed in Forbes at $7 billion – because this was less than he claims "to be worth".

> Never mind that he has his own 747, in which he sits on a throne during flights. Never mind that his "main palace" has 420 rooms. Never mind that he possesses his own private amusement park and zoo and, he claims, $700 million worth of jewels. Never mind that he's the richest man in the Arab world, valued by Forbes at $20bn, and has watched his wealth increase by $2bn in the past year. None of this is enough. There is no place of arrival, no happy landing, even in a private jumbo jet. The politics of envy are never keener than among the very rich. (Monbiot, Enough Already, 2013)

A genuine theory of well-being in the tradition of Veblen would encompass the psychopathologies of economic actors including the craziness of "successful people". It would include a study of how the operation of the market creates psychological pathologies which then enter into the way that those markets work.

Chapter 12

The attention seeking economy, information and the manufacture of ignorance

Information is lost as well as gained during the processes of economic development and change. There is a great deal of difference between direct knowledge and knowledge that is taken in through a variety of media. Much of what we take for granted is actually better understood as "consensus trance". To orientate to the world properly we need to have a proper feel for the huge amount of what we don't know – and there are multiple categories of unknowing.

Information is lost as well as gained

Given the cultural and psychological degradations to which our society has been subject, it is not surprising that we are in danger of passing on a barbaric worldview to the next generations. In their book *Ecological Economics* Joshua Farley and Herman Daly point out that we are all born ignorant and that knowledge can be lost as one generation succeeds the next. It is an illusion to believe that information, ideas and knowledge are expanding all the time.

> It is a gross prejudice to think that the future will always know more than the past. Every generation is born totally ignorant, and just as we are only one failed harvest away from starvation, we are also only one failed generational transfer of knowledge away from darkest ignorance. Although it is true that today many people know many things that no one knew in the past, it is also true that large segments of the present generation are more ignorant than were large segments of past generations. The level of policy in a democracy cannot rise above the average level of understanding of the population. In a democracy the distribution of knowledge is as important as the distribution of wealth. (Daly & Farley, 2004, p. 41)

What I have sought to show in the preceding discussion is where there has been such a huge loss, and indeed, a degeneration of the possibility of knowing, because of the rise of non-indigenous societies that have displaced and are now dominating indigenous societies. The non-indigenous societies have evolved market forms unconstrained by any kind of ethics and infested with sophisticated psychologically informed manipulation. This has been brought about by people who have a mind-set that focuses on the measurable above all else, a mind-set that makes count what can be counted only and above all counted by money. The guiding ideology, we might almost call it the religion of this world view, is neoclassical economics.

Although there are hopeful signs in the biological sciences that some of the possibility of knowing can be recovered, it is useful to explore why it will be such an uphill struggle. How and why has it come about that non-indigenous knowing in market societies is now so detached from incredibly threatening ecological realities. How is it that a lot of people are most ignorant in the very fields of knowledge where they most of all need to be informed if humanity is to have a future.

Elsewhere in this book I draw attention to the way in which competent scientists are publishing peer reviewed studies saying that the environmental crisis e.g. in the form of the climate crisis, represents a life-threatening global emergency for humanity. Yet most people do not accept or are even unaware of the magnitude of the threat. Billions of people are reluctant to look at the "inconvenient truths" thrown up by environmentalists. Instead of integrating these truths into their "rational expectations" for themselves and their children, they are turning instead to "reassuring lies" created for them by the public relations industry. It is also necessary to look to how it is possible for a number of ultimately futile corporate agendas to capture the mass discourse about sustainability and turn them to their short run financial advantage. For example, by forming coalitions around fruitless approaches that waste time and valuable resources.

Direct knowledge and media-ted knowledge

Economists are fond of telling us that they describe the world as it is, and not as one might want it to be. So let's describe the world as it is in regard to how public attitudes are shaped.

When people had, or still have, a life gathering, hunting, cultivating and harvesting from the landscapes and waterscapes around them from places that they were, or are, managing as natural commons, they had and have an intimate daily knowledge of their natural environment. They feel responsible for that landscape – indeed they may feel a kind of love and care for it. Nature is regarded as kin. In these circumstances people feel and experience themselves as part of nature. They belong to the land and to a place more than the place and the land belongs to them.

This direct experience and knowledge can be contrasted to the kind of "media-ted knowledge" of the urban market society in which non-indigenous peoples live. This is a society in which knowledge is taken in from written texts, from televisions and from computer screens.

In the new complex urban societies where land is private property and people have no intimate relationship with it, the connection that generates vernacular knowledge of the land has been largely broken. Daly and Farley's idea of lost knowledge applies here. But knowledge takes a different form too. Knowledge is now media-ted knowledge. There are knowledge and information providers who are often different from knowledge users or consumers.

Most of the things that we think we know we have got from others via a medium of communication, not from direct experience. There has been a choice of someone to write and publish information about something in the hope, the belief, or the expectation that it will capture the attention of an audience, a readership or viewers. Secondly, there are the choices of readers, viewers, or listeners to decide to devote attention to the information that has been provided.

To be sure, there are still stories, rituals, ceremonies and people who wear badges and uniforms to signals their allegiances. However, these dimensions of knowledge are mostly detached from land based natural processes and increasingly colonised by the mass media and other forms of knowledge management. For example, information about a variety of processes is generated by experts in a technical language that is difficult to fathom unless one has the relevant expertise. This will often lead to another link in the chain between information provider and general public – a journalist who acts as a simplifier, a populariser or the pop science publications of academics.

In the previous chapter I introduced a concept called "the economy of attention" and related it to the onslaught of the marketing industry as it battles to steal our attention at every opportunity. At this point, it is necessary to add that it is not just brand marketers that attempt to grab and manage our attention. There are a quite a range of other processes that try, and succeed, in managing what we devote our attention to.

When we are involved in paid work our employer can oblige us to focus our attention on the work tasks in our job description. On many other occasions we must devote our attention in a variety of public institutions and public duties. For example, children *must* give their attention to their teacher, now and then I must give my attention to the tax office by filling in their forms.

In other circumstances we have a degree of discretion and choice what we devote attention to. We can, if we are so minded, decide to devote some of our attention to political tasks, like the green movement, out of a sense of community and collective responsibility, if you like, out of a sense of citizenship.

For most people, everyday life means that they must routinely devote most of their attention to their domestic tasks, maintaining the house, looking after the children and other dependents, getting the shopping in, and to their work. What they allocate their attention to is therefore partly "drilled". Much of the corresponding personal relationships therefore have a rather automatic, routine, character. At the end of the working day most people are often tired. They are not really able to devote their attention to highly complicated issues. Because so much is asked from them in their work, in their consumption and domestic activities and in the raising of children, they are continually under time pressure. That has the consequence that they have often no more mental energy to do other than sit in front of the TV and give themselves over to the simplifications that the mass media "gives" them.

This business of "allocating attention" therefore happens everywhere in society. Naturally the print, and even more the electronic mass media function as attention capturing, directing and channelling agencies. The radio and TV media are the attention capturers and channels of our society par excellence. There is a huge interplay between them and politics and economics. One might even say that political power is the power to have priority access to the mass media to set the agenda for policy and to frame political debates. Political and economic activity are sub sets of a bigger process of allocating focused attention alongside attention given to various diversions, sports, game shows, celebrity gossip, dramatic entertainment and so on.

The politics of attention in our society has therefore become rather like a one way street – or at least it was until the internet gave people a limited power to speak back. The power structures want people to devote this "scarce good" that measures up the units in which our lives are measured, exclusively to their agendas. They oblige people in their jobs to devote their attention in a particular direction, and in their free time too they make what is a theft of their time. This happens through bombardment with advertisements and the domination of the mass media discourse. They spread sweet dreams or broadcast programmes which function to tranquilise, to reassure and to escape. Hollywood is a dream factory.

In the circumstances it is not really surprising that people are vulnerable to having their opinions and understandings shaped by campaigns planned in the public relations industry which, together with the advertising agencies, work closely with the media organisations.

By and large, conventional economic theory does not consider where people get their information and ideas. It is just assumed that people have fixed, not malleable, tastes; that they act individualistically and rationally with all the information that they need; that they are not swayed by the influence of others. What is missing is any exploration of the way that opinions, values and tastes are shaped collectively by a mediated and selective presentation of reality and by the framing of issues in the media. What is also absent is the possibility that opinions, values and tastes could be largely moulded in such a way as to match the interests of powerful people in society. This alternative critical viewpoint is not really compatible with economic models or the ruling ideology in which "the voters" and "the consumers" are really taking the ultimate decisions.

To understand the mechanisms by which non-indigenous "homo economicus" are trashing the planet we need to escape from the facile idea that consumers have independently formed innate preferences and that these innate preferences also inform their political thinking. A good start to understanding what happens in the real world is to take a quote from Edward Bernays. He was a nephew of Sigmund Freud and drew on his uncle's ideas, and those of other psychologists interested in group psycho-dynamics and crowd psychology, to establish the "propaganda industry" in the 1920s. This was later renamed "Public Relations" to disassociate it from the successes that Dr Goebbels had had using the same techniques to enrol mass support for the Nazis in Germany. (Bernays, 1928). As Bernays put it:

> If we understand the mechanism and motives of the group mind, is it not possible to control and regiment the masses according to our will without their knowing about it? The recent practice of propaganda has proved that it is possible, at least up to a certain point and within certain limits. (Bernays, 1928)

Crucial to this control of the group mind and the regimentation of the masses is the ability to create and manipulate what has been called "the consensus trance". According to psychologist Charles Tart, groups agree on which of their perceptions should be admitted to awareness (hence, consensus). Then they train each other to see the world in that way and only in that way (hence trance). The emperor without any clothes is an example of this idea. Another example is explained by Tart himself:

"Suppose we are talking with several co-workers at the office. On the surface level we are friendly but on another level we may be rivals competing for promotion. As a result, our conversations have hidden agendas, such as an implicit contract that we will focus on the surface friendliness and not notice the hidden rivalries in order to smooth our interactions, thus, avoiding the extra stress that would be generated through open rivalry. A second hidden agenda might be to preserve our self-concept about not being aggressive. A third might be to spy out information about our rival's intended actions that might be useful to us. An atmosphere of friendliness might make it more likely that a rival will be lulled and say more than he or she might say if he or she remembered our rivalry. A fourth hidden agenda might involve demonstrating our own superiority by being relaxed about a rival" (Tart, 1994, p. 202)

As a result there is a surface veneer of friendliness where no one looks too deeply underneath.

What often sustains the group trance is the fear of ostracism. There are taboo things that one cannot say or question – among business, government and most economists the very idea of questioning growth is not allowed otherwise one is banished to the group of tree huggers and eco-freaks who are not to be taken seriously.

With their approach that simply adds up the actions and ideas of individuals, economists have no way of making sense of "the group mind". If, as Margaret Thatcher said, "There is no such thing as society" then the very idea of a "group mind" is absurd. Even while, desperate to be seen as a loyal member of the inner circle of power, the economists, politicians and mandarins develop a keen sense of what they can and cannot say to each other and in public. The desire to belong is a strong one, especially for ambitious people, so even while the official's theory pictures all of us acting as independent minded individuals, the reality in the centres of power is very often abject conformity and sycophancy to the ideas and opinions of those who are more powerful than oneself.

Meanwhile, in society as a whole a great deal of effort and a lot of money is spent on managing collective perceptions and mass opinion. The operations of the PR industry are crucial to understanding mass ignorance and mass values on the environment. In 2010, science historians Naomi Oreskes and Erik M Conway published a book called *Merchants of Doubt* which drew parallels between what has been happening in the discussion of climate change and other public policy debates about smoking, acid rain and the hole in the ozone layer. A number of contrarian scientists were working with conservative think tanks and private corporations to "keep the controversy alive" on these issues and challenging the scientific consensus. The PR industry was at work. (Oreskes & Conway, 2010)

There is a certain irony in all of this as conservative economists like to claim the superiority of the market because it is supposed to best produce what corresponds to the aggregation of individual preferences. How these preferences are formed is supposed to be of no business of economists. Yet here we have a lucrative market served by companies and foundations that seek to shape the preferences of the public by creating doubt where the scientific consensus is that no such doubt exists. In other words this is a market sector that exists to distort the accurate formation of preferences...

But then to the faithful among the neoclassical, since the market is *the* optimal way of organising resource allocation, if any problem arises which the market cannot resolve without significant intervention from outside, then it must follow, inevitably, that the problem is not real.

What we might be witnessing here is an ideological consequence of market fundamentalism. In other words there might be a sort of collective denial of aspects of reality by a group of fundamentalists to avoid cognitive dissonance. What suggests this is a study of the past careers of a number of climate contrarian scientists. Earlier in their lives they were fierce anti-communists involved in research on the atomic bomb or on rockets to deliver atomic bombs. If you have a mentality prepared to contemplate fighting a thermonuclear war, climate catastrophe is probably a price worth paying in order to retain a market economy uncomplicated by state enforced mitigation policies.

For many people the best way of coping with cogent critics is to ignore them and there have been lots of cogent critics of market economics over the last two centuries. I don't expect therefore that many will read this book – though a few might skim it looking for something that they are convinced is wrong which will then allow them to put it back on the book shelf.

Even when prominent neoclassical economists are forced to admit that a key part of their thinking is in error, the textbooks still reproduce the error and not the criticism... However, were a neoclassical economist to be reading this piece then I would imagine that they would say that this is all about politics, social psychology and not economics.

This way of putting reality into boxes that protect something by splitting off the difficulties into another box is familiar to therapists. Bankers do it too – things that might damage a company's reputation, or are particularly risky, are placed in another company, "a special purpose vehicle", registered in an offshore tax haven, so they "don't really count" as a part of the bank that set them up.

Yet the problem of acquiring accurate information cannot be expelled from economics as if the insights of other subject disciplines don't count. Since information is heavily mediated by agencies that select and shape it for their clients, there is no way around the fact that information, and its half-brother "misinformation", arises in a field distorted by power structures. An analogy would be the way that the path of light is bent by the gravitation of objects of great mass in physics. Finding the truth to make economic decisions is problematic because interests are at stake.

The fact is that, in order to take decisions as to whether or not to buy a commodity, consumers need to know about that good. If they are environmentally aware, or concerned about social issues, they will, for example, want to know about the so-called "external costs" which, to repeat, are all pervading. That will make it in someone's interest to try to control that information.

Managers too will want to know about many things and it will often be in someone's interest to mislead them. For example a business purchasing drilling rights will want to know the likelihood that the well will turn out dry or how quickly it will deplete. This information is likely to be subject to distortion. A company that knows that a gas field they bought is not as productive as they had originally hoped, and that depletion rates are quick, will probably want to get out if they can. However, to liquidate their investment they will want other suckers to believe that the gas field is productive, and worth paying money for. The same logic applied when Goldman Sachs' traders offloaded securities that they privately labelled as "toxic waste" while misleading those buying them to believe that they were valuable.

Governments too will want accurate information. It is their job to know when production processes are risky, dirty and costly to keep serviced if they are to take rational decisions about public infrastructure. But it will frequently not be in the interests of companies to be fully upfront about these things. The fact that a quiet small town is going to be subject to an onslaught of heavy trucks passing through it, or the fact that jobs promised by a development will be taken by staff back at their HQ thousands of miles away, or what chemicals are being used in an industrial process, may be things that companies would rather the politicians and the public did not know.

Instead of a fairy story that economic decisions are taken by people appraising all the available information in conditions of "rational expectations", realism demands that we acknowledge that decisions are likely to be taken in a variety of "states of knowing/unknowing" – developed from: (Witte, Crown, Bernas, & Witte, 2008) :

Known unknowns – things/situations that you know you don't know about;

Delusions and wishful thinking – errors in which you (and perhaps your group) have an emotional investment which are thus, difficult to shift

Denials – things which are too painful to know so you ignore information that confirms them

Informational asymmetry – unknowns for some people that are known to others (vested interests blocking information flow);

Costly information – situations where getting to know costs so much so that that partial or inaccurate knowing or even ignorance may be chosen instead

Deception and secrecy – hiding knowns from others and/or fostering errors or delusions (by using secrecy jurisdictions and tax havens for example)

Technical information – information that is difficult for lay people without a specific competence to interpret

Taboos – things/situations that a peer group/the law/ company business culture think you should not try to get to know

Paranoias – hypotheses about the nature of unknowns that impute motives by others that are to be feared

Granfalloons- system of group belief to pursue a purpose that is ultimately futile, even destructive, but profitable for members of the coalition pursuing it.

Choosing definitions that hide and distract from problems – e.g. saying that there are no cases of shale fracking causing water contamination – by defining fracking to exclude very common drilling and well integrity failures as well as very common surface accidents and spills.

Attentional manipulation – deliberately directing attention to one process so that victims do not devote attention to some other process which remains unseen (see the cover of the book)

(Some things will be *"unknown unknowns"* – but by definition we cannot articulate them until "after the event" as this information emerges during the course of activity)

Accurate information is hard to come by, particularly in societies managed by sociopaths. Even when one tries to actively research for the information that one needs it will often be available only from and through media (ted) sources. It will be open to distortions by vested interests. It may turn out to be "misinformation". "Rational decision making" is a concept, an idea, that deviates a long way from everyday reality.

Getting at the truth is not straightforward – and not only because of crude manipulation by spin doctors. Mass opinion is also formed by the taken for granted way that the media and "experts" present and prevent real deliberation by pre-supposing the conceptual frames in which information about issues are chosen, researched and presented. Academic discourse is a powerful force for affecting the way that issues are framed. In the case of the environment and climate change the issues are typically framed using concepts adapted from mainstream economics.

For example, by framing issues to do with climate change in economics language a powerful taboo is implicitly imported into any discourse, a taboo that does not have to be made explicit, because it is "understood" as self-evident: on no account can any options be considered that do not involve continued economic growth.

Using neoclassical economic theory as the concept system imposes a set of presumptions that limit democratic deliberation of issues. Economists enforce a view in which a mathematical procedure is supposed to give us the answer to what to do about questions like climate change or biodiversity loss, not debate and contestation of different views and value systems. Because supposedly the calculation of what people are prepared to pay is all that counts it automatically follows that the money perspective wins. As Professor of public policy, Clive Hamilton puts it in a criticism of one climate economist, Richard Tol:

> The only preferences that Tol regards as legitimate are those expressed by consumers in the supermarket and never those expressed by citizens at the ballot box. This is perhaps the ultimate conceit of mainstream economics, the equation of market behaviour with democracy itself. (Hamilton, 2010, pp. 59-60)

What then tends to happen is that an economic mind-set takes control over the decision-making in a way that particularly favours people of wealth. The key information used to assess environmental issues are in the form of measurements that economists make. The relevant variables are the kind that economists will recognise. Financial measuring rods are judged to be the right ones. The research procedures take for granted value systems and processes of judgement that are preference utilitarian i.e. they do not necessarily reflect and respect the widely different ethical systems used by the public which are not all utilitarian at all e.g. rights based ethics.

Having destroyed democratic debate in the framing of the issues, the economists then frame the allowable solutions. Business and other "economic actors" e.g. consumers must be incentivised to behaviours that protect the environment. This is achieved by "giving nature (or its attributes like "eco-system services") a price" and "hardwiring it into financial markets" (UNEP).

The critique of this way of doing things is found elsewhere in this book. Suffice it to say here that this situation allows what is called "environmental policy" to be colonised by corporate agendas which have very little to with saving the world from environmental destruction and everything to do with corporations gaining strategic control of value chains - for example in genetic and technical information, in production processes and resources in energy, biomass, water and land. A techno-innovation juggernaut is constructed with the help of the state... the destruction of the environment continues and economists give their blessing.

In conclusion, the emergence of non-indigenous market based societies has powerfully undermined the very possibility of acquiring the kind of adequate knowledge, connected to the necessary purposes and belief systems, that are needed to protect nature and the environment. Indigenous societies are fighting back, desperately. However, the global economic system that is destroying the environment has not just lost access to knowledge known in earlier centuries, it has evolved institutions whose role is to actively block the population from knowing and to lead them away from the knowledge that they need to protect themselves from the perilous state of the ecological system.

Chapter 13

Inequality, Epidemiology and Economics

Public health is an alternative indicator of well-being and is strongly correlated to levels of equality or inequality. Greater equality means greater well-being for everyone and a smaller need for the state - yet inequality has been increasing dramatically.

My father was called a "public health inspector", later, an environmental health officer and, although I trained as an economist, I have, for many years of my life, worked on the fringes of the health and social services - having dealings both with mental health services and also with the public health services. During and after this time it always seemed blindingly obvious to me that health statistics provide a far better indicator of improvements (or deteriorations) in well-being than increases in GDP. After all, GDP can rise because business for undertakers is booming and prescriptions for anti-depressant pills are soaring.

As a matter of fact, it is the business of public health professionals to address themselves to what makes a society and community healthier, physically and mentally. They look into this with epidemiological studies to identify what needs to change for positive improvement. They have another way of looking at the issue of what constitutes "improvement" – and arguably a much more tangible one than that of neoclassical economics.

Over time, as social and economic conditions have changed, what public health professionals have addressed has changed too. In the early nineteenth century it was necessary to battle to clean up urban areas and install an infrastructure to improve public hygiene and sewerage disposal – services which proved to be far more effectively developed by innovating local authorities than by the free market.

In our own times however, epidemiological research has shown that improvements in public health require something that free market economists don't like to hear about – greater income equality. Inconveniently for neo-liberals, there is a great deal of evidence for this – and perhaps even more surprising for them, the well-being of the better off groups in society tends to be higher in more equal societies too. This may seem counter intuitive to people with a neoliberal way of thinking about things but the evidence exists. As a society becomes more equal the health and quality of life of the better off also improves.

The book "The Spirit Level" by two professors of epidemiology, Richard Wilkinson and Kate Pickett gather together a large amount of evidence. (Wilkinson & Pickett, 2010). Since what they have discovered is an unwelcome finding for many academics they have been accused of cherry picking their data but, as they explain in rebuttals of their critics in the second edition of the book, they chose data sources on strict criteria to ensure that genuine comparisons were possible between countries. As they explain too, their findings have been common knowledge among epidemiologists for decades. They quote the editors of the *British Medical Journal* in 1992 who wrote:

> The big idea is that what matters in determining mortality and health in a society is less the overall wealth of that society and more how unevenly wealth is distributed. The more evenly wealth is distributed the better the health of that society. (Wilkinson & Pickett, 2010, p. 81)

Evidence for a correlation between poor health and income inequality exists for physical as well as mental health and drug addiction. Lower life expectancy, higher rates of infant mortality, shorter height, poor self-reported health, low birth weight, AIDS and depression are all higher in more unequal societies.

Many non-health issues are also correlated with the degree of inequality. Indicators of educational attainment, violence, measures of imprisonment and punishment all vary with the degree of income inequality. Some critics have alleged that these are just statistical correlations and that Wilkinson and Pickett have not proven causative connections. Perhaps a book that causes severe cognitive dissonance is not one that they want to read closely for the allegation is not true.

But how does it come about that the better off also have their health and life quality improved if a society moves towards greater equality? One of the first achievements of public health practitioners in 19th century Britain, the improvement of public hygiene and clean water supplies, not only turned out to be good for the poor, it turned out to be good for the relatively well-off too. Wealthy people too had died in the cholera epidemics. They too suffered from the stench of the drains and the failure to clean the streets.

There are multiple knock back effects of income inequality too. Earlier in this book the evidence about consumerism and "affluenza" draws attention to the way in which people with extrinsic values, who pursue income related purposes and status ends, do not achieve happiness. How could they?

The consumer culture systematically muddles things that are not at all the same – if you seek and achieve status then you put yourself above other people. If people look up to you because of your wealth and power then you separate yourself from them and create a treadmill for yourself to maintain or even increase that distance. You may indeed then surround yourself with sycophants – neoclassical economists are good at fulfilling this role for rich people – but the emotional quality of your relationships will not be very high. You may, of course, create stylised rituals with any people who are prepared to believe that they are your inferiors – your butler, chauffeur or chamber maid. Within the constraints of those relationships you may feel the comfort of familiarity as someone gets to know you and appears to accept you for what you are. However, these are not exactly close relationships. You will not be able to share feelings of vulnerability and loss which are bound to occur in life, nor warmth and human closeness. The inability to empathise with others, which is what Adam Smith described in his *Theory of Moral Sentiments* as the foundation of morality, will be closed off to you. (Smith A. , The Theory of Moral Sentiments, 1759)

You will also have to accept a great many restrictions to your life, for example, living in a gated community; the need for extreme care and for a personal body guard. All this in addition to the inability to understand why your life still feels empty, and the fear of sharing that with anyone which will all degrades your quality of life.

I recall when I worked in Germany in the 1990s, one of my colleagues was a Brazilian professor of architecture from the University of Rio de Janeiro who was on sabbatical leave. She loved it in Germany because she felt safe there. She would explain to me how, in Rio, she would choose a different route to work each day, at a different time, because she was terrified of armed young men hijacking her car or kidnapping her. This was a common occurrence and a relative of hers had been murdered when he resisted having his car stolen. Her life in Rio was thus, one of chronic gnawing fear. Rio at that time was one of the most unequal cities in the world with extreme wealth and extreme poverty coexisting side by side.

Meanwhile I live in Nottingham which, a few years ago, was one of the leading cities in the UK for gun violence. It was, and still is, a city with an economic development strategy based on its being the regional shopping capital. Nottingham has had a policy of promoting itself as a major centre for night clubs for the relatively wealthy young people who were at, or had just graduated from, the two universities. The city centre is an "in your face" consumer centre – for those who can afford it. Meanwhile, over many years, the working community of Nottingham, the people who had worked in Raleigh's bicycle factory, Boots the Chemist, the textile industry, telecommunications and the local pits – and who had lived in the inner city, lost their jobs. Many of them lost their homes too as estates were broken up in slum clearance programmes which in turn broke up supportive extended family relationships and scattered people into new estates on the edge of the city. Many of the young people in these estates, unemployed and without qualifications, looked from the outside at the party in the city centre that they had little money to join in with and developed strategies of their own. Many either sold drugs or took drugs - or both – and then fought turf wars with guns to be top dog. And/or they ended up on psychiatric wards and the drug addiction unit. The (probably very temporary) city centre success story has a dark shadow.

The implications of the Wilkinson and Pickett research, and that of their colleagues, is profound. However, you look at it, the evidence is that greater well-being is to be found through greater equality and that, without it, societies become highly dysfunctional. The fact that this idea does not occur to most economists, indeed that it an anathema to them, is no doubt because of the very false set of concepts and values that the economic religion has implanted in their minds. Margaret Thatcher expressed their mind set when she claimed that "there is no such thing as society". And indeed, if you read most economics textbooks it is pushing it a bit to describe them as "social" science. Because the "methodological individualists", take tastes and preferences as givens and do not delve deeper into how these preferences are formed it is easy for them to be left with the impression that it is as if people calculate their individual interests in isolation. If you amputate the social and institutional processes of preference formation from your theory of the world then you will indeed end up believing that there is no such thing as society because you let no consideration of social processes ever pollute the purity of your individualist theoretical construct. Ignoring leads to ignorance.

But of course "methodological individualism" is a complete nonsense. Much of advertising is to encourage people to show off via their consumption. It is the encouragement of a toxic kind of social relationship but a social relationship it is nonetheless. And we influence each other in many other ways too.

One should also say here that, even in a very conventional economic sense, the inequality research has multiple economic implications that have scarcely begun to be explored. For example, if more equal societies have better educational attainments then that has major implications for economic performance and efficiency. Whatever view you have of the economic future, whether you think of it in conventional mainstream terms in terms of a growing "knowledge economy" or whether you think of it, as I do, in limits to growth terms, a better educated labour force is good news. It suggests that economic efficiency is actually encouraged by more equality – an idea that you won't find many economists exploring.

Greater equality means a smaller need for the state

Yet the idea is plausible, as is, on first impression, the surprising idea that greater equality would probably lead to a smaller state and ultimately to lower taxes. Adam Smith put his finger on the key issue at stake here:

> Civil government, so far as it is instituted for the security of property, is in reality instituted for the defence of the rich against the poor, or of those who have some property against those who have none at all. (Smith A. , The Wealth of Nations, 1776)

From this follows that the greater the gulf between rich and poor the bigger the government, the more it has to do and the greater the expenditure it will need. As Wilkinson and Pickett explain:

> Greater inequality actually *increases* the need for big government – for more police, more prisons, more health and social services of every kind. Most of these services are expensive and only very partially effective, but we shall need them for ever if we continue to have high levels of inequality that create the problems they are designed to deal with. Several states in the USA now spend more on prisons than one higher education. In fact, one of the best and most humane ways of achieving small government is by reducing inequality. Similarly the assumption that greater equality can only be achieved through higher taxes and benefits, which presumably led the Tax Payers' Alliance to publish its criticism of *The Spirit Level,* is also a mistake. We have been at pains to point out that some societies achieve greater equality with unusually low taxation because they have smaller earnings differences before taxes. (Wilkinson & Pickett, 2010, pp. 294-295)

Sadly, arguments on their own are not enough. As the gulf between rich and poor widens, the possibility of any communication of ideas and social feedback across the growing divide gets smaller and smaller. So too does the chance of communicating with a state set up to defend the rich and pre-occupied with their own interests.

Growing inequality

At the time of writing, the gulf between rich and poor in most countries globally is now very wide indeed. There are good reasons to believe that the gap could get wider. One of very few economists to actually study inequality in depth is Thomas Picketty, a professor at the Paris School of Economics, in a very large tome published in French in 2014 and in English translation in early 2014.

Picketty argues that the history of inequality cannot be reduced to purely economic mechanisms:

> The history of inequality is shaped by the way economic, social and political actors view what is just and what is not, as well as by the relative power of those actors and the collective choices that result. (Picketty, 2014, p. 20).

The social and political mechanisms were particularly visible in the shocks during and between the world wars roughly in the period from 1914 to 1950. In this period, inequality fell dramatically in many European countries and to some degree in the USA. This was largely through taxation regimes to pay for the war as well as political responses to the aspirations of mobilised populations.

At other times, economic trends within capitalism have pulled in contradictory directions. There have been those processes that have tended to increase inequality and opposite processes tending to reduce it, such as, the increasing diffusion of knowledge and skills. It is However, the forces for inequality that have tended to prevail.

The chief driver of increasing inequality according to Picketty is a rate of return on capital, r, which is greater than the rate of growth, g. In shorthand r > g. This is because the very rich get most of their income, not as a payment for employment (including for management) but as a return on their capital, whereas, most others are earning an income from their work.

> When the rate of return on capital significantly exceeds the growth rate of the economy... then it logically follows that inherited wealth grows faster than output and income. People with inherited wealth need save only a portion of their income from capital to see that capital grow more quickly than the economy as a whole. Under such conditions it is inevitable that inherited wealth will dominate wealth amassed from a lifetime's labour by a wide margin, and the concentration of capital will attain extremely high levels... (Picketty, 2014, p. 26)

His book is full of statistics which make his point about rising inequality – although not as high as it would have been had not "the shocks" of the interwar periods occurred. In that period, inherited wealth took a hard knock in many countries. Throughout most of history, most people have lived in poverty in their old age and then died with little or no wealth at all. However, as society becomes more unequal, the rich are at their most wealthy in their old age and at death and pass on their inheritance. This is observable by comparing the average wealth of people in their fifties to people in their eighties. During the crises early in the 20th century, the ratios changed dramatically. On the eve of the First World War, in France, octogenarians were two and a half times as wealthy as people in their fifties. In 1930 they were only 50% wealthier and by 1947 the people in their 50s were actually 40% wealthier than those in their 80s. (Picketty, 2014, p. 396)

After a period of reconstruction following World War Two, inequality has been on the rise for several decades. In ball park figures, global GDP has grown at about 3.3% pa and average world wealth per adult has grown at about 2.1% pa per adult after allowing for inflation. However, the average annual growth rate of income for the top 1/ (100 million) highest wealth holders has been more like 6.8% pa and average. (Picketty, 2014, p. 435)

Other studies at slightly different dates give other figures for income inequality and wealth inequality. The figures differ but they are all huge – greater than at any time in human history. A 2006 study by James Davies of the University of Western Ontario together with Anthony Shorroks and Susanna Sandstrom of the United Nations University – World Institute for Development Economics Research, found that the richest 2% of adults in the world owned more than half of global household wealth. Wealth here is taken to mean net worth - the value of physical and financial assets less debts.

The same study found that the richest 1% of adults alone owned 40% of global assets in the year 2000, and that the richest 10% of adults accounted for 85% of the world total. In contrast, the bottom half of the world adult population owned barely 1% of global wealth. (Davies, Shorrocks, & Sandstrom, 2008)

Since 2006, there has been the global financial crisis of 2007 and its aftermath. This crisis has not stopped the concentration of wealth increasing and concentrating even further. The super-rich have governments and central banks to look after their interests. If they get into trouble they are mostly bailed out. It is the rest of us that have picked up the losses... and our increased vulnerability makes it even easier for the super-rich to rip us off.

As growth falls off, the rich are still able to continue to take a rising cut of world income so inequality is likely to rise even further in the absence of equalising political intervention. The processes that limit growth, like depletion of fossil fuel sources, are creating new opportunities for the elite as they corner the increasingly scarce natural capital resources and make everyone else pay high prices for them. This is very clear for example in the high and rising price for oil and natural gas. As the cost of bringing new production of oil and gas rises, much existing production in remaining oil and gas fields will have a lower production cost and will make a big rental income from the difference between the oil and gas price and their lower production costs. This money will likely flow into funds and part of these will be used to buy up other natural capital assets...

Of course we can try to tell these wealthy that they would be better off in a more equal world. However, they are now so far away from us ordinary mortals that it is doubtful that most of the super-rich, and the organisations that work for them, are any longer within communication range. A very large part of their wealth (and operations) is hidden in tax havens and secrecy jurisdictions. According to some estimates to a value of between 10 and 30% of global GDP. (Picketty, 2014, p. 466)

It was this fact that the rich have opted out of responsibility to the community that they dominate that brought the eruptions of the Occupy movement - which was then met by closed minded thugs in uniforms, armed with pepper sprays.

The classic Chinese oracle, the I Ching, says of revolutions: "*The object of a revolution must be the attainment of clarified, secure conditions to ensure general stability on the basis of what is possible at the moment.*" (Wilhelm(Tr) & Baynes (Tr), 1984, p. 49)

What is possible at the moment are the creation of "lifeboat projects" for a world in crisis. Federated and networked together these can constitute a "solidarity economy" to attract millions of people as the world of the super-rich hits the rocks of ecological limits. No doubt they will try to solve the resultant crises at our expense and we must also devise joint strategies to counter a further increase in inequality in an aggressive and yet constructive way. Then again, violent revolutions in a world armed to the teeth will destabilise rather than stabilise.

These political economic issues are discussed further later...

Chapter 14

The centrality of externalities to economic understanding

What economists call "externalities" are not unusual or a special case, they are ubiquitous. They are rooted in private property and the relationships of market society. The way in which non market societies protect bio-diversity through totem arrangements is described.

Private property means that a single owner has the right to do with a resource as s/he sees fit. However, what they decide about these "resources" affect communities of people and communities of species (eco-systems). Very often, the effects are not positive. John Ruskin, a 19th century art critic who also wrote on economics, coined the term "illth" to describe the destructive effects imposed on society and the environment by the economy of his day.

Economists have had to adjust their theories and have come up with the concept of "externalities", that is, the benefits or costs of an allocation decision that arise for non-owners. In a later chapter I critically examine the idea that these externalities can be managed by those people affected by them coming to a deal with those causing them. This would involve finding "the right price" for the externality and then doing a trade. The purpose of this chapter is to look at the institutional and property relationship contexts in which these "externalities" arise, and thus, to show how and why, in some kinds of society, there are no "externalities".

The word, "externality", conveys the impression that this is a footnote to economic theory, a sort of additional point. Actually, externalities are ubiquitous. There cannot be any kind of resource allocation decision involving matter or energy without externalities. "The economy" is embodied and embedded in physical and energetic processes in the physical world. It involves "stuff" processed by energy conversions. This stuff, the matter, can neither be created nor destroyed, though it can change its form. Likewise, energy changes its form when used. It follows from this that what are used as "economic resources" must have come from somewhere originally where these resources had an original function and/or were part of some other system or structure. These resources must also go somewhere after they are embodied in products and/or where they are wholly or partly turned into wastes. Extracting resources from places has consequences and dumping wastes and pollution has consequences. Over several centuries, this extraction and dumping has usually been out of, and back, into the commons.

The fish on your plate was originally a part of the marine eco-system and, after it is processed by your body, will become sewerage that may go back into the marine eco-system. The heat from the cooker is from gas that was in the ground and getting it out of the ground changed the geological structure of a place. This process might affect underground water flow bringing contaminants to the surface, as it does in the case of fracking. Burning the gas will change the characteristics of the atmosphere.

Because production processes are embedded and embodied in the physical world, nothing of substance happens without "externalities". Climate change illustrates this clearly. No productive activity takes place without the use of energy. Almost all energy in developed economies, as well as a large amount of energy in "developing" economies, involves generating greenhouse gases. The greenhouse gases arise when producers use oxygen in the atmosphere to burn fuels with and thus, generate CO_2. This is an all pervasive process and what is all-pervasive should be integral to production theory, which it isn't in neoclassical theory. In mainstream economics, climate change economics is a topic for a tiny number of specialists. It is almost as if climate change is some kind of special case.

> Externalities are ad hoc corrections introduced as needed to save appearances, like the epicycles of Ptolemaic astronomy. Externalities do represent a recognition of neglected aspects of concrete experience, but in such a way as to minimize restructuring of basic theory. As long as externalities involve minor details, this is perhaps a reasonable procedure. But when vital issues (e.g. the capacity of the earth to support life) have to be classed as externalities, it is time to restructure basic concepts and start with a different set of abstractions that can embrace what was previously external. (Daly & CobbJr, For the Common Good, 1994)

Protecting bio-diversity through totem arrangements

A crucial question is then whether or not the other people affected by so-called externalities get to have any say in the resource allocation decision – and if so, how much say or influence do they have. Some indigenous peoples "represent" particular species, get to know all about them, and therefore protect them in their totem arrangements. In this way, the "community" becomes more than its human members. "Non-human persons" are represented indirectly too.

The following is an example of how this works. In modern economics we would speak of there being an "externality" if trees are cut down and if this, in turn, results in maggots from those trees getting everywhere. In Australian aboriginal arrangements this is prevented by a specific man's totem responsibilities, rooted in the aboriginal religious code:

> I am boss for *Mpwere* [Maggot] Dreaming. My worship is maggots and witchetties and flies... and itchy grubs – those hairy caterpillars that line up- and those *angente* [sawfly] grubs that attach themselves in a mass to the river red gum trees. Those trees can't be cut down or there will be lots of maggots- maggots everywhere. Wenten Rubuntja quoted in (Gammage, 2011, pp. 129-129)

Here are community members who know how their eco-system works and by "representing" other species in their community's decision-making they prevent particular kinds of "externality" arising.

It would be wrong to over-idealise indigenous societies but it is also important to recognise skills, knowledge and practices which "modern societies" have lost and forgotten. Customary and commons based societies often do not have a problem of "externalities" if the community is functioning properly because everything is internal to the community. If the community is long standing and has a deep knowledge of the local eco-system then environmental impacts on all "people actors" and "other species actors" are taken into account in its decisions.

Buen Vivir or Sumak Kawsay – the "Good Life" without externalities

Similar arrangements can be found among other indigenous peoples. In a society where harmony between the people, and between the people and the ecological system, is the desired norm there is an ethic and a belief that emphasises balance rather than "improvement". This means that all community interests (and all species) are taken into account and accommodated in whatever decisions are made. For example, the first nations living in the Andes region had and have a philosophy of *Sumak Kawsay*, translated into Spanish as *"Buen Vivir" or "Good Life."* (Fatheuer, 2011)

We must beware of understanding this in a non-indigenous, consumerist idea of a *"Good Life"*. It is only conceivable in the social context in which people live. It involves striving for harmony and balance rather than dominance. This is important because the concept has plurality and a co-existence based on respect – both of human communities and of Nature – integral to it. It is also the opposite of "development" as conventionally understood. Eduardo Gudynas explains that "Buen Vivir rejects the idea of a predetermined historical linearity in which 'development stages' must be followed by all nations (imitating industrialised nations) but rather defends the multiplicity of historical processes" The dominance of western ideas are not rejected by seen as one among many options in an approach that has been called 'interculturality'. (Gudynas 2014).

Its features are:

- Harmony and balance of all and with all
- Complementarity, solidarity and equality
- Collective well-being and the satisfaction of the basic needs of all in harmony with Mother Earth
- Respect for the rights of Mother Earth and for human rights
- Recognition of people for what they are and not for what they own
- Removal of all forms of colonialism, imperialism and interventionism
- Peace between people and with Mother Earth

When people live as members of human communities, in communities of species, decisions about "resources" accommodate multiple users and therefore multiple uses. Externalities don't arise in so far as this accommodation occurs effectively.

In a commons and other social arrangements, to allocate community resources one would expect that efforts would be made to accommodate all interests so that extreme either/or allocation decisions are not made. However, private property is precisely defined by the power of the property owner to ignore and overrule consideration for other people and species. This has allowed the accumulation of wealth by stealing from the commons in one of two ways described by American author Peter Barnes:

> Enclosure, in which property rights are literally taken or given away, is half the reason for the commons" decline; the other half is a form of trespass called externalizing —that is, shifting costs to the commons. Externalizing is as relentless as enclosure, yet much less noticed, since it requires no active aid from politicians. It occurs quietly continuously as corporations add illth to the commons without permission or payment. The one-two punch of enclosure and externalizing is especially potent. With one hand, corporations take valuable stuff from the commons and privatize it. With the other hand, they dump bad stuff into the commons and pay nothing. The result is profits for corporations but a steady loss of value for the commons. (Barnes, 2006, pp. 19-20)

Extractivism and the "invisible elbow"

"Externalities" are therefore particularly the result of a breakdown of community management arrangements when private property displaces common property. As we saw earlier, private property arrangements tend to be associated with large scale specialist uses of land and resources which displace the diversity of community and species uses. The resulting resource use practice is sometimes described as "extractivist". The "Ricardian" specialism imposed on localities by their private owners focuses upon single uses which displace others. This enables large scale production for distant markets while at the same time necessitating further marketisation. In the world as recommended by Ricardo, if your area is now entirely given over to producing wine everyone living and working in that area has to buy in all their other food and other needs because there are no longer any local sources for other foods, fibre crops and clothing and so on.

The resulting "de-localisation" in this kind of world then also gives rise to pervasive "externalities" because they make it increasingly difficult to see dishonest, cruel and destructive practices which occur during the production of what you buy. When you purchase clothing and other goods produced outside your own area, you cannot possibly know in any detail or with any certainty the conditions under which the purchased in products are created. You can see the product and you can know what its price is, however, the fact that it was produced by child labour, or in a factory that was in danger of collapsing, is likely to be unknown to you.

Smithian economists make much of the "invisible hand"; of the self-organising market in which prices give people the information they need in order to make their buying and selling decisions. What is suggested here is that prices can tell you all that you need to know. But there is a flaw in this argument that economist Michael Jacobs called "the invisible elbow":

> If consumers had to suffer all the pollution caused by the products they bought, they wouldn't buy them in such damaging quantities. It is precisely because costs are passed on to third parties that we let them occur. Environmental degradation is a genuine case of passing the muck...

environmental problems occur through the combination of millions of individual economic decisions. These decisions are taken privately, without reference to what everyone else is doing, because nobody can know what everyone else is doing. Added together, market forces generate an overall result which no-one can predict. This is the "invisible hand" which the economist Adam Smith argued brought general prosperity. But it can equally be an "invisible elbow" which brings the earth's precarious ecological balance crashing down like a pile of cans in a supermarket. (Jacobs, The Price of the Future, 1990)

Chapter 15

Ethical Disconnection and re-connection – corporations as "people" and NGOs

Externalities involve ethical choices. The mechanisms that allow corporate actors to distance themselves from responsibility from their anti-social and anti-environmental choices are described – for example the role of corporate personhood and evasions of regulation, taxation and control. NGOs and Civil Society Organisations have evolved to counter unethical corporate choices. Unfortunately they are often co-opted and neutralised.

Externalities as ethical choices in a globalised world

There is a great irony that Adam Smith, a professor of Moral Philosophy, should become the apostle of an economic order that degraded people's inclination to take moral decisions in their economic arrangements. Further, an economic order which has helped "externalities" to multiply until the point where we have a veritable social and ecological crisis. Loving your neighbour is a fine and practical ethical principle but almost all of the products that we use are not produced by our neighbours at all, but by people elsewhere in other countries and, to an increasing extent, on the other side of the world.

Distance matters - the greater the geographical and institutional distance between decisions and the people bearing the consequences of those decisions, the more difficult it is for the decision-maker to know about these consequences, good or bad. In addition, the more difficult it is for a person suffering the consequence of decisions to know who the decision-maker was and their motives. Distance erodes feedback, accountability and responsibility.

As a Professor of Moral Philosophy, Adam Smith wrote not only the "Wealth of Nations" but a book called "The Theory of Moral Sentiments". In the latter he argued that human morality is based in the capacity of human beings to conceive what they would feel if they "were in other people's shoes" in conditions of happiness or misfortune.

> As we have no immediate experience of what other men feel, we can form no idea of the manner in which they are affected, but by conceiving what we ourselves should feel in the like situation. Though our brother is on the rack, as long as we ourselves are at our ease, our senses will never inform us of what he suffers. They never did, and never can, carry us beyond our own person, and it is by the imagination only that we can form any conception of what are his sensations. Neither can that faculty help us to this any other way, than by representing to us what would be our own, if we were in his case. It is the impressions of our own senses only, not those of his, which our

imaginations copy. By the imagination, we place ourselves in his situation. (Smith A. , The Theory of Moral Sentiments, Chapter 1, 1759)

What we can say that our imaginative capacity to mirror the feelings of others depends, according to Smith, on the vividness of our observation. This involves either seeing the fortunes or misfortunes that effect people first hand or through the vividness and detail of a description. It follows from this that our ethical sense is most finely tuned to the love and care we feel for people that we know very well, or, if not, those people for whom we take a detailed interest and about whom we have much information. These are people to whom we are "close" where the word has a rather literal meaning. We are "in touch" with these people and what Smith says makes sense for our relations with people like this.

It also follows from this that, for Smith, our moral sense, rooted in a sympathy for the people and places that we are familiar with, can only extend so far:

> The administration of the great system of the universe... the care of the universal happiness of all rational and sensible beings, is the business of God and not of man. To man is allotted a much humbler department, but one much more suitable to the weakness of his powers, and to the narrowness of his comprehension: the care of his own happiness, of that of his family, his friends, his country... (Smith A. , The Theory of Moral Sentiments, 1759)

But Smith's idea here throws up the question of how morality operates in a globalised economy or even whether it is possible in such a world. The scholastic economists had said that we give to those we love and we exchange with strangers. But strangers are those with whom we have no immediate sympathy arising in closeness, in familiarity and vivid personal experience of their world. We cannot so easily conceive of how strangers will feel, nor with the experiences that might affect them. Indeed, when we go into a shop we buy products almost entirely made by strangers we will never meet. We have no idea who they are nor under what conditions they worked to deliver the product to us.

Clearly, if we are producing goods for ourselves we are likely to be a little bit careful about the use of toxins in the production process. It is a similar case when we produce for loved ones or for local customers we have got to know and who buy from us every week. But does it apply in the same way to strangers on the other side of the world though? Strangers who may buy from us only once? The ethical issues are actually the same, but the emotional sense of loyalty to loved ones, friends and people we know, compared to unknown people far away, do not feel the same. Nor are the structures of accountability the same. Prior to the financial crash of 2007, many financial securities that Wall Street "insiders" knew to be worthless and described using words like "toxic waste" were sold to pension funds on other continents. Did they care? These were anonymous people on the other side of the world. Clearly, if Smith was right then a global economy is highly vulnerable. Only at a local level are people's sympathies likely to be strong enough, and loyalties powerful enough, to maintain ethically healthy economic relationships where economic actors actually buy into regulation.

It is important to make this argument because "externalities" are ethical choices. When a company pumps its toxic waste into a river, that is not just an economic act it is an ethical choice by its managers and/or its owners.

Ethical disconnection – the role of corporate "personhood"

To make (un)ethical choices easier, economic history has been full of processes and institutional arrangements constructed to allow the people making the production and supply decisions to distance themselves spatially and institutionally from their ethical responsibility to a wider society and to a clean environment. In the nineteenth century, the creation of limited liability companies and the development of corporations enabled responsibility for debts to be transferred to "corporate persons" and away from individuals who put their money into these companies.

It was not always so. For example, after freeing itself from British colonialism and for the first half of the 19th century, US states kept a close control on business corporations. In a book by Thomas Hartmann we learn how in most US states during this period corporations were required to have a clear purpose, to be fulfilled but not exceeded.

- Corporations' licenses to do business were revocable by the state legislature if they exceeded or did not fulfil their chartered purpose(s) or misbehaved.
- The act of incorporation did not relieve corporate management or stockholders/owners of responsibility or liability for corporate acts. Corporation officers, directors, or agents couldn't break the law and avoid punishment by claiming they were "just doing their job" when committing crimes but instead could be held criminally liable for violating the law.
- State (not federal) courts heard cases where corporations or their agents were accused of breaking the law or harming the public.
- Corporation charters were granted for a specific period of time, such as twenty or thirty years (instead of being granted "in perpetuity," as is now the practice).
- Corporations' real estate holdings were limited to what was necessary to carry out their specific purpose(s).
- Corporations were prohibited from making any political and other kinds of contributions, direct or indirect.

All corporation records and documents were open to the legislature or the state attorney general

(Hartman, 2010)

But in 1886, after a series of cases brought by lawyers representing the expanding railroad interests, the Supreme Court ruled that corporations were "persons" and entitled to the same rights granted to people under the Bill of Rights. Since this ruling, America has lost the legal structures that enabled people to control corporate behaviour.

From this time onwards, "ethical responsibility" has been set up in an institutional and legal structure that made the companies accountable to the owners only. The companies, the supposed "corporate persons", have a fiduciary duty to make maximum profits. Unlike real human beings, who act from a range of motives including the empathy and sympathy of which Adam Smith wrote, corporations are supposed to be exclusively self-interested. This means that they are effectively supposed to rob the commons if it is legal to do so. As investor Robert Monks put it very eloquently in the film "The Corporation":

> The great problem of having corporate citizens is that they aren't like the rest of us. As Baron Thurlow in England is supposed to have said, "They have no soul to save, and they have no body to incarcerate"... The corporation is an externalizing machine, in the same way that a shark is a killing machine. (Achbar and Abbott, 2004)

To whom do these companies owe loyalty? What does loyalty mean? Well, it turns out that that was a rather naïve concept anyway as corporations always owed obligation to themselves to get large and to get profitable. In doing this, it tends to be more profitable to the extent that it can make other people pay the bills for its impact on society. There's a terrible word that economists use for this called "externalities".

People who are subjected to military training are subjected to various psychological management techniques to make killing easier for them. For example a firing squad puts a blindfold over the eyes of the person to be shot – not only for the sake of the victim, but for the sake of the soldiers doing the shooting. In addition one or more rifle may be loaded with a dud bullet so that the soldiers may never know whether they actually killed when they pulled the trigger. Killing is easiest done at a distance and easiest if shared – one person loads the guns, another person gives the order to fire, another pulls the trigger. (Grossman, 2013)

The destructive dynamic of the modern economy is organised rather like this: in their relationship to these supposed corporate "people" the shareholders of companies listed on the stock markets have no personal involvement in what the companies actually physically do in the world. At the same time, capital market institutions exist for shareholder owners so that they can move their wealth into and out of companies with great rapidity, and in ways that are entirely impersonal and enhance the ethical disconnect. The very concept of "shares" lends itself to building up portfolios with a small spread across many companies and securities. This makes it even more impractical for wealth owners with a reasonably well spread portfolio to actually know what each of these companies are up to in the real world, even if they were interested – which mostly they are not. Further, the biggest companies operate trans-nationally across multiple continents. It is again impossible to know what they are doing in detail in each place.

To complete the arrangements to "distance" wealth owners from any responsibility for what the companies that they own actually do, there are tax havens and secrecy jurisdictions operating in the global network of asset and financial markets.

Evading regulation, taxation and control

In theory "externalities" can be corrected in a variety of ways: by regulation; by state subsidy for adjustments to production arrangements; by taxing harmful activities or by setting quotas that limit harmful activities. However, unable to tax their richest citizens, most wealthy states are increasingly at the mercy of international lenders and finance houses who call the shots when it comes to policy. Indeed, it has become an accepted practice for governments to compete by offering companies ever more lax or non-existent regulatory regimes. (This idea is explored in more length in the chapter about co-opted states).

To sum up the argument so far, not only are externalities ubiquitous, there has also been a logic that has expanded them. If, as neo-liberal economists claim, it is in the interests of private property owners to solely pursue their own interests then it is in their interest to externalise as many costs as they can get away with.

So far, this chapter has considered the circumstances in which people and companies cause "externalities". In what follows I want to consider what happens to the people who suffer them, and what opportunities they have to deal with them or get some kind of restitution.

After enclosure, after colonial and post-colonial expropriation, after marketisation, de-localisation and the institutional arrangements just described, the possibility of challenging and influencing the destructive dynamic of the economic system have declined dramatically. With the shrinking of the commons, the vernacular familiarity, understanding and control of ordinary people over their natural and economic environment has been radically reduced. In a society where technologies do not change from one generation to the next, ordinary people are more able to accurately judge the consequences of productive decisions. As technologies evolve very rapidly this becomes very difficult. It becomes difficult too because many modern processes deploy technologies whose destructive effect is either hidden and/or evolves over a long time frame.

To take decisions about resources you have to privately own them. It is true however, that a limited number of remedial decisions are sometimes taken by states when private decision-making is particularly damaging. Therefore, as a generality, decisions have become either market decisions – taken by private businesses and consumers - or citizens' decisions. Citizen influence over decisions about land and resources that they do not own are possible via land planning or by regulation. Nevertheless, the basic philosophy is to keep economics decision-making by citizens to a minimum and leave this to corporations.

It is also true, in some cases that negatively affected people can resort to the courts, for example, using tort law to claim the perpetration of a nuisance. However, this requires action that will be costly in a variety of ways. Thus, to repeat, the property owner is in a relatively favourable position to ignore externalities and is likely to be "ignor–ant" of the problems they are causing.

As should thus, be clear, citizens' attempts to influence the "allocation of resources" in such a way as to prevent negative externalities entail a struggle with institutional hurdles and geographical distance. Free market economists like Ronald Coase envisaged models for dealing with pollution in which there is a single polluter and a single pollutee. In fact, there are corporations which are well resourced and well connected with the state, have access to PR machinery and can get the best lawyers... alongside often hundreds of thousands or even millions of unorganised victims with very few resources, if any, to put up against the polluters. They need representation – they need organisation and agents to be able to find out what is going on, draw attention to it, lobby and develop a countervailing power to the power of the corporations.

The role of Non-Governmental Organisations and Civil Society Organisations

In recent decades, a very large number of civil society organisations and non-governmental organisations have appeared all over the globe trying to resist destruction unleashed by the unrestrained market and by states whose policies have been largely co-opted to serve the agendas of corporate actors. In a book describing the civil society organisations that have been set up everywhere to resist the trend of destruction, Paul Hawken guesstimates that there are probably over one million, maybe even two million, organisations working towards ecological sustainability and social justice. (Hawken, 2007, p. 2)

Note – this is not one to two million individuals. This is one to two million organisations.

Hawken writes:

> This movement... doesn't fit the standard model. It is dispersed, inchoate, and fiercely independent. It has no manifesto or doctrine, no overriding authority to check with. It is taking shape in schoolrooms, farms, jungles, villages, companies, deserts, fisheries, slums – and yes, even fancy New York hotels. One of its distinctive features is that it is tentatively emerging as a global humanitarian movement from the bottom up. Historically social movements have arisen primarily in response to injustice, inequities and corruption. Those woes still remain legion, joined by a new condition that has no precedent: the planet has a life threatening disease, marked by massive ecological degradation and rapid climate change. (Ibid p 3)

No matter how good they are NGOs and CSOs will always have been an imperfect substitute for what was lost when communities lost collective control over their living environments. The problem for this vast "movement" is that it can be subverted, co-opted and undermined by the corporate sector - particularly as organisations in this movement are often dependent on corporate and state funding to allow them to function.

The actions and messages of NGOs and civil society organisations often take place in conditions in which the large corporate actors determine the terms of the debate. Insufficiently critical NGOs and CSOs often act in ad hoc ways responding to immediate humanitarian or environmental problems without any deep analysis of where these problems come from or vision of how to produce the fundamental change that would actually get to the roots of where the problem lies. Without thinking about the issues in depth many NGOs accept conventional wisdoms and ideas like those of "development" naively accepting the corporate and economist's narrative that poor people and poor countries are poor because they have been "left behind" and now must be "helped" to develop, to improve their economic arrangements. Given this as their starting point, the actions of NGOs can be dysfunctional, damaging and condescending, particularly as they are often "outsiders" to problems, and they can end up doing more harm than good.

> The problem is that most NGOs treat us as if we are babies still drinking from feeding bottles. They speak for us and design projects for us. Most times they are the main beneficiaries of the projects "for the communities". In Paraguay there are hundreds of NGOs who, by obtaining the compliance of some Indigenous individuals, believe that they possess the right to decide on behalf of entire Indigenous communities. In other cases, not even acceptance by a few is required for advancing what outsiders view as solutions to our problems.

> I have seen this with my own eyes. Once, an NGO came to our community. The NGO had designed a project without ever asking us what we wanted. When funding for the project was granted by an international donor, the NGO sent a musicologist to oversee the project. What we needed badly at that time was an agronomist, for the Yshiro-Ebitoso had been hunters, gatherers and fishers. We do not know how to plant very well, what seasons correspond to each crop, and so forth. We asked that this NGO send us an agronomist, but there is always this attitude of not listening to our voice. They sent us a musicologist, as if in our poverty what we need is just to go on singing. "An agronomist, not a musicologist, is what we need", we said to them, "Yes, yes. Sure, sure", they said but later on sent us a veterinarian. He was probably a friend of the NGO's director. We do not have animals! This is shameful. The projects never work out well because those who organize and direct them will not listen to us. (Barras, 2004, p. 49)

Co-opting and neutralising NGOs

It is then easy for NGOs to get sucked into "consultative arrangements" which offer a place at the table where they end up thinking very much like the corporations and the governments and having very little real influence. Thus, the NGOs' presence in consultative processes can serve to endorse the practices of the polluters and human rights abusers whose PR strategies successfully enrol NGOs to give a seal of approval.

Even worse is when CSOs and NGOs end up intellectually and conceptually co-opted and framed in a mainstream economic discourse that assumes the very problems and approaches that are problematic. Namely, that:

1. The goal of (un)economic growth is a given
2. That environmental problems should be dealt with in a cost benefit framework where

deliberation and debate between all affected parties is replaced with a supposedly "objective calculation" to work out the optimal outcome

3. Policy instruments should ideally be market based.

These are critiqued in more depth elsewhere in this book. Suffice it to say here very briefly, that if NGOs accept these typical pre-conceptions for environmental and social decision-making they will have given up on protecting the eco-system and communities in the face of the economic onslaught.

If one accepts economic growth then one accepts that in about 21 years as much economic activity will take place as in all of world history up to now – for this is the doubling time at a 3% rate of compound growth. The idea that the ecological system has both the resources and the sink capacity to survive that onslaught is complete madness.

Secondly, using cost benefit analysis to deal with externalities pre-empts and prevents democratic deliberation and is an implicit claim that a mathematical procedure gives us a correct answer rather than debate and contestation of different views and value systems. To the economist the preferences to be regarded as legitimate are those of people when they spend money – not people in democratic processes. As Clive Hamilton has argued "this is perhaps the ultimate conceit of mainstream economics, the equation of market behaviour with democracy itself". (Hamilton, Requiem for a Species, 2010) To allow "cost benefit analysis" to be the procedure for assessing and dealing with externalities is to allow economists to take over the process of deciding about them and set up a procedure that assumes people think with money focused value systems and it allows economists to describe the options, the goals and choices as they, the economists, think appropriate.

Thirdly, market based policy mechanisms implicitly assume that good environmental behaviour has to be made to pay, in money terms – which implies that money is the ultimate end/ way to measure "preferences" and environmental protection is to be framed as a means to a money end. But if money is the ultimate aim then actors will also game environmental policies, or manipulate or avoid them if doing so pays more – the fact is that it is this very mentality, which one does not find in communities who regard themselves as protectors and stewards of nature that is destroying the ecological system on which we all depend.

Fortunately there are those in the NGO/CSO community who realise these dangers and are concerned to develop a smarter and more critical way of operating. They realise that what they are doing must be rooted in values and ethics and that, if they are to escape an ad hoc incoherence, they must situate their actions in a narrative for the future of the economy and society which makes a bigger sense and represents a new vision for society, a "Great Transition". These ideas are explored more fully in the final chapter.

PART TWO
Economics, Land
and Nature

Chapter 16

Indigenous Economics

Mainstream economics regards environmental protection as a matter of finding the "right price" for environmental preferences. This is not how indigenous people think about environmental issues. The chapter contrasts the mentalities of people that belong to places vs the mind-set of the population when places belong to people. There are differing epistemes in different societies and "traditional environmental knowledge" is a totally different way of knowing to that taken for granted by economists.

This section of this book is devoted to several chapters on a set of themes almost entirely neglected by contemporary economists – land. For decades economists have been uninterested in the topic. Their heads are in the clouds – spinning theories about the worlds of high finance – without their feet being on the ground. Yet a very large part of the financial securities that the economists theorise are ultimately based on income streams that derive from land and locations. The financial economy must derive its income from real sources. Financial assets are titles to income streams but where does this income from? To a very large extent the answer is from mortgages, loans to property companies and capitalised rental streams – payments for places. Economist Michael Hudson has a name for the dominant part of the modern economy – the FIRE sector. FIRE stands for Finance, Insurance and Real Estate. They are very closely integrated which will be explored later in this book. The point here is simply to indicate that if land appears to have disappeared from economics, it is because "finance" is obscuring the view.

This is a critical situation because the most serious problem facing humanity is the damaging relationship between the economic system and the ecological system. As regards this most serious crisis mainstream economists have no explanatory framework worthy of intellectual respect.

Finding the "right price" for the environmental preferences

If we follow standard economic approaches to the environment then the appropriate way to protect it is to elicit the strength of people's preferences for nature (or its different attributes). This is done by finding out how much people are prepared to pay to maintain it. In other words, how much money they are prepared to accept in compensation for its destruction for economic purposes. It is all a matter of finding the right price. (See chapter 26). However, this implies that people have already formed preferences and that, in turn, implies that they actually know about the environment, or aspects of the environment that are being threatened. In practice:

> Most people have limited experience in assigning monetary values to environmental goods, because this requirement does not occur in everyday life. One may also question whether people

have preferences for all environmental goods. For example, can we have preferences for a species threatened by extinction, if we never knew it existed? If we have preferences for the species, they must have been created rather quickly and are likely to be far from stable over time. Therefore it is important to take the process of preference formation seriously. (Johnsson-Stenman, 2002, pp. 112-113)

In this chapter it is my intention to explore what ought to be blindingly obvious. That is, that the everyday life of many people precludes them getting much information about ecological systems and nature, or forming deep "preferences" that would result in their having the will to protect it. For billions of people, nature and the eco-system have become "out of sight and out of mind". The evolution of market society has progressively cut off whole populations from the possibility of knowledge about the environment. In fact, society has evolved institutions and practices that actively try to prevent them being adequately informed about the perilous state of the ecological system; actively try to mislead them about how dangerous things are and actively encourages participation in a system of consumption that uses resources without considering ecological consequences. This is a system intent on shaping peoples values in an anti-ecological way.

While the economists tell us that what makes a market society so wonderful is that it caters to people's preferences, allocating resources according to the signals in market valuations, the deeper reality is that the most powerful players in the economy seek to shape what value we place on things like ecological system reality. They do so in their own interests and in ways that foster ignorance or indifference to ecological destruction.

To consider the full range of issues relevant here is to delve into the realms of religion, society, culture, psychology and human personality. Neoclassical economic theory wants to say that humans can be conceptualised as calculating machines, taking decisions based on "rational expectations" in market dealings and using available information which will usually be sufficient for their purposes. The problem with this view is patently obvious once one begins to look at the ecological crisis. Huge numbers of people are ignorant and utterly unconcerned about the health of the ecological system and that is a large part of the problem.

Indigenous peoples and the environmental crisis

If we then ask which sections of society are concerned about the environment, the answer is largely people in the least developed societies; the indigenous populations - or the remnants of them; tribal societies and first nations in Canada. As Noam Chomsky has pointed out, these are the societies trying to do something about the environmental crisis:

In fact, all over the world – Australia, India, and South America – there are battles going on, sometimes wars. In India, it's a major war over direct environmental destruction, with tribal societies trying to resist resource extraction operations that are extremely harmful locally, but also in their general consequences. In societies where indigenous populations have an influence, many are taking a strong stand. The strongest of any country with regard to global warming is in Bolivia, which has an indigenous majority and constitutional requirements that protect the "rights of nature". (Chomsky, 2013)

Why is this the case? To give an answer is to describe what disappeared, what was forgotten, when economics developed. It is to describe the culture and belief systems that economics has claimed to replace. To think about people's relationship to the ecological system, as economists do, primarily as being about "preferences" about how "clean" these people want the environment to be, will not help us resolve environmental problems. On the contrary, this mentality is a sure indicator of why we have an ecological crisis in the first place. It is a symptom of a dislocated and displaced culture. In a quite literal sense it is the pathological world view of a non-indigenous society whose members are not rooted in a place, who are almost entirely blind to nature and quite unaware of their own ignorance of it, as well as their dependence on it.

In arguing that many indigenous peoples have, by definition, a closer relationship to, and understanding of, their sustaining ecological systems, I do not mean to imply that indigenous societies always got it right and never damaged their own eco-systems. Clearly some indigenous peoples prior to European colonialism did make catastrophic ecological errors.

Easter Island is a famous example where a community made disastrous mistakes in the management of their ecological system. When settled in 800 AD, Easter Island was covered by tropical forests and, at its peak the population rose to an estimated 10,000. However, the rate of forest clearance was greater than that of its regeneration and the system passed a threshold, a tipping point, in which soil erosion was high and the forests could not regenerate. By 1600, their famous statues could no longer be built and (more significantly) canoes for catching large fish and marine mammals could no longer be constructed either. The population collapsed to an estimated 2,000 people. (Brian Walker and David Salt *"Resilience Thanking"* Island Press 2006, p.60) (Walker & Salt, 2006, p. 60)

Nevertheless, it is clear that communities that inhabit a place for a long time and live off the surpluses of a fluctuating eco-system are likely, over many generations, to have a better understanding of what is sustainable and what is not. In most "developed countries" the very nature of development has led to society losing that ecological knowledge.

To undo our cultural ignorance of these issues is a massive task. It involves questioning and rejecting foundational ideas in our culture and beliefs. It involves going back a long way in history and then rethinking what has happened. In fact, we must go back to so called "hunter gatherer" societies and try to understand them on their own terms, rather than seeing them as "primitive".

In the last few decades, anthropological research has challenged the assumption that remaining hunter gatherer societies, which had not embraced settled "agriculture", were somehow "backward". On the contrary, they were managed on a very sophisticated basis and anthropologists like Marshall Sahlins have gone so far as to claim that they were the "original Affluent Societies". He argues that such societies cannot be understood using economic principles which reflect western values. Going further, Sahlins poses the radical idea that the agricultural (Neolithic) revolution cannot be said to have brought unquestioned progress. (Sahlins, 1972)

Stone Age Economics

The existence of these "original affluent societies" challenge the foundational assumptions of economics. To quote Sahlins:

> There are two possible courses to affluence – either by producing much or desiring little. The familiar conception... makes assumptions peculiarly appropriate to market economies: that man's wants are great, not to say infinite, whereas his means are limited, although improvable... But there is also a Zen way to affluence, departing from premises somewhat different from our own: that human material wants are finite and few, and technical means unchanging but on the whole adequate. (Sahlins, 1972, p. 2)

If you live a nomadic existence then possessions are weight that hold you down, they are a burden. Imagine packing your possessions in a big suitcase and having to take it with you wherever you go.

> The hunter, one is tempted to say, is an "uneconomic man". At least as concerns non subsistence goods, he is the reverse of that standard caricature immortalised in any "General Principles of Economics", page one. His wants are scarce and his means (in relation) plentiful. Consequently he is "comparatively free of material pressures", has "no sense of possession", shows "an undeveloped sense of property", is "completely indifferent to material pressures", and manifests "a lack of interest" in developing his technological equipment. (Sahlins, 1972, p. 13)

The "principles of economics" were not lived by hunter-gatherer societies. As a result, many of these societies *were* sustainable, in contrast to our own, which very clearly is not.

This sustainability was rooted in a very deep understanding of the ecological system and respect for it. If we take as an example the way of life the Australian aboriginal people before the white colonists arrived. It was one in which land care was the main purpose of life. Gammage quotes Bill Stanner:

> No English words are good enough to give a sense of the links between an aboriginal group and its homeland. Our word "home" does not match the aboriginal word that may mean "camp", "hearth", "country" "everlasting home" "totem place" "life source" "spirit centre" and much else all in one. Our word "land" is too spare and meagre. (Gammage, 2011, p. 145)

Aboriginal society was permeated by ecology, just as our society is chiefly characterised by its absence. In his book about aboriginal land care in 1788, historian Bill Gammage explains how aboriginal people in Arnhem Land in Australia classified the countryside with a deep awareness of the ecological associations between animals and plants - what that meant for their food supply; the woods needed for spears and for resins and fibres, at any season of the year. (Gammage, 2011, p. 145)

This kind of relationship to "land" (in an expanded sense) for the indigenous person can be understood as "belonging" to a homeland. The concept of home is not fixed at an exact location but covers an area of landscape. Gammage quotes Edward Eyre:

> Another very great advantage on the part of the natives is, the intimate knowledge they have of every nook and corner of the country they inhabit; does a shower of rain fall, they know the very rock where a little water is most likely to be collected, the very hole where it is longest retained... Are there heavy dews at night, they know where the longest grass grows, from which they may collect the spangles, and water is sometimes procured thus, in great abundance... (Gammage, 2011, p. 146)

Note again the remark that English words are not good enough to express the relationship between aboriginal people and homeland. There is a "lexical void" – a lack of words to express an idea - because the largely European cultures, both in Europe and in those continents to which the Europeans migrated, produced "economics" with missing cultural components. That is, all those features of thought which occur when a people belong to a place but which are missing in the thought of a dis-located culture.

The different relationship: people that belong to places vs places that belong to people

The crucial distinction here, and it cannot be found in economic textbooks, is between places belonging to people (and corporations) and people belonging to places. Indigenous people belong to places have lives bound into traditions connected to deep knowledge of those places; their landscape and ecological features; the species that live there and a sense of inter-generational responsibility for place and people. This is a spiritual commitment and is what went missing when the "economic religion" of the mercantile conquerors became the criteria by which the use of people and places were judged.

Indigenous people do NOT see the earth as a resource store that belongs to them. Instead, they often see themselves as part of the earth, as walking and living pieces of the earth. They do not have an anthropocentric world view with humans as the peak of creation and its owner. Conversely, their view tends to be nature centric with humans merely participants and parts in this world.

This is not homo-economicus style thinking. It bears no comparison to preference utilitarianism. The difference in mentalities between people belonging to the land and the land belonging to people is much deeper. When people belong to the land, then the land has a spiritual dimension for them. They carry responsibilities in a way that private property owners do not. This different way of being includes the other living species as non-human persons. It involves deep practical knowledge and acts as a guide.

In contrast, economics describes a world in which private property owners take "decisions" about the use or "management" of their "resources" which are "inputs" used to produce "outputs". The language reflects a particular mentality that matches a way of doing things within a particular kind of society. Economics is not some kind of universal truth applicable for all time – it is the product of dislocation and displacement. It is a religion for non-indigenous people, people whose ancestors were displaced and dislocated who now, in the modern world, move regularly, who have little attachment to place and little sense of inter-generational responsibility for their descendants in a place.

By contrast, for most of the history of humanity, communities of people lived with each other in a community of species (an eco-system in a landscape and/or a waterscape). The diversity of the landscape and the diversity in the community needed to be maintained in balance, in harmony. In communities, driving the private interests of particular people at the expense of others in that community leads to tensions and conflict. Furthermore, to use the eco-system in one way only is to undermine a variety of species and uses of the landscape. Tension and conflict lies that way.

The difference can be illustrated by the following quotes:

> I fought nine years to obtain property titles for my community. Bureaucrats and ranchers showed me papers and more papers to demonstrate that our lands were privately owned. I did not care because in that land our grandparents are buried. They showed me papers. I showed them bones. When I received the titles to our lands, the bureaucrats and the ranchers who had laughed at me asked, "How did you obtain the land?" "With the bones of my ancestors", I replied. (Barras, 2004, p. 50)

"When Canadian government surveyors first ran across Gitskan people in their traditional territory, the Gitskan asked, "What are you doing here?"

"Surveying our land," answered the surveyors.

Incredulous, the Gitksan responded: "If this is your land, where are your stories?"" (Rasmussen, 2013)

De-territorialisation in non-indigenous societies

Economics, by contrast, is the product of a non-indigenous culture. Belonging to places did not always mean belonging to an egalitarian society. In the European Middle Ages, belonging to a place came to involve a set of obligations to a feudal lord who imposed duties on the serfs outside his castle walls. Many people had good reason to run away and the medieval period ended partly because, in this process of moving and running away, multiple geographical and mental boundaries dissolved. A process of "de-territorialisation" took place in which people found a relative freedom from feudal exactions by living in towns, or by travelling to faraway places as the trade routes opened up.

However, the process of change was one in which places came to belong to people instead of the other way round – particularly via the enclosure of the commons. Land grabbing took place by people who wanted to profit from the new mercantile connections; people who mostly lived in the towns and who were well connected politically. This took place over several centuries and completed and transformed

European society whose adventurers then went on to transform global society. Many of the people expelled from the land ended up as vagabonds and were either herded into the new factories, or into punitive workhouses. They either migrated voluntarily or through transportation. A European diaspora began and took a colonial form.

Now, several centuries after enclosure, people in towns and cities get their water through a tap and food from a supermarket, while the supermarkets jointly manage the countryside in many countries working together with global agri-business corporations and the financial markets. Meanwhile, many people in the cities change their location every few years in order to keep themselves in paid work.

Economics is a theory developed by and for people who feel themselves as belonging nowhere in particular... although they may, opportunistically, pretend to belong in tax havens.

Economists claim that, in order to protect "land" or eco-systems (the living network of beings in a place and the community that lives there) it has to be owned as private property. The United Nations Environment Programme tells us that, in order to protect nature, we must give it a price and "hardwire it into financial markets" – whose actors are global and who buy and sell assets often in minutes.

The truth of the matter is the other way round. To protect a natural environment a community must belong there, be rooted there, have understood and know all the details of that place for generations and intend to pass that place, with all their knowledge, down to their descendants.

Many indigenous communities have a variation of the axiom that one must consider one's actions up to the seventh generation – that is the generation after one's grandchildren's grandchildren. That is what it means to belong to a community that belongs to a place. It is not an idea compatible with the economist's assumption that all people take long term decisions using an interest rate with which they discount the future in favour of the present.

> ... those who are embedded tend to look after a place; those who are disembedded do not. A non-indigenous civilization is a complete rupture with the entire arc of human history. By the way, that doesn't mean all indigenous civilizations were saintly or nice. It just means they were rooted. They may have uprooted others, enslaved peoples, created empires, but every human civilization—Inuit, Roman, Egyptian, Mayan, Haudenosaunee, Anishinaabeg, and so on—has had a homeland somewhere. Every civilization has had a particular place on earth that generation upon generation felt beholden to...... Until now." (Rasmussen, 2013)

We are now in a much better position to answer the question: "How does it come about that it is indigenous and tribal peoples who are the ones who are fighting to save the environment?" In theory, much scientific and ecological information is available to the people in "developed societies" but these are societies made up of non-indigenous people. We non-indigenous people live a life which we take for granted and do not see it as at all peculiar. But we are dis-placed and "belong no-where". Aboriginal culture and land care in Australia lasted at least 8,000 years and possibly as much as 50,000 years. In that time the possibilities for getting to know the ecological system were infinitely greater than anything that was possible after the agriculture developed to feed the towns where the intellectuals developed the knowledge system and theorised for the merchants in the emerging age of commerce.

Differing "epistemes" for different societies and "traditional environmental knowledge"

What we are describing here in the contrast between indigenous and non-indigenous world views is something that is a lot deeper than different "paradigms" of the world. What we are describing are different conditions of possibility for knowledge, different "epistemes". "Epistemes" is a term suggested by Foucault, in his 1970 book *The Order of Things* to describe the different foundations for the way different societies think, that creates the "conditions of possibility" for knowledge. An episteme is "that which makes knowledge possible". (Birkin & Polesie, 2013)

In recent years, there has been a recognition by some economists and academics (who are mostly from dominant non-indigenous communities) of what is called "traditional environmental knowledge" or TEK for short. There has been a dawning realisation that indigenous cultures which were previously barely given any attention by economists, actually possess valuable information relating to local eco-systems. An example of this occurred when economists and policy makers realised that it would be valuable to construct "vulnerability indices" for so called "less developed" societies, like "New Caledonia". This was in order to gain a better understanding of the reasons for the increased rate of natural disasters occurring in those societies. Such vulnerability indices are an innovation in economics because they admit the existence of natural limits on economic activity and represent a movement away from a concern for growth, and development, to a concern for resilience and sustainability. Significantly, when this occurred researchers suddenly discovered that indigenous people were a rich source of knowledge and information.

> The context and importance [of the practical activities of] villagers had not been understood". Whole areas of knowledge had previously been unknown to the colonising outsiders – traditional medicines, control of pests and diseases, and the agricultural calendar where decisions about timing "was one of the most important aspects of Melanesian life. "the research survey concluded that while New Caledonian's (Kanak) knowledge of nature and the environment was very large indeed little of that rich heritage had been recorded... (Harries-Jones, 2004, pp. 290-291)

A convergence of concerns and purposes produced the discovery of knowledge by people whose experience had not been recognised or been found interesting to researchers. This knowledge in turn led to researchers recognising that "They had to reform the standard terminology of GDP in order to accommodate their focus on risk, vulnerability and its alternatives" (Harries-Jones, 2004, p. 291)

It is important to make clear, however, that "Traditional Environmental Knowledge" is the way that non-indigenous thinkers (like economists) conceptualise the knowledge of indigenous people. For indigenous people the knowledge is not understood in the same way. It is framed differently and arises from a different "episteme".

The Spiritual Significance of land and places

The term "Land"... is not restricted to the physical environment only. It has a much broader meaning, used by indigenous people to refer to the physical, biological and spiritual environments fused together. The closest scientific equivalent of the "Land", taken without its spiritual component, is "ecosystem".

Traditional knowledge is practical common sense, good reasoning, and logic based on experience. It is an authority system (a standard of conduct), setting out rules governing the use and respect of resources, and an obligation to share. For example, it tells people that they do not have the right to hunt all animals of a species, as in wolf kill programmes. The wisdom comes in using the knowledge and ensuring that it is used in a good way. It involves using the head and the heart together Traditional knowledge is dynamic, yet stable and is usually shared in stories, songs, dances and myths. (McGregor, 2004, pp. 78-79)

Traditional environmental knowledge comes, therefore, out of a different episteme. The economist lives in a world where, if s/he recognises nature at all, this recognition consists of thinly understood species that are either crops or weeds, live**stock** or pests and general wildlife. In other words, species already classified as to their market significance, as resources, or even as "eco-system services", assessed in relation to their use for humans. "Information" is framed in economics speak – which is absent of any sense of responsibility, any spiritual content, any loyalty, any feeling for other species.

By contrast, a large proportion of the poorest people on the planet, are struggling to keep it alive because they experience and know it as being alive. They know and experience the eco-system as communities of human and non-human beings, each of which is actively interpreting their environment where this largely means interpreting each other and acting on their interpretations.

In his writings about the Nunavut and Greenland Inuit Peter Harries-Jones compares the perspectives of scientifically trained ecologists and hunters. The Inuit regard animals as "non-human persons" who are able to build up knowledge about their environment so that skilled hunters can rely not only on their own interpretations of the environment but that of animals interpreting other animals in interaction with the environment.

The behaviour of fish and seals not only gives signs about the location of fish and seals to Inuit hunters in Greenland but indicates the behaviour of whales, glaciers, winds, water temperatures and other physical aspects of the environment... Greenland Inuit are able to observe and account for animal movements and other aspects of behaviour in a systematic way because they believe that animals have their own semiotic interpretation of their environment. (Harries-Jones, 2004, p. 291)

This sense of nature as being animated, as being alive, of being a place of "inter-being" by "selves" of different species is not compatible with the neo-Darwinistic/neo-liberal bio-economic vision of selfish genes, or of biology as competing survival machines that underpins much of non-indigenous economic thinking.

The Inuit view is, however, compatible with the emerging thinking in biology which envisages the biological world as organisms which, as feeling, interpreting and intentional selves, are involved in a process of self-creation or autopoiesis.

According to biologist Andreas Weber:

> Natural history should no longer be viewed as the unfolding of an organic machine, but rather as the natural history of freedom, autonomy and agency. Reality is alive: It is full of subjective experience and feeling; subjective experience and feeling are the prerequisites of any rationality. The biosphere consists of a material and meaningful interrelation of selves. (Weber, Enlivenment. Towards a fundamental shift in the concepts of nature, culture and politics, 2013)

If the biosphere - and the economy too - are made up of an "interrelation of selves" that have a degree of autonomy, freedom and agency it makes sense to grasp and understand this kind of world through stories. There is, to be sure, a place to understand things through science based on measurement and mathematics but stories and narrative give a different kind of understanding (which is why telling the story of economics, the people who thought it up and the conditions in which they did so, gives us a different perspective about it from reading a textbook written as if economics was a finished product).

There are some mysteries we cannot ever understand. The Tao that can be told is not the eternal Tao. The Great Spirit is the Great Mystery. Deborah McGregor quotes Elder Annie Catholique:

> When the government people talk about land, I find it very funny, talking about all the things we use, all the things we survive on like animals and caribou and those things. When I think about land, I think about the Great Spirit. (McGregor, 2004, p. 79)

It should be remembered that stories as explanations and as guides for living are often the creation of peoples whose cultures are non-literate – and there is a danger for literate people to assume that the non-literate must be ignorant as it is assumed that knowledge must be stored somewhere external, on paper, or in digital form, "to count" and to be taken into account. However, an oral tradition has its own features and possibilities of knowing and of passing on knowledge. It has other ways of people remembering together while, at the same time, bestowing significance to what is important, anchored into the rhythms of life.

Rituals, ceremonies and totems

A practice repeated, perhaps on a seasonal basis by a community, becomes a ritual. Other ways in which people can synchronise their feelings and thoughts are through ceremonies. These help ideas and practices to be remembered.

The point about such rituals and ceremonies is that they create continuity and stability – they fix things. In this context it is understandable that a community can come to believe that the failure to perform a ritual, or the failure to perform it correctly, will throw the world into chaos. It will become formless and void again. To the Australian Aborigines, it was when the creator ancestors did these things for the first time that the world was created out of the void.

To remember how to cross a landscape safely without maps and service stations a community evolves songlines. I express this in non-indigenous thought. To the Aboriginal people the landscape was created by the creator ancestors who sang the landscape into existence. These "songlines" were based on the landscape and the creatures in that landscape with their ecological associations. Thus, for example, sites along a "red kangaroo songline" matched the best habitat for the red kangaroo – a description of the landscape from a red kangaroo perspective, including a hunting ban at the major sites. Thus, the creator ancestors had decreed a conservation imperative when they sang the landscape into existence which meant that kangaroos had refuges. In bad seasons they had somewhere to breed and recover. Only when their numbers built up again, and they moved off the refuges, could they be hunted.

(Gammage, 2011, p. 135)

Proximity to animals and species that one has a need to understand creates more than conceptual involvement – it engages emotions. It creates identification and involvement which are inconceivable to people who connect to animals as packaged meats or to plants trimmed, cooked, tinned and on a shelf.

Totems are thus, more than badges and labels – they are allegiances. Once again we must grasp the right direction meant when the word "belonging" is used. Gammage comments that, in English, a totem can simply be a badge, however, for aboriginal people a totem is a life force stemming from and part of a creator ancestor. Thus, an emu man is of the same soul and flesh as an emu and must look after it and its habitat, just as it must care for him. It is not his totem, he is of its totem.

This is nature and its species as kin. With this mind set and with spiritual relationship to land, it was a requirement of all people to care for the land and its creatures, regenerating the land through ceremonies, protecting totems (species) and their habitats. This in turn made land care purposeful, universal and predictable – even in what seemed to European settlers to be untouched wilderness. (Gammage p 117)

This is nothing like an "environmental preference" in a utilitarian sense, symbolised with a badge. With different members of the community having different totems, and those community members knowing everything about their totem species in great detail, the community has biodiversity protection built into the belief system and into the social structure.

Chapter 17

Colonialist economics - the contrast with indigenous land care principles

Many, though by no means all, indigenous peoples practiced sustainable land care and used concepts that contrast strongly with modern economics thinking. Much economic thinking is intrinsically ecologically destructive.

To describe the European merchant adventurers as "discovering" the rest of the world is a mis-description. What they thought they had discovered were "primitive" peoples – people who were virtually a part of the wildlife – to be driven out of desirable land areas or tamed and used as work animals. They attacked and took over and were aided, not only by their weaponry and ships but also by the diseases that they took with them. The invaders had some immunity to these diseases, but the populations of the "Americas" particularly, did not.

We cannot describe what subsequently happened around the world as the result of superior economics but rather as the outcome of successful military campaigns and organisation, together with luck for the invaders and the devastating effect of disease on the indigenous peoples. Millions of people of the first nations died in the Americas. In Africa millions were enslaved. In Australia campaigns of genocide were waged against aboriginal peoples. In India millions starved. Back in Europe the Irish starved too – while food was exported to Britain. History is not a story in which the good guys always win. The story of European colonialism was a story in which the mass murderers triumphed.

It therefore seems justified to describe the period that followed the writings of the scholastic economists as ones in which criminal gangs, who had earlier taken over as rulers of a number of European countries, who had stolen the rights of ordinary people in order to use the surrounding landscape by enclosing the common lands, now expanded their murderous businesses and practices into the rest of the world.

They had good PR techniques, one must acknowledge that. In order for gangs of psychopaths to justify their entitlement to murder and steal, a cloud of ideas, as well as much theatre and fancy clothing, complemented the intimidation. In medieval Europe, the gang leaders honoured themselves with titles like "King", had crowns put on their heads, were robed in the finest clothes and exercised their power with a large amount of theatre. For example, "coronations" were held, preferably in buildings which had been standing for a few centuries, and involved being blessed on behalf of the sky god by priests who were also dressed up for the occasion. When you could do that over several generations your family has definitely made it...

Over time, pageantry and intimidation were not enough. Although helpful, you needed philosophers and thinkers to back you up too. The philosophers argued that the violence and theft perpetrated on people around the world was good for them. Furthermore it was incredibly useful to work to get colonised people to think in the same way as the colonisers. The central idea was that their subordination involved arrangements that were not only an improvement but that these arrangements were inevitable, they were desirable, they were progress.

That was where economics came in. Adam Smith helped with one of his formulations in which history was inevitably a progression towards "An Age of Commerce". First came the age of hunters, then of pastoralists, then of agriculturists and then the Age of Commerce.

Nowadays, there is a slightly different formulation. There are "developing countries" and there are "developed countries". The most recent words conceptually frame the fate of a number of countries very nicely. It makes clear that the people in "developing countries" are second class and that they need "help" to "develop". They need multinational corporations to help them to do this – as well as NGOs.

However, the kind of development to which many societies and their supporting eco-systems have been subjected has often thrown the ecological system out of balance. Many pre-colonial ecological systems had a greater diversity - an interplay of different uses and different users. This was replaced by a smaller number of cultural types (plant and animal species) in a more specialised landscape with monocultures operating at a large scale. The resultant systems were sometimes pushed across ecological thresholds into a different state from which there is no simple turning back.

Economic principles that were ecologically destructive

What is certainly clear is that invading European colonists made plenty of ecological errors. The reasons for these errors are instructive. They show us clearly that the "principles of economics" as formulated by Smith, Malthus, Ricardo, Bentham and later economic theorists were contrary to the principles employed by many indigenous peoples and that they were, in fact, ecologically destructive.

Let us take again, an example from Australia from the book by Walker and Salt on Resilience thinking. The example concerns the Goulburn-Broken Catchment which is a sub system of the Murray Darling Basin. European settlers moved in from 1830, cleared the land for dairy pasture and horticulture and then, because of the vagaries of drought and flood, started to develop irrigation on a progressively larger scale. Dams were built and extended after each period of drought and the area became very prosperous – at first. However, an "ecological system threshold" was eventually reached because of the scale of irrigation. The water table rose to within 5 to 6 metres of the surface and there were rising problems of salinity. The problem has subsequently been addressed in an expensive fashion by pumping the groundwater but much of it is salty and this shifts the problem to somewhere else. (Walker & Salt, 2006, pp. 38-52) Over the last few decades the situation has been increasingly precarious.

127

As the ecological system has lost its resilience what can we say about the colonial "improvement"? Clearly that is was not sustainable – and what is not sustainable eventually comes to an end.

Having described what has happened Walker and Salt ask the question:

> An interesting hypothetical: if the early settlers had been forewarned of the problems that would be faced some one hundred years later, and been in the possession of the information we now have, would they have made different decisions on how they developed the region? Probably no. A delay of one hundred years between an action and its consequences makes it difficult to take those consequences seriously. Humans have both high discount rates and an enormous capacity in believing the future will generate solutions to problems that don't have to be faced in the foreseeable future. (Walker & Salt, 2006, p. 49)

But what kind of "humans" are Walker and Salt writing about?

As the two authors note, almost in passing, without further thought, the first occupants of this land were Aboriginal people who have been present for 8,000 to 10,000 years, possibly longer. The Aboriginal people had managed the grassy woodland during that time with periodic fires and during their time the water table was 20 to 50 metres below the surface. Were they not "humans" too? During their 8,000 to 10,000 years would the water table have been raised if they had had the technologies that were available to the white settlers?

Contrary to what Walker and Salt assert, as if writing about a universal human nature, the answer is "NO". As a matter of fact, aboriginal people did use dams in water management but nothing on the scale used by the white settlers. Had they known that dams would be destructive of the ecological balance there is no question that they would not have used them.

When Walker and Salt assert that "humans" inevitably develop things and "can't stop themselves" taking a short term view that sacrifices the interests of future generations for present ones, they are expressing the values and mind set of the European settlers and their "economic religion" but the religion of the aboriginal people was different. Like many other indigenous people, they had an ethic of land care that was integral to their spirituality and their way of life. This was based on a multi-generational care for the land – which is precisely what Walker and Salt imply is impossible given their economist-compatible assumptions about "human nature".

Aboriginal land care practices were described in the previous chapter. What the Europeans at the time did not notice or realise... or perhaps found it in their interests to deny... was that the patchwork mosaic of species in the landscape, and the predominance of grassland, was a result of the management practices of the Aboriginal people who had lived there and cared for the land for thousands of years. The idea that Aboriginal peoples had created themselves a landscape that enabled them not to have to work very much did not match contemporary concepts of political economy. The European "civilisers" stole this landscape and degraded it by their unsustainable practices but were convinced that their kind of "development" was an improvement. Not understanding the practices and skills of Aboriginal people in the controlled use of burning, the settlers allowed grasslands to revert to forests. As the decades have passed it led to catastrophic fires that regularly occur in Australia. Had aboriginal landcare not been displaced this would not happen.

In theorising about efficiency and the management of resources with a western European mind-set, many "great thinkers" were unable to see efficiency when it was right in front of them, so steeped were they in a hubristic assurance of their own cultural superiority. Charles Darwin is an example. He described the aboriginal people as "harmless savages wandering about without knowing where they shall sleep at night and gaining their livelihood by hunting in the woods". For all his powers of biological observation, he did not realise that the woods were part of a mosaic of land uses, created and maintained by fire management, to suit the needs of different species and intended to maintain biodiversity.

Had the settlers realised, or been prepared to acknowledge, the truth, it would have created serious problems for them - and for political economy. It would have undermined the principles that justified taking the land. Philosopher John Locke had argued that God gave the world to men in common but the justification of private property rights was that the land was to be used by "The industrious and rational" with "Labour to be the title to it". Property was justified by the rational industry and improvement brought about by work. Had the settlers recognised that aboriginal people were industrious and rational, that they were managing the land, indeed that they had created the best land, then they would have had to have recognised that they themselves were interlopers and had no rights to the land. The settlers' ignorance – or state of denial - prevented them acknowledging themselves for what they were - thieves – whose mission of "improvement" was destructive of a finely tuned eco-system.

The aborigines *were* industrious and rational. The needs of multiple species were taken into account. Their landcare was ecological system management, not just land management for a mono-culture. The thinking behind the burn patterns took into account the habitat needs of possums, wombats, birds, insects, reptiles and plants. Laying out the countryside to suit species, using burn patterns, led to highly complex landscape management, requiring great care over many generations and a knowledge not just of the needs of animals but the cycles of plants. (Gammage, 2011)

Fortunately for the aboriginal people, they did not think or behave with the market mind-set. When we look at how they did think and behave, without assuming European cultural superiority, their actions and thinking made a good deal of sense. Thus, contrary to the assumptions and assertions of the Reverend Thomas Malthus, Australian aboriginal people did not have a population that kept on growing in numbers until it reached the limits of food production. In 1788 they had what they thought of as abundance and could satisfy their needs with less work than all but the privileged Europeans because they practiced population control as a precautionary measure for their society. (Gammage, 2011, p. 151)

Contrary to the ideas of Adam Smith, the aboriginal people were not obsessed by the notion of scarcity and by technical improvement to overcome it. Like the societies described my Sahlins they regarded themselves as living in a state of abundance.

A further point is that aboriginal patterns of production never really matched Smith's ideas about the "stages" of human economic evolution which were supposed to pass from hunting, to pastoralism, to agriculture, to commerce. The aborigines had refined living as "hunter-gatherers" and they included a mix of ways of hunting, gathering, cultivation and pastoralism all together, without fences or fixed residential settlements. The mix even included a limited place for trade but, above all, focused upon sustainability and what today we might term a "steady state economy".

Aboriginal people did not think using economic categories

Not that the aboriginal people would have described or thought of what they did in the terminology of economics, ecological or otherwise. They did not worship efficiency and technology. Instead they had a relationship to ancestor creators and to a God who expected them to maintain the landscape, the creatures and plants in it, as it was and as they were. Whereas the Europeans were driven by a faith in change, in development, the aboriginal people saw themselves as duty bound to maintain things as they were.

So Salt and Walker are wrong in their assumptions of "humans". There were humans that knew how to manage for the long term and did so effectively for thousands of years. The weakness on the Salt and Walker argument is to start their story where the white settlers arrived and to take the ideas of economics on faith – when it is just these ideas that are the problem.

In their land care too, aboriginal people made "land management decisions", contrary to the assumptions of another economist, David Ricardo. Ricardo noticed that, in his own society, the best land was allocated for cultivation first and that the competitive demand for the best locations enabled the owners of the most productive land and/or the most desirable locations to charge a rent for it. The starting point for Ricardo's theory of rent is the idea of the differential productivity of natural resources and the tapping of the best resources, or those easiest to access, first of all. This idea was later adapted by other economists and turned into the notion of declining marginal productivity. More generally, all economists assume that the natural resources that are easiest and cheapest to extract get used first.

Yet aboriginal people related to their landscape according to a different logic. Bill Gammage quotes the observations of a settler called Carnegie, about Helena Springs in the desert northwest of Lake Mackay. Helena Springs is the best water for hundreds of miles and Carnegie notes how it was much used by birds and animals. However, "Curiously enough, few native camps were to be seen, nor is this the first time that I have noticed that the best waters are least used... These desert people... have some provident habits, for first the small native wells are used, and only when these are exhausted are the more permanent waters resorted to." (Gammage, 2011, p. 255)

In the Aboriginal System the aim of the game was not to maximise production it was to maintain the ecological balance. Since nature always fluctuates in some way living through maintaining a balance means culling or taking from that which is temporarily in surplus... while not taking from animals and plants that are in need of regeneration. Gammage quotes Latz, who explains:

In the desert you've got to have this system because you have really bad droughts and so on. You've got to have a sanctuary from where your animals can expand back after a drought. Not a single animal was allowed to be killed in this area. Not a single plant was allowed to be picked. These sanctuaries were scattered all over the landscape - wherever there was important Dreaming there was a sanctuary area. (Gammage, 2011, pp. 284-285)

What we call, using our westernised minds, two centuries further on from Adam Smith, "an economic system" is not really how other societies and cultures thought about their arrangements for living. In the language of economics, we think of "resource management arrangements" but there is a danger of only thinking in these terms because these words reduce and limit our understanding of the arrangements of other societies.

"Resource management arrangements" are what we have **after** the land has been fenced off by settlers and **after** there has been a process of colonial expropriation. It is what we have at the point that "economics" starts to be used to explain decisions about land. But "economics" cannot be used to adequately express what came before because there are no words in economics to express the full extent of what was taken away.

It is not merely "resources" that are taken away when land is expropriated, fenced off and subject to "improvement". It is a way of life; spiritual responsibilities; individual and group identity; relationships to ancestors; relationships to contemporaries; relationships to successive descendants; to other species; relationship to the "Great Spirit" as inter-being which enfolds and unfolds all of these in and out of itself.

Why is this so?

Chapter 18

Concepts for a fenced off world

Private property in land means enclosure and exclusion. Economists typically assume that economic choices involve inevitable trade-offs. However, it is not true that alternatives must always be forgone. There is often a potential for sharing and mutual accommodation that is being ignored. Not all choices are rivalrous.

The answer is because the fenced off world described by Adam Smith and David Ricardo is a world of specialisation and that means a radical reduction in diversity of users and diversity of uses at each place, in each unique eco-system. Dragged into the global market, the eco-system in each place became "dis-located" and the community of people who belonged there were "dis-placed".

Managing land and places to maintain diversity has an entirely different logic to managing for specialism and private use. Ultimately managing places for specialist uses, while excluding other people and species, requires that property owners need to back up their rights by access to violence. This is the role for the state in market societies. As Adam Smith recognised:

> Civil government, so far as it is instituted for the security of property, is in reality instituted for the defence of the rich against the poor, or of those who have some property against those who have none at all. (Smith A. , The Wealth of Nations, 1776)

Private Property in Land means enclosure and exclusion

A private property regime in land means that "resource use" decisions are private decisions. "Resource use" is not subject to deliberation by multiple people in a community where different interests need to be accommodated in order to maintain social harmony. In the form of private property, the resource owner has "dominion" over resource use. It is his or her choice how they are used and not the business of anyone else. "Alternative resource uses" are therefore more likely "to be forgone", at the expense of others, when resources are owned as private property.

For this state of affairs to come about the single users must be able to *exclude* other people from being able to use the resource. If the resource was previously available to a community, but is now only available to an individual, there must have been a process of "enclosure".

The word "enclosure" expresses a historical process in which *institutions for exclusion* have been set up. This means not only fences and hedges – but laws, courts and law enforcement arrangements. If they cannot exclude other people using them e.g. taking fish on the high seas, then resource appropriators do not really have dominion or private property in the resources and we call this an *"open access regime"*.

In this situation, multiple owners and multiple uses that accommodate everyone's needs, are more likely. In other words, issues of what resources are used for (allocation decisions) are usually entangled with issues of who is the beneficiary of the resource use (distribution decisions). The creation of private property means a reduction in the variety of resource users and a reduction of the variety of resource uses at the same time. Private property is associated with more specialisation and greater inequality at the same time.

Given single owners with the power to exclude others, it is more likely that single uses will prevail. In a study of the historical process of enclosure in the UK Simon Fairlie describes how powerful interests drove the land grabbing, typically declaring that the areas that they took over were worthless – but that when they owned this land they would be able to "improve" it.

This was usually a lie:

> An acre of gorse — derided as worthless scrub by advocates of improved pasture — was worth 45s 6d as fuel for bakers or lime kilns at a time when labourers' wages were a shilling a day. On top of that, the scrub or marsh yielded innumerable other goods, including reed for thatch, rushes for light, firewood, peat, sand, plastering material, herbs, medicines, nuts, berries, an adventure playground for kids and more besides. No wonder the commoners were "idle" and unwilling to take on paid employment. (Fairlie, 2009)

And Fairlie quotes a contemporary, William Cobbett:

"Those who are so eager for the new inclosure," William Cobbett wrote, "seem to argue as if the wasteland in its present state produced nothing at all. But is this the fact? Can anyone point out a single inch of it which does not produce something and the produce of which is made use of? It goes to the feeding of sheep, of cows of all descriptions... and it helps to rear, in health and vigour, numerous families of the children of the labourers, which children, were it not for these wastes, must be crammed into the stinking suburbs of towns?" (Fairlie, 2009)

More decisions took on "either/or" characteristics under the enclosing regime of exclusion because decisions were no longer being made by communities seeking to share use between people and between uses. As an infrastructure for trade developed, like better means of transport, the new private owners started to use the land, not to provide for any local needs at all, but to produce for lucrative distant markets. The process of exclusion and fencing off was accentuated and accompanied by an accelerated collapse of sharing.

Are trade-offs inevitable, must alternatives always be forgone?

This brings us to THE standard economic concept – that of "opportunity cost". This is the assumption that whenever a resources is put to use it always inevitably entails a forgone alternative – that there is always a trade-off. Thus, for most economists it seems to be utterly self-evident that the environmental crisis can be formulated this way: either nature *or* economy is an inevitable choice. If we want pristine nature then we will be left with fewer resources for economic activity. If we want more resources for economic activity the alternative forgone is less pristine nature.

But it is not, and was not, always an inevitable choice. We should be wary of allowing economists to foist their assumptions on us. (This is the idea that the cost of using a resource one way is the best alternative forgone).

If we start with the assumption that choices about the use of resources have an "either/or" character and "have to be made" in this way, then the inevitable consequence is a lost opportunity for another possible use. However, before we leap to the conclusion that this is inevitable we might first consider whether, in many situations, *a more economical solution would be for some way to be found to avoid the choice altogether.* Can some way be found to accommodate two or more options?

In an essay which challenges the assumption that economic choices are inevitably trade-offs, philosopher Alan Holland, writes:

> Perhaps the situation can be recast to avoid the choice altogether... People have learned to be wary, for example, of the choice that is sometimes presented between jobs and wildlife, and are suspicious of the ideology that informs such a "choice". Failing that, there are different pathways through. Here it is not, or not only, a matter of minimising losses and residues, but a matter of doing justice to the various claims, where considerations of appropriateness are to the fore... (Holland, 2002, p. 31)

The Potential for Sharing - subtractable, rivalrous and dividable choices

There are, however, influences that incline economists to pose the either/or question implied in the concept of opportunity cost. There are resources whose characteristics Elinor Ostrom called *"subtractability"*. Use by one person limits the opportunities for others to use the something but not necessarily in an all or nothing sense. In most economics texts such goods are termed *"rivalrous"* and the word implies people have to compete for their use and that one person's gain is the other person's loss. This is in the sense that if I drink a glass of water then you cannot drink it. If I eat the whole of an apple then you cannot eat it. However, drinking water and apples can be described using another word, *"divisibility"*, which suggests a different way of reacting to the nature of the resource and the nature of the relationships associated with the good. I can drink half a glass of water and you the other half. I can eat half the apple and you the other half. Rivalrous goods can often also be shared - albeit in a subtractive way.

The potential for sharing will vary according to the nature of the resource, the intensity with which it is used as well as the ingenuity and preparedness to co-operate of those sharing it. For example, an area of land zoned for building can be shared by more people by constructing additional stories upward. Again, sharing what is impossible at any one point in time may be possible by allocating time slots. An individual book can only be read by one person at any one time, but can be borrowed and used by many different people at different times. That's what libraries are for. Not all resources can be shared, of course. In the act of production some resources change their form and become embodied or converted during production or subsequently through consumption. Land can be shared in various ways because it is durable but flour used in baking disappears into the product.

For the dynamics of a community the potential for sharing is crucial. In medieval times, lands were shared in different kinds of ways, including land for arable crops. These were periodically re-assigned to different individuals in the community. When land is owned by a community but, in practice, best cultivated by individuals it made sense that people took it in turns to work with the better and the worse patches. Otherwise, the privileges of having the best plot would undermine the community. You could always compensate people for improvements when they left.

Sharing resources fosters supportive human relationships based on reciprocity. It helps to develop trust and thus, well-being. If people go to a therapist it will not be to consult about how to be happier by having more but how to improve or repair emotional relationships. Families share the use of resources and so do communities. If you believe some economists then human well-being is to be found in the possession and consumption of goods and services. Relationships are "reciprocal services" where people are spared the cost of keeping accounts about what each person has provided the other (Becker has this view). For most people sharing is a crucial dimension in their integration in a network of relationships.

Non-rivalrous resources

There are also resources that can be shared in a non-subtractive way. They are non-rivalrous and you don't have to "divide them" - indeed it would not make sense to do so. This is true of knowledge and information. We don't reduce information by using it, the reverse is the case. By using knowledge, we increase its availability. Sharing knowledge is generative. By refining, amending, checking, developing, adapting and sharing with others, non-subtractively, we increase knowledge. There is no "alternative forgone" when the resource is used.

Chapter 19

Commoning

This chapter explores the features of sustainable commons and the extent of commons today. It describes the practice of commoning as a possible response to the ecological crisis.

By definition colonial settlers were non-indigenous people. They were displaced and dislocated people already because of enclosure and warfare in Europe in the centuries leading up to the European invasion of the rest of the world.

In 1649, at the time of the English Civil War, Gerrard Winstanley wrote: "England is not a free people until the poor that have no land, have a free allowance to dig and labour the commons". But by the times Winstanley wrote he was advocating an attempt to reclaim land that for many of his contemporaries had already been lost for several generations.

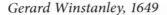

"England is not a free people, till the poor that have no land, have a free allowance to dig and labour the commons..."

Gerard Winstanley, 1649

17th century drawing of forcible land enclosure and expulsion

"Improvement" – the justifying mantra

The history of enclosure took place over many centuries and, at some points in this process, it slowed down and was even put into reverse. For example, during the Tudor era, there was great fear of the destabilising consequences for society as people lost their jobs and homes and became vagabonds so that Acts of Parliament were passed against enclosure. In this period, large landowners took arable land for their sheep for the developing wool trade. This was very lucrative for the noble thieves but it is scarcely possible to argue that the transformation of arable land to sheep pasture was an "improvement".

In later centuries "improvement" became the justifying mantra in England. The rise of the towns created a demand for arable food products while the introduction of cotton reduced the demand for wool and hence for sheep grazing. Other drivers were the trend of aristocratic landowners to take over forests and wooded areas for their parklands.

The enclosure process accelerated in the 18th and 19th centuries with the landowning class using their control of the state to push through enclosure by act of parliament and by force.

As always, the argument was that enclosure would enable the improvement of the land. It is exactly the same today when corporations in so called "developing countries" grab land with the claim that they can use it better.

But claims of improvement as a justification for land theft have always been questionable. For example, we should ask whether "improvement" might have subsequently taken place anyway, under common ownership regimes, or whether improvement under common ownership might have evolved in another direction, or whether the benefits of the improvement justified the costs in human misery.

According to Simon Fairlie:

> ... a number of historians have shown that innovation was occurring throughout the preceding centuries, and that it was by no means impossible, or even unusual, for four course rotations, and new crops to be introduced into the open field system. In Hunmanby in Yorkshire a six year system with a two year ley was introduced. At Barrowby, Lincs, in 1697 the commoners agreed to pool their common pastures and their open fields, both of which had become tired, and manage them on a twelve year cycle of four years arable and eight years ley. Of course it might well take longer for a state-of-the-art farmer to persuade a majority of members of a common field system to switch over to experimental techniques, than it would to strike out on his own. One can understand an individual's frustration, but from the community's point of view, why the hurry? Overhasty introduction of technical improvements often leads to social disruption. In any case, if we compare the very minimal agricultural extension services provided for the improvement of open field agriculture to the loud voices in favour of enclosure, it is hard not to conclude that "improvement" served partly as a Trojan horse for those whose main interest was consolidation and engrossment of land (Fairlie, 2009)

What is beyond doubt was that this was "theft" on a grand scale, sanctioned by the state. What is also clear is that the early economists were among the loudest in their applause and among the most vicious when advocating the destruction of the rights of poor people. Thus, many contemporaries were aware that a huge injustice was being perpetrated. In the face of this onslaught, people not only resisted but counter-posed alternative ideas of their own.

In 1775, inspired by a grass roots campaign to stop enclosure of Newcastle Town Moor, a self-taught radical called Thomas Spence published his penny pamphlet *Property in Land Every One's Right*. It was re-published as *The Real Rights of Man* and was being distributed over a hundred years later. In it he proposed the establishment of Parish Land Trusts and a programme that included:

> The end of aristocracy and landlords; all land should be publicly owned by "democratic parishes", which should be largely self-governing; rents of land in parishes to be shared equally amongst parishioners; universal suffrage (including female suffrage) at both parish level and through a system of deputies elected by parishes to a national senate; a "social guarantee" extended to provide income for those unable to work; and the "rights of infants" to be free from abuse and poverty. (Dickinson (Ed), 1982)

It was clear that many people were uneasy about the misery that enclosure was causing, even if they were not always as radical as Spence. One solution proposed was to give the poor their own smallholdings, in other words allotments. Mainstream economists were having none of that However,...

> In the face of such a strong case for the provision of smallholdings, it took a political economist to come up with reasons for not providing them. Burke, Bentham and a host of lesser names, all of them fresh from reading Adam Smith's Wealth of Nations, advised Pitt and subsequent prime ministers that there was no way in which the government could help the poor, or anybody else, except by increasing the nation's capital (or as we now say, its GDP). No kind of intervention on behalf of the landless poor should be allowed to disturb the "invisible hand" of economic self-interest — even though the hand that had made them landless in the first place was by no means invisible, and was more like an iron fist. At the turn of the century, the Reverend Thomas Malthus, waded in with his argument that helping the poor was a waste of time since it only served to increase the birth rate — a view which was lapped up by those Christians who had all along secretly believed that the rich should inherit the earth. (Fairlie, 2009)

The same thinking continued right into the second half of the 20th century. On 13th December 1968 Garrett Hardin, an academic working in the Malthusian paradigm, published an article in the journal *Science*. His article had a very catchy title which might partly explain why it was subsequently cited so much. The theme explored was the unfitness of commoners to manage commons. *The Tragedy of the Commons* expressed the case for private property rights using ideas straight out of neoclassical economic textbooks. Hardin illustrated his ideas with the example of a commons on which herdsmen graze their stock:

As a *rational being*, each herdsman seeks to maximize his gain. Explicitly or implicitly, more or less consciously, he asks, "What is the utility to me of adding one more animal to my herd?" This utility has one negative and one positive component. The positive component is a function of the increment of one animal. Since the herdsman receives all the proceeds from the sale of the additional animal, the positive utility is nearly + 1.

The negative component is a function of the additional overgrazing created by one more animal. Since, however, the effects of overgrazing are shared by all the herdsmen, the negative utility for any particular decision-making herdsman is only a fraction of - 1.

Adding together the component partial utilities, the *rational* herdsman concludes that the only sensible course for him to pursue is to add another animal to his herd. And another... But this is the conclusion reached by each and every *rational* herdsman sharing a commons. Therein is the tragedy. (Hardin, 1993, pp. 131-132)

According to historian Peter Linebaugh, the reference to a rational herdsman is a fantasy because in history the commons is always governed. Thus, "the pinder, the Hayward, or some other officer elected by the commoners will impound the cow, or will fine this greedy shepherd who puts more than his share onto the commons." (Linebaugh, 2013, p. 117)

As a matter of fact, as he explained in his essay, Hardin borrowed his argument from an Oxford Professor of Political Economy who was a Malthusian, William Forster Lloyd, in one of his *Two Lectures on the Checks to Population* from 1832.

Like Malthus, Lloyd was opposed to "having all things in common". Linebaugh quotes Lloyd:

(a) state of perfect equality by its effect in lowering the standard of desire and almost reducing it to the satisfaction of the natural necessities would bring back society to ignorance and barbarism. (Linebaugh, 2013, p.118)

Hardin later admitted that he had been mistaken and had been describing unmanaged 'open access regimes'. However, challenging errors can lead to some useful work. Another academic, Elinor Ostrom. Ostrom conducted her own research on the commons, together with her husband, Victor. Over many years, she helped develop a network of academics to create a "knowledge commons" about the commons. (Wikipedia is an example of a "knowledge commons" defined as, people voluntarily donating their time and effort to develop a free knowledge resource).

Research by Ostrom and her network of collaborators showed that commons were widespread. Many had survived as successful management regimes for centuries. They were far from being tragic – they were actually a model for sustainability, for protecting the interests of future generations and not degrading natural environments.

Features of sustainable commons

The particular focus of the research of Ostrom and her collaborators was to find out what made for a long lasting commons. What was it that enabled them to survive? She came up with this list:

1. Clearly defined boundaries (effective *exclusion* of external unentitled parties);
2. Rules regarding the appropriation and provision of common resources are adapted to local conditions;
3. Collective-choice arrangements allow most resource appropriators to participate in the decision-making process;
4. Effective monitoring by monitors who are part of or accountable to the appropriators;
5. There is a scale of graduated sanctions for resource appropriators who violate community rules;
6. Mechanisms of conflict resolution are cheap and of easy access;
7. The *self-determination* of the community is recognized by higher-level authorities;
8. In the case of larger common-pool resources: organization in the form of multiple layers of nested enterprises, with small local Common Pool Resources at the base level. (Ostrom, 1990, pp. 90-91)

Using these principles many commons have survived for centuries. For instance, drawing on the research of Robert McC. Netting, Ostrom cited the case of Swiss mountain farmers in the village of Toerbel. They farm private plots for vegetables and other crops in the valleys but **choose** to hold upper Alpine pasture as a commons resource. The costs of maintenance and management arrangements for upper pastures are shared for summer grazing. "Cow rights" are assigned and no more cows than a farmer can provide hay for overwintering in the valley are allowed during summer grazing on the common pasture. This is to prevent overgrazing. The regulations to this effect dated back to 1517. Cheese from the whole herd is then divided up according to the number of each farmer's cows in the herd. (Ostrom, 1990, p.61-62)

Not all commons are land based. There are examples of centuries old community managed irrigation systems that exist in Valencia in Spain that go back even further than the Toerbel arrangements.

> For at least 550 years, and probably close to 1,000 years, farmers have continued to meet with others sharing the same canals for the purpose of specifying and revising the rules that they use, selecting officials, and determining fines and assessments. (Ostrom, 1990, p. 69)

What are the potential tensions within irrigation commons that might break them up? Irrigation system maintenance costs labour and/or money so where several farmers are taking water there might be a temptation to cheat by taking more water, or water at the wrong times, as well as not contributing to the upkeep of the system. Those downstream ("tailenders") would be the losers. Their failure to get water at the time they need it could disincentivise helping upstream farmers ("headenders") maintain a whole system.

Inherent tensions of these sorts raise the question whether "government" and its agencies could do a better job by taking over the provision and management of common pool resources. It has proved possible to research this because information can be found for comparable government managed schemes. A study by Ostrom and Gardner looked into the record with 86 farmer managed irrigation systems (FMIS) and 26 agency managed irrigation systems (AMIS) in Nepal. The agency managed schemes were run by agencies on behalf of the government. What the figures showed is that when farmers organised a commons irrigation system themselves they did a better job.

Table 1
Water Adequacy[a] by Type of Governance as Arrangement and Season

Season of Year	% of FMIS with Adequate Water at the Head	% of FMIS with Adequate Water at the Tail	% of AMIS with Adequate Water at the Head	% of AMIS with Adequate Water at the Tail
Monsoon	97	88	92	46
Winter	48	38	42	13
Spring	35	24	25	8

[a]Water adequacy was measured on a four-point scale from adequate to nonexistent based on structured coding of field visits and case studies.

(Ostrom & Gardner, Coping with Assymetries in the Commons.
Self Governing Irrigation Systems can Work, 1993)

For a commons to work it must be based on a participative structure, a culture of interdependence, a deep knowledge of the state of the "resource" being governed and set of ethical principles based on fairness between participating parties – it requires a practice of "commoning" among those involved. What we might call an "ethics of environmental conservation" is embedded in relationships with a close community and neighbours, people who one would see every day, where families have relationships generation after generation. That's why two contemporary advocates for the commons, Silke Helferich and David Bollier write that "It is more accurate to talk about 'commoning' or 'making the commons' than 'the commons' as a thing. Commons don't just fall from the sky. They aren't simply material or intangible collective resources, but processes of shared stewardship about things that a community (a network or all of humanity) possesses and manages in common, or should do so" (Helfrich and Bollier 2014)

This is a description of sustainability with a proven track record. But economic history over the last few centuries has seen a relentless drive to break up these kind of arrangements through processes of "enclosure" in order to develop capitalist land and labour markets.

The extent of commons today

Because they are still widespread commons are of more than historical interest. Given the positive record of many commons the continuance of the process of enclosure is just as controversial as it always has been. The poorest people of the world still largely make their living on and with common lands - Liz Alden Wiley has attempted to calculate the amount of common land still existing – lands which are now under intense global commercial pressure. Her estimates are that the rural per capita availability of people's commons per global region are: for the Middle East/north Africa 1.567 hectares; for Sub Saharan Africa 2.695 ha; for Central America/Caribbean 1.549 ha; for South America 13.161 ha; Asia 0.45 ha; North America 11.287 ha; Europe 6.582 ha and Oceania (incl. Australia) 69.75 ha. (Wily, 2011, p. 26)

For example, in sub-Saharan Africa 75% of the land area is held by communities under customary law, almost all as collectively held forest and rangeland, used to hunt, gather or graze animals on. In most of Africa, private title covers only on average between 2 and 10% of the land. However, the colonial legacy led to the rest of the land being considered "without owner", when in fact these vast areas were and are held by communities under common ownership systems. By describing this land as "without owner", colonial powers justified expropriating it. A situation that has been maintained by many African states after independence. (Wily, The Law is to blame. Taking a Hard Look at the Vulnerable Status of Customary Land Rights in Africa, 2011)

What happened earlier in England, during the Highland clearances and after Cromwell in Ireland, was driven by mercantilist and then industrial backed colonialism globally. It continues. As we have already seen in other chapters, the pressure to expropriate the collective owners has come about because of the rise of commercial society with its claim that it can improve these lands. This has been coupled with the economist's theology for market society with its assumption of moral superiority because of its technological prowess embodied in fossil fuel powered machines and devices. Technical "progress" brings about increased production. As a result, there is less scarcity and it is taken as self-evident that this means was improvement and progress even though it is based on displacement, dislocation, ecological degradation and land theft. The owners and beneficiaries of the technologies are strengthened in their neo-Darwinian assumptions that they have triumphed because they are the strongest and fittest – and are destined to call the shots.

Commons, the ecological crisis and the future

As we reach the limits to economic growth, the economic system runs up against the host ecological system. The limits to economic growth are then expressed, in the reducing language of economics, as shortages of "natural capital" – much of which is still under collective and common ownership. Grabbing common lands is described as a way of developing the "green economy"; as a way of responding to the ecological crisis when, in fact, it is a way of intensifying it. For centuries, communities have preserved fragile ecological systems, forests, landscapes and waterscapes and now multinational corporations claim that these lands cultivated to produce crops for bio-fuels represent an alternative green future. People who have managed landscapes sustainably find that huge damns are to flood their land in the interests of what is claimed as "green energy" (even though the flooding will be likely to produce methane emissions and accelerate the climate crisis).

The people with big money and rapacious appetites adapt to changing times. As their economy degrades the ecological system "natural capital" i.e. productive and still fertile land, forests, sources of minerals, fresh water supplies, becomes scarce. At the same time, profitable places for investment are scarce and, with the banking system in crisis, there is a need for places to put the huge amounts of money that the banking system creates. The place to put this money for maximum returns is in the acquisition of the natural assets that are becoming scarce and on which they will be able to charge a "scarcity rent". Thus, completing the expropriation of remaining commons by private interests in the name of progress, even while they are completing the destruction of communities and living systems of the planet.

You can see the mentality at work in this quote from William Buiter, the chief economist of the global banking corporation Citigroup in July 2011:

> I expect to see a globally integrated market for fresh water within 25 to 30 years. Once the spot markets for water are integrated, futures markets and other derivative based financial instruments... will follow... Water as an asset class will, in my view become eventually the single most important physical commodity based asset class, dwarfing oil, copper, agricultural commodities and precious metals. William Buiter, chief economist, Citigroup July 2011 (Lubin, 2011)

Yes indeed, Professor Buiter. And as governments frack huge areas for shale gas the demand for water will increase even more, while the amount of fresh water will decline dramatically because of the contamination created. Obviously a good investment.

Chapter 20

"Improvement" through bio-diversity collapse

Ricardian development involved not just specialisation of labour but specialised uses for land. Specialised uses for land have destructive ecological consequences and are only possible with much energy consumption. The increasingly destructive impact on ecological systems is approaching a global tipping point.

In 1750, global economic activity was probably only 1% of what it is now so it is easy to assume that what subsequently happened was a success story for the improvers and for economics. Yet the truth is that we do not know what would have happened if the common lands had been protected and agrarian innovation had taken a different course.

At the end of the 20th century radically different approaches to cultivation, called permaculture which is based on ecological design principles, are being pioneered in some places. They are based on fostering optimally combined biological communities of plants and animals AND fostering human community relationships. Permaculture would have been compatible with maintaining the commons and could have been another kind of development. What if ecological design principles had been explored and adopted two centuries ago? What if, on "discovering" Australia, a serious attempt had been made to get to understand the aboriginal people, respect them as equals and learn from them? What if similar encounters on other continents had led to serious learning that changed the way people thought about how to cultivate and design growing environments? It would have been entirely compatible with advancing knowledge. The suggestion is purely hypothetical but it is legitimate to make it in order to question the assumption that Europe took a route of "progress" over the last few centuries. In the older idea, "progress" was a moral idea and economics was a part of moral philosophy. So what kind of progress or improvement was it when millions died, were enslaved and dispossessed?

At the beginning of the 21st century we must ask too whether this "improvement", if that is what it was, is any longer sustainable. It certainly does not have a track record like the arrangements of the aboriginal people that lasted 8,000 to 15,000 years.

Starvation in the "Age of Reason"

So what did happen? We start this story in 18th century Europe. This is often called "the Age of Reason" – but during this period, in the period 1740 to 1743, for example, Europeans died in their millions due to famine and because of hunger related diseases brought about by arctic winters and summer droughts. (Davis, 2002, p. 281). In addressing what to do about this European thinkers of the time had a choice:

either to see the role of the state as existing to help people who were in desperate straits. Alternatively, to take the view that state intervention was part of the problem that was holding agriculture back.

An influential group chose to believe the latter view. Physiocratic theory was developed by people who were relatively well off, educated people who had prospered and were relatively secure. Many of them lived in towns and cities – which had the wealth to import food from afar if local harvests failed. In the 18th century, they were the optimists about the potential for what they called "improvement". They saw this as requiring the removal of the protection of the commons from ordinary people so that "improving farmers" could increase production. At the same time they were keen to ensure that landowners, who played no part in the production process but creamed off a part of its product as rents, be subject to the taxes that were necessary to support the state. In this way, taxes on labour and capital would not be necessary.

As we shall see, they only had very partial success against the landowners but mostly succeeded in disinheriting working people in the countryside, whose lives were made even more vulnerable. The theorists were not carrying the same kind of risks as those affected by their recommendations – people whose lives became a nightmare if the harvest failed. Those who are comfortable can afford to be complacent about risks – because other people carry them. (This is probably why Kahneman and Tversky's Prospect Theory, which recognises that people make risk averse economic decisions and that people are motivated for security as well as for "improvement", has taken such a long time to become recognised in economic theory. Elites are usually secure, they are making other people take the risks).

Land Specialisation vs Land Diversity

In an earlier chapter, the implications of the increasing division of labour for an increasingly specialised use of land was described. Human labour specialisation has had the consequence of spatial specialisation or monocultures. A tightly integrated small scale specialisation for local needs is one thing – specialisation producing single products in bulk for distance markets is another.

Two possible kinds of structure can be represented by schematic diagrams. A, B, C and D can be thought of as products. These products also imply specific types of land use producing those products. If they are agricultural products then they can be thought of as species – either crops or animal species (live "stock"). (Fleming, 2004)

The first diagram is intended to represent 4 districts which are relatively self-sufficient. Each area produces all four products, namely A, B, C and D. There is trading between the four districts (the dotted arrows) but not with great intensity because most needs are provided for by local production in each place. There is a local diversity of production and diversity of land uses.

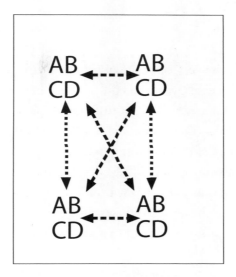

A local agricultural economy where there is greater diversity of products and is a locality with little external trade, is also likely to be more biologically diverse. One can thus, interpret the first diagram as describing a place with a bio-diverse landscape. ABCD might even be species designed to grow together as a "guild". A guild is a grouping of plants, animals, insects and other natural elements that work together to survive, grow symbiotically, and help one another reach their fullest potential. This is the basis on which "companion planting" works.

Although Adam Smith praised the advantages of the division of **labour** or labour specialisation, there are advantages in NOT having a divided use of **land** or land specialisation, but having "designed diversity". This diversity then requires, in turn, non-specialised labour to manage it.

Land is a lot more than simply being a space for injecting inputs into and extracting products out of. It is a living community of organisms re-generating life in multiple forms. To be healthy it must be diverse, not specialised, and for ecological health, the most appropriate way to cultivate is to support, use and work with nature's diversity. For example, Native American gardeners planted squash, maize and beans together – the so called "Three Sisters". The maize provided something for the beans to climb up, the beans provided nitrogen for the soil and the squash plant spreads across the ground – their leaves smothering weeds, retaining moisture in the soil. Together they also provide a balanced diet.

Diversity (instead of monocultural specialisation) works because particular plants and animals can and do help each other. Their roots might be at different depths and thus, not in competition for nutrients, while some plants attract beneficial insects for pollination and/or attract insects or birds that keep other plant predators at bay. The advantages of non-specialist multi-functionality applies to structures too. A hedge that separates animals and provides fodder for them, can also be a place for wildlife to nest; act as a wind break and sun trap on one side while providing for shade loving plants on the other. Of course, if land and structures are designed to be diverse, the labour required to create and maintain them must also be varied i.e. non-specialised. There is plenty of specialisation in nature but it only works efficiently at far smaller scales than typically found in market driven specialist monocultures.

Permaculture

There are good rationales for doing the very opposite of monoculture i.e. creating closely integrated systems that mimic how natural processes work. In contrast to specialisation as the economic principle, permaculture works with the idea that every element fulfils multiple functions and every function is performed by multiple elements. Multi-functionality should realise all the sustainable potentials of unique locations as integrated wholes. If there is going to be a hedge to separate areas, then the hedge can also function as a windbreak, a suntrap, a wildlife corridor and place for beneficial insects. If there are going to be chickens in a system, they can also clear and manure ground that will later be planted and their body warmth can be used to heat greenhouses. In the right kind of system design all the species characteristics of plants and animals are put to good use rather than being suppressed.

If the use of resources one way involves a loss of alternatives, there is a good chance that there has been a design fault. Ecological productivity arises from an interacting community of species appropriate to a particular set of conditions and the cycling of each other's products and wastes. Further, planting a diversity of seeds also expresses a different economic principle to "improvement", namely resilience, because sowing many types of species involves risk spreading. With weather and other growing conditions (like the prevalence of pests and diseases) being unpredictable, it makes sense to have a variety of species so that, if some are hit by unfavourable growing conditions, others plants still thrive and can be harvested securely.

What is described here, and codified in design systems like "permaculture", is an opposite principle to land specialisation. It is designed diversity. Ecological cultivation and ecological building are ideally developed together and related to the features of unique places in order to take advantage of specific micro-climates; specific patterns of drainage and water flow; particular kinds of soils; land formation and topology. Not only are the cultivation spaces designed according to the location, the buildings are too. They work with building materials available according to the local timber or plants, or available from the local geology and specific rock formations. (Bell, 2004)

This approach to the design of production is utterly different from what we have today. It is a totally different paradigm – a different way of thinking based in ecological logic. It revives the idea that nature needs community – communities of species and communities of people. It would be compatible with the revival of a commons based use of landscape and waterscapes.

Ricardian Development – monoculture and outwards focused development

In the 18th century, the enclosures were bringing in another kind of agricultural development – monocultures. What took place instead, and what was theorised and promoted was a "Ricardian" form of development reflected in this second diagram.

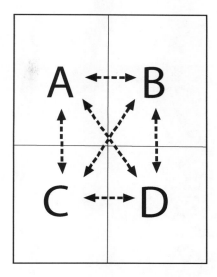

Now each of the four places must trade to get their needs met and production in each place has been scaled up not only into a division of labour but into a division of land use which becomes a "mono-cultural" use of land in each of the 4 districts.

Economic development in this form has to involve inward imports and outward exports to each separate area so that the diversity of needs in each district can be catered for. This is a schematic representation of the form of "development" that favours merchants and which feeds the growing and influential urban centres. It requires trade. A farmer who grows nothing but wheat is not in the business of self-supply but of selling the wheat to either accumulate money and/or to buy in their other needs. A large amount of transport is needed, and with this, fossil fuel use. The transport is needed not only to deliver the farm produce to the market, but to bring back soil nutrients and other inputs to the fields to replace the nutrients extracted by the monoculture growing practices.

Large scale cultivation also de-links the fields from the places of consumption and that reduces the chances for returning nutrients to the land. Where there is a tight integration of residential areas and growing areas, food wastes, as well as composted human wastes (faeces) can be returned to the fields relatively easily. The short distance helps to maintain phosphorous and other essential soil nutrients. By contrast, when food sources become separated by distance from food consumption, sewerage ceases to be an available resource. The plumbing and sewerage arrangements of urban areas frustrate a circular arrangement with agriculture. Sewerage goes into waste water systems where it is mixed with runoffs from streets and industrial toxins and therefore is contaminated and no longer available as a soil nutrient except at great treatment cost.

Energy intensive agriculture

This kind of economic arrangement is extremely energy (and carbon) intensive. As time has gone on, the fossil fuel intensity of farming has massively increased. Folke Gunther, a Swedish academic and farmer explains the basis of modern farming in a simple diagram.

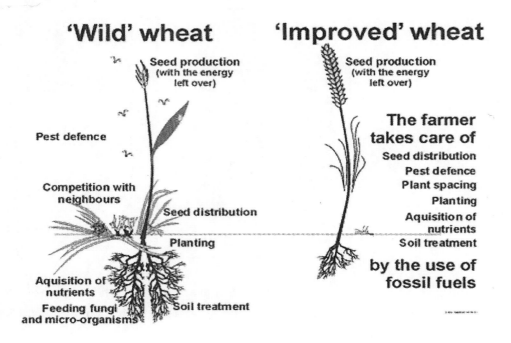

Reproduced with the permission of Folke Guenther

In order to survive and propagate, a wild plant has to carry out a considerable amount of "work" with the solar energy that it acquires. Only a fraction of this "work" is necessary for the domesticated plant. The rest is done by the farmer, with the use of fossil fuels. This means that the domesticated plant can put much more energy into seed production. It is this seed that is then harvested as grain and appropriated for human use. (Gunther, 2003, p. 246)

This looks unambiguously like progress. But is it sustainable? *Only* if energy continues to be abundant and cheap *and* if humanity can find a cheap and effective way of mitigating the associated carbon emissions, can we feel confident about this way of cultivating. There is nothing else in nature that works by homogenising the countryside using lots of cheap fossil energy. Using solar energy alone compels a different approach. If human economic systems are to work with nature, rather than against it, then economics must recognise the rationales and logic of those different approaches.

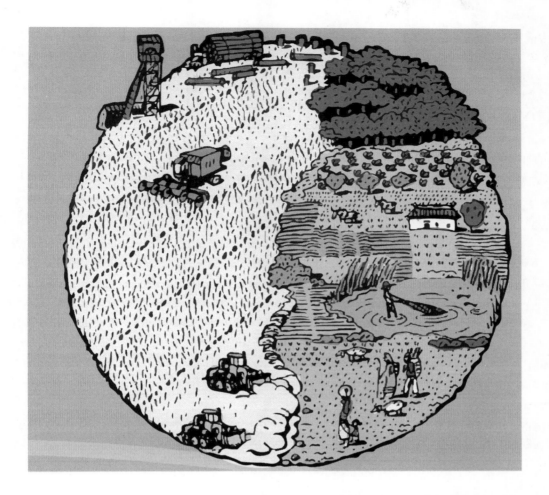

Graphic of two types of land use from International Land Coalition reproduced with permission

Scaled up means scaled up waste, pollution and vulnerability to diseases and pests

There are further consequences of monocultures. When any production process is scaled up it has consequences for the surrounding eco-system, whether it be an agricultural or an industrial process. All scaled up processes produce large amounts of waste and pollution which are more likely to overwhelm the capacity of local sinks. To take an example - if an area has an increasing concentration of pig farms – it will have an increasing concentration of pig slurry.

Another negative outcome of scaling up is greater vulnerability to crop diseases and pests. Crop concentration is an attractor for insects or animals that live on plants. This has led to a chemical war against these creatures. A war which evolves over time as "pests" acquire immunity to the measures taken against them. Concentrations of plants or animals are also vulnerable to infectious diseases passing quickly between them. Monocultures and factory farms then deploy means like antibiotics but these too lose their effectiveness over time, including as a human medicine. (Young, Cowe, Nunan, Harvey, & Mason, 1999) We have thus, ended with a race between the laboratories of corporations to preserve their product sales and industrialised agriculture techniques and a variety of pests and diseases.

151

In order to attack the pests with even higher doses of chemicals the plants themselves must be modified to be able to survive the greater toxicity of the herbicides and pesticides. Genetic modification of the plants is done to enable farmers to plant with increasingly toxic chemicals. (Swayne, 2012)

Killing the Planet

The clunky arguments of production economics do not begin to have an explanation of these deeply destructive processes because the economics of cultivation, food growing and the land is not grounded in species characteristics or ecological realities. We are describing living systems here and economics and economists have no understanding of living systems, only a mechanistic idea in which "factors of production" are combined in different quantities and in which production arrangements are supposed to be more economical at scale. The fact is that, when species of plant and animals are forced into monoculture production arrangements and factory farming, the scale of specialisation leads to totally unnatural environments for living beings. These environments are a mismatch for the species characteristics of the plants and animals which become vulnerable, get ill and, in so far as they are sentient beings, suffer a great deal during a highly artificial, cruel and short life. The increase in production, "the efficiency," is thus, achieved at the same time as an increasing vulnerability, a loss of resilience and a race to prevent sickness and disease.

In the process, nature is destroyed as a diverse and living integrated system. Adam Smith's "Age of Commerce" and the Ricardian specialisation in regard to land use and biological processes is killing the planet.

Because human activity is on such a scale this is of incredible importance. As one group of authors puts it:

"In Genesis, God blesses human beings and bids us to take dominion over the fish in the sea, the birds in the air, and every other living thing. We are entreated to be fruitful and multiply, to fill the earth, and subdue it (Gen. 1:28). The bad news, and the good news, is that we have almost succeeded." (Sanderson E. W. et al. 2002)

Most of the terrestrial biosphere has now been altered by human residence or agriculture. Even before settled agricultural systems were established humans had sent many species to extinction and therefore radically transformed the ecological system. There is no "Nature" uncontaminated by humans and whether we like it or not humans are now "stewards of nature" for good or bad.

According to the study by Sanderson just quoted less than a quarter of the earth's surface can be considered "wild" and unaffected by human use with these "wild" lands producing a mere 11% of the Planet's net primary production. "Net primary production" is a term used by biologists to describe the production of chemical energy in organic compounds by living organisms – mostly by converting the energy of the sun. In other words a mere 11% of the planetary "production", or growth, of plants and animals happens in wild areas. Humans now consume about one third of all terrestrial net primary productions. They move more earth and produce more reactive nitrogen than all other terrestrial processes combined.

"Nature" is really a "Human-Nature" *joint system*. The question is whether the stewardship of this joint human-nature system is heading towards a tipping point, a point of catastrophic collapse or whether human society can transform itself and the natural system, pulling back from the brink Can humans transform the nature-human system into something more benign – for example, using what are learning about ecological systems to reclaim and develop productive ecological landscapes rather than creating toxic wastelands and deserts?

Is destructive "improvement" approaching a tipping point? Are we heading into a "perfect storm"?

There are many reasons to believe that the "improvement" delivered to us by "development" in its present form is highly precarious and is approaching a tipping point at a global level. These reasons include:

1. Climate change, leading to a rise in surface temperatures and a decline in crop yields of 10% per every degree C rise in global temperatures.
2. Declining regional water availabilities. There are falling water tables in countries populated by half the world's peoples. According to figures quoted by Lester R. Brown, 175 million Indians consume grain produced with water from irrigation wells that will soon be exhausted.
3. Soil degradation and erosion are bringing increasing desertification. Top soil is eroding faster than new soil formation on perhaps one-third of the world's cropland.
4. Increased urbanisation and non-farming activities are out-competing food production for land and water use.
5. Fossil-fuel depletion is impacting fertiliser/pesticide availability and costs, reducing access to the inputs that have increased yields over the last few decades.
6. There is a decline in the biodiversity of food crops, bringing vulnerability to disease just as pesticide costs rise.
7. Crops are being used increasingly to feed animals rather than humans as affluent meat-based diets become more common.
8. Biofuels; grains and crops are used to feed cars rather than humans.
9. Depletion of global phosphorous inputs. According to the European Fertiliser Association, phosphorous may begin to run out in the second half of the century. And without phosphorous, crop yields will fall by 20-50%.
10. Global diseases and poisoning of bee pollinators leading to serious problems for bee pollinated crop yields.
11. Rising world population, increasing at 1.14% per annum or an extra 75 million per year (Wikipedia). The cultivated area per person fell from 0.6 hectares per person in 1950 to 0.25 hectares in 2000. (Limits to Growth 30 Year Update, p. 62)
12. The bulk of global grain market in the hands of just three companies. Development of

"terminator" seeds to concentrate all seed sales in the hands of a corporate elite.

Economists often use a principle called *"ceteris paribus"*. They look at a complicated situation, change one variable and examine what would happen, *ceteris paribus* – all other things remaining the same. However, at the limits to economic growth, all other things are not remaining the same – many are getting worse simultaneously. The phrase "the perfect storm" is sometimes used to describe this combination of many unfavourable conditions at the same time. It is compounded by "vicious cycle" feedbacks. Hunger creates discontent which feeds into political instability and conflict, which makes cultivation more difficult and thus creates more hunger. Political and social institutions collapse. In conditions like this diseases like Ebola are more likely and less manageable. Such diseases feed back further chaos because they lead to a failure to continue cultivation and thus lead to more hunger.

Mainstream economics is very little help in situations like this – particularly as its prescriptions of letting the market operate with private property owners pursuing their individual interest. We can see this if we trace back and look at the original economic thinkers about agriculture.

Chapter 21

Releasing "improving farmers" from community constraints - the Physiocrats

The Physiocrats were early exponents of the idée fixe of laissez faire economists – that by freeing up markets "improvement" will occur. The assumption here was that production increase should take priority over security for poor and vulnerable parts of the population.

Landed Estate Management

As we have seen, economics had started as the economics of the household – but in very unequal societies the large households of rich people, in their agricultural contexts became estates. An estate supplied on a bigger scale and surpluses were produced to be sold in order to buy in other types of goods and services. The earliest text on economics, around 362 BC, was called *Oeconomicus* – The Economist. It was written by Xenophon and is mostly about the management of an agricultural estate. In it Socrates describes a conversation with a farmer called Ischomachus. We don't learn a lot about nature but we do learn a lot about how Ischomachus trains his wife and trains and manages a division of labour among his slaves. (That familiar punishment and reward model so beloved by elites – rather like the sort theorised by Bentham). (Xenophon & Dakyns(Tr), 2013)

If we now fast forward to Sir William Petty in the 17th century we have his reflections on the place of nature, in the specific form of land, as a "factor or production". "Labour is the father and active principle of wealth, as lands are the mother" he wrote in 1662.

If land is the mother of all wealth then, to become wealthy, a gentleman, or a state, had to have land available to apply labour to. Ten years before penning his thoughts about the role of land and labour, Petty had gone to Ireland with Cromwell's invading army and secured a contract to survey the country. Those who had lent money for the military campaign were to be repaid in land and Petty's survey was to facilitate the confiscation. Such were the skills of 17th century economists. (Webb, 1878)

Petty's ideas influenced others. In France, trader and banker, Richard Cantillon familiarised himself with the writings of English political economists and adopted and developed his view. In an essay written around 1730, he modified Petty's assertion that land is the mother of wealth and labour its father: "The Land is the Source or Matter from whence all Wealth is produced. The Labour of man is the Form which produced it." It is upon the surplus—or, as Cantillon calls it, the "overplus"—produced on the land that all non-agricultural professions subsist. Thus,: "All the classes and inhabitants of a State live at the expense of the Proprietors of the Land." Only the landed proprietors could be said to be truly independent members of society; all others were dependent upon the surplus product of the proprietor's land and upon the latter's expenditure of the revenue they receive from ownership of land. (McNally, 1988, p. 96)

Note that there is no mention here of "capital". People who worked on the land would work with animals and with hand tools – but not, as today, with expensive powered machinery or with petro-chemical based fertilisers and pesticides. As such it seemed obvious to think of the costs of production that ultimately determined prices if markets were competitive, as being determined by the cost of the human labour input measured in labour time.

In effect, Cantillon was lobbying for the French state to do more to support agriculture rather than focusing on the mercantilist accumulation of wealth through trade. His focus was "improving agricultural production" which he assumed would be best brought about by promoting the kind of large capitalist farms in to be found England. These were run by improving entrepreneurs who ploughed financial capital into agriculture. This was not the same as supporting the absentee landowners who were taking rent and spending it in the towns on a leisured urban lifestyle, rather than investing in agricultural improvement.

Freeing up markets – the idée fixe of laissez faire economists

Cantillion's priority for agricultural improvement, as he saw it, was in turn taken on by Francois Quesnay and the Physiocratic school. Quesnay theorised that agriculture production supported "sterile" economic sectors which effectively gave nothing back to the further improvement of agriculture. To set agriculture free agricultural markets should be opened up to allow entrepreneurial farmers to make money from expanding production. He advocated dismantling a mass of exactions and market interventions by the state to "free up the market" to encourage production.

This idea has occurred repeatedly in the history of economics and, at that time, it ran up against older notions – moral restraints on markets to protect the poor.

> The most difficult question for those advocating liberalization of the grain trade was the freedom to export grain. It followed logically that such freedom should be granted if the object was to expand the market for grain to maximize demand and, thereby, the incentive to produce... But an unqualified right to export grain required accepting the view that even in cases of dearth or famine (which most economic liberalizers discounted as a serious possibility under conditions of free trade) the state would not intervene to assert the priority of subsistence over liberty of commerce—a position which required aggressively asserting the absolute freedom of markets regardless of the conditions of the poor. Yet this was precisely the position taken by the growing "liberty lobby" of the 1750s and 1760s, as well as that taken by the Physiocrats. Moreover, the government itself adopted this position for a time in the 1760s and again in the 1770s—before an aggressive campaign on behalf of traditional policy forced the government to retreat. (McNally, 1988, pp. 94-95)

In Europe's "Age of Reason" sound economics meant that the poor should starve in order that markets be allowed to stimulate food production. Laissez faire and "liberty" meant letting that happen.

Chapter 22

Agricultural empires, public works and the protection of the peasantry

In contrast, agricultural policy in India and China at the time of the Physiocrats protected the peasantry.

It is interesting to compare agricultural policy, in the same epoch, with practices in India and China.

Chinese and Indian experience shows that improvement of the rural economy, and intervention in times of dearth to protect the poor, did not have to be counterposed. There did not have to be a trade-off. On the contrary they could have complemented each other - using different approaches in different circumstances, according to harvest and weather fluctuations. In modern day terminology, the priority for resilience was not at odds with the priority for "improvement" (nowadays "growth").

In 18th century China, the peasantry were regarded as having a human right to guaranteed subsistence (**ming sheng** is the Chinese term). The empire went to immense lengths to ensure that they did not starve. In 1743 and 1744 disastrous harvests threatened the lives of millions of people but they were supported by the Confucian administration of Fang Guancheng. For several months, huge quantities of grain were transported by canal to the designated disaster counties that were suffering from drought. There was no labour requirement imposed on the peasantry in exchange for relief. (Davis, 2002, p. 281)

The Mughal rulers in India also thought that it was their job to protect the peasantry:

> Like their Chinese contemporaries the Mogul rulers Akbar, Shahjahan, and Aurangzeb relied on a quartet of fundamental policies – embargoes on food exports, anti-speculative price regulation, tax relief and distribution of free food without a forced labour counterpart – that were an anathema to later British utilitarians. (Davis, 2002, p.286)

So, in both the Mughal Empire in India and during the Quing dynasty in China, the respective emperors saw themselves as having an obligation to support the poor during times of dearth and did so effectively. The rations were not stingy and, what's more, they did not even require the poor to work for them. Both emperors took the view that if people starved on a large scale, that undermined the rural economy and they would be more likely to rebel.

India and Chinese agrarian systems were, however, differently organised to Western European agriculture. In Europe the farms were largely rain watered. There were some irrigation systems – for example in Spain – and these were organised by individual farmers or as water commons. However, by and large, farm production and farm labour was not characterised with a deep division of labour. In complete contrast, along the river valleys of the Middle and Far East, irrigation and flood control systems involved large scale public works. This entailed a complex division of labour spread across large areas of the countryside.

In the terminology of Karl Wittfogel these were "hydraulic societies". The large scale organisation of labour across wide areas meant that, from very early in history, states developed the organisational and technical ability to construct navigation canals, aqueducts and reservoirs. Having developed these organisational capabilities they went on to construct other large scale public works - highways, large walls for defence, palaces, temples and tombs. They were thus, also able to put large and complex armies in the field. (Wittfogel, 1957)

Apart from the periods of chaos between dynasties, the states of the hydraulic societies were competent and flexible developers of agriculture. A 2,000 year old system still provides irrigation that covers over 5350 square kilometres in the province of Sichuan in China. During the Quin Dynasty, in 246 BC, the Zheng Guo Canal was opened connecting the Jing and Lo rivers. It was 124 kilometres long. In the Sui dynasty, in 605 AD, a giant north-south waterway was constructed to guarantee supplies to the capital and over the next centuries extended to be 2,000 km in length. (Griessler, 1995, pp. 65, 69, 136)

In order to achieve these immense public works the empires appropriated to themselves a very large part of the agricultural surplus – that part of production above the immediate consumption needs of the cultivating population. Some of this became a source of food to protect against harvest fluctuations. At other times it fed the workers who were engaged in the public works. It paid for armies too.

The system advocated by the "Physiocrats" in Europe was not the same. Their idea was to put cultivation in the hands of prosperous improving farmers. For them, the part of the agricultural surplus that was going, as rent, to the landlord class and that which was being spent in the towns was sterile because it was not coming back to improve agriculture. It made sense to see these land rents as the appropriate source of taxes for state revenues – to take the tax burden from others.

In theory, the creation of a space for "improving capitalist farmers" cut two ways. At the cost of working people in the countryside who were subjected to greater insecurity, and also, very much in theory, in taxes to be imposed on a parasitical landlord class. The subsequent fate of the landowners varied from country to country, in France, some of them lost their heads in the revolution. They also lost some protection in the United Kingdom when the Corn Laws were abolished after the Napoleonic wars. However, while the new ideas of political economy justified a campaign which took away protection for the poor, the landowner class had more social power and were able to protect their position.

The situation of the USA was different again. Over most of the 19th century, European settlers moved westwards grabbing land as private property from the First Nations. By the end of the 19th century, though the lands had all been taken, at that point a struggle broke out regarding the power of big landowners. The idea of a land value tax, based on earlier ideas from Smith and Ricardo surfaced and caused considerable controversy, leaving their mark on economics.

Chapter 23

Who are the parasites? The radical implications of classical economics

Henry George and Karl Marx developed alternative radical theories out of the ideas of Adam Smith and David Ricardo.

The classical economists did not mince their words. As Mason Gaffney puts it:

> ... classical political economy was a remarkable phenomenon. Its major writers in England were able to portray the dominant class of rent-takers as idlers and superfluous drones. One surmises they got by with this because the idlers were proud of it. In their value-system, labour was not respected; conspicuous leisure was. Saving was regarded contemptuously as stinginess: conspicuous consumption was the mark of a gentleman and aristocrat. (Mason Gaffney, "the Corruption of Economics". (Gaffney, 1994)

Ricardo and land rent

The Physiocrats, Adam Smith and especially David Ricardo theorised land rents as the ideal source for taxation. Ricardo's key insight was that economic rent is not a cost of production. No one produced the land, it was a free gift of nature so there was no cost involved in using it for production. Landowners could charge rent for its use because of their ownership alone. Their income was not really a cost, it was a re-distribution of what had been produced but without the landowners doing anything at all, except diverting some of the produced income to themselves "unearned". The value of a location is not the result of anything that the landowner does – the landowner reaps where they have not sown.

In Ricardo's definition, rent arises in the difference between the costs of production from different acreages of land. Some acreages are preferable as locations because the soil is better, or these locations are closer to market and to sources of inputs that have to be transported in. At the preferable locations, more money could be made by farmers but landowners could ask more rental, siphoning off the monetary benefits of the advantageous location from the farmers into their own pockets because of competition between farmers.

The classical economists realised that if the landowners had their rental incomes taxed, they could not add the tax charge to the rental charge since renting farmers were already being charged up to the maximum that they were prepared to pay. If more rent was demanded from the farmers in order to pay for the tax that had been imposed on the landowner, it would be in the interests of the farmer to move. The tax would have to be paid out of the rent and could not be added on top of it. That was the theory anyway – if there's going to be taxation, then it should be on land rents was their message. The trouble was that the landowners were politically powerful and able to block taxes being placed upon rents.

This is a recurring theme in economics. Economists have an idea – but the political power of interest groups is so powerful that the idea remains of purely theoretical interest. What did However, happen early in the 19ᵗʰ century was a successful campaign against landowning interests organised by the Corn Law League. Tariff protection to prevent cheap grain being imported into the UK had kept grain prices high. This, in turn, had enabled a high rake off by landowners who could charge higher agricultural rents from their tenant farmers who were getting a good price for their grain. The people who paid were workers whose food prices were higher than they might otherwise be, and their employers who had to pay higher wages. Eventually the Corn Laws were swept away – a success for the growing industrial employers and for the economics of free trade - in the UK at least.

Henry George

Apart from their defeat by the Corn Law League in the UK, the landowners in many countries were able to hang onto their power and influence in the 19ᵗʰ century. However, towards the end of that century a campaign by American journalist, turned tax activist, Henry George, used the ideas of Ricardo and the classical economists, and gave landowners in a number of countries a serious scare. He succeeded in popularising the idea that taxes should focus on land rentals. What's more he popularised a view of social inequality that focused on landownership as the cause. In the view of George, landowners acquired property titles that enabled them to channel the increasing wealth of society into their own pockets even though they made no positive contribution to the development process. Economic development inevitably takes a spatial form. It happens somewhere and if the landowners own that somewhere they can make money without doing anything else.

For instance, consider a railroad that joins a city to a town on the coastline. Now city people can travel to the coastal town with relative ease for holidays and recreation. The smart money will then move to buy land around the coastal town. When people want to build hotels they will have to pay rentals to the landowners. It is the landowners who are able to make the wealth that the railroads bring about by building and running hotels and the other facilities of a seaside resort. They don't have to lift a finger to earn this rent. They just have to buy up the land – which they can often do cheaply because they have insider information and realise before anyone else what is being planned. Then the work of other people, developing a tourist resort, will make their newly acquired land valuable.

Towards the end of the 19ᵗʰ century, economists were pre-occupied, indeed obsessed, with analysing the sources, determinants and social rationales of interest and other income returns to private property. Apart from theorists and campaigners like Henry George, who focused in landowner rental income, the trade union and socialist movement were emerging and developing their own critical and challenging ideas. Influenced by theorists like Karl Marx, the very legitimacy of property income was in question. Answering Marx was a strong motivation for many economists. (Tobin, 1998)

Karl Marx

Marx's key idea was that the source of property incomes was "surplus value" produced by labour. What workers and their families needed as wage income, in order to reproduce and maintain their own "labour power", was less than the full value of what they produced. In effect, workers spent part of the day working for the wages to maintain themselves and their families (the next generation of workers) while the rest of the day they produced exchange value that was paid out to others as property income - distributed as profits, interest and rents.

For Marx, therefore, the division of income was explained in terms of the power asymmetry underlying the social relationships of capitalists and workers. Workers were driven to work for the employing class. They had no choice but to work on terms largely favourable to their employer because they, or their ancestors, had lost access to the means of production though processes like the enclosures. Their only hope was to organise for greater bargaining power and try to enhance their bargaining position by engaging in class struggle. (The working class were obliged to exchange their labour power on a market for wages but this was a market where there were trading under an institutionalised form of duress. Without access to means of production to work for themselves there was a structural power inequality underpinning the labour market).

On the question of land rents, both Marx and George agreed that they should be spent on public purposes. Though George did not agree on the nationalisation of land, it was enough for him to tax away the land rental from the landowners.

The first demand of *The Communist Manifesto* by Marx and Engels was the nationalisation of land and the devotion of its income to public purposes.

For a time, the ideas of Marx and those of George were competing forms of radical thought that located contemporary problems either in the capitalist class or in the landowning class. Both strands of radicalism had their roots in classical economic theory and conservative economists decided that classical economic ideas needed to be neutered. That is largely why we now have neoclassical economics. The conclusions that were being drawn from classical economics were suddenly very threatening to propertied people. As Gaffney explains in relation to George:

> The menace George posed to rent-takers is clear from how he viewed them. To George, the landowner *per se* is non-functional (unproductive), a layabout drone, a drain on the hive, a transferee, a welfare case. Worse than that, he or she often makes the land itself lay about, too: then he or she is *dys*functional or counterproductive, a double-dipper. Worse yet, landowners become triple-dippers when they use their discretionary income and wealth to dominate politics and drain away yet more treasure through subsidies, public works and services, protections from

competition, cheap credit, and so on. Often they are not just passive drones, but active predators. (Gaffney, 1994)

Landowners in the USA funded academic economists in order to put up a counter argument while using their influence in the universities to ensure that academics who supported George were fired. In this way, the others got the message in an era in which there was no such thing as academic tenure. It was a period in which businessmen, landowners and wealthy people were replacing clerics on the boards of colleges. Economics began to change. Classical economics became neoclassical.

Chapter 24

Marginal Productivity Theory

This chapter describes the "marginal revolution" of neoclassical economics. The idea of marginal productivity and payments to "factors of production" was developed for ideological reasons to counter thinkers like Marx and George. The theoretical framework learned by generations of students is contradicted by the evidence. The ideas of capital and land in neoclassical economics are incoherent.

Economists tell us how consumers on the market, "voting" with their purchasing power got what they wanted and wealthy landowners got the economic theory that they wanted. It was economists like J.B. Clark that were necessary if your economics department was to become well-funded. Clark moved to Columbia University in 1895. The university was blessed by funding from Wall Street banker J. P. Morgan.

The key idea for theorists like Clark was that "factors of production" earned what they added to production "at the margin". If adding an extra worker to the payroll adds more to production, sales and revenues, than that worker costs to hire, then it was in the interests of the employer to hire the extra worker. The same logic continued to apply as long as each additional worker enabled more money revenue to come in from extra production and sales than they cost. The process of adjustment by hiring more workers would stop at the point where the last worker (marginal worker) was adding as much to enterprise revenues as they were costing. Now what could be fairer than that? Employers would employ more workers until a point where each worker is being paid the same amount of money as the value they have added to production can be sold for.

The same logic is applied to explain the income being earned by the other "factors of production", namely, an amount equal to the revenue from the sale of their marginal products. This idea was an ideological construction that suited business interests nicely.

Critics have pointed out the flaws in this reasoning. A technical argument about where a business person will no longer find it worthwhile, under tightly defined conditions, to add more and more labour to his capital, has been fudged as an ethical argument justifying the income distribution between that business person and his employees and ignoring the underlying social relationship between the wage labourer and the capitalist.

In the words of Joan Robinson:

The very essence of the theory is bound up with a particular institution -- wage labour. The central doctrine is that "wages tend to equal marginal product of labour". Obviously this has no meaning for a peasant household where all share the work and the income of their holding according to the rules of family life; nor does it apply in a [co-operative] where, the workers" council has to decide what part of net proceeds to allot to investment, what part to a welfare fund and what part to distribute as wage. Joan Robinson quoted in (What is Wrong With Economics, 2009)

Neoclassical economics thus, emerged, originating in an ideological imperative, namely, the justification of property incomes. This new approach concocted an elaborate fiction that was subsequently fed to each generation of students which purports to describe how companies decide how much they are going to produce.

If you ask most business people what determines how much they produce they will probably say that they are limited by how much they can sell or how much capital they can raise to expand production – which will also depend on them convincing a capital provider of how much they can sell. To the neoclassical economist, however, what limits what a firm will produce is not only that it may have to reduce its prices if it tries to sell more but that, as the firm increases, its production its costs will rise.

In the textbooks there is a picture of what happens in the production arrangements of companies which goes like this: If a company wants to expand its output "in the short run", it will find itself unable to alter the availability of some "factors of production" like its premises and its capital equipment. However, it will be able to vary the input of other factors of production like its labour force. But adding more and more workers to the fixed quantity of capital equipment will eventually lead to "diminishing returns". The neoclassicals want us to believe that output will increase but at a diminishing rate. The reason is that the ratio of workers to capital equipment becomes less than optimal after a certain point. Indeed at some point adding another worker would lead to no extra output at all. The last worker would simply get in the way and might even reduce total production.

The implication of "diminishing returns" from the variable factors of production (e.g. labour) is that if companies try to expand output they find that their costs will rise. Let us illustrate by imagining a company in which, in the early stages of an expansion process, there is little labour and much capital equipment. In this company, in order to expand production by 10 units a week it would require one extra worker costing an extra £100 a week to hire. An example of what "diminishing returns" would mean is that, to produce a further 10 units a week beyond this might require 2 extra workers costing £200 to hire. An extra 10 units a week again might cost 4 extra workers at £400. This being the case, if this imaginary company is to be induced to produce more and more, its owners will want to be able to sell the greater number of units at higher and higher prices so that they can cover the higher and higher costs. Since the company is unlikely to be able to get consumers to buy more at higher prices its expansion will be choked off by the diminishing returns which has led to rising costs.

Well, that is the textbook story anyway – but it is a conceptual house of cards which was dreamed up for ideological purposes in order to justify the distribution theory. The idea of diminishing returns is important because, if you think about it, it implies that to employ more workers the labour force must take a wage cut. In the imaginary story an employer who employs more people is getting less and less additional product for each additional worker. To induce him to do this, he has to be able to pay them less to make it worth his while. It's obvious then, isn't it that, if there is unemployment in the economy, it is because wages are too high. Wouldn't you know it - once again the poor have only themselves to blame.

Steve Keen quotes Galbraith:

> Neoclassical economics can be summed up, as Galbraith once remarked, in the twin propositions that the poor don't work hard enough because they are paid too much, and the rich don't work hard enough because they are not paid enough. (Keen, 2011, p. 119)

What all of this has got nothing to do with, however, is the real world. This theory has been tested against empirical research over a hundred times and shown not to be true. If the theory were true it would be demonstrated by rising costs as companies try to expand, but these are not the findings. A few companies have cost structures like this but the vast majority don't. The evidence is in cited in Keen's book *Debunking Economics*.

For example, a study by Alan Blinder surveyed 200 medium to large US firms which collectively accounted for 7.6% of America's GDP admitted that:

> The overwhelmingly bad news here (for economic theory) is that, apparently, only 11% of GDP is produced under conditions of rising marginal cost... Firms report having very high fixed costs – roughly 40% of total costs on average. And many more companies state that they have falling, rather than rising marginal cost curves. While there are reasons to wonder whether respondents interpreted these questions about costs correctly, their answers paint an image of the cost structure of the typical firm that is very different from the one immortalised in the textbooks. Blinder 1998 quoted in (Keen, 2011, p. 126)

Blinder's research is not alone. Steve Keen mentions 150 empirical studies. Every study found the majority of firms acting in a way that contradicts the textbook theory. (Keen, 2011, p. 125)

The reason is that the idea of "diminishing returns" is wrong. It is far more accurate to describe short term expansion (or contraction) in an industrial economy as involving "constant returns" as production is scaled up or scaled down. The "constant returns" occur at the same time as an increase or decrease in capital utilisation.

Here is another imaginary example that is a little more realistic. You wish to set up a business in the clothing trade employing (mainly) women who each work with a single sewing machine. You do it by acquiring premises and putting a number of sewing machines in the factory. The price of the premises, the sewing machines and other equipment are your fixed costs. As you start up you may use only half of the sewing machines and half of the production space of the factory, depending on the size of the market but if your product becomes more popular you hire extra women to sew using the otherwise unused sewing machines and the previously unused factory space. The sewing machines and space brought into use do not cost any more. These are fixed costs that were already being paid for and are now being spread across a larger volume of production. Nor are there any "diminishing returns" to the increased labour input, because, just as before, each worker works with one sewing machine and in the same amount of space, specifically for their work.

Fact is that production in an industrial economy requires an often tightly defined specialisation of labour functions and/or a specific relationship of workers to production equipment. There is no point in varying the worker to sewing machine ratio. Two or more workers per sewing machine at any one time makes no sense at all. Likewise, at any one time, just one lathe will be used by just one worker. A blast furnace has just so many workers with specific functions. The technical ratios between specialist workers in teams and between the workers and machines cannot be varied. To have flexibility one must have spare capacity – and then employ that capacity in the appropriate ratios that make for team work and relate workers with specific trade skills to specific kinds of equipment. The capacity, unused and used, represents a fixed cost that, when spread over increasing production, brings unit costs down. Because expansion is an expansion of all factors of production in a technically defined and fixed ratio, no such thing as diminishing returns occurs. What occurs is that capital utilisation rises or falls spreading the fixed costs over a varying output.

All this was largely worked out by a critic of the neoclassical school, Piero Sraffa in a paper written in 1926 that was published in the *Economic Journal* (Sraffa, 1926). It forms the basis for the chapters in Steve Keen's book from which I have taken this very brief account.

Keen quotes Sraffa:

> Business men, who regard themselves as being subject to competitive conditions, would consider absurd the assertion that the limit to their production is to be found in the internal conditions in their firm, which do not permit of the production of a greater quantity without an increase in cost. The chief obstacle against which they have to contend when they want to gradually to increase their production does not lie in the cost of production – which, indeed, generally favours them in that direction – but in the difficulty of selling the larger quantities of goods without reducing the price, or without having to face increased marketing expenses. (Keen, 2011, pp. 116-117)

This way of explaining things helps to explain the rise and rise of the marketing industry. If, as neoclassical economists claim, it is diminishing returns and rising internal costs that prevent companies selling more and more then why would they bother to advertise? If the adverts worked they would be pushing themselves into a zone where rising internal costs would choke off further production anyway. On the other hand, if unit costs fall as production expands, then as long as the price is greater than that unit cost the company will make more the more that it sells. What limits the company then is the ability to sell its product. If the company reaches full capital utilisation then what limits it is the ability to raise new capital to expand – and that partly depends on being able to convince an investor of increased sales in the future.

Capital in neoclassical theory

The fact that the theory does not match reality does not stop marginal productivity theory and diminishing returns being reproduced in the textbooks because it is useful ideologically as an "explanation" of income distribution. "Land", "labour" and "capital" "get what they contribute at the margin" according to the theory when things are presented in this way. It is not within the scope of this book to go into these ideas in depth because I am trying to review the foundational issues that underpin economics in a simple way. Unfortunately, it is not possible to ignore them either and, in fact, there is a whole set of questions about "capital theory" where Ricardian economists in Cambridge in the UK and neoclassical economists in Cambridge in the USA (at the Massachusetts Institute of Technology) clashed about how to understand the "returns to capital". These are described in Steve Keen's book *Debunking Economics* where he does a good job in describing a very complex debate in which neo-classicals like Samuelson eventually acknowledged that the Cambridge economists in the UK had established their point. In effect, the UK economists challenged the idea that profit is the reward for capital's contribution to production.

For neoclassical theory to be a complete picture of income distribution in society it has to scale up from how individual firms operate. This meant that economists needed to assume that units of labour and "capital" were identical or homogenous entities that move between economic sectors and firms as they adjusted continually to try to achieve their optimal outputs. Now, that idea is understandable when it comes to labour moving from one company or economic sector to another. But a loom cannot "flow" into work as a lathe. A lorry is a piece of capital equipment that cannot flow into use as a computer. Land cannot flow either. It is stuck where it is.

Economists have had lots of fun over the years dreaming up metaphors to try to get around this problem. Much effort has been devoted to creating "models" where "capital" as a physical entity is thought of in malleable terms in order to rescue neoclassical distribution theory. Capital in a "putty" form, or models using capital that could be reconstituted in a different form like Meccano, have been put forward. This was all in order to have "capital" that could move from sector to sector.

J B Clark started the process with what was called the "jelly theory of capital". Naturally, Clark recognised that capital goods differ from industry to industry and from time to time. To cope with this conceptual problem, he regarded capital goods as being specific and transient embodiments of a general and permanent "essence of capital". This is the fund accumulated by the economy's savings up to any point in time and ploughed into specific capital goods.

Mason Gaffney describes this way of thinking as "endowing capital with a Platonic essence". The ancient Greek philosopher Plato thought that what we experience in the physical world is an imperfect reflection of eternal perfect "forms" that exist somewhere. Ideal objects that capture the "real essence" of the things dimly reflected in our imperfect everyday physical existence. Thus, particular machines – lathes, looms, tractors – were an imperfect reflection of the "essence of capital". The rationale of thinking in this way is something like this: capitalists use their resources in processes that "turns over" capital. Assuming they are involved in production they start with money, go on to buy machines, buildings, materials and hire workers, organise a production process and then sell the products to make a "return" which brings their money back with, as they hope, more money than they started. In this process, and over time, they will hold back some of the money returned to replace and buy new machinery. (Gaffney, 1994)

However, the only thing that looms, lathes and lorries, as items of capital equipment have in common is the fact that they have a money value. Neoclassical economists ignore the differences and just count the money value of the different kinds of machines as the common element making for comparability and measurability. But there is a problem of using price as a common way of counting different kinds of capital goods. The price of capital goods depends on the rate of profit and the rate of profit is the very thing that you are trying to explain. What one can do, however, is think of "capital goods" as commodities which enter into the production of other commodities. With this idea, Piero Sraffa at Cambridge UK succeeded in showing that you could make calculations based, not on money prices, but from calculating commodity inputs into the economic process as "dated labour inputs". Ultimately, any lathe, loom or lorry is made with labour and with other inputs. These other inputs were made from labour and even earlier inputs. The earlier inputs were made from labour and other inputs made even further in the past and so on. If you go back far enough, you only have labour inputs – but you have to adjust your calculations to allow, at each stage, for a profit rate which has been taken out; and for the fact that different kinds of commodities enter into the production of other kinds of commodities in variable ratios.

What this exercise establishes is that, rather than the rate of profit depending on the amount of capital used as neoclassical economists would like us to believe, the measured amount of capital depends upon the rate of profit.

This, in turn, grounded the idea that the distribution of income is not the result of impersonal market forces but reflects the power relationships between different social classes as well as the technical capabilities of factories.

In later chapters I will explore ideas about production not developed by either Cambridge, England or Cambridge, USA – to explore the idea that the production of society depends on one input in addition to labour that enters into absolutely all economic activity – energy. Since energy is a commodity that enters into the production of all commodities, it is absolutely crucial and, as we will see, if the amount of energy needed to produce energy rises, and if the amount of energy needed to produce other raw materials rises too, then society will be in deep trouble.

Land in neoclassical theory – or its absence

J B Clark was not just interested in providing ideological cover for the property income to capitalists. He was concerned about landed income too. Perhaps conscious of the need to counter the arguments of Henry, George Clark described "land" as just another purchased input, another form of capital.

Adding land to the picture of capital as Clark did was, as Tobin pointed out, a step that destroyed the equation of the capital stock being equal to the society's accumulated savings. One may save resources (hold back from consuming them) in order to create machinery instead, but no one saves up to create land. Leaving aside polders and other reclaimed land, land is already there.

No matter – for Clark capital could "transmigrate" into land – a metaphor that made land and capital the same kind of stuff. This theoretical sleight of hand had the useful function of getting rid of the Ricardian theory of rent and provided the appearance of an answer to Henry George in the process.

Henceforth, most economists just focused on "labour" and "capital" as concepts to explain production. Land, with its distinctive features – spatial, temporal and environmental, largely disappeared from economic theory.

Thirty years after Clark, John Maynard Keynes wrote his *General Theory of Employment, Interest and Money* and declared that the influence of land was restricted to an agricultural age. It was capital and particularly, financial capital, which was the important influence in the modern age (cited in Harrison, 2005, p. 142)

Trying their best to be helpful to the elite, the idea of rent was also muddled by creating a new definition for it. "Economic rent" is now said to be the difference between what each factor of production is paid and how much it would need to be paid to remain in its current use – a definition of rent that rests upon the idea of opportunity cost.

Taking land out of economic theory meant that economic theory was "dis-located" or "dis-placed". The conceptual category of "land", and the linked concept of "rent", represented real influences in the world that the system of ideas called "economics" was struggling to represent. Making these categories disappear from the constellation of ideas that made up economic theory had serious implications. The theory lost dimensions of inclusiveness and clarity. It was impoverished. More events could now happen in reality than the concept system had terms to explain. What was disappearing from theory when the concept of land was fudged into the concept of capital was the likelihood of further investigations into the distinctive features of land – spatial, temporal, environmental and ecological – all those things that I have tried to put back into this book. Even considered in narrowly economic terms, land as a very distinctive kind of asset because it is one of the main forms of collateral for the banking and finance system.

Discussions of production as the relationship between capital and labour were no longer "grounded". The embodiment of economic activity in the physical world disappeared. The sense that it entails natural fertility; specific production locations; the extraction of matter and energy sources from out of the planetary crust and, consequently, putting wastes back into the earth; into the rivers and the atmosphere. All these kind of things were effectively out of sight of the theory and out of the mind of the theoreticians.

Out of sight and out of mind was exactly how the landed elite liked it – particularly in Britain where the power and inequality involved in landed property has been deliberately hidden by an aristocracy anxious to avoid the threat of a land value tax and to enjoy their privilgeses undisturbed. Kevin Cahill's book *Who Owns Britain* sets out the figures starkly: the UK is 60m acres in extent, and two-thirds of it is owned by 0.36% of the population, or 158,000 families. In Scotland it is even worse – 432 individuals own half the private rural land. In contrast 24 million families live on the 3m acres of the Britain's "urban plot" – and then buy into the idea that Britain is a severely overcrowded country in which land is extremely scarce. (Adams, Tim 2011)

"Much of this can be traced back to 1066. The first act of William the Conqueror, in 1067, was to declare that every acre of land in England now belonged to the monarch. This was unprecedented: Anglo-Saxon England had been a mosaic of landowners. Now there was just one. William then proceeded to parcel much of that land out to those who had fought with him at Hastings. This was the beginning of feudalism; it was also the beginning of the landowning culture that has plagued England – and Britain – ever since." (Kingsnorth , Paul 2012.)

However, in the last few years a large amount of landed property in the UK has been purchased by the moneyed members of the global elite from the descendants of early medieval gangsters. The astronomic house prices and rents in London as well as in some of Britain's country estates is because the property magnates of the world are buying up the place. (Adams 2011)

Concluding remark – different meanings of "diminishing returns"

It was Ricardo who first utilised the concept of "diminishing returns". He realised that different areas of land as a resource had different fertility and different degrees of desirability in other senses too e.g. distance to markets. He used this idea of differences in desirability in his theory of rent. Ownership of the most fertile land nearest to market meant the ability to charge more rent than in less fertile and more out of the way places. What happened was that the neoclassicals tried to adapt Ricardo's explanation for rent for other factors of production by claiming diminishing returns in different circumstances - where factors of production were used in differing ratios with each other. As we have seen, this was not an appropriate thing to do in most industrial production processes but the idea of diminishing returns is useful in some contexts. As we will see, it is useful in office work and service contexts and it is, above all, useful in describing the relationship between the economic system and the ecological system.

As the size of the economic system expands in relation to the fixed size of the ecological system, there are indeed diminishing returns. When the best sources of fuels, minerals and soils are used first, depletion means that the cost of extracting increasing amounts for economic use increases. More resources have to extract resources. Furthermore, if wastes and pollution from production increase then more resources have to go to deal with the consequences. This is diminishing returns. Those problems are the limits to economic growth. Ironically neoclassical economists seem unable to acknowledge these diminishing returns as a problem.

Chapter 25

Georgist Macro-Economics and the Land Value Tax

The ideas of Henry George are still very relevant for economic theory. A site value tax would help to stabilise property market cycles and promote greater spatial efficiency. However, while helpful, market mechanisms like a site value tax will not, on its own, fully resolve the environmental crisis.

Why the real estate market plays an integral role in macro-economic conditions

Given the way that land was dismissed out of the theory, including in the writings of John Maynard Keynes, it was not that surprising that it has been left to a few economists working in the Georgist tradition to explore and unravel the interplay between the banking system and the real estate, housing and land markets in the explanation of the economic cycle. For example, (Harrison, 2005) and (Anderson, 2009)

The link between real estate and finance is clear and obvious. A great deal of the collateral underpinning bank lending is real estate and housing. In the UK about 70% of bank collateral is tied up in this way, with a similar large proportion in many other industrial countries. It is therefore not surprising that there is a close relationship between the economic cycle in the real estate market and financial crises.

Because it is "embodied", any form of economic development has a spatial dimension. It "takes PLACE". Economic development involves the need for locations - for factories, offices, roads, railways and housing. Some sites emerge as particularly favourable - particularly when opened up by infrastructure investment – often paid for by taxes. The wonder of the market economy is claimed to be that if prices signal that something is profitable more of that thing will be created. But you cannot increase the amount of land, and each location is always unique. So, during economic development booms, the land price soars in specific locations (the capitalised rents for owning particular locations). Recognising which locations to get hold of is a way of making a lot of money. You do this by getting credit to buy up land and property and then persuading politicians to spend tax money on infrastructure to boost the value of the purchased locations.

Tycoons can make serious money like this – as long as landowners can ensure that the value that they capture remains untaxed. A modern day example can make this point clearer. London's extension of the Jubilee Tube Line to Canary Wharf cost £3.5 billion but increased property values by an estimated £13 billion along the route. Landowners did nothing to earn this windfall except owning the land. (TransportforLondon, 2004)

So who does create this rising value of land? What people are prepared to pay for a location reflects the value of adjacent amenities which are either public goods financed out of taxes or advantages created by the surrounding population living there, for example, social networks; a rich job market; services and cultural activities. These collective amenities incur costs and need to be maintained so it is only fair that the landowners should pay for them in taxation. When no taxation occurs, landowners get the desirable features for free and someone else pays, wealth is transferred into landowner pockets – as well as enriching the banking sector. (Lyons, 2012, p. 104)

The chief economics commentator for the Financial Times, Martin Wolf, put it succinctly when he described the gains made by landowners, as **"the reward of owning a location that the efforts of others have made valuable"**

Property market cycles and their bubbles

By making money for themselves like this from other people's efforts, the finance and real estate sector also seriously destabilise the economy. Property market cycles tend to be about 14 years in length. The long run rate of interest is about 5% and, bearing in mind the rent that people pay, affordable house prices work out at a sum which is equal to about 14 years in rent. If land, house and property prices are bid any higher, debts become unserviceable and the housing and property market grinds to a halt.

Economic cycles tend to end in "bubbles". The rising price of particular classes of assets like land or property creates a collective euphoria or mania. People borrow to buy this asset, or invest all their savings in it on the anticipation that they will make more money as its price continues to rise. Their credit inflated purchases chase up the price until the price of the asset and the servicing of debt become unsustainable. Confidence falters and the crash occurs. The big money is to be made by getting in a bubble early and getting out early. Banks are left with debtors who have lost money and cannot pay up who then have the collateral seized from them.

None of this would happen if the original idea of the Physiocrats, Smith, Ricardo and George had come to pass – that the landowners forfeit the rising land values (capitalised rental values) through a tax. A land value tax would remove the incentive for land price speculation pumped up by bank credit creation. There would be no point in speculation because gains would go to the taxpayer. There would be no point in buying and hoarding land and then leaving it unused, on the anticipation that its value will rise. Hoarded land would have to pay tax, and if it was unused, it would still pay a tax, thus, speculative holding of idle land would lead to loss. A site value tax would release land onto the market and actually bring down land prices.

Spatial inefficiency

The failure to impose a site value tax has far reaching knock-on consequences for the natural environment because of spatial inefficiency. If, for example, we look at Ireland we can see that the speculative property boom that led to the financial collapse of 2008 led to a lot of building that was never completed, as well as a dispersed settlement pattern that is very inefficient in the use of space, infrastructure and resources. In the absence of land value tax, the system of land planning was abused to zone inappropriate areas as development land. Rezoned land went up in price and was sold on to developers for a windfall profit in which local authorities revenues were also swollen. The resulting spatial allocation of building resources made no sense. Ireland is now one of the most car dependant societies in Europe. Spread out like this, many Irish people have a sedentary and car based lifestyle which is partly why 61% are overweight or obese. (Osbourne, 2012, p. 134)

This car use also generates greenhouse gases making Ireland vulnerable to oil depletion and rising fuel prices.

Had there been a site value tax, landowners would have had to pay for vacant sites as well as used ones. They would have had an incentive either to use empty urban spaces or sell these spaces to those who would use them. This would have protected the countryside by making urban sprawl unnecessary. Cities and towns would have used urban space more efficiently and compactly. The need to travel distances would have been reduced and more people would be able and willing to get around by foot or by bicycle.

Arguments like these are persuasive – they suggest that smart taxation will go some way to help resolve a number of serious economic, environmental and social problems. It is why it is so encouraging that, in late 2014, the Scottish government are considering land reform and measures such as a land value tax. (Hunter, J. Peacock P. Wightman, A. Foxley M. n.d.)

This has led some thinkers to conclude that if "land" (expanded as a concept category to mean all "natural resources") is given a price, either as a tax, or through some other mechanism like auctioning permits to authorise natural resource use, then all will be well. Humanity will be able to resolve the environmental crisis solely with market mechanisms. In the next few chapters we will examine why it is not as simple as that because this is still framing human-nature interactions inside an anthropocentric view. If we frame things through markets driven by what humans find desirable we are still seeing nature as a "resource" which is only of instrumental value. This is very reductionist, and human centred attitude *is itself* a major part of the problem.

Chapter 26

lllth rights for sale

Anthropocentric views of nature are very different from the "nature as kin" viewpoint of many indigenous societies. In the anthropocentric view nature is converted it into "environmental goods" for which people have "preferences" of varying strengths.

Anthropocentric views of nature versus nature as kin

So far we have looked at economics as a conceptual framework that reduces "nature" to being a "factor of production". This is an extended version of the classical economist's concept of "land". Economists in more recent years are more likely to use a different terminology. When they write they are more likely to use words like "natural capital" and "eco-system services".

No matter, all these conceptualisations are "anthropocentric". This is a word that conveys the idea that nature is there for human use. There is an argument that it is this attitude that is at the root of the environmental problem and that only when humans take a nature centric view will their protection of the earth stand some chance of being adequate. As Luck et al. put it:

> To regard nature as a provider of services is one particular metaphor that carries different kinds of value connotations. For example, it promotes valuing nature primarily through the benefits that humans derive from ecosystems and places these benefits in the same context as those delivered through human activities... Adopting an economic language and metaphor to frame human–nature relationships implies the idea of possible equivalents (i.e. certain components of nature can be replaced completely by other components or human-derived alternatives). For example, an implication of possible equivalents is that the loss of a species and its various contributions to ecosystem function is completely compensated for by other species in the system or through human alternatives (e.g., the loss of biological control agents compensated for in all contexts through the use of pesticides)... As the Ecosystem Services concept increases in prominence, it becomes arguably even more important to contrast its core metaphor of nature as a supplier of services with alternative metaphors and ways of valuing nature (e.g., nature as kin...) (Luck et al., 2012)

"Nature as kin" can be taken as a reference to the belief systems of many indigenous people. For example, the idea of "mother nature" or Pachamama, or again, the totem identifications of indigenous peoples with particular species of plants and animals. This is a way of mentally and emotionally framing human-ecosystem relationships that earlier chapters examined in more depth. It involves thinking of our place in nature in spiritual and cultural terms, seeing ourselves as pieces of the earth - which bears no point of similarity with the stream of consciousness in the head of a typical economist. For now, however, I will use the anthropocentric viewpoint to illustrate this mentality of the mainstream economist.

Looked at from an anthropocentric view, the environmental crisis is framed as a management problem about "resource use". It appears as a question of how to "allocate natural resources and ecological system services". Since resources are supposed to be best allocated by competitive markets, the environmental crisis then appears to be the result of a failure of markets. The solution for this problem, in turn, is to make markets work better or, alternatively, to mimic the way markets work but within government policy making processes.

"Environmental goods"

What these words, in turn, mean is either bringing "environmental goods" into actual markets by an extension of tradable property rights so that they have a real price, and are bought and sold, OR constructing "shadow prices" for the environmental goods to produce valuations that guide policy makers as if there were markets.

A well-meaning example of this approach was a study by Robert Costanza in Nature in 1997 where he (and his research team) put a financial figure on the value of the planet's eco-system services at $33 trillion dollars. (Costanza et al, 1997). In line with his study, Costanza has more recently argued that to protect the features of the planet that he and his team had valued, people would be motivated primarily by money:

"I do not agree that more progress will be made by appealing to people's hearts rather than their wallets." (Costanza, Letter: Nature: ecosystems without commodifying them, 2006)

As was shown in an earlier chapter, the Costanza view assumes that extrinsic motivations, in this case the desire for money, are the essential incentives to sort out environmental problems. For pragmatic and rhetorical reasons, many ecologists and environmentalists have gone along with this point of view in recent years. They collaborate with economists doing calculations that conceive of nature in money terms and construct money directed institutions in order to rescue it. This way of going about things is, for example, the theoretical underpinning of the recent United Nations Environmental Programme approach, called "The Economics of Eco-systems and Biodiversity" (TEEB). (UNEP, 2013) (Spash, 2011)

According to the TEEB, money values represent "A common language for policy makers, business and society". The person heading the TEEB research process, a manager of the Deutsch Bank, Pavan Sukhdev argues that "You cannot manage what you cannot measure". For people like Pavan Sukhdev, there is an assumption that he shares with neoclassical and Austrian economists, that where a common unit of calculation is absent, rational choice is not possible. Rational choice consists of "trading off" costs and benefits through this common unit of comparison. Rationality requires commensurability – indeed, in market logic it requires *money* commensurability.

Not everyone agrees. Sukhdev's view brings to mind a quote from Einstein

"Not everything that counts can be counted and not everything that can be counted counts."

Capitalist ratio-nality

Unfortunately, Einstein's viewpoint is not shared by the economic priesthood. Schumpeter put their view when he wrote:

> Capitalism develops rationality and adds a new edge to it... It exalts the monetary unit... into a unit of account. That is to say, capitalist practice turns money into a tool of rational cost-profit calculations... and thus, defined and quantified for the economic sector, this type of logic and attitude or method then starts its conquerors" career subjugating – rationalizing – man's tools and philosophies, his medical practice, his picture of the cosmos, his outlook on life, everything in fact including his concepts of beauty and justice and his spiritual ambitions. (Schumpeter, 1987, pp. 123-124)

"Rationality" as understood here is a word meaning a set of mechanical procedures for making calculations about ends that are perceived as given. The great virtue of the market on this view is that, through the universal unit of money, it offers an algorithm for calculating the ratio of benefits and costs. The underlying assumption of this, in turn, is that money enables a common measuring stick to compare benefits and costs so that decision-making becomes essentially a mathematical exercise.

The implication is that having priced nature it can then, and should be, "hardwired into financial markets". The argument goes that unless nature has a price it will get overused because it will be taken and used for free.

The completely opposite point of view is to say that if "nature" has a price then that will not protect it because it is being put up for sale. The idea that a price will discourage use needs to be considered in the light of the fact that the banking sector creates money when it lends. For example, it could well afford Costanza's $33 trillion at 1997 prices because it can create the money that it needs to buy up any natural resources.

According to the opposite logic, instead of putting nature up for sale to protect it, communities should take nature out of the market so that it cannot be sold. This would mean giving nature rights, making these rights defensible in the courts, or ensuring that nature remains in the possession of communities who treat it as kin, who have a culture of protecting it, and managing it protectively, in commons. Outside of academe, and outside of the urban offices, peoples who live close to nature, whose security is dependent on it, have a vernacular knowledge of local environments on which they depend and do not make the mistake of merely viewing nature as existing only for human use – as an "input" or as a "resource". The viewpoint of nature as a resource inevitably reduces and, in the reduction, leads to ignorance of the multi-dimensional character of natural processes, to a narrow-minded instrumentality and to complacency

Of course, many economists, outside of their professional role, as ordinary people, are not totally unaware of the existence of nature as a multi-dimensional life process that cannot be reduced to inert resources to be extracted. Nevertheless, the key idea of their discipline is that nature is there for human use. It is there as a source of materials and energy for the economy, as a provider of "services" and as a place to dump wastes, as a sink. Alternatively, it is there as a collection of sites to be developed in a variety of ways. There is, of course, nothing wrong with thinking of the natural environment in this way – except where this becomes the sole way of thinking about nature, and/or this way of thinking about nature is assumed to be the most important way of thinking about it that trumps all others.

Why this might be so is suggested by a metaphor of our relationship to our mothers. It is of course true that our mothers are providers of a variety of parental services to us but if we conceive of our mothers only in this way then our relationships with them, and with others too are likely to be toxic. If, on the other hand, we have an attitude to nature that is one of awe and wonder then we are more likely to see our existing knowledge as limited and in need of enlargement given our immersion in natural processes that are much bigger than ourselves.

Economics books have to have graphs and here are some...

Now let's have a few graphs. No economics would be complete without graphs – preferably graphs that cross each other to show a "point of equilibrium". No neoclassical feels comfortable without such graphs because it is one of the underlying assumptions of economics that there is an optimal point of balance somewhere, a Goldilocks point, where interacting market actors with different interests eventually arrive by making a number of small adjustments to their behaviour ('marginal adjustments' to use the jargon).

The Holy Cross of economic theory (drawing by author)

This isn't really how I see things but I am using these graphs here to show how environmental economists conceptualise the economics of biodiversity as measured by the number of species alive each year and the costs and benefits of either keeping them alive or driving them to extinction.

As said before, environmental issues like "species provision" is framed in terms of benefits and costs, in particular "marginal" benefits and "marginal" costs so it is important to be clear what these "costs" and "benefits" really consist of. People unfamiliar with economics may struggle to comprehend what the words mean until they grasp a crucial idea. This is that economists are not talking about anything to do with the biology of species, or about ecological relationships, they are talking about the purely subjective attitudes of human beings towards the species or the ecological relationships. The word "benefits" in an economic analysis means the subjective satisfaction that arises because of species e.g. the pleasure of a birdwatcher that endangered species are protected and thus, available for view. At the same time the word "costs" means the forgone satisfactions that arise from doing without things that we could have had e.g. the satisfaction from the food that could have been grown in an area had it not been designated a protected environmentally sensitive area.

Everything in this analysis is anthropocentric. It is what counts for human beings that discounts any inherent value in nature or its attributes as such.

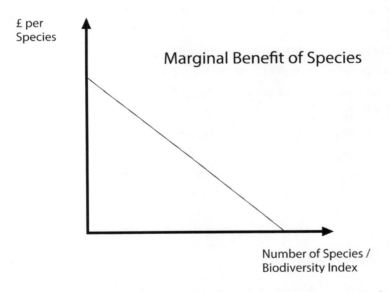

So firstly, here is a graph which is intended to represent the mainstream economist's view of a declining marginal benefit of species, measured in money terms. (The £ sign could be dollars or euros according to circumstances). What this graph is intended to show is that, if there are only a few species, then one species less again would represent a big loss of economic benefits, denominated in money terms – so the graph starts high up on the left hand side. However, if there is a high level of biodiversity and there are lots of species, then the loss of one species represents a much smaller loss of economic benefits, again measured in money terms – thus, the graph falls towards the right hand side. "How many spiders, slugs and weeds do we need anyway?" might express this attitude. There can be a variety of ways in which one defines economic benefit. The use of a species directly, its indirect use, the value of holding open its survival as an option for future use.

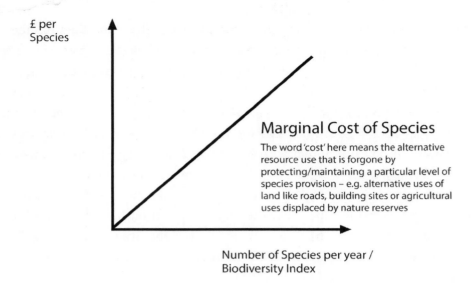

Marginal Cost of Species

The word 'cost' here means the alternative resource use that is forgone by protecting/maintaining a particular level of species provision – e.g. alternative uses of land like roads, building sites or agricultural uses displaced by nature reserves

In the next graph we express the idea of the "marginal opportunity cost" of species provision. If we are going to let species continue to live, they will need habitats which we might otherwise use to build roads on, or use for growing agricultural crops. The more species we try to preserve, the higher the costs for keeping one more species alive will be. Putting the same idea in the jargon, the marginal cost, the cost of one more species protected, rises as we try to protect successively more species.

To the great pleasure of most economists, the marginal benefit and marginal cost curves can be shown in such a way that they cross at some point, representing a certain number of species. At that number of species the economists can declare that there there is "optimal species provision". To understand in what sense this is regarded as "optimal" imagine that we were at a point above the "optimal provision" – point C on the graph. At this point, the cost of protecting the species at the margin, the last species, can be seen to be more than this species yields in benefits. The cost of protecting the marginal species is AC but the benefits are less, namely BC. Thus, it follows that there would be a net gain to humans in removing that protection until the optimal point is reached (taking more lands away to grow wheat on it because those orchids, although nice to look at, are not as beneficial as all that).

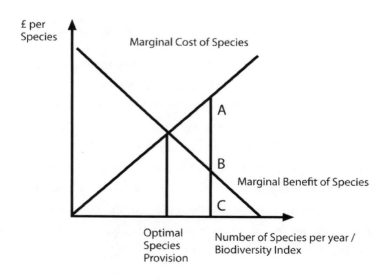

The problem is that markets don't always work well to value species benefit. For example, they might only take into account what farmers think about the benefits of species on a particular area of land and not what birdwatchers and nature lovers think. There is a difference between the private assessment of benefits and costs by the people with rights to use the land economically and a wider social assessment of benefits which is reflected in the next graph. The next graph is supposed to represent the idea that, in addition to the assessment of say, private economic actors like farmers of the benefits of "species provision", there is a wider environmental and social benefit reflected in a higher level of benefits per number of species.

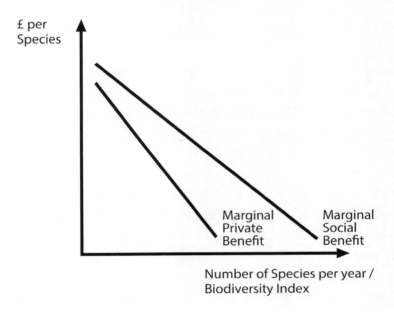

In these circumstances the "optimal species allocation" would appear to be larger than what private markets would, on their own, provide and some kind of state policy action is required to correct the "under provision" of species. This is achieved by some kind of state action to correct the prices at which the environment goods (in this case a level of biodiversity) are provided. This requires an increase in the price achieved by "commodifying" the social and environmental benefits. This is shown in the next diagram.

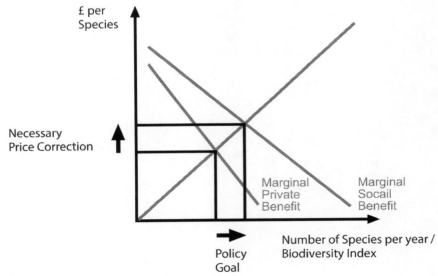

In these examples, the valuing of biodiversity, measured as the valuation of rate of species extinction/protection, has been taken as an example of "valuing nature".

There are many other dimensions to the human – environment relationship to which money valuation methods can be applied. Another example would be the recreational and leisure values of different natural environments. These can be measured in monetary terms in a reasonably straightforward way by the "travel cost method". In practice people do demonstrate how much they value a place in money terms by how much they pay to travel to it. In this case, one can make a reasonable case that visitors are, in a sense, "consumers" of a natural environment.

Other approaches to measuring costs and benefits, and working out, in practice, what the "price" for "nature" and its attributes and services should be, have been theorised too. For example, there is the so called "benefit transfer method" which estimates economic values by transferring existing benefit estimates from studies already completed in regard to another location or issue which is thought to be comparable.

These valuation approaches represent a very particular way of thinking about the human relationship to the environment. It is an approach that assumes that we all have preferences for the various "attributes of nature" and that the concepts of "benefit" and "cost" refer to the degree of satisfaction in meeting, or not meeting, these preferences. The "optimum" aimed for is the peak level of satisfaction (utility) that is available given all the constraints. The environment, in the graphical case biodiversity, is treated as an "environmental good", the protection of which has costs and benefits and it is as if people "consume" the biodiversity provided by nature.

Many people struggle with this way of thinking and it is not surprising that they do. My argument here is that economists have tried to stretch their concepts into realms where they do not make a great deal of sense. OK, I can acknowledge that the travel cost method gives a money valuation that recreational users of the natural environment have put on the places that they have paid money to visit. However, there are value measures of other "environmental goods" which make no sense at all.

Chapter 27

Contingency valuation – and what it tells us about neoclassical economists

Environmental economists "value nature" in whole or in parts using techniques designed to find out how much people are prepared to pay to protect it, or prepared to accept as compensation if it destroyed. There are many flaws in this approach. Cost benefit analysis is an undemocratic process rigged by economists and there are better alternatives.

Willingness to pay and willingness to accept

Contingency valuation is particularly controversial and there is a large literature arguing rival points of view on it. A contingent valuation of an aspect of nature is supposedly found by asking people what they would be prepared to pay (WTP) to avoid "loss of an environmental good" in a given scenario e.g. what they will pay to protect a species from extinction. Alternatively, people can be asked what they are prepared to accept as compensation for losing "an environmental good" e.g. for losing a clean environment and having to put up with pollution.

Note that there is a difference between willingness to pay (WTP) and willingness to accept (WTA). Although there is a principle that "polluters pay", so that they "internalise" the "external costs" of their activities, the assumption of the willingness to pay approach is that the public must pay up if they want an environmentally destructive activity or situation to be rectified or to be reduced or stopped.

The difference is important. Studies have shown that there can be quite a lot of difference between the two. Willingness to accept figures are a lot higher than willingness to pay figures. As is blindingly obvious you cannot pay more than your level of income and level of wealth permits you to do if you are forced to bid to keep a clean environment. Willingness to pay has been shown to be limited by people's income, whereas in regard to willing to accept, people can hold out for what they truly think that they deserve in compensation. There is no restraint with WTA so that people are able settle for what they think is an appropriate figure.

Despite the fact that willingness to accept is more in tune with the principle of "polluter pays", and more likely to be "accurate" as a reflection of preferences, economists show their true loyalties and tend to favour willingness to pay approaches. They say that this is because the figures are then likely to be "conservative" i.e. the environmental valuations are likely to be lower. Wouldn't you know it - economists favour the polluters over the polluted. What a surprise!

This was the case, for example, with the so called "experts" panel of the National Oceanic and Atmospheric Administration (NOAA) in the USA who were appointed in the early 1990s to produce a set of rules and "best practice" for conducting contingency valuations. Spash states:

> Despite acknowledging that WTA is the theoretically correct measure for damage assessment, the NOAA Panel recommended the universal use of WTP as a "conservative" estimate. Strong criticism of this decision has failed to impact peer practice. (Spash C. L., 2002, p. 206)

When importing the methodology for contingency valuation into the UK at the Department of Transport similar "conservative" methods were used – namely willingness to pay instead of willingness to accept. (Spash C. L., 2002, p. 206)

In point of fact, the "pay the polluter" principle was enshrined in the European Union's Emissions Trading System (ETS), perhaps because it was designed by business and this was a way of buying off opposition. In the early stages of the ETS, "permits to emit" were handed out for free on what is called a "grandfathered" basis. In other words, the number of permits to be distributed to particular companies was calculated on the basis of the pre-existing proportions by which companies are already emitting CO_2. The permits given to the companies had a market value - at least they did when the scheme was having a minimal effect, before the carbon price dropped to virtually nothing. Thus, giving the companies the permits was giving them a gift with a money value. Having booked the value of these gifted permits into their accounts, the subsequent use of the permits when they emit was then described as a cost of their operations and companies put their prices up to claim cost of the permits back from their customers. The result has been, in effect, a "pay the polluter" principle.

As already explained, the underlying logic of contingency valuation is a cost benefit calculation looking at the consequences of different levels of "environmental destruction" in order to identify the "optimal level". To enrol people into contingency valuations they are recruited into surveys and are then asked willingness to pay or willingness to accept questions which are supposed to measure how much they value the benefits of "environmental goods". When they do this, neoclassical economists assume that the people they are questioning understand the questions in the same way that they, the economists, do. They assume that people think within a philosophical framework of consequential utilitarianism. This means that the economists are assuming that what matters to the people being asked are the consequences of their choices and that those being surveyed are measuring the strength of their preferences as regards these consequences by sums of money that they are prepared to pay or prepared to accept to "pay for" environmental goods.

Unfortunately for the economists, there is evidence that when it comes to decisions of this sort, many people don't think in this kind of mental framework at all. Early research on contingency valuation by social psychologists Kahneman and Knetsch came to an alternative view of how surveyed people were mentally framing the valuation questions. Surveyed people did not see themselves as "paying for" environmental goods but rather as making charitable contributions. Further studies have tried to get to the bottom of what motivates people and how they approach it:

Overall, the results from the standard contingency valuation method survey approach to WTP question design support the concerns in the social psychology literature about the importance of a range of motives for giving... Human value formation with respect to the environment appears to be far more complex than economists have previously assumed, and combines both attitudes and ethical and economic values. (Spash C. L., 2002, p. 219)

Research shows that a lot of people do not think in the way that economists think they do – the results throw a fascinating insight into how wrong economists often are when they make assumptions about human motivations and actions. Whereas the economists see what is happening as people "paying for" their preferred amount of environmental goods, many people being surveyed regard the environmental issue as one of rights e.g. of species and duties e.g. to protect those species.

The reaction of economists to people who do not think like they do is also revealing. Because they have a different way of thinking about the issues, some contingency valuation survey participants refuse to play ball in the manner expected by the economists. Survey participants enter "protest responses" e.g. zero bids or refusals to bid, even though they appear to show strong support for the "environmental goods" in question. These "protest responses" are probably best interpreted as a refusal to betray a moral commitment by assigning to it a money value... The response of the economists has then several times been to interpret the protests as "irrational" and excluded these responses from their analysis. (Spash C. L., 2002, p. 205)

You could not get a better picture of a profession who, when their belief system is challenged, damn those who don't share their world view as irrational and expel them from further consideration.

Economists engaged in corruption

Not all economists are as small minded. For example John O' Neill gets to the heart of what is at stake when the principle is "willingness to accept":

> Ethical "preferences" are not like non-ethical preferences... If preferences for environmental goods are matters of ethical principle then such commitments are exhibited by a refusal to betray them when offered cash. One should no more accept a price where issues of environmental value are concerned than one should on issues of abortion, euthanasia, commercial surrogacy, hanging or any other issue of principle. To engage in monetary valuation in these arenas would be quite properly rejected as inappropriate, to ask willingness to pay questions an exercise in corruption. The proper mode of resolution is public debate in which utilitarians have to state their case with others – as they do in issues of abortion, euthanasia, commercial surrogacy, or hanging. (O'Neill, 2007, pp. 38-39)

In economic theory there is nothing to be found about why people arrive at their preferences and thus, how much they are willing to pay for things. So, in the case of willingness to pay studies, there is an issue of what, if anything, you tell people in framing the question about paying. If you don't tell people anything about the issues, what you get is a sort of beauty contest in which pandas do well in terms of willingness to pay. However, uninformed people are less inclined to pay to maintain bio-tops with lots of bamboo, which the pandas need to have something to eat. Creepy crawlies, snakes, spiders and insects don't do very well either – even if they play an important role in eco-systems. Nor would one expect much willingness to pay for species that people don't even know exist, like soil organisms and microbes that are nevertheless integral to the ecological process.

It must be admitted that this does represent a certain economic reality, even if not any kind of ecological logic. To the extent that if zoos become the last refuge for species in danger of extinction then the willingness of zoos to take and try to breed species will be very influenced by what the paying public wants to see. And it may not be creepy crawlies. However, this is not eco-system maintenance. It is the end of the road for species if they only survive in zoos.

To return to the issue at stake, that of preferences for "environmental goods" - it seems reasonable to expect that preferences, when measured, should be informed preferences. However, in this case the price that people are willing to pay depends on the information and presentation rather than anything else. There is too, a philosophical problem when we try to express the value of objects as arising in our informed preferences about them. That is, that you cannot count as fully informed unless you perceive the value of the object to your purposes which means that there is a circularity in the reasoning. O'Neill quotes James Griffin:

What makes us desire the things we desire, when informed, is something about them... their features or properties. But why bother then with informed desire, when we can go directly to what it is about objects that shape informed desire in the first place? If what really matters are certain sorts of reasons for action, to be found outside desires in the quality of objects, why not explain desires in the qualities of the objects, why not explain well-being directly in terms of them. (O'Neill, 2007, p. 40)

Would this not take us away from the idea of utility back to the old idea of use value?

The distributional consequences of willingness to pay for the poor

To continue the critique further there are important issues to do with the distributional justice of the benefits and burdens of nature conservation within a market framework. Perhaps it is not an accident that the UNEP want to "hardwire nature into *financial markets*" after they have turned it into a collection marketable instruments. After all they could not sell nature to ordinary people because ordinary people would not have enough money to buy it. On the other hand, ordinary people who have been driven into poverty by the actions of the financial markets are the people who are the most likely to feel under pressure to sell what natural resources they possess. This is a cruel irony because it has been (cash) poor people whose care of landscapes, waterscapes and forests under customary arrangements that has sustained these landscapes for centuries. As Martinez-Alier notes, people in need are willing (or forced) to accept lower sums of money for Ecosystem loss. (Martinez-Alier, 2002)

An undemocratic process rigged by economists and the alternative decision-making processes

We should remind ourselves that when such studies are done, what is happening is that economists are taking a decision-making process about the environment and the economy into their own hands and using a calculation procedure in which they claim to have expertise. In the process they are taking it out of the hands of stakeholders. As we have seen, this procedure has been shown to misrepresent the points of view of many of these stakeholders who, if they protest against the process (by making protest zero bids), may be disqualified altogether because, the economists claim, they are "irrational". Quite apart from the fact that, even in preference utilitarian terms, the process is rigged in favour of polluters (because willingness to pay is mostly used rather than willingness to accept) it is profoundly undemocratic.

According to many economists, there are no alternatives to their approach (which is why they see people who do not think like themselves as irrational) but, as Spash puts it, the idea that there are no alternatives is "blatantly false".

There are a range of methods for decision-making about economic developments that impact on natural process and communities using multi-criteria analysis which can allow for incommensurability. There are also participatory approaches for deliberating on environmental issues like citizens' juries and consensus conferences. Community activists have also developed tools like "planning for real" and from the global south techniques like "rapid rural appraisal" have been used. The most important issue in these techniques for decision-making is to make the process participatory and deliberative – to get the stakeholders learning about and thinking about the issues. This is a major theme in a book by John O'Neill, *Markets, Deliberation and Environment*. Having described the literature on deliberative policy formation, O'Neill acknowledges that they have problems too (power asymmetries among stakeholders) but argues that deliberation is still a much better approach than spurious cost benefit analysis.

Ad hoc arrangements of deliberative democracy may have much to recommend them but the more fundamental approach, to the extent that it is possible, is to re-create "long term management of natural resources" by affected communities. The evolution of human-nature interactions requires a return to commons forms of organisation where communities re-establish living relationships to their natural environment organised collectively. Nor is it impossible to see how this might come about. Fracking communities are finding that unless they come together to protect their living environment, the water, the air and the soil, are all threatened by a coalition of the energy sector, government and unscrupulous landowners. Effectively, people need to come together to collectively protect their eco-system or there may be lasting damage done to where they live. This implicitly raises the importance of the re-establishment of collective control by communities if they are to prevent having where they live made unliveable – a sort of a re-run of the enclosure and expulsion that happened several centuries ago.

To conclude, in this chapter I have tried to present the viewpoint of mainstream economics about the environment. As we have seen, the key idea is anthropocentric. It is about people's preferences in regard to the provision, protection or destruction of "environmental goods". It purports to value "nature" and the environment on this basis so that what the economist claims are "rational decisions" can be made about its use as a resource. The aim of the exercise is "efficient use" which means, given the circumstances, getting optimal benefits which are conceived of in utilitarian terms as preference satisfaction. However, there are lots of problems with this approach. Where it is the approach of choice for dealing with environmental-economic interaction, then it is an extraordinarily complacent way of going about things. While it makes some sense to use this methodology to assess how much time and money should be spent on clearing up litter, to use it for issues like climate change is completely inappropriate.

Contingency valuation and cost benefit analysis, as recommended by neoclassical environmental economists, is not at all the same as acting according to the precautionary principle. Acting according to the precautionary principle is a way of thinking about the environment in which current uses have possible, albeit often uncertain, negative effects in the future whose magnitude cannot always be known for sure. There is enough scientific evidence that many environmental problems carry a risk of pushing the ecological system beyond "tipping points" that are irreversible and which might lead to catastrophic changes. The task of the ecological economist is therefore first and foremost to get clear the capacity limits in the ecological system beyond which those tipping points may occur, and then to ensure that equitable policies are in place to stay inside them.

In short, an alternative kind of economics would start, not with preferences, but with ecological magnitudes measured in physical units. For example, at the current time, many climate scientists are telling us that unless emissions of CO_2 fall by 6% to 7% per annum for the foreseeable future, the chances are very high indeed that the earth's climate system will go into a "partial runaway" through its own reinforcing feedbacks. It is an urgent task to prevent that happening – contingency and cost benefit analysis gets in the way when we need to slam on the economic brakes.

PART THREE
Households and Lifestyles

Chapter 28

Household economy

Do households exist to service the economy or vice versa? The composition of different kinds of households will depend on demographic structures which have profound political and economic consequences. Household arrangements can become out of balance and re-creating efficient habitats can be seen as a legitimate economic goal. The time spent in households versus the time spent in paid work time is a central feature of any pattern of economic arrangements.

Although economics started, quite literally, as the study of the management of households this dimension of the subject has, over several centuries, been relegated to virtual non-existence. Households are still there, just about, in textbook diagrams that represent "the circular flow of income and expenditure". Money income passes from the company sector to households in payment for "factors of production" which are shown as labour and "capital" – whatever "capital" is. Then households spend the larger proportion of the income on consumption products of the business sector and save the rest. The diagrams typically show the savings eventually being channelled by financial intermediaries to businesses as resources to be spent on "investment". More complicated diagrams add taxes and government expenditure as further "leakages" out of and "injections" into this circular flow.

Feminist economics

Little is said about households however. This has led feminist economists to point out that a good deal of activity takes place in households that reproduces the next generation of workers and provides services for the current labour force; and make the point that without this activity no economic activity in the larger economy would take place. At the same time, the point is made that what has largely evolved as "women's work" is not paid a wage, largely not noticed and not socially valued either. It is just taken for granted. To the extent that, while concerns arising in the "household sector" become part of public and political concern, they do not arise in "economic policy" but rather in "social policy", "child welfare", "health and mental health", "education" and so on... and all of these are typically subordinated to economic policy. (Floro, Grown, & Elson, 2011) (Picchio A. 2014)

It is almost as if there is an assumption that people come into existence and live their lives in order to be available to the economy beyond the household. It is what the "beyond the household economy" "can afford" that determines what is available for state expenditure on welfare, education and health.

In short, the household economy started off in history as being the original focus of economic activity. Its extension was the commons which people managed together as communities. However, with the rise of the market economy, the production and other activities beyond the household are now dominant. Accordingly, for several centuries, the masters of industry, commerce and finance have sought to entrain the household to their rhythms, their world view and their priorities.

People are not born to be part of "labour supply"

Yet the fact is that, because people are not born to be "labour" they persist in actions, activities and ways of living which defy how they are supposed to behave in a market economy. For example, for most markets the theory is that if you put the price of something up you get more of it. Yet it cannot be taken for granted that there is an "upward sloping supply curve for labour" i.e. that if wages are higher people will offer to work longer hours. This is because, when they find that they have a higher income, many people may decide they would now prefer to work shorter hours.

In the early days of the industrial revolution, employers would be very frustrated that many working people only worked as much as they required to meet their immediate needs and then wanted to knock off until such time as they needed more money. You could not run an industrial economy like that. People as "labour inputs", as factory "hands", had to be disciplined to be punctual to clock time, which was a new experience and way of being for people before the commercial age. Punctuality and working hard was a new morality to be internalised by a population who did not regard themselves as "labour" but as human beings.

The labour force, being people, also needed somewhere to live, to eat, to sleep, defecate, give birth, bring up children, to be ill, recuperate and, if not, then to die. The early industrial masters were largely only interested in these things in so far as their workers could not survive at all without a wage to pay for these "physiological overheads" and they wanted this wage to be as low as possible for hours of employment that were as long as possible.

The household economy has thus, come to be viewed as an appendage of the production economy beyond it. Although in more recent times, the flood of consumer goods could not find a market unless at least a large part of the population had an income large enough to buy them. (An alternative solution has been to get people into debt to pay for them – naturally this solution only works for a few years.)

Do households exist to service "the economy" or the other way round?

The widespread way of perceiving households and people as if they are there largely to "service the economy" belies the reciprocal nature of a central relationship. Economists and politicians appear to believe that what can be "afforded" in the way of "social welfare" depends upon how prosperous "the economy" is. However, "the economy" to which they are referring is just one side of a total system that is sustained by contributions from another vast pool of human activity without which "the economy" would not function at all.

For current economists and politicians it is as if only the commercial economy is "productive" and that the household economy depends upon it in a one way flow. Actually, the reverse is every bit as true and, indeed, one way of perceiving the crisis occurring in modern societies is that the commercial sector has become dysfunctional precisely because it no longer plays an adequate role to support and provide for households, but, rather parasites upon them and renders them unable to function as places where people can effectively manage and live satisfying lives.

Household activities and typologies

If we are to survive and avoid some of the worst of these scenarios for the future it will in large part depend on how we organise the household economy, for that is where we spend most of our lives and where most of our activities take place.

The household sector is where children are brought up and they are (largely) not cared for in the paid work sector – although children are supervised and under the care of nurseries and teachers at school for part of the time. At the other end of the age spectrum, elderly people are also not, in general, in paid work, though they may or may not play valuable social roles. There are unemployed people, ill and disabled people outside of the paid work sector too. Of course, employed people also spend a large part of the day in the household when they are not actually actively in their employed role. They must sleep, eat, change and launder their clothes. So they must shop for food, cook or access catering arrangements, they must supply and maintain their households with a variety of products. If they are to bring up children, or support elderly or disabled dependents, then they need time for these roles, without which society could not reproduce itself. We need to add all these categories up to get a sense of the total time allocation to the household sector.

When household arrangements become out of balance

Mainstream economics does not generally have much interest in all of this. There is a lot written and thought about the management of "the economy" but how the "household economy" is managed is no longer given any real attention in mainstream economics - only, for the most part, by feminist economists and ecological economists. In this sense the economic mainstream has abandoned its original role and function and the result has been catastrophic. This is particularly the case for individuals where the management arrangements for their households run out of balance – where there are, for example, health and relationship problems.

To repeat, economics was originally about the management of a habitat and relationships together. People have to hold in balance their emotional and dependent relationships within the practical activities involved in habitat arrangements. They need to make habitat arrangements work in a way that can be matched up with the time that they have available after paid work and other commitments, as well as to match the money that they get from working, or from pensions or from financial support from their loved ones.

If they cannot make their habitat and household arrangements sustainable through time, then they also will not be able to function in the formal sector of the economy as a "labour input" either. This is because their lives will start to evolve in a chaotic fashion, in a vicious circle in which problems pile on top of new problems. Thus, once debts become unsustainable, desperate people take risks - they put themselves into the hands of loan sharks and the interest rates on their debts spiral. Again, once people are unable to pay their housing costs and lose their homes, their relationships and support networks are also likely to break up under the strain. Or again, once the sheer impossibility of maintaining a habitat and relationships has eroded people's emotional strength, their mental capacity is likely to breaks up too. Now they will no longer be capable of functioning and turning up to work. What is more, as their lives devolve more and more chaotically, and out of control, they may end up on drugs, legal (prescribed by GPs and psychiatrists) or illegal (brought from a local pusher). Either way, a chemical dependency will rob them of the remaining emotional energy to do anything about their situation and add another twist to the downward spiral in their lives.

The original idea of a social security net was to provide a support system to prevent this kind of comprehensive breakdown. It was, and is necessary because society had enclosed the commons – the resources beyond the household that people could access to meet their needs, if often rather precariously. This appears to be completely lost on those who manage social security, social welfare, employment and health policy. They have forgotten that economy is about the management of households – including the households of the people who they are only able to see as "labour inputs". The result is that, instead of managing the paid work economy to ensure that households are made easier to manage and made more viable, current policy appears to believe that people as "labour inputs" are infinitely flexible in their ability to cope with any situation and can be compelled by markets and punitive policy to adapt to the demands of paid work no matter how impoverished and chaotic their home situation.

Re-creating efficient habitats as an economic goal

It is this kind of analysis, it should be said, that gives a social rationale for the ecological transformation of the household, community and local economy. The case for local economics, as opposed to the trend to global specialisation, is not only to save energy and carbon on the transport of goods by supplying them closer to home. Nor is it just about taking advantage of the unique features of local climate, soils, water and wind flow in an ecological re-designed local economy. It is also to recreate efficient habitats for human beings to live in - so that managing the practicalities of life and relationships, that part which makes up 80 to 90% of our lives, is easy, pleasant to manage and efficient (in the sense of requiring few resources).

This entails making housing energy efficient and neighbourhoods places with common resources that can be accessed by all local people so that the consumption economy becomes unnecessary and so that people can form relationships and develop a value system of mutual aid. But for a redevelopment of a community economy to be possible it is necessary too that the rest of the economy becomes the appendage of the habitats, of the households, rather than vice versa.

The term "provisioning economy" has been used for a different vision of what the economy might be about – and provisioning in this context is about returning to the original idea that the economic activities beyond the household and its extension into the community are there to be at the service of communities. (I may say that it requires too a variety of complementary policy approaches, otherwise, the operation of the market as it currently is will undo any change in a positive direction. For example, neighbourhoods that are easy to live in as a result of community development strategies could find that their rentals rise – as landowners who have done nothing at all to improve a place cash in on the benefits. There is thus, a requirement for site value taxation to recycle the money benefits back to communities.

So, let it be repeated, for people to manage the household economy they need time and they need resources. The usual words to describe the resource flow through households is "consumption" and consumption is usually expressed in economics using monetary measures. However, it is possible to do a bio-physical analysis of consumption, not in monetary terms but in physical measures like quantities of energy denominated in Joules, litres of clean water or, coming out of the household, the weight of refuse.

A bio-economic methodology can be used to analyse these issues, to analyse time allocation and to see if more energy and devices (like "labour saving devices") might help resolve any dilemmas. This approach has been given the snappy title "Multi-Scale Integrated Analysis of Societal and Ecosystem Metabolism" (MuSIASEM)". It is an accounting framework that relates the "stock" of total human activity to flows like energy throughput, water use, waste flows and other physical measures. (Giampietro, Mayumi, & Sorman, 2011) (Giampietro, Mayumi, & Sorman, 2013)

Thus, for example, it is possible to analyse the total energy throughput of society measured in Joules, TET, against the total number of hours of human activity, THA, to get a societal average for the exosomatic energy metabolic rate for society as a whole, EMR_{SA}. ("Exosomatic" refers to devices that use energy outside the human body – like cars, computers, vacuum cleaners etc. - as distinct from energy that passes through the human body, initially as food which is an "endosomatic" flow).

$$EMR_{SA} = THA/TET$$

An analysis like this can be done at different scales i.e. whole economy, sectors, and sub sectors and so on. Thus, we can relate the total energy throughput for the household sector of the economy against the total number of human hours spent by a society in household activities in order to get the exosomatic energy metabolism for the household sector.

$$EMR_{HH} = THA_{HH}/ TET_{HH}$$

We can measure consumption in energy and material throughputs. Energy here means both food throughputs into human bodies as well as energy that flows through the devices that ensure that households are warm, dry, clean and comfortable places to live in; that are used for cooking food and for performing a perform a variety of other necessary functions. In theory too, it is possible to create disaggregated figures for different aspects of household activity, for example, residential energy use and energy use for private transport. However, statistics are not always easy to come by.

That in turn allows us to calculate ratios or energy throughput per hour of human time in the household (not in paid work) to see how intensively the household sector uses energy. In Western Europe for example about 90% of all human time is spent in the household sector (not in paid work) and the energy metabolism is between 2 and 8 MegaJoules per hour in different countries. This is very low compared to energy metabolic rate in the two paid work sectors of the economy: in the services and government sector at 30-100 MJ per hour and 130-1,000 MJ per hour in the production sector of the economy. (Giampietro, Mayumi, & Sorman, 2011, p. 265)

Household time and paid work time compared

As we might supposed from the prior discussion of demographics, it is no surprise that different countries have very different figures for the proportion of human time spent in households and in paid work. For example, in 1999 "an average person" in China spent 80% of their time "in the household sector" whereas in Italy it was 92.3%. This "average person" is obviously a statistical entity, a composite figure that is calculated according to the actual number of old and young; the unemployed; the people who are ill; the hours of employment for those in work etc.

As one would expect too, it is possible to disaggregate the figures for households into types of households according to the number and type of people in them i.e. households with a single adult; households with a couple of adults and two children; households with differing numbers of adults (shared households with students for example); households with a single retired person and so on. (Giampietro, Mayumi, & Sorman, 2011, pp. 291-292)

Much of the research on these issues has been at the University of Barcelona in Catalonia so statistics for Catalonia have been published which can probably be taken as broadly indicative of what is likely to be the case in many other "developed" societies. Thus, it is possible to give a finer detail of time allocation outside of paid work, as well as the energy usage associated with it, helping our understanding of issues central to the quality of life. One study by Giacomo D'Alicia and Claudia Cattaneo breaks down time allocated in Catalonian society into the component activities as follows:

PO – physiological overhead which are hours allocated to sleeping, eating and personal care. In Catalonia this is 48.1%, nearly a half.

UW – unpaid work. These are hours allocated to household chores like cooking and home maintenance, caring for children, clothes, shopping, gardening, voluntary work and meetings. In Catalonia this is 10.9% of time and compares with paid work (PW) which is 10.8% of total human activity – a fact which leads D'Alicia and Cattaneo to conclude that, in terms of hours, unpaid work is equal to paid work to guarantee the Catalonian standard of living. As they also point out, this 10.9% for unpaid work also produces things not available on the market that cannot be purchased by money "such as the feeling of being important for somebody, encouragement, recognition and the meaning of life".

Of course, there are also human activity hours devoted to study (School, University and Free learning – which can each be separately accounted for). This takes up 2.3% of total time in Catalonian society. Transportation and commuting use up 5.1% of time and last, but by no means least, leisure and entertainment makes up 22.8%. (D'Alisa & Cattaneo, 2011)

Other uses for the MuSIASEM approach enables the observation that different kinds of households, clustered differently in different kinds of residential areas, have totally different kinds of features in regard to proportions of time in paid work; energy, food and water throughput and amounts of waste to be collected and disposed of. It enables the profiling of the physical and energetic metabolism of households in different areas of cities and the countryside. It enables us to observe too, that certain patterns are obviously much more energy and materials efficient than others. Heating shared between two people can be virtually a heating bill halved and carbon emissions halved. That means that a society with an increasing number of elderly single people will struggle to bring down emissions at the household level unless it plans appropriately

In this regard, the idea of co-housing has much to recommend it as a means of sharing and making households more efficient arrangements for living. It is a household typology which, in many cases, is better suited people's needs. It enables the sharing of household chores, space and appliances. It saves space and energy and increases possibilities for socialisation. It thus, increases life quality and reduces consumption at the same time. It has been shown that co-housing can save 31% of space, 51% of electricity and reduce consumption of general goods by 8%. (D'Alisa & Cattaneo, 2011)

Chapter 29

Demographics

As John Maynard Keynes put it: "In the long run we are all dead". Economics has to include consideration of the long run trends of births, deaths, migration and of the age composition of societies. As we reach the limits to economic growth the death rate may start to rise. Globalisation may make the spread of diseases very rapid. Preventing novel diseases like Ebola may prove expensive and the health and well being of the population at large may become dependent on some of the most exploited and devalued people in our society – cleaners, carers and grave diggers.

Obviously all households are different and yet we can generalise by grouping households into types. There are households composed of couples with children; single parent households; single elderly persons and so on. Clearly the mix and types of households will reflect the demographics of a society – the proportions of the population falling into different age groups and migration patterns. Migrants tend to be young and single, and are often male. They often live together in homes in multiple occupation. An ageing society is likely to have more single person households after the death of a spouse, with a preponderance of women as the life expectancy of men tends to be shorter.

Awareness of the demographic composition of a country is important to understand what is going on in its household economy and figures that average across all age groups can be seriously misleading. To illustrate the potentially misleading character of averages, Giampietro, Mayumi and Sorman give the example of the average amount of nutrition in developing and developed economies. (Giampietro, Mayumi, & Sorman, 2011, pp. 23-24) In many poor countries, the calorific intake is much less on average than in richer countries and it is easy to draw the conclusion that this is the result of the wealth and income difference. No doubt there is truth in the idea that diets in poor countries are inadequate. However one must also grasp the significance of the differing demographic compositions. Infants and children have lower weights and eat less on average than adults. "Developing" societies with a high proportion of infants and children therefore have a per capita food requirement that is less than the food requirements in "developed" societies with a higher proportion of adults.

... we should note of course that, as the young population grows up, its food requirements will expand considerably and faster than the growth of population...

We cannot properly understand what is happening in a society without grasping its demographic structure, recent demographic trends and how the demographic structure is likely to evolve in the future.

In the recent past, discussions of demographic trends have understandably been about the so called "demographic transition". Three centuries ago, countries tended to have a high death rate, low life expectancy and a high birth rate to replace many people, including the large proportion of children, who died young. Over two centuries in North America, Europe and Japan improved diets, public health and medicine led to a higher life expectancy so that death rates fell slowly over time. A fall in birth rates occurred too, however, this was after a time lag. Thus, for a long time, birth rates exceeded death rates and population rose, albeit, affected by the world wars which particularly led to the slaughter of many young men.

If birth rates are higher than death rates and children are surviving, the average age of the population will get younger as the total population grows. However, when the birth rate falls below the death rate, this reverses. In recent decades, the birth rate in North America, Europe and Japan has continued to fall so that it is below the "replacement rate" of 2.1 in many countries. This means that, unless there is inward migration, population falls and, on average, the population gets older.

Since World War II, a similar transition has been occurring in many countries in the global south. Death rates have been falling fast while birth rates have remained high so that population has been rising quickly and the populations of many countries in the global south are very young.

There are exceptions however. There have been lower birth rates in countries like China. The one child policy in that country stemmed the birth rate to below the replacement level for the population. In other countries too, like Thailand and North and South Korea there is a sub replacement level of the birth rate.

How the demographic situation will evolve in the future is crucial to many aspects of its future economic and ecological situation. As is obvious, the size of the population; its age profile and different profiles in rich or poor countries, will affect future labour supply; the age profile and size of the employed and non-employed dependent population; energy, materials and other forms of consumption; greenhouse gas emissions; rates of resource depletion and thus, overall ecological impact.

Clearly the age profile of a society says important things about how it is likely to allocate the time of the population. This age profile can be represented graphically by a chart in which the number of people of a particular age group, are represented by a horizontal bar – stretching out to the left for males and to the right for females. The bars are then stacked on top of each other with the older age groups at a progressively higher level. An illustration is shown for Japan in different years. (Smil, 2007)

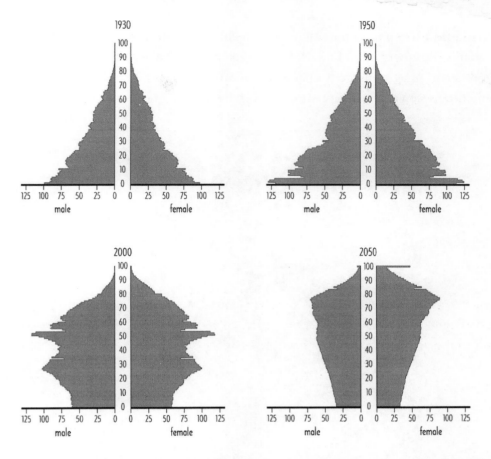

A crucial thing to interpret the charts is to look for where the bars are longest – for this is the age group which is currently predominating in any society. The higher the bulge, the older the age profile of the society. Most developed societies tend to be old and most so-called developing societies are "young" with the wider bands, of dependent children nearer the bottom. In a few years' time, a "young society" with a high proportion of children, will find that it has a lot of young adults looking for work, source of income and nutrition. In an ageing society there is a high proportion of dependent elderly people. Although, in a few years' time the bulge of elderly people will, so to speak, be "spat out" at the top when that group dies. The progression from a "young society" to an "elderly one" can be seen clearly in the Japanese data.

Obviously, the demographic composition of a society will be crucial to understanding what proportion of the time of the population is spent in paid work i.e. in what is more conventionally thought of as the formal economic sector, and therefore *not* spent in the household sector.

Population Projections and the death rate

Obviously a projection of population is an attempt to second guess the future. Most projections that one sees clearly assume that population growth will continue for the next few decades at least – but not all believe this. The famous *Limits to Growth* study modelled population as part of a one hundred year projection into the future. The "business of usual" scenario 1 shows a peak in life expectancy early in the 21st century, after which life expectancy falls as human welfare falls and overall global population starts to fall from about 2030 onwards. The rising death rate in this simple model is because of a global agricultural crisis leading to poorer nutrition and a decline in medical services. In real life it may involve other things too like the emergence of novel diseases like Ebola; the declining effectiveness of antibiotics that have been misused in agriculture so that diseases can no longer be knocked out by antibiotic drugs; increased conflicts between and within nations and civil strife.

Albrecht Durer, *Four Horsemen of the Apocalypse*. Woodcut Image 1497 Public Domain Image

We cannot rule out population catastrophes such as occurred in the past due to what were pictured in popular mythology as the '"The Four Horsemen of the Apocalypse" – famine, disease, war and therefore mass death. Such catastrophes are already an everyday hell in parts of the world characterised as "failed states" and could spread into the "developed societies" threatening to drag all countries and societies into the same horror as suggested in the foreword. (Brown L. R., 2011)

At the time of writing this book two developments illustrated this uncomfortably well. One was the development of a new cold war between Russia and the western powers and the other was Ebola. I will not cover the first here except to note that at the beginning of 1914 few people expected there to be a war and when it did break out few people were seriously worried about it because they all expected to win and that the war would be over quickly. This illustrates well how people can misestimate a profoundly dangerous situation and the failure to appreciate the danger meant that the statesmen of Europe "sleep walked" into a catastrophe which left 20 million dead.

What I will briefly mention here is Ebola because that has already had serious economic impacts in western Africa and may have more far reaching implications that illustrate other issues in the book. The implications of Ebola are further explored in the chapter on resilience and collapse.

What makes Ebola particularly vicious is not only the fact that it kills a very large percentage of those that it infects. It is also the fact that its method of transmission exploits human care relationships. It is the fact that the healthy look after the sick, clean up after them and then, if and when they die, people who loved the dead want take their last leave of the body. All this makes the carers and people in close relationships vulnerable to the virus. It is no accident then that women, as the chief care givers are particularly vulnerable to Ebola.

It also makes for a terrifying irony that must be addressed if the disease is to be controlled – that we are all dependent on some of the most exploited parts of our society doing their job well under dangerous conditions if the disease spreads – cleaners. In a globalised economy the cleaners in many major institutions – hospitals, universities, transport infrastructures, offices – are often sub-contracted migrant workers. They work for low pay under conditions which maximise profits for the companies that they work for and increasing the chances that cleaners will be infected in an Ebola outbreak.

At the time of my writing this newspaper report was published describing a potential front line against Ebola and the people who might have to fight it:

"About 200 airline cabin cleaners walked off their jobs at New York's LaGuardia airport on Thursday, to protest what they say are working conditions that do not protect against potential Ebola contraction.

"When I do bathroom, I come in contact with tampons which I have to grab with my hand, with a glove that's so cheap that it breaks easily. I come in contact with faeces, a lot of faeces and vomit. And we have to clean those bathrooms spotless because they audit those planes," Wendy Arellano, one of the workers, told the Guardian.

"They expect us, that if a little bit of faeces stays on the toilet, that we remove it with our hands because [if not] they will say that bathroom is dirty. And I refuse to do it because I think it's disgusting and I don't have the appropriate attire, and because I don't know what that person has.

"We come in contact with a lot of stuff that is dangerous for our health and obviously they don't give us the appropriate tools to work with."

"Workers set up picket lines overnight, by non-unionized Air Serv cleaners near Terminal D. The one-day strike forces airline crews to clean planes themselves." (Gambino Lauren, 2014)

How does it come about that parts of the economic system puts these cleaners at risk, and through them all of society, and yet does not give them the appropriate tools to work with? As we have already seen in this book many economists would answer that this by describing it as a problem of "externalities" – companies employing cleaners consider how to make profits for themselves and do not necessarily take into account all the costs and benefits of their decisions to the wider society. In other words ethical issues with immense implications for everyone are translated into cash issues.

Another issue that Ebola throws into relief is how globalisation has made the spread of diseases difficult to control and potentially very rapid. If you look at the roots of the term, "quarantine", it originates from words that meant an isolation period of 40 days and this, or a "trentine" of 30 days, was a method used in earlier epochs to try to prevent the spread of infectious diseases. Travellers and traders from areas where a plague was rife would be required to wait on an island, or a ship would be required to rest at anchor offshore for the required period before being allowed to travel dock at a local port.

When the 19th century English economist David Ricardo argued the benefits of free trade he could not have foreseen that the global economy would eventually be bound together with air travel. He could not have foreseen that, to re-create long lasting quarantine arrangements between nations, would be impossible in an era of international production systems, using just in time global supply chains, without major disruption.

It is not very nice to admit some potential developments. Economic textbooks claim that, when they are theorising, economists are seeking to describe the world as it is, rather than making value judgements about how they think that the world should be. This seems easy enough and uncontroversial when describing how people make choices between tins of beans and tins of spaghetti hoops – but when we start theorising about rapidly rising death rates and the economic implications of quarantine and health care systems, then describing the world as it is can involve emotional effort because it can be frightening.

What is particularly frightening is recognising and acknowledging those periods in history where, as individuals or as communities, we might lose control and where our very existence might be at stake. There are powerful psychological blocks against acknowledging that we might be in such situations. That is the same mentality which says: "there will not be a war" or "it will all be over by Christmas". It couldn't happen here is a message that politicians are keen to convey. This is the consensus trance at work and it is the same state of mind that holds away the idea of climate change, not giving it much or any attention in the same way that we give little attention to the idea that one day we will all die.

In his novel, **the Plague**, written in 1947, Albert Camus describes the early stages of an epidemic that befalls an Algerian town called Oran and he describes how a number of characters and the townsfolk in general react to it. It is full of deep psychological observation, including the description of the sense of unreality at the beginning of the plague process. There is anxiety but it is mixed with confidence. Yet there are situations in life where the confidence subsequently proves misplaced.

In this passage Camus writes about real people – not the fantasy of "rational decision makers" that economists typically describe:

".......the citizens of Oran were like the rest of the world, they thought about themselves; in other words they were humanists: they did not believe in pestilence. A pestilence does not have human dimensions, so people tell themselves that it is unreal, that it is bad dream which will end. But it does not always end and, from one bad dream to the next, it is people who end, humanist first of all because they have not prepared themselves. The people of our town were no more guilty than anyone else, they merely forgot to be modest and thought that everything was still possible for them, which implied that pestilence was impossible. They continued with business, with making arrangements for travel and holding opinions. Why should they have thought about the plague, which negates the future, negates journeys and debate? They considered themselves free and no one will ever be free as long as there is plague, pestilence and famine." (Camus, 2013)

At the time of writing this book I have no idea whether Ebola will spread globally and whether it will have any effect on the world economy. I am still assuming a future and a place for journeys and debate. There have been other terrible diseases that seemed to be running out of control that humanity has partially tamed in some parts of the world – like HIV/Aids, like SARS. Great efforts are being made to develop vaccines to tame Ebola. Nevertheless it is conceivable that Ebola could spread and the number of cases could grow - eventually perhaps across the world. This would certainly be the case if the number of cases continued to double every month as was the case at the beginning of the outbreak in western Africa.

It will readily be seen that if the doubling every month were to continue, there will be powerful forces to close down international travel movements - but that is not, in fact, as easy as it seems for reasons already explained. We live in a global economy. For example Liberia is a major source of rubber to go on the tyres of the world. The Firestone company source materials there. Everywhere across the world there are supply networks and just in time delivery schedules exporting and importing the components and raw materials of the products of the global economy. The epidemic in West Africa has already led to severe disruptions in the economies of those countries - and attempts to control its international spread could have a devastating effect on global trade and communications, including in food and food products - as well as on the international financial flows and financial institutions associated with them.

As John Maynard Keynes put it "In the long run we are all dead". He died at 62 of a heart attack.

Chapter 30

Time and Temporal Inequality

Temporal inequality is a little noticed feature of our society. Poor people wait for things – the well-off are waited on. Temporal inequality is crucial to understanding people's time choices.

The typologies for households may also help to map particular kinds of social and other problems in particular kinds of areas and the infrastructure and services that will be needed in an area. For example, it seems obvious that a family, and even more single parents, with young children are going to be struggling with time pressure because the demands of childcare, housework and earning enough money to pay the bills all has to be done in the 24/7 week.

In recent years, much has been made about what is called the "work-life balance". To understand this issue properly we really need to know both what kind of household type people experiencing this problem are in. It is obviously not single elderly people living on their own, who may have many problems but not this one, because they are not in paid work. It is also obvious that, when human beings allocate their time between different activities, there is not a simple choice between paid work and leisure. We allocate time in a very complex choice between paid work; multiple kinds of household work; travel to work time; care work; physiological overheads (eating and sleeping)... and leisure if we are lucky.

Economics tends to focus on our welfare with the assumption that that this arises from the satisfaction that we get from what we buy in the shops. However, there is a slightly different, but arguably more relevant idea, that well-being arises from a broader range of issues and life contexts. Absolutely central to well-being is the quality and quantity of our time and the conditions in which we are forced to allocate it. (Davey, Pathologies and Policies of Time, 2001)

In this connection, inequality has not only a monetary dimension, it has a time dimension too.

Temporal inequality and well being

As social critic Ivan Illych once put it, powerful social groups have an energy guzzling "well-sped" life style. With speed they get more things sold (higher turnover), they produce things "more cheaply" (in money terms - the energy use is not cheap to the environment) and they get to the scenes of battles first and shoot quicker than their rivals.

> High speeds for all mean that everybody has less time for himself as the whole society spends a growing slice of its time budget on moving people. Vehicles running over the critical speed not only tend to impose inequality, they also inevitably establish a self-serving industry that hides an inefficient system of locomotion under apparent technological sophistication... From our limited

information it appears that everywhere in the world, after some vehicle broke the speed barrier of 15 mph, time scarcity related to traffic began to grow. After industry had reached this threshold of per capita output, transport made of man a new kind of waif: a being constantly absent from a destination he cannot reach on his own but must attain within the day. By now, people work a substantial part of every day to earn the money without which they could not even get to work... (Illich, 1973)

In their consumption the rich are well sped too. Consumption takes time – a car needs to be cleaned, maintained, repaired, and refilled. A large house and possessions likewise requires more cleaning, looking after, and security arrangements. The rich, as well as the poor, only have 24 hours a day. But they have servants, secretaries, chauffeurs, gamekeepers, estate managers, personal assistants, researchers, au pairs, nannies, housekeepers, doormen and residential schools to send their children to.

If a lot of us cannot keep up it is partly because synchronising lives as members of the underclass, with the time needs of our well sped betters, becomes more difficult and burdensome as they become what can be appropriately described as more manic.

The well sped elite of a well sped society wants its service class to be flexible with their labour times. The worse jobs are not only worse in pay - they tend to be inferior in their temporal features. As a general rule people do not choose to do night shift work. They take on such work when their life circumstances leave them little other choice. A German study concludes:

> Shift work is not voluntarily chosen. Coming to terms with the bad work conditions is necessary to survive. It is the material pressure to feed one's family, to pay off debts, to finance housing costs, or to save for a house, that forces people to accept the conditions of shift work. Alheit P. Dausien B and Flörken-Erdbrink quoted in (Kasten, 2001, p. 150. The author's translation).

There is plenty of evidence that it is working women that find time pressures hardest of all to manage. The study by D'Alicia and Cattaneo mentioned earlier shows that Catalonian men work more in the market – on average 3.16 hours a day compared to 1.5 hours a day for women. However, women do more unpaid work – 3.99 hours a day compared to 1.6 hours a day for men. Overall, it will not surprise women readers that Catalonian women work on average 1.09 hours a day more than men. Although this gender inequality in workloads is changing, and is less among younger age groups, the work burden for women in the 25-44 age group is "almost unsustainable" and women have to sacrifice at least one hour personal care and/or leisure to carry the greater burden than men.

Nor can this situation be resolved using the technology of what are, supposedly, "labour saving devices" in the household. If anything the reverse is the case. Microwave ovens, washers and driers, food processors, disposable napkins and purchased childcare do not reduce unpaid work time. They increase its intensity because the technical changes generate new activities and standards. This increases the level of psychological stress at the same time as it increases the energy consumption used in, or making, the devices and products. If there are an increasing number of single person households, then this is even more the case. However, household arrangements like co-housing could help a lot in resolving some of these issues. (D'Alisa & Cattaneo, 2011)

In the absence of adequate household arrangements to lift the burden, a woman's work is never done. Women's perceived double responsibility to their family, as well as to an employer, is further complicated when work times are required to be more flexible to suit the irregular needs of employers. This makes it difficult to co-ordinate with family and domestic commitments. When the opening and closing times of schools, childcare and other facilities do not match up together, it all gets very complicated. There is a continual struggle to make ad hoc arrangements with relatives and friends to collect the children from school. Low paid shop workers, who are mostly women, live in a continual "time dilemma" trying to relate work times to other key times, like when child care is available. Time planning becomes a major stress in its own right.

Even though people may be employed "part time", when that part-time is moved around to different times of the day and week it is even more difficult to establish a manageable routine. I know from my past experience that working a three day week in a five day world was very difficult to manage satisfactorily. Full timers wanted to organise meetings on the days that I was supposed not to be working. By turning up to meetings on those days, and then taking time off somewhere else in the week, I ended up with a less than satisfactory arrangement. My "free time" ended up fragmented and unpredictable. I may have had as much "quantitatively" but it was not as usable. It was thus, not the same "qualitatively".

In the underclass, what often happens is that people who cannot manage to synchronise their lives to keep up with the pace and routine (or flexible availability) required by the synchronisers of the economy end up with no activity at all. They end up with plenty of time - they end up unemployed.

Social psychologists have confirmed by research what, to many people, will be obvious: too much time pressure leads to stress but too little time pressure leads to boredom. (Freedman & Edwards, 1988)

Psychological studies (again quoted in Levine) show that the unhappiest people of all are those who are under no time pressure at all. A psychologist called Mihaly Csikszentmihalyi kept track of a number of people with a radio telephone and asked them repeatedly what they were doing and how they were feeling. Those who were occupied by a moderate amount of activity gave the most positive reports of their feelings, those who were trying to do several things at once were stressed. However, those who were doing nothing at all, had no feeling of time flow and seldom reported that they felt well. This latter group were the unhappiest. That's another dimension of well-being that you won't find in the economic text books. (Levine, 2001, pp. 275-276)

From this perspective, the experience of unemployment is a psychological nightmare for many people. After they first become unemployed, and after, typically, they have spent their redundancy money redecorating the house, the problems for newly unemployed people begin to set in. Relationships with other family members are put under strain by the changed interpersonal time patterns. More time may be spent together with a spouse at home, for example, but with less to do together so that friction occurs.

Where repeated attempts to find a job fail, the unemployed person often loses a future horizon. It is typical too, of unemployed people to slip out of clock time into event time. They live when something is happening and/or when they can see other people. This is often the evenings. They start to get up late and go to bed late - living in a later cycle.

Inequality expresses itself therefore, not only in money but in time spent waiting. At the top of society people are **waited on**. They are waited on by their drivers, they are waited on at home and in hotels, in the office and in restaurants - so that time is easier to manage. A large part of the fragmented time in the underclass is spent in **waiting for.** The lower in the social hierarchy you are the more you wait for transport (for buses); in employment department; social security and housing benefit queues; at post office counters; in doctors surgeries and on waiting lists for operations (when one cannot pay for private treatment); in hospitals on mental health orders; in police cells; courts and in prisons.

Socially excluded people are often spatially distant from the centres of power - something that has temporal implications. To get from your village or your part of the city by bus to visit a relevant government office may be a time commitment that you can ill afford. To get to a good supermarket selling cheap food may take too much time, so you buy in the more expensive corner shop with less choice. Thus, even though nothing much happens in the lives of socially excluded people, the time they live is still committed time and it is still a time that is hemmed in by constraints that reduce life quality.

Despite unemployment, or perhaps because of the lack of an imposed work time rhythm, socially disadvantaged people tend to pass their days fragmented in event-time. This different quality of time in and for the underclass is incredibly important to understanding and explains why it is often so difficult for public and voluntary agencies to synchronise with poor people and form trusting and dependable relationships with them. No doubt, to the kind of incurably comfortable person whose opinion counts among those in government, the underclass are feckless and unreliable and so deserve the discipline of the market to get them to sort themselves out and pull themselves up by their own bootstraps. A closer look, however, reveals why it is almost inevitable that poor people have such a chaotic lifestyle. It is difficult for them not to have one. They do not have the resources in money; available non-fragmented time; relationships with people who are themselves not living chaotic lives and secure living environments to make dependability possible.

Chapter 31

Life Management, Stability and Life Transitions

Lifestyles and routines can be considered as "packages" of elements which must be held in balance one with another like income, habitat, relationships and activities. Lifestyle transitions involve moving from one "package" to another. There are different kinds of transitions including downshifting and upshifting. Downshifters can sometimes be part of a pioneering minority in a society that is facing the limits to economic growth.

If you open any economic textbook you will find a theory of how decisions are taken by businesses. The theory is wrong and ideologically driven – but it is a sort of a theory. You can also find a heroic narrative about "entrepreneurs". Again it is an idealisation, largely to celebrate and justify. But there is no real theory of households any more – just a theory of what is supposed to happen when individuals go shopping.

But when it comes to households, or indeed, when it comes to individuals, can we not say anything more than people "seek to maximise their satisfaction with their purchasing power" when they go shopping?

The work of Daniel Kahnemann that was mentioned earlier stressed that most people taking economic decisions, and most households too no doubt, are risk averse. What this suggests is that an important motivation in people's resource allocation decisions is the maintenance of stability.

Routines

Of course, a stable life has its draw backs. It may not be that exciting. In its routines it may get boring. Nevertheless, as Arnold Bennett, the British novelist and playwright put it

"The great advantage of being in a rut is that when one is in a rut, one knows exactly where one is"

Kahneman referred to the reference points that people judge situations against: Being averse to risking what they have already. Being In a rut the reference points are clear.

Let me therefore suggest something that might seem so obvious that it does not usually get any attention. This is that, for most of the time, most people live in routines which are the constants, the stability in their lives. It is very difficult not to - no individual and no society could function if all its members were constantly on the move, constantly changing jobs, constantly changing instrumental and work relationships. Although nomadic lifestyles and a range of agricultural and pastoral skills can make for great variety, these skills too must be exercised in known locations. They must involve arrangements between people in conformity to routines imposed by the seasons and nature - the need to sow and to harvest at the same times of the year. Matching temporal rhythms are also necessary if people are to sustain relationships - to be in a relationship people must not only spend time together they must, to a degree, synchronise their emotional states and practical inclinations. (Boscolo & Bertrando, 1993)

It follows from these obvious things that, to find and express their identity, people must hold in balance a habitat with all its domestic arrangements and chores of eating, sleeping, toilet and hygiene with their work and income and their network of instrumental and emotional relationships. These are constituted as inter-dependent patterns - as a generalisation we cannot have a large habitat without a large income. The number and quality of our relationships will depend upon the size and type of household partly, which will need to match the size of our habitats if people are to live together. Our income will depend partly on our work and skills. Our work, skills and incomes will determine our relationships. These in turn will affect our state of health, our morale and aspirations. How these arrangements are managed together depends on our age, gender, state of health and disability. They are also embedded in spatial, economic and cultural arrangements which will affect what kind of neighbourhood or settlement we live in; how it organises the supply of essential means of life and how far we must travel to work. All of these will fit into the household typology that we mentioned earlier.

Lifestyles considered as "packages" and lifestyle transitions

As the different elements in our lives have to be managed as a package - as interrelated elements which must be consistent with each other - the routines and the ordinary features of our lives can be thought of as having an inertial character. To be sure, even a routinised lifestyle will have some variety and novelty in each day, up to a point. However, beyond that point, adjusting one aspect of our lives even further will mean that we must adjust other elements in our lifestyle package. In turn, this is likely to bring with it a degree of uncertainty and unpredictability. For example, if we decide to move from where we live then we will be faced with different financial circumstances and that will have a consequential effect on work, relationships and so on. (Davey, The De-Growth Economy and Lifestyles, 2008)

As is obvious, periods of comprehensive lifestyle change are of different types. There are some changes which are inevitable age specific processes. The obvious cases being during late adolescence and early adulthood when most people start living independently, move from education to a job (if they are lucky) with an independent income and develop their own adult sexual relationships. As they are doing this all at once it is a difficult and challenging time - but it is happening with all the others of their age group. At the other end of life, there are the challenges associated with retirement. In between there are also typical lifestyle transitions triggered when children leave home, parents die, people evaluate their lives so far and perhaps have a mid-life crisis, deciding if they really want to live as they have been doing for the rest of their lives. As should be clear, there are situations where a life style shift is happening to all one's peers, for example, when a firm goes bust and there is mass redundancy which affects an entire community. There is the rather different situation in which only one person, or a family decides to launch out in a change of direction. There are situations too which are willed, which are entered into

209

deliberately and those which are entered into because people are forced to change - as in the redundancy situation.

It is clear that what all these situations share in common is that they involve launching out into the unknown. All these situations involve risks. As the English author Arnold Bennett expressed it "Any change, even a change for the better, is always accompanied by drawbacks and discomforts."

At its worst, a change in life launched into with insufficient skills, resources and friends can go badly wrong. Indeed there are arguments that mental breakdowns sometimes have this character. The stresses, tedium and limitations of an existing lifestyle may become too much and a person decides to launch into new territory. This might involve risks leaving a job without a new one; risks changing where they are living; risks leaving a relationship and giving up a secure habitat in the process. To others this seems like a crazy choice as the person acting does not have the resources and skills and support to make the move - and indeed may fall in the process. Their emotional turmoil therefore becomes greater. This is described by the psychiatrist Anthony Storr in psychological terms:

> Suppose that I become dissatisfied with my habitual self, or feel that there are areas of experience or self-understanding which I cannot reach. One way of exploring these is to remove myself from present surroundings and see what emerges. This is not without its dangers. Any form of new organisation or integration within the mind has to be preceded by some degree of disorganisation. No one can tell, until he has experienced it, whether or not this necessary disruption of former pattern will be succeeded by something better. (Storr, 1994, p. 35)

This is a very good description of how madness might arise in a lifestyle transition that goes wrong. Sometimes the new surroundings and new setting are not better and the people in the old relationships resist or counsel against the change. Sometimes the change, which has financial implications, is badly managed. Sometimes the new surroundings require skills and an orientation that we do not have. In those circumstances, the psychological stresses that have impelled our movement become even worse in our new surroundings. To those who observe the process it appears that we have gone mad, that we have chucked ourselves recklessly into a new lifestyle for which we are not suited and not equipped.

Obviously, the idea of lifestyle transitions is relevant for whether households are adapted to "sustainable living" or not. Some people who are concerned about the ecological crisis have joined cultural and practical movements whose aim is to go a good deal further than changing to low energy light bulbs. They have decided to go for bigger changes – including moving away from consumerism altogether – perhaps embracing ideas like "degrowth".

In so far as the idea of "degrowth" becomes a cultural movement that inspires people to change their lifestyles, it is enormously helpful that there are other people who are treading the same path and helping each other along the way. This gives some sense of what to do and what to expect. In this sense degrowth as a movement, with complementary and similar movements like permaculture, can be a powerful support for change. The risks are that much less when one is not on one's own in the change process. It is perhaps for this reason that movements that form around causes can be so intoxicating. Although one knows that change will be challenging and discomforting, the fact that other people are making these changes in the services of a cause is actually making it easier.

"A cause may be inconvenient, but it's magnificent. It's like champagne or high heels, and one must be prepared to suffer for it." Arnold Bennett

Without such causes, the danger of being stuck in a rut is that one does not explore sides of oneself and that, by staying in situations of safety, one limits what one can become.

"The real tragedy is the tragedy of the man who never in his life braces himself for his one supreme effort, who never stretches to his full capacity, never stands up to his full stature." Arnold Bennett

It is in this way that one can understand the attraction and the possibility that people would decide to adjust their lives and be prepared to sacrifice their income and purchasing power to be able to do so. The attraction of degrowth is clearly that, by having less income and purchasing power to acquire consumer goods, one will be able to get certain experiences and satisfactions in life that money cannot buy directly. Perhaps it is more time to spend with one's children as they are growing up. Perhaps it is to learn a new trade that is regarded as more interesting, more challenging and more socially responsible. Perhaps it is to engage with social and community responsibilities. At such times, the absence of work and contractual obligations may free people up to be more creative and use their time better. The purchase of freedom by less money is often a very good bargain.

Downshifting and upshifting

In the last few years, a significant number of people have made a decision to change their lifestyles with more time for themselves purchased by taking a lower income. This is called "downshifting" and in his book *Growth Fetish*, Clive Hamilton reports a number of studies on its extent in different societies. Not long before Hamilton's book was published, 19% of the US adult population declared that over the previous five years they had voluntarily decided to make a change to their lives that resulted in making less money. This excluded those taking a scheduled retirement. A similar survey in Australia found that 23% of 30-60 year olds had downshifted, citing as their reasons a desire for more balance and control in their lives, more time with their families and more personal fulfilment. (Hamilton, Growth Fetish, 2004, p. 206)

For all of those people who have chosen to make a lifestyle change of this type there will be others who want to make this kind of change but who, whether because of a lack of support, knowledge or resources may lack the will to take the plunge. Perhaps, with more support, they can be persuaded to do so. However, there are also people who will be trying to change their lives in the other direction- perhaps they will just be starting adult life or consolidating a lifestyle which is fundamentally growth focused and within the mainstream values of the current economic system. After all, there are powerful forces encouraging them to do so. Perhaps they will be too tightly bound into the messages and values of the growth system, its routines and its obligations - particularly debt and a consumption lifestyle - to be aware of or consider a degrowth approach to life.

At the moment, this group probably constitutes the majority of the population. A lot of people like this are only amenable to change messages at those points in their lives where they are going through fundamental changes, like moving job or house, or having a child. It is during such fundamental changes that people are compelled to re-evaluate what life means for them and how they might live it.

Growth and mainstream institutions

A large majority of people are bound into a relationship with the mainstream institutions of our society which can run most smoothly if the future is predictable and organised in bureaucratic routines. Growth gives the arrangements and routines of an increasingly complex society leeway for adjustment and for coping with stresses and change. Access to additional resources is typically seen as the way to solve problems and these resources are seen as arising out of extra income, extra production or through borrowing.

When borrowing occurs, extra resources to solve problems are generated by shifting payment into the future and paying interest to buy the right to do this. However, any macro growth of output and real income is ultimately only possible through an increase in physical energy available to the economy multiplied by the efficiency with which the energy can be applied to the production process. Once the amount of energy available in society is no longer rising the scope for real output growth eventually dries up. There may be some scope for efficiency increases for a time but this will be limited. At some point, solutions for problems cannot be found in extra resource availability but must be found in greater ingenuity for improvised solutions working with the same or less. This means more psychic work and stress levels are likely to rise.

Downshifters as a pioneering minority

As a result of the limits to economic growth, we are entering a period of time when a majority of people are likely to get increasingly stressed and challenged by the difficulties of the economy without yet realising the extent of the changes required. In contrast, the people who have decided to change their lives in a degrowth direction are currently a small minority whose orientation to wider developments means that they are anticipating and pioneering new life styles. They are the people who are creating the community gardens, the social enterprises, the community exchange systems, the cultural arrangements which provides seeds for a new degrowth economic order. Hopefully, those who have voluntarily changed their lives will have created "lifeboat institutions and arrangements" which can later support millions who find that they are being compelled to change when the existing economic system hits increasing difficulties.

As is obvious, some life transitions are not voluntarily entered into. Sometimes abrupt lifestyle shifts take place across society that most people do not want. In the early stages of wars and economic catastrophes, people may watch with interest the novelty of things going seriously awry. They may even, perversely, celebrate in the hope that change will make a normally humdrum existence more exciting and dramatic. However, grim experience may take away the excitement, replacing it with unwanted and unpleasant experiences that had not been expected. Fundamental change may confront a lot of people with painful and frightening challenges.

This possibility cannot be avoided. Most people are likely to be forced into degrowth lifestyle changes that they have not wanted. They may enter the process enormously stressed, very angry, frightened and unhappy. This would be very dangerous. Historical experience suggests that millions of people can be mobilised by channelling their emotions of frustration and fear against scapegoat minorities and foreign enemies. We are already seeing how shortages of oil and gas are being conceptualised by governing elites and the media as "energy security" issues in which nations are pitted against each other. Military intervention to secure oil and/or gas fields and pipeline routes has inflamed and polarised cultural and religious divisions. Such conflicts are in the short term interests of armaments manufacturers, aerospace, military logistics, security companies and the builders of gaols. Opportunities for profit in these circumstances will increasingly arise out of what Naomi Klein has termed "disaster capitalism" or "shock capitalism". The degrowth movement will have its work cut out to develop a positive alternative to this frightening scenario of increasing conflict and destruction.

PART FOUR

Production in the Paid Work Sector

Chapter 32

Energy in the economic system

The production economy is embedded in the physical world and thus, subject to the laws of physics. Concepts like "entropy", "sources" and "sinks", are useful to help us understand the embedded and embodied character of economic activity. Energy is converted through our bodies and through technical devices. The idea that economic development has meant a movement from an "empty world" to a "full world" is useful – but we must take care to acknowledge that we label the earlier state of an "empty world" which was often a sustainable low impact way of living by an indigenous society.

All economic activity is embodied and embedded in the physical world. We therefore need an understanding of the different ways that energy flows through, or is converted, inside human societies and economies. This fact, ignored by most economic theorists, is central to ecological economics. Indeed near the beginning of their textbook on "Ecological Economics" Herman Daly and Joshua Farley describe an economy thus,:

> An ordered system for transforming low entropy raw materials and energy into high entropy waste and unavailable energy providing humans with a psychic flux of satisfaction in the process. (Daly & Farley, Ecological Economics, 2004)

The ***circulation*** of money in the economy can continue indefinitely but not the flow of ***throughput***. It is possible to recycle materials but never 100% and it takes energy to do so. Meanwhile, energy is not (usefully) recyclable at all. Its usefulness and order decreases as it is used so that it becomes what physicists call "bounded energy".

Thus, the ***throughput*** of the economy moves from being useful raw materials and available or free energy derived from ***sources***, both of which have low entropy, and they are turned into high entropy wastes and bounded or unavailable energy in ***sinks***.

Daly and Farley follow in the footsteps of one of the founding fathers of ecological economics, Nicholas Georgescu-Roegen, who related resource use in economics to the second law of thermodynamics. The formulation of this law arose at the time of the industrial revolution when scientists became intrigued by the idea of a machine that could be fuelled by the same heat it generated while it worked. What they were looking for was, effectively, a perpetual motion machine. That would have meant free energy – it would have meant machinery running on nothing – or power for free. (Georgescu-Roegen, 1993)

No such machine was ever found to be possible. Sadi Carnot realised that a heat engine could only perform work by taking heat from one reservoir and transferring it to another reservoir at a lower temperature. Once heat is dissipated in the general environment, the energy is still there but it is no longer available for work.

The message in the second law of thermodynamics is that, as far as physics is concerned, we can't get something for nothing. The energy that is available for work as coal, for example, can no longer power anything when once that coal has been burned and the heat from combustion has dissipated in the general environment. As Georgescu-Roegen put it "All kinds of energy are gradually transformed into heat, and heat becomes so dissipated in the end that mankind can no longer use it".

He also proposed that *matter too* was subject to a natural tendency to disorder – it rusted, dissolved, rotted, dispersed, broke down, aged. In "economics-speak" it *depreciated.*

This produced a way of thinking about the ultimate source of the resources that are available for human purposes, a way of thinking that is rooted in physics. The common denominator of all usefulness is low entropy matter-energy – which can be used up but cannot be created.

Energy through our bodies and energy through devices - endosomatic and exosomatic energy flow

Thinking of the economy in these physical dimensions it is clear that a part of the total energy flow is going through conversions and processes in human bodies, while amother part is converted in powered devices and machines. The part that is taken in and converted in our bodies as nutrition is turned into the activity of muscles, internal organs and mental activity. This is called endo-somatic flow. The part that flows through machines and devices external to the body is called exo-somatic flow.

We can express these flows in terms of metabolic rates – as per capita endosomatic flow and per capita exosomatic flow and we can compare the two in different kinds of societies. Thus, in a developed society the metabolism of endosomatic energy lies in the range of 10-12 MJ per capita per day, whereas, the metabolism of exosomatic energy (measured as primary energy resources used for human devices and machines) can be estimated at 500 – 900 MJ per capita per day. Thus, the exo/endo ratio of developed societies is typically about 50/1 to 75/1. By contrast the same ratio in pre-industrial societies is typically only 5/1 – where the energy used for exosomatic devices is energy used for cooking, heating and illumination – and includes energy provided by work animals and local sources of mechanical power such as waterfalls or windmills. (Giampietro, Mayumi, & Sorman, 2011, p. 187)

This is a diagram that expresses the endosomatic conversions occurring through the human (and work animal) bodies of a pre-industrial economy, before the introduction of fossil fuel driven devices.

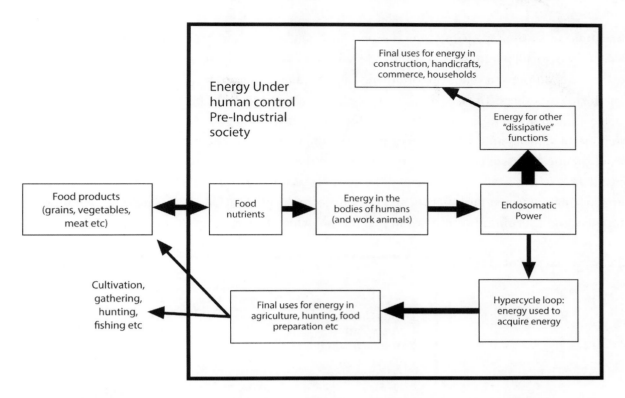

Redrawn from Giampietro, Mayumi, & Sorman, 2013, p. 123 with permission from Taylor and Francis

Human activity in the form of cultivation, gathering, hunting and fishing gives rise to grains, meat, vegetables etc which are the nutrient intake converted in human (and work animal) bodies into physiological energy that powers body functions. A large part of that energy then goes back into cultivation, food and fuel gathering, hunting and fishing in a loop – described here as the "energy for energy loop". The other part of the energy i.e. the net energy that is left over after the energy for energy loop, goes into other activities – into the household, construction, energy used in handicrafts and energy used in a limited amount of commercial activity (production for exchange).

In his description of industrialisation, Adam Smith and the early economists focused particularly on the organisation of the division of labour and specialisation which they saw as the reason for the increasing productivity of labour. However, the point about this specialisation was that it simplified work processes. This subsequently, led to the possibility of mechanisation. Machines could not initially be designed to do many complex processes but they could be designed to do a single process. These mechanical devices then came to be powered by steam engines using coal combustion.

So, from the industrial revolution onwards, what we had were production processes where people did not work with their muscles but used their minds and hands to guide machines powered by the burning of fossil fuels. Of course, some of these powered machines could also be applied to the extraction of fossil fuels which meant that the production of fossil fuels could be expanded enormously.

For the next 200 + years, there was then a continuous process of technological innovations - some of them incremental product improvements; some of them radical departures in products; some of the innovations in clusters spanning several economic branches and some of the innovations changing the whole techno-social paradigm. The innovations were in waves or clusters because some innovations created the conditions or platform for others. In particular, innovations in the energy system acted as platforms for others. Thus, coal, iron and steam power provided the basis for a revolution in transport through the railway age. Later, oil and petroleum based power created the platform on which motor vehicles and ships could be powered differently, petrochemicals could be developed and agriculture mechanised. Electrification then created the basis for the white goods industries, household conveniences which in turn transformed the domestic economy and helped create the conditions for a large number of women to enter the paid labour force. Electrification also created the conditions for computers and telecommunications and the internet which brings us up to current times.

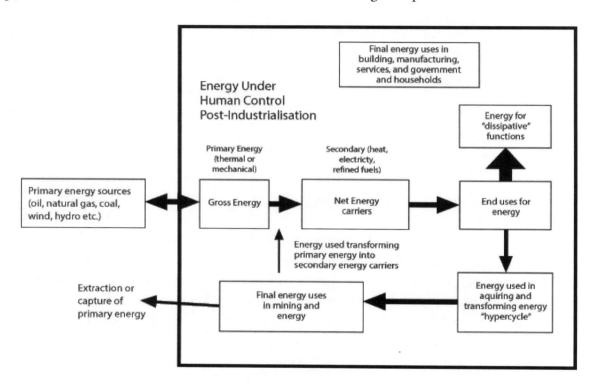

Redrawn from Giampietro, Mayumi, & Sorman, 2013, p. 91 with permission from Taylor and Francis

This brings us to this schematic representation of an industrial economy. The diagram is also from a book by Giampietro, Mayumi and Sorman about the energy metabolism of society. The extraction (or capture) of fossil energy, with some nuclear, hydro and other primary sources of energy, gives rise to a primary gross energy supply which is converted, or refined, into secondary energy sources like electricity, heat or refined fuels. A portion of these secondary net energy carriers are then re-applied in the energy and mining sector to extract and capture more energy in what is termed a "hyper-cycle".

If that were all that were to happen the energy supply would get bigger and bigger until its sources were depleted. However, that does not happen because there is a very high net energy available for other functions in the rest of the economy where some of the energy is "dissipated". This is not meant in a negative way – merely that they do not build the energy supply further in a direct physical sense. The net energy that goes to the dissipative sector is used in manufacturing, in building, in agriculture – and also in services and government which have a co-ordinative, management and distributive function, and in households. These parts of the economy are also necessary in their own way – for example some of the energy flows through households and are used in cooking, washing, hot water, keeping people warm and dry and so on. Without these functions people would not be available to work in, or supervise, the energy sector or any other part of the economy.

What should perhaps be clear from this is how much current standards of living are dependent on a high energy throughput. One way of thinking about all this is to take the amount of power output an average human body can achieve when working with its muscles as a reference measure – this is about 7 kW continuous energy work for 12 hours a day, 7 days a week. We can use this as a sort of yardstick or to say that in the average lifestyle it is as if we had 30 energy slaves working for us when we use devices such as motor cars, computers, household appliances, delivery vehicles etc.

The problem is that these energy devices have been run mainly by combusting fossil fuels which (a) deplete (b) change the climate (c) overwhelm the eco-system with wastes from the deluge of products once they thrown away, as well as the toxic wastes of fuel based chemicals.

It isn't just a problem of climate change – the scale of human activity is now overwhelming the planet's eco-systems in a number of different dimensions and threatens to do so in others.

The idea that growth could not go on forever and that fossil fuel based technological civilisation had its limits has now been around for a number of decades. One of the earliest ecological economists, Kenneth Boulding (1910-1993) put it succinctly - "Anyone who believes that exponential growth can go on forever in a finite world is either a madman or an economist".

The full world and empty world concept

Fortunately a few economists are not mad and have modelled other ways of seeing the relationship between the economy and the ecological system and how it has evolved over time. Herman Daly and Joshua Farley, two ecological economists, describe the last few centuries as the movement of from an "empty world" to a "full world". The throughput of matter and the conversion of energy in the economic system have, however, now reached a critical scale when compared to the enclosing ecological system.

A Macro view of the Macroeconomy

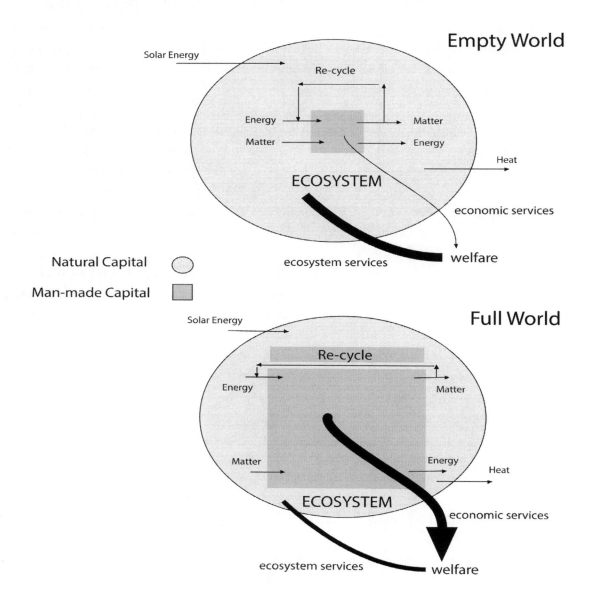

From *Ecological Economics*, by Herman E. Daly and Joshua Farley. Copyright © 2004 Herman E. Daly and Joshua Farley. Reproduced by permission of Island Press, Washington, D.C.

The vision of what has happened that is portrayed here is reasonably clear - the economy cannot go on expanding in what Daly and Farley term the "full world" situation. The availability of "natural capital" sets restraints on how much the economy can expand both in regard to sources of materials and energy and in regard to "sinks" – which are the places and processes where the wastes of economic activity are absorbed by the planet.

In the Daly pre-analytical vision energy conversion is crucial because energy is an "input" that enters into **all** economic activity, powering all the machines and devices of modern civilisation. However, because of the second law of thermodynamics energy cannot be "recycled". It always changes its form in a way that involves a change in "entropy"- which is its degree of usefulness for human purposes. It is true that materials like metals can be recycled but this takes energy and there is always some net loss. Moreover most energy is currently fossil energy and is non-renewable. One cannot recycle energy and there is evidence that it is becoming more costly, in energy terms to access fossil energy (coal, oil and gas). At the same time there are absolute limits on the amount of renewable energy too, which, because it is less dense and intermittent, is not such a convenient source to power the machinery of modern society.

Daly's pre-analytical vision draws attention to the limits to growth and has much to recommend it as long as it is not misinterpreted to reinforce the idea that in "an empty world" the influence of humanity was absent over large areas and that nature existed there untouched by human management – until it came to be "developed". Such an account can lead to an underestimation of the human impact on nature going back a long way in history. Even before the development of agricultural civilisations humans were a cause of significant extinctions across several continents which led to considerably altered landscapes and transformations in the biosphere. The concept of an "empty world" can also miss the way that some indigenous communities have lived with nature – managing landscapes with a light touch, with approaches that were generative of the biosphere, rather than undermining it - using techniques that colonising Europeans did not notice or appreciate.

Chapter 33

Using Energy to extract energy – the dynamics of depletion

The "Limits to Growth Study" of 1972 was deeply controversial and criticised by many economists. Over 40 years later, it seems remarkably prophetic and on track in its predictions. The crucial concept of Energy Return on Energy Invested is explained and the flaws in neoclassical reasoning which EROI highlights.

The continued functioning of the energy system is a "hub interdependency" that has become essential to the management of the increasing complexity of our society. The energy input into the UK economy is about 50 to 70 times as great as what the labour force could generate if working full time only with the power of their muscles, fuelled up with food. It is fossil fuels, refined to be used in vehicles and motors or converted into electricity that have created power inputs that makes possible the multiple round-about arrangements in a high complex economy. The other "hub interdependency" is a money and transactions systems for exchange which has to continue to function to make vast production and trade networks viable. Without payment systems nothing functions.

Yet, as I will show, both types of hub interdependencies could conceivably fail. The smooth running of the energy system is dependent on ample supplies of cheaply available fossil fuels. However, there has been a rising cost of extracting and refining oil, gas and coal. Quite soon there is likely to be an absolute decline in their availability. To this should be added the climatic consequences of burning more carbon based fuels. To make the situation even worse, if the economy gets into difficulty because of rising energy costs then so too will the financial system – which can then has a knock-on consequence for the money system. The two hub interdependencies could break down together.

"Solutions" put forward by the techno optimists almost always assume growing complexity and new uses for energy with an increased energy cost. But this begs the question- because the problem is the growing cost of energy and its polluting and climate changing consequences.

The "Limits to Growth" Study of 1972 – and its 40 year after evaluation

It was a view similar to this that underpinned the methodology of a famous study from the early 1970s. A group called the *Club of Rome* decided to commission a group of system scientists at the Massachusetts Institute of Technology to explore how far economic growth would continue to be possible. Their research used a series of computer model runs based on various scenarios of the future.

It was published in 1972 and produced an instant storm. Most economists were up in arms that their shibboleth, economic growth, had been challenged. (Meadows, Meadows, Randers, & BehrensIII, 1972)

This was because its message was that growth could continue for some time by running down "natural capital" (depletion) and degrading "ecological system services" (pollution) but that it could not go on forever. An analogy would be spending more than one earns. This is possible as long as one has savings to run down, or by running up debts payable in the future. However, a day of reckoning inevitably occurs. The MIT scientists ran a number of computer generated scenarios of the future including a "business as usual" projection, called the "standard run" which hit a global crisis in 2030.

It is now over 40 years since the original *Limits to Growth* study was published so it is legitimate to compare what was predicted in 1972 against what actually happened. This has now been done twice by Graham Turner who works at the Australian Commonwealth Scientific and Industrial Research Organisation (CSIRO). Turner did this with data for the first 30 years and then for 40 years of data. His conclusion is as follows:

> *The Limits to Growth standard run* scenario produced 40 years ago continues to align well with historical data that has been updated in this paper following a 30-year comparison by the author. The scenario results in collapse of the global economy and environment and subsequently, the population. Although the modelled fall in population occurs after about 2030 – with death rates reversing contemporary trends and rising from 2020 onward – the general onset of collapse first appears at about 2015 when per capita industrial output begins a sharp decline. (Turner, 2012)

So what brings about the collapse? In the *Limits to Growth* model there are essentially two kinds of limiting restraints. On the one hand, limitations on resource inputs (materials and energy). On the other hand, waste/pollution restraints which degrade the ecological system and human society (particularly climate change). Turner finds that, so far it, is the former rather than the latter that is the more important. What happens is that, as resources like fossil fuels deplete, they become more expensive to extract. More industrial output has to be set aside for the extraction process and less industrial output is available for other purposes.

> With significant capital subsequently going into resource extraction, there is insufficient available to fully replace degrading capital within the industrial sector itself. Consequently, despite heightened industrial activity attempting to satisfy multiple demands from all sectors and the population, actual industrial output per capita begins to fall precipitously, from about 2015, while pollution from the industrial activity continues to grow. The reduction of inputs to agriculture from industry, combined with pollution impacts on agricultural land, leads to a fall in agricultural yields and food produced per capita. Similarly, services (e.g., health and education) are not maintained due to insufficient capital and inputs.

> Diminishing per capita supply of services and food cause a rise in the death rate from about 2020(and somewhat lower rise in the birth rate, due to reduced birth control options). The global

population therefore falls, at about half a billion per decade, starting at about 2030. Following the collapse, the output of the *World3* model for the *standard run* (figure 1 to figure 3) shows that average living standards for the aggregate population (material wealth, food and services per capita) resemble those of the early 20th century. (Turner, 2012, p. 121)

Energy Return on Energy Invested EROI

A similar analysis has been made by Hall and Klitgaard. They argue that to run a modern society it is necessary that the energy return on energy invested must be at least 15 to 1. To understand why this should be so consider the following diagram from a lecture by Hall.

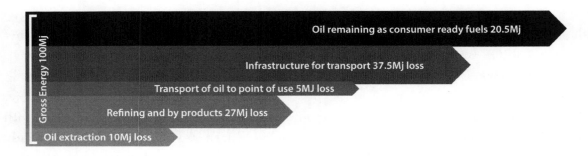

(Hall, 2012)

The diagram illustrates the idea of the energy return on energy invested. For every 100Mega Joules of energy tapped in an oil flow from a well, 10 MJ are needed to tap the well, leaving 90 MJ. A narrow measure of energy returned on energy invested at the wellhead in this example would therefore be 100 to 10 or 10 to 1.

However, to get a fuller picture we have to extend this kind of analysis. Of the net energy at the wellhead, 90 MJ, some energy has to be used to refine the oil and produce the by-products, leaving only 63 MJ.

Then, to transport the refined product to its point of use takes another 5 MJ leaving 58MJ.

But of course, the infrastructure of roads and transport also requires energy for construction and maintenance before any of the refined oil can be used to power a vehicle to go from A to B. By this final stage there is only 20.5 MJ of the original 100MJ left.

We now have to take into account that depletion means that, at well heads around the world, the energy to produce energy is increasing. It takes energy to prospect for oil and gas and if the wells are smaller and more difficult to tap because, for example, they are out at sea under a huge amount of rock. Then it will take more energy to get the oil out in the first place.

So, instead of requiring 10MJ to produce the 100 MJ, let us imagine that it now takes 20 MJ. At the other end of the chain there would thus, only be 10.5MJ – a dramatic reduction in petroleum available to society.

The concept of Energy Return on Energy Invested is a ratio in physical quantities and it helps us to understand the flaw in neoclassical economic reasoning that draws on the idea of "the invisible hand" and the price mechanism. In simplistic economic thinking, markets should have no problems coping with depletion because a depleting resource will become more expensive. As its price rises, so the argument goes, the search for new sources of energy and substitutes will be incentivised while people and companies will adapt their purchases to rising prices. For example, if it is the price of energy that is rising then this will incentivise greater energy efficiency. Basta! Problem solved...

Except the problem is not solved... There are two flaws in the reasoning. Firstly, If the price of energy rises then so too does the cost of extracting energy – because energy is needed to extract energy. There will be gas and oil wells in favourable locations which are relatively cheap to tap, and the rising energy price will mean that the companies that own these wells will make a lot of money. This is what economists call "rent". However, there will be some wells that are "marginal" because the underlying geology and location are not so favourable. If energy prices rise at these locations then rising energy prices will also put up the energy costs of production. Indeed, when the energy returned on energy invested falls as low as 1 to 1, the increase in the costs of energy inputs will cancel out any gains in revenues from higher priced energy outputs. As is clear when the EROI is less than one, energy extraction will not be profitable at any price.

Secondly, energy prices cannot in any case rise beyond a certain point without crashing the economy. The market for energy is not like the market for cans of baked beans. Energy is necessary for virtually every activity in the economy, for all production and all services. The price of energy is a big deal – energy prices going up and down have a similar significance to interest rates going up or down. There are "macro-economic" consequences for the level of activity in the economy. Thus, in the words of one analyst, Chris Skrebowski, there is a rise in the price of oil, gas and coal at which:

> The cost of incremental supply exceeds the price economies can pay without destroying growth at a given point in time. (Skrebowski, 2011)

This kind of analysis has been further developed by Steven Kopits of the Douglas-Westwood consultancy. In a lecture to the Columbia University Center on Global Energy Policy in February of 2014, he explained how conventional "legacy" oil production peaked in 2005 and has not increased since. All the increase in oil production since that date has been from unconventional sources like the Alberta Tar sands, from shale oil or natural gas liquids that are a by-product of shale gas production. This is despite a massive increase in investment by the oil industry that has not yielded any increase in "conventional oil" production but has merely served to slow what would otherwise have been a faster decline.

More specifically, the total spend on upstream oil and gas exploration and production from 2005 to 2013 was $4 trillion. Of that amount, $3.5 trillion was spent on the "legacy" oil and gas system. This is a sum of money equal to the GDP of Germany. Despite all that investment in conventional oil production, it fell by 1 million barrels a day. By way of comparison, investment of $1.5 trillion between 1998 and 2005 yielded an increase in oil production of 8.6 million barrels a day.

Further to this, unfortunately for the oil industry, it has not been possible for oil prices to rise high enough to cover the increasing capital expenditure and operating costs. This is because high oil prices lead to recessionary conditions and slow or no growth in the economy. Because prices are not rising fast enough and costs are increasing, the costs of the independent oil majors are rising at 2 to 3% a year more than their revenues. Overall profitability is falling and some oil majors have had to borrow and sell assets to pay dividends. The next stage in this crisis has then been that investment projects are being cancelled – which suggests that oil production will soon begin to fall more rapidly.

The situation can be understood by reference to the nursery story of Goldilocks and the Three Bears. Goldilocks tries three kinds of porridge – some that is too hot, some that is too cold and some where the temperature is somewhere in the middle and therefore just right. The working assumption of mainstream economists is that there is an oil price that is not too high to undermine economic growth but also not too low so that the oil companies cannot cover their extraction costs – a price that is just right. The problem is that the Goldilocks situation no longer describes what is happening. Another story provides a better metaphor – that story is "Catch 22". According to Kopits, the vast majority of the publically quoted oil majors require oil prices of over $100 a barrel to achieve positive cash flow and nearly a half need more than $120 a barrel. But it is these oil prices that drag down the economies of the OECD economies.

For several years, however, there have been some countries that have been able to afford the higher prices. The countries that have coped with the high energy prices best are the so called "emerging non OECD countries" and above all China. China has been bidding away an increasing part of the oil production and continuing to grow while higher energy prices have led to stagnation in the OECD economies. (Kopits, 2014)

Since the oil price is never "just right" it follows that it must oscillate between a price that is too high for macro-economic stability or too low to make it a paying proposition for high cost producers of oil (or gas) invest in expanding production. In late 2014 we can see this drama at work. The faltering global economy has a lower demand for oil but OPEC, under the leadership of Saudi Arabia, have decided not to reduce oil production in order to keep oil prices from falling. On the contrary they want prices to fall. This is because they want to drive US shale oil and gas producers out of business.

The shale industry is described elsewhere in this book - suffice it here to refer to the claim of many commentators that the shale oil and gas boom in the United States is a bubble. A lot of money borrowed from Wall Street has been invested in the industry in anticipation of high profits but given the speed at which wells deplete it is doubtful whether many of the companies will be able to cover their debts. What has been possible so far has been largely because quantitative easing means capital for this industry has been made available with very low interest rates. There is a range of extraction production costs for different oil and gas wells and fields depending on the differing geology in different places. In some "sweet spots" the yield compared to cost is high but in a large number of cases the costs of production have been high and it is being said that it will be impossible to make money at the price to which oil has fallen ($65 in late 2014). This in turn could mean that companies funding their operations with junk bonds could find it difficult to service their debt. If interest rates rise the difficulty would become greater. Because the shale oil and gas sector has been so crucial to expansion in the USA then a large number of bankruptcies could have wider repercussions throughout the wider US and world economy.

Renewable Energy Systems to the Rescue?

Although it seems obvious that the depletion of fossil fuels can and should lead to the expansion of renewable energy systems like wind and solar power, we should beware of believing that renewable energy systems are a panacea that can rescue consumer society and its continued growth path. A very similar net energy analysis can, and ought to be done for the potential of renewable energy to match that already done for fossil fuels.

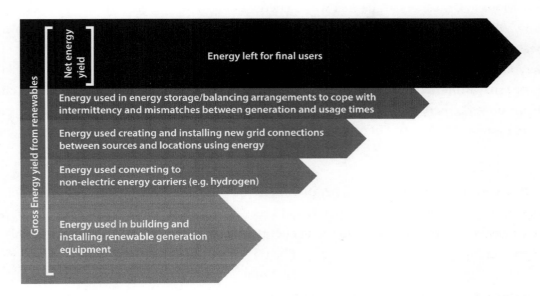

Before we get over-enthusiastic about the potential for renewable energy, we have to be aware of the need to subtract the energy costs particular to renewable energy systems from the gross energy that renewable energy systems generate. Not only must energy be used to manufacture and install the wind turbines, the solar panels and so on, but for a renewable based economy to be able to function, it must also devote energy to the creation of energy storage. This would allow for the fact that, when the wind and the sun are generating energy, is not necessarily the time when it is wanted. Furthermore, the places where, for example, solar and wind potential are at this best – offshore for wind or in deserts without dust storms near the equator for solar - are usually a long distance from centres of use. Once again, a great deal of energy, materials and money must be spent getting the energy from where it is generated to where it will be used. For example, the "Energie Wende" (Energy Transformation) in Germany is involving huge effort, financial and energy costs, creating a transmission corridor to carry electricity from North Sea wind turbines down to Bavaria where the demand is greatest. Similarly, plans to develop concentrated solar power in North Africa for use in northern Europe which, if they ever come to anything, will require major investments in energy transmission. A further issue, connected to the requirement for energy storage, is the need for energy carriers which are not based on electricity. As before, conversions to put a current energy flux into a stored form, involve an energy cost.

Just as with fossil fuels, sources of renewable energy are of variable yield depending on local conditions: offshore wind is better than onshore for wind speed and wind reliability; there is more solar energy nearer the equator; some areas have less cloud cover; wave energy on the Atlantic coasts of the UK are much better than on other coastlines like those of the Irish Sea or North Sea. If we make a Ricardian assumption that best net yielding resources are developed first, then subsequent yields for will be progressively inferior. In more conventional jargon – just as there are diminishing returns for fossil energy as fossil energy resources deplete, so there will eventually be diminishing returns for renewable energy systems. No doubt new technologies will partly buck this trend but the trend is there nonetheless. It is for reasons such as these that some energy experts are sceptical about the global potential of renewable energy to meet the energy demand of a growing economy. For example, two Australian academics at Monash University argue that world energy demand would grow to 1,000 EJ ($EJ = 10^{18}$ J) or more by 2050 if growth continued on the course of recent decades. Their analysis then looks at each renewable energy resource in turn, bearing in mind the energy costs of developing wind, solar, hydropower, biomass etc., taking into account diminishing returns, and bearing in mind too that climate change may limit the potential of renewable energy. (For example, river flow rates may change affecting hydropower). Their conclusion: "We find that when the energy costs of energy are considered, it is unlikely that renewable energy can provide anywhere near a 1000 EJ by 2050." (Moriarty & Honnery, 2012)

Now let's put these insights back into a bigger picture of the future of the economy. In a presentation to the All Party Parliamentary Group on Peak Oil and Gas, Charles Hall showed a number of diagrams to express the consequences of depletion and rising energy costs of energy. I have taken just two of these diagrams here – comparing 1970 with what might be the case in 2030. (Hall C. , 2012) What they show is how the economy produces different sorts of stuff. Some of the production is consumer goods, either staples (essentials) or discretionary (luxury) goods. The rest of production is devoted to goods that are used in production i.e. investment goods in the form of machinery, equipment, buildings, roads, infrastracture and their maintenance. Some of these investment goods must take the form of energy acquisition equipment. As a society runs up against energy depletion and other problems, more and more production must go into energy acquisition, infrastructure and maintenance. Less and less is available for consumption, and particularly for discretionary consumption.

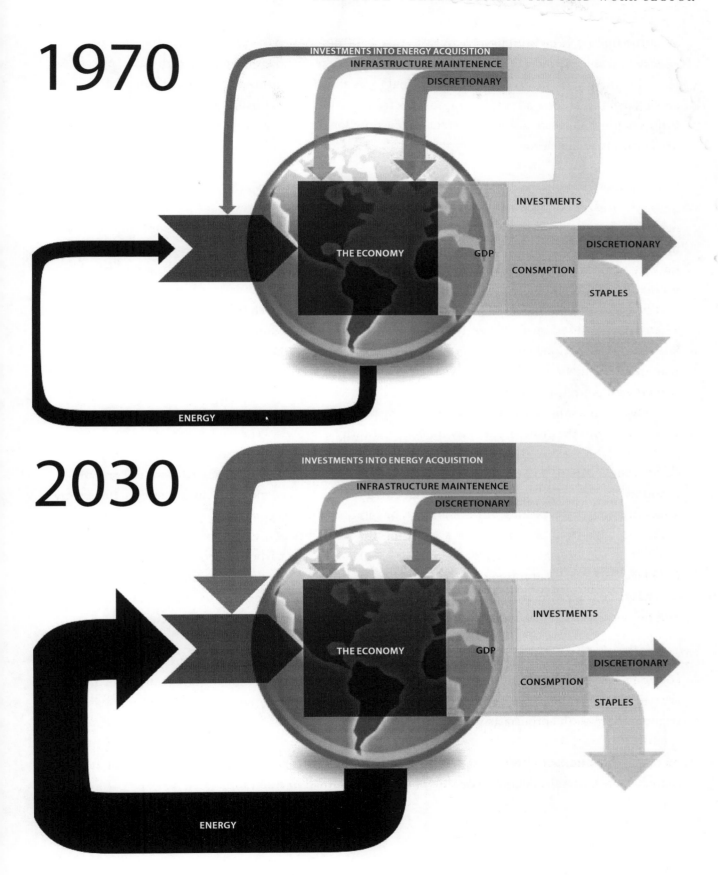

(Hall, C A S, Powers R and Schoenberg W. 2008 – Graphics reproduced with permission)

Whether the economy would evolve in this way can be questioned. As we have seen, the increasing needs of the oil and gas sector implies a transfer of resources from elsewhere through rising prices. However, the rest of the economy cannot actually pay this extra without crashing. That is what the above diagrams show – a transfer of resources from discretionary consumption to investment in energy infrastructure. But such a transfer would be crushing for the other sectors and their decline would likely drag down the whole economy.

Over the last few years, central banks have had a policy of quantitative easing to try to keep interest rates low. The economy cannot pay high energy prices AND high interest rates so, in effect, the policy has been to try to bring down interest rates as low as possible to counter the stagnation. However, this has not really created production growth, it has instead created a succession of asset price bubbles. The underlying trend continues to be one of stagnation, decline and crisis and it will get a lot worse when oil production starts to fall more rapidly as a result of investment cut backs. The severity of the recessions may be variable in different countries because competitive strength in this model goes to those countries where energy is used most efficiently and which can afford to pay somewhat higher prices for energy. Such countries are likely to do better but will not escape the general decline if they stay wedded to the conventional growth model. Whatever the variability, this is still a dead end and, at some point, people will see that entirely different ways of thinking about economy and ecology are needed – unless they get drawn into conflicts and wars over energy by psychopathic policy idiots. There is no way out of the Catch 22 within the growth economy model. That's why degrowth is needed.

Further ideas can be extrapolated from Hall's way of presenting the end of the road for the growth economy. The only real option as a source for extra resources to be ploughed into changing the energy sector is from what Hall calls "discretionary consumption" aka luxury consumption. It would not be possible to take from "staples" without undermining the ability of ordinary people to survive day to day. Implicit here is a social justice agenda for the post growth - post carbon economy. Transferring resources out of the luxury consumption of the rich is a necessary part of the process of finding the wherewithal for energy conservation work and for developing renewable energy resources. These will be expensive and the resources cannot come from anywhere else than out of the consumption of the rich.

It should be remembered too that the problems of depletion do not just apply to fossil energy extraction coal, oil and gas) but apply across all forms of mineral extraction. All minerals are depleted by use and that means the grade or ore declines over time. Projecting the consequences into the future ought to frighten the growth enthusiasts.

To take in how industrial production can hit a brick wall of steeply rising costs, consider the following graph which shows the declining quality of ore grades mined in Australia.

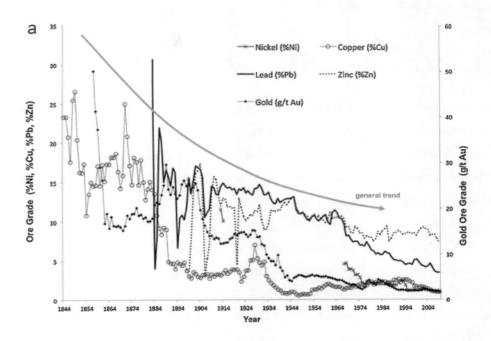

(Prior, T., Giurco, D., Mudd, G., Mason, L., Behrisch, J. 2012) Diagram reproduced by permission of Elsevier.

As ores deplete there is a deterioration of ore grades. That means that more rock has to be shifted and processed to refine and extract the desired raw material, requiring more energy and leaving more wastes. This is occurring in parallel to the depletion in energy sources which means that more energy has to be used to extract a given quantity of energy and therefore, in turn, to extract from a given quantity of ore.

Thus, the energy requirements to extract energy are rising at the very same time as the amount of energy required to extract given quantities of minerals are rising. More energy is needed just at the time that energy is itself becoming more expensive.

Now, on top of that, add to the picture the growing demand for minerals and materials if the economy is to grow.

At least there has been a recognition and acknowledgement in recent years that environmental problems exist. The problem is now somewhat different – the problem is the incredibly naïve faith that markets and technology can solve all problems and keep on going. The main criticism of the limits to growth study was the claim that problems would be anticipated in forward markets and would then be made the subject of high tech innovation. In the next chapter, the destructive effects of these innovations is examined in more depth.

Chapter 34

Convivial Technology versus Granfalloons

Technological innovation is considered the source of 'salvation' in economics. However, there are different kinds of technology and in recent years "convivial technology" has been developed to conform to more people and environmental friendly principles than those of the technological mainstream. Unfortunately, even convivial technologies are often developed in hybrid and mixed conditions using infrastructure platforms from the economy of the corporations, as well as sometimes reflecting consumerist values. At the same time, the "green technology" in the economic mainstream is not at all that it seems. The increasing complexity of products and societies leads to increasing unpredictability. There is actually no such thing as a sustainable company or product because sustainability is society-wide. Rebound effects often render environmental innovation futile. Efficiency improvements have limited effectiveness in a growing economy. Granfalloons are vested interest coalitions formed around illusory and futile innovations like biofuels which are sustained by the optimism bias of techno-enthusiasts.

Salvation through technological innovation – but which type of technological innovation actually?

If we conceptualise economics as a belief system that is, in some respects, akin to a religion then what is its concept of salvation? What will redeam us? What is the solution to all our problems? The answer of the economists is, as we have seen, specialisation and technology. If we have problems, the message is that markets will solve them by bringing forth new technologies.

We have now had over 200 years of this technological 'progress' since the "industrial revolution" and it appears to be, if anything accelerating. This technology mostly gets a good press and there are good things that one can say about it. For billions of people, technology appears to have removed many material insecurities – until now. Unfortunately, technology has also brought many environmental and other problems – and the solution to these problems is typically conceived as more of the same – new technologies incentivised by market dynamics.

The magic 'hurrah word' to describe the process by which these new technologies come about is "innovation".

Without the razzmatazz, innovation means doing things in a new or different way. However, the word 'change' does not evoke the same heroic feeling that celebrates and congratulates the cleverness of technologists and the dynamism of the risk-taking entrepreneurs who are backing them. Innovation is what is achieved by the heroes of the modern age. They are the celebrities like Bill Gates and Steve Jobs, the managers of cutting edge technological companies. Under their lead the growth economy boldly goes where humans have never been before...

But the technologies that we depend upon in our highly complex society can fail us and make our problems worse. In the end, technology is a means to an end and, when the ends that prevail in society are growth of profits, growth of wealth and power, and growth of the egos of entrepreneurial celebrities, then it is not surprising that the technologies that are there, supposedly for green purposes, may nevertheless fail to deliver.

There are different types of technology just as there are different types of motivation, different types of entrepreneurialism and different types of development. It is important to compare them and be clear which type one is considering.

In this regard, much thought has been devoted by the visionaries of an ecological society about what the technology of the future should be like. For these thinkers, the issue is not simply one of resource efficiency, still less considerations of profitability and self-aggrandisement, but the effects of technology on society, on the local (and global) environment and its appropriateness for communities. Thus, while there is a mainstream technology, there are also "alternative" technologies whose developers start from a different ethical standpoint. At the time of writing, it is possible to observe three different trends which, when taken together, can be described as the promotion of a kind of "convivial technology" after the ideas of Ivan Illich. (Deriu, M. 2014). These three trends are Open Design; Re-usable and adaptable technologies and technologies evolved to be constructed, maintained and repairable in "Do it Together" sessions in community workshops and settings.

Guidelines for People Friendly Technology

Manipulative Technology	Convivial Technology
Effects on social relationships	
Promotes and requires competition	Promotes and requires co-operation
Orientated to capital not to need	Connects people
Top down developed and constructed	Offers direct user/developer contact
Assumes strong hierarchies for its use	Developed in network structures and can be used in non-hierarchical systems

Justice

Cannot be used by all	Offers available to all
Tends to exclude according to gender	Is gender inclusive
Difficult to learn how to use	Simple to learn
Assumes elite knowledge in production and use	Assumes only easily available knowledge for production or use
Intellectual property based and thus, not readily available	Allows freely distributed knowledge
Expensive	Cheaply available

Autonomy

Can only be repaired or maintained by experts	Easy to maintain and repair
Limited useful product life	Durable
Cannot be adapted to other use	Open to adaptation
Connected to large scale national infrastructures	Can be adapted to local use and suitable to local infrastructures
Expensive in the use of time	Saves time
Can only be built with special knowledge or machinery	Can be made through DIY

Health

Poisons or degrades soil	Raises soil fertility
Poisons water	Improves water quality
Emits air pollution	Promotes air quality
Destroys eco-systems	Helps maintain and create eco-systems
Carries high risks of unknown harms	Known to be safe in operation

Resource Use Intensity (efficiency)

Inefficient	Efficient
Consumer non renewable resources	Uses renewable resources
Uses distantly accessed raw materials	Uses local materials
Not recyclable	Recyclable
Works against natural processes and givens	Uses local givens
Requires the use of fossil energy	Requires renewable energy

(Vetter, 2014)

This table is by no means an idealistic, purely theoretical set of principles. Real products have been designed and developed with principles like this. One such is LifeTrac, a tractor which belongs to a "Global Village Construction Set" comprising of a Lego like kit set of 50 machines currently under development that communities need "in order to build a small civilisation".

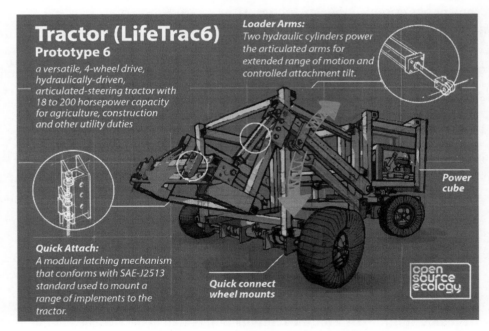

Source http://opensourceecology.org/portfolio/tractor/

According to the website set up for Open Source Technology:

The Global Village Construction Set (GVCS) is a modular, DIY, low-cost, high-performance platform that allows for the easy fabrication of the 50 different Industrial Machines that it takes to build a small, sustainable civilization with modern comforts. We're developing open source industrial machines that can be made at a fraction of commercial costs, and sharing our designs online for free. http://opensourceecology.org/gvcs/ (Open Source Ecology Website. Webpage Machines: Global Village Construction Set)

The construction instructions are Open Source, an idea developed by computer software programmers that has been extended into "Open Design", which involves the design and production of physical products untrammelled by the hindrances of an intellectual property regime. "Rent" is charged for the use of knowledge slowing down the transmission and development of ideas. In this kind of economic system there are no patents because the guiding principle is co-operation rather competition. The Peer to Peer (P2P) production system is envisaged as a new form of economy and society, with intellectual commoning extended into the production system. In this framework, As Andreas Vetter explains, the open source tractor is built in a modular way so that people in another place can more easily develop locally appropriate substitute and additional components. It is simple to build and repair, otherwise it would never be built at all. Its size can be changed and adapted to local circumstances. The material used in production should, ideally, be producible locally or can be re-used locally. With products like this, it is possible to envisage local communities sharing equipped facilities in "micro-factories" where products like this are produced, repaired and maintained for shared community use.

There is state support for this type of economic development too from the Government of Ecuador. Ecuador's government has critiqued the destructive path of what they term "extractivist economics" and neo-colonial growth in favour of peer to peer production systems and open source commons. Their ideas are not "western imports" but are based on the philosophical system of indigenous Andean communities. This philosophy incorporates the ideas of "buen vivir" or "sumac kawsay", roughly translated as "good living" or "life to the fullest". This strategy is described in an article by David Bollier who quotes from the Ecuador "National Plan for Good Living 2009-2013":

> The Andean indigenous peoples have contributed to this debate [about development] by applying other epistemologies and cosmos-visions. One of their greatest contributions is the notion of sumac kawsay, 'life to the fullest.' The notion of development is inexistent in these people's cosmos-vision since the future is behind us because the concept implies something we do not look at or know. In the Andean cosmos-vision, the past is in front of us; we see it, we know it, it is ours and we walk with it...

> The concept of "good living" necessarily resorts to the idea of "us". The community shelters, protects, demands; it is the basis for the reproduction of that collective subject that each and every one of us is. That is why humans are conceived as one part of a whole that cannot be understood only as a sum of its parts. The whole is present in each being and each being in the whole. "The universe is permanent; it has always existed and will always be here; it is born and dies in itself and only time can change it." (Kichwa saying). This is why harm to nature is to harm ourselves. Sumak kawsay, or life to the fullest, transmits this cosmos-vision...

Comments Bollier:

> This is taking "development" back to basics. It does not simply assume—as the "developed world" does—that more iPhones and microwave ovens will bring about prosperity, modernity and happiness. The report goes on to critique the philosophical errors of neoliberal political philosophy and to set forth specific objects for fostering "social and territorial equality, cohesion, and integration with diversity". (Bollier, 2013)

The hybrid and mixed character of current strategies

Technological strategies of this sort seem to stand a better chance of creating a really sustainable society, and represent a view of how things might be in the society and economy beyond the limits of economic growth. However, a note of caution is also needed, since no technological system can evolve in a vacuum. In current conditions, most alternative technological developments have a hybrid character. They are not entirely disconnected from the technologies and economic processes of the wider capitalist market.

Thus, many, perhaps most, developers of open source technologies do not fully embrace commons, environmental or community enhancing principles, and may focus on the development of products, like open source racing cars, which reflect the values and priorities of growth and consumer society. Much open source freely available design is appropriated by capitalist corporations. The real power is shown in the way that, although the use of internet systems has facilitated networking and intellectual commons of various kinds, the infrastructures on which these intellectual commons are based, are still developed, owned and controlled by profit making corporations. These corporations capture the potential to create money value, particularly by selling the ability of the systems to channel mass attention as platforms for advertising and public relations strategies. One has only to think, for example, of *Facebook,* to see that a powerful tool for networking and the development of horizontal networks, is still programmed and run for profit by a capitalist corporation for these purposes.

This has led some thinkers to question how peer to peer production and intellectual commons might protect themselves from private sector parasitism. What institutions and what property systems can reinforce collective and commons values? For example, is it possible to adjust the intellectual property rights so that peer produced knowledge is freely available but only to those who are themselves using it for a purpose that is itself open and collective? The result ideally would be that freely available knowledge enhances the peer process and the knowledge commons through flowing back into collective processes.

At this time, the development of alternative technological systems is best understood as a mixed process in which, although we can theoretically disentangle the convivial from the manipulative, the alternative from the mainstream, in real life, is sometimes much more difficult. Thus, much of the open source approach is dependent on the rapid development of the internet, which is in itself a major consumer of energy, both in the production of the hardware and in the use of the information technology devices. In order to properly account for the overarching energetic and ecological effects of the whole process, positive and negative, it would be necessary for global society to have processes of governance that set limits on the volume and types of use of certain critical resources used. For example, the volumes of pollution like CO_2 generated during would be set within severe reducing limits. Unfortunately, no such processes of global governance currently exist.

Iterative strategies – successive approximations to partially unknown places

It is indeed very difficult to envisage the kinds of processes that would bring about a comprehensive change for the better including the technologies that are needed.

If there were agreement among stakeholders about environmental problems arising from economic activity, and if there were clarity and certainty about the science in regard to the magnitude and nature of the cause and effect relationships, then the problems would be simple to solve.

Usually, however, environmental and social problems are characterised by radical disagreements among stakeholders largely because, as we have seen, they have very different ethical and value systems and contradictory purposes. In addition, there are bound to be considerable uncertainties in regard to cause and effect relationships. This includes different assessments that arise because people have different purposes and, therefore, tendencies to denial and wishful thinking that characterise the way people think in the light of their purposes.

Taken together, the problem of disagreements among stakeholders and different assessments can be expressed by this diagram called the "Stacey Matrix", after the academic who first formulated it.

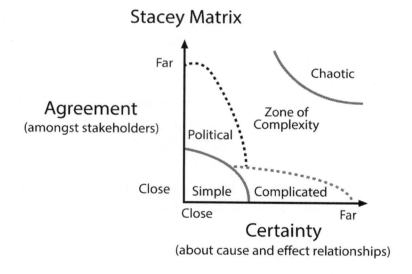

(Stacey, 2012) Diagram reproduced with the permission of Ralph Stacey – but see text.

Stacey first used this diagram in a textbook in the mid-1990s but later came to regret the "matrix" which became very popular. When I wrote to him asking permission to use it he wrote back to explain why by quoting something else that he had written:

Presenting things in this way suggests that managers can decide which kind of situation they are in and then choose the appropriate tools. This is typical of a number of contingency approaches to tools and techniques, approaches of which I am now highly critical. This contingency approach contradicts the whole point of the book which stresses unpredictability and tight limits to the ability of managers to identify what situation they are in and choose outcomes in instrumental, rational ways. Conditions close to certainty and agreement hardly ever occur in human interaction. The diagram proved to be very popular and a number of writers took it up and amended it in a number of ways – it came to be referred to as the Stacey Diagram, which is unfortunate because I came to see how problematic this kind of contingency approach is. My colleague kept telling me that people liked the diagram so much because it collapsed the paradox of certainty and uncertainty and doing so enables people to carry on thinking as before when I thought I was challenging them to think in a different way. I resisted this criticism for some time but then eventually saw the point and dropped the diagram altogether only to find that it had developed a life of its own whether I liked it or not, as others adapted and used it.

(Stacey, R. 2012)

The world that we live will always be subject to rival interpretations and rival interests. The future cannot be known with certainty and many developments arise as unforeseen consequences of earlier decisions. Unavoidably we are usually forced to live in a "Zone of Complexity" and, whether we like it or not, we sometimes find ourselves in a zone of chaos. In the so called 'Zone of Complexity' the questionsthat we face are best thought of as using a terminology all of its own, as 'wicked problems' where it is difficult to know how to conceptualise what is going on, difficult to understand, and difficult to find appropriate solutions.

From this follows a need for different kinds of strategies which are more trial and error based. They need to be iterative, approaching solutions through successive approximations, accepting that there can be no "ideal right answer". However the "error" in "trial and error" is usually difficult for governments to admit, for companies to finance and for managers, officials and politicians to agree on.

This is connected to a scale problem. Trial and error is possible in a world where companies and technologies are small scale. It becomes more difficult where companies and technologies are trying to operate on a mega scale. The error is even more catastrophic when it occurs, not at local government level in one or two places, but at a level promoted by multinational corporations and international institutions. Thus, while there is a case for trial and error, in many cases, this ought to be tempered by a need for caution – which means adhering to the precautionary principle.

These are considerations that are very pertinent to so called "green innovation"... whatever that is supposed to be. The conditions in which it might be developed are contested and often very complex. It should not surprise us that, for all its importance as a way out of humanity's current dilemmas, there has been a great deal of difficulty tying down what "green innovation" really consists of. Even though "convivial technologies" give us important clues of what green technologies might be like, the way that convivial technologies can be tied into an energy guzzling internet platforms suggests difficult paradoxes, which are likely to frustrate those looking for technological panaceas.

Complexity entails unpredictability

A further reason for the elusive character of "green technologies" is the sheer complexity of global economic relationships, which makes for greater difficulty in predicting all the consequences of innovations.

It is in the very nature of the ecological perspective that we take an interest in the whole picture – but once we do that, the knock on consequences of any localised techno-innovation are difficult, indeed impossible to predict. This is partly because "innovation" usually adds more complexity to an already complex picture where complexity is part of the problem.

The point here is that the more elements in a situation, the more complex it is, the more difficult it is to explain how that situation has arisen and and what its knock-on consequences will be. Predicting how large systems will behave, for example how they might break down, is more difficult than predicting what might happen with small systems. In a larger systems there are more interactions and feedbacks to transmit consequences between and within sub-systems. In a small system there are fewer elements and interactions between them that can go wrong.

Innovation, which of itself leads to greater complexity, also adds a higher level of uncertainty as to how systems will evolve. As they evolve under the stimulus of innovations at some point in the web of interconnections, knock-on consequences may be neither predictable nor helpful.

There is no such thing as a sustainable company or product

In this context, it is important to grasp that there can be no such thing as a sustainable company, product or service, only a sustainable economy or society. Also, that the very same innovation, in different contexts, can be either beneficial to human/nature interactions or destructive.

When most corporations are using buzz phrases about 'green innovation', what they usually mean is greater materials and energy efficiency. The game is to get more output with less input of various kind of stuff. It is described with lots of words beginning with "re"... re-use, recycle, repair, re-manufacture and so on. Then there are words to describe the facilitation of waste streams circling back into production processes - industrial ecology, drop-off and buy-back centres and so on.

Many of these ideas about materials and energy efficiency make a lot of sense but there's a hitch with them, which is referred to as the rebound effect, or the Jevons effect after the 19th century economist Stanley Jevons.

The rebound or Jevon's effect

The problem with improving energy efficiency is that it tends to lead to an increase, rather than a decrease, in aggregate energy used. People find that their low energy light bulbs are cheap to run, so they leave them on all night. Or, with the money that they save through cheaper energy bills, they fly to Spain on holiday. The business that very successfully saves money on its energy and materials bills uses the savings, which appear as increased profits, to expand production lines or develop new products. It's a growth economy and the faster materials and energy efficiency increases, the faster the economy can expand.

Increasing energy efficiency also facilitates new product features. A more energy efficient phone is a technical device that can be used to do more and different kinds of things. Customers, including other businesses, are encouraged to upgrade the technologies they use and, in the process, the amount of energy used increases again.

A striking example of this is energy usage by small consumer electronics and information technology products such as mobile phones, IPads and the like.

> ... these products now account for approximately 15% of global residential electricity consumption. While efficiency improvements have been made, savings have been cancelled out by the demand for equipment which provides more functionality, or is larger or more powerful, and therefore uses more electricity. (OECD/IEA, 2009, p. 21)

International Energy Agency projections predict that the energy use by these kind of gadgets will double between 2009 and 2022 and increase by 3 times by 2030.

Thus, it is because the energy efficiency of these products and the internet increases that energy consumption increases. The energy efficiency makes possible new pieces of equipment and new applications. Customers acquire upgraded equipment which, require much more background electronic information storage to run, and the data stores guzzle vast quantities of energy.

To make this situation even worse, it seems some studies show that after the consumption of more ethical products (like the use of more energy efficient cars) some consumers feel that they are then titled to consume more unethical products. (Santarius, 2014 p14)

It would be wrong to knock energy efficiency as a problem solving strategy. In order to be able to deal with the environmental crisis it is obviously necessary to promote it. The point is, that energy efficiency on its own is not sufficient. Other policies are necessary and in most cases the policies that are needed are absolute limits on allowed production imposed as "reducing caps". The absolute allowable ceilings need to be reduced as rapidly as possible.

With fuels, there needs to be a policy that limits the amount of carbon that can be burned and brings this amount down very quickly. This would not be administratively difficult – one could simply ban the production and original sale of carbon fuels without permits. The number of permits would be limited each year and the ceiling reduced each year. For climate stability, there needs to be about 6% per annum to avert catastrophe. Permits would allow a quantity of fuel which contains the specified amount of carbon embedded in it, something that is known with reasonable accuracy. Fossil fuel suppliers would have to buy the permits and the money from selling the permits to them would go to all of us equally

The problem is not of administrative difficulty, it is the hostility of fossil fuel suppliers and their lobby influence. However, without a reducing cap like this, increasing energy efficiency improvements will not do the job needed. Because of the rebound energy efficiency improvements without a cap serve to stoke the growth of resource and energy use.

Efficiency improvements are non-linear – eventually costs rise very steeply

A further point of great importance to understanding the limits of technological innovation is the non linear way in which materials efficiency improvements occur. Take the abatement of Nox from car exhausts for example. The marginal costs of reducing 80% of Nox are reasonable, but the costs of reducing the last 20% are very high. The consequences can be understood in this way. If one doubles the amount of car use and abates 50% of Nox from each car, there will be the same total amount of Nox emissions. Do that again, and there will again be the same total amount of Nox emitted. However, repetitions that put one in the zone above 80% abatement and the costs of further abatement rise very steeply. The Nox problem comes back with a vengeance as one tries to continue growing the number of cars.

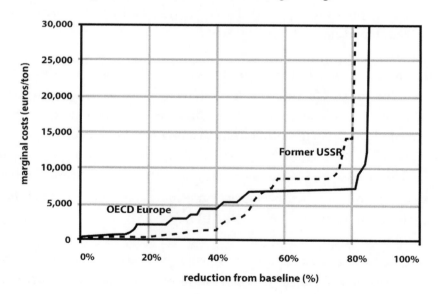

Non linear costs of pollution abatement
The air pollutant NOX can be removed from emissions to a significant degree at low costs, but at some level of required abatement the cost of further removal rises precipitously. The marginal cost curve for NOx removal for 2010 for OECD Europe and the former USSR in euros per ton.

(Van Harmelen et al. 2002) Reproduced with permission from Elsevier.

The fact that some forms of "Green Innovation" are futile when evaluated against stated intentions does not mean that they are unprofitable. On the contrary, they may be very profitable. When "green innovation" is very profitable but futile or destructive, it can be very difficult to stop. This is because vested interest coalitions can form around the futile strategy and it is in their interest to hide or deny the truth. The process of truth denial can be organised in a very aggressive fashion. Coalitions of interest groups can form around these toxic forms of innovation – like industrial groups, academics, officials and policy makers and even misled NGOs.

Granfalloons

The author Kurt Vonnegurt invented the term "granfalloon" to describe a specious belief system that brings people together in his novel "Cat's Cradle". Some ecological economists find the word useful to describe coalitions around practical innovations and beliefs that appear to provide solutions to environmental problems but, in reality, raise false hopes and waste resources.

Unfortunately, getting the general idea of what granfalloons are, does not necessarily make it easy to recognise them. Indeed, there are some disagreements among ecological economists about what constitutes a "granfalloon". For example, Giampietro, Mayumi and Sorman are of the view that the idea of "degrowth", considered as a voluntary reduction by a society of the use of energy in an economy, is a granfalloon and they mock the very idea. They describe "degrowth" using a metaphorical image in which a football team is sent out to play a match having previously been put on a diet in which they have access to only half the usual calorific input. They argue that that is not something any team would do voluntarily. A response would be that it would be very appropriate to put a team on half the calories if they were overweight. (Giampietro, Mayumi, & Sorman, The Metabolic Pattern of Societies: Where Economists Fall Short, 2011, p. 334)

The ingredients for a granfalloon suggested by Giampietro, Mayumi and Sorman are:

1. A culture that believe strongly in silver bullet techno-fixes
2. The desire of politicians to have something to point to that will reassure the public in the face of problems like climate change
3. Information uncertainties and unknowns and very complicated technical discourses that make it difficult for most people to penetrate the issues involved in evaluating a particular policy and product
4. Strong path dependency when it comes to the evolution of a particular product that has been involved in a particular policy agenda – more specifically the difficulties of recognising, acknowledging and writing off investment in unsuccessful R and D strategies once they have been started. (A typical narrative is to suggest "these are just teething problems" or "generation two technologies will solve these problems")
5. Source of subsidies for industries and academics

Case Study - Biofuels

The coalition promoting and producing biofuels is an example. The fact that bio-fuel production is not understood as being futile is because the production process is not being evaluated properly i.e. by using an adequate energetic, bio-physical methodology. As a result, policy makers, academics, and people who ought to know better, do not see that bio-fuel production is only viable in current conditions because it is being subsidised by relatively cheap inputs of fossil fuels.

The aim of bio-fuel production is to replace fossil fuel production. Thus, to evaluate them properly, one needs to assume that there are no fossil fuel inputs going into their production. That means that a proper evaluation should assume that the fuel inputs that go into making bio-fuels should themselves be bio-fuels. Evaluating bio-fuels on that basis reveals them to be completely futile as a replacement liquid fuel source.

Mario Giampietro and Kozo Mayumi calculate typical figures for the production of corn ethanol from one hectare of land in the USA and sugar cane ethanol from one hectare in Brazil. They assume that the fuel inputs needed to produce a new batch of biofuels is all taken from previous bio-fuel production. This enables a comparison of inputs and the outputs for the two sources of ethanol.

US corn ethanol production is a highly mechanised process, both in the fields, and in the subsequent processing of crops. Mechanised production processes consume a lot of energy to power the machinery used. In fact, so much fuel is used that net bio-fuel output per hectare is tiny. Most of the bio-fuel output has to be used as an input to enable the next round of production. The resulting *net* yield of fuel per hectare is very low and that means, in turn, that huge land areas would be needed to produce a meaningful net output.

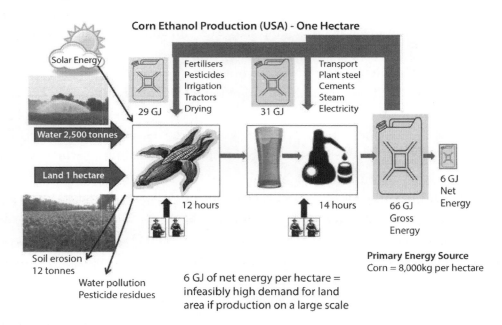

(Giampietro, Mayumi, & Sorman, 2013) Diagram redrawn and used with permission of Routledge/Taylor and Francis.

As can be seen with corn ethanol production, 60 GJ of fuel is needed to make 66 GJ of fuel on one hectare. So, a great deal of fuel is needed as inputs in fertilisers, pesticides, irrigation, tractors and drying and then in the processing of the corn into enthanol. With such a small net yield per hectare, a huge number of hectares would be needed to get a meaningful amount of ethanol.

In the case of Brazilian sugar cane ethanol, the production process is not highly mechanised and, as a result, it is possible to get a meaningful net supply of ethanol from a comparable area of land (i.e. one hectare). However, this is possible only through the employment of a huge amount of labour. The constraint in this case is the labour intensity of the process. In fact, figures given by Giampietro, Mayumi and Sorman, show 210 hours are needed for the cultivation of the sugar cane for every hectare and 90 hours of labour are then needed to convert the harvested cane into ethanol. Although it is possible to produce 117 Gigajoules of net energy from each hectare of land, this requires 300 labour hours. To expand the supply of ethanol under these production conditions, the high labour intensity requires that labour time is taken from other parts of the economy on a scale that is infeasible for anything except a small addition to production.

To conclude, biofuels are a granfalloon delusion because they require too much labour and/or too much land. For Italy to supply 30% of its transport fuel by biofuels without fossil fuel inputs, it would require an estimated 94% of the labour supply to work in agriculture and around 7 times the agricultural land in production according to Giampietro and Mayumi.

Biofuels do not increase energy security, they drive up food prices, and they drive up fuel prices. They also use a lot of land. Land use changes are known to increase carbon emissions because the carbon in the soil and forests is released to the air when the land is being prepared for production. So, when the land use changes associated with conversion to bio-fuels is taken into account, there is a net increase in carbon emissions. To make a bad situation even worse, bio-fuels use a huge amount of water. One third of global water withdrawals are now used to produce bio-fuels, enough water to feed the world according to Maude Barlow. (Barlow M. , 2012)

Yet biofuels are still vigorously promoted with the idea that these problems will be ironed out later, that they are just teething problems.

Climate policy being used as Trojan horses for corporate agendas

Economic ideology implies that businesses can be incentivised to more benign environmental practice. The reality is that there are plenty of examples of climate policy being taken over and used as "Trojan horses" for corporate policy agendas. This is the case, for example, with the so called "bio-economy" agenda of chemical/pharmaceutical, GM, seed and bio-tech corporations like Monsanto, Proctor and Gamble, Chevron and BASF.

Companies like these take over and use the "green economy" strategy to secure state sponsorship; public finance for R & D; support for intellectual property protection etc. For the corporations, this is less about saving the world from climate change and far more about gaining strategic control of value chains, specifically, in genetic and technical information and production processes and resources in energy, biomass, water and land. The aim of the techno-innovation is to concentrate power in their hands as humanity approaches the limits to growth.

If one has the eyes to see it, the bio-fuel example demonstrates nicely a point made by the authors of the ***Limits to Growth*** studies. They argued that if humanity finds a solution or an apparent solution, to lift or resolve one of the limits to growth, but tries to continue growing the economy, then it will soon hit other limits. The example shows - biofuels promoted by the corporations and co-opted governments are leading humanity into a land crisis, a soil erosion crisis, a water crisis and a food crisis. As the Limits to Growth authors say "In a complex, finite world, if you remove or raise one limit, and go on growing, you encounter another limit. Especially if the growth is exponential the next limit will show up surprisingly soon. There are layers of limits". (Meadows, D., Randers, J., & Meadows, D. 2005 p 222)

Putting more resources into problem solving
– carbon capture and storage

According to the original authors of the ***Limits to Growth*** study, the ultimate limit, the one that finally brings the system crashing down, is what they called "the ability to cope". In their model, the ability to cope runs out where there is no more industrial output that can be put to use producing new technical fixes for emerging problems. Eventually, it becomes clear that the technical solutions that seemed like a good idea never get much further than the drawing board or as prototypes.

At some point, it becomes obvious that a greater proportion of society's resources is being invested in remedial problem solving – taking up arms against a sea of troubles – rather than providing a service that the public actually wants. As society becomes more complex there comes a point where the compexity becomes too great. The society and its political and economic institutions can no longer cope with "stress surges" i.e. disease outbreaks; wars; breakdowns in critical infrastructure and institutions and harvest failures. It is not the "stress surges" on their own that are problems, but the crumbling ability of an over-complex management system, deploying a huge proportion of social resources, trying to find adequate responses to the stresses.

Carbon capture and storage is an example of a technology which uses up resources and energy, but brings no direct benefit to humanity while attempting to deal with the immense amount of CO_2 that comes out of current fossil fuel power stations. The idea is to devise technological processes that capture CO_2 after combustion of the fuels, the purification and liquefaction of the CO_2 and then arrangements to pump it to places where it can be injected underground into safe storage for, it is hoped, the next few thousands or millions of years.

There are a number of problems However,. 5% of the CO_2 emissions associated with a power station occur in the mining and transport leading up to the delivery of the fuel. Because CCS reduces the efficiency of the power station there will have to be a lot more mining and transport. Something like

30% more coal is thus, needed. When one takes that into account, the real reduction of CO2 may begin to look more like 78% of the CO2 (starting from an assumption of 88% capture at the power station itself). In addition, extra methane is released during the additional mining of the coal, so the greenhouse gas reduction, measured in CO2 equivalents, is more like 68%. (Fischedick, Esken, Luhmann, Schuewer, & Supersberger, 2007 p.22-23)

A further problem is leakage when the gas is underground. Leakage, in the case of gas wells, has already been explained in this text and carbon capture and storage also has potential to lead to a contamination of ground water. It would not necessarily happen in all places, but how much can we trust the companies given their record? (Little & Jackson, 2010)

Ironically, some of the places that the gas industry wants to deploy its recent technologies to extract "unconventional gas" are the most promising for carbon capture and storage but fracking would make this impossible. (Elliot & Celia, 2012)

Other peer reviewed scientific studies have concluded that the whole idea is impractical. One study, in the Journal of Petroleum Science and Engineering argues that:

> Published reports on the potential for sequestration fail to address the necessity of storing CO2 in a closed system. Our calculations suggest that the volume of liquid or supercritical CO2 to be disposed cannot exceed more than about 1% of pore space. This will require from 5 to 20 times more underground reservoir volume than has been envisioned by many, and it renders geologic sequestration of CO2 a profoundly non-feasible option for the management of CO2 emissions. (Ehlig-Economides & Economides, 2010)

A further problem is one of time scales. Even if CCS were possible on a large scale it would take several decades to roll out. But, given the urgency of the climate crisis, humanity does not have that amount of time.

Optimism bias

In point of fact, Carbon Capture and Storage is a good example of "optimism bias". This has been recognised as a problem in business planning by business studies experts, but it can be argued that it is a widespread problem in the culture of technology and engineering. Technical solutions to problems are put forward that, on closer inspection, would cost far too much to implement and take far too long to bring to fruition. A few years ago, we heard PR and media statements about impending carbon capture and storage projects as the coal power industry fought to re-create its future given the threat of climate change. However, from early in the hype about CCS more cautious experts were admitting that it would take at least 20 years to develop on a commercial scale, that would make a difference, and there is not that amount of time.

The fact innovation has become a hurrah activity to be celebrated does not help. Over and agaInst those who have been sceptical of technology and who are subject to the accusation of "Luddism", there is 'technicism' – an over-confidence that technology is chiefly a benefactor of society, that new or newer must be good and then better. To question techno-innovation can involve being critical of the people who promote it. For the techies it can be taken as a personal affront to their competence, to their implicit belief system and to their wallets.

In point of fact, there is a lot of literature about "optimism bias" in business. It is connected to an observation made by Daniel Kahneman – that people take decisions from what they know, and routinely fail to take into account that there is always more out there in the world to be sorted out, to cost money and to delay completion. Even some governments have been forced to recognise this tendency. Internal guidance notes by the UK Treasury advise officials as they appraise tenders for capital projects by engineering companies that:

> There is a demonstrated, systematic, tendency for project appraisers to be overly optimistic. To redress this tendency appraisers should make explicit, empirically based adjustments to the estimates of a project's costs, benefits, and duration...

"Nonstandard civil engineering" projects are typically 3% to 25% optimistic as regards duration. Projects of an "equipment and development" character have typical duration overruns between 10 – 54%. (HMTreasury, 2013)

There is also always more out there in the world to cause accidents, spills and disasters. There is plenty in the world that one might not notice, if one doesn't want to, that can render one's plans futile. That was why the precautionary principle was formulated. However, the precautionary principle is likely to be a personal insult to some brave innovator, perhaps threatening the already committed investment of time and money of some heroic entrepreneur and venture capitalist with friends in high places.

Extreme technology and technological hubris

Meanwhile, as humanity reaches the limits to economic growth, technology becomes more "extreme". More energy is deployed, more violently, on a bigger scale to extract energy and ores that are only available at lower and lower grades and thus, require the shifting of more and more rock. Deep sea drilling, or fracking for shale gas and oil are examples of a trend to taking on ever greater technological challenges with ever bigger risks. But, as we have seen, belief in technology has many of the characteristics of a religion. It is an integral part of modern culture. The idea that that human technical ingenuity might fail us is a challenge to a faith that few are prepared to contemplate.

It follows from the strength and intensity of this faith that when, eventually, it does fail, the disorientation, the sense of being lost, of being utterly unable to understand what is happening, in large parts of the population is likely to be profound. The contraction or crash after the limits to growth will not only be a period of economic difficulty or chaos, it will be a cultural or even a quasi-spiritual crisis.

Another God will have died and the disorientation in the political economic elite will probably be greatest of all.

Economics is a subject that tells us that rational people pursue their individual interests in conditions where they are well informed. In this book, I am challenging this idea and trying to create a more realistic understanding of people, with all their frailties, and the difficult and uncertain conditions in which they act. To conclude this chapter therefore, I want to consider technologists and the companies that they run or work for as ordinary human beings operating under conditions of uncertainty and conflicts of interest and see how that might give us a different view of current technological and economic trends.

I start with an assertion - it hurts to have one's professional competence challenged and it hurts even more to have to acknowledge that one is in error. I know, because I've had things pointed out to me that ought to have been in my area of expertise which I did not know. It will hurt even more if other people have been damaged by one's error. In these circumstances, perhaps one's job and one's status is at stake. When such personal risks are at stake, the ability to service one's own debts, the ability to pay for one's house and sustain relationships may all be put in jeopardy. The temptation not to acknowledge one's personal errors, or those of one's company or industry are going to be great in circumstances like these. Whole groups of upstanding people make mistakes and then dig themselves into deeper holes by elaborate conspiracies to cover up the truth, using their connections to do so. One has only to look at the way that large numbers of police contrived to cover up their errors at the Hillsborough Football disaster. In 1989, 96 Liverpool football fans died in a crush due to errors in crowd control, and the police conspired to direct the blame for this away from themselves onto the football fans.

There are a variety of collective and individual psychological manoeuvres that make it possible for people to live with the injury that they might impose on other people, or have already imposed on other people. If we follow the ideas of Adam Smith that moral behaviour comes about when people are able to empathise, and can see in another person's fate what might happen to them, then it is necessary to create a distance between oneself and the "other". To be able to live with what would, otherwise, be the worry of putting risks upon other people for one's own benefit. To see "the other" as an inferior whose feelings and needs can be dismissed will help. It will help too to see relationships with people and communities in strictly instrumental terms. They are "things" to be managed, technical problems not intrinsically different from engineering problems. The German philosopher Martin Heidegger reflected upon the philosophical roots of technology and viewed it as a process of conceptually "enframing" our understanding of "being". The mentality ends up "enframing" human beings as just another "standing stock", which are Heidegger's words for "human resources", or people conceived only as means to ends. (We are here to serve the economy, "cogs in the machine", rather than the other way round). (Heidegger, 1950)

One of the great insights that psychotherapists have uncovered in the 20th century is the way that our adult personalities are powerfully influenced by what emotional challenges we face as infants and children and the way that we manage these and come to understand them. As a massive generalisation we can say that if we are "made to feel small when we are small", if we are humiliated for our vulnerability, this will be reflected in our later adult thinking and behaviour. All the trappings of "being grown up", of being able to exercise the power and influence that as a child one did not have, will be extraordinarily important. Getting attention as a child only when one "performed" in the way expected by parents may be an unrecognised driver of adult people's behaviour too.

These may help us to recognise that the choice of a career path may reflect what has happened in earlier life. For small boys who have now grown up, engineering and technology might provide a variety of paths where they can immerse their attentions, emotions and energies manipulating complex things and abstract processes as an alternative to the bewildering, confusing and frustrating world of people, whose unpredictability and emotional responses are the sorts of thing that they had too much of as a child. People like this may have highly developed "hard skills" but poor "soft ones". The hard skills entail qualifications and experience with a high level of technical detail and expertise which in effect commit them to continue to follow a career in a field that is damaging to human society. Examples would be those engineers and ancillary professionals engaged in extracting more fossil fuels who do not deeply question the ethical implications of this, for that would entail questioning the purpose of their life.

From this point of view, the assertion by NGOs, civil society organisations and communities that proposed technological developments are a risk to them that they do not want to carry, might be considered, on the other hand, an affront to the technological competence of some of the engineers, a statement of the anti-scientific and emotional anti rationalism of tree huggers, fools and weirdos. The engineers and company managers might feel themselves to be the true grown-ups because they know what they are doing... thank you very much... and the people who confront them are just another irritating problem to be managed in meetings with other real grown-ups like policemen and politicians.

From this point of view, one can see why the managers of engineering and technological companies might routinely over estimate their own competence and routinely discount the problems and the costs of their endeavours.

Or perhaps not... one of the features of the oil and gas industry for a number of years now has been the dawning realisation that the work force is ageing and approaching retirement age. There is a shortage of young personnel to replace them – perhaps because young people are smart enough to be able to see that it is not in their best interests to join up to a declining industry. On this optimistic view, the current enthusiasm for shale gas and mega technologies is the final, yet very destructive, thrashing around of a dying industry, promoted by old men who are better off consigned to retirement. Smarter young people are trying to pioneer and develop smaller scale and local technologies that are more realistic in the times that we live in – the convivial technologies with ethical features that respect and match local communities and local ecological systems.

Chapter 35

Unconventional Gas as a Granfalloon – A Case Study in Hubris and Optimism Bias

The drive to develop unconventional gas sources illustrates multiple concepts developed in this book: the centrality of energy, the limits to economic growth; the interpenetration of economics and politics, the use of PR and deception by corporate actors. Technologies for "unconventional gas" extraction like shale gas fracking, coal seam gas de-watering and underground coal gasification are granfalloons pushed by a coalition of economic actors. The evidence is beginning to come in that the public health and environmental costs of these innovations will exceed their benefits.

The development of the unconventional gas industry is fascinating for the way that it so clearly and graphically reveals many of the themes of this book. If we want to understand how the economy works in the real world, then we need to understand the close integration of the political system and the economic system at the highest levels. In the case of the gas industry, reflecting the strategic importance of the energy sector to the economy. We need to understand how and why risk management at the highest levels takes second place as a priority to growth. We need to understand how appearances and information are managed and massaged to manipulate public perceptions and policy. We need to understand the way that public institutions are co-opted by industry and their staff compromised and undermined. We need to notice and trace out the vested interest coalitions and the power asymmetries in who has influence in government and who has not. All of these have been on display during the development of the unconventional gas industry. Above all, the development of this industry illustrates how hubris can occur in economic policy.

"Hubris" is not a word that you will read often in economic textbooks, but if economics is to describe the world as it is, rather than as we would like it to be, then hubris should be a key part of the concept framework. Derived from an ancient Greek word it means extreme pride or arrogance. Hubris often entails a loss of contact with reality, an overestimation of one's competence and capabilities and it is commonly found in people who are occupying positions of power... like, for example, the people managing the companies in the oil and gas industry, who have friends in government. As a "hub interdependency" in society, the management of oil and gas has become strategically vital for political and economic life and most of life's practicalities. That makes the managers of that industry very powerful in government too and they are used to getting their own way.

As a result, what we are seeing at the time of writing, when the oil and gas industry is faced with severe problems as a result of depletion and the onset of peak oil and gas, is not a reduction in their political power, but paradoxically, an increase. This is because governments and industry are seeking a way of maintaining "business as usual" through what they have been doing for the last two hundred years – developing new technologies.

These new technologies – given the generic term of "unconventional oil and gas" – are very much the "Granfalloon" du jour.

The Vested Interest Coalition

As already explained, granfalloons involve vested interest coalitions. Even though a granfalloon ultimately involves a futile agenda the members of the coalitions can certainly be sectional beneficiaries. So who are members of the unconventional gas granfalloon?

Firstly, obviously, there are companies from the oil and gas industry. This includes the exploration and development companies who look for, then extract the gas and sell it on. However, we should not assume that they are always the chief beneficiaries. There is a saying: "in a gold rush sell shovels". Whether there are hydrocarbons in the ground or not, the companies that sell or hire the equipment can make money. This means the directional drilling rigs, the pipelines, the installations that clean the gas prior to being sent on, the places where the gas is compressed to be pushed down the pipelines. What these companies need is not so much gas as the belief that there is gas, or that there is very likely to be gas. They thrive on confidence, on the famous "animal spirits" and, if they can convince governments to take the risks away from the industry, then they are onto a winner. In the USA, these are companies like Schlumberger, Halliburton and Baker Hughes who are able to make a lot of money as long as the capital keeps on flowing into the development of the gas fields.

This brings us to the finance sector which is also part of the granfalloon coalition. But what do they get out of it? First of all, the finance sector needs to believe that new technologies will always come to the rescue of the growth economy, otherwise the stability of the whole system is threatened. Unconventional Gas has played a role in keeping that faith alive. Secondly, the finance sector is needed to provide the money for the capital installations to keep the industry developing. Shale gas wells deplete very rapidly, so in the USA, 7,000 new wells are needed annually just to keep overall production stable. This requires a lot of money - $42 billion a year in capital investment in 2012 just to offset declines. However, when you take into account that the market value of all shale gas produced in 2012 was only $32.5 billion it does raise the question – how on earth is this process going to be profitable? (Rogers, 2013) At the beginning of 2014, quite a few exploration and development companies in the USA had been making losses and were forced to write down their capital. Towards the end of the same year recessionary conditions in the world economy was bringing down the oil and gas price and high cost producers of shale gas were concerned. Would they be able to service their debts? Would the junk bonds of the sector be re-classified as "distressed debt"? Would this distressed debt drag down the whole finance market?

The finance sector are part of the coalition but, if the gas boom is a bubble, many in it may not turn out to be beneficiaries at all. As explained elsewhere in this book, we can never know the future exactly but there will often be ways of constructing an optimistic view of it – as a bull rather than as a bear. For example, the losses of the shale gas industry in the USA can be interpreted as the result of the low gas price. However, if installations are constructed to export gas to elsewhere in the world where it will fetch a higher price, it is possible to believe that the current losses are only temporary. In the end, the most successful financial operators who are closest to the industry like to believe that, if they are investing in a bubble, they will realise when it is time to get out – selling the shares and assets to the last suckers who, taken in by the confidence to the last, then take the losses.

Other parts of the coalition are connected professions and institutions. There is work, prestige and political influence as long as the "unconventional gas" bandwagon stays on the road. Academic departments of petroleum engineering; geologists and their institutions; engineering consultancies and regulatory officials also earn a living and have their social standing from a prosperous oil and gas sector. If the oil and gas sector goes into decline, whether through depletion or through climate policies, these professions and organisations would have little future. They are not taking that prospect passively but actively working against it. For ancillary professions and institutions like these, unconventional gas has been a bonanza – not only in attention but also in research grants, government contracts and the like.

Both the oil and gas industry, and its supporting professions have been aided and abetted by governments desperate to keep energy flowing, partly as a source of tax revenues and partly to ensure the sources of cheap energy that are key to keeping the economy growing. Because the energy supply is a "hub interdependency" that has to be kept running, stabilised and even, if possible, growing, it is inevitable that all aspects of the energy sector should have a tight integration with governments.

Everywhere one looks in the world, either the state owns and controls the energy companies or the other way round. The relationship runs through multiple aspects of state policy. Where a huge amount of energy in all forms is traded internationally, there is not just a relationship between energy companies and energy departments of government, but between energy companies and foreign ministries too, not to mention military and security institutions. Close work and personal relationships are formed between the senior managers in the energy companies, the politicians, officials, and senior military and intelligence personnel. It is inevitable that the relationships often involve a "revolving door" between the companies and government. (Klare, 2008)

Wherever you look the evidence stares you in the face. The administration of George W. Bush was an administration rooted in the oil and gas industry. Dick Cheney, the Vice President, was the CEO of energy services company Halliburton and its various offshoots. In the UK, such was the tight relationship between BP and the British Cabinet Office under Tony Blair that, when George Brown, at that time the British Chancellor, was asked who the most powerful person in the UK was, he did not reply that it was his boss, Prime Minister Blair, his answer was Lord Browne, CEO at that time of BP. It was BP officials who drafted the proposals for the European Emissions Trading System which is supposed to be the basis of European climate policy. In Russia, there is a tight relationship between the energy sector, and in particular Gazprom and the government, run for most purposes by the FSB, the Russian secret services.

Economic textbooks that do not reflect these realities are irrelevant to understanding resource allocation in the real world. The political-economic elite is closely tied into carbon energy sources and banking and it has been aware of a developing crisis for some time. The elite have been aware of oil, gas and coal depletion and the rising energy costs. A report in the London Guardian in 2009 admitted that the International Energy Agency, which co-ordinates and researches the energy interests of the major oil importing economies, had seen a crisis coming but had not been saying so loudly in order not to frighten the financial markets. (Macalister, 2009)

This powerful group of people are well aware too that rising carbon emissions are a problem.

An apparent answer to the prayers of naive politicians

That is why, at first glance, shale gas, as well as methane extracted from coal seams, has appeared as an answer to the prayers of many of the politicians of energy importing countries.

If there is a crisis, the economists tell us, rising prices will bring forth new technologies to solve it. The truth is, however, that it has been state sponsorship that has paved the way for the development of this industry, far more than the market price. The preparedness of the elite to ignore the damage that will be done to communities and environments is also crucial to its success.

Over a number of years, the oil and gas industry has learned to do more sophisticated things than just drill downwards. They can drill horizontally along shale gas formations or along coal seams deep underground. Some busy politicians, who know a small amount about lots of things, but who have little time to explore any issue in depth, may have thought that what is called "unconventional gas" would be a new source of energy, the extraction of which could both reduce carbon emissions and solve the problem of rapidly depleting oil and gas wells. The gas industry had a lot of money at their disposal to fund publicity and lobbying and they have certainly influenced the US and UK governments around to this point of view. No doubt they were helped in this by the oil and gas connections of the previous administration of George W. Bush and Dick Cheney who were a lot savvier about the dirty reality.

In the space of a few years, after the 2006-2007 spike in energy prices, a glut of gas from these new sources in the USA brought natural gas prices down. The USA started to be regarded as the new Saudi Arabia. It has been claimed that the USA has enough natural gas to last another hundred years at current rates of use. Preparations are being made to liquefy it and sell shale gas for higher prices on world markets. And this energy source is supposed to be cleaner than coal too! A miracle had occurred. Obama was jubilant and politicians like David Cameron and George Osborne in the UK, cheered on by Lord Browne in his new role as shale gas promoter, wanted a part of the action by promoting unconventional gas in the UK too.

In this respect, the UK politicians were looking to get out of an increasingly difficult economic position brought about by the decline of oil and gas fields in the North Sea. A quick history of the UK's primary energy supply is that "peak coal" occurred in the UK about the time of the First World War and has been in decline ever since – though the Thatcher government accelerated that decline. What made the Thatcher policies possible was that, from the 1970s, an economic bonanza from North Sea oil and gas helped turn the UK economy around. It gave sterling the status of a petro-currency. It brought in plenty of tax revenues too. It was this development, not the supposed policy success for Margaret Thatcher, which temporarily arrested the economic decline of the UK. But the North Sea peaked in about the year 2000 and the decline since then has been steep. The push for unconventional gas in the UK has been about giving the oil and gas industry a future by developing it onshore – instead of government policy acknowledging the long run trend to depletion and therefore seeing a need for a fundamentally different economy and way of living.

The Technologies

There are in fact not one but three "unconventional gas" technologies. They are:

- Shale Gas fracking
- Coal bed methane (coal seam gas) involving the "de-watering" of coal seams.
- Underground coal gasification

As regards the first of these, shale gas, it should be explained that shale is an impermeable rock and the gas which cannot be extracted without effort. It has to be explosively fractured, the fractures "propped open" (with sand) in order to allow the gas to escape back up to the wellhead with the flow back water. The water used per frack per well is the equivalent of about 3 to 5 Olympic swimming pools of water laced with toxic chemicals with a variety of functions in the fracking process. For example, one chemical is there to "lubricate the water" so that it slips down the narrow pipe with less friction as it is pumped underground at pressures as much as 15,000 pounds per square inch. The pressure will be supplied by perhaps ten 1,000 horse power pumps. Of all the water being forced underground, 25 to 75% will be returned to the surface, the rest will remain underground. The gas will then be separated out from the produced water that comes to the surface.

"Virgin coal bed methane" or "coal seam gas" as it is called in Australia is another technology. Methane is held in place in cleats (small fractures) in the coal which is saturated by water deep underground. By "de-watering" the coal seam through pumps, the pressure holding the methane in place is released and the methane flows out with the water. This process sometimes involves fracking but, at time of writing, more usually does not.

The underground gasification of coal is yet another process. A cavity is created along a coal seam by direction drilling which is connected to the surface by bore holes at both ends. The coal is ignited and air and water to control the process is pumped down at one end while, at the other end, gases that have resulted from the partial burning process are taken out of the ground. The partial combustion process creates synthesis gas not unlike the old town gas. It contains carbon monoxide, hydrogen, methane as well as CO_2 - a mixture that can be burned, for example, to drive electrical power generation.

The harms of shale and coal seam gas

There are a considerable number of serious risks and harms. However, it is communities and the environment that pick up the costs while the benefits, in the form of revenue and profit streams, are picked up by people elsewhere.

Unconventional gas is spatially extensive. Well pads, a network of connecting pipelines, compressor stations and cleaning installations industrialise, fragment and change huge areas. When a company called Dart applied to develop coal bed methane in Falkirk in Scotland, the result was that the land take for pipelines was 4.5 times that for the well pads. All this is not easily compatible with other land uses – whether agricultural, leisure, nature reserves, or residential.

There is, for example, evidence from peer reviewed studies that farm animals are made sick by the unconventional gas fields. One study, based on interviews with animal owners living near gas wells in 6 states in the USA "strongly implicates exposure to gas drilling operations in serious health effects on humans, companion animals, livestock, horses and wildlife". (Bamberger & Oswald, 2012)

One of many reasons for a clash with residential and agricultural uses for land is the sheer volume of heavy vehicle movements. A figure of 17 - 51 HGV movements a day per well pad over a 73 - 145 week period is repeated several times in an environmental assessment by consultants commissioned by the UK government. The higher number is more likely when water has to be taken to the well by road and the produced water taken away by road too. It should also be taken into account that a gas field is likely to have many well pads close to each other. (AMEC Environment and Infrastructure UK Ltd, 2013)

There is a lot of noise, activity and light 24/7/52 with exhaust fumes from pumps, installations and heavy goods vehicles. "Fugitive natural gas emissions" are another problem. There is a great deal of methane leakage during and after the process, as well as flaring and venting from compressors and cleaning stations. All of these create characteristic "gas field haze" and a marked reduction in air quality, life quality and an increase in ill health. The Associated Press recently reported that Wyoming's air quality is worse than Los Angeles' due to gas development. (Gruver, 2011).

Scientific studies show that gas field air pollution is associated with acute and long term health problems for people living nearby. A peer reviewed study by the University of Colorado found that local residents were exposed to trimethyl benzenes, aliaphatic hydrocarbons, and xylenes, all of which have neurological and/or respiratory effects. The effects included eye irritation, headaches, sore throat and difficulty breathing.

> We also calculated higher cancer risks for residents living nearer to the wells as compared to those residing further [away]... Benzene is the major contributor to lifetime excess cancer risk from both scenarios. (University of Colorado, 2012)

Fugitive methane emissions

A great deal of academic literature now exists about the leakage of methane and other gases. This occurs through improperly sealed bore holes, from faulty equipment and during transport, or simply from fissures and faults so that the gas comes out of the ground away from the wellhead.

It also occurs through venting. During drilling, flow-back, and after each stage of fracking, when capture of the gas is not yet possible, the gas is either vented or flared. Drillers often hit pockets of shallow methane which flows directly into the well. This early methane also must also be vented or flared. (Howarth, Santoro, & Ingraffea, 2011)

The industry has been quick to attack these findings claiming that methane found, for example, in local water supplies or observed bubbling up in rivers or in the air, is "naturally occurring". The idea is that it was there already but was previously not noticed. However, academic research in Australia (in coal seam gas fields) and in the USA suggest otherwise. The evidence is that methane concentrations are higher nearer gas wells and less when more distant. This is true for water borne contamination (Osborne, 2011) and also for air borne contamination (Tait, Santos, & Maher, 2013) (Thompson, 2012) (Tait D. R., Santos, Maher, Cyrnonak, & Davis, 2013)

There is now an increasing literature about why gas wells leak (water, chemicals and gas). The oil and gas industry have wrestled with leaking wells since the very beginning of the industry. (Dusseault, Gray, & Nawrocki, 2000) (Ingraffea, 2013). A global study of leaking oil and gas wells in the journal *Marine and Petroleum Geology* found that "The percentage of wells that have some form of well barrier or integrity failure is highly variable (1.9% to 75%)".

Of specific relevance to UG are statistics for gas fields in Pennsylvania:

> Of the 8030 wells targeting the Marcellus shale inspected in Pennsylvania between 2005 and 2013, 6.3% of these have been reported by the authorities for infringements related to well barrier or integrity failure. In a separate study of 3533 Pennsylvanian wells monitored between 2008 and 2011 there were 85 examples of cement or casing failures, 4 blow outs and 2 examples of gas venting. (Davies, 2014)

If you take the smaller figures for failure rates there might at first sight seem to be little cause for concern. A 1.9% failure rate seems like a low risk. However, a gas field is likely to have hundreds or even thousands of wells. So even a small gas field is highly likely to have some failure where the health and environmental effects can be very serious. To make this situation worse, the number of oil and gas wells that leak increases over time, including when the gas fields are no longer in use.

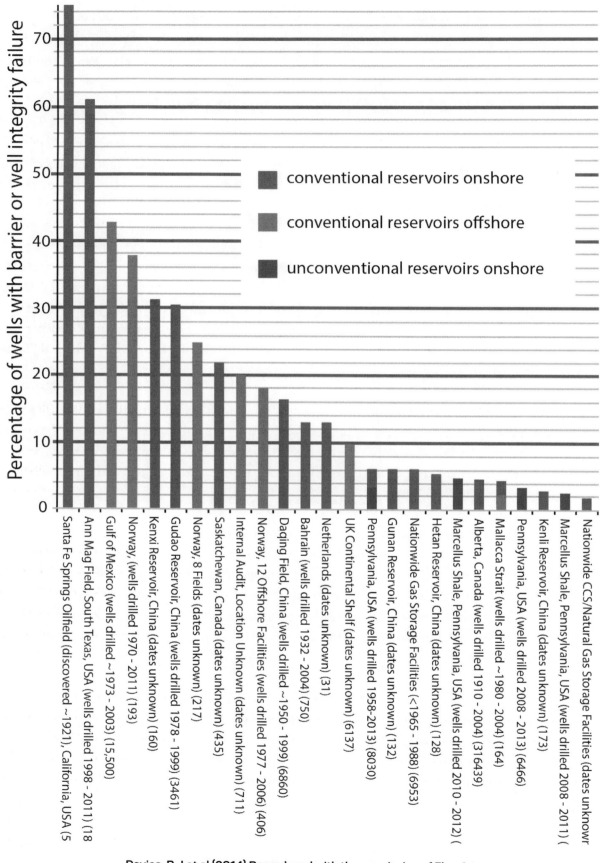

Davies, R J et al (2014) Reproduced with the permission of Elsevier.

The rate at which methane leaks is absolutely crucial to the greenhouse gas implications of the unconventional gas industry. It is sometimes claimed that, because natural gas, when burned, gives rise to less CO2 than the combustion of coal, that natural gas is climate friendlier. This is an argument often put forward by the industry to promote the production of shale gas. The argument neglects the following However,. Firstly, methane is a much more powerful greenhouse gas than CO2 (100 times worse over a 20 year time span) so the existence of fugitive emissions from leaking gas wells and pipelines may make it more greenhouse damaging than coal depending on the rate of leakage. Estimates of typical rates of leakage and the effects vary. According to the US Environmental Protection Agency, the average rate of leakage is about 2.4% per annum. Many experts believe it is much more than this. For example, Howarth, Santoro and Ingraffea of Cornell University estimate it at 8% pa (Howarth, Santoro, & Ingraffea, 2011) Tom Wigley found that unless leakage rates could be kept below 2% substituting gas for coal is not an effective way of reducing greenhouse gas emissions. (Wigley, October 2011, Vol 108 (3))

A crucial finding here is that measurements of leakage from gas installations, the so called "inventory measures" are much smaller than findings taken by flying planes over gas fields. "NOAA researchers found in 2012 that natural-gas producers in the Denver area "**are losing about 4% of their gas to the atmosphere** — not including additional losses in the pipeline and distribution system." In another 2013 study, 19 researchers led by the NOAA concluded "Measurements show that on one February day in the Uinta Basin, the natural gas field leaked 6 to 12 percent of the methane produced, on average, on February days." The Uinta Basin is of special interest because it "produces about 1 percent of total U.S. natural gas" and fracking has increased there over the past decade." (Sweeney & et.al., 2013)

In response to these studies, defenders of the oil and gas industry have challenged the higher leakage rates with a study of their own produced by academics at the University of Texas. This study claims a very low figure of 0.42% leakage of gross annual natural gas production. (Allen et al., 2013)

Other academics have cried "foul" on that study since the gas industry self-selected whether they wanted to be in it or not – so it is to be expected that it was the companies and sites that have a low leakage that were prepared to come forward in what is also a very small sample. The Texas study has also been criticised because it does not mention gas leakage in infrastructures. Nor do the authors discuss the discrepancy between their findings and those of the researchers who took field measurements. (Shonkoff, 2013)

Secondly, even if it were the case that gas was more climate friendly than coal, it would only be helpful in reducing greenhouse gas emissions sufficiently if gas actually replaced coal and is not used additionally to coal. In the USA, increased natural gas production has led to some coal being exported instead of being used domestically. A part of this has been to the UK where low coal prices have led to UK power generators using more coal. The carbon intensity of UK power generation rose in 2013 because of this.

Thirdly, to avert a climate catastrophe the International Panel on Climate Change is arguing for a carbon budget to prevent global temperature rises overshooting a 2 degree increase. This means, effectively, a 6% per annum reduction in emissions for the next few decades. For this speed to be achieved, it is not only necessary to radically reduce energy use but to transform the energy system directly over to renewables, not to go through some intermediate process via an allegedly slightly more benign fossil fuel. According to research led by the Grantham Research Institute (under the leadership of Lord Nicholas Stern):

Between 60-80% of coal, oil and gas reserves of publicly listed companies are already "unburnable" if the world is to have a chance of not exceeding global warming of 2°C. (Carbon TrackerInitiative and Grantham Research Institute, 2013)

Since methane is a combustible gas there are fire and explosion risks. There are many examples of explosions and fires at wells, in compressor stations and during transport. It even includes several cases of exploding trains. One derailment in Quebec killed 47 people. Accidents involving ruptures and leaks of equipment are common, as are heavy truck crashes. The fatality rate among oil and gas workers in the United States is more than 8 times the all-industry fatality rate. (Lohan, 2014)

Contaminated Water

This draws attention to many contaminated water leaks and spills. The industry is keen to point out that fracking occurs a long distance below aquifers and sources of drinking water. It claims that, because of this distance, water contamination is most unlikely. However, much contamination occurs from water that is brought to the surface *after* fracking in leaks and spills, or, if we describing coal bed methane de-watering, with the produced water that is the result of the de-watering process.

Gross and associates have demonstrated that surface spills or leakage into the shallow water formations is a critical event and could account for most water quality issues associated with hydraulic fracturing. Chemicals can potentially leach into groundwater through failures in the lining of ponds or containment systems most of which are constructed near the well sites to temporarily hold flowback/produced water. Between 2009 and 2010, of the 4,000 permitted oil and natural gas wells in Marcellus Shale in Pennsylvania, there were 630 reported environmental health and safety violations of which half were associated with leaks and spills of the flowback/produced fluids. (About 8% of the wells). (Chen, Al-Wadei, Kennedy, & Terry, 2014)

Various chemicals are mixed into water to create fracking fluid depending on operating conditions. Many of the chemicals used in the USA, Australia and Canada are carcinogens known to cause liver and/or kidney failure; are irritants, cause birth defects and affect the respiratory system. (Kassotis, Tilitt, Davis, Hormann, & Nagel, 2013) (Conoco-Phillips Canada Resources Corporation, March 2013) (BC Oil and Gas Commission, 2013)

An issue that has received less attention are the toxic chemicals used immediately prior to the injection of fracking fluid. Shortly before the water is pumped down, explosive charges are used to punch holes through the well pipes and into the surrounding rock formations. A patent filed by Halliburton, which is available on the net, proposes the use of unstable compounds of heavy metal mixed with an oxidiser. This means that substantially all of it will be oxidised and atomised in an explosion as the rock is penetrated and fractured. If a perforation gun like this was used, then oxidised and atomised heavy metal particles will be washed into the fracking fluid and presumably a large part will come back up to the surface in the flowback. The heavy metals listed as possible for use include zinc, aluminium, bismuth, tin, calcium, cerium, cesium, hafnium, iridium, lead, lithium, palladium, potassium, sodium, magnesium, titanium, zirconium, cobalt, chromium, iron, nickel, tantalum, and depleted uranium. (Barlow, Le, & Barker, 2009) Many of these would have serious health effects if they get into aquifers or into the water supplies via spills or by well leakage.

One material in particular stands out in this list because it is very hard and very cheap. Depleted Uranium is a waste product of the nuclear industry. That industry is always on the look-out for some way of putting it to use and some way of selling it. Most uses so far have been military ones i.e. for hardening shells so they can penetrate concrete bunkers or the metal armour protecting tanks. There is a growing literature that suggests that acute or chronic exposure to DU dust has serious health consequences. Watch this space...

As important, are the toxic chemicals that come to the surface from the rocks that have been fracked. They would have no control over this and, on the basis of previous experience are likely to include BTEX – Benzene, Toluene, Ethyl- Benzene and Xylene – all of which are highly toxic and carcinogenic. (Chen, Al-Wadei, Kennedy, & Terry, 2014)

Surface water management is a particular problem of coal bed methane extraction because the process of extracting methane involves de-watering the coal seam. The extraction of large volumes of groundwater to de-pressurise the coal seams may reduce the water resources in connected surface and groundwater systems and flows as water is drawn down into the areas that are being pumped out. Taking water from the coal seam may also lead to subsidence which may also affect surface-water systems. (Williams, Stubbs, & Milligan, 2012, pp. 42-55)

If large volumes of water, including treated wastewater, are released to surface-water systems they are likely to alter natural flow patterns and water quality of rivers and wetlands. Injection of extracted water or treated wastewater into other aquifers has the potential to reduce the beneficial use characteristic to these aquifers. (Williams, Stubbs, & Milligan, 2012)

Injection can also cause increased seismic activity. One of Oklahoma's biggest man-made earthquakes, caused by fracking-linked wastewater injection, triggered an earthquake cascade that led to the damaging magnitude-5.7 Prague quake that struck in November 2011. Many of the quakes triggered by unconventional gas activities are very small, but they can have serious consequences if they damage the wellbore and lead to a well leaking contaminated water and/or gas. (Oskin, 2014) In mining areas, subsidence may already make potential fracking areas seismically unstable.

A crucial assumption of those who argue that these processes are safe is that there is no connection between where the coal seam is being de-watered and other water systems underground. However, not only are their naturally occurring faults, but in many cases, there are one or two centuries of old mine workings in coal areas, which have been long abandoned and which create that connection. Very often, the underground mine workings are not well documented as they are very old.

Reductions in the quality of life become reflected in falling house prices. As explained in another chapter, if an area becomes less desirable, people are prepared to pay less to live there so property prices fall. This deprives people of the resources that they would need to move if they have to sell their houses to be able to buy somewhere else. (Insley, 2012) The only compensation is that a transient oil and gas workforce moving into some areas need accommodation too, so some short term rents may rise. However, a transient workforce has no commitment to an area, no relationships there and the costs of local policing may rise too. (This remark applies in the USA, Canada and Australia. In the UK, it is likely that since the country is relatively small, if the industry develops, then many oil and gas industry workers will commute a relatively short distance to the gas fields while living in the nearest city).

Underground Coal Gasification

The potential harms of the underground coal gasification require treatment all of their own. Partly because they are, if anything, even more extreme, and partly because they exemplify the well-known adage that insanity is to repeat the same mistakes over and again and expect a different result.

The idea for UCG has been around since 1868 and was, indeed, championed by Lenin in the Soviet Union. It has been tried repeatedly but each time abandoned, usually because of environmental pollution and public safety issues. No doubt, the champions of UCG feel the reasons that UCG has never been widely adopted was always the problem of creating a passage along a coal seam through which the partial combustion process could take place without all the capital and work that is involved in full scale mining. Now that the oil and gas industry has developed directional drilling, this technical problem has been removed. However, the more serious problems are the health, safety and environmental ones and these have not been solved by a long way. Unfortunately, the danger to other people's health is not the first thing on the minds of fossil fuel companies. The dangers revealed in repeated failures of this approach have not permanently warned off adventurous engineers – making this a case of technological hubris. No doubt, there is something in human psychology that wants to pull something off that no one else has succeeded in doing. But it is more than a little unfortunate when the health and well-being of communities, and indeed the whole planet, is put at risk by a drive for engineering glory.

A history of repeated failure is not usually a promising start for any industrial development but higher and higher energy prices, as well as the relentless decline of conventional coal mining, have kept the engineering dream alive. This is connected to the coal industry's attempt to secure a new future - climate change or no climate change. The capital and careers invested in the coal industry just will not give up, which means that each failure is seen as part of a learning process, subjected to PR treatment with the aim of getting continued research funding and state support for the next attempt.

The earliest experiments with UCG started in the Soviet Union in Angren, not far from Tashkent, Usbekistan in the 1930s. This is the only place in the world where UCG has been operated over a substantial period of time. Usbekistan is the third worst country in the world for its environmental record according to an index produced by Yale and Colombia Universities. There is no environmental monitoring there and official health data is restricted. The effect of UCG on the population is therefore not known, but anecdotal reports from local doctors suggest that cancers and respiratory problems are very common. (IWPR, 2012)

Apart from Usbekistan, there have been sporadic trials in the USA, in Australia, in Belgium, Spain and the UK. This experience suggests that UCG processes are difficult to control underground, can be unstable and can easily run out of control. The partial burn can create a cavity that collapses creating subsidence above. Large volumes of carbon monoxide are dangerous if they come to the surface in an uncontrolled way. The heat and the pressure caused by the partial burn process is a force tending to spread the pollution. Highly contaminated water containing BTEX is produced by the partial combustion process that comes to the surface with the syngas and pollutants. Of three recent test projects in Australia, two have been shut down following toxic compounds being released into the biosphere. (Rowling, 2010) (Sustainability Support, 2010). Of 30 trials in the USA, 2 released contaminants – a fact reported by researchers as if that was a good result – although it does not seem likely that this would be a chance that nearby communities would want to take. (Burton, Friedman, & Upadhye).

Perhaps the most serious of the possible problems associated with UCG would be if fires started underground could be extinguished. In the areas where UCG is likely to be tried there are also likely to be underground coal mine workings. The British Isles are littered with underground mine workings and natural faults. If a supply of oxygen through uncontrolled sources like old mine workings reaches the combustion process, which is supposed to be partial, the coal seam could catch fire and burn indefinitely.

Coal seam fires are not uncommon around the world. They release toxic fumes at the surface; can ignite grass and brush or create forest fires; cause subsidence under surface infrastructure like roads, pipelines, electric lines, bridge supports, buildings and homes. They have been known to burn for decades, even centuries, are extremely costly and difficult to extinguish and are unlikely to be suppressed by rain. Whole settlements have had to be abandoned because of such fires in the vicinity. Global coal fire emissions are estimated to include 40 tons of mercury going into the atmosphere annually, and make up three percent of the world's annual CO_2 emissions (Coal Seam Fires, 2014)

Also disastrous, is that UCG potentially expands the reserves of exploitable coal by a factor of 5 – an extra 4 trillion tonnes. If all of that were burned, it would emit 15 trillion tonnes of CO2 into the atmosphere to give 2000ppm – with the safe upper level being, perhaps at most 350ppm. (House, 2010)

Chapter 36

Regulation = Permission: The Precautionary Principle Betrayed

It is unlikely that regulation will make technologies for unconventional gas extraction safe. The development of unconventional gas appears to be comparable to a number of industries and products where early warnings about public health and/or environmental dangers were downplayed because the industry had powerful allies in government

In the face of the overwhelming evidence of the harms, or if you like the costs, of unconventional gas, the development of this industry is a useful case study to contrast the real world with the textbook fantasy world.

For a start there are, as far as I am aware, no examples of governments or industries trying to apply a Kaldor-Hicks compensation test to unconventional gas development. On first appearance you would think that this is an ideal opportunity to try the idea. Here you have economic activities in which one group of people are the beneficiaries and another group of people are the losers. So why does the government not supervise a process to ascertain whether the loss to the losers could be fully compensated out of the gains to the winners in order to make sure, with all the externalities, that there is a net benefit to society?

I ask "tongue in cheek" and it wouldn't happen. For a start, most governments are more closely allied with the fossil fuel industry than with its victims. Even if they were more even-handed, they could not possibly organise a public process to find out what is the appropriate level of monetary compensation for the harms of unconventional gas and then *not* ensure that this compensation was actually paid. (It will be remembered that the K-H test says that total social well-being is increased if winners can compensate losers satisfactorily and still be better off - but that they don't actually have to pay the compensation. However, in the real world, if they did not actually pay the compensation, the losers would be more than a little upset. In the real world social injustice causes powerful "disutility" – a theoretical point that Kaldor Hicks ignores.)

I suppose this could be solved by setting up the policy process on a "willingness to pay" basis. Economists could be employed to ask the victims of the unconventional gas industry what they are willing to pay not to be polluted in order to prevent their health and quality of life being ruined. But how many economists would be brave enough to do that? They might be able to do research about how much people are prepared to pay to save endangered species, but not how much they will pay to keep the gas industry out of their neighbourhood. A "willingness to accept" exercise would be more palatable to the victims but might open up a can of worms. Communities would probably want such a large sum of money that it would prevent the industry going ahead anyway.

Of course, it all rather depends on what stage of the process such an exercise take place. The history of unconventional gas so far shows that it gains initial acceptance only because of a huge information asymmetry where residents only realise after the event, when the industry is established and in operation, that their life has become a hell. By this late stage, their bargaining power has already collapsed and they are more or less prepared to accept anything in order to get out. For the industry, therefore, it is important to manage the PR very carefully into disguising or hiding the future impact, by massaging appearances, giving out misleading messages and old fashioned lies. A great deal of effort goes into trying to prevent people living in affected communities from making "rational choices".

The issue at stake with unconventional gas is whether it makes sense as a collective process, taking into account all its effects upon all the affected stakeholders including the wider environment and future generations. However, the asymmetry of power among the stakeholders and the concentration of benefits upon the pro-lobby is what makes government and industry so "gung ho" – because it will be at other people's expense. It is what makes this a granfalloon. In a situation like this, one group, the pessimists (and realists), want to assert the pre-cautionary principle, while another, the industry and its allies, are under the influence of what psychologists call "optimism bias".

Optimism bias is considered in an earlier chapter but to state briefly here, it is an observed tendency to think that business and other plans will turn out better than they actually do. It not only applies to the projected cost outcome of activities which are commonly under-estimated, and the time it will take to achieve them which are underestimated too, but also to the health and safety and environmental risks. These risks too are underestimated. It will be recalled how, as Daniel Kahneman puts it, people tend to take decisions on what they know and what they know is always less than what there is. Since the world is always more complicated, since the geology in each place is always different, since operating conditions, staff, institutional arrangements and other things vary, the variety regularly produces surprises and sometimes very unpleasant surprises. This is called Murphy's Law – if something can go wrong, then it probably will do.

There is also always more out there in the world to cause accidents, spills and disasters – but government at the highest level doesn't want to acknowledge that. That was why the precautionary principle was formulated. However, the precautionary principle is a personal insult to brave innovators, and it threatens the already committed investment of time and money of heroic entrepreneurs and venture capitalists with friends in high places.

One way of understanding hubris is that it is a particular example of **"optimism bias"** which comes about when people have got used to having it their way, when they have had a lot of personal luck and good fortune that they assume as a norm, and when they are shielded from personal costs by their resources and connections. The late David Fleming describes the experience and thinking of some senior decision-makers when he wrote about the "Survivors Fallacy"

The fallacy that the experience of survivors is relevant to that of non survivors. The most obvious example is the case of smoking; lifelong smokers who assert that smoking did them no harm, and therefore could not harm anyone else either, bias the argument because those for whom smoking was lethal are not around to put their side of the case. (Fleming, 2004)

It is this kind of situation that predisposes fortunate people, who have made it up the hierarchies of power, to lack the caution that ordinary people learn in the school of hard knocks. Fortunate people tend to be complacent. They do not get the idea of a precautionary principle because they have never been kicked in the face by real life when it is at its most vicious. The economist's idea that people are rational agents lacks this sense that different people's rationality will vary widely according to previous experience. Very often, the "rationality" of senior decision-makers lacks the key dimension of pre-caution because they have never learned to need it. A privileged background makes one highly unqualified to exercise power in troubled times. An easy rise to power is likely to leave one with insufficient experience of misfortune – ask the members of the Bullingdon Club.

In these circumstances, what is actually happening is *not* that the individuals who make government decisions are designing policies to adjust the market to reflect the "externalities" of the oil and gas industry – but the very reverse. Governments are going out of their way to incentivise the development of the industry by taking as many of the risks off the industry as they can, and loading them onto communities instead. At the same time they are keen to give the reassuring appearance that the government is acting to protect the public and thus, to disarm rational community resistance. They are two faced. They speak with forked tongue – which is not to say that the kind of characters that end up governing us are self-aware enough to notice that this is what they are doing.

Given the huge amount of information that is now available from the USA and from Australia in particular, it is now very difficult to hide how destructive the industry is. The British government acknowledges the potential harms of unconventional gas because it can do very little else. There is just too much evidence out there on the internet. Thus, to gain acceptability of the industry, they claim that regulation in Britain is more stringent than in other countries and that it is possible to prevent the negative impacts. They do not argue that unconventional gas is safe – they argue that it can be made safe.

However, over a century of health and safety regulation in the UK and in other countries gives no ground for confidence. On the contrary, in the UK, just as in many other countries, there has been repeated shameful disregard for public health and the environment. Industrial and commercial interests have repeatedly overridden the right of the public to be protected. Thus, with unconventional gas we have the beginning of the replay of a tragedy that has already happened many times in different forms – potentially on a more destructive scale than ever.

Late Lessons from Early Warnings

A good place to review what really happens under the regulatory regimes both in the UK and elsewhere is a 200 page peer reviewed study by 20 authors and an editorial team of 5 people published by European Environment Agency in 2001. The study is titled "Late Lessons from Early Warning – the precautionary principle 1896 – 2000" - hereafter called the PP study. (Gee, Vaz, eds. et al., 2002)

This study draws on European and US experience to explore what lessons can be drawn from catastrophes like acid rain, BSE, asbestos, benzene, halocarbons and the ozone layer, hormones as growth promoters and so on. In each case, there were early warnings of threats to the environment and public health – but in each case there was a long delay before an adequate response was taken.

Why? The histories of a great deal of suffering and destruction that continued longer than they should have done give us warnings about what is now likely to happen in regard to fracking unless communities act to protect themselves independently of government. (Or unless a collapse in the oil price undermines the fledgling industry).

Here is an example – asbestos. As early as 1898 there were strong grounds for suspecting that white asbestos was a serious hazard – and some UK Factory Inspectors said so. It was not until 100 years later, in 1998 that it was banned in the UK. Was this a triumph for British health and safety regulation?

Why the repeated history of delay? Lessons written up in the PP study bear ominous similarities to the rush to defend unconventional gas as "safe if well regulated".

Firstly, what often happens is that those making the risk assessment assume that the technologies, their protective measures and their regulatory arrangements will happen as they are supposed to happen. Technologies will perform to the specified standards. People will keep to the rules, the equipment will work as it is supposed to. The gap between theory and real life is not taken into account here. As the PP study makes clear this is one more example of ***"optimism bias"***:

> ... real life practices can be far from ideal; and it may be a long time before we realise that this is the case. Sometimes actions are taken that appear to be in defiance of prior experience. The leakage from petrol station storage tanks was underestimated in the US regulatory appraisal of MTBE and so led to an underestimation of the resulting exposures. Although storage tanks can be redesigned to reduce the chance of leakage, this benefit can be lost by incorrect installation. (Gee, Vaz, & al., 2002)

Risks that can be reduced in theory nevertheless occur regularly

As regards unconventional gas (UG), the United Nations Environment Programme, therefore, has a much more realistic view of things when, in a briefing about UG written by Pascal Peduzzi and Ruth Harding, it says:

Even if risk can be reduced theoretically, in practise many accidents from leaky or malfunctioning equipment as well as from bad practises are regularly occurring. This may be due to high pressure to lower the costs or to improper staff training, or to undetected leaks leading to contamination of the ground water. (Peduzzi & Harding, 2012)

A peer reviewed editorial in the *British Medical Journal* makes a similar point. It was written and published in April 2014 in response to a report on the public health implications of shale gas by Public Health England, an agency of the British government. The PHE report declares that in Britain it will all be different because of regulation that will impose best engineering practice and that fracking can be made safe. The BMJ editorial disagrees. It is subtitled "Mistaking Best Practices for Actual Practices" and in it the BMJ authors write:

> A focus on mostly hypothetical regulatory and engineering solutions may mistake best practices for actual practices, and supplants the empirical with the theoretical. (Law, Hays, Shonkoff, & Finkel, 2014, p. 8)

The UNEP authors and those who were writing for the BMJ live in the real world. By contrast, the authors of a report written for the British government by AMEC, a firm of engineering consultants, live and write in "Spin World". In order that the UK government can fulfil its obligations to the European Union, they have to do a "Strategic Environment Assessment" about the development of UG in the UK. AMEC was commissioned to draft this report. (AMEC Environment and Infrastructure UK Limited, 2013)

The AMEC report authors do not deny the problems of unconventional gas fields and refer to issues with water, public health, land use, air quality, visual amenity, soil conservation, biodiversity, disturbance to communities, traffic, noise and light pollution. Yet over and again in relation to these problems, the report uses the same phrases: "it is expected", "it is anticipated", it is assumed", "it can be expected"... that planning controls and regulation will mitigate or resolve the problem sufficiently so that the situation is "not unacceptable".

Unlike the UNEP report that assumes that if things can go wrong they will go wrong, AMEC writes a litany of phrases like "It is assumed that current controls are enforced by regulators and followed by operators" and "assuming (the use of) the best available technology".

Yet what was found by PP study was that very often there was a big gap between the regulations and regulatory compliance. For example, there was, and has been, a large amount of illegal disposal of PCBs and, in the UK, unrealistically optimistic assumptions were made about implementation of changes to UK slaughterhouse practices as a crucial part of the response to the BSE crisis. (Gee, Vaz, & al., 2002)

We know from the UK already what happens when a fracking company is trying to cut costs and has friends in high places. The film "The Truth about the Dash for Gas" makes the point that exploratory drilling by Cuadrilla unleashed an earthquake that was 2.3 on the Richter scale. This damaged the bore hole with potentially serious consequences for ground water. Despite this, Cuadrilla did not tell the Environment Agency for 6 months. (Jackson, 2014)

Another incident in the film about fracking in the UK explains how Cuadrilla disposed of "naturally occurring radioactive water" that had come back up the frack well by putting it through a sewerage works that was not equipped to deal with radioactivity. (No sewerage works are equipped to deal with radioactivity). (Jackson, 2014)

The failure to maintain regulatory independence – foxes in charge of the hen house

One of the key lessons from the PP study is to "maintain regulatory independence from economic and political special interests". As it says:

> There is evidence in the case studies that interested parties are often able to unduly influence regulators. As a result decisions that might reasonably have been made on the basis of the available evidence were not taken. Benzene was demonstrated to be a powerful bone marrow poison in 1897; the potential for acute respiratory effects of asbestos was first identified in 1898; and the first cases of PCB-induced chloracne were documented in 1899, with effects on workers known by the late 1930s. Yet it was not until the 1960s and 1970s that significant progress began to be made in restricting the damage caused by these agents. One factor in the slow UK response to BSE was that the governmental regulatory body was responsible first to the industry and only second to consumers. (Gee, Vaz, & al., 2002)

In the case of unconventional gas, there is nothing like "regulatory independence" from economic and political special interests". On the contrary, the government has allowed the oil and gas industry to write the regulations and the policy.

The role of Lord Browne is particularly central. He is a former CEO of BP, a former non-executive director of Goldman Sachs and is currently (Feb 2014) head and major shareholder of the fracking Company Cuadrilla. No one has cast a single vote for this man in an election and yet he has been appointed to the Cabinet Office to advance the unconventional gas agenda.

Lord Browne has a long track record of steering British politics from behind the scenes. During the Labour Blair administration, BP's management team under Lord Browne had a close relationship with the Cabinet Office. Thus, it was BP who largely designed the European Emissions Trading System and launched it via their influence in London and Brussels.

Under Lord Browne's management, BP was responsible for multiple health and safety catastrophes, particularly in the USA. This led to after-the-event regulatory action by the authorities there including the largest criminal fine ever for an air quality violation in history. This was after an explosion at a Texas refinery that killed 15 people and injured 170, as well as a catastrophic oil spill in Alaska that killed a worker and injured two others. (US EPA, 2007)

These catastrophes, including more recently the Deep Water Horizon spill, has prompted people in the USA to examine the BP record, much of it under the management of Lord Browne. Their conclusion, according to this review in the St Louis Post – Dispatch:

> BP's actions are facing unprecedented scrutiny, thanks to a years long history of legal and ethical violations that critics, judges and members of Congress say shows that the London-based company has a penchant for putting profits ahead of just about everything else... A review of BP's history, however, shows a pattern of ethically questionable and illegal behavior that goes back decades. (Mauer & Tinsley, 2010)

It is the manager of this same company who headed the Royal Academy of Engineering (RAE) when they produced a report, together with the Royal Society, claiming that fracking can be done safely if properly regulated. This was at a time when Browne was head and 30% owner of Cuadrilla, the UKs leading fracker. Browne was also a member of the Royal Society, joint publishers of the same report. The report, which is regularly cited by politicians who defend fracking and is on the website of DECC, is created by an organisation that is part funded by the oil and gas industry. In the last 3 years, the RAE has taken £601,000 from oil companies with links to fracking and awarded cash prizes to BP engineers for their work in hydraulic fracturing. (Caddie, 2012) ("Fred", 2012)

The frackers in government appoint the officials, write the regulations and design the tax breaks

This unelected member of the Cabinet office has parachuted his appointees into a variety of government ministries. These include 4 appointees in senior positions in DEFRA, the ministry that oversees the regulators (Iain Ferguson, lead non-executive Board Member; Paul Rew; Sir Tony Hawkshead and Catherine Doran – all non-executive Board members). With their help, the Environment Agency is being prepared ready for fracking – for example "streamlining" the procedure to get a permit to dump contaminated water from 6 months to 2 weeks. (As when Cuadrilla's radioactive water was dumped in the Manchester Ship Canal). (Jackson, 2014)

Meanwhile, Browne has parachuted 3 appointees Into the DECC. In theory, DECC has a responsibility to address and lead Britain's policy for climate change mitigation and the reduction of fossil fuel consumption. However, it now has this policy: "DECC is committed to ensuring that we maximise economic recovery of the UK's hydrocarbon resources, and support industry in pursuit of this". (The Unconventional Hydrocarbon Resources of Britains Onshore Basins, 2010)

Finally, Browne put 4 appointees into the Treasury – including Baroness Hogg an independent director of the BG group – whose fracking in Queensland Australia has created a public health crisis there. Hogg's expertise in the management of fracking should be assessed against the fact that, when the

Queensland government were finally persuaded to look into claims that the BG group's gas field in Tara were leaking, they inspected 58 gas wells in the field and found 26 of the 58 were leaking. In one case, above the lower explosion limit of methane and, in a further 4 cases, close to that limit. (The State of Queensland, Department of Employment, Economic Development and Innovation, 2010)

Appointees like Baroness Hogg have been put in the Treasury to ensure that fracking is given generous financial support. Sure enough, a package of financial support aimed at stimulating the shale gas industry was unveiled in the 2013 budget. This included a new shale gas "pad" allowance, ring fenced for up to 10 years thus, halving the tax the Shale gas industry will have to pay. In addition, shale gas producers will be able to offset their exploration and development costs against tax for a decade. The budget report also stated that the government will consult on whether these measures should also apply to other forms of onshore unconventional gas including coal bed methane and the highly controversial underground coal gasification. Further, the budget also "committed the government to develop proposals to ensure that local communities will benefit from shale gas projects in their area". We now know that this means financial measures to incentivise cash-strapped local authorities to accept gas fracking in their areas – contrary to their responsibilities to look after the interests of local communities.

The "regulatory independence" advocated as a key lesson of the PP Report published by the European Environment Agency, therefore, looks like a completely lost cause as far as the UK is concerned. What is happening in government is consistent within a long and shameful history of British public authorities betraying their responsibility to look after the health and safety of the general public because the regulatory process has been captured by business interests.

One can see this, for example at the *Health and Safety Executive* who, theoretically have a responsibility to keep workers and communities safe. On 18th November of last 2013, the HSE issued a press release about a revision of the workplace health and safety regulations of 1992. In their press release, they explained that the revised regulations would "make it easier for employers, building owners, landlords and managing agents to understand and meet their legal obligations and so reduce the risks of over compliance." (O'Neill, 2013)

(One can imagine the court scene: "Do you plead guilty or not guilty to polluting this community?"... "Not guilty – to have done any more would have been over-compliance with safety regulations")

Frackers marking their own homework – the regulatory farce in Lancashire

The Prime Minister claims that "the regulatory system in this country is one of the most stringent in the world. If any shale gas were to pose a risk of pollution, then we have all the powers we need to close it down". At the same time, the Environmental Agency (EA) has been allowing drillers to "mark their own homework" – effectively to self-certify their own compliance with the regulations.

A report in *Private Eye* gives a real life view of how tightly Cuadrilla is being regulated, and cites the way that they have handled "produced water" from fracking that is radioactive because of contamination by the rocks underground. Naturally occurring radioactive materials are common in the oil and gas industry.

The *Private Eye* article illustrated how Cuadrilla had hired specialist firms to provide supervised radiation protection and deal with radioactive waste. One of these firms had no previous knowledge of dealing with radioactive waste until approached by Cuadrilla, and yet, was able to be used as a reference that Cuadrilla's plans for dealing with radioactive waste were "optimal". The other company gives just one day training courses for Cuadrilla's employees to turn them into "radiation protection supervisors". When Cuadrilla produced excessive radioactive water, the Environment Agency allowed them to dump it. (Fracking -The Great Debate, Private Eye 1347, 2013)

Mike Hill is an oil and gas engineer who supports fracking but only with adequate regulation. He has pointed out how the Office of Unconventional Gas and Oil is at one and the same time cheerleader for the unconventional gas industry and its regulator. This is the exact opposite of the recommended principle in the PP study which argues for independence for the regulators from the industry itself. It is not surprising then that what regulations exist are modelled on the offshore industry where countryside and a residential community do not exist. The Environment Agency never visited the Cuadrilla wells at all to ensure that the wells were constructed as agreed. The EA does not inspect the chemicals used to verify what they are and in what quantity. Nor is the flow back verified. (Hill, 2013)

Hill thinks that the regulations are utterly inadequate. He points out the way that the Environment Agency appears to believe that flow-back water is non-hazardous waste. This convenient idea would allow the EA to give permission to waive regulations on dumping safely. Hill comments:

> Environment Agency consider flowback fluid non-hazardous! Lead at 1438 times drinking water, Cadmium 36 times, Chromium 72 times, Arsenic 20 times, NORM at 90 times max permissible limit. This is "non-hazardous" according to UK competent authority! (Hill, 2013)

Suppressing the truth

In these circumstances, where is unpolluted information likely to come from? The answer is that communities and workers are aware of issues first because they suffer from them. As the PP study shows, it is often workers and affected communities who become aware of problems before regulators. Workers and communities are often aware too how real world conditions deviate a long way from "what is supposed to happen" if the technology functions perfectly and the regulations are adhered to.

> "One prominent contribution from lay knowledge relevant to the regulatory process

> Concerns workplace awareness of emerging patterns of ill health. The histories of usage of asbestos and PCBs provide examples where workers were aware of what regulators subsequently

recognised to be a serious problem. Similarly, local communities may become aware of unusual concentrations of ill health before the authorities, such as the Love Canal example cited in the Great Lakes case study.

Another aspect of lay knowledge is where workers know that real practices do not match the theoretical assumptions of risk assessors. The UK slaughterhouse rules over BSE separation of "specified bovine offal" from meat were widely flaunted, yet failures in the inspection regime meant that this was not drawn to the attention of the regulators. In this case, workers in the industry in question were apparently better informed about the operational realities than were high-level regulatory advisers and officials." (Gee, Vaz, & al., 2002)

It has been communities in the USA and Australia who have raised issues about their health and well-being and what actually happens in a fracked gas field. But what happens to these people who do resist what is happening and try to draw attention to the dangers? The PP Study is once again revealing – it shows that there has been a repeated tendency of politicians and the vested interests who have bought their support to try to "shoot the messenger" bringing bad news, to shut them up and to try to force self-censorship.

Gagging orders on victims and health professionals

This is again matched with the gas fracking experience. For example in the USA, people whose lives have been ruined by the gas fracking industry find that they can get financial compensation, help with their medical bills and assistance with obtaining clean water. However, the price for doing so is by agreeing to be bound by gagging orders – even imposed on their children for the rest of their lives.

Two young children in Pennsylvania were banned from talking about fracking for the rest of their lives under a gag order imposed under a settlement reached by their parents with a leading oil and gas company. The sweeping gag order was imposed under a $750,000 settlement between the Hallowich family and Range Resources Corp, a leading oil and gas driller. It provoked outrage on Monday among environmental campaigners and free speech advocates.

The settlement, reached in 2011 but unsealed only last week, barred the Hallowichs' son and daughter, who were then aged 10 and seven, from ever discussing fracking or the Marcellus Shale, a leading producer in America's shale gas boom.

The Hallowich family had earlier accused oil and gas companies of destroying their 10-acre farm in Mount Pleasant, Pennsylvania and putting their children's health in danger. Their property was adjacent to major industrial operations: four gas wells, gas compressor stations, and a waste water pond, which the Hallowich family said contaminated their water supply and caused burning eyes, sore throats and headaches. (Goldenberg, 2013)

Of course, when there are widespread health problems they turn up in doctors' surgeries. Doctors and vets start to ask questions about what is going on in the communities that they are serving. This led one general practitioner in Australia to do a study of people living in the Tara Gas field run by the BG group in Australia. She found a pattern of symptoms which pointed to neurotoxicity – with a high proportion of children affected. (McCarron, 2013)

In the case of unconventional gas, the evidence gathered by doctors in the USA and Australia has not been quickly followed up. Indeed, in the USA, there have been attempts to gag what doctors can say too. The *Los Angeles Times* writes about a law introduced in Pennsylvania as follows:

> The law compels natural gas companies to give inquiring healthcare professionals information about the chemicals used in their drilling and production processes — but only after the doctors or nurses sign a confidentiality agreement.

> Some physicians complain that the law is vague and lacks specific guidelines about how they can use and share the information with patients, colleagues and public health officials, putting them at risk of violating the measure. But refusing to sign the confidentiality agreement denies them access to information that could help treat patients. (Banerjee, 2102)

Compromised public agencies, compromised professionals

In the UK, we already have indications that doctors and public health professionals will be leaned on to prevent them speaking out, as is their professional and ethical responsibility. Or, if they do speak out, they are ignored in favour of a more compliant "expert opinion". This can be seen by the way that Public Health England produced a report which is being used by government in their propaganda offensive to declare fracking safe. (Public Health England, 2013)

What happens in a number of these reports is cherry picking of the issues where it is easier to reassure the public with other issues left unexamined and unaddressed

Paul Mobbs, an independent environmental investigator, has also looked into the PHE and makes the following comments about the way that it breaches principles of impartiality in a completely cavalier fashion. Among many criticisms that show how PHE cherry picked the data to fit the governments desired conclusion, he points out how the available peer reviewed evidence is misrepresented:

> If we examine the human health assessments considered by PHE, and cited multiple times, they do not argue that unconventional oil and gas are "low risk". Some consider the risks to be high, while others consider they are presently indeterminate – and much more research is required before any certain case might be made. If we widen the search and look at other public health sources, we also find either uncertainties, or warnings of uncertain but arguably significant impacts. That Public Health England were able to jump from the evidence presented in these various studies, to a position of stating "currently available evidence indicates that the potential

risks to public health... are low if the operations are properly run and regulated", is an absurd deduction from the available information. (Mobbs,P. 2014 (b))

Further to this, Mobbs shows that much evidence is ignored, including any evidence published after 2012, with far more peer reviewed literature being available in 2013 than in previous years.

The conclusion that Mobbs comes to is shared by the *British Medical Journal* which comments on the PHE report

> Unfortunately, the conclusion that shale gas operations present a low risk to public health is not substantiated by the literature. The correct conclusion that Public Health England should have drawn is that the public health impacts remain undetermined and that more environmental and public health studies are needed. (Law, Hays, Shonkoff, & Finkel, 2014)

Declaring that Britain has the most stringent regulations in the world while cutting the regulators

The de-regulation agenda matches the government's programme of financial and staffing cuts. Owen Paterson's Department for Environment, Food and Rural Affairs was hit by cuts of ten per cent in 2010 with further drastic cuts in the spending review for the period to 2015/16. This led political analysts to see "an uncertain future for Britain's fracking watchdog". (Stevenson, 2013)

In the meantime, while David Cameron tells us we have the most stringent regulations in the world, his government has fought off European Union attempts to regulate fracking – probably because they would really be more stringent!

It is no surprise then to read in the study of the PP how Britain delayed action on acid rain caused by sulphur emissions from coal fired power stations in the UK because the impact was perceived as being mainly abroad. It affected other people so it was politically possible to ignore and deny.

Some professions dominate the risk assessment process – others get ignored

In an ideal world that really took the precautionary principle seriously, inter-disciplinary perspectives on potential environmental and health risks would be fostered and information being raised from sources like this would be taken seriously and looked into further. However, the experience written up in the Precautionary Principle study shows that particular professions, with particular perspectives and concerns dominate the risk assessment process and they are often not the most appropriate ones to judge.

> For both asbestos and ionising radiation the setting of standards was strongly influenced by the preoccupation of medical clinicians with immediate acute effects. In both cases, the toxicology

and epidemiology of long term chronic effects remained relatively neglected. The introduction of MTBE was based on bodies of knowledge concerning engines, combustion and air pollution. The water pollution aspects associated with persistence and significant taste and odour problems were essentially disregarded, though the information was available. For sulphur emissions the regulatory appraisal was initially focused on human health concerns. When ecological effects became apparent, a regulatory process constructed to address health issues experienced problems assimilating and reacting to these. (Gee, Vaz, & al., 2002)

The geologist view and the British Geological Survey

In the case of unconventional gas, geologists have carved themselves out a particularly prominent role. The British Geological Survey is constantly being mentioned in relation to fracking. It is not without significance to note therefore that the BGS takes a large part of its funding from the oil and gas industry and it is not without significance that about one half of geologists go to work in the oil and gas sector. The BGS is therefore very much a part of the "granfalloon coalition" and although there will doubtless be people at organisations like the BGS who are aware of their ethical responsibilities it is difficult to see the BGS as "fully independent".

It is important to note here that the BGS have created their own specialist department for the safety and environmental issues and are profiling themselves as experts on the safety of fracking. A key theme that they have ended up studying is seismic activity as a result of fracking, particularly as they were asked to help investigate a small earthquake as a result of Cuadrilla's activity in Preese Hall in Lancashire. The BGS were instrumental in recommending a so called "traffic light" system in which drilling is halted for further investigations if seismic activity is detected above a particular magnitude. Cuadrilla recommended 1.7 as being that magnitude with an additional 0.9 magnitude post even rise for operational purposes if it appears safe to continue. However, the BGS argued that 0.5 would be a more acceptable level. So far so good for the BGS... but the BGS then argued that this 0.5 could be adjusted up to a magnitude of 3.0 maximum later if conditions appear to justify this.

This has led community members at Preese Hall to point out that the 0.5 appears to be a magnitude designed to appease community concerns at first. Later, when the industry has sunk a lot of capital into different landscapes, when there are hundreds of wells with thousands of fracks occurring, the commercial pressure to turn a blind eye will be very powerful. The likely tendency then to allow the acceptable level seismicity with its associated level of well damage and contamination to be screwed upwards will be very powerful. (Jackson, 2014)

According to David Cameron, if it appears that a fracking company is putting people's health at risk, the regulators have powers to close things down. However, as we have already seen, what happens in the real world is rather different. When well-connected people with friends in government, in the media and among regulators, have sunk huge amounts of their own money, and bank money, into business ventures, there is an extremely powerful pressure to make that money pay. The whole history of regulating industry shows an extreme reluctance to close down processes which would impose big losses on business. This is especially true when the people being hurt are just "little people" without the same connections and friends. That's why the BGS's idea that the level of acceptable seismicity may be allowed to rise later is so dangerous for ordinary people (and convenient for the industry).

Another issue that the BGS have taken up is water contamination. One of the things that they are doing is gathering evidence prior to any fracking. The rationale is that baseline figures for water quality before fracking are necessary in order to prove whether or not fracking subsequently gives rise to contamination. This seems like a thoroughly good idea until you wake up to the fact that, if the BGS do discover contamination after fracking, then it will be too late to do anything about it at the location concerned. In other words, the BGS is not advocating the precautionary principle be applied – for this would be an argument not to frack in the first place because of the danger of a negative impact and the consequences of that impact.

In their own presentation of the risks, the BGS are focusing on how deeply the fracking occurs and what separates the shale or layer to be fracked from aquifers above. Repeatedly, we hear their argument that fracking is often a mile underground and so, it is argued, a long way below a level at which contamination can occur.

This way of presenting the problems focuses where the industry appears to have the stronger arguments. I write "appears" because a peer reviewed study by Duke University academics has shown that fracked groundwater systems in the US pose risks to other groundwater systems that were thought to be, but were not, hydraulically separate. This study clearly shows the risks in some groundwater geologies of cross-contamination. (Warner, et al., 2102)

Moreover, in focusing on the distance between layers to be fracked and aquifers, other issues of potential contamination get neglected. These issues include those covered earlier in this chapter i.e. engineering failure; fractures in well casings and failures in cement seals; as well as accidents and spills occurring at the surface.

These other kinds of issues ought to be picked up by other types of professions like water engineers, but these other professions have to be prepared to take up the dangers. In fact, there is already intense pressure being exercised to "manage" potential difficulty from other professional groups and institutions, for example, water management and environmental management professional groups.

Is the water industry compromised too?

It is pertinent here to point out that the Water Industry was privatised under Margaret Thatcher and keeping us safe from profit-driven irresponsibility by the water industry is now the responsibility of the Drinking Water Inspectorate which is another offshoot of DEFRA. Yet, as we have seen, DEFRA have been pushed by their political masters to be gung ho promoters of fracking. Meanwhile the private companies who run the water industry do not inspire a great deal of confidence that they are going to look after the public interest. It is not reassuring to find water companies being prosecuted for supplying water unfit for human consumption and being fined for this. (Drinking Water Inspectorate, 2014)

The Chartered Institution of Water and Environmental Management

It is the Chartered Institution of Water and Environmental Management that profiles itself as an ethical guardian for the water industry. It is a registered charity and is another "royal" organisation as the charter in question is from the monarch. They have produced a document called "Shale Gas and Water" which was compiled after consultations and a conference. It is a very detailed document and there is a lot that is valuable in it. However, it still raises fundamental issues of professional ethics. It looks as if the "Chartered Institution" has fallen in line with the "consensus trance" that the regulation can keep us all safe.

Here are some excerpts:

> There has been widespread public concern over well failure with an industry report estimating that by the time a gas well is 15 years old there is a 50 per cent chance of failure, and two out of four of Cuadrilla's wells in Lancashire have failed. These are alarming statistics, however, in spite of any drilling-related difficulties; the term failure does not necessarily mean any indication of leakage of contaminants to the environment, and this was not the case in Lancashire." Well failure" refers to the failure of any barrier element within a multiple barrier system and is reported to the appropriate regulatory agency. Failure to pass a barrier test does not mean that a leak to the surrounding environment has or will occur and rigorous well testing can help to identify any potential problems that can then be repaired. The multiple barrier system enables the optimum level of protection through the geology within which the bore is drilled. (Shale gas and Water, 2014)

Weasel words – whoever wrote "does not mean that a leak has or will occur" appears to be trying to wriggle out of acknowledging the bitter experience in the USA and Australia. Although well failures do not necessarily lead to leakage, they very often do, as the evidence from earlier in this chapter shows clearly.

The chief problem with any barrier system is that there is always a contact with the rock strata, no matter how many barriers there are, and that point of contact with the strata is cement. If and when the cement fails to make a bond with the rock, there is a fissure which can widen for a variety of reasons and then eventually migrate upwards. That can happen for several reasons, including seismic activity, perhaps induced by the fracking itself, as happened in this case.

These are the words of Mike Hill:

> Fracking fluids contain substances that if contaminating the aquifer then will spread over a large area (100s of km2) and pose a significant threat to agriculture, wells and livestock – i.e. the food

278

chain... One well will leave 10 million litres of fracking fluid in the ground. Just one exploratory well leaking has the potential to cause widespread damage to the environment and poses a risk to public health... Just the one and only well fracked in the UK so far (PH-1) 200m from Weeton Village and 5 Km from Blackpool (pop 250,000) caused two tremors at 1.4 and 2.3 ML and damaged the well over a very large interval with severe deformation for 240 feet. (Hill, 2013)

Independent examiners – the rating agencies of the oil and gas sector???

These do not inspire confidence. Despite this kind of evidence, which should set the alarm bells ringing at the Chartered Institution, their report says:

> Responsibility for the monitoring of well integrity, and ensuring the competence of those doing so, lies solely on the well operator as duty holder. There is also an independent well examiner. Monitoring of well operations during construction are based on weekly operations reports submitted to HSE by the well operators to ensure the construction matches the design, alongside both planned and subject to ad-hoc site inspections. The HSE's role is one of sampling to verify that regulations are complied with and taking appropriate enforcement action where they are not. (Hill, 2013)

Earlier in this chapter, I drew attention to the way that, in November of 2013, the HSE appeared to be chiefly concerned not to burden employers and businesses with "over compliance" when it came to health and safety regulations. As for the independent examiners - one has to ask if they would be anything like the independent examiners of the finance industry who gave AAA ratings for what industry insiders for financial products were calling "toxic trash", and whose rating could be bought by payments from the issuers of that toxic trash? There are "independent examiners" on North Sea oil rigs too and yet 34% of oil and gas wells show anomalies (i.e. failures of integrity) in the UK's North Sea sector. That is hardly a figure to inspire confidence in "independent examiners" who, after all, would have come up through the industry. Their peer group would be those they are regulating.

Regulations for Traffic and Flaring

There is plenty more involved in fracking than what happens underground. According to Mike Hill, regulation is needed for flaring and traffic too. The number of tanker trips to take flow back water from a standard traffic pad would amount to 3,384 standard trips and with 120 pads and 3,000 wells (proposed in PEDL 165 in the area between Preston and Blackpool) this would involve over 400,000 initial tanker trips. (Hill, 2013)

There comes a point, however, where one has to ask if the amount of regulation, the energy costs, the disruption and the magnitude of risk, justifies the energy yield – also bearing in mind the climate implications. Continuing down a hydrocarbons route means that the harms exceed the benefits and this whole charade is only possible by ignoring harms – because the carbon money lobby is so powerful in government. It has to be admitted however that, if fracking were banned, with the North Sea fields in decline, there would be no future for many currently employed in the oil and gas industry, nor for many employed in ancillary departments of government and a very large number of people in professions like geology. This, I fear, is a large part of the current problem.

Digging in for a long fight?

The failure to take major health and environmental risks seriously occurs repeatedly in regulatory institutions and has done so for over a century. There are repeated cases where the precautionary principle fails because industry vested interests prevail so that politicians, regulatory agencies and professional bodies fail to do their job of protecting the public.

> Difficulties can also arise where the regulatory agency becomes part of the issue through its past decisions. Both situations are illustrated by BSE, where identification and recognition of the problem was influenced and delayed as a consequence of wider policy considerations (the economic impact on farming) and the concern that lack of consistency would undermine the credibility of government and agencies alike. (Gee, Vaz, & al., 2002)

Governments and regulatory agencies do not like to do U turns because it makes them look fallible, incompetent or even corrupt – which they often are. We can't have the public authorities looking like that can we? The problem then persists until the industry dies an economic death anyway. What does not happen is anything that remotely resembles what is in a textbook of economic theory.

What kind of environmental regulation?

Environmental "resources" like water and the air are shared. For example, the water system is a common pool resource that ought to be managed in the interests of everyone AND taking into account ecological system realities. The "interests of everyone" means – people for residential purposes (drinking, cooking, washing etc.), different industries (brewing, agriculture, leisure sailing, angling etc.). Taking into account ecological system realities means that the needs of wildlife, plants, drainage, rivers and streams, hydro-geological functions etc. also need to be taken into consideration. There are a variety of users for water, a variety of uses and a variety of ecological realities all of which must be harmonised. Rational organisation would be about achieving that. The unconventional gas industry and government want to use brutal economic and political power to allow ONE business group – the oil and gas industry – to override and put all other users and uses for water in jeopardy. They want to go to the head of a queue for their dangerous and toxic use of water which puts into question the long run abilities of communities living in ecological systems to continue to function.

This incompatibility with other land and residential uses can effectively mean that the residents of an area are being expropriated once it has been decided that the gas industry will move in their area - unless they can stop it happening - in a process reminiscent of the enclosure process. In this case it is not commoners who are being displaced but less powerful private property owners pushed out by more powerful actors who have their own use for the land, and who are backed up by the central state. It is particularly ironic that this is happening in Australia, the USA and Canada on land originally taken from aboriginal people and the first nations.

The answer is to counter-pose the establishment of a water commons which would be managed by informed negotiations between all water users of appropriate uses for water at a local and regional level. That is, I believe, what we need to construct as we get to know what uses and users for water that there are and come together across water sheds to organise the defence of shared resources against poisonous extraction by one branch of industry. (Barlow, 2012)

Final Comment - Ethical culpability

It is debateable how much and whether the differing protagonists for these technologies are aware of the undoubted dangers and damages to the environment and to communities living in the gas fields. No doubt, in the vested interest coalition pushing the various unconventional gas technologies, there will be proponents of unconventional gas who really believe that, with regulation, it will be sufficiently safe to be "not unacceptable". No doubt, people suffering from hubris and optimism bias sincerely believe that their judgement is reliable. Certainly, there are promoters of unconventional gas who want to believe that it is safe, who are prepared to accept the reassurances of the industry and its public relations helpers and to repeat the "official line" of "not-unacceptability".

It is interesting to note, however, that when senior members of the oil and gas industry find that they themselves live close to a proposed unconventional gas field, they can change their minds quite rapidly. This was highlighted in the United States when the CEO of Exxon Mobil was involved in an anti-fracking lawsuit because the fracking was proposed where he lives. It was interesting too, that a retired Mobil executive who had come out against fracking wrote him an open letter about this saying:

> No one should have to live near well pads, compression stations, incessant heavy truck traffic, or fracking water towers, nor should they have their water or air contaminated. You and I love the places where we live, but in the end, if they are ruined by fracking or frack water tanks, we can afford to pack up and go someplace else. However, many people can't afford to move away when they can no longer drink the water or breathe the air because they are too close to one of your well pads or compressor stations. (Abrams, 2014)

Chapter 37

Resilience and Collective Psychology – fast collapse or slow disintegration

Will a failure in hub interdependencies lead to economic and social disintegration? The connection between the energy and finance institutions, as well as the state of public health are explored to examine whether there might be a "cross contagion" of cascading collapse between some combination of a public health crisis, difficulties in the financial economy, the energy sector and supply networks which run into and reinforce each other. (Textbox on the Eurozone Crisis)

A repeated theme of this book has been that, in concentrating on the improvement of production (i.e. the increase of production), economics has systematically neglected issues of safety, vulnerability and resilience. We saw in an earlier chapter that the research of Kahneman and Tversky suggests that people are risk averse. However, economic decision-making is driven by powerful companies and governments who are frequently able to impose risks and costs on others while taking gains for themselves. There are however other risks which occur, not at local or company level, but in the system as a whole. There is a need to explore what might happen after the limits to economic growth are reached, and whether humanity will face a manageable contraction or a variety of catastrophic collapses. In this chapter, I want to look at some of the conceptual thinking about these issues as they relate to the beginning of the 21st century.

The decline in Resilience

As explained by the late David Fleming:

> The resilience of a system is its ability to survive without loss of diversity and complexity despite shocks. The diversity and complexity are essential: resilience is an empty concept except when they are implicit in it. The surface of Mars, or a dead coral reef, are resilient in a trivial sense – resilient, since they do not change under assault. There is no loss of diversity and complexity, but that does not make them resilient, since there is no loss of diversity and complexity to lose. (David Fleming, "The Lean Economy" p113 of a draft sent to the author)

To get a grasp of the issues it is necessary to contrast and counterpose the idea of resilience to that of productivity and efficiency. For most of the history of humanity, what people were concerned about has been ecological (and economic) resilience rather than production increase and efficiency. From the eighteenth century, the efficiency and "improvement" advocated by Adam Smith and later economists was all about more production by an increased division of labour and increased complexity. But this has brought reduced resilience.

This idea of "resilience" in complex systems has been the subject of much inter-disciplinary study by a group of thinkers who have evolved an interpretation of transformations in nature and human society which they call "*Panarchy*". (Gunderson and Holling 2002)

The word "*Panarchy*" can be understood by breaking it into its two parts "Pan" and "archy". The Pan word is meant to evoke the idea of Pan, the god of Nature, as well as the word part "pan" as in "panorama" - an overview vision. The word part "archy" is as in "anarchy" or "hierarchy".

The framework described in *Panarchy* is one in which transformation of human and natural systems occur through "adaptive cycles". An adaptive cycle evolves in three dimensions:

1. Productivity and potential: the amount of energy and resources embodied and embedded in the system and its ability to capture and use energy for its purposes.
2. Connectedness: the level of interconnectedness of its parts (e.g. a transport and communications network – the supply chain and financial interdependencies of which David Korowicz writes).
3. Resilience: the ability of the system to withstand or respond to shocks – at its most fundamental by reinventing itself.

Schematically we can apply this to human societies and eco-systems by describing a cyclical process which goes through 4 to 5 phases:

1. Starting with a pioneering phase where, depending on the type of system, human groups or species, manage to survive a collapse and thrive, beginning to develop a new kind of system using the resources and elements released by the collapse of an old one.
2. A structure begins to take shape as connections between these pioneering groups, or species take, place and they begin to develop a new system.
3. The system moves into a consolidation phase and forges its chief structures which become dominant. However, the system now starts to evolve more complexity and "round-about" ways of doing things. In the process, the structure becomes rigid and loses its resilience.
4. Stress surges bring on collapse – the rigid complexity of the system cannot cope with a variety of challenges and problems and breaks down, its productivity and connectedness collapsing with it.
5. The disconnection and decline eventually leads into a new pioneering phase and the emergence of the next social or ecological system – though in our own age it might not....

An example of this cycle in a natural system is provided in the spruce fir forests of eastern North America. An insect called the spruce budworm will defoliate the trees to the point where they die off over extensive areas. Prior to human harvesting and management this occurred in a cycle of 40 to 130 years when a mature forest acquired such a dense volume of foliage that the effectiveness of insectivorous birds that kept the budworm under control was diluted. The budworms spread out of control and the forest died. (Holling C S 2002)

Turning to the human economy the analogous vulnerability is the complex network that must be kept going to produce almost everything. In his book, *The Lean Economy*, the late David Fleming placed a particular focus on what he called the "intermediate economy" in his description of the Panarchy cycle. The intermediate economy is where the increasing complexity occurs. It encompasses all those processes that are not wanted for their own sake. They are the increasingly complicated means to a final end. For example, the transport sector is not wanted for its own sake – it is the goods that transport delivers that are wanted, not transport as such. The transport sector is the means to get the inputs and raw materials delivered to production processes as well as the necessary means to get consumer goods to the end consumer. The expanding intermediate economy is where the "internet of things" inflates in phase 3 of the Panarchy cycle.

Technology consists of a great many devices that are powered by energy. These devices process and transform input materials and provide, in turn, outputs and components for other devices to process. There is a dense web of interdependencies all of which depends on infrastructures of finance, trade and energy to keep the networks humming. If the finance, trade and energy hubs fail, then techno civilisation could be in deep trouble. That would feed into a public health crisis and make things worse. An alternative scenario is of a public health crisis being the initial origin of a crisis in the other infrastructures.

A colleague of mine in the think tank Feasta, David Korowicz, has studied the potential for catastrophic breakdowns. He writes about what he calls a "cross contagion" between the financial and the trade/ production networks leading to a supply chain collapse. He argues that if such a collapse persists for a sufficient time period it would not be possible to get the system up and running again – and that period is not very long. He draws upon real life events like the United Kingdom fuel blockade by lorry drivers in the year 2000 and the events following the Japanese earthquake and Tsunami of 2011 to make his point about the possibility of breakdown, which gets progressively worse and leads into a collapse, because of multiple domino breakdowns, cascading through "hub interdependencies". (Korowicz, 2012, p. 5)

Crucial to understanding the degree of vulnerability of our economic system is the extraordinarily high level of complexity and interdependence in global production systems. There is not only of internet of information there is, so to speak, an "internet of things".

> We can catch a fragmentary glimpse of this via Eric Beinhocker who compared the number of distinct culturally produced artefacts produced by the Yanomamo tribe on the Orinoco River and by modern New Yorkers. The former have a few hundred, the latter, tens of billions... Consider that a modern auto manufacturer has been estimated to put together 15,000 individual parts, from many hundreds of screw types to many tens of micro-processors. Imagine if each of their suppliers put together 1,500 parts in the manufacture of their input to the company (assuming they are less complex), and each of the suppliers to those inputs put together a further 1,500. That makes a total

of nearly 34 billion supply-chain interactions (15,000 x 1,500 x 1,500), five times the number of people on the planet. This is a highly imperfect example but it signals the vast conditionality upon which modern production depends. (Korowicz, 2012, pp. 4-5)

It is possible to question this view – another colleague of the author, Dr Nick Bardsley of the University of Reading, points out that David Korowicz might be better to use the words "supply web" rather than "supply chain". Webs contain multiple pathways, if one node breaks down, other connections between can be made that route around the breakdown. There is greater resilience in a web than a chain. Bardsley agrees though that commercial concentration tends to turn webs into more vulnerable chains. It is also true that the break-down of hub interdependencies like the financial system would have catastrophic consequences.

Cross contagion vulnerabilities of techno-civilisation

Techno-innovation has brought humanity a long way in terms of production possibilities – but how resilient is this production system? How vulnerable is it? While many experts are, with very good reason, concerned about a catastrophic transformation of the climate system because of the greenhouse effect of fossil fuels, others are concerned that even before a climate crisis has done its worst, the technological infrastructure of society could break down catastrophically in a linked financial, supply chain and public health collapse. For example, at the time of writing in 2014 the spead of Ebola in West Africa shows what a devastating effect diseases can have when they spread through the inter-dependent networks of an economic structure. What I am drawing attention to here is the potential of "cross contagion" between different sources of vulnerability.

While techno civilisation is vulnerable to depleting sources of energy and materials, society is also potentially vulnerable to the disruptive effect of public health crises. In addition there are other sources of instability – for example the growth of the finance sector, and therefore of indebtedness. In the longer term there will also be the effects of climate change. Each of these individually can reduce resilience – together they could interact in ways that are particularly catastrophic

Hub interdependencies and the dynamics of cascading collapse

The dense interrelated complexity of the modern world means that chain reactions or cascade of problems can pass through the entire system when one problem (i.e. an abnormal state that falls too far outside the organisational routine) leads, domino style, to another one, in a progression of vicious spirals. This is particularly the case if failures occur in "hub interdependencies" – systems that connect everything together like the transport networks, the power supply system, the money system – and also, a connecting "system" that is often unnoticed while everything is operating well, public health.

To take public health first – this is not normally thought of as a connecting thread that holds our society together but we can see what happen when a serious contagious disease like types of avian influenza or Ebola spreads through society. It is not only that people are ill directly, it is also that fear, behaviour change, and the measures taken to prevent the spread of the disease, have extremely disruptive effects on economic activity.

This is discussed in an autumn 2014 study on the economic impact of Ebola by the World Bank. The study emphasises two channels of impacts. Firstly there are the direct and indirect impacts of sickness and death which consume resources in health care and take people out of the labour force – either permanently if they die or temporarily. These disrupt planting and harvesting in agriculture as well as the transport of food and other products to market. This in turn leads to rising food prices, to hoarding and speculation in food products.

The second impact is the result of widespread fear and behavioural changes that come about as a result of that fear. As repeatedly argued in this book, and as explained by Kahnemann and Tversky, people are risk averse and this has major economic consequences. In this case the fear of association with others reduces labour force participation, disrupts transportation, markets and government services. Fear also discourages people seeking medical treatment for other diseases and problems and this has knock on health consequences of other kinds. There are effects on trade, travel, commerce, tourism and the hotel sector. Investors and people with a stake in an area where the illness is raging lose confidence, put their plans on hold and perhaps close down economic activities like mining and evacuate their staff.

Governments find themselves in deficit because of the additional costs of containing and treating the outbreak yet have falling tax revenues. They are forced to divert dwindling resources into combating the disease.

The World Bank authors quote studies which suggest that, in regard to the impact on the economy it is the behavioural change brought about by fear which has the largest effect. "In the recent history of infectious disease outbreaks such as the SARS epidemic of 2002 and the H1N1 flu epidemic of 2009 behavioural effects are believed to have been responsible for as much as 80 to 90 percent of the total impact of the epidemic" (World Bank Group. 2014 The Economic Impact of the 2014 Ebola epidemic. October 7th 2014).

We should remind ourselves that when economists write about "impact" they reduce the meaning of impact to what happens to income. For those in the middle of the nightmare the greatest "impact" as a lived experience is most likely to be the trauma and horror of the disease itself, the chilling effect on human relationships, traumatised abandoned and orphaned children, the experience of living continuously in great fear and whether ones loved ones and oneself lives or dies. However the income impacts do indeed feed back into the epidemic in a vicious spiral.

This matches the experience of previous epidemics. In his 1722 *"Journal of the Plague Year,"* a fictional description of the plague in London in 1665, Daniel Defoe wrote of the poor who

> "might be said to perish not by the infection itself but by the consequence of it; indeed, namely,
> by hunger and distress and the want of all things: being without lodging, without money, without

friends, without means to get their bread, or without anyone to give it them; for many of them were without what we call legal settlements, and so could not claim of the parishes, and all the support they had was by application to the magistrates for relief, which relief was (to give the magistrates their due) carefully and cheerfully administered as they found it necessary, and those that stayed behind never felt the want and distress of that kind which they felt who went away in the manner above noted.

"Let anyone who is acquainted with what multitudes of people get their daily bread in this city by their labour, whether artificers or mere workmen—I say, let any man consider what must be the miserable condition of this town if, on a sudden, they should be all turned out of employment, that labour should cease, and wages for work be no more.

"This was the case with us at that time; and had not the sums of money contributed in charity by well-disposed people of every kind, as well abroad as at home, been prodigiously great, it had not been in the power of the Lord Mayor and sheriffs to have kept the public peace. Nor were they without apprehensions, as it was, that desperation should push the people upon tumults, and cause them to rifle the houses of rich men and plunder the markets of provisions; in which case the country people, who brought provisions very freely and boldly to town, would have been terrified from coming any more, and the town would have sunk under an unavoidable famine. " (Defoe, 1722. Project Gutenberg EBook #376)

In a similar manner the epidemics in West Africa have reduced food supply and increased poverty and the people are now dependent on international support.

At the time of writing it is unclear how well the so called "developed countries" will do to avoid these kind of impacts because they are able to keep Ebola out of their populations. Governments confidently state that they are well prepared. Even *if* this proves to be true the protection for populations in the global north is likely to prove highly expensive. The cost of the successful treatment of one person in an isolation clinic in Eppendorf near Hamburg was about 2 million Euros according to the news magazine *Der Spiegel*. This was partly because the patient vomited over expensive ultrasonic equipment and a mobile X ray machine.

Holding Ebola at bay, to the extent that it is possible, is going to be resource intensive. Consider, for example, what it took the health authorities in Nigeria to manage the situation when the virus was "imported" by a single traveller who flew into Lagos in 2014. From this single traveller there were 19 confirmed cases of further infection. 8 of these resulted in death. So how did the Nigerians contain the situation, for now at least? (December 2014). The answer is that they had a polio eradication programme using similar procedures and skills. This programme had spare capacity because of its success and could be reassigned to contain Ebola. However, containing Ebola created when just one man entered Nigeria required 1,800 health staff. These had to be properly trained and equipped with safe wards to fall back on. They had to be able to make 18,000 visits to check on 900 people.

As long as the disease continues to grow in West Africa it can be expected that "exports" of cases to other countries will become more frequent. A lot of resources may be required in tracing and in managing at risk contacts. It is easy to imagine situations where a cluster of cases overwhelms the wafer thin resource available in some countries to contain the disease. (Tomori, O, 2014).

The current confidence about controlling Ebola transmission in developed countries like the UK is based on the assumption that it will be possible to keep the reproduction number of the virus below 1. The reproduction number is the number of people an infected person infects. At the moment the reproduction number in West Africa is about 1.5 to 2 or more additional infections for each infected person which is why the number of cases has doubled every month.

If something doubles every month it means that if you throw resources at that problem then, in a months time your resources might be only achieving one half as much as a month earlier if their positive impact is not fast enough. Studies suggest that at this level even improved contact tracing, new medication, lower infection rates occurring in hospitals and lower infections through better burial practices is likely, at best, to slow the growth of the disease. (Rivers CM et al 2014)

The danger is then that the growth of the disease in West Africa will also spread through cross border "exports" - both in Africa itself and trans-continentally – perhaps into the densely populated slums of other cities. If there is double the number of cases in the countries in which Ebola is originating and you would expect double the number of "exports" unless rigid quarantines can be enforced. In three months if you double the number of cases, double it again and double it again you have 8 times the number of "exports", all other things being equal. In 6 months the epidemic would be 64 times the size.

The point here is that if the resources available for the response are swamped by its growth rate then the control response will break down. At some point along a process of this kind the possibilities for standard public health measures for control of the disease by "importing countries" could disintegrate - and not just because of the increasing numbers of "exports" - also because of the growing geographical spread of sources from which infectious "imports" would be coming. Here is why:

If you look at the advice of agencies like the UK government organisation "Public Health England" what they do is talk about control measures for people who are exhibiting particular symptoms – e.g. fever, headaches, vomiting, and diarrhoea - AND who come from the currently most affected countries in West Africa. If a person comes from Germany, or Japan or most other places and they have those symptoms they can be pretty much ruled out as having Ebola. This is tremendously useful as a lot of possible cases can be ruled out as too unlikely to warrant committing resources for someone who one can confidently predict is not going to be an Ebola case.

However, the more countries that Ebola spreads to the more difficult it would - or will - become to rule out an Ebola diagnosis for each of these people. So the number of cases that "might be" Ebola will increase and, after a certain point, the resource requirements of contact tracing and then the monitoring of all these people for up to 21 days would become quite impractical. The epidemic would overshoot resource availabilities and preparedness.

On top of the control costs there are the fear and behavioural consequences. The first case of Ebola in New York chilled financial markets in the USA and Asia. Stocks in hotel operators, airlines and holidays fell. The word "contagion" in an interdependent world can therefore have non-medical meanings. Public health threats and fear contaminate economic processes.

Other Vulnerabilities in 'Hub Dependencies'

Ebola is not the only reason to be concerned. It is one of a number of vulnerable interdependencies in our society where a breakdown would have far reaching consequences. One has only to see what happens when the electricity supply grid breaks down for it to become clear how vulnerable we could be to a collapse of a "hub-interdependency". Of course, many organisations will have their own power generators as "back-ups" for emergencies but, should these run out of fuel, the mechanisms of our complex civilisation would grind to a halt. An overlapping network of intermediate economy and state functions would break down - computer and telecommunications, lighting; traffic management and transport; production systems and food delivery arrangements; water and sewerage... In the resulting public health crisis the health service would be hard pressed to manage, dependent as it is too, on a dense network of complicated arrangements and energy intensive hospitals.

Another potential vulnerability is transaction, payment, money and accounting systems. There are circumstances in which they could fail too. If they did, nothing in our civilisation would be able to move and that, in turn, would unleash another kind of public health crisis.

Cross contagion – the energy crisis, the financial crisis, public health and collective emotion

There is a connection between the crisis in the production and energy system and the crisis in the financial system, and it is not only because electronic payments systems require electrical power. People and companies have to service their debts and they must also pay their fuel bills. One reason the world's central banks have been desperate to drive down interest rates is that high energy costs make it difficult for people and companies to service their debts and if interest rates were high the debt servicing burden would become unsustainable and the finance system would collapse.

In his article reviewing the 40 year evidence about the *Limits to Growth* study, Graham Turner explores the links between the "general financial crisis" and the other limits to growth trends, although financial problems were never part of the original *Limits to Growth* modelling. Although the immediate causes of the financial crisis of 2007 appear to have been massive defaults on high risk debts like sub-prime mortgages, a contributory factor was the very high oil and food costs which made debt servicing very difficult for low income earners. This is one connection between the financial system crisis and the energy and production crises. One analyst who explored the connection between oil prices and economic activity found that

> Whereas previous oil price shocks were primarily caused by physical disruptions of supply, the price run-up of 2007–08 was caused by strong demand confronting stagnating world production. Although the causes were different, the consequences for the economy appear to have been similar to those observed in earlier episodes, with significant effects on consumption spending and purchases of domestic automobiles in particular. Absent those declines, it is unlikely that the period 2007Q4–2008Q3 would have been characterized as one of recession for the United States. This episode should thus, be added to the list of U.S. recessions to which oil prices appear to have made a material contribution.

> (Hamilton, 2009)

There is an end of the technological road that humanity is currently following. Techno-optimists claim that new technologies can provide the answer to our problems. It is true that we desperately need science and technology to provide answers. However, many new technologies involve a further clever use for energy in further more complicated arrangements.

Ultimately, no one can exactly foresee the future, yet from analysing what has already happened we can see potential developments. Consequently, it seems likely that a central determinant of how fast a crisis might evolve lies in the inter-play between the financial markets, developments in the energy sector, public health and mass emotion.

The financial sector is hugely inflated in the form of loans and derivative contracts which can only be serviced and honoured in conditions of general prosperity. All financial securities ultimately derive their worth from claims to a share of the income arising in the real world of production and service provision and, if that world of production and services is not growing, the ability to service debts declines and disappears. Since growth in the general economy is largely dependent on the growth of the energy supply, the implications of energy depletion for the financial markets are rather obvious – the financial sector is in trouble. A deflationary melt-down could also come about as a result of changes in mass behaviour as a result of novel diseases.

That said, some players in the finance sector might still identify investment options. The more catastrophes, the more assets can be purchased cheaply. The more conflicts over scarce resources, the more weapons can be sold. The more desperate people, the greater will be the market for tranquilisers and illegal drugs. The more epidemics the greater the desperation for vaccinations produced by the pharmaceutical companies. Furthermore, when we reach the limits to economic growth, that means that "natural capital" will be scarce – land and water, for example. So there is money to be made by buying these scarce assets and then charging very high prices to desperate people for their use. Uneconomic growth, even collapse, is full of opportunities, including for vulture capitalists. A sort of growth could continue – with a growing market for undertakers.

Over the last few years much thinking has gone into the interplay between the "energy descent" and financial market instability. Would a rapid slide in the production of fossil energy mean a collapse in financial market confidence? On a day to day basis, the financial markets depend on trust and confidence for their operation. However, these have been known to evaporate virtually overnight, producing a chain reaction, a domino crisis in which interest rates rise, debts are called in and those people and companies operating with high leverage suffer huge losses. Unable to honour their debts, they then ruin their counterparties who, in turn, are unable to honour their commitments to others. In a crisis like this, credit and payment systems can freeze up and, if banks go down, then the entire system might go into shock. You can't buy your groceries at the supermarket because your bank card won't work and the supermarket can't pay its suppliers because its payment arrangements will be paralysed too.

The question then arises – how fast and in what way will the financial markets take in the idea of the limits to economic growth, of the depletion of energy source? How serious could an infectious epidemic and its consequences get? I have colleagues who think a collapse could happen very quickly with shocking and near apocalyptic consequences.

Perhaps they are right - though other futures seem possible too. I have been at pains to explain in this book that faiths, particularly collective ones, do not always shift very rapidly. They are subject to considerable inertia. After over 200 years' growth, there is an argument that it will take some time for very powerful institutions and individuals to take in the idea that that growth is over. Neoclassical economics, growth, technology are salvation faiths which many people are extremely reluctant to abandon, even in the face of a huge amount of evidence. These faiths are their general orientation in the world, the way that they make sense of things. To abandon them will not be easy – indeed it could be terrifying.

This helps us to contextualise the shale gas boom, as well as other processes like ripping apart Alberta in Canada for its tar sands, biofuels and all the other granfalloons. Despite all the evidence about the immense risks and damage done by shale gas, despite the very rapid rate of depletion of shale gas wells, shale gas is central to the strategic thinking of a large part of the elite. It and the other technologies have a function in the systems of faith – they foster the belief that there is life yet for the carbon economy and for the oil and gas sector. They have not reached the end of the road. The rock strewn dirt track at the end of the road is not a mirage, it is a viable way forward. Growth is still possible. America will become the next Saudi Arabia of gas. The diseases can be contained by new vaccines. The financial markets are safe.

Humanity, at least that part that lives in the rich countries, has found new technological ways to rescue its way of life.

Yes – maybe….or maybe not. At the end of 2014 the surge in production of shale oil brought about by fracking in the US coincided with a faltering with the powerhouse of the global production economy, China. A glut in supply met a fall in demand. The price of oil fell and the Saudi Arabian elite were not inclined to cut production to keep the oil price up. They needed the money from continuing to sell oil to pay for their state expenditures and if the falling oil price undermines the US high cost producers, the Iranian economy and the economy of Russia, then for the Saudi elite so much the better. However, over a number of years a lot of Wall Street's money, available at very low interest rates because of Federal Reserve policy, has gone into junk bonds to fund the fracking bubble. Many of these bonds have now become "distressed debt".

Whoops...

Text Box On the Eurozone Crisis

Things are not always as straightforward as they seem. It is sometimes difficult to make out the connection between particular developments and the larger picture. Thus the Eurozone crisis is often presented as if it were due to inadequate financial discipline by states. i.e. governments have spent too much and not taxed enough so they have needed to borrow and the debt has got out of hand. In this narrative governments need to adopt policies which cut expenditure, raise taxes and privatise assets instead of spending and borrowing so much. The story is that this would not be so difficult without a massive amount of corruption and cronyism by the elite which protects itself first of all so that the burden falls on those least able to bear it. This is no doubt true – but the accusation could equally, if not more apply, to corruption in the elites of the creditor countries. Wall Street is not noted for its ethics while the City of London has survived as a global financial centre with its network of offshore tax havens by catering to those who want to evade financial regulations.

An alternative way of understanding the Eurozone crisis is as a symptom of the decline in resilience in the context of slowing economic growth. It is part of the bigger picture. To use a metaphor, it is very difficult to stay balanced on a bicycle unless it has forward momentum. Likewise a growing economy can cope with the debts that arise between partners if both partners are prospering and growth is occurring. However, when growth falters imbalances and inequalities are exacerbated by debt – then debt grows until that point where it becomes unpayable. This is illustrated in the Eurozone crisis which is better understood as the inevitable outcome of imbalances and competitive stresses between economies in Europe as the global economy has faltered.

In the common currency zone Germany has out-competed the peripheral countries but they are no longer in a position to devalue their own currencies. Before the common currency was introduced countries that could not compete with Germany (and other countries in the Eurozone) retained competitiveness because their separate national currencies could be depreciated against the deutsche mark.

For example, if Italy was importing more goods from Germany than it was exporting back to Germany the lira could be depreciated against the deutsche mark. In that situation for Italians to continue buying German goods meant more lira had to be offered for the German currency and for the German goods which would thus become more expensive in Italy. By contrast, as the lira depreciated against the mark, Germans buying from Italy would get more lira for their deutsche marks and this would be encourage them to spent more in Italy. Imports of German goods would fall and Italian exports to Germany would rise and the imbalance situation would be rectified.

In the common currency zone this adjustment can no longer happen. Imbalances actually got worse instead. A common currency zone enhances existing inequalities. In 2012 it was being suggested that many southern Europe peripheral countries were 30% overvalued compared to Germany but could not devalue. Greece was probably 60% overvalued.

For a time the peripheral countries borrowed from Eurozone banks to pay for their import surpluses. However that is a temporary solution. The German economy is undermining the economies of its competitors who are also its customers. This also had knock-on effects on property markets and then on state finances in the peripheral countries. Property development was one field where foreign competition was limited because you can't trade buildings and the property market was also partly pumped up by European Union infrastructure spending which was added to the bank loans. Eventually the property bubble burst. The broken banks passed their property market losses over to governments who passed the losses onto populations impoverishing them further (e.g. in Ireland and Spain).

Falling incomes created government deficits because tax receipts fell and welfare and unemployment benefit payments rose. The import surplus of German goods made state funding even more of a problem. Healthy domestic businesses from which tax revenues could be raised are fewer because of the northern European competition while people have needed to claim welfare and unemployment benefits because they could find no work. (Until these benefits were cut too). These developments were added to the fact that over a number of years most peripheral countries had reduced taxes on the rich, as well as on property and real estate, and put taxes on ordinary people and labour instead.

This situation led to a "sovereign debt crisis" with soaring interest rates payable on the debts of government like Greece. Higher interest rates had to be financed out of state budgets so lead to more tax on ordinary people (though not on elites), cuts in services and privatisations. These austerity measures reduce income and spending as people and companies cut back more, reducing the tax take again while elites took their money to tax havens like Switzerland or London's offshore tax havens. Government deficits got worse. Rating agencies downgraded country debt ratings again and interest rates rose further.

Riots, strikes and protests eventually mean that governments fall. The choice is then to accept "technocratic" politicians - i.e. unelected rulers - usually former bankers and their associates or politicians of a more radical persuasion. Bankers who have "insured debt" against default lean on politicians behind the scenes lest they have to pay out on default insurance and this creates pressure for further austerity on the people. People who cannot pay don't pay – so the prospect of default looms anyway. Banks fear bankruptcy and a domino chain of failures as state bonds are downgraded and their assets lose value. The crisis got worse until the European central bank adopted a more relaxed approach to creating money to buy up the debt of the countries in difficulties, much to the frustration of some German economists who are fixated on questions of monetary discipline.

Whatever. The policies of the European Central Bank merely bought time and nothing has really been resolved. Countries that have joined the Eurozone have been told that they can never leave...

Chapter 38

Employment in theory and in real life

The economic theory of the labour market bears little resemblance to what really happens in the labour market. Workers don't just make material products, they arrange things and attend to people. As society has evolved and become more complex, the office has becomes the more common workplace and work is largely conceptual and intangible. Mainstream economic theory has little to say about intangible work in bureaucratic empires. As the economy becomes more unstable, paid work becomes a nightmare for many people and the temptation to work longer hours for little extra return is great.

Services and Government in a world in difficulties

Despite the fact that people do not come into the world for the specific purpose of becoming a "human resource", conventional economic theory regards the labour market as a market not unlike any other.

The supply of labour

Perhaps the most important element to the supply of labour will be the number of people in the population who are of "working age", as well as their education and skills, hence their ability to perform in particular job roles. This is largely a feature of demographics as well as education and other policy. Obviously, what matters is not only the size of the population but its age profile – the proportion of "working age". Further to that, the so called "participation rate" is that percentage of the population of working age in employment - bearing in mind that people will take time out of paid work for a variety of reasons, even if they are of employment age. This includes women parenting young children; people whose illness and disability which prevents them working (sometimes through stigma and exclusion more than real inability); people who have given up looking for work because they have become demoralised and adjusted to long term unemployment; as well as people caring for older or ill family dependents.

This is part of a macro picture of the economy. Many textbooks also give a micro analysis of the labour market and portray the supply of labour by describing the choices for individual workers responding to the price of labour. In other words, adjusting the time worked to changes in the wage rate. The supply of labour is described in the textbooks as involving a choice for the worker of how many hours they want to work depending on the wage rate on offer – even though in practice many people have to work a fixed time on a "take it or get out basis".

When labour supply is described in this micro-economic way, the words sometimes used are of individuals choosing between "leisure" and "consumption". This is highly misleading. A good deal of the time that is not spent in paid work has to be committed to domestic labour and to the re-creation of the physiological ability to work again by sleeping, eating, cleaning and other activities belonging in the household – not to mention the time needed to attend to the care of children and other dependent people. Thus, "leisure" is usually only a fraction of the non-paid-work time. As was explained earlier, figures for Catalonia were that about 22.8% of time goes on entertainment and leisure, far less than on sleeping, eating and personal care – which is about half. This is to say, that much of the time not spent in production is spent in reproducing labour power, either that of the worker and/or of their children who are future generations of workers.

A further obvious point is that people do not just choose do paid work only in order to have the money to purchase consumer goods. If they are lucky, employment also brings job satisfaction; interests; a life narrative; purposeful activity; a structure to the day; meaningful relationships with colleagues and a role in the wider society. In the simplistic account, these things are not mentioned, although they clearly will influence how much time people allocate to paid work as opposed to free time. Thus, in a job where there is plenty of job satisfaction, one might expect someone to put in a lot of overtime – perhaps even unpaid overtime - just because they are enjoying what they are doing. On the other hand, people may also put in a lot of overtime, not because they are enjoying their work at all, but because of loyalty to colleagues, ambition to get along on a career path and other kinds of non-monetary motivation.

Of course, neoclassical and Austrian economists are not interested in all of this. "Methodological individualism" assumes that workers make "rational choices" based on their preferences and prices. Thus, how they come to their preferences about employment is of no interest to the economist. The mainstream economist thus, limits her or his interpretation of the world to cut out of consideration some of the most profound issues influencing human well-being. All that economists are interested in, as one would expect from a conventional economic analysis, is the wage rate – the price of labour per unit of time – and how much time people want to work for that rate. If the wage rate goes up, then there is supposedly an additional incentive to work longer hours because one can get even more consumer goods in the shops. This is counterbalanced by the incentive to "buy more time" as "leisure" because at the higher wage rate one can, in theory, work fewer hours and still have the same amount of purchasing power in the shops. (With a 5% wage rate increase one could have the same take home pay working 5% fewer hours).

This, anyway, describes the micro economic theory of the labour supply. A few moments thought is all that is necessary to become aware that it has little basis in reality anyway, because most people most of the time are not able to pick and choose how many hours that they work according to the wage rate. In most formal employment, conditions and hours are fixed contractually in order to stabilise routine and continual working procedures at fixed times in factories, offices and shops. Although sometimes, workers are able to make a choice to switch between part-time and full-time working. In addition, work times are often largely task determined so that they cannot be adjusted easily whether to respond to changing wage rates or anything else. As I shall argue later, what people are contracted to work and what they actually do work are often very different. In many professions, for example, people find they cannot fulfil all that is expected of them in their contracted hours and feel obliged to work a lot longer for no extra pay. A lot of this time is not visible because it is done at home or at another place than the official place of work. This has nothing to do with the wage rate and is far more due to a sense of obligation.

In other employment situations there is an increasing global trend to informal employment, which gives employers the flexibility to impose whatever times they wish. A large number of poor people are trying to sell their labour power in a buyer's market for labour and are forced to accept conditions where they have no ability to choose their hours because they must take what work they can, whenever they can get it.

The demand for labour

The theory of the demand for labour is equally fanciful and, again, often far from the reality. In many textbooks the demand for labour is described as a derived demand. There is a demand for apples and therefore a demand for apple pickers. The "marginal productivity" theory was described earlier in this book. As explained, the theory is that employers' demand for labour will depend on what each additional worker will add to production (the marginal physical product) multiplied by the price of the product.

The problem with this way of thinking, however, is that there is no "physical product" for about half of all paid employees in the world! Almost half of global employment is in the services or government sector – or, if not, in the offices and support activities of the production sector and not directly connected to production. Indeed, services and government is the part of global employment that is growing most rapidly. Although many routine standardised services can be quantified so that it is possible to measure the work that people do – haircuts, the processing of standard applications for services etc. – there are also many types of work where routines and standardisation cannot be done so easily – e.g. neighbourhood community work; psychotherapy; artistic creation; any form of investigative work; research and development activities.

In their social metabolic analysis, Giampietro, Mayumi and Sorman calculate the magnitudes. Giampietro is at the University of Barcelona and he gives figures for Catalonia in 2005 which can be taken as a ball park figure for all "developed" societies. Of all human activity in Catalonia, 9% is in paid work and 91% is in the household. Household activity includes sleeping, eating, recreation, the time of children, of the retired, unemployed people and sick people etc. Of the 9% of human activity in paid work, 65% is in services and government while 35% is in the production sector which is making "stuff". (Giampietro, Mayumi, & Sorman, 2011 p. 207).

It will be immediately recognised that, when it comes to employment, services and government are far more predominant than production in terms of hours worked.

Even in countries like China where employment in material production makes up a much larger proportion of paid work activities, the trend is towards a rapid development of services. Thus, while agricultural employment has shrunk as a proportion of total paid labour time, service employment has grown more rapidly than industrial employment. Between 1980 and 1999 the fraction of human activity in paid work that was employed in agriculture fell from 68% to 47%. The fraction of human activity working in industry, energy and mining, slightly decreased from 18% in 1980 to 17% in 1999. However, the fraction working in services and government increased dramatically from 14% in 1980 to 36% in 1999. (Gowdy, Giampietro, Ramos-Martin, & Mayumi, 2009, p. 214)

This has considerable implications for how one thinks about some kinds of "employed work" and in many cases makes approaches to theorising "human resources" in the standard economics form irrelevant or misleading. Approaches that assume that one can always quantify work can prove to be highly problematic. By this I mean there are large areas of work where the act of quantification, which occurs in order to try to improve management control, efficiency and to reduce costs, does not produce "improvement" but actually leads to a damage to effectiveness.

Often enough, quantification assumes features that are not there. This is particularly where a lot of what is happening is "emotional labour" which cannot be measured without rendering relationships insincere and inauthentic; where many activities are non-routine and one-off so measurements and "continuous improvement" is a meaningless goal; where people are involved partially voluntarily and it is unreasonable to measure up their involvement; where measurement demonstrates a lack of trust and thus, erodes and sours working relationships; where achieving one goal undermines another connected one and where measurement draws resources from things that are not measured, which then deteriorate, in favour of things that are measured.

Fear in the office

The typical workplace in the so called "developed world" and in many so called "developing countries" are not factories or workshops but offices. The predominance of offices as places of employment may not survive the limits to growth but as economists we ought to theorise about where people are actually employed. In fact there are an increasing number of people who are not even employed in an office - they are actually not located anywhere in particular but are continually on the move. The work done involves *the* institutionalised maintenance of health, education and social welfare (functions that used to be fulfilled in households, families and local communities but which are now increasingly institutionalised), a variety of state regulatory functions and, in the private sector, the planning, co-ordination and organisation of distant production processes, together with arrangements for PR and marketing.

To these places of employment should be added the development of financial management and services which is a huge area of expansion deserving of recognition. The communications and information processing media are part of the infrastructure for all these services.

A large proportion of these activities require a highly educated labour force.

In a book titled *The Collapse of Complex Societies,* archaeologist Joseph Tainter, argues that civilisations inevitably get more complex over time as they try to solve problems by the use of increasing complexity. If there is a problem, societies set up rules and regulations, specialist jobs, companies and government departments to deal with them. This complexification is successful at first, according to Tainter, but the returns diminish over time. At some point, increasing complexity means that responses to stress surges, in the form of wars, diseases, crop failures, monetary crises which become so difficult to organise that the complex society collapses. It is not then the stress surge on its own that brings about the collapse, but the failure of the over complex society to be able to manage them. (Tainter, 1988)

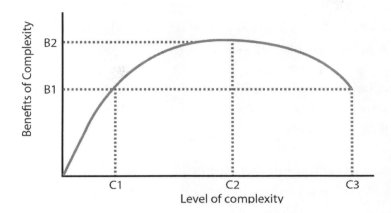

The collapse is then the enforced return to a lower level of complexity, through much chaos and confusion.

It is possible to argue that the growing size of the state in all advanced societies, as well as the growing size of the service sector, is a reflection of these processes. Adam Smith and Ricardo thought that an increasing division of labour would bring about increasing wealth and prosperity and perhaps they have for now, though at a tremendous delayed cost that has often not been noticed or counted (like the still to be felt impacts of climate change).

However, the huge increase in specialisation over two centuries has also brought about the need to have a vast services and government sector to co-ordinate and regulate production and reproduction (households). The resources to sustain this vast expansion in services and government come from the energy and materials that are produced by the production sector of the economy which services and government are, in turn, supposed to manage and facilitate.

This is not always how people think about public services and government in particular. In the media, a lot of the discussion about the growing complexity takes the form of discussions about taxation and the size of the state. Business people think that they "are taxed too much" and argue for less regulation, less welfare and less "nanny state". The truth is though, that in the private sector too, i.e. inside large corporations, there is also a vast inflation of co-ordination activity, and it could not be otherwise if international production arrangements with "just in time" production systems are to be kept running. All of these activities then require a very large allocation of human labour time, a very large number of electronic devices to assist the labour force and a not inconsiderable throughput of energy to keep the services and government sector working.

The scope for mechanisation and using energy in powered devices in the services and government sector is less than in industrial production. Therefore, it comes as no surprise that of the 1,120 Petajoules that flowed through the Catalonian economy in 2005 just 14% was used in the household sector while 86% was used in the paid work sector. Of the energy flowing through the paid work sector, 28% is devoted to services and government sector while the rest, 72%, is devoted to the production sector.

All of this helps contextualise what happens when a society hits a crisis because it discovers that its energy system is toxic (the effects of CO2 emissions on climate). In any case, depletion of energy sources means that fewer resources are available to sustain the services and government needed to co-ordinate and regulate a hyper complex, hyper interdependent division of labour.

As energy costs rise, we have seen how, because energy is needed for all functions in society, there are fewer resources for discretionary activities. People cannot service their debts and pay their energy bills and that is a problem for government too.

The resulting crisis in services and government then takes the form of a terror that a large number of people will lose their jobs and, as is obvious, losing a job is likely to send life into crisis for millions who are already in debt and struggling with their bills.

For those who keep their jobs, life inside the office is likely to become crazier given the specific features of office work.

When work is largely conceptual and intangible.

That is because, for many people, work has become increasingly conceptual and intangible. This, in turn, makes supervision very different from the factory system in most cases. It makes it impossible to give detailed directive supervision of many work tasks - much work must be delegated to workers to get on with on their own initiative.

This means that techniques of management are not so much telling people what to do but negotiating and discussing context setting arrangements. Management is indirect - via mission statements, performance standards, quality controls, good practice guidelines, SMART targets and the setting of procedures. Then, workers are left, day to day, hour by hour, to get on with it and try to work it out as best they can, staying within what are often infuriatingly irrelevant or off the mark targets, trying very hard to be seen to be doing their job.

The fact that many work activities have intangible outputs and outcomes has psychological consequences. With factory production work, one can see a material product taking shape as a result of the labour, and therefore, measure productivity increases in a very tangible way. However, in many service sector and office work settings, measurable outputs and outcomes are very difficult to show. This can make workers anxious that their contribution is not being noticed in conditions of increasing job insecurity. That, in turn, is a powerful force magnifying extrinsic motivations, for example, doing things to be seen, to get noticed, rather than for their own sake. If one is not noticed, then one might lose one's job in the next round of cuts and life management of habitat, debt servicing, relationships would all unravel.

Productivity increases to intangible work - what does it mean?

A further difference from work in the factory system is that, whereas in the factory system the investment in (fuel powered) machinery led to visible and tangible increases in the productivity of labour, as well as labour displacement, many service sector jobs cannot be mechanised in the same way.

As we have seen, perhaps a third of the energy that goes into the paid work sector goes through services and government in "developed countries". There has been scope to mechanise things like mailings lists with computer generated address labels from data bases, and the pressure is on to try to standardise as much as possible. However, you cannot mechanise so easily the work of a teacher, or social worker or surgeon nor the work of advertising agency staff. As a result, many "tertiary" jobs, particularly those which involve person-to-person interaction, cannot demonstrate continuing increases in productivity to justify why people should keep their jobs in hard times. Let alone justify continued salary increases which people need in order to service their debts.

Despite this, the economic ideology of promoting "continuous improvement" remains all-pervasive. As a result, whatever a worker is doing is never good enough - in a situation where startling increases in productivity arising from investment, whatever that means, are ruled out. In person-to-person services, there is no investment or automation that will obviously increase output in a continuous way, nor automated means to increase quality. In many cases, the only way to get improvement, it seems, is to put in longer and longer hours. And yet, longer hours do not increase outcomes at all. After a point, it reduces output as workers become tired, make mistakes, and morale slumps. In the tertiary sector, there really are diminishing returns when tired workers increase their input of time. Even if working longer hours did improve outcomes as people work harder, would anyone notice anyway?

"Presenteeism"

One result of this is "presenteeism". It is the opposite of absenteeism. A few years ago, 1 in 6 British workers were still at their desks after 10.00pm at least once a month. Some employers are becoming aware that presenteeism rarely results in real output increases and are trying to discourage it. However, workers practise presenteeism because they were anxious about job security and want to be seen to be keen. A recession where people have even more reason to fear for their jobs will probably make this kind of situation worse - it certainly has in Japan over the last decade of recession.

Not that all problems of overworking are a simple result of social cost pressures and government cuts. In some material that I have seen from the Austrian based organisation Verein zur Verzoegerung der Zeit, which was analysing the same phenomena, other motivations are suggested.

Some people prefer the office to their homes. For example, they are so busy with being the manager at the office they cannot switch out of this role at home. Their spouses and children find it hard to cope with them when they do come home. As work is given priority over family, the relation with family deteriorates. When the dedicated worker finally does go home, they experience such hostility that they get caught in a vicious circle of preferring to stay away longer. ("Society for the Deceleration of Time")

Work as motivation and massaging appearances

Many modern jobs are about massaging appearances, about motivating people and controlling them or trying to alter their behaviour. This is true, for example, of the PR industry and advertising, as well as, in a very different kind of way, true of the burgeoning counselling and therapy industries. It is obviously true too, for the media industries. Some jobs are about mystification and some about clarification. Some of us are employed to find ways to motivate people to eat a more healthy diet, others are employed to motivate people to eat out of burger bars and fast food restaurants. Graduates are coming straight out of the same university departments of psychology and other human and medical sciences and, in effect, working against each other. The so called Information Economy is not about neutral information at all - it a contested space where rival interpretations, exhortations, motivations jostle with each other for our attention and choice. The biggest players often have the loudest voices through their access to mainstream institutions and the mass media.

What is important in this world is to get noticed - to have your narrative about your work taken into account. This is not necessarily the same as doing a good job. It is more about good PR.

The importance of being noticed

One strategy for the problem that your work is not being noticed by the people that might matter is to make sure that you are seen. This entails turning up to, or even better, calling a large number of meetings. There is safety in numbers and, the more managers or officials that tag along to your meetings, the higher your outcome targets are, as well as the more you are likely to be perceived as a busy and important person. You will be "well-connected", advance your career or, at least, be safe from the next round of cuts. It's an excellent personal PR strategy.

Fluctuating Workloads - taking on more work in quiet periods overhypes the peaks

Much work is unstable - there are troughs as well as peaks. In the troughs, if one spends time doing background reading, or reflecting, it would seem that one has been doing nothing and there are those who dare not give this appearance. So, rather than take advantage of the troughs to relax, they anxiously seek out new work. The problem then is that, as their work picks up again, they hit workload peaks with the old work and the new agenda they have now added - and they simply cannot control their workloads getting into a frightful state.

"Emotional labour"

Far from being about producing "physical products" as suggested in economic theory, a large amount of employment is of a person-to-person character. It is also frequently about motivation, and an increasingly large element is best described as working with emotions.

Emotional labour is when your employer requires you to have a particular set of feelings that will please the customer or public. At home, and in our personal relationships, therapists tell us we should get in touch with our feelings and not bottle them up. When you are feeling angry, frustrated and irritated, or when you are feeling frightened, you need to be able to get out what it is that is bothering you and negotiate your relationships with those around you. You need to be able to recognise their feelings too, respect them, and work with them. But can you do that if, for example, you work at a call centre? What exactly do you do with the impatient and rude caller who is steaming with rage because his computer isn't working and he's having to pay a telephone charge to get your advice to fix it? He might be the tenth of such aggressive callers in the last day. Are you expected to express what you are really feeling to him? Hardly... among other things the caller might actually be an agent of your employer checking up on your telephone manner. (Hochschild, 2012)

Workers in health and social welfare also do *emotional labour*. They are employed to empathise, or keep their cool, under difficult conditions. On the corporate mission statements, for example, it says that staff will deal with users of services with politeness and respect. Yet these may be the very same users who, because of the time they have had to wait, as well as the intensity of their needs, are very often aggressive and angry.

Insincerity becomes the norm. Avoiding the truth is ordinary.

Working without a clear workplace

A further feature of contemporary work is that, because it is person-to-person work, conceptual, organising, logistics and persuading work, the labour process often *doesn't have to be fixed in place to a particular machine and location*. Computers, phones, iPads have all been developed as mobile options so that you can move around with them. But this loss of a fixed location for your work can carry anxieties with it. It can mean that you are no longer **seen** doing the intangible things that you do. At least in the office, people saw you making phone calls and typing letters - now how are your superiors to know that you are there and still doing things? You are out of sight and possibly out of mind. Until possibly, you are remembered at the time of the next reorganisation and round of cuts and, perhaps, therefore the victim of the next staff downsizing. How many calls on the mobile are really about reminding the office that you still exist and are an important part of the operation?

A further complication - Co-ordinating and synchronising with the underclass

Working in dispersed locations has stresses of its own, particularly for health and other workers co-ordinating to be available when people are actually in. Many workers have a problem of finding a time when people are in their homes so that they can arrange a time to help them. It's a problem not only of agreeing a time, but of actually sticking to it. Vulnerable client groups often have no daily routine and they probably often have no diary to help them to remember. In the "underclass" are people whose chaotic lives mean a succession of crises so, even that if they remember the appointment at their house, there's still no guarantee they will be in. They may be at a doctors' surgery; summoned to solve a housing benefit crisis or they may have run away, too embarrassed to let anyone in to see their shambolic and sordid circumstances.

Working without clear work times

When a clear notion of work place begins to dissolve, so too often enough, does the notion of a defined time of work. If your work involves a lot of thinking and you are always contactable on your mobile - when exactly does work stop and when does it begin? If you go to sleep thinking about unresolved dilemmas at work and wake early thinking about them - are you even at work in bed? It's all a long way from "clocking off" from a shift in the factory, or at a large care institution with fixed shifts, where you left behind fixed routines, "switching off" psychologically as well.

There are powerful pressures to overwork in this kind of world. If you are insecure about it then, to compensate for the invisibility and intangibility of your work, you do that bit extra... attending a meeting that isn't otherwise really necessary, just to make sure your bosses are still aware that you are there.

Specialised work that no one else understands

Yet another feature of work nowadays is the use of narrower specialities. As the home and local community are emptied of more production and service functions, everyone wants to be a graduate expert in the resultant externally organised institutions. For most of history, *Jacks and Jills of all trades* provided for the bulk of their own needs, DIY style, with the help of their neighbours in small local communities. Nowadays, millions of highly educated specialists are trying to live together and co-ordinate immense bureaucratic empires, each of which are themselves, focused only on a narrow range of activities. For example, education specialities; social work specialities; market niche specialities; computer software specialities; art niches; media niches... The likelihood is, that only a tiny number could understand what you are doing in your job anyway, because only a few have had your ten year training. So on what criteria can your managers judge your work and appreciate it anyway?

The growth of bureaucratic empires

The more specialities, the more complicated and complex the resultant co-ordination between them, the more referrals, the more departments and the more liaison and referral arrangements, the more committees needed to manage them all. This is Tainter's dynamic of increasing complexity in spades.

The bureaucracies and managerial structures also blossom because they cover larger geographical areas. The larger the organisation, the further away senior managers are, the more to co-ordinate and the more bureaucratic layers. As senior managers get to be further away in geographical and organisational space from the operational level, so too, a breed of manager takes over that has no experience of "coming up through the ranks" and no idea what is involved "at the coal face". This breed also has no personal interest, loyalty or commitment to local staff or local services who they never meet regularly, nor get to know. The probability is, their background will be in accountancy, business studies and "economics" and they will know a lot about costs and record keeping - but little about practical operations.

What senior managers do in order to appear to be useful - measurement and reorganisation

Tainter's dynamic of increasing complexity is linked to another feature of modern work, that of the phenomena of permanent reorganisation with all its unstable and unsettling effects. Our betters need *to be seen to be doing something too,* to be seen to be improving things, lest we forget how much we need them. A lot of the things we have to do is really about reassuring them that *they* are really needed. This goes for managerial reorganisations, for example, and for the ever increasing volume of quantitative performance returns.

The consequences of senior managers feeling the need to be seen to be doing something can be negative when the most important thing to be done is thinking about things - or resting. Thinking and resting are not unproductive activities. Thinking, reflecting upon things, is the very stuff of intelligent management - even if you can't see it when it is happening. Nor is resting an unproductive use of time. Rest and recreation is re -creation. It is the re-creation of the capacity of the human body and mind to function - it is like the recharging of a battery. It is biological time in which, to be sure, you cannot see anything taking place, but something very important is happening nonetheless. Without the recharge process there will be no long run effectiveness.

Alas, to an insecure manager (or politician) things may not appear like this. If they must be seen to be doing something (when, in reality, it would be better to do nothing) then senior managers or politicians always have one option they can turn to - reorganising the managerial structure itself, its funding and monitoring regimes and/or its fundamental policies. Too often reorganisations are a substitute for thinking up any new ideas. Thus, it will often be necessary to bring in consultants from outside to give the ideas.

Consultants and reorganisations

The consultants, significantly these are typically from accountancy organisations, will usually understand the situation even less but have the necessary rapacious arrogance to assume that their MBA qualifies them to recommend for any situation. There are then rarely any improvements to the quality of the work done, at ground level, "at the coal face". (Craig & Brooks, 2006, pp. 111-132) However, such reorganisations still have two advantages. Firstly, they convey the appearance that senior management (or politicians) are active and in control, while, secondly, it takes up the time of subordinates and stops them finding the time to take their own initiatives. (Which might often be more focused and relevant because subordinate initiatives would be derived closer to coal face realities).

If reorganisation involves lots of partnerships it ties up a wider circle with consultations about the bigger agenda, rather than allowing the junior partners to find the time to develop agendas of their own. And it all adds to the time pressure down the line, as everyone goes to the meetings about the latest good idea about a yet bigger and more complicated management system, rather than setting up meetings of their own about what concerns them. Furthermore, as every dictator in history has realised, regular reshuffles and reorganisations of the bureaucratic hierarchy prevents trust relations, allegiances and alliances being formed out of which opposition, or even new bids for power, might be made.

Measurement and paper trails - drugs for insecure managers?

Another option for insecure managers who need to be seen to be busy, is to measure things. Since managers are paid to manage, it follows that they are paid to improve the performance of their subordinates. Politicians are keen to claim that the public sector, and particularly its bureaucracy, can be made more efficient. The use of public money must be closely scrutinised, particularly as the public services keep growing. Money paid in taxes must not be wasted. To prevent skiving and waste by officials they are put under scrutiny by auditors, management consultants and put under pressure to justify whatever they do. Needless to say, this does not reduce the amount of work and resources used, it increases it. In proportion to the implied lack of trust, the anxiety about the need to prove what one does increases, and the need for managers to keep records that will cover their backs likewise rises. This leads to a snowball effect in the amount of paper work, form filling and record keeping. Everywhere, there are instructions, procedures, best practice guidelines, measurable targets to be met.

Measurement and the decline of trust relations

This increased paperwork does nothing to improve services - indeed it takes the time resources away from their improvement. Their improvement can usually only come about through practitioners having time for reflection about the coal face practice. Allowed some space for leisurely strategic thinking about day to day to operational problems - but away from these problems, not in the middle of them, while the phone is ringing. To this must be added the need for senior managers to then trust in the judgement and suggestions of their subordinates - letting them implement their strategic ideas. However, in this regime of neurotic management and paper trails, trust is just what is lacking. To develop trust requires time and stability in work groups. However, not only is there no time for reflection in the work, there is no time for "time wasting" on developing trust relations, mutual understanding and communication inside work groups themselves, or between them and higher decision-making bodies.

Neglected time needs

Those who have to struggle with these social neuroses of our betters as services and government become places of screaming stress, have to draw up descriptions of work in the new fashionable forms: with project milestones, with specific, measurable, achievable, repeatable, time bound targets and so on. Typically, the things that go missing are target times for pausing, for reflection on the work, times for the development of good relations in the office - the creation of a work group common spirit.

If you want targets for these things, then you have to remember to put something in the budget for training and consultancy, and you pray that you will actually find the time to actually do them. We call such times "time out" which says a lot about how we see them, that is, as a sort of additional luxury. In fact, if a group or an organisation is really to function and develop as a team, it must devote time to the structure itself and the human relations between people. From this point of view, "times out" are crucial to functioning - building trust, relationships and understanding between members.

(Anyone who has been on a good away weekend will find out how much you learn about other people and how much it serves to bring out issues and team spirit. This is really quite crucial but is often neglected. Time is needed for such things, yet too often, time is only available for people to work together as if they were mere automatons - operators of a collection of kinds of technical expertise).

Different management styles

Managers are individuals. One cannot generalise. Some of them are interested in, and care about, their work. They understand their job as being about working with people - with colleagues, clients and citizens who they seek to understand as individuals, as well as seeing them as "human resources" i.e. as means to organisational ends. Other managers are more interested in, and care about, their career paths. Being a good manager and being on a successful career path are not the same. When you are interested in, and care about the people, as well as about the work, you accumulate a deeper understanding. You remain open in attitude to the ideas of colleagues to whom you may feel a certain loyalty and responsibility. When you are interested in your career path and promotion, what you are interested in are measured results. Your relationships to the "human resources" are less important as you don't intend to hang around long anyway. You are aiming for promotion to head office.

How the ambitious manager benefits from situations to demonstrate firefighting skills

Increasingly chaotic time, like the ones we are in, are heaven made for a certain kind of ambitious manager. If they are lucky, they get promoted when there are plenty of problems to be sorted out - and they can rush around firefighting. If middle managers get their faces seen resolving problems, their self-esteem, morale and reputation are on a rising curve. Thank goodness society is in crisis! Just think of what might happen if ambitious managers were to get caught in the nightmare of everything going well! If everything is functioning reasonably smoothly, subordinates looking after themselves effectively, well able to sort out problems among themselves, then who is going to notice that the ambitious middle manager is even there? The same paradox goes for senior managers. To get yourself noticed you need to be firefighting, so you need a good crisis. If you haven't got a crisis you can provoke one - set up a new project or discover the need to reorganise things.

The overall picture - absurd jobs, mentally unhealthy workplaces

In summary, as we approach Tainter's point of collapse. A not untypical worker in large parts of the office/service sector, will be tangled in a large, bewildering bureaucracy whose senior managers know and care little about the front line operational staff, clients or the main activities of their organisation. Such staff may be struggling to recover from the practical and emotional turmoil of the last reorganisation and/or are confronted by a new one, which adds to their sense of job insecurity and expendability. Their work may involve conceptual and intangible activities that no one else fully understands, and they may have difficulty showing what tangible outcomes they create. They may, therefore, find it difficult to prove that the outcomes of their work are improving over time - even though this is what is expected of them. What will make their lot more difficult is that they will be operating in a world where the competition for appearances are everything to one's security and advancement. The situation then arises that profiling oneself by being seen and heard, particularly by attending a lot of meetings, is more important than actually getting on and doing the job. The likelihood is that their employer has a PR strategy and a mission statement about the supposed representation of the interests of all stakeholders which is far from the realities. At least part of the strain is knowing this, or even being one of those inauthentic people responsible for the maintenance of the facade. The problems may appear unresolvable and follow the unhappy worker home, with tasks to do on the lap top and while they are on call. Only by making a big enough space between themselves and their work, by flying abroad on holiday, do they really feel they "escape". (However, your work may follow you on holiday too, if you take your mobile). In short, what is called "work stress" is based on a pervading sense that much of their work is actually absurd or futile, a profound sense of insecurity and a sense that they are living a lie.

Very few people seem to be asking *whether this system development might not itself be creating new kinds of pathologies and problems - particularly in the field of work related illness and mental illness*. In these new structures, work problems are no longer experienced so much collectively - in a way picked up by trade unions as collective bargaining issues, they are more and more experienced individually. The psycho-dynamics of work in the new bureaucracies is experienced as conflicts and tensions between individuals and particular colleagues, supervisors and customers (and volunteers). The problems lie in coping with the tensions arising from: aggressive clients; envious or hostile colleagues who are floundering in their jobs; with knock-on effects of both an emotional and performance character; harassment by supervisors and/or floundering supervisors and failing support mechanisms; failure to meet targets because these targets are meaningless, unrealistic or contradictory. Finally, there is a pervading sense that no one at senior levels really cares, that whatever the PR and the mission statement say, the real mood is one of cynicism, powerlessness and hopelessness which makes it difficult to live with the gulf between the institutional PR narrative and the down to earth reality.

Institutional Contexts - When Resource Problems become time problems

Often enough, particularly in the public and not for profit sectors, managers put themselves and other people under time pressure because they are trying their best to solve or ameliorate a mountain of health, social and environmental problems and the misery and pain associated with these.

Far too often, the sheer volume of these problems in relation to the available time resources, is so great, that "care" takes the form of a form of processing that uses fixed procedures with little room for tuning into individuals. The time does not exist and the supplicant for institutional help must subordinate themselves to the time availabilities and rhythms of the institution. Resource problems reveal themselves too in waiting lists. A certain kind of over-conscientious manager and pressured staff may succeed in achieving shorter waiting lists. Although they probably die younger and make more mistakes too. This is the consequence where public services are squeezed through lack of public funding. An example would be in education, where teachers are required to put in more time on the cheap, doing more paper work, working with bigger classes, less classroom help and more disturbed and demanding children. The public sector and voluntary sector is then literally worked to death - because stressed and conscientious workers have more heart attacks and strokes.

Obviously, the time management problems that exist at the interface between public and voluntary sector organisations and citizens in need are not simply waiting list problems. Particularly at the bottom of the social structure, where health, care and environmental problems are concentrated, there is a much greater difficulty of synchronising with public and voluntary services. This difficulty is getting worse now that services are more located in the community.

In conclusion

The identification of an appropriate pace and amount of work is, it should be said, only useful if a worker can then decide that s/he will not work beyond that pace. This requires a personal decision - and/or a group one. Sometimes, this confronts workers with the necessity to contemplate the possibility of leaving their job altogether when it is necessary to set a marker, beyond which they are not prepared to work under any circumstances. Without this decision, that one has a "bale out point", one has no natural or obvious limit beyond which one will not keep on trying to do more, even though it is futile.

An important contribution to a sustainable society is made when overworked people decide to drop out, or radically reduce, the amount they work. If necessary, they reduce their income and consumption at the same time. The process is described as "downshifting". Much consumption is, in any case, akin to comfort eating, a sort of psychological compensation or substitute for living. Since high consumption is also a burden to the ecology of the planet and greater well-being is probably to be found in a lower energy, lower income and lower work life style for those who are currently overworked, overweight and over tired; giving up ambitious ideas about what we can achieve personally, giving up our ambitions might be just what is needed.

None of this, however, should be interpreted as meaning that dealing with stress is a matter for workers themselves. Stress cannot be dealt with by setting up a stress industry of counselling and other services, telling workers to work less but maintaining the pressures on them by ceaseless reorganisations and performance management pressures. Something has to give. As the limits to growth kick in and many jobs become even more like hell, there will be a lot of people forced to recognise that their only realistic option is to drop out or reduce their workloads. Society will need support arrangements for people to do so - despite our betters saying that "work" is a duty.

PART FIVE

Entrepreneurs – Anti-social and Social

Chapter 39

Entrepreneurship – the narrative of destructive creation

In the religion of economics, the entrepreneur is a hero engaged in a narrative of destructive creation. Entrepreneurs are tragically noble figures on a treadmill of competition – but who is really making the sacrifices? Often it is the entrepreneur's family or other "stakeholders" who are carrying the costs and risks. What motivates entrepreneurs and what are "animal spirits" anyway? As their organisations develop, the role of the entrepreneur changes and, at their most powerful, they seek to co-opt officials and politicians for their agendas. Management can be exercised through over centralised control freakery or via distributed decision-making systems. Many entrepreneurs and managers are psychopaths, and criminals are entrepreneurs too. In the modern world, control fraud i.e. looting your own company is not uncommon. The City of London as tax haven and secrecy jurisdiction is one of a number of places to hide out.

"Capitalism is the astounding belief that the most wickedest of men will do the most wickedest of things for the greatest good of everyone." John Maynard Keynes

In economics, particularly economics of the Austrian school, we not only have a story about the satisfaction of needs and wants, we also have a story with a hero. The hero is the entrepreneur.

The entrepreneur is celebrated because the entrepreneur takes risks. They advance some resources that they already own, their property, in anticipation of a successful venture in which they hope that they will make profit. However, the future is always uncertain. The best laid plans of mice and men often go awry so the entrepreneur can make a loss too.

One of the earliest theorists of this was Richard Cantillon, an Irish refugee in France, whose *Essai sur la Nature du Commerce en General* has been claimed by the Austrian school of economics as the first economic treatise (in other words before Adam Smith) and also the first example of Austrian economics. He is one of their heroes. (Thornton, 2010) (MisesWiki, 2013)

Cantillon wrote about how economic actors, lacking control over the market, had to operate in conditions of uncertainty in which losses as well as profits were possible.

> The price of these products will depend partly on the weather, partly on demand; if corn is abundant relative to consumption it will be dirt cheap, if there is scarcity it will be dear. Who can foresee the number of births and deaths of the people in a State in the course of the year? Who can foresee the increase or reduction of expense that may come about in the families? And yet

the price of the Farmer's produce depends naturally upon these unforeseen circumstances, and consequently he conducts the enterprise of his farm at an uncertainty.

The unsuccessful entrepreneur will live poorly or go bankrupt, while the successful entrepreneur will obtain a profit or advantage and cause entry into the market, "and so it is that the undertakers of all kinds adjust themselves to risks in a State." The entrepreneur brings prices and production into line with demand; in well-organized societies, government officials can even fix prices of basic items without too much complaint. (quoted in Thornton, 2010)

It is through such stars that the world is "improved", production is increased and jobs are created. Since the ultimate problem, as conceived by economists, is scarcity, the entrepreneurs preparedness to risk their wealth is an act to be celebrated by people who effectively become our saviours.

The narrative of the intrepid entrepreneur is closely tied with the romance of "innovation". The entrepreneur is able to see the value of a new technical process or product and their visionary placement of their resources, their organisation of the productive process, and its transformative effects keeps society "moving forward". This "dynamism" is self-evidently "a good thing".

Other societies have existed that see things differently. They prioritise sustainability and resilience which are not at all the same thing as production increase and resource use efficiency. Indigenous people typically see themselves as having a responsibility to think of the consequences of major change for their descendants – sometimes for seven generations in the future. Their traditions are about preserving tried and tested approaches to living within the capacity limits of local ecological systems.

If a generation is 30 years then 7 generations are approximately 200 years. We are only now beginning to see whether the entrepreneurship and innovations of the industrial revolution can really be counted as "a good thing". If we look at how damaging climate change already is, as well as at the rate of species loss, the situation is not looking very good.

It may be therefore that the plucky entrepreneur has a tragic destiny. Austrian economists wearing bow ties have been telling them that their creative destruction is wonderful for humanity when, all along, and without realising it, the profit seekers have been leading humanity into hell.

The tragic nobility of entrepreneurs on the treadmill of competition

At the time of writing, very few conventional entrepreneurs are likely to recognise this. They will be far too busy. An important part of the story that many entrepreneurs themselves like to believe is already tragic, but very noble. This is, that they can never rest in their ceaseless quest for improvement. The creative soul has a tragic but noble destiny because their successes bring imitators who erode the gains which come from being at the head of the field. So they are on a treadmill. Society benefits, however, in the form of increased efficiency and new toys that they did not know that they needed. As the entrepreneurs' investment grows, it must be continually transformed or it will suffer at the hands of competitors, perhaps entering from other parts of the interrelated web of changes in the process of "creative destruction". The entrepreneur that rests satisfied may find his assets are the ones whose value is destroyed by the next round of innovations introduced by pioneering new competitors. It is a neo-Darwinian world – destroy your competitors or they will destroy you. The successful entrepreneur is the long run survivor in this world.

There is no doubt that bringing something new into existence, where the processes of doing so are complex and involve a lot of unknowns can be tough. This is particularly the case for young beginners when they are wrestling with the problem of business start-ups. The Buddhist idea of what causes suffering is where people want the world to be different from the way it is - and when people set out with an idea or a plan to bring forth a business and a product that has not existed before they can easily end up going round in circles. There will be times in the process when they will be under enormous pressure to give up – perhaps at the point that others begin to lose faith in their ability to realise their idea, and withdraw their previous commitment.

To successfully carry through the start-up, the entrepreneur may see themselves as needing an entire organisation, at least in embryo, but find this difficult to achieve. They will need the product or service AND the market AND the people to produce the product AND somewhere to produce it AND a functioning bookkeeping and management system AND an awareness of regulations AND a legal framework. All these elements will have to match together. Achieving each element of the complete package BEFORE being able to start seems like a formidable challenge requiring a considerable faith in oneself.

A common mistake in the early stages is to keep on thinking of more elaborate ideas and to try to achieve too much in the architectural mind-set just described. For very often, the best way of developing a company or small organisation is NOT to try to assemble all the elements together before starting.

If all elements of an organisation are to be evolved, then this must be through the smallest steps at first because small steps are achievable and bring a team together around practicalities, experiment and learning. To take a banal example, if you're setting up a business selling pickles you would be advised not to try to go into serial production at first but to experiment on a very small scale with a single batch production made in a borrowed kitchen with friends and sold to friends too. Such small experiments become learning exercises, get people working together, synchronising their times and developing complementary roles. It enables an emergence process, where each step organically leads to a larger and more complex one that is closer to the complexity of a continually functioning organisation.

What is clear is that "entrepreneurs" are rarely doing things on their own. Their ability to achieve anything at all depends on their ability to bring a functioning team together, as well as to establish relationships of other sorts with suppliers, regulators, colleagues and customers. That's why the idea of the heroic entrepreneur is a bit misleading if one takes it to mean that an individual is carrying the whole emotional and financial load of the process.

Entrepreneurs and their families – who is really making the sacrifices?

For a start, if, for example, a business has to be initially conducted from people's houses, then a partner and children may also be carrying a part of the load and will also perhaps be soaking up the emotional frustrations of "the entrepreneur" (i.e. husband and father – perhaps wife and mother) as they hit obstacle after obstacle. One crucial aspect of the life of the entrepreneur may well be not being there mentally and emotionally for their children. Since this will have long run psychological effects, should we not also include these effects in our assessment of who is carrying the emotional load of "entrepreneurship"? These are not the only possible effects.

> "Kyle" recognized fissures in his marriage before he launched an electronics manufacturing company. Afterward, those fissures widened into canyons. Kyle admits he neglected his wife, poring over business plans when she wanted to chat. For her part, his wife didn't take him seriously; she openly doubted that the company would ever support them.

Again

> One test of the entrepreneur's motivation is how much of the family's collective life he is willing to sacrifice with little payoff. Tony, a software and media entrepreneur, admits subjecting his wife to "eight years of damn-near abject poverty and suffering" while he struggled to produce and sell a TV show. Finally, "She couldn't take it anymore," he said. "Two kids in diapers and wondering where next month's mortgage payment was coming from." Tony's wife delivered an ultimatum: the TV show or her. "I said, 'The TV show'", he told me. "That was the day the love died." The marriage died with it. (Hirshberg, 2010)

Although the entrepreneurial process is hard, and not just hard for the entrepreneur, it is not going to be equally hard for everyone. For people who are well connected, who have resources and a track record, the process of drawing together the ingredients of a successful venture are bound to be easier. Start-ups by what might be called members of the "corporate aristocracy" will not have the same "heroic characteristics" as young unknowns just out of university. Although middle aged managers working through their mid-life crisis by striking out on their own again might like to imagine so. It is obviously going to be easier because with greater resources one can draw together the necessary package of elements to make for a functioning project. There will be easy access to the office facilities so that it will not be necessary to work in the bedroom. There will be easier access to the skilled people, the money, the advisers and the political connections.

Getting others to pay the costs – unrecognised stakeholders sharing risks

As often as not, many others are therefore sharing in the burdens and risks of the entrepreneur's decisions. While Austrian economists celebrate heroic individuals, the truth is, that all business ventures are dependent on the participation of others, sometimes willingly involved and sometimes not. Many

18th and 19th century business ventures in "the colonies" required labour, and since voluntary labour was scarce slavery was resorted to. This was one way in which large amounts of capital were raised that was subsequently risked.

The development of limited liability and corporations as fictional persons, has also been all about reducing risks for individual entrepreneurs – which means, pari passu, imposing those risks on other people - creditors of various kinds and workers.

Nor should we forget that risks are also carried by communities and ecological systems. As already argued, the whole idea of "externality" is utterly ideological because it appears that externality is somehow exceptional, a special case. Yet ALL economic decisions involve taking materials and energy out of the environment where people and other species live. All economic activity ultimately involves wastes going back into the environment. NO economic activity takes place without these "externalities". No entrepreneurs have ever, or can ever, produce and sell anything without "externalities". Thus, a very large part of the long run unknown costs of economic activity are actually not born by the entrepreneur at all but by the environment, by communities and by future generations. The destruction in the "creative destruction" is therefore not just of "capital", or of jobs... the destruction is of ecological systems, species, and the stability of the Earth's climate.

Over the centuries, entrepreneurs have also spent a lot of time thinking how they can shunt losses arising from uncertainty, including about the environment, onto the state and therefore onto today's taxpayers and onto future taxpayers. No doubt, this doesn't quite match the economist's ideology but it is what happens. The successful entrepreneur needs to be "well connected". By intensive lobbying of politicians and officials, as well as parachuting their people into government offices to write draft legislation, it has been possible, for example, for the carbon aristocracy to offload the risks of developing "unconventional fuels" like shale gas in the UK government's energy strategy. You get lots of "enterprise" if there are no risks when taking investment decisions because the state/taxpayer are backing them. We've also seen that state backing for "too big to fail" financial institutions has led to a reckless "entrepreneurialism", partly because banks expect to be rescued when they come unstuck.

The repeated experience, through economic history, of market bubbles which are characterised by collective euphoria, tells us something very powerful about "entrepreneurship". It enables us to "get real" about the people who play leading roles in the economy. Although it is true that entrepreneurs are making decisions which involve committing resources in the face of an unknown future, the main method most managers use to guess the future is to try find out what everyone else thinks – it is to "go with the herd".

At least then, if everyone gets it wrong, one cannot be singled out as any more blameworthy than anyone else. In a newspaper like the Financial Times, journalists - typically called "market strategists" - collect opinions from people in companies about what the market trends are. That way, they get a bit of fame while their peers get a sense of what others in the market are thinking.

To sum up thus far, "entrepreneurship" is a category covering a multitude of circumstances, a multitude of actors and a multitude of behaviours. Some of these may certainly approximate the challenging obstacle race that justifies the romance. But a closer look reveals a range of often unrecognised stakeholders sharing the risks, many of whom are unwilling participants; that by no means all entrepreneurial actors have it difficult and those who are well connected and well-resourced may get the state to hold their hands. In addition, it is by no means self-evident that a restless increase in production is in the long term interests of a sustainable and resilient society. Nevertheless, there are plenty of people out there who are desperate to prove themselves, to prove that they can "perform", to "achieve" – who are not asking themselves from whence this inner drive comes.

Motivations - what drives entrepreneurs?
What are "animal spirits" anyway?

Childhood neglect perhaps? Only being noticed when they were "a credit for the family?" Having to "earn" love?

Before going further, let us have a look at the psychological roots that drive people to want to be entrepreneurs. While economists would say that the motivation of the entrepreneurs is the profit, more particularly the rate of return on the capital that they risk, there is clearly usually more going on than this. The famous phrase used by John Maynard Keynes to describe the preparedness of entrepreneurs to venture into the unknown and to try to shape the economic future was "animal spirits". This description does not really tell us anything in depth, but it does not convey a feeling of the rational calculation of future profit probabilities. The phrase evokes something more emotional and perhaps driven.

Over a lifetime in an entrepreneurial role, people's motivations are likely to change too. Indeed, some entrepreneurs may lose interest in their entrepreneurial role once the company that they have helped to found is well established. After a point, it will become possible to move on without any loss of income because they have accumulated enough capital. Thomas Picketty points how the fortune of Bill Gates, the founder of Microsoft, has continued to grow just as rapidly since he stopped working for that company. A very rich person can plough back virtually all their income into further investment so their wealth will grow with no effort at all. (If there is any connection between effort, ability and wealth it disappears altogether at this point. A point that is even more evident in the case of people who inherit their wealth and put in no work to earn it at all.) (Picketty, 2014, p. 440)

As I have attempted to convey already, the superficial idea that you might get having read too much economics is that new entrepreneurs are responding to market opportunities to make money and, in particular, to maximise the rate of return on capital. However, this kind of thinking about motivations doesn't get us very far. Certainly, if one looks at the literature that tries to motivate people to set up their own businesses, the potential rate of return is not the only or even the main motivation mentioned. Being one's own boss and having the scope to realise one's creative impulses are also there. No doubt, many people have experience of how institutions and companies run and want to show how it could be done differently and, as they see it, better. Then there are those who "want to prove themselves".

Companies are set up by human beings and human beings are more complex and varied than one will learn from economic texts. The rate of return on capital is only the way of keeping score in a choice of "life game" in which the deeper motivations need to be uncovered. It is possible to conceive of many different motivations to be an entrepreneur, but there is clearly a difference between those whose motivations are extrinsic and those who are intrinsic.

The intrinsically motivated entrepreneur is interested in what they are trying to sell or produce for its own sake. They are the producers of a particular product because that product interests them, or they believe in it and they are only secondarily interested in it as a way of making money. Some of these kind of entrepreneurs may work together with peers to innovate forms of social and environmental enterprise and/or strive to develop a co-operative or a community business. In many cases, money making is merely a means to another end.

An extrinsically motivated entrepreneur is not really interested in the product or service that they sell as such. They are interested in it chiefly because it makes money and it allows them to profile themselves in a status role, in short, as a vehicle for attention seeking and social cache. The entrepreneurship is about proving to other people something about themselves. This kind of entrepreneur has what the therapist Erich Fromm called a "marketing personality".

For some entrepreneurs the exercise is about "being" and involves factors such as work satisfaction; the exercise of creativity; the engagement with something that interests them; the development of working relationships; contribution to a local community and protection of the environment.

For others it is about "having", that is, purchasing power; celebrity status; the ability to prove to those that doubted them in the past that "they can make it" and that they can be really grown up.

This distinction makes sense of a phenomenon noticed by John Kay, which he explains in his book, *Obliquity*. The companies that tend to do best in terms of financial performance are often the ones in which the managers are not striving for best possible financial returns, but have other motivations – which business partners and customers perhaps sense and respond to positively – sensing a greater concern for quality and trustworthiness, sensing shared values. (Kay, 2010)

The "legacy problem"

Evidently, a person can make a transition from one kind of entrepreneurship to another, and they do.

Organisations can also change. They can start from an idealistic vision and lose that as they grow larger and find it difficult to manage the complexity of relationships in the organisation in a non-hierarchical way, finally resorting to conventional command and control top-down management systems. This changes the entire spirit of the venture and culture of the organisation. As it degenerates away from its ideals, it starts to follow much more conventional extrinsic goals.

Another pressure to change identity and purposes lies in the difficulty that small organisations often have of expanding because they lack finance. Perhaps the team that started up the company finally resorts to a "venture capitalist", which leads to a powerful player coming into a business with a different value system. This person has no loyalty to original colleagues or original ideals, but plenty of concern about his money stake and a desire to prove that he is smart when it comes to business. His money stake turns out to be the purchase of the right to push around an "old guard" who are not regarded as equal partners because, as the newcomer sees it, they lack the savoir faire in cut and thrust, the ruthlessness of the market, possessed by the man with the money. He turns into the new boss... very much like the old boss that the initiators of a company were running away from when they set up their new company in the first place.

Yet another process is where the originator of an organisation is ready to move on, either because of tiredness, age, or for some other reason. A successful organisation is likely to be eyed-up by money junkies as a desirable acquisition and, as the founder moves on, the time to move in arrives.

The name for these kinds of transitional crises is the "legacy problem". It is not just communism that degenerated and disappointed expectations. Many idealistic business ventures do as well. Nothing lasts. (Kelly, 2012, p. 157)

One interesting and little known fact is that there are more people employed by co-operatives in the world than there are employed in large corporations. We can ponder why the successes of co-operative are so little recognised. Perhaps it is because they make less fuss about themselves and their managers. Partly this is because, in co-operatives, people are likely to share management decisions, or at least the managers are unlikely to stand out. Perhaps also it is because there are people and co-ops who do not want to grow their organisation larger and face the legacy problem. Co-operative managers are more likely to be in the background.

The idea can be expressed the other way round. In capitalist corporations where extrinsic motivations are uppermost, it is more important to the managers that everyone knows that they are there. This might be regarded as narcissism but also their way of justifying their large remuneration. Thus, rather than their fabulously productive role accounting for their income, it might be the other way round. Their fabulously large income accounts for their very visible role and also meets a "look at me" need to be recognised as a very smart operator in a fast changing environment.

The changing role of entrepreneurs as their organisations develop

If a start-up is successful – and one in three fail in the first 3 years in the UK – then the entrepreneur who has been there from the beginning will progressively move into a different role. As an organisation grows in size it will also grow in complexity. Entrepreneurship becomes a different kind of process, namely, how to manage and steer in conditions of growing size and increasing complexity.

As explained above, the development of organisations in a competitive environment is a struggle to grow larger in order to survive. A transition from flexible pioneers with the freedom of action that comes from having few ties, to highly networked and highly integrated bureaucracies with many stakeholders and many different elements to co-ordinate through necessary changes.

Economists like to argue that markets are the best way to manage complex systems. The different nodes in a network of productive interrelationships (suppliers and customers) can best be organised by independent actors who organise specialist production and services, a fragment of a larger whole, and then buy and sell with the rest of the whole network. Prices are used as the signal that co-ordinates the information needed for successful insertion in the wider whole. That is how it is supposed to work. Yet the modern world is characterised by vast multinational economic empires that co-ordinate a huge amount of productive activity "in house". While economists denounce economic planning by the state, a huge amount of highly complex economic activity is effectively planned "in house" by corporations.

The reasons for this are not hard to find. "In house", a company has more control over potentially destabilising variables – like untrustworthy and unreliable suppliers of crucial components and materials if they have to be purchased. Through the market the so called "transaction costs" are higher – investigating the reliability of retailers and suppliers, drawing up contracts etc. Every business operates in a larger environment which is a source of potential instabilities and unpleasant surprises. One way of trying to master the risks and uncertainties arising in this unknown environment is to swallow it up, take it in and make it part of the company.

Co-opting governments

For very large companies, the final end of this process is to co-opt government too, as we can see when large companies move from being on the consultation lists of officials, to a position where these companies parachute their staff into government ministries and are consequently allowed to draft regulations and legislation. This enables "entrepreneurs" to rope in taxpayers to underwrite their activities and pick up their risks, at the same time as undermining the rights of citizens to resist the environmental and community costs of "enterprise". (A recent example has been the policy to promote the development of shale gas in the UK).

It was Mussolini who described fascism as the unity of the state with corporations.

Entrepreneurship at this level is something else again from that described earlier in the case of small pioneering start-ups. At this level, it is quite impossible for business leaders to have a knowledge of all that is going on in their companies. In fact, they can at most have a tiny amount of knowledge. The "allocation of resources" inside large corporations consists of decisions distributed to many people across many parts of the organisation.

Control freakery

Whether the personality of the "entrepreneur" will allow this to happen is another matter. The history of some organisations, some businesses, and some states, is dominated by sociopathic control freaks whose personalities drive them to take all the detailed decisions and to be seen to take all the detailed decisions so that they can also take all the credit. Such people are narcissistic – self-absorbed, arrogant and domineering. Their behaviour reveals outbursts of petulance and rage if they are not deferred to and it is clear that what they crave is to be able to exercise control over people that are supposed to admire and worship them. It is often said that psychopaths are very charming and charismatic and thus, appear, at first sight to be ideal leaders – but the charisma and the charm is merely one of a repertoire of control tools.

What kind of childhood and upbringing predisposes a person to develop into this type of personality is outside the scope of an economic anti-textbook, but a realistic theorisation of "entrepreneurship" is incomplete without a description of the type – for entrepreneurship, management, politics and military service are typical favoured launching pads for the rise of such creatures.

If it is not clear enough already, perhaps I should spell it out in simple words. Economics gives us an abstract description in which entrepreneurs seek to maximise the rate of return. In fact, business is made by people and people have all sorts of different kinds of personalities and motivations. If this complex picture cannot be synthesized into a single clever mathematical model, then tough for the model builders. It is easy enough to see what is going on and write the story in words.

Reality also includes people who are flexible enough to be able to delegate without feeling desperately emotionally insecure and/or getting into a rage. There are people who are able to share management functions and control with others without having what my mother would have called the "screaming hab dabs". There are lots of people who are not dependent for their self-esteem on other people admiring and adoring them, or having them as an audience. There are people too who are quite content to work in the background, and not seek the limelight in any way. Not everyone wants to live in a soap opera like Dallas. There are people who have intrinsic motivations and who are able to live a life that, while not always blissfully happy, are nevertheless able to be authentic, true to themselves

In these circumstances, it is possible to conceive of organisations that are not necessarily going to be those where an "entrepreneur" tries to oversee as many decisions as possible. Indeed, as I have already explained, there are more employees of co-operatives in the world than there are of corporations. If we don't hear of this very much it is probably because the co-operatives get on with what they do and don't make a fuss to get noticed in the same way that the corporations and their very important managers do.

Distributed management – the viable systems model of Stafford Beer

So, there are organisations in which it is possible to conceive of different kinds of management arrangements. Organisations where the managers are prepared to acknowledge when they do not know, and when someone else knows better, because that other person has more experience and more day to day contact with the issues in question. Another way of putting this is that a well-managed organisation is one that has the right balance of autonomy in its specialist parts with arrangements to make the specialist parts cohere together in a larger whole.

This idea was elaborated by the management theorist, Stafford Beer, in his so called "Viable Systems Model". His co-ordination approach is a tool for management of complex arrangements. It is based on two overarching principles: maximised self-determination for the participants in the specialist activities of a larger structure balanced against arrangements to ensure overall coherence between these specialist activities. (Walker J. , 2006)

Coherence arrangements between the specialist activities are ensured by the provision of 4 types of co-coordinative functions to ensure that the specialist departments "remain in each other's loop", are accountable to each other and work together effectively for the same greater purpose.

These 4 types of co-coordinative function are:

1. Harmonisation
2. Mutual enhancement
3. Strategic external orientation
4. Maintenance of joint purpose

Maximised self-determination of specialist departments is balanced in the interests of co-ordinated coherence in a negotiated and periodically updated structure. There is also agreement regarding what information is required to keep track of the overall structure in meeting its goals.

The basic principle is that the people taking management decisions about specialist tasks should be the people involved in the specialist tasks and therefore knowledgeable about them. They agree with the larger organisation what specialist objectives their part of the organisation will seek to achieve and how they will be monitored on these achievements. To avoid interfering micro-management, they are then entitled to be left to do the job as they see fit as long as results are adequate in relation to what has been agreed.

Coordinative service functions are only activated in the interests of the common purpose, with specialist departments compelled to be involved in pre-agreed circumstances.

These circumstances are where:

1. Departments are at odds with each other and their activities need harmonisation (conflict resolution and stabilisation)
2. By mutual agreement, joint action between specialist functions will achieve more than working separately (arrangements to realise synergies)

3. External orientation intelligence reveals emerging opportunities and threats (strategic orientation to an evolving external environment)

4. There appear to be differences in agreed purposes and values (work to ensure that the organisation maintains a common culture, identity and values)

The viable systems model was meant by Beer to describe not only business organisations but any system that had staying power, including, for example, the human body. For any viable system to be able to persist, it must always exist nested inside a larger viable system. Thus, a company exists in an economic sector which, in turn, is part of an economy which is part of the human-ecological system. In the "other direction" the specialist parts of a company, say, are themselves nested sub-systems e.g. the sales department; the production department; the purchasing department.

When organised in this way, the structure is **not** one in which the entrepreneur is taking the crucial decisions as a heroic individual. The structure is aimed to distribute decision-making to the appropriate places in an organisation, namely to the people who are doing the work and who are best informed about locally specialised decisions. Further, while coordinative decisions can and are taken for specialist departments to ensure that they are properly integrated into the larger whole, these coordinative functions are not "the boss" but services which negotiate with the specialist work departments, in the interests of the whole organisation.

Properly conceived of, this is a structure that does away with "the entrepreneur" because the decision-making is taken by everyone in an organisation according to their place in it. This is why it has been described as an ideal organisational framework for workers' co-operatives and for federations of co-operatives. (Where the federation is the next level of recursion in the system). See Jon Walker: *The Viable Systems Model. A guide for co-operatives and federations* at (Walker J. , 2006)

Management by psychopaths and their loyal followers – University of Chicago trained

Not only can the entrepreneur be thought of as disappearing in this structure, so too can any form of top down command and control management. But this is profoundly threatening to any structure of the authoritarian type. In the early 1970s, Stafford Beer was invited to go to Chile to help design a management system for the Chilean economy using the VSM as a participative model. It came to an end when a murdering psychopath called General Pinochet organised a coup against the elected government, supported by a team of economists trained at the University of Chicago.

One of the writings of Stafford Beer is titled *Designing Freedom* (Beer, 1973) but freedom for those they regard as their social inferiors is the last thing that psychopaths are able to contemplate. What's more, there are plenty of people who have grown up, adapted to living with and surviving under control freaks. These people are frightened of freedom because they want someone to tell them what to do, and what to believe. The secret of surviving as such a person is to be able to manage your emotional responses in such a way as not to offend your "betters", to give them the loyalty and admiration that they demand,

and to use the power that they give you to manage your emotions. Naturally, to be in an inferior position to your betters is humiliating and demeaning and one has feelings that arise from this situation that are not very nice. But loyal bullies can always channel their feelings into kicking around people who they feel to be their social inferiors. The loyal bully notices these people because they are troublemakers and/ or layabouts. They show disrespect to the better class of people, as well as the institutions that promise stability and efficiency, and so need to be kept under surveillance. If necessary, the trouble makers can be given a good thumping, or even killed, if the circumstances are that extreme. Loyalty to the machine gives meaning, simple explanations and things for loyal bullies to do in troubled times. When conditions are chaotic, the simplest explanation is that social pests and nuisances are not doing what they are told and law and order must be restored. What the Nazis did when they came to power in Germany was to introduce a policy of "Gleichschaltung" – a German word that conveys uniformity, bringing into line and total conformity. It is an engineering view of society and life as if everyone were components in a machine and should do exactly and only what they are told. Any person, society or nation external to the "engineered harmony" is automatically a source of disorder to the machine and, since this world view matches quite well with the viewpoint of the military, they are seen as enemies to be subordinated and brought into conformity.

As already pointed out, Mussolini defined fascism as the combination of the corporations and the state. In order to crush dissent on behalf of the state-corporate alliance, fascism works with people of this type. No doubt, the personality type was also enrolled under the bureaucratic dictatorships of the soviet type too. However, when such societies collapsed the opportunities for sociopathic entrepreneurs and loyal bullies blossomed.

Criminals are entrepreneurs too

According to a senior fellow at the Washington based Center for International Policy, in the 1990s "Russia suffered the greatest theft of resources that has ever occurred from any country in a short period of time, $150 billion to $200 billion in a decade. This is the low end of the figure which goes as high as $350 billion" (Raymond Baker, quoted in Loretta Napoleoni *Rogue Economics).* At the same time, the collapse of the East European economies was extremely good for entrepreneurs in the sex trades.

> A strong correlation exists between the supply of Slavic prostitutes and female unemployment; to an extent, they show identical geographical patterns. (Napoleoni, 2008, p. 13)

> ... the new sex trade was only the tip of the iceberg. Globalisation allowed the exploitation of slave labour at an industrial level, reaching an intensity never seen before, not even during the transatlantic slave trade. From the cocoa plantations of West Africa to the orchards of California, from the booming illegal fishing industry to counterfeit producing factories, as I found again and again during my research, slaves have become an integral part of global capitalism. (Napoleoni, 2008, p. 1)

Once we recognise that many entrepreneurs are psychopaths, we must also acknowledge that criminals can be very entrepreneurial too. Of course, not all entrepreneurs are criminals – just a large proportion.

Central to the economics as a belief system is the idea that looking after oneself, the pursuit of self-interest, leads through the magic of the market process, to a greater good. The idea has always been garbage, as we have seen, but even its proponents will admit that it assumes that everyone is playing by a set of rules. At least the state can impose a set of rules, even if the entrepreneurs don't like them.

But why should we believe that this happens when there is so much evidence that many entrepreneurs go to a lot of trouble to evade regulation and to hide what they are doing? If economics is supposed to explain the features of the world as it is, rather than how we would like it to be, then economists need to explain what the captains of industry and finance are hiding when over 80% of international loans are routed through secrecy jurisdictions, more than half of world trade passes (on paper) through these same jurisdictions, virtually every major European company and the majority of American companies use secrecy jurisdictions for a variety of unspecified purposes. Also, when at least $21 trillion of unreported private wealth was owned in tax havens by private individuals in 2010 – equivalent to the size of the United States and Japanese economies combined. (Henry, Christensen, & Mathiason, 2012)

Control fraud – pursuing self-interest by looting your company

A crucial assumption in much economics is that there is an alignment between the interests of the companies and their managers. In recent years, however, there has been a recognition that if people see "their rational interest" in making as much money as possible, then it might be in the interest of the entrepreneurs to loot their companies – to run them for maximum gain for the managers until they run into bankruptcy.

William K Black is an economist who has studied this in depth, particularly as it applies in the US finance sector. After his experience as investigator and prosecutor of crimes committed in the US Savings and Loans scandal of the late 1980s, Black developed the concept of "control fraud".

According to Black:

> Individual "control frauds" cause greater losses than all other forms of property crime combined. They are financial super-predators. Control frauds are crimes led by the head of state or CEO that use the nation or company as a fraud vehicle. Waves of "control fraud" can cause economic collapses, damage and discredit key institutions vital to good political governance, and erode trust. The defining element of fraud is deceit – the criminal creates and then betrays trust. Fraud, therefore, is the strongest acid to eat away at trust. Endemic control fraud causes institutions and trust to become friable – to crumble – and produce economic stagnation. (Black, 2005)

What is taking place here is that the senior managers run companies (or other organisations) in their own interests and against the interests of all the other stakeholders – not just shareholder and creditors, but also employees and communities.

The problem is not just to be found in the United States, obviously. Similar examples of looting by elite entrepreneurs were revealed across the globe by the financial crisis of 2007-2008, including in banks in the UK, Ireland, France, Germany and Iceland.

In order to loot your company in the finance sector, you get it to grow rapidly to maximise short term profits and thus, your own bonuses and executive pay – but in so doing you run it over a cliff edge. This is because rapid growth means lending with no heed for proper standards of prudence and without regard for risk. As much as possible, you grow the company by borrowing money from others to fund your lending (i.e. you don't risk your own money). You don't set aside reserves for inevitable losses because the accounting for that would reduce short term earnings. You pass the risk parcel to other suckers where possible. This happened just before the 2007 crisis when big financial institutions were selling financial assets with AAA ratings that they were privately describing as "toxic waste". (Black, 2005)

You then get your friends in high places to bail you out and block prosecution. As in the game, Monopoly, you get your "Get out of Jail Free" card. Control fraud of this type is often covered up with the support of corrupt friends in government.

After the Savings and Loan Crisis in the late 80s and early 90s, a thousand people were convicted of financial fraud by prosecutors like Black. By contrast, after the crisis of 2007/2008 the elite criminals in the US financial sector have largely walked away with their fortunes and very few have been prosecuted.

This is true of the UK too where, despite warnings, the regulators i.e. the Financial Services Authority, allowed reckless lending at two banks, namely, Halifax and Bank of Scotland (HBOS) and the Royal Bank of Scotland (RBS), and then failed to properly investigate. (Fraser, 2011) (Murray, 2011)

The City of London and its network of tax havens sells itself as a place that sees and hears no evil

The "light regulatory touch" in the City of London has not been accidental. It is part of a political-economic strategy. In his book *Treasure Islands,* financial journalist Nicholas Shaxon explains how, at the end of the British Empire, the City of London had to re-invent itself as a financial centre. In the late 1950s, the euro-dollar market enabled London to offer the evasion of Federal Reserve Regulation on dollars held in London instead of in the USA. This strategy of making London into a place to evade financial regulation was then extended geographically through a network of tax havens and secrecy jurisdictions in Britain's dwindling network of colonies and "dependencies", for example, in places like the Channel Islands, the Isle of Man and, above all, the Cayman Islands. The process took place with the help and connivance of the gentlemen at the Bank of England and the City of London. (Shaxon, 2011)

As Nicholas Shaxon documents, the function of these islands is to launder the profits of international crime syndicates; arrange finance associated with gun running and the arms trade; park money looted from countries by their oligarchies; evade financial regulation; provide havens for the shadow banking sector and to facilitate tax evasion. Since the evasion has been on a substantial scale, that is one of the little stated reasons for a crisis of government finances in many countries, the problem of fiscal deficits, financial instability and the austerity attacks on ordinary people. The chief purpose of these places is to create places where the global business elite can operate as "unknown unknowns".

According to the Tax Justice Network:

Writing about the predominance of British "overseas territories" (OTs) and "crown dependencies" (CDs) in the financial secrecy index (FSI), the Tax Justice Network comments:

> If the Global Scale Weights of just the OTs and CDs were added together (24% of global total), and then combined either with their average secrecy score of 70 or their lowest common denominator score of 80 (Bermuda), the United Kingdom with its satellite secrecy jurisdictions would be ranked first in the FSI by a large margin with a FSI score of 2162 or 3170, respectively (compared to 1765 for Switzerland). Note that this list excludes many British Commonwealth Realms where the Queen remains their head of state. (TaxJusticeNetwork, 2013)

In simple terms, the City of London and its network has retained its global financial presence by becoming the chief haven for crooks and tax cheats.

Elite fraud causes intensifying economic, political and moral crises but, for some difficult to explain reason, it does not a figure much, if at all in neoclassical economics. According to William K. Black:

> Economic theory about fraud is underdeveloped, core neoclassical theories imply that major frauds are trivial, economists are not taught about fraud and fraud mechanisms, and neoclassical economists minimize the incidence and importance of fraud for reasons of self-interest, class and ideology.

> Neoclassical economics" understanding of fraud is so weak that its policy prescriptions, if adopted wholly, produce strongly criminogenic environments that cause waves of control fraud. Neoclassical policies simultaneously make control fraud easier and more lucrative, dramatically reduce the risk of detection and prosecution by maximizing "systems capacity" problems, and encourage crime by making it easier for fraudsters to "neutralize" the social and psychological constraints against deceit and fraud. Thus, the paradox: neoclassical economic triumphs produce tragedy... (Black W. K., 2010)

Chapter 40

Entrepreneurship in the Social and Solidarity Economy

Co-operatives have been described as freshwater fish in a saltwater environment. In the 1930s, the co-operative sector in many countries was very powerful but it was destroyed by fascist and communist regimes. What was it that the authoritarians found so threatening in co-operation? Alternative economic models like co-operatives and social enterprises are explored, together with the arrangements that can help sustain them, like co-operative federations and support networks. However, there are no panaceas – co-ops and social enterprises fail too.

As I have been at pains to point out, the role of the entrepreneur is an idealisation and there is not a simple picture. While a very large proportion of entrepreneurs are crooks, especially in elite positions, this is by no means true of everyone. For example, a book by Claudio Sanchez Bajo and Bruno Roelants, shows that, during the economic problems of the last few years, co-operatives have had fewer problems. This is because there are less perverse incentives and co-operatives have less scope for control fraud by their managers because of the shared ownership, participative management and better integration with communities and other stakeholders.

> Cooperatives tend to have a longer life than other types of enterprise, and thus, a higher level of entrepreneurial sustainability. In [one study], the rate of survival of cooperatives after three years was 75 percent, whereas it was only 48 percent for all enterprises... [and] after ten years, 44 percent of cooperatives were still in operation, whereas the ratio was only 20 percent for all enterprises. (Bajo & Roelants, Capital and the debt Trap. Learning from Co-operatives in the Global Crisis, 2011) (p. 109)

The fact is then, that entrepreneurs are of many different types, with many different motivations and standard economic theory tells us almost nothing that would help to understand them. In a study based on 26 Czech and 45 British social enterprises, Nadia Johanisova finds that the most important success factor is motivation. The motivation of social entrepreneurs is not for money or fame but more for self-fulfilment, commitment to place where they have roots and an opportunity to make a difference. Johanisova comments:

> This casts doubt on economic theory which assumes financial motivation to be the principal incentive for work....The social enterprises profiled in this report defy conventional economic wisdom in other ways as well: (1) by definition their remit stretches beyond the financial to the social and/or environmental, (2) they are need as well as market driven and may juggle diverse activities instead of specialising, (3) more than half do not particularly wish to grow beyond their

current size... Yet they survive and sometimes thrive in an unforgiving environment. (Johanisova, 2005, p. 93)

Co-operatives would have been a lot further forward had not their gains been brutally repressed, particularly in the 1930s and 1940s, by the fascist and communist governments. In her book, Johanisova describes the incredible achievements of the Czechoslovak co-operative movement up to the 1930s. Over decades, small credit co-operatives in rural areas called Kampelika had become an important part of village life. Despite the voluntary and amateur nature of the administration of the Kampelika, they were efficiently run and were able to eliminate rural usury, educate farmers about accounting and thrift, purchase farm machines for members, install scales in villages to check weights, plant trees and organise cultural events. They complemented other co-operatives i.e. marketing, processing, flour mills, distilleries and so on. They also played a major role in the development of an electric grid connecting 15,000 villages. (Johanisova, 2005, pp. 28-29)

The psychopaths strike back – what they find so threatening in co-operation

This entire movement then disappeared almost without trace because of the Nazis and then, subsequently, the communist regime. Pat Conaty and Michael Lewis draw on a book by Johnston Birchall to describe how similar set-backs occurred in other countries in the interwar period. In Italy, Mussolini seized the assets of 8000 Italian co-ops and took them over, killed leaders and burned shops. In Russia, Lenin repressed them but allowed them to revive before Stalin destroyed agricultural co-operatives (providing 65% of food provisions) in favour of forced collectivisation. Urban co-ops were then closed in 1935. In Germany, Hitler seized their assets and nationalised 1100 consumer co-ops, 21,000 credit unions, 4000 co-op savings banks and 7000 agricultural co-ops. In Austria, where one out of every 3 three households had been members of consumer co-operatives, Hitler's invasion led to the leaders of the co-ops being replaced by fascists while their assets were seized and handed over to private business owners. In Spain, Franco arrested and killed many co-op leaders while many others took exile in Latin America. (Conaty & Lewis, 2012, pp. 220-221)

One may ask why this happened. One answer, when co-operative assets were seized and passed over to private owners, or to the fascists, was that the co-operatives had been too successful for the private economy and the real basis of economic power in society was being revealed - violence was being used to re-stabilise the private sector. There is a deeper answer too. All entrepreneurial activity, all business activity, is based on an ethical and a value system, and that ethical and value system, whether consciously or not, implies a vision for society. As regards Czechoslovakia, the co-ops were a threat to the dictators – fascist and then communist - because they represented a self-organised society where people took decisions for themselves and were well-organized to do so.

A form of economic organisation and entrepreneurship that tries to embody and embed democratic principles implies a deeper form of political democracy too. Not least in the sense that co-operatives imply practical participation in economic decision-making by ordinary people who thereby develop skills for a genuinely participative political democracy. John Stewart Mill realized the implications when he wrote:

> *We do not learn to read or write, to ride or swim, by being merely told how to do it, but by doing it, so it is only by practicing popular government on a limited scale, that the people will ever learn to exercise it on a larger. (On Liberty)*

This is why this movement has always been an anathema for autocrats who reserve for themselves alone the power to decide what they deem in the best interests of society. On the other hand, Mill's insight helps to explain why generations of heretical economic thinkers and social philosophers have tried to revive the social justice tradition of the guilds, recreating the commons and an economics based on co-operation and community.

Alternative economic models in India

The attempt has been international – and not just confined to Europe or the Anglo Saxon world. Gandhi's vision for economic development for an independent India was as a co-operative path promoting self-sufficiency and self-rule (Swaraj). In his vision, economic activity involved people "developing themselves", including in a spiritual, self-transformative dimension. (Schroyer, 2009, pp. 82-85)

After Gandhi's death in 1947, Vinoba Bhave and JP Narayan organized a Bhoodan (land gift) and then a Gramdam (village gift) movement because, without land, there was no way that the village poor in India could be self-sufficient and participate in economic life. The basic idea of both movements was therefore to urge large landlords to gift part of their land to the rural poor. Although significant acreage was donated, the movement ran up against the problem that the rural poor did not have enough money or access to low cost finance. When recipients of the land gifts borrowed, using the land as collateral, much was repossessed.

The village gift movement learned from the repossessions. The amended idea envisaged gifted land organized through village trusts to overcome the risk of repossession. Overall Bhoodan and Gramdan secured 5 million acres over 20 years. The idea spread internationally. Experiments like these inspired Martin Luther King and then a Community Land Trust movement in the United States and elsewhere. (Schroyer, 2009, p. 85) (Conaty & Lewis, 2012, p. 87)

Co-operatives and social enterprises today

At the present time, at least one billion people on the planet are members of co-operatives, though you would never know that from mainstream economic textbooks. In over 800 pages, Mankiw and Taylor's economic textbooks never discuss co-operatives at all. They only mention "co-operation" as an economic phenomena that they consider is unlikely to happen but which does so occasionally nevertheless. If you are educated in Harvard where Mankiw teaches, you might never find out, therefore, that co-operatives employ more people than the multinationals and provide services to 3 billion people weekly. That is about 40% of people on the planet.

Co-operative federations and support networks

There are remarkable success stories. In the Basque country in Spain, the Mondragon Corporation has evolved from small beginnings in 1956 to a business group with 80,000 employees, operating transnationally in finance, the manufacture of industrial goods, retail and knowledge – the latter being linked to the Co-operative University of Mondragon. Mondragon is a network that has evolved its own federated support institutions and infrastructure which is crucial to the success of the associated co-operative businesses.

The fact is, that for hundreds of years, and in our own time, huge numbers of people have tried to organise business on ethical, community focused and co-operative principles. However, they have operated in a hostile business environment. As Professor Jaroslav Vanek of Cornell University puts it:

> If you go to a bank and ask for a loan to start a co-op, they will throw you out. Co-ops in the West are a bit like sea water fish in a freshwater pond. The capitalist world in the last 200 years has evolved its own institutions, instruments, political frameworks etc. There is no guarantee that another species could function if it had to depend on the same institutions. In capitalism, the power is embedded in the shares of common stock, a voting share. This has no meaning in economic democracy. Economic democracy needs its own institutions for one simple reason. Workers are not rich. Let's face it, most working people in the world today are either poor or unemployed. They do not have the necessary capital to finance democratic enterprises. Hence, we need some instruments and institutions which make this possible. Why? Because we know that once democratic firms are organized, or even if they have all the elements of democratic principles, they work far better than capitalist enterprises. (Vanek, 1995)

However, while the Mondragon Corporation as a network is a powerful example of what is possible when communities and workers federate, it does have its problems. At the time of writing, Fagor, one of the largest of the Mondragon co-operatives, has had to file for protection against its creditors as it tries to re-organise. The co-operative Bank in the UK has also been in difficulties at the time of writing. It took over the Britannia Building Society that had too many bad debts.

It is therefore necessary to inject a note of caution into the discussion of co-operatives – and into thinking about the whole social economy.

There are no panaceas – co-ops and social enterprises fail too

Co-ops and social economy enterprises fail too. Nothing is eternal, conditions of uncertainty apply to co-ops too and poor decisions are taken by people no matter how ethical or community orientated they are. Nor are the motivating values and ethical systems that apply in co-ops and social economy enterprises always what they seem to be. One may think that the social entrepreneurs are motivated by the ideals of co-operation, the love of their fellow human beings and the environment, indeed they can loudly proclaim that they do. Yet, in practice you sometimes find people who are actually motivated to **be seen** to be virtuous - and a lot more virtuous than anyone else. These top dogs and leading experts in co-operation may turn out to be condescending micro-managers who always know what is in everyone else's best interests. Now and then, unfortunately, one meets virtuous people who see themselves as so much better at co-operation than anyone else. Stated values may not align with realities when people are lacking in self-awareness about their holier than thou stance. Such narcissists may be inclined to petulance and even vindictiveness if and when challenged – as can easily happen because they are such a pain to work with or under.

No organisational form, no ownership regime, is a cure all. It is impossible to design a system that will solve all problems. Karl Marx once wrote that we make our own history but not in conditions of our own choosing. Some of the conditions that may not be of our own choosing include the personalities of our colleagues and co-workers. As therapists will tell you, people's personalities can be changed slowly – but it takes time. People need to want to change and they are rarely open to therapeutic suggestions from their colleagues.

Freshwater fish in a saltwater environment

Other conditions constraining organisations in the social and ecological economy are those kind of institutional mismatches that Jaroslav Vanek refers to. It does not help that co-operatives, social enterprises and not for profit organisations exist in a market, institutional and cultural environment that is not set up for them. It is clear, for example, that the current difficulties of Fagor of Mondragon are related to the Eurozone financial crisis and the catastrophic economic conditions in Spain. (Written early 2014). These, in turn, were largely the result of real estate speculation pumped up by the Spanish banks, which are hardly the fault of Fagor, though it is now a victim of the fall out.

There is a deeper lesson here. Co-operatives and social economy organisations can be pulled down in the collapse of the general economy. Indeed, the closer they are aligned with and integrated into the economic mainstream, the more likely this is to happen. Workers' ownership and control will not prevent this happening on its own.

This brings me to the example of the John Lewis Partnership. This is the largest worker owned company and third largest private business in the UK with over 70,000 partners. It is sometimes held up as wonderful example to show how successful a trusteeship model for a business can be. For example, by Lewis and Conaty in their book *The Resilience Imperative* (Conaty & Lewis, 2012, pp. 280-283) or by Marjorie Kelly in her book *Owning our Future* (Kelly, 2012, pp. 177-184). As with the Mondragon Corporation, the gains of the John Lewis Partnership are shared between the worker partners. The Partnership has mechanisms to hold management accountable, to debate and suggest policies in a transparent and accountable system, while power is shared in a federated system of councils which

Lewis and Conaty describe as "reminiscent of the guilds". Like Mondragon, the Partnership has secured its growth through self-financing thereby avoiding the instability and speculation of the capital markets.

Yet for all of these successes, there is a tremendous paradox with the John Lewis Partnership. In an era of consumer capitalism where the economic system is banging up against the Limits to Growth and millions of people are groaning under unsustainable debts, the John Lewis Partnership runs a chain of stores that are veritable temples to consumerism. There is no doubt about it – the partners do sell these consumer goods very successfully, but are these purposes a contribution to sustainability and the future of humanity? According to Marjorie Kelly, the JLP are stepping up their environmental commitments. Under pressure from Greenpeace, the JLP recently backed down from a tie up between its associate company, Waitrose, and Shell. Despite this, the JLP focus on growth means that its carbon emissions are still growing in absolute terms.

In her book, Kelly describes asking someone from the JLP the very pertinent question: "How can a department store chain shift into a low-consumption, no growth economy?" and says of the person that she asked "He doesn't have an answer. Maybe none of us do." (Kelly, 2012, p. 184)

Indeed! The purpose of department stores simply does not match a future of energy descent and degrowth, whether they are owned by their staff or not.

Perhaps a better model for the future is provided in Italy, where there has been a 20 year explosive growth of co-operatives providing social services in ways that integrate the participation of disadvantaged groups. In 2013, these Italian co-operatives employed 360,000 paid workers including 40,000 people from disadvantaged groups, with over 31,000 volunteers. They now provide for almost 5 million people and have a turnover of 9 billion euros. These co-operatives also illustrate again the importance that has developed at Mondragon – a level of supportive "enterprise ecology" where there is co-operation among co-operatives – networks and an infrastructure shared between organisations with common values and purposes. (Conaty & Lewis, 2012, pp. 251-257)

The specific client focus of the Italian co-ops is relevant too. In an era of stagnation and even collapse in the so called "developed countries", when a bulge of elderly people are reaching retirement and will have plenty of needs in their last years, in an era when many others are being thrown into unemployment, poverty and ill health, what the Italian co-operatives are doing will need to be a major direction for the social economy.

The central point is this – companies that focus solely on return on capital alone cannot do a number of jobs, despite all the "invisible hand" clap-trap. The ethos of extrinsic motivations gives rise to types of enterprise culture that are antithetical to authentic care for people and places. Co-ops and social enterprises can be formed to work for intrinsic motivations, rather than for monetary rewards – but that does not mean, of course, that they can neglect attention to covering their costs. They are not necessarily profit focused if they are trying to make a surplus in what they do so as to ensure their long run financial stability.

Further, much more radical models exist which turn away from consumerism. Throughout Germany, one can find centres set up with equipped workshops which people can use to develop skills to make things DIY. There are also "repair centres" and networks so that people can give away or exchange used products, not to mention community gardens to grow your own food - all a little bit different from John Lewis and its associate organisation, upmarket supermarket Waitrose. (HEi, 2014) (Verbund Offener Werkstaetten (Association of Open Workshops), 2013)

PART SIX
Money and Finance – Credit Discredited

Chapter 41

Money, finance and credit creation

The history of the financial sector goes back a long way. Usury was long regarded as ethically unacceptable but both Calvin and Adam Smith tried to justify it with arguments that are still suspect. The finance sector played a role in financing wars and it evolved, strongly linked to the real estate market. This chapter looks at the functions of money and how bank credit creation creates debt money. It explores risk management and the tendency of the finance sector to turn into a casino. When collective confidence goes too far, prudent lending standards go out of the window, and there is a great deal of criminal activity. In the modern world the financial sector is on a collision course with ecological reality. (TEXT BOX – Discounting – Financial Logic misapplied to sustainability)

> The study of money, above all other fields in economics, is one in which complexity is used to disguise truth or to evade truth, not to reveal it. The process by which banks create money is so simple the mind is repelled. With something so important, a deeper mystery seems only decent. John Kenneth Galbraith

Adam Smith and Calvin on usury

When Adam Smith wrote his little homily about a butcher, a baker and a brewer, he did not mention a banker, although he was well aware that banking and finance was an important part of the business scene. For that reason, the "Wealth of Nations" contains lengthy discussions about how the banks at that time created paper money, about the function of bills of exchange meeting the credit needs of commerce, about the role of the Bank of England and what determines the rate of interest. There was a discussion about the ethical issues too, and what Smith thought of the centuries old prohibition on usury and interest charging. His view was that the prohibition of usury was a lost cause, though he did see a role for setting a legal rate of interest at slightly above the lowest market rate. This, he argued, would prevent money being lent to speculators ("prodigals and projectors"):

> In some countries the interest of money has been prohibited by law. But as something can everywhere be made by the use of money, something ought everywhere to be paid for the use of it. This regulation, instead of preventing, has been found from experience to increase the evil of usury; the debtor being obliged to pay, not only for the use of the money, but for the risk which his creditor runs by accepting a compensation for that use. He is obliged, if one may say so, to insure his creditor from the penalties of usury....... In a country, such as Great Britain, where money is lent to government at three per cent and to private people upon a good security at four and four

and a half, the present legal rate, five per cent, is perhaps as proper as any. (Smith A. , The Wealth of Nations, 1776, pp. 195-196)

Smith's comment that "As something can everywhere be made by the use of money, something ought everywhere to be paid for the use of it" is particularly important to understand. In the pre-industrial economy where the moral condemnation of usury prevails, production and incomes did not grow over the long term. In these circumstances, the rate of interest could usually only be paid by a transfer of the proportion of income in society from debtors to creditors and that was socially corrosive. However, in a growing economy, interest was seen differently. Interest was paid on money lent in order to finance a venture like a trading expedition or the building of a factory and the interest was a share in the increased wealth brought about by the venture.

This was an idea that Adam Smith had got from John Calvin (1509-1564), who had unpicked the arguments that Christian theologians had thrown against usury. Lending to people who made money was not the same as lending to exploit the poor. However, as Ann Pettifor argues:

> ... both Calvin and Smith err in their analysis, they ignore the fact that lenders can make a profit, or a capital gain, even when the enterprise makes a loss. And while profits can rise or fall, the interest on the loan remains fixed.... Loans should be considered ethical if they are evidently repayable; and lenders should be held co-responsible with the debtor for determining the repayability of a loan. In other words, lenders and borrowers should share in both gains and losses. (Pettifor, 2006, p. 131)

Paying for wars – the role of finance

Quite apart from the ethics of either sharing or not sharing losses, I think we can legitimately ask: what was real source of the "growth in income and wealth" at the time of Adam Smith that was shared with the financiers? As already explained, much of this original growth in incomes and wealth actually came about by stealing goods, from enclosing common lands, disinheriting those who had depended on it, and enslaving indigenous peoples for forced labour in conquered colonies. The early financial industry made their money by financing wars as rival factions in the European elite vied in carving up the world. This was hardly like banks funding the expansion plans of Smith's small town butchers, bakers and brewers.

> A king or a prince would borrow by issuing securities – debt acknowledged by the principality or government which were then bought by the banks in exchange for their bank notes. The notes were spent by the government and the debt paid for out of future tax revenue. So the ruler's ambitions were easily financed. It has been suggested that the great Rothschild banking concern's Paris office lent generously to Napoleon whilst in England its English office was providing funds for Wellington, and that just one condition was attached: loans were approved to either side on the understanding that the victor assumed responsibility for the loser's debt!. (Anderson, 2009, p. 65)

The ease with which the finance sector had made it possible to pay for wars cannot be described as an advance for human well-being, and little has changed from the early days. In order to finance the illegal invasion of Iraq, the US Treasury issued $80 to $100 billion in bonds which were bought by the banks, pension funds and insurance industry.

The finance sector, elite crime and real estate

From start to finish, the history of the finance sector has been a history of criminality. That corruption has been the norm has been revealed repeatedly by the frauds and scams that came to light at the time of each financial bust – 2007 and 2008 inclusive. The only thing that has changed is that, if anything, the chances of banksters ending up in jail seems to be declining. When the United Nations Environment Programme makes a case for "hardwiring nature into financial markets" it is difficult not to draw the conclusion that they are arguing for selling nature to crooks. Considering the number of scams in the carbon markets, there is plenty of evidence for this point of view.

> One thing that stands out when you read US economic and banking history is the extent of political corruption, which can only be described as utterly rampant. Today's African dictator has nothing on a few of yesterday's US politicians. Much, though by no means all, of the corruption was connected to real estate, railroads and banking. (Anderson, 2009, p. 116)

For example, describing the politics of 1857 in the USA, Kenneth M Stamp explains how:

> Most of the financial corruption resulted from the temptations dangled before politicians by land speculators, railroad promoters, government contractors and seekers after bank charters or street railways franchises. Often the politicians were themselves investors in western lands, town properties, railroad projects, or banking enterprises, and the distinction between the public good and private interests could easily become blurred in their minds. (Quoted in Anderson, 2009, p. 117)

A crucial source of wealth to underpin the expansion of credit in the early days, and still today, was land and property transfers out of the public domain, out of the commons, into the hands of the finance sector as we have already explained in the chapter on land economics. Over and again in the history of the banking sector, we find a close connection between financial instability and the bursting of speculative land price bubbles. Credit has not only been created to expand production, but to allow elite insiders to cash in on government granted licences and privileges, the most important of which have been land values. Most of the collateral for bank loans is based on commercial and residential real estate - houses, offices, factories and the value of the locations under them. The finance sector is integrated into the real estate sector.

The functions of money

To understand financial markets and the role of the money in the economy, we must go back to basics. What exactly is money?

Firstly, it is used as a unit of account. It is used as a sort of measure. In the textbook accounts, money makes exchange possible by making commodities comparable. As already explained, many economists think that money can be used as a proxy measure for welfare because he amount of units people are prepared to pay is thought to be a measure of the strength of preferences. Money's function as a common unit of account is behind the assumption of commensurability, the type of "rationality" that thinks that all things become comparable when one is able to say how much they are worth. This is the core mentality of economics and of the money society.

Secondly, money is a means of exchange which serves to overcome the limitations of barter. In the process of barter, there needs to be a correspondence of wants and offers between two people, and that is often problematic.

The formula C – M – C expresses the sequences in which money is used as a medium of exchange. "C" stands for a commodity, a product intended for sale, and "M" for money. Thus, the sequence C – M – C means an exchange sequence in which an economic actor starts with one or more commodities, sells them for money and then uses the money to purchase one or more different commodities. The intended end is the acquisition of a commodity. (Daly & Farley, Ecological Economics, 2004, p. 246)

However, money has another function, that of a store of value, or more accurately, as a store of purchasing power. Money can be held or hoarded for expenditure later – allowing the time management of purchasing power.

Many macro-economic problems (problems that affect the economy as a whole) can be traced back to this – for if people hold onto their purchasing power, then they are not spending it. And if they are not spending it, other people and companies will not be earning it. If, for example, people expect the future to be one of government austerity and poverty, they are likely to try to hold back some of their money "for a rainy day". However, in cutting back their spending, what is called the velocity of circulation of money will fall, the aggregate demand for the goods and services on sale in society will fall and national income will fall too. There will be a self-fulfilling prophecy – expectation of difficult economic times leads to actions which bring on difficult economic times.

Thus, we note that the "means of exchange" function of money and the "store of purchasing power" function have an inverse relationship.

As a store of value or purchasing power, money can also be borrowed and lent, therefore creating options in the time management of money. Credit enables borrowers to bring forward their purchases for a fee. That fee is the interest rate that they must pay out of lenders.

As many critical economists, including Karl Marx, have noted, the fact that money can function as a store of purchasing power has an important consequence. It has changed the means-ends relationship when money and goods are in circulation. Whereas, in early economic history, a very large number of people exchanged mainly for the purpose of ending up with other goods that they wanted nowadays most exchange is focused on the end goal of making more money. The goal of exchange is no longer primarily the acquisition of other commodities. Most money is put into circulation with the intention of making more money.

This can be expressed like this: M - C - M"

M" is different from M – there is more of it and that's what's intended.

Accumulating money has become an end in itself. When something becomes an end in itself, and that end takes priority over all other ends, one describes those people fixated on that end as addicts. To understand contemporary society it is not too far from the truth to describe it as being run by money junkies. The way they measure things, their unit of account, takes priority. In psychiatric literature we can read how destructive it is when getting the next fix takes priority over everything else. Is the following any different?

> I was probably one of the biggest currency traders in the world, including the banks. It was very exhausting because it was already a 24 hour market. When I went to sleep I would wake up every two hours to check the market as it opened: Australia, Hong Kong, Zurich and London. It killed my marriage. Quoted in (Kreitzman, 1999, p. 26)

The trader's marriage took second place to his money-making and he presumably, therefore, found it impossible to synchronise his emotional and family life with his partner - because he was synchronising himself instead with the money markets.

In the financial markets, the evolution of money circulation has now gone one stage further.

M – M"

A sector of the economy has emerged that has no direct connection with producing any tangible good or service but, instead, deals exclusively with money itself. One may truthfully say that this financial sector is now the dominant part of the economy. The tail is wagging the dog. It is to this sector that the United Nations Environment Programme says nature should be delivered for sale.

Bank credit creation creates money – debt based money

To understand how the banking sector works, the key thing to grasp is that when banks give credit they create the money that they are lending. Money is not backed by gold – it is backed by the agreement of a customer of the bank to repay the bank with interest. In other words, it is backed by debt. (Ryan-Collins, Greenham, Werner, & Jackson, 2011, pp. 17-18)

When a bank lends, what happens is that, on the asset side of the bank balance sheet, a new loan to a customer is created. On the liabilities side of the balance sheet, the bank writes the equivalent amount of money into a customer's account, which the customer can spend e.g. on a house. New money is now in circulation.

If the customer repays the bank, the assets of the bank are reduced by that amount. The loan, an asset for the bank, is extinguished. At the same time, because the customer will have repaid the bank out of their account, their account balance will fall. The reduced account balance for the customer is a bank deposit that just shrank. The money supply and bank assets are reduced together. (Under some loan agreements one is penalised for paying back early).

It's that simple.

95% to 97% of money in circulation is loaned into existence by the banks on the expectation of repayment in the future and interest payments in the meantime. However, the payment of interest on top of repayment is possible over the long term only if incomes are rising. The debt money system pre-supposes and requires growth in the economy in order to be viable.

The financial sector on a collision course with the ecological reality

The implications of this have been realised for a long time. The banks and finance sector has an interest in expanding the money and credit supply and growing its own wealth by compound interest. This, in turn, puts the requirements of the financial sector on a collision course with the real economy which cannot grow indefinitely on a finite planet. A Nobel Prize winner in chemistry called Frederick Soddy made this point in the 1920s. Economists told him he did not know what he was writing about. (Daly & Farley, Ecological Economics, 2004, p. 256)

Nowadays, there is still much debate among economists on the consequences of the debt based money system. Many mainstream economists argue that borrowing and lending merely shifts purchasing power from lenders to borrowers - and back again when lenders are repaid. As such, they maintain, borrowing and lending does not substantially change purchasing power but merely redistributes it.

This ignores the way that banks create *new* money when they create credit – which means that banks are effectively creating new demand. (It is common to portray the banks as if they were harmless intermediaries). When the process is working the other way, so that more debt is being repaid than new credit is being created, the process of money creation is working in reverse. Money is disappearing. Demand is being destroyed and the debt money in circulation is shrinking.

Confidence, trust and the management of risk

Which of these processes predominates depends, on balance, on confidence and levels of trust. The word credit comes from a Latin word which meant "to trust". When confidence and trust is high, so is credit and thus, money creation. There is, to use the jargon, lots of "liquidity". In a crisis of confidence, when the trust that others will be able to repay disappears, money and liquidity "dries up".

The confidence and the trust relates to general market conditions as well as to circumstances particular to each lender and borrower. There is a crowd dynamic and there are individual circumstances. One very important problem during a period of generalised confidence and trust is that there tends to be a high level of crime, fraud and gullibility, which is then revealed in the subsequent period of crisis.

That said, there are many ways to try to manage the risks of the recipient-financial provider relationship. Understanding risk management techniques is pretty much the key for understanding the way the finance sector works. Lending and borrowing is self-evidently a risky activity because circumstances change, people misjudge and repayment may not be possible. One of the key themes in financial relationships is, therefore, how the risks are managed and, in particular, which party bears the risks.

People tend to think of usury as old fashioned lending arrangements when a very high interest rate was demanded. Actually, there was more to it than that. What also characterises usury is that lenders seek to put all the risk onto the borrower. They do this with collateral. This is property that is forfeited by the borrower if repayment and interest payments are not paid, as in the contract.

The usurious relationship can be contrasted to capital provision in an "equity relationship" where risks are shared. If the capital recipient loses money during their business venture, the loss is shared with the capital provider.

There are many ways in which different specialist institutions of the financial sector "manage" different kinds of financial risk. That is obviously the role of the insurance sector but it is also the basis for a number of other financial services. For example, the future markets agree a price for the buying and selling of commodities at some time in the future, or they create options to buy or sell a commodity at an agreed price at an agreed date in the future. It will be readily appreciated that this could be convenient for business people like farmers, for example, who want to be able to plan with the assurance of knowing what price they will be able to get for their growing crop.

Or that is the theory anyway. Sometimes in economics a theoretical idea gets outgrown by a different reality. Nowadays, the actors in the futures markets have ceased to be solely or mainly people actually involved in production trying to manage their risks. Instead, there are very large financial institutions who are actively gambling, particularly on foreign exchange transactions. From being a helpful service, the market has taken on more of the characteristics of a casino.

This is a general problem in the finance sector when it comes to risk management and always has been. If the financial sector is to be stable, then you would imagine that prudence in lending and other risky financial transactions would prevail. There are indeed standards and practices to ensure that financial transactions of various kinds are conducted on a prudential basis. For example, in theory, careful lenders will check that a person borrowing a substantial amount of money, perhaps to buy a house, has a secure job and an adequate income to repay what they borrow.

It would be relatively easy to fix this by the so called Tobin Tax, a sales tax on cross border foreign exchange trades most of which are for speculative purposes. The tax would make this kind of trade (or the trade in other assets for speculative purposes) unprofitable, but since almost all establishment politicians are co-opted by the financial institutions and elite there has been little progress over 4 decades towards implementing the idea since it was first proposed in 1972, by James Tobin. In the last few years, there has been some suggestion that a Tobin Tax might be introduced by some countries in the European Union to arise tax revenues in countries with very difficult state finances. However, countries like the UK and Luxembourg, who function as safe havens for international finance, have been opposed. (Thompson M. , 2013)

Leverage – the temptation to throw prudence goes out the window

The problem is, however, that prudential practice goes out of the window in so-called "bubbles". To understand bubbles, it is helpful to understand the temptation that leads to recklessness because of what the money men call "leverage". (They usually are men. Studies show that women in the financial sector tend to be more careful).

Leverage is the mechanism that it makes it possible to make lots of money when asset prices are rising.

An example would be that I buy an asset for £100m using £99m borrowed money and one million of my own. Let's assume that the asset value now rises by 1% so it is worth £101 million and I sell the asset and repay the money. Leaving aside the interest payment on the loan I've doubled my money. I started with an investment of £1 million and ended up with £2million.

This way of making a lot of money with borrowed money can easily create a collective euphoria. A lot of people lose their heads. If everyone assumes that markets will continue to rise, they speculate on the assumption and borrow money to do so. A self-fulfilling prophecy occurs because everyone's expectation of a rising market means that there is a preponderance of buyers and this bids up asset prices.

"The Way to Grow Poor" Currier and Ives, Cartoon of 1875. Public Domain image

Typically, this process occurs in and through the property and land market. Economic development has an inevitable spatial dimension. It takes PLACE somewhere. Particular sites become desirable for the development of housing, factories, offices, shops and transport networks. Site values and land rents are bid up and a property boom is unleashed with the banks creating credit to make it happen. Prudential lending standards slip.

There is, therefore, a big difference between a period of credit expansion and a period of credit contraction. Periods of growth are made possible because there is a "virtuous circle" in which easy credit is spent into the economy, and the rising demand creates confidence which in turn leads to more credit being given and taken.

In the good old days a few decades ago, some of the credit expansion would be used to pay for investment in capital goods by companies that produce real things. Thus, a real expansion in production would then take place and incomes would rise. There was enough cheap fossil energy whose production could be expanded to facilitate this expansion. The rise in incomes enables people to service debts and to repay them. In more recent times, however, only a very small part of credit created in the finance sector has actually gone into productive investment to expand the real economy. With energy costs high and rising, there are simply not the profitable investment opportunities in the "real economy". Instead, individuals and institutional investors who are looking for somewhere to invest money find that the return on investment is very low unless they take increasing risks. At the time of writing (June 2014), an article in the news magazine *Der Spiegel* describes how, on the lookout for higher returns, money is flowing into collector's item such as, teddy bears, porcelain, and fine wines. Above all, however, it is flowing into land and into the property market. (Reiermann & Seith, 2014) This looks to be a repeat of the ten years before the financial crisis of 2007 when, in the UK, 40% of bank lending went into loans to buy property i.e. into the bubble – and only 13% was invested in businesses. From the banks point of view, business lending in "the real economy" appears more risky. Businesses often have limited liability and that limits the ability of the banks to reclaim what they have lent if these businesses go bust. Towards the end of a boom in production, new opportunities for making profit through expanding production dry up so that people and institutions with money to invest start looking around for other kinds of investment and become more inclined to take risks, igniting a speculative spiral.

Expansion of credit creates new demand by "borrowing from the future". When the future arrives, debts need to be serviced and paid back. When the repayments being made to the banks are greater than the new credit being created, money and demand is being destroyed. As credit shrinks, so does aggregate demand. It creates a "deflationary spiral" – a vicious circle. When debts cannot be repaid, then neither can the credit instruments and obligations based on those debts. If mortgages cannot be serviced, then the mortgaged backed securities that they have been packaged into also lose their value. A game of musical chairs takes place. When the music stops, only the big players are left with their capital protected – because the government bails them out if need be as they are "too big to fail" (and too big to jail).

Crime waves - globalising financial fraud and mania

Modern electronic telecommunications has globalised these collective manias and depressions and made them more difficult to control. Whereas, a local bank manager could know the circumstances of local businesses, it is not possible to know the underlying financial health of borrowers/debtors on the other side of the world. There is, in the jargon, a large information asymmetry, which means some people know and understand what's going on a lot better than others. The practice of relying on ratings agencies to assess the risks of lending has arisen in consequence. Unfortunately, judgements by these rating agencies can be bought too.

Much that is called financial innovation is a way of hiding risks, pulling the wool over the people's eyes and passing the risk parcel onto more vulnerable and less in-the-know actors.

In the first decade of the 21st century, ethical standards across the entire financial sector slipped catastrophically. In the years leading up to the financial sector crash of 2007/8, William K Black estimates that about half a million felonies took place in predatory and reckless lending. Financial sector workers made money, the more money that they lent. The loans that they made were being packaged up into securities and being sold on, so other people picked up the risk that the loans would never be repaid. Just before the crash, bankers were well aware that the securities that they were selling were "toxic trash". (Black W. K., 2010)

It is to this sector, the sector that commits half a million felonies and thinks nothing of selling financial "toxic trash", which the United Nations Environment Programme suggests we must deliver nature, packaged up in financial instruments.

As billions of people are now finding to their cost, even when the financial sector takes huge risks and commits mammoth crimes, the governments and official agencies have rushed in to rescue with tax payers money. States are terrified at what will happen if financial sectors topple over in a domino chain of collapses. The pyramid of inter-related debt is now so gigantic.

For the financial assets to retain their value, they must be able to maintain their claim to a revenue stream in the so called "real economy". This is the context in which we are being told that "Nature Inc." must be "hardwired into financial markets". It is this bunch of crooks that we are led to believe must be "incentivised" to protect nature. The idea is that carbon credits, bio-diversity credits, wetland credits, can be created as "products" and traded in the financial markets. Then the purchase of permits (pardons) for the destruction of nature somewhere can be offset by paying corporations to "protect" nature somewhere else - where it is cheaper to protect – typically in "developing" countries. And how do you "prove" you are protecting nature in these other places? You turf local people out of their commons lands – even though many of them are from communities that have been protecting the eco-systems on these lands for centuries...

Let me conclude these thoughts about finance and nature with some comments on discounting – and then another text box on the eurozone crisis.

Text Box: Discounting – Financial logic (mis)applied to sustainability

If you think about it, sustainability is an issue of inter-generational distribution. For centuries, people expected their grandchildren to be living at roughly the same level of wealth and income as they did. Indeed, as we have seen, indigenous people often saw it as their responsibility to ensure that things stayed the same. However, all this changed with the industrial revolution. From this time onwards, in the industrial economies the assumption was that savings ploughed into investment was a sacrifice that would bear wealth for future generations. The sustainability discourse has put that assumption into question for those who believe in the limits to economic growth – but not for those who expect growth to continue.

The point here is, that if growth continues, then future generations will have more resources to cope with climate change and other environmental problems. Landscapes may be degraded, there may be fewer singing birds, but there will be plenty of substitute satisfactions to be had in the shops and online.

On the other hand, if you think the economy in the future is doomed to shrink, the issues look different. It follows from this that the ethical choices now are dependent on a judgement of the future. Will, or can, growth continue and can it provide for increased well-being?

As a general rule, ecological economists are more sceptical that growth will or can continue and derive ethical conclusions from this. Their ethical conclusions are sometimes called "strong sustainability rules". The duty is on current generations to preserve an adequate amount of resources – particularly non-renewable and renewable at no more than maximum sustainable yields. Neoclassical economists, in contrast, call for a cost benefit approach in which the future and present are compared using inter-temporal discounting. The higher the discount rate, the less emphasis and priority is put on environmental mitigation whose costs are experienced now but will have its main benefits in the future.

So what is discounting? The logic of discounting goes as follows:

1,000 euros in ten years can be earned by 386 euros now at a 10% compound interest rate. Thus, asset values of 1000 euros in ten years are held to have a *present value* of 386 euros at a 10% interest rate.

By the same logic, one million euros in one hundred years' time is worth only 75 euros now. To compare the future and the present we discount the future with "an appropriate" interest rate.

But what is this interest rate a payment for actually? It is typically described as a payment for time preference. In theory, people would rather have things (including money) now. There are several reasons. The future is uncertain. We might die before the future or otherwise be unable to enjoy our money then. We are impatient and then there is an argument based on the idea that the richer we are, the less extra money will mean to us, and because we are getting richer the future sum of money will mean less to us. (In the jargon, a lower marginal utility obtainable for a sum of money after our incomes have increased when we are in the future).

These arguments are dubious for interest payable on bank credit. If interest is because we are forgoing the pleasure and advantage of having money now in order to lend it out, it might make some sort of sense. But, let's remember that most banks are not forgoing anything when they lend - they created this money out of thin air to lend. It is not as if the bankers had something else to do with money in their vaults and are diverting it from these other purposes which they can no longer pursue, to repeat, the banks create the money out of nothing, afresh, when they lend it.

Whatever, there are other reasons to question the logic used when discounting is applied to the calculations of costs and benefits of environmental mitigation. (Daly & Farley, Ecological Economics, 2004, pp. 271-276)

What is particularly dodgy about the discounting idea is that it applies a notion that might conceivably have some relevance for the thinking of an individual, to a decision that relates to society as a whole, and the relationship between generations, most of whom have not even been born. An individual might apply discounting thinking for their time preferences for money in a project over their lifetime – but does the same logic apply to society as a whole? Does it apply to non-market goods? Can it be right to apply it to inter-generational decisions where some of the parties to this process are not even born?

Recognising the validity of some of these questions has led some (but not all) economists to acknowledge the case for a "social discount rate", which is different from the private one, making a mathematical choice for a lower discount rate to reflect an ethical judgement.

A further point to consider is the possibility that the future might be poorer than the present. If one accepts the limits to growth idea this looks highly likely. In this case, the rationale for a positive discount rate disappears altogether. In fact it more than disappears. If the future will be poorer than the present, then discount rates will be negative. There is a case for prioritising investment now because unless we get on to fix things now, with the greater quantity of resources that we have, the people in the future will not be able to.

A more general critique of discounting is that what is happening is the familiar economic practice of considering ethical issues as mathematical calculations. Future well-being is being calculated with money as the unit of account, which implies that well-being is something that you can buy. As is usual with economics, the assumptions of money junkies are taken for granted when it is these very assumptions that need exploring and questioning. The discounting approach is framed within a set of assumptions that, as humanity moves into the future, the world is a better place if there are more opportunities for consumption events – where people can maximise their utility.

In this reduced and highly impoverished view of what it is to be human, the mathematics to calculate well-being through the consumption events are not even seen as being connected together. To make this view of the world tractable, in a mathematical sense, economists make an assumption that is called "additive separability". This means they simply add up the positive consumption experiences, and the sacrifices people have made as unconnected events. As Ramsey (1926) expresses it "Enjoyments and sacrifices at different times can be articulated independently and added".

If life was simply and only a succession of separate shopping and work events this might make sense – but people make sense of their lives by connecting the events in their lives with stories, with narratives. Without these narratives and stories, life has no possible meaning or purpose. Indeed, it is quite impossible to take decisions in relation to well-being outside of narratives. John O'Neill gives examples in his book *Markets, Environment and Deliberation*. Imagine a situation where health and social services are confronted with a choice between placing an elderly farmer in a care home and supporting him in the farm house he spent his life developing. Cost and benefit calculations cannot ignore what the farm means to him, given his life narrative and hence his identity. "Additive separability" would mean maintaining the continuity of his life narrative would have no importance. (O'Neill, 2007, pp. 79-88)

To conclude, the narrative of indigenous peoples is typically to decide important issues in such a way as to ensure that, 7 generations in the future, the people will still be taken care of. This is based on the narrative of a particular community in a particular place which has a spiritual dimension to it, rooted in responsible ecological system care. But when they enclosed and privatised land, that is precisely what disappeared. As many people at the time, who criticised the commercial society from a civic humanist tradition, feared would happen as a result of enclosures. As John O'Neill explains "the disruption of historical narrative by market norms lay at the heart of the debates about land and commerce in Britain in the seventeen and eighteenth centuries. The civic humanist criticism of commercial society was founded on claims concerning the relationship between civic virtues and the ownership of property. Commercial society, by mobilising land, undermined the link between generations." (O'Neill, 2007, p. 89) Looked at from this ethical and spiritual perspective, discounting is an ethical disgrace that reveals the fraudulent character of most policies for "sustainability" which are supposed to protect future generations. On the contrary, the future generations are systematically betrayed by neoclassical economic based policy.

Chapter 42

The Psycho-dynamics of the financial market

Mental health problems and debt finance are strongly linked. People in debt have a higher incidence of psychiatric problems, and there is a higher rate of psychiatric symptoms among the people working in the finance sector too. During a bubble, egos are pumped up with asset values – and, when the bubble bursts, reputational collapse occurs with corresponding psychological effects.

When we look at the financial markets from an emotional and mental health angle, we don't find optimal equilibrium states and rational people adapting to them. Instead, we come across a large number of unhappy, dysfunctional and disorientated people. Let's look first at the debtor – creditor relationship from a mental health point of view.

Mental Health and Debt

For a start, there is a striking correlation between mental ill health and debt - on both sides - lenders as well as borrowers. Among other things, it is now well documented that self-reported anxiety increases with the ratio of credit card debt to personal income; that the onset of mortgage debt has a negative impact on mental health on males; that of people receiving debt advice, a high proportion (62% in a UK study) reported that their debt led to stress, anxiety and depression which they are likely to consult their doctor about; that there is a relationship between debt and post natal depression; that debt is the strongest predictor of depression; that difficulties in repaying debts are strongly connected with suicidal ideation and self-harm; that debt is associated with feelings of shame, social embarrassment, a sense of personal failure, negative self-identities and is implicated in isolation, social exclusion and strained relationships. (Fitch, Chaplin, Trend, & Collard, 2007)

Now let is turn to look at the situation on the other side, among the people who lend money, or at least those who manage and direct the credit markets. Mental health problems can be severe in the heat of financial competition. Drugs and alcohol are commonplace on Wall Street.

> In a study of 26 men ages 22 to 32, all prestigious Wall Street brokers, researchers at Florida's Nova South-eastern University examined how work stress affects brokers" physical and mental health. Led by John Lewis, Ph.D., a psychology professor at NSU, the study found that a broker's average workday was 10 to 12 hours long, and that those earning the most also slept the least. The participants rarely missed work, calling in sick an average of twice a year but suffering from the flu or a virus at least twice as often. And despite being wealthy, the brokers were unhappy. Thirty-eight percent met the criteria for subclinical major depression, while 23 percent were clinically

diagnosed with major depression—shocking, considering only 7 percent of men are currently depressed in the U.S., according to the National Institutes of Mental Health. (Gorrell, 2001 update 2009)

A few years ago, during the financial crisis of 2007-2008, New York newspapers revelled in stories about stressed-out traders reaching breaking point. One broker, Christopher Carter, was charged with assault for throwing a hedge fund manager, complete with an exercise bike, at a wall in an Upper East Side gym. The hedgie's offence? He grunted and shouted, "You go, girl!" too loudly during a spin class.

In London, a hedge fund manager, Bertrand des Pallières, made news during the time of the financial crisis because he was so busy shorting stocks that he didn't notice for three months that his £80,000 Maserati had been towed away.

Jim Cramer, a hedge fund manager turned television stock picker, told the New York Times that drugs tended to reinforce traders' inability to spot a looming downturn: "Prozac and all those other drugs banish the 'this is the end of the world' thoughts. Which means you are not as anxious as you should be about an obvious downside." (Clark, 2008)

During the panic, therapists reported that there was an epidemic of psychological illnesses in the finance sector, while some of the managers used some of the oldest of psychological strategies for coping - avoidance, denial, switching off mentally in the heat of the crisis. An example was James Cayne, chief executive officer of the Bear Stearns bank.

The German news magazine *Der Spiegel* described Cayne's work style thus:

> Even in times of the greatest crisis the boss of investment bank Bear Stearns did not let himself be distracted from his hobbies. Last July, as one of his Hedge Funds broke down, the head of the board travelled undisturbed to a several day long bridge tournament in Nashville, Tennessee. While his troops fought for survival Cayne was not contactable. He had turned his mobile phone off. Its ring could have disturbed the many times American bridge champion. " (Die Bank Raeuber, 2008)" - translator author.

Even a cursory glance reveals therefore that, from the point of view of community mental health, the credit system is highly dysfunctional. Of course mental health workers meet desperately unhappy people living absurd lives all the time. Meeting people trapped in belief systems that, from the outside, seem crazy goes with the job. Normally, to be unlucky enough to qualify for a mental illness diagnosis, the apparently strange belief system that you have, and your strange way of making sense of the world must be unique to you. It will be seen as part of your inability to communicate with others. Then a psychiatrist can damn you with a variety of diagnostic labels like "thought disorder" which are said to be the symptoms of something deeper.

Over the last couple of decades, it has become clear that a lot of these strange thoughts are actually interpretable with a bit of effort. Psychologists, therapists and counsellors who become good at this quickly note emotional response patterns in society at large - the common cultural assumptions that help form collective emotional responses made by whole groups of people. There is nothing new in this. Freud applied his ideas out of the consulting room in observations about the wider world and his ideas were picked up by the advertising industry in the manner already described. Using what we know about group emotions, it seems to me that it ought to be possible, and would indeed be valuable, to integrate the knowledge of group psycho-dynamics into our understanding of the way that markets evolve, including financial markets.

As explained in the previous chapter, using borrowed money during a boom phase, as long as asset values continue to inflate, it is easy to make money using borrowed money. This is called leverage and the point about leverage on the way up is that it can get out of control. Betting that asset values will go up with borrowed money creates a further pressure pushing those values up even more in a self-fulfilling prophecy. Such self-fulfilling prophecies are common in mental health - confidence leads to success and builds confidence even more. However, where there are no limits to mood enhancement, it leads into mania – and that includes on the financial markets...

Egos get pumped up at the same time as assets values

In the circumstances of a leveraged boom it is not only asset values that get pumped up but egos. Ordinary mortals who, in other circumstances would see themselves as no more or less important than anyone else, suddenly become very rich and acquire the symbols of social success that are so important to "marketing characters". It is thus, not only bank balances that swell in size when bonuses are announced.

Trading rooms are fiercely competitive places and the action is fast and furious. In finance, just as in any other branch of life, the more one devotes one attention to the matter at hand, the better one will do. The broader and deeper one's knowledge is, the more edge one will have over everyone else. However, this has some resemblance to addictive behaviour. In an addiction, everything and everyone takes second place to the addiction. The guru who understands the markets better than anyone else probably understands the other things in life less well - and certainly gives them lower priority. For the finance experts, it will probably seem self-evident, ultimately, that the way out of problems is to buy one's way out. This will not make for happy relationships. (Kreitzman, 1999, p. 26)

Earlier in the book, I quoted the example of the currency trader whose marriage was wrecked because of the way that he tried to keep track of the 24 hour currency market and woke every 2 hours to keep track as markets on the other side of the world opened. This is the kind of thing that a manic person will do. The fact that other people in the financial markets are living in the same crazy way is likely to mean that it is not interpreted as mania, but it does not change its essential character. The euphoria of mania is like the excitement of a small child the day before its birthday. This child cannot sleep because the next day will bring a pile of presents, a party and lots of attention. The manic person cannot find a way to switch their feelings off and is constantly on an adrenalin high. Often enough, in these circumstances more and more commitments are taken on. What is missing is the idea of a personal limit to one's practical and work capacities.

In the life of a person who is not wealthy, these practicalities and the urgent adrenalin-charged character of their relationships will eventually mean that they come unstuck. Making ever more commitments means that they over-reach. Complications are not foreseen. Other people do not play ball with grandiose designs. If one does too much one doesn't have time to wash one's clothes and do the washing up. Life, practicalities, projects and relationships fall apart as one goes past one's limits.

A rich person may not have some of the complications of ordinary life which would floor a manic person. Their money can buy servants and, with enough wealth, sex (though not love) is no problem either. Many of the practical problems in life can be solved with money or a credit card - until the crash.

The whole history of the market economy tells us that a crash comes eventually. Euphoria impairs judgement. The overconfidence of rich and powerful people, because it cannot be held in check by the countervailing power of those who are not as strong economically or politically, nevertheless, reaches a point beyond which it cannot go further. As I once argued in a Psychotherapy Journal:

> The ancient Greeks already knew how to describe situations like this. This was a job for the Goddess Nemesis whose role it was to maintain equilibrium on earth "rebalancing" happiness from time to time. In fulfilment of her role, Nemesis had a tricky relationship with the goddess Tyche - who was irresponsible in handing out Luck and Fortune, indiscriminately heaping her horn of plenty, or depriving others of what they had. In particular Nemesis would wreak havoc on those favoured by Tyche if they failed to give proper dues to the gods, become too full of themselves, boasted of their abundant riches or refused to improve the lot of their fellow humans by sharing their luck. (Davey, What Future?, 2007)

People who become too full of themselves eventually believe that they can get away with anything in the pursuit of their addiction. In the literature about the financial crisis of a few years ago we could read over and again that the banks did not trust each other. When trust breaks down, we have a very specific kind of psycho-dynamic occurring between people.

A Professor of Organisational Ethics at the Cass Business School, Roger Steare, undertook integrity tests on more than 700 financial services executives in several major firms and came to the conclusion that: "There is a systemic deficit in ethical values within the banking industry. This will not change by hanging a few people out to dry".

The results of these tests indicate that, as a group, they scored lower than average in honesty, loyalty and self-discipline. Steare compared traders to "mercenary hired guns", who regularly switched firms to maximise earnings. (Hunt, 2008)

Reputational collapse

Behind the technical language of "liquidity", is a language that distances us from the deeper reality. The truth about the credit crunch was that it was a reputational collapse of the participants of an entire economic sector - the people running this sector overreached themselves. The really damaging thing has been that most of them have been able to get away with it because governments feel that they must bail them out. This means that the whole charade will happen again... and again... until society organises a fundamental root and branch reform of this sector.

The road that has brought humanity to this crazy point has been one where there have been, and still are, plenty of illusions. These are little different from the illusions that a manic person would create. Cassandras who try to express the folly of pushing beyond the limits are ignored.

In the case of the financial markets, because the manic process is a collective one, the illusions are repeatedly embodied in institutions and are dignified with words like "financial innovation". Rather as a mad person will split off the part of their personality that does not fit their cosy self-image, that is, the murderously angry and hateful self, so the financial institutions split off the financial junk that earns them fees making predatory loans to people who cannot afford to pay them back or are in other ways dubious ethically and financially. The splitting hives securities off balance sheets into "special purpose institutions". Rather as the mad person will wishfully believe what they want to believe rather than hard realities, the banks have paid other organisations to give AAA ratings to the worthless pieces of paper that they issue so that everyone, including themselves, can believe that everything will be OK.

Such strategies have their parallels in mental mechanisms of avoidance - the pathologies unravelled by clinical psychology. But then, to use the terminology of Freudian analysis, the repressed truth, the reality that has been held at bay, returns. The worthless assets have to be taken back onto the books. Reality bursts through the illusion.

To conclude, it would be valuable to integrate into our theorisation of what happens in the course of the credit and other economic cycles and events, the emotional changes of the people involved as they act and live through these events. Very often, people live with their emotions but barely notice them. They have no language or concept systems to describe their emotional responses and we may describe them as emotionally illiterate. Not having reflected deeply on their own emotional responses and those of others, they may act in ways which are unconscious, lacking in self-awareness. As explored in other chapters, this kind of person lives through what the therapist Erich Fromm called a "marketing personality".

Chapter 43

The Reform of the Financial System and Techniques for Debt Cancellation

Money experiments took place during the financial crises of the 1930s. Although these were repressed by central banks, the need to control the finance sector during and after the world war was recognised so that the 1940s and 1950s was an era of "tamed banks". It would be possible to write off debts and clip the wings of the banks without collapsing the financial system in today's world too. In the absence of a political will to do this, other reforms and DIY financial initiatives are possible. Community finance needs to be part of a solidarity economy

There is little point in analysing in depth the problems arising from the financial sector but then not proposing what is to be done about it. It will not surprise readers to learn that, over the centuries, there have been many attempts to change the money system and many proposals for reform. Some of these proposals have even been tried, in practice, in local experiments and found to work very successfully. To prevent these success stories catching on and spreading they were then closed down by the national monetary authorities.

It is said that the banker Mayer Amschel Rothschild (1744 – 1812) remarked, "Give me control of a nation's money and I care not who makes its laws" while his son, Nathan Rothschild (1777-1836) is said to have remarked, "I care not what puppet is placed upon the throne of England to rule the Empire on which the sun never sets. The man who controls Britain's money supply controls the British Empire, and I control the British money supply."

The authenticity of these quotes has been questioned but we have enough evidence from our own time to see how impervious to reform and change the financial and monetary system is. The financiers can buy the politicians. They have always been a very powerful lobby and still are. (Protess, 2011) To see that really successful experiments in money reform were closed down in the 1930s thus, comes as no surprise. The financial elite were not going to give up control of the money supply without a gigantic amount of resistance, and will not in our own time either - no matter how much destruction their system wreaks upon people and planet.

Despite the odds, people have repeatedly taken on this challenge and struggled with what, in retrospect, appears to be a labour of Sisyphus – the Greek hero condemned by the gods for his defiance to roll a rock up a hill eternally only to see it roll down again – because the Gods decreed it so.

Money experiments of the 1930s

Given the economic turmoil of the 1930s, it is not surprising that there was considerable interest in money experiments. One experiment in particular had remarkable success at the end of the 1920s and the beginnings of the 1930s, the idea of "Freigeld" (free money), which was tried at a local level initially in Germany and then in a number of other countries. It worked with a negative interest rate called "demurrage" and was intended to be democratically accountable and managed locally. The idea of a negative interest rate was to discourage hoarding and greed. To maintain the validity of the money, a fee had to be paid regularly by buying a stamp to put on the money. In the last chapter, it was explained how the store of value function of money is contradictory to the means of exchange function. If you use it as a value store, you are not spending it. So, to discourage hoarding, holders of "Freigeld" had to pay to maintain its validity and this encouraged people to spend it. (Conaty & Lewis, 2012, pp. 60-64)

These experiments were inspired by the writings of a German entrepreneur called Silvio Gesell who had, in turn, taken his inspiration from reading about the practice of re-minting money in medieval times. In German speaking areas of Europe, as well as in France from the 12th century onwards, rulers would call in local coins for re-minting every 4 or 5 years - but 3 coins would be returned for 4 handed in. The withheld coin was a tax by a local ruler. This depreciating currency appears to have stimulated trade.

The most famous example of the success of the depreciating currency in the 1930s was tried in the town of Woergl in Austria which was suffering from a 30% unemployment rate. In 1932, the local authority introduced 40,000 "free schillings" to pay the salaries of municipal staff. It had to be revalidated every month at a 1% reduction of its value, 12% per year. In the first year, the velocity of circulation was 13 times that of the national Austrian currency.

> Within the first year new homes were built and old ones repaired; municipal buildings were improved; streets were repaved; a reservoir, a bridge and a ski jump were built; and forests were replanted. Unemployment ended. A year later 200 Austrian towns were gearing up to adopt the reform. (Michael Lewis and Pat Conaty **"The Resilience Imperative"** New Society Publishers, 2012, p.63)

Meanwhile, in the United States, economist Irving Fisher thought Gesell's ideas were a brilliant approach to solving the problems of the Great Depression. In 1932, a number of American towns were also circulating free money and Fisher proposed free money be distributed to each state in proportion to its population. He produced a book to help local communities set up their own local stamp script currency.

The Austrian central bank declared the free schilling illegal. Within a year, unemployment in Woergl was back at 30%. Meanwhile in the United States President Roosevelt banned stamp script money in March 1933. (Conaty & Lewis, 2012, p. 63)

The era of tamed banks

Within a few years of the bankers demonstrating their political power to prevent a rational response to their destructive system, the world had been tipped into a global war. The failure of elites led to them attempting to "solve" economic problems by increased authoritarianism and by turning mass discontent against scapegoats. However, the subsequent war radicalised many people and, in a number of countries, ushered in a new epoch with a massive expansion of state involvement in the economy and a transformed relationship between state, society and banks. The 1940s, 1950s and 1960s were an era in which bankers appear to have been tamed, interest rates were at or below 2.5%, relatively high taxes were imposed on the rich and a welfare state was introduced in a number of countries. For a time Keynesianism reigned supreme.

This showed that financial reform is possible, but it takes extraordinary times to achieve it. Sadly, the reforms were reversed eventually. There was a cruel paradox in this – the stability made people forget the need for close control of finance.

Self-Reinforcing Deflationary Spirals

At the time of writing, we are again entering what are likely to be extraordinary times. As we reach the limits to economic growth, the banking and finance sector is becoming increasingly unstable. Without economic growth, there is not the increase in income with which to service the interest on debt finance. The Finance Sector can still make money – but in conditions of stagnation it is only possible to do so by transfers of wealth and income from the rest of society. When the finance sector makes gambles and loses, and when it then become insolvent, it can only be kept alive by transfers of wealth and income from the rest of society, which the rest of society do not have the increasing income to provide except by increasing impoverishment. Central banks are trying to rescue a debt based system by creating more debt and by quantitative easing.

The danger in these circumstances is of a downward debt deflation spiral that is self-reinforcing. With aggregate demand not sufficient to buy all the produced goods, stocks of unsold goods will rise and companies will be tempted to reduce prices to shift these goods, so as to get the cash that they desperately need to service their debts and pay the bills. There will be an increasing number of "fire sales" of goods and assets as households do likewise. Yet, if the overall price level starts falling, the economic system tips into a vicious circle. Anticipating falling prices, hard up people and cash strapped companies delay their purchases in the anticipation that they can buy what they wanted later, at a lower price. But this delaying reduces aggregate demand even further, reduces incomes further, means more laid-off workers and bankrupted companies and drives the economy deeper into recession. As the price level falls, it means too that debts become more burdensome. Debts are denominated and fixed in money terms. If prices fall in aggregate to half of their previous level, then a £1million debt will have now become equivalent to a £2million debt at the previous price level.

From the summer of 2014, central bankers in the Eurozone have been frightened that such a debt deflationary spiral could start to happen. An article in the German news magazine *Der Spiegel* said:

> Nothing frightens central bankers more than continuously sinking prices. The phenomena can push the economy into a downwards spiral. If people believe that prices are falling then they hold back on purchasing in the expectation that they will be able to get things cheaper later. The consequences are fatal - consumption expenditure collapses, people lose their jobs which means that demand falls even more and so more people lose their jobs.
>
> To prevent this vicious circle taking place the money policy makers regard it as decisive that companies and consumers should have an expectation of a stable rate of price increase. The European Central Bank and the Bundesbank make it known therefore that their inflation goal is 2% per annum.
>
> But prices changes are a long way from that in the Eurozone. The actual rate is a mere 0.5% per annum. Because interest rates are also near zero at the moment the central bankers have little room for manoeuvre. The money policy makers in Frankfurt fear that if expectations of the inflation rate fell even more the downward spiral could start. (Der Spiegel 30/2014: 58-60)

The response to the threat of deflation has been "Quantitative easing". This means that central banks have created money to buy bonds, driving down the interest rates to ultra-low levels for the banking sector itself. At the same time, and on the other hand, over the last few years many nation states that have been tipped into economic crisis have had to pay very high interest rates when they want to borrow. This is really rather extraordinary when you consider that governments could, in theory, get central banks to create new money and make it available directly to the government without the government's having to borrow it and pay an interest rate to the banks. What prevents this happening is pure economic ideology. We are told that if central banks print money for governments it will create inflation. Yet, when private banks create debt money and it is used to bid up house prices, creating inflation in the housing and asset markets, this is, for some reason, quite acceptable. The Treaty of Maastricht was written in such a way as to ensure that it is the private banks who get to create new money, not governments. Nor is it true, if there is widespread unemployment that creating new money for government programmes would create inflation. It is more likely that it would reduce unemployment – although rising energy prices are something to be concerned about in current circumstances. At any rate, what has happened several years into this policy has been that central bankers have pushed stagnant economies closer to serious depression. Their policies have done nothing to address the real long term cause of stagnation. In the "real economy", the cost of energy has risen because of depletion of oil, gas and coal. As energy costs enter into everything we do, this has held economic activity back and the financial system has been more precarious as a result. Without growth, there is no extra wealth being produced for the financiers to share in. As they are belatedly waking up to this, some governments are panicking and going hell for leather in favour of forms of "extreme energy" like fracking for shale gas that do more damage to the environment, communities and society, than they do good. The elite have run out of ideas and are disorientated as to our true collective dilemmas.

In the meantime, central banks have created cheap money to bail out the private banks. The banks have then used the ultra-cheap money for a new round of speculation – driving up asset prices and putting a lot of money in risky ventures that seemed to promise high returns, like fracking for shale gas and oil. The risks of this became evident when oil prices fell towards the end of 2014. No doubt the finance sector will expect to be bailed out again, but not their customers. In so far as there are collateral assets to be claimed the transfer of wealth will continue but not the underlying problems. That's the game being played by the elite.

Such policies must be turned on their head for social justice and for long run sustainability. The politics to aim for, against incredible odds, is to cancel a substantial portion of the debts of bank customers – but in a way that does not completely collapse the banks. At the same time, it is important to address the crisis in the energy system.

"And forgive us our debts, as we forgive our debtors" Matthew VI 12, King James Version

Given the nature of debt and its use as a tool of oppression by elites there are records at least as far back as the Bronze Age of protest movements aimed at cancelling unjust debts – for example in Mesopotomia, ancient Greece and ancient Rome.

In more recent times there have been several international campaigns aimed at cancelling debts by the governments of the poorest countries of the global south. These have not been without success – in 2006 Norway cancelled the debts owed to it by 7 countries. In 2007 Ecuador's Public Credit Audit Commission conducted an audit of Ecuador's debt and declared the debt to be illegitimate.

Government debt audits sometimes have civic participation and there are also cases of purely civic audits of debts. The aims of the audits are to determine how debts came about , who was responsible and what effects the debts produce. In Spain a Citizen's Debt Audit Platform performs general analysis of Spanish national debt at different administrative levels and in regard to different sectors. All parties are allowed to request information, not just "experts", demand government explanations, share relevant information, denounce irregularities and propose alternatives. (Cutillas, S. Llistar, D and Trarafa, G 2014)

These audits apply to government debts. But what about the cancellation of private debts?

How to write off debts without collapsing the banking system

The first thing to say about this is that, merely writing off debts for bank customers would leave a few problems and isn't even that fair. As a simple solution on its own, it would it leave the banking system broke. If the banks were broke, they would have to suspend payments and there would be no money coming out of the cash machines. What's more, people like me, the author, who have never been in debt

358

in our lives, would wonder why people who had been reckless and imprudent with their money were being rewarded and not those who had been more cautious.

Despite reservations and problems there is, however, a way that debt cancellation can be done fairly. There is an approach that would leave the banking system to some degree intact. Although after the banking system has been cut down to size through a jubilee, wiping out most of the debts, it should have its wings permanently clipped through a thorough going reform so that it cannot get us into the same mess again.

However, before describing this solution, let us get a proper understanding of what the problem is. Why is it not possible to just unilaterally cancel all debts?

The answer, simply, is that a large part of the bank sector would go bust. Since almost all of the money in circulation is created by banks, when they lend, it follows that almost all the money is backed by debt. If you cancel the debt, this bank money is backed by nothing. The banks would go bust and would not be able to pay out when you put your card in the machine in the wall. Notes and coin would still be available but they represent a very small proportion of the money in circulation.

There seems to be a "Catch 22" here which has politicians and officials going around in circles. If we want to have a functioning finance system, then at the present time we must keep the banks healthy. That's a nice situation for them to be in and they are using this dilemma at our expense. They can gamble in international finance markets and if they win they keep the profit. If they lose then we pay – because they have to be bailed out by taxpayers.

But this cannot go on. In the recent past, taxpayers in many countries have been on the hook for so much money that states have come close to going bust too – and the next stage in this game has been that banks have gambled against those states going bust.

To let this continue to happen is crazy. As Steven Keen argues in the second edition of his book *Debunking Economics*:

> When borrowing is undertaken to speculate on asset prices debt tends to grow more rapidly than income. This growth causes a false boom while it is happening, but results in a collapse once debt growth terminates – as it has done now.

> Though borrowers can be blamed for having euphoric expectation of sustainable capital gains, in reality the real blame for Ponzi schemes lies with their financiers – the banks and the finance sector in general – rather than the borrowers. That is blindingly obvious during the Sub-Prime Bubble in the USA, where many firms wilfully wrote loans when they knew – or should have known – that borrowers could not repay them.

These loans should not be honoured. But that is what we are doing now, by maintaining the debt and expecting that debtors should repay debts that should never have been issued in the first place. (Keen, 2011, p. 354)

But Keen then recognises that this would not be easy to implement as it would bankrupt much of the finance sector. So is there a way out?

The answer is "yes". As I have just explained – the current dilemma is that if you cancel debts then the bank deposit money created by lending is no longer backed by anything and the banks goes bust. However, this is solvable if the central bank creates an equal amount of non-debt money to replace the deposits that are no longer backed by anything.

In order to solve this dilemma, my colleague, the late Richard Douthwaite, devised an idea that he called "deficit easing" which is an alternative to "quantitative easing". Put simply, he proposed that the European Central Bank (or any other central bank) create non-debt money and give it to governments to spend. (Douthwaite, 2011) As part of this idea, he suggested that some of the money might be given straight to individuals so that they could either pay down their debts or use it to invest in green projects. This is the core idea which I wish to propose here.

Note the idea that some of the money could be used by households to invest in green projects. This is important both for reasons of social justice and of ecological efficiency. It is not only the banks who would not be happy if ALL debts were simply cancelled. While some people are very much in debt, some people have little debt and others have none at all – like me for example. There are many reasons for this disparity and I dare say that, in my case, it was partly good fortune. For example, I completed my higher education at a time when there were student grants and not loans. However, I am not in debt because I do not own a house, I do not own a car and in fact I own very little. I do not have a consumerist lifestyle. I don't mean to be "holier than thou" but, at least in part, the reason some other people are deeply in debt is surely because they took on the consumerist values which are so damaging to the ecology of the planet and also because some of them burned their fingers speculating. To use the more moralising terminology of Adam Smith, some of the debt is by "Prodigals and Projectors" and their use of finance has not been good for the economy or the environment. Bailing each individual out for up to the full amount of their very different levels of debt does not seem to me very fair either – and might even be seen to reward prodigality and recklessness.

Instead, we need a scheme with a pattern of rewards and incentives that is more appropriate to the times that we live in. This could be achieved by giving people the wherewithal to reduce their debts, if they have debts. Additionally,

Giving the same amount to people who have no debts, or have low debts, which they could use too – not on a consumption binge, but on green investment to bring down our ecological debts (the carbon intensity of our lifestyles).

So how would this be organised? Here's how it might work (in the UK – you could adapt it to your country if you don't live in the UK).

Every adult individual gets a voucher for, say, £25,000 (in the UK) – or some other sum...

On the voucher it explains that the voucher can be used by the person to whom it is addressed in one, or both, of two ways:

To repay debts or money owed to any lender organisation or company in the UK registered with the financial authorities (Prudential Regulation Authority) – all such lenders will be obliged to take early re-payment on receipt of a voucher up to the whole value of the voucher, or whatever percentage of it that the voucher holder wishes to use for debt repayment purposes. PRA registered lenders receiving re-payments with the vouchers can then claim cash from the central bank, which will be paid into accounts set up for them at the Bank of England.

And/or

The vouchers could be used to make payments for invoiced services or products for energy efficiency or renewable energy work from companies or organisations already existing as at the point in time when the scheme is introduced. This would be with the proviso that the companies or organisations concerned were part of recognised industry trade associations like the Energy Systems Trade Association, the Federation of Environmental Trade Associations, the Energy Institute and the Renewable Energy Association etc. Some people do not own their homes, so alternatives would be needed too. For example, allowing people to invest in bonds that support renewable energy development. The green economy sector could be invited to submit proposals for what would qualify.

The requirement for these to be pre-existing organisations registered with trade associations is to prevent "cowboys" getting in on a bonanza. Over time, proposals might be worked out for accreditation to allow new firms to set up with suitable skills. Companies wishing to apply for this work, or for a source of capital, will be obliged to register their interest with their trade association and will submit proof of payment of a voucher or part of a voucher to their trade association which will maintain an account with the Bank of England.

Vouchers must be presented for repayment of debts within so many months of receipt of the voucher.

Vouchers (or parts of vouchers) used for energy efficiency, renewable energy work or investment in clean energy can be redeemed over a longer time period – as it would take time for suppliers to gear up and increase their capacity to deliver.

In his original article, Richard Douthwaite suggested that if governments are timid, lest money creation and use sparks inflation, there is the option of doing it in incremental stages. So, in my example, this might mean something like £10,000 per individual now, £10,000 next year, and £5,000 the year after, with the state and monetary authorities feeling their way. If a recession or a depression is starting, the creation of new money would be no bad thing to help to prevent the downward slide. When banks do not lend and people and companies are paying back their loans, they do so by using their deposits to pay back to the bank so the money in circulation actually falls and deflation sets in. The scheme as described here would work against this.

When the central bank redeemed the vouchers, they would do so by paying non-debt money into accounts of financial authority registered lenders at the central bank. So bank assets in the form of loans would fall but bank assets in the form of money reserves at the central bank would rise by an equal amount. There would now be £25,000 more than previously in each individual's account, equal to the non-debt money created by the central bank.

The bank reserves of newly created central bank money would be inactive and not in circulation unless and until the banks start lending again. On the other hand, households whose debts were reduced would now be paying much less in debt service charges and be more inclined to spend a higher proportion of their income.

So the banks will find themselves with lots of cash but far fewer remaining loans outstanding from households. Because the banks make their money through loans, the profitability of banks would fall but they will still be solvent as they will be sitting on lots of cash. Unlike a straight bank loan write-down, this will mean that most banks would probably survive. However, they would shrink in size and importance as their importance is based on the debt they own. When debt is being paid off, their power would shrivel. Conversely, and at the same time, the burden on households would be reduced. Although those imprudent enough to borrow very large amounts would still be on the hook for some of their earlier borrowing.

Over the last few years, quantitative easing has not led to increased lending to the real economy by the banks because economic activity and confidence has been low. The banks have feared to lend and businesses have feared to borrow. Households are still too indebted to want to take on new debt given the insecurity. Thus, the part of aggregate demand which was previously based on debt creation is no longer there. However, with this scheme described here, aggregate demand would be lifted because people would be relieved of their debt servicing costs and because of spending some of the vouchers to transform the energy sector. (At the time of writing, the UK government has very stupidly tried another approach to encourage people to borrow more in the housing market which could start another housing bubble).

Having written off a large proportion of the debts – how to clip the wings of the banks

Having brought the banks down to earth, they must permanently have their wings clipped so that we do not have this situation arising again. There is a famous quote that we should take to heart. It is from a 1927 lecture by Sir Josiah Stamp who became Director of the Bank of England in 1928. Although the veracity of the quote has been challenged, it matters not here. The point is, that it accurately tells us what the situation might be if bank debts were paid down by the kind of scheme proposed here without further measures:

> The modern banking system manufactures money out of nothing. The process is perhaps the most astounding piece of sleight of hand that was ever invented. Banking was conceived in inequity and born in sin.... Bankers own the earth. Take it away from them but leave them the power to create money, and, with a flick of a pen, they will create enough money to buy it back again.... Take this great power away from them and all great fortunes like mine will disappear, for then this would be a better and happier world to live in.... But, if you want to continue to be the slaves of bankers and pay the cost of your own slavery, then let bankers continue to create money and control credit.

Whether Stamp really did say this, or not, is less important than the fact that it is true... If people repay their debts to the bankers but the banking system remains in its current form, within a few years we would probably be back in the same situation again. A permanent solution is needed and that permanent solution is provided by applying and adapting ideas currently being put forward by the Positive Money campaign in the UK. (PositiveMoneyCampaign, 2013)

The Positive Money Campaign makes a number of proposals, but the one which concerns me here is the one that takes away from bankers the right to create money when they lend. What this would mean, if implemented at this time, is that the cash that the bankers now have from repaid debts could be used by them to make loans – but it would not be allowed for them to "leverage" it many times. It could **not** be used in a fractional system to create ten or twenty times the level of credit and new money that they were left with after the debt repayment Jubilee.

No doubt, the banks will do everything that they can to prevent this happening. But what is being proposed is an arrangement where they should be grateful that they would be allowed to receive a pay-back payment for cancelled debt at all. In the reformed banking arrangements, they would have to risk their money if they then lend it out again. If they wanted to lend the "pay-back money" out again, the accounting procedures would be different from before. When they lent it, that money would leave their accounts and enter the accounts of the borrower. The banks would only get the money back when the borrower repaid. It would not be possible to lend a multiple of it as is the case at the moment.

Other Reforms and DIY initiatives

Much more needs doing to sort out the financial sector. In particular, the money and the banking sector needs to be localised and become a servant of ordinary people during the difficult period of energy descent and degrowth that lies ahead.

There are plenty of precedents for ordinary people initiating financial innovations. These successfully demonstrate that it is possible for communities to take their destiny into their own hands. While the big financial institutions operate increasingly impersonally with credit scores, and focus mainly on business with corporations or very rich individuals, an increasing range of tools and strategies are being evolved around the world in order to assist smaller financial projects aimed at people and environments in need.

There is nothing new about this. Building societies (savings and loan associations in the USA) emerged out of what were originally financial clubs called "terminating societies" early in the 19th century. (Conaty & Lewis, 2012, p. 59) People saved together and used the money pool to buy houses. The order in which people got the money with which they could buy houses was determined by lottery. When all the member had acquired a house the club disbanded. It was important that the person who received the first houses continued to contribute to the general fund and the last person who got a house was willing to continue paying until he did so. At a 5% interest rate this typically took 14 years. (Harrison, 2005, p. 30)

The economic crisis of the 1930s also generated a great many innovations – some of which have survived and flourished. One example is the JAK bank in Sweden, a co-operative that is fully owned by its members. There are 35,000 of them and the bank has $163 million in assets and $147 million in loans (2012). JAK members agree to pool their savings and then lend them to one another, interest free, for mortgages, home improvement, student loans etc. This is done using a system of "savings points" to balance saving and borrowing. As Anthony Migchels explains:

> The JAK has a very low default rate, for which there are several reasons. Interest free loans are obviously much easier to repay. Members are far more committed than "customers". And JAK requires its members to save to obtain the right to borrow. Savers are known to be good debtors.

> How can it be interest free? Well, very simple: instead of interest savers are rewarded with interest free loans for themselves. Most people would rather have interest free loans than interest on savings, especially if they actually did the math. (Migchels, 2012)

Costs are covered by fees and, to keep them low, JAK staff train community based volunteers in interest free lending principles and practices. (Conaty & Lewis, 2012, p. 74)

At the time of writing, in the years after 2008, there are broadly speaking two different trends happening in the world of "alternative finance". Firstly, there are initiatives from organisations which see their role as evolving and advocating for changes in the existing system of finance, accountancy and money. Secondly, there are those trying to create new approaches directly, for example, peer to peer lending arrangements through the internet and locally based alternative currencies. There is a lively exchange of ideas and approaches between these different groups. For example, the "Finance Innovation Lab" exists as a network of NGOs, financial providers, trusts and think tanks to develop ideas and bring innovators together. http://thefinancelab.org/ (What is the Finance Innovation Lab, 2012)

In a world threatened with collapse as we reach the limits to growth, financial sector innovation at the local level, combined with reform at the national and international level, will be crucial. This is because, to make profits in a time of collapse, the financial sector has already shown that it will become increasingly predatory, fixing on the vulnerabilities of millions of people whose lives are being thrown into turmoil by the crisis. Credit cards commonly charge compound rates between 20 and 40%. At a 36% compound interest rate you will be paying back double what you borrow in just 18 months. In fact in the UK, pawnbrokers can legally charge 80% for secured loans, while payday lenders can charge 2,000% or more. This is a return to old fashioned usury with a vengeance.

Security through relationship and community building

One dimension of the needed transformation is to fight predation by developing alternative financial institutions based in communities. Their aim is to restore "credit" to the literal and original meaning of the word in the Latin, referred to earlier, *"credere"* i.e. "belief" and "trust". Belief and trust can only be based on local and intimate knowledge based in real relationships.

Financial organisations need to be rooted in and be there to serve local communities – both individual households and community businesses. They need to be part of a wider "enterprise ecology" for social enterprises, co-operatives and solidarity economy organisations. Ideally, they will collaborate with other organisations, so that their lending can be connected to financial, welfare and tax advice, training in money management skills and, where appropriate, business planning and development skills. When finance is an arrangement between people in a community, some of whom are earning more than they are spending while others are at the times of their life where they need to borrow, arrangements can be made which reflect mutuality, enhance relationships and share risk and rewards. They can be part of a community development and building process.

Without the supportive networks and services, things are more likely to go awry. What does not work well is the mixing of systems where different motivations and principles are at play. Features like mutual support arrangements, the sharing of local knowledge and so on are not usual parts of finance services in the mainstream economics way of thinking. Orthodoxy pictures finance in an entirely impersonal way. There is no place for a concept of "trust", interpersonal feeling or loyalty. The lesson drawn from Smith's "invisible hand" in the mainstream is that greed is good and that each individual economic actor can make an individual calculation of what is in their own personal interest. Then, miraculously the market will do the rest.

The global market and institutional developments have created ever more institutional, geographical and conceptual space between financial actors. It is totally impractical on a global scale to form trusting relationships based on long lasting interpersonal knowledge. In that sense, there is an inherent "moral hazard" arising out of a spatial dispersion of economic actors. The result is that the finance sector is now driven by people who feel no loyalty to anyone. They take decisions based entirely on mathematical algorithms and rely on computer checked statistical calculations about clients and partners.

However, it doesn't work very well when you take the personal relationships and trust out of finance - or rather it only works because there is an ability to rely upon the state as a source for a bail out. If you follow William K. Black's ideas, (Black W. K., The Best way to rob a bank is to own one. How corporate executives and politicians looted the S&L industry, 2005). The senior managers of the biggest finance institutions do not even feel any loyalty to the organisations they are governing and run them to maximise their personal income, even though this leads these institutions into forms of extreme imprudence and insolvency - control fraud as Black calls it.

Finance as part of a solidarity economy

So, to repeat, in a "solidarity economy", cheap credit arranged by organisations serving the poor are ideally linked to a variety of services. For example, the SEWA Bank and the Working Women's Forum in India have developed a broad range of services that go well beyond stand-alone microcredit. Through organising a "horizontal co-operation" they have forged links between trade unions advocating for just pay, market co-operatives for the self-employed, bulk purchasing cooperatives for buying supplies, and community and social finance services to address a number of business and household finance needs. Over 1.6 million members in different urban and rural sub-regions of India have been inspired to collaborate and innovate solutions for a wide range of challenges." (Conaty & Lewis, 2012, pp. 194-195)

This is far from the approach of the International Monetary Fund and the World Bank which have little to say on community level approaches. Their links have been with global banks that simply provide wholesale capital to micro-finance institutions without any links to supportive services and institutions. The result is a reproduction of usurious lending practices, high interest rates and borrowers who end up killing themselves.

Standard economic presentations of interest rates present the issues as a purely abstract issue of supply, demand and the "price" of borrowed money as if the issues are entirely impersonal. On the contrary, the practice of lending and capital provision is a relationship between people in which ethical and moral choices are being made in conditions of shared uncertainty and risk. The fact is, there is nothing abstract or impersonal about an interest rate – the medieval Christian theologians who, up until Calvin, regarded usury as moral failing saw things clearly.

So too did Mohammed who regarded profit sharing as permissible as long as a capital provider was prepared to share losses with the capital user if a venture did not go well. In the Islamic religion, the relationship between borrowers and lender who both face an uncertain future is interpreted as being connected to the relationship with Allah [God]. The taking or giving of interest, *Riba*, is forbidden because it is:

> ... sometimes understood to infringe upon Allah's sovereignty. In this view, the charging of interest is said to guarantee a rate of return in the future. This is considered blasphemy since only Allah can guarantee or know the future. To set a fixed interest rate upon a loan is to put oneself in the place of Allah. (Wilfred J Hahn quoted in Pettifor, 2006, p. 132)

PART SEVEN
The Climate Crisis

Chapter 44

Climate Science and the Market in Delusion

Vested interests who wish to deny the climate crisis have created a dishonest PR sector fostering delusion about a huge threat to humanity. This chapter presents a thumbnail sketch of climate science and then explores issues of civic epistemology – how to handle public debate about a complex controversial issue where most people lack the expertise to assess the facts. The chapter explores why climate science upsets the market faithful and whether a production and finance system collapse would be terrible but might actually save humanity from an even worse climate catastrophe

A thumbnail sketch of climate science

Although I am not a climate scientist it is not possible to understand "climate economics" without a limited understanding of climate science. Basically, the combustion of fossil fuels and much agricultural activity, deforestation and land use change has built up the proportion of CO_2 and other greenhouse gases, like methane and nitrogen dioxide, in the atmosphere. As solar radiation hits the earth, including the seas, much radiates back into space as infra-red radiation but a proportion is reflected back again and held back by the greenhouse gases. This leads the earth, including the oceans, to warm up.

The story is made somewhat more complicated because light is also bounced back into space by "aerosols" which are dust and other particles, including those given out during industrial processes. Solar radiation bounces back too off lighter reflective surfaces like snow and ice. Initial "forcings" also give rise to other changes in the climate system which are described as "feedbacks". Some of the feedbacks are dampening – like the tops of a greater number of clouds reflecting back sunlight into space, or rising temperatures drying up some wet areas that had been a source of methane. Some of the feedbacks are reinforcing or amplifying – like melting ice changing the albedo (reflectivity) in the arctic so that the melted sea water and tundra, which are darker, absorb more heat and no longer reflect back solar radiation into space. Another reinforcing feedback is the methane release from melting tundra and from underwater methane hydrate crystals turning into gas as the water warms at the sea bed. Since methane is a greenhouse gas its release into the atmosphere reinforces the warming trend.

A predominance of reinforcing feedbacks causing "an avalanche" or "snowball effect" of self-accentuated processes. The planet is perilously close to a threshold beyond which a process of runaway climate change is likely to occur. Quite where this threshold occurs is unknown, and we may already be over it, but a political target appears to have been set for rhetorical purposes that humanity should not exceed a 2 degree temperature increase over the pre-industrial. There is an argument that staying below a 1.5 degree increase would be a better target and with a 2 degree C increase. There is little doubt that reinforcing effects would make it impossible for humanity to prevent further temperature increases of between 2 and 4 degrees. There would be many impacts with a 2 degree increase. Not the least is the melting of the Greenland ice sheet which, on its own, will eventually raise global sea levels by 7 meters. To this should be added the melting of Antarctic ice sheet.

> The important point is that the uncertainty is not about whether continued rapid CO2 emissions would cause large sea level rise, submerging global coastlines – it is about how soon the large changes would begin. The carbon from fossil fuel burning will remain in the climate system for many millennia, ensuring that over time sea level rise of many meters will occur -- tens of meters if most of the fossil fuels are burned. That order of sea level rise would result in the loss of hundreds of historical coastal cities worldwide with incalculable economic consequences, create hundreds of millions of global warming refugees from highly-populated low-lying areas, and thus, likely cause major international conflicts. (Hansen, Kharecha, Sato, Masson-Delmotte, Ackerman, & et al. 2013, p. 9)

Sea level rise is just one of many catastrophic impacts. Another would be mass extinctions. At 1.6°C above preindustrial temperatures, the International Panel on Climate Change estimates 9-31 percent of species will be committed to extinction. With global warming of 2.9°C, an estimated 21-52 percent of species will be committed to extinction. (Hansen et al p 11). (Hansen, Kharecha, Sato, Masson-Delmotte, Ackerman, & et al. 2013, p. 11)

The effects on human health would likewise be overwhelmingly negative. While there would be some positives, like fewer deaths from cold, the negatives would outweigh these and include (i) increased malnutrition and consequent disorders, including those related to child growth and development, (ii) increased death, disease and injuries from heat waves, floods, storms, fires and droughts, (iii) increased cardio-respiratory morbidity and mortality associated with ground-level ozone. (Hansen, Kharecha, Sato, Masson-Delmotte, Ackerman, & et al. 2013, p. 13)

These facts ought to be the starting point of an emergency policy response, but nothing remotely adequate to the scale of the challenge and the threat is being planned anywhere. Many scientists agree that a "safe" level of CO2 in the atmosphere has to be some way below 350 parts per million, but we are already at about 400ppm and continuing to rise. To make a difference, in other words to have a reasonable chance of stopping emissions rising by... and then have emissions fall by 6 to 7% per annum. Given that we are already over 350ppm, it is also necessary to find ways to take CO2 out of the atmosphere in some way by improving carbon sinks.

Climate Science and the Market for Delusion

The 5th Assessment Report of the International Panel on Climate Change was published in 2014. It is the consensus assessment of the world's scientists of the state of their knowledge about climate change and what they think is likely to happen. What happened in the mass media at this time, and even in statements by a government environment minister in the UK, Owen Paterson, was a clear attempt to downplay the message of the scientists and the impact of the report. In the opinion of Paterson:

> People get very emotional about this subject and I think we should just accept that the climate has been changing for centuries... I see this report as something we need to take seriously but I am relieved it is not as catastrophic in its forecast as we had been led to believe early on. What it is saying is that it is something we can adapt to over time, and we are very good as a race at adapting.

Climate scientists responded angrily – for example, Professor Kevin Anderson of Manchester University and the Tyndall Centre for Climate Change Research:

> It's a deliberately partial reading of the report. Either that or he has not read the report properly or does not understand the significance of the emissions scenarios. These tell us that business as usual will give us a 50:50 chance of a 4C temperature rise. His view that we can muddle through climate change is a colonial, arrogant, rich person's view. Many people will die in the developing world where the changes will be felt the most and it is irresponsible and immoral to suggest that we as a species can adapt to climate change. (Bawden, 2013)

The market for delusion

If we are, as neoclassical economists claim, "rational individuals", then you would think that all of us would put a lot of weight on the research findings of such a large number of scientists and the rigour of the process that is gone through. There were 209 Lead Authors and 50 Review Editors from 39 countries. Over 600 Contributing Authors from 32 countries. Over 2 million gigabytes of numerical data from climate model simulations. Over 9200 scientific publications cited. The final draft for governments received 1855 comments from 32 Governments. In total there were 54,677 comments from 1089 Expert Reviewers from 55 countries and from 38 Governments. That is a lot of "rationality" that has gone into the process. (WorkingGroup1, IPCC, 2013)

As regards climate science more generally, one study searched the university accessible "Web of Science" for peer reviewed scientific articles about climate change published between 1 January 1991 and 9 November 2012 that had the keyword phrases "global warming" or "global climate change." The search produced 13,950 articles. Only 24 of these rejected global warming – 0.17% of the studies. (Powell, 2012)

The fact that a large number of people do NOT accept the overwhelming scientific consensus in these circumstances is therefore interesting because it is evidence that challenges the neoclassical economist's view of what people are like. Clearly, a very large number of people are NOT rational. Ironically, a key reason that people appear unable and/or unwilling to accept the science is connected to markets supplying pseudo confirmations of non-scientific views of reality.

This can be put in another way – there is a market for delusion. The market supplies a stream of messages that create "doubt" about the climate science, even when none exists among the scientists themselves. The US Union of Concerned Scientists show how many apparently independent organisations that spread doubt about climate change are, in fact, bankrolled by the fossil fuel sector. For example, the American Enterprise Institute received $3,615,000 from ExxonMobil from 1998-2012, and more than $1 million in funding from Koch foundations from 2004-2011. Americans for Prosperity received $3,609,281 from fuel billionaires Charles and David Koch from 2007-2011. The Cato Institute received $5million from the Koch brothers between 1999 and 2011. The Competitive Enterprise Institute likewise receives funding from the Koch brothers and from Exxon Mobil up to 2008. Also, the Heartland Institute, Heritage Foundation, Institute for Energy Research all received money from the Koch brothers and Exxon Mobil. The aim of all this funding is to:

- Raise doubts about even the most indisputable scientific evidence
- Attempt to portray opposition to action as a positive quest for "sound science" rather than business self-interest
- Access government to block federal policies and shape government communications on global warming.

(Global Warming Skeptic Organisations, 2013) (Gibson, 2012)

Given the scale on which they are being funded, there are now a lot of delusionary ideas out there: the climate has changed before; it's the sun; it's not bad; there's no consensus; its cooling; the models are unreliable; the temperature record is unreliable; animals and plants can adapt; it hasn't warmed since 1998; Antarctica is gaining ice... the contrarian arguments are generated in a factory whose aim is to mislead and confuse. All of them have been refuted - but how is the average citizen to know or keep track of the barrage of misinformation that big money keeps generating? (Global Warming and Climate Change Myths, 2014)

In the current situation, the IPCC Assessment Report 5 draft has generated a huge controversy around the idea that "it has not warmed since 1998". In the 15 years from 1998 to 2012, the actual surface temperature increase was 50% slower than the average on the model runs. However, 1998 was a particularly hot year to start measuring a trend from. If the trend between 1992 and 2006 had been chosen it would have shown a surface temperature increase that was much faster than the IPCC average of model runs. Climate scientists refer to natural variability i.e. temperature fluctuations around the trend over relatively short time periods. This natural variability can be accounted for by factors such as the way that the ocean has absorbed a lot of the heat, as well as variability in aerosols, particulates in the atmosphere from industrial pollution and volcanic eruptions that reflect solar energy back into space. Perhaps the most plausible explanation for most of the recent variability is the fact that there has been a lack of temperature readings to gauge Arctic temperatures which have been rising much more rapidly than have previously been estimated. Now that more accurate estimates of Arctic temperatures are available, the so called "pause" in global warming largely disappears. (Connor, 2013)

Post Normal Science and Civic epistemology

These are complex issues for a lay person to assess and it is easy to understand that people would feel bewildered by the arguments. It has been argued that what we are dealing with in situations like climate change goes beyond what "normal science" can cope with. Because the climate system is so vast and complex with multiple feedbacks there is bound to be some uncertainty and this complicates a situation where multiple stakeholders have different values and motives. At the same time the stakes are very high and decisions are urgent. This has been described as a situation where "normal science" still has an important role but is not in itself enough. There is a case for a "post normal science" where the "expert scientific community" has to be extended to a wider group of people with differing concerns and perspectives who are in a position to articulate different perspectives to inform a consideration of the issues and exercise quality assurance over the science. (D'Alisa G. and Kallis G 2015)

This is a sensible principle for trying to get an understanding of complex issues but it does assume that participants are not in the process in order to wreck it. It presupposes that they share a sufficient common starting point to work together co-operatively, respecting each other's perspective for what they can learn from each other. It assumes that they are not, for example, trying to use "uncertainties" in a discussion in order "to prove" that there is no problem at all that needs dealing with.

For those people not familiar with certain issues bewilderment can be exploited. In fact, there is a whole topic of "civic epistemology" which can guide approaches to questions where people feel out of their depth in the face of "expert knowledge". For people who are concerned to maintain a rational approach to controversial matters, when they are not themselves experts in the specialist field concerned, there are criteria, shall we say "diagnostics" that can be used to assess the issues. In this connection, the evidence that underpins any belief can be examined from "procedural" as well as "substantive" grounds.

"Procedural" means looking for consistency of the evidence with due scientific process – this is the quality control in academic production. Is the evidence appearing in a peer reviewed journal? Has the evidence been replicated by other peer reviewed research processes? Is the research by a scientist operating in the field in which they have been trained and in which they have expertise?

Of course, there are a lot of other sources of information out there – academic monographs; investigative journalism; data and reports from government agencies; data collected by corporations; research and reports by NGOs, charities and think tanks; consultants reports and press, radio, television and internet blogs. All of these are potential sources of accurate information – or potential sources of errors and deliberate obfuscation. A politically literate person will sift these sources of information according to quality control criteria. Thus, a newspaper article written by a scientist who has published peer reviewed articles in the field, who is highlighting findings from peer reviewed literature, can be taken as credible. Whereas, someone who has no qualifications as a scientist, or is a "scientist" but not from the field in question, has retired and/or ceased publication, has not written peer reviewed articles in the field in question but casts doubt on peer reviewed literature, is a highly dubious source. Especially if you find, as is very often the case, that they are being sponsored by money from fossil fuel companies.

As part of the tobacco companies' war to deliberately create doubt about the health consequences of smoking, politically sympathetic physicists published articles in non-peer reviewed journals to help the tobacco companies hold off regulation. (Oreskes & Conway, Merchants of Doubt., 2010)

If climate science wrecks your religion then obviously you are not going to believe in it... In the world of ancient Greece, the word "idiot" was used to refer to people who did not contribute when they were entitled to do so in the democratic process. Instead the idiots devoted their time to their own private interests and wealth. From Adam Smith onwards, mainstream economists have told people that, by pursuing their private interests, a greater social good is brought about by the "invisible hand of the market". After Smith, the idiots – naturally I am using the word in the ancient Greek sense - could feel reassured and work to accumulate private wealth. They could feel secure in the idea that, while the state was there to protect them, it was supposed to keep out of their self-interested dealings because their "self-love" was being converted into social well-being quasi-automatically – particularly by stimulating clever technologies. This simple mantra is what I earlier described, following Richard Norgaard, as "economism" and it has become the religious faith of the modern age with the economists as the priesthood.

Actually, it is not at all the case that the market works as a socially coordinative system because people are pursuing their self-interest. What makes the market "work", to the extent that it does, as a coordinative system, is only that everyone is playing the *same* life game. The drive for money as a common criteria for social action leads to a common life style. The way people play or are obliged to play the same money making game glues society together on a particular path of development. Because a predominant grouping is playing the same game in terms of motivations, criteria and measures of success, interdependency in capitalist social relationships is made possible.

Why climate science is upsetting to the market faithful

With economism functioning as a foundational religion underpinning the general orientation of market based society, it is incredibly unsettling to the faithful to hear the message of climate science because it implies that the free market does not, after all, automatically deliver collective well-being. The evidence for this is provided by psychological studies which show that the more people identify with "free market principles" the more likely they are to reject the findings of climate scientists. A study in the USA surveyed the views of a representative 1000 people and found that a market based worldview constituted an overwhelming barrier to the acceptance of climate science. A similar finding applies to the science associated with smoking. The study, by a team led by Professor Stephan Lewandowsky chair of cognitive psychology at the University of Bristol in the UK, is titled *The Role of Conspiracist Ideation and World Views in Predicting Rejection of Science* and is published in the journal *PLOS ONE*. (Lewandowsky, Gignac, & Oberauer, 2013) Commenting to a Guardian journalist about these findings Lewandowsky says:

> I cannot be sure of the causality, but there are multiple lines of evidence that suggest that the
> involvement of worldview, such as free-market principles, arises because people of that worldview

feel threatened not by climate change or by lung cancer, but by the regulatory implications if those risks are being addressed by society. Addressing lung cancer means to control tobacco, and addressing climate change means to control fossil-fuel emissions. It's the need to control those products and their industries that is threatening people with strong free-market leanings. (Readfearn, 2013)

Faced with a choice between what science is telling them, or a fantasy, a large number of people prefer the fantasy, and there are plenty of vested interests from the fossil fuel industry keen to fund publicity for their delusions. The irony here is that, while economists model reality on the assumption of rational individual's market ideology, there appears to be a powerful influence in favour of irrationality – while powerful vested interests are happy to fund a variety of dangerous delusions.

In the 1999 film, *The Matrix*, the chief character is asked whether he wants to take a red pill that will show him the painful reality or take the blue pill and remain in the simulated reality. The economics profession are mostly in business helping to produce the blue pills. Neoclassical economics is a menace - it is a generator of collective psychopathology, in a society dangerously out of touch with reality.

Getting on a plane that is 95% likely to crash, because there's a 5% chance that it won't crash

But is there not a chance that climate science is wrong? Might it not be the case that climate change is not the result of human activities and that it does not repay the effort to do anything about it? While the climate scientists go to immense trouble to express their degree of confidence in their findings, the climate deniers don't bother to do the same thing. So yes, even the climate scientists admit that they might conceivably have got it wrong. There is a chance that this is so, but on the core issues that chance is a very small one indeed.

Thus, if one reads the IPCC 5th Assessment Report Summary for Policy makers there are a mass of findings about climate change with regard to atmospheric changes; ocean temperatures; the cryosphere (ice sheets); sea level; carbon and geochemical cycles; drivers of climate change; quantifying the system and so on. Each of the findings under these headings are assigned a confidence level. For example, when it comes to the attribution of climate change there is this statement:

> Human influence has been detected in warming of the atmosphere and the ocean, in changes in the global water cycle, in reductions in snow and ice, in global mean sea level rise, and in changes in some climate extremes. This evidence for human influence has grown since Assessment Report 4. It is *extremely likely* that human influence has been the dominant cause of the observed warming since the mid-20th century. Working Group 1 Contribution to the IPCC Fifth Assessment Report *Climate Change 2013: The Physical Science Basis* Summary for Policymakers (IPCC, 2013, p. 15)

Note the words "extremely likely". This is defined elsewhere in the same report in this way: "extremely likely: 95–100%". So yes, the scientists are acknowledging that there is a small chance that they might have got it wrong. But think of it this way – would you get on a plane that is 95% likely to crash because there is a 5% chance that it will not do so? No rational person would if they had a choice - unless they were being misled by a criminal misinformation.

A production and finance system collapse to "save" us?

There are other senses in which some predictions based on climate science might be wrong. There has been some argument about whether, or how much, the rising energy and money costs of extracting fossil fuel resources because of depletion might lead to a future fall in emissions because the fossil energy might not be there in sufficient quantities, extractable at a commercial cost, leading to the worse emissions growth scenarios coming about. This is the view of Graham Turner, in the study mentioned in an earlier chapter that reviewed the evidence 40 years after the famous Limits to Growth study commissioned by the Club of Rome.

> The corroboration here of the Limits to Growth standard run implies that the scientific and public attention given to climate change, whilst important, is out of proportion with, and even deleteriously distracting from the issue of resource constraints, particularly oil. Indeed, if global collapse occurs as in this LtG scenario then pollution impacts will naturally be resolved, though not in any ideal sense. (Turner, 2012, p. 123)

This is another kind of argument, about the other limits to economic growth kicking in faster than climate change. It is a view shared with some other ecological economists, for example, Giampietro, Mayumi and Sorman in their book *The Metabolic Pattern of Societies* go so far as to argue that all the fuss about climate change is a "granfalloon" because the effects of peak oil will kick in much quicker. They might be right. However, the speed with which it will be necessary to reduce emissions to have a safe future climate is so dramatic that both issues need to remain on the agenda. (Giampietro, Mayumi, & Sorman, The Metabolic Pattern of Societies: Where Economists Fall Short, 2011, pp. 328-329)

No one has a magic ability to accurately predict the future. We are still condemned to make predictions to manage our lives. As we reach the limits to growth, some nasty surprises – and perhaps even some nice ones - may be waiting to take history in an unexpected direction. At the time of writing, the United States government appears to be self-destructing because Tea Party market fundamentalists in the USA are unwilling to pass a budget. Were this to go on, I dare say it could damage global economic activity seriously and lastingly - and thus, perhaps bring down emissions. A war in Syria which might have escalated into a major global conflict was only narrowly averted - that too might have disrupted the flow of fossil fuels. Various diseases are becoming a major threat because of the declining effectiveness of antibiotics. Perhaps that might create a population crisis and again bring down emissions. The future is one that no one can foresee. None of these things make climate change any less important as a major threat to humanity that justifies being taken any less seriously.

In this chapter, the climate crisis is taken as a case study to illustrate the insanity of "economics thinking". The aim is to illustrate how economists flounder with perhaps the greatest problem facing humanity. My aim is not to present the climate science because I am not a scientist – rather it is to portray how economists have reacted to climate science, to the limited extent that they have, which is not much.

In an earlier chapter, I showed how what are called "externalities" are not exceptional but ubiquitous – and you cannot get more ubiquitous than carbon emissions in societies that have "developed". Since all economic activity involves the use of energy, and virtually all post-industrial energy sources are based on burning fossil fuels, the production of CO2 is all pervasive. The consequences of that CO2 are therefore properly a mainstream economic problem. In the report commissioned by the British government on the economics of climate change and written by a team under the leadership of Nicholas Stern, climate change was characterised as the greatest market failure that the world has seen. You would think that this would make climate change a big deal for the university departments of economics. It ought to be at the core of the subject.

Not so... it is when they are wrong that the leaders of a subject discipline most recent criticism. If they can get away with it, the favoured response is to ignore an issue like this one. It is necessary for the old duffers to retire and the next generation to take their place before a problem on this scale can be dealt with. This is more than unfortunate because humanity doesn't actually have very long before a dangerous problem becomes a catastrophic problem. In the meantime, economics and economists do not actually help us get to grips with climate change for reasons summarised succinctly by Stephen J Decanio:

> Economics is not a useful language for discussing climate change policy for three main reasons:
>
> Cost-benefit analysis requires unrealistic assumptions about human preferences, technological possibilities, and property rights. Traditional economic assumptions tend to bury important ethical and moral questions beneath technical details. Because speaking in economic terms requires specialized knowledge, fewer people can participate in the political area, narrowing the public policy discourse. (Decanio)

Chapter 45

The Climate Crisis as seen by the economics mainstream

Mainstream economics frames the climate crisis in a particular way but this approach is not at all helpful. There have been a variety of controversies which show clearly how economists think – like the "price of a life" controversy. The findings of the Stern Review were widely quoted but how were they calculated? Much of the controversy about the Stern Review among economists was about the discount rate to be applied to future projections. These issues are explained.

Although the effects of climate change seem to be near to apocalyptic over the long term, over the short term taking significant action to cut emissions also appears to be a tremendous challenge. The magnitude of this challenge is indicated by a statement in the Stern Review of *The Economics of Climate Change* "Experience suggests that it is difficult to secure emission cuts faster than 1% per year except in instances of recession..." (Stern, 2006, p. 231)

When the Soviet Union was wound up the Russian economy collapsed. Between 1989 and 1998, fuel related emissions fell in that country by 5.2% per annum because economic activity halved. However, this was no model to copy. It was a period of deep crisis. The death rate, particularly among young Russian men, soared. (Stern, 2006, p. 232)

How mainstream economics frames the climate crisis

This brings us to the climate policy response so far, or the lack of it, and how mainstream economists frame the climate debate.

- Any policies have to be consistent with **growth**
- Optimal policies are supposed to be based on **cost benefit calculations** in which gains and losses for different people through time are held to be commensurable in money terms
- An **appropriate discount rate** must be charged when making policy calculations
- It is assumed that climate change, its impacts and their costs are predictable, at least in probability terms, and controllable. The assumption of policy is that we are facing **calculable risks instead of "Strong uncertainty"**
- The appropriate goal of policy it to find the **"correct carbon price"** imposed by a carbon tax and/ or cap and emissions trading systems to **drive the evolution of techno innovation solutions**

The game that neoclassical economists think that they are in is one of finding the best deal for humanity in regards to "costs" and "benefits", calculable in a money unit of account, on a continued growth path. The neoclassicals see themselves as trying to find the optimal trade-off between states of the climate system and states of economic system which can be thought of as a kind of "optimal insurance deal". This is one huge global cost benefit calculation in which to get it wrong entails one of two possible outcomes – either the "insurance premiums" (ambition and scale of the mitigation costs) are set too high, or they are set too low when compared to the damage costs caused by the climate impacts that are eventually suffered.

Two examples can be given of the cost benefit approach, that of William Nordhaus and that of the Stern Review. The latter was the report produced by a research team commissioned by the UK Treasury under the leadership of Nicholas Stern, now Lord Stern.

The approach of Nordhaus is called a Dynamic Integrated Climate Economy model, or DICE for short. The underlying assumption of DICE is that the degree to which climate change takes place depends upon the magnitude of mitigation efforts. For each degree of possible climate change, there will be a degree of impact damages with a corresponding cost of these impacts. The averting of these costs by mitigation efforts (e.g. technological change in the energy system) can be thought of as the benefits of mitigation. However, mitigation efforts also entail implementation costs. The aim of the exercise with DICE is to calculate all the costs and benefits arising from different amounts of mitigation, now and in the future. The costs and benefits of different levels of mitigation ambition are calculated and discounted back to current monetary values using an appropriate discount rate. (Hamilton, 2010, pp. 60-61)

The greater the mitigation effort the less the climate change impact costs (the greater the benefits in averting these impact costs). However, the greater the mitigation efforts the greater the money costs of mitigation. So for Nordhaus, the aim of the exercise is to do the sums and find the level of climate mitigation effort that minimises the costs of climate change AND the costs of mitigation when added together – all discounted back to present values. This is the optimal trade off point.

In a paper of 2008, Nordhaus argues that a business as usual policy (i.e. no climate mitigation) would give rise to damages of $23 trillion. However, by spending $2 trillion on mitigation climate impact costs would fall to $18 trillion, $5 trillion less. Thus, the world would be saved $5 trillion minus $2trillion = $3trillion net in climate impact costs. According to the Nordhaus calculations, this is the optimal trade off point - minimising cost of mitigation and cost of climate change impacts together.

Clive Hamilton is not impressed:

> By any reasonable criterion Nordhaus's analysis is mad. He behaves like the ultimate economic technocrat with his hand on the global thermostat, checking his modelling results and fiddling with the knob, checking again and adjusting further, all so that the planet's atmospheric layer may be tuned optimally to suit the majority of human inhabitants (Hamilton, 2010, p. 62)

A key point in Hamilton's critique is the delusion that it is possible to predict and calculate the impacts of climate change for the century ahead - indeed the assumption that it is precisely controllable like a thermostat. This ignores the many unknowns in climate science, how these will translate into actual historical events and the possibility of dynamic reinforcing feedbacks.

As Hamilton puts it the climate is "more like a wild beast than a thermostat that can be controlled".

The "Price of a Life" controversy

For the Nordhaus approach to have any meaning all, things must be comparable and measurable in money terms. Money must be trusted as an appropriate unit of account which is able to make all things commensurable. Changes in health, education, and environment are all reduced down to changes in income that is measurable in GDP terms. Thus, the underlying ethical choices are hidden behind mathematical calculations of various categories of loss and gain. For example, Nordhaus speculates that there will be some benefits of extra recreation in the US from a warmer world, but some loss of life elsewhere. Another ecological economist, Clive Spash, explains how a methodology like this, that aggregates gains and losses in money figures, means that dead people in China and India are compensated for by extra golfing holidays in Florida.

This has not been well received in poor countries. Great controversy arose at the time of the 1995 International Panel on Climate Change Report when some economists varied the "dollar value of life" in their climate calculations on the basis of income differences which meant that a rich person's life was valued at 15 times the value of a poor person's life. "On this basis if you kill 14 poor people to save one rich person there is a "net gain". (Spash C. L., 2008) (Thematic Guide to Integrated Assessment Modeling of Climate Change [online]., 1995)

Why Kaldor Hicks doesn't work for climate economics

The method used assumes the Kaldor-Hicks compensation principle. However, as already explained, Kaldor Hicks does not require that losers actually get any money or goods in real compensation payments. The "potential" ability to compensate is supposed to be enough.

Quite apart from the evident injustice of this approach, there are other reasons why this "lowest common denominator utilitarianism" does not work for climate policy. In so far as climate change policy is about the relations between people living in different time periods, the required Kaldor-Hicks transfers are physically impossible. People living in the future cannot send goods back into the past to compensate present day individuals who may have to give something up to avert dangerous climate change. Those living in the present can to some degree determine the future's endowment of produced and natural capital but causation in the reverse direction cannot happen.

Meanwhile, in the here and now, golfers in Florida need not worry that they will be paying extra taxes to compensate families dying from droughts, floods or sea level storm surges in the third world. As long as golfers are judged better off by more than the families of the dead (and the dead themselves) are worse off, that is all that matters. Clearly, asking the opinion of those involved is not on the agenda." (Spash, 2008)

The quote by Spash reminds us what is involved in the neoclassical style of reasoning. Mainstream economists replace what should be a subject for human communication – between various communities of affected people, who are winners and losers, in a process of deliberation – with a calculation by a professional priesthood in which the real ethical issues and power relations are hidden behind obscure calculations. The premise of welfare economics is that the utility gains and losses of people (measured in money) must be aggregated and it is assumed that the gains of some can be added to the losses of other people.

Equity calculation weightings

It will be recalled from earlier in this book that neoclassical economists set great store by the idea of declining marginal utility. This is notion that as one gets more of a good the additional satisfaction or utility from each additional unit possessed declines. The fifth slice of pizza does not add as much to satisfaction as the first. The logical corollary of this is that an additional dollar to a rich person, who already has plenty of everything, will not add as much as a dollar to a poor person who has very little. Applying this kind of logic to climate change impacts and costs implies the need to recognise that marginal gains or losses to a poor person are greater than to a rich person. Yet most climate cost benefit analyses ignore this and implicitly assume that the income distribution in society is justified. "This means if a person who lives on $2 a day loses $1 and a millionaire gains $2 the world is a better place" (Baer & Spash, 2008)

There are, however, a few studies that make calculations to adjust climate cost benefit analyses with an "equity weighting". These include a study by Nordhaus and Boyer. The effect of adjusting with equity weighting leads to a significant change in the quantification of climate damage. In a Nordhaus and Boyer study, the measure of damages at 5 degrees C increases from 6% to 8% of GDP. A 2002 study by Richard Tol found that damages double at 5 C degrees when an equity weighting adjustment is made. (Baer & Spash, 2008, p. 17)

The Stern Review

The Stern Review received much international publicity. It was published in 2007 after a number of studies, like those of Nordhaus and Tol, had suggested that the cost of climate change impacts was likely to be relatively small. A study by Richard Tol had even claimed that there could be overall benefits for small increases in temperature, particularly in rich countries. Stern, however, found that the cost of climate impacts would be much larger and came to the conclusion that it was worth paying 1% of world gross production each year in climate mitigation investment in order to prevent overall costs of climate change equivalent to losing at least 5% of world GDP each year, now and forever.

The 5% loss figure related to global per capita consumption, and Stern noted it would increase further if three other issues were taken into account:

"Non-market" impacts on environment and human health which would bump up the 5% of global GDP to 11%; the effects of reinforcing feedbacks in the climate system which could further increase the impacts – increasing the 11% to 14%; and an equity weighting figure reflecting the greater impact on poorer countries which would increase the overall impact figure from 14% up to 20%. (Stern, 2006, pp. 161-162)

The abatement cost conceived of like an insurance premium

Stern later increased his cost figure for necessary mitigation from 1% costs to 2% of world GDP. He described this abatement cost as being like an insurance premium.

What are these figures and where do they come from? As we saw with the critique of Nordhaus, using aggregate GDP numbers measures life by the ability to consume. Stern approached the issues in much the same way. He too is primarily calculating "consumption" – though the idea of consumption is an expanded one, including health, education, the environment and the like. Here again is the assumption of commensurability made possible by money valuations. Although, to be fair, there is a lengthy discussion of the ethical issues of doing this - adding up, aggregating, the monetary measures of the consequences of climate change.

> The stripped down approach that we shall adopt when we attempt to assess the potential costs of climate change uses the standard framework of welfare economics. The objective of policy is taken as the maximisation of the sum across individuals of social utilities of consumption. Thus, in this framework, aggregation of impacts across individuals using social value judgements is assumed to be possible. In particular, we consider consumption as involving a broad range of goods and services that includes education, health and the environment. The relationship between the measure of social well-being – the sum of social utilities in this argument – and the goods and services consumed by each household, on which it depends, is called the social welfare function. (Stern, 2006, p. 33)

So, the authors of the Stern Review were aware of the criticisms and difficulties of their approach, for example, of how to value health. They were aware of the debates about the "value of a life". They were aware that characterising "broader dimensions of welfare" in money terms "should be viewed with circumspection".

However, after making their caveats, they went ahead and used the approach anyway.

The appropriateness of equity weightings to adjust aggregate figures was also acknowledged. However, the Stern team said that they lacked the time to do their own equity weighting calculations. Instead, the review quotes adjustments in the study by Nordhaus and Boyer as "indicative" of the sort of change that they too should be make. This led to their assertion that a reasonable equity weighting change in the estimate of maximum damages would be an increase from 14.4% to 20% of GDP. (Stern, 2006, p. 187)

Baer and Spash comment:

> The Stern Review follows Nordhaus in producing a figure (for damages) with a calculated deceptive precision which is simply arbitrarily rounded up to another number. (Baer & Spash, 2008, p. 18)

Results that are "illustrative only"

The figures from the Stern Review are "ball park", little better than guesstimates of what might happen in a largely unknown and unknowable future. Stern seeks to tame uncertainty by turning his future projections into a range of probabilities about future climate states and their impacts. To do this, he used a model called PAGE 2002 (*Policy Analysis of the Greenhouse Effect 2002*) with 30 crucial inputs, each of which has a supposed "probability density function". (Inputs are things like the ratio of climate damages in different regions for each temperature increase, or the figure to calculate the sensitivity of temperature increase to different levels of CO_2 increase). (Stern, 2006, pp. 173-175)

In practice, as Spash argues, only the "climate sensitivity" has any significant scientific literature. (Climate sensitivity is a figure for how much global temperatures increase for a doubling of CO_2 in the atmosphere). For the other inputs the PAGE authors used their judgement based on scanty evidence. Guesstimates are subjected to a sophisticated mathematical process and, to cover their backs the researchers write caveats that few people will read:

> Integrated assessment models can be useful vehicles for exploring the kinds of costs that might follow from climate change. However, these are highly aggregative and simplified models and, as such, the results should be seen as illustrative only. (Stern, 2006, p. 124)

This did not stop these results being used as headline figures in many mass circulation newspapers, TV and radio reports. Anyone not knowing might have thought that the figures that got the press coverage were grounded in precise science.

Climate policy and the discount rate

It was the discount rate used in the Stern Review that really upset a lot of economists. They thought it was too low and they were not impressed by a chapter where Stern discussed the ethics of discounting.

It will be remembered that when calculations occur for situations evolving over time, economists like to discount future money values in order to make them comparable with current money values. Discounting assumes that people have time preferences for money now, rather than money in the future, and that is what the payment of interest is all about. It is a payment for relinquishing money to a borrower and only getting it back later. The practice of discounting is very controversial when it comes to making comparisons across different generations, which is what climate change and sustainability is all about. I argued earlier that the mind set of many indigenous peoples would reject this practice.

There is a lengthy ethical discussion in the Stern Review on the topic of discounting which concludes:

> ... while we do allow, for example, for the possibility that, say, a meteorite might obliterate the world, and for the possibility that future generations might be richer (or poorer), we treat the welfare of future generations on a par with our own. It is of course possible that people actually do place less value on the welfare of future generations, simply on the grounds that they are more distant in time. But it is hard to see any ethical justification for this. (Stern, 2006, p. 35)

The significance of future generations being richer or poorer is explained below, but the strange reference to a meteorite perhaps needs to be explained too. The idea contained here is: why be concerned about future generations if there is a chance that they might not be there anyway? This would be the case if a meteorite hits the earth and wipes everyone out. It's only a small chance perhaps, but that small possibility needs to be counted in as part of the calculation.

Stern, therefore, decided to use a discount rate of 1.4%. This was lower than rates used in other climate studies so William Nordhaus and Richard Tol became very upset. Nordhaus argued that the present generation will have to forgo a large amount of consumption now for the benefit of future generations, who will be much richer than the present generation.

If future generations are richer, then they will be able to afford to carry the costs of climate change impacts. This gets to the heart of the issue. At the risk of over-simplifying, behind all the sophisticated mathematical projections about the future the differences of view can be described as either "degrees of complacency" or "degrees of alarmism" depending on which side you stand.

To the "growth optimists", whatever happens to the climate, the economy will continue growing and future generations will be in good shape to cope in terms of technology, resources and human made capital (if not natural capital). In this view, it seems justified to calculate with a high discount rate. This will tend to discourage spending now to achieve future mitigation benefits which, when they are heavily discounted, don't appear to be worth a lot. The rationale is that, after all is said and done, the future generations are going to be fabulously wealthy and should easily be able to cope.

On the other hand, to those like the current author, whose world view is framed within a "limits to growth" perspective, climate change is one of a number of problems that threaten to lead to, or already are leading to, a dangerous ecological overshoot. In this perspective, future generations may not be better off at all. They are likely to be much worse off and in a much inferior position to cope with the climate problems bequeathed to them. This is the case for dealing with the problem now to head it off.

Huge problems facing humanity are given to the economists to judge. Perhaps after all, Gregory Mankiw is right. The economists are like wizards with magical divinatory powers. They look at huge existential threats facing humanity and, instead helping to organise collective deliberative processes to draw in all of society to discuss how to cope with a vast common threat, the economists withdraw to do complicated mathematical calculations. They re-emerge having performed the calculations in accordance with the magical rites.

If you look closer though, what they have mostly done is pulled ball park guesstimates out of a hat, applied a discount rate that is completely subjective and entirely inappropriate to protecting future generations, and published reports with deceptively precise figures. The reports may contain caveats about the figures in the small print but only a tiny number of people notice.

Having performed the magical rites on our behalf, which most people are nowhere near qualified to understand let alone do, the media reassures the masses that our betters are still in control and know what they are doing. The consensus trance remains intact. It is yet closer to midnight and nothing has actually been done to reduce emissions.

Seven years after the Stern Review

Seven years after the Stern Review little has changed. Nicholas Stern, now a Lord, is playing a leading role in a "Global Commission on Environment and Climate"(GCEC) which involves ex-heads of state, bankers, leaders of international organisations like the World Bank and a team of mainstream economists to back them up. Late in 2014 they produced a lobbying document titled *Better Growth. The New Climate Economy* ahead of the UNFCCC Conference of the Parties to be held in Paris in December 2015. (GCEC. 2014.) The hope is that, inspired by this 15 year strategy, civil society organisations will fall in line and back the technocratic solution.

The chief priority of this group is already clear from their document title. As it says on page 9, "In the long term, if climate change is not tackled, growth itself will be at risk" (page 9)

With small differences the thinking is the same as that of the Stern Review. In a critique of the "Better Growth" document Clive Spash draws attention to the familiar features of mainstream economics. What follows draws heavily on the critique of Stern by Spash. (Spash, Clive L 2014)

The approach frames the issues in a "risk management" perspective. It is as if the costs are to pay for an "insurance deal" – all of which is based on the confident assertion that risks are predictable. This is contrary to a 'strong uncertainty' view of climate change and its effects. As Spash explains, string uncertainty "calls for precaution and avoided pathways that lead to disastrous scenarios, not deliberately walking down them on the basis of a gamblers role of the risk management dice."

The approach is based on the consequentialist utilitarian perspective. This conceptually reduces harm to innocent victims as lost output that can be measured with income statistics - a form of 'commensurability' that allows calculation and comparison of losses and gains, costs and benefits. As Spash comments: "Economics has become a profession where more dead people can be compensated by better growth, that is a net benefit can be calculated if the value of the growth in output makes consumption goods worth more than the people killed in their production"

There is the usual fixation on growth – with the assumption that its benefits will trickle down, the arrogant belief that the kind of development delivered by the corporations is what the poor need and the complete failure to question what vision for society is needed – as Spash puts it "inequitable material affluence in a competitive individualistic society or human flourishing which enables a good life in communities of sharing and caring for others".

Given its authorship it is not surprising that the climate crisis is assumed to be best understood as market failure in which 'external' climate costs and benefits have not internalised by market actors. A predictable carbon price is needed and carbon trading arrangements are needed to deliver this price. Who is to blame for the market failure? Ironically, it is the states that are at fault because weak politicians have not shown enough political will to intervene in the market. What is neglected here, of course, is the ubiquitous character of externalities and the sheer scale of the task of changing them all - as if we had all the information needed to know what the adjusted prices should be. The report also ignores the power of the corporations to block these market corrections when it does not suit their interests – a power that has rendered carbon markets completely ineffectual anyway.

Meanwhile there is effectively nothing in this report about the Jevons paradox or rebound; about the scarcity and depletion of particular raw materials like rare earths that would be needed to extend out the technological options envisaged; about energy return on energy invested; about global real-politik and strategic military contests for resources; about the problems associated with fracking and so on.

So what is it that really agitates the groups that are behind this document? Since 2007 it has become increasingly clear that if climate change is to be tackled then most fossil fuels will have to remain in the ground – and there has been a recognition too that this would mean a lot of very big, very influential companies losing a lot of money. The fossil fuel reserves are their assets and their value would have to be written down. Many companies would go bust. As explained earlier in this book because there is a strong interpenetration between the state and the energy companies many states would lose out too – for example on important sources of taxation. This is why the question of how to deal with the "carbon bubble", as it is called, has become a concern for those in the elite who do recognise that something must be done. As the finance report of the GCEC says:

"The financial impact of stranded assets is not about lost production, but lost value.

For example, under our evaluation scenario, even oil producers whose output is

Unaffected by the [GCEC recommended] transition could see the value of their oil production fall by up to 60% due to falling wholesale oil prices that result when demand declines." (GCEC 2014b)

What then is the solution? Surprise, surprise! It is technological innovation by the big corporate players achieved by "getting the market prices right" as well as channelling resources raised through taxation to subsidise and encourage techno-innovation and R&D. Carbon capture and storage has been the big idea so far but it looks as if it will be too expensive and has been effectively shelved by Britain and Norway. However, as Spash explains the view of the "Better Growth" authors:

"Promoting massive R&D holds the hope that a miracle technology will appear and all those toxic fuel assets will suddenly be valuable again".

This is what a group of powerful people look like when they lose touch with reality. As we have already seen the techno-innovations that are supposed to mitigate climate change are largely granfalloons. The elite fantasy of growth combined with R&D and techno-innovation to resolve the climate crisis can do a lot of damage by diverting us from the reality of the catastrophe that humanity faces.

Chapter 46

The Climate Crisis and Economic Policy Choices

A major issue in climate economics is whether it is possible to halt the growth in carbon emissions and to achieve, instead, a rapid reduction. It concludes that carbon emissions will never fall at a sufficient rate in a growth economy. Unfortunately, the EU operates a climate policy framework, the EU Emissions Trading System, that was designed by BP and it doesn't work. Policies that might work were the political will there are described. However, the fossil fuel industry still has a stranglehold on policy.

An entirely different way of thinking about climate issues is needed, one that is consistent with the limits to growth paradigm. The alternative way of framing the climate debate is:

- Humanity is faced with the **high likelihood of a catastrophic ecological tipping point and this crisis is part of a general crisis at the limits to economic growth**
- There are **many unknowns** exactly where that tipping point – beyond which might be runaway climate change because of feedback
- This tipping point imposes the **need for an absolute limit** on what can safely be emitted and what must be clawed back out of the atmosphere – given the uncertainty with a need for a high margin of safety
- This **limit trumps any growth agenda** because the danger is so great and ecological scale limits must be imposed in physical quantities (e.g. of allowed carbon emissions) before the market can be allowed to operate
- The limits to economic growth require that climate policy be part of a more general transition of society and economy for which efforts must be made to enrol everyone.
- Techno-innovation may have a role in the transition but will not be the sole or even the main method of reducing energy consumption – moral, cultural, behavioural and other changes are also needed.
- Limits need to be imposed as equitably as possible as part of the larger transition
- We need to get on with this task now, as a matter of urgency

Decoupling – relative and absolute

Central to the alternative approach is a focus upon what is called "de-coupling" also sometimes described as "de-materialisation". The question at stake here is whether it is possible to grow the economy and, at the very same time, achieve an absolute reduction in the throughput of energy and materials, that is, to decouple growth from increased material and energy usage. More specifically, in relation to the climate crisis, is it possible to grow the economy and reduce carbon emissions at the same time? Various proponents of degrowth do not deny that it is possible to increase the efficiency with which energy and materials are used in the economy. They do not deny that the amount of carbon emitted per unit of output can be decreased and that "relative decoupling" can occur. What they do not believe is that absolute decoupling can be made to work – and certainly not on the scale necessary to avert the danger of runaway climate change.

No good or service can be produced without energy – even "information" requires energy to run the computers or make and print books, magazines and newspapers. As the economy grows it requires more energy and, because virtually all energy in our society is generated by burning carbon fuels, that means more CO_2 emissions. The figures show clearly that for decades, carbon emissions and economic activity fluctuate together in lockstep. This is a key concept already discussed in the chapters on production and technology but, to refresh the point, here are two graphs compiled by Gail Tversky, drawing on GNP calculations by Angus Maddison, energy calculations by Vaclav Smil, supplemented by information from BP, EIEA and USDA. (Tverberg, 2012)

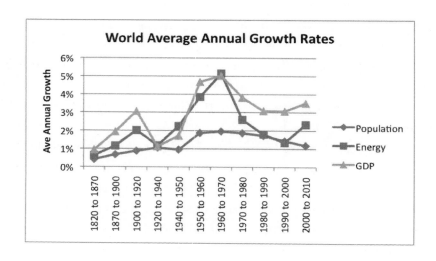

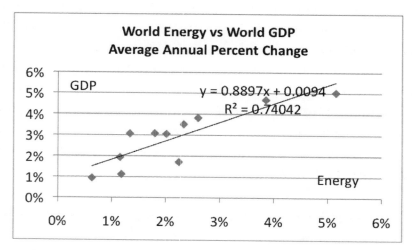

Graphs reproduced by permission from Gail Tverberg (Tverberg G. 2012)

The graphs show that energy production and world GDP are highly correlated and, since most of the energy is derived from fossil fuels, this involves increased emissions. Unless the connection between growth of production and growth of emissions can be broken, and to a sufficient extent, there can be no reduction of carbon emissions without an end to growth – indeed without contraction.

At this point, a reminder is necessary. It may be that depleting fossil fuel supplies and the production crunch brought about by rising energy and material costs that was described in an earlier chapter, will achieve a considerable turn down in carbon emissions anyway. This would not be a particularly pleasant resolution of the crisis but it would certainly change the conditions in which the climate crisis would have to be resolved. On the other hand, the global power elite appear to be hell bent on continuing to extract and use carbon based fossil energy if they can, so we cannot totally be sure if things will evolve into this kind of crunch. This is despite the fact that in 2012 the International Energy Agency acknowledged that 2/3 of recoverable carbon in fuels needs to stay in the ground up to 2050 to have any change of staying below a temperature increase of 2degrees C. This matches findings from the IPCC working group 3. (IPCC.WG3.Final Draft AR5. Presentation 2014)

There is plenty of carbon here to bring greenhouse gas concentration levels well above 600 ppm. As we have already seen, fracking for shale gas is just one of several options being pursued to get new fossil energy sources out of the ground in the face of the depletion gradients, bringing with it the threat of high fugitive methane losses. Underground gasification of coal is another technology based on extracting the energy from deep coal seams by partially burning it underground to extract the energy in the form of syngas. When it comes to the surface, syngas can be burned to generate electricity. If this can be made to work, there are unfortunately very large reserves of coal in the world that can still be used as energy sources.

Worse still, attempts are being made to tap "frozen" methane from the oceans called methane hydrates. This is a dangerous process because methane hydrate unfreezes from its crystalline form directly into methane gas and, when it does so, it enormously expands in volume. The process is thus, very unstable and explosive. However, Japanese technologists claim to have been able to do it and might be able to turn this into a commercial venture. (Reuters, 2013)

The description of the situation at this point in the analysis is to use what is called the *Kaya identity* after a Japanese energy economist Yoichi Kaya, who proposed a way of breaking down the different components to explain the growth (or reduction) in total emissions. These components are growth of the economy measured as GDP per capita (GDP/population); growth of the population; the energy intensity needed per unit of economic output (energy/GDP) and the emission intensity of that energy (CO_2e/energy).

It can be readily appreciated that emissions from the last two components can be reduced as a result of:

- *Increasing energy efficiency* - the amount of energy used per unit of economic output/service is reduced brought about by more insulation in buildings, lighter more efficient vehicles, machinery etc.

And

- **Decarbonising energy sources** - the amount of carbon used in generating energy is reduced by switching to renewables - wind, solar, tidal, wave etc. It also requires changes to the grid to balance for "intermittency" as well as switching to an electric infrastructure (e.g. electric cars)

At this point, the distinction needs to be drawn out between relative decoupling and absolute decoupling. Relative decoupling means that for every unit of output less carbon emissions are generated. Another way of saying this is that the "carbon intensity of output falls".

In his book *"Prosperity without Growth"*, Tim Jackson gives figures which show that the global carbon intensity declined by almost a quarter from just over 1 kilogram of CO_2 per one US dollar output in 1980 to 770grams of carbon dioxide per US dollar in 2006. (Jackson, 2009, pp. 48-50) The fall in CO_2 intensity per unit of economic output did not mean, however, that the absolute volume of carbon emissions fell. Because growth of production per capita and population grew even faster, the total amount of carbon emissions went up – even though, due to "relative decoupling", carbon dioxide emissions rose at a slower rate than GDP. To sum up, this was relative decoupling but not absolute decoupling. (Jackson, 2009, pp. 50-53).

As a rule of thumb, absolute decoupling will only start to occur when the rate of relative decoupling is greater than the rates of increase of population and income combined. Thus, with global population increasing at 1.3% and the global per capita income increasing at 1.4% per year in real terms, the required technical improvement (reduction) in carbon intensity is greater than 2.7% (1.4% + 1.3%) per year. So what has the rate of technical improvement been? As Jackson computes the figures, carbon intensity has only been improving at 0.7% per annum. Thus, emissions have been increasing at 2% per annum.

Since Jackson's book was published, more up to date figures published by the IPCC's Working Group 3 for the 5th Assessment Report shows that the situation has deteriorated. This is not only because of growth in population and per capita growth, but also because the emission intensity of energy has increased. (IPCC. WG3. Final Draft AR5 Presentation 2014)

While the efficiency with which the global economy uses energy, as measured by the energy/GDP ratio, has continued to improve, the slow decarbonisation of the global energy supply has been put into reverse. The carbon intensity of energy is actually increasing, particularly as more coal is being used. The fact that there is so little sign of hope appears to be because, as depletion has driven up oil and gas supplies and prices, coal is being turned to instead, as well as more emission intensive sources of oil and gas (like Canadian tar sands and shale).

The scale of the challenge – the necessary rates of emissions reduction

These figures should be compared with what a team of climate scientists have calculated is the necessary rate of reduction.

> Keeping global climate close to the Holocene range, we will conclude, requires a long-term atmospheric CO2 level of about 350 ppm or less, with other climate forcings similar to today's levels. If emissions reduction had begun in 2005, reduction at 3.5%/year would have achieved 350 ppm at 2100. Now the requirement is at least 6%/year. Delay of emissions reductions until 2020 requires a reduction rate of 15%/year to achieve 350 ppm in 2100. If we assume only 50 GtC reforestation, and begin emissions reduction in 2013, the required reduction rate becomes about 9%/year. (Hansen, Kharecha, Sato, Masson-Delmotte, Ackerman, et al. 2013)

Another climate scientist, Kevin Anderson, argues that to stand an outside chance of not rising more than 2 degrees C, global emissions will have to stop rising at the latest by 2020 and will then have to fall by 10% per annum thereafter. (Kevin Anderson, "Pick a card – any card... How in funding targets to meet politically palatable goals, climate scientists undermine issues of equity and fairness", Presentation to the Joseph Rowntree Foundation, March 2013 and available at *http://kevinanderson.info*)

The graph below shows Anderson's presentation of the options – the continuation of business as usual trends would mean a 4 to 6 degree C increase.

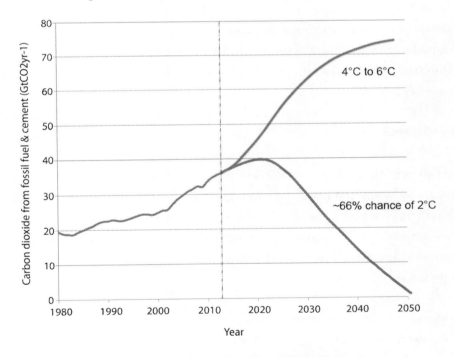

Reproduced with permission from Kevin Anderson.

Just to stop global emissions growing, if GDP growth rates are 2.7% pa then carbon intensity must reduce at 2.7% per annum, which is nearly 4 times the current rate of improvement. In order for emissions to fall at 10% per annum, if growth continued at 2.7% pa, this would require carbon intensity to improve (reduce) at 12.7 % per annum. This is 18 times the current rate of improvement. (Anderson K. 2013)

Such a fall seems inconceivable in a growth scenario so that Kevin Anderson and his colleague Alice Bows had already in 2008 taken the view that:

> ... dangerous climate change can only be avoided if economic growth is exchanged for a period of planned austerity within Annex 1 nations at the same time as there is a rapid transition away from fossil-fuelled development within non-Annex 1 nations. *(Anderson & Bows, 2010)*

The climate crisis is still on...

In his March 2013 presentation to the Joseph Rowntree Foundation, Anderson has moved on with the recognition that the necessary reductions barely affect a very large proportion of the world's population. The austerity has to be carried by the elite. Perhaps 1% of the global population accounts for 50% of all emissions and if we take the top 5% we are talking about the 60% of emissions. It is above all the carbon intensity of the lifestyle of the global elite that is taking us all to climate hell and it is the lifestyle of this elite that needs to be tackled.

So how can this be done – and as part of a larger societal response to the limits to economic growth?

- Try to calculate (with a very safe margin for error) the small amount of additional carbon that can be emitted to stay well back from the runaway tipping point
- Only permit that very limited amount of carbon to be released – and let the market set a price for that amount of carbon
- Do this in a way that affects everyone but hits the richest the most because they are responsible for most of the emissions

Of course, saying this begs the political question of how such a policy can be brought about, but we will park that question at this point and come back to it later. The assumption for now is that some organised agency can be found with the political will and power to set an absolute ceiling on the amount of carbon based fuels that are allowed into the economy. Or, put the other way around, an agency is created with the power to keep most remaining fossil fuels in the ground untouched. This will then, in turn, force a number of other processes such as:

- **Lifestyle changes** – eating less meat which is an energy and carbon intense foodstuff; cycling and walking more and less travel; more growing your own food; voluntary reductions in consumption with a culture of "sufficiency" reductions.
- **Energy efficiency** in buildings, production, transport **plus...**
- **Renewable generation** – wind; solar voltaics + thermal, concentrated solar power; hydro, tidal, wave power; some bio-

- **Technologies to complement renewables** – electric storage technologies and grid balancing
- **Land use changes, ecological design, organic agriculture** with protection against deforestation and degradation of peat lands *and*
- *Enhancement of carbon sequestration in land and biomass*

Effective cap and ineffective caps – how the EU operates a policy designed by BP that doesn't work

But is it possible to impose a carbon price (or a cap)? How is it possible to drive a process of decarbonisation? What can be done about emissions from land use changes and deforestation? What is to be done about other sources of global warming like black carbon, methane emissions, N2O emissions, HCFCs and so on? There are lots of questions in climate policy that need answers. It is not straightforward by any means.

Taking the question of the cap first. At the time of writing, the very idea of a "cap" is greeted with scepticism by many climate activists because current policies of "cap and trade" have been so ineffectual. But, to be fair, the word "cap" has been abused. A "cap" should mean an absolute limit but in current policy frameworks it is no such thing. The so called "cap" operated by the European Union does not function as a real restraint. It has been designed to leak because fossil fuel business interests had control of the policy making process and the policy making implementation. The problem is not with the idea of a cap. The problem is the power of the fossil fuel lobby that has made a nonsense of its practical implementation. If a carbon tax was used instead of a cap, the very same problem would still be there. The fossil fuel industry would do everything in their power to undermine an effective tax too if it hit their profits and power, which an effective tax would. This is the fatal weakness in the ideas of James Hansen and others, including economist Jeffries Sachs, who call for a carbon tax, as a solution.

It should not surprise that the cap and trade policy in Europe has failed. As we have seen repeatedly in this book, policy is written by the polluters for the polluters and when the European Union's Emissions Trading Scheme was set up, it was no exception. For a long time, the major fossil fuel suppliers had resisted any restraint on emissions but, at the end of the 1990s, some of them changed tack. Recognising that some policy was inevitable, companies like BP in Britain, moved to take over the policy making process and thus, turned it to their own advantage. BP first experimented with an internal emissions trading scheme which was started in 1999. In 2002, the BP model was scaled up with the support of the UK government's Department of the Environment and 34 other voluntarily participating companies. This UK scheme, in turn, became a model for the European Union's Emissions Trading Scheme. This was despite the fact that, from very early on, it was evident that the BP scheme was ineffectual. The supposed "cap" that it used did not really restrain emissions. Some of the later problems of the EU's ETS were already visible in the earlier BP/UK government experiment. However, such was the lobbying power of BP and its corporate allies, that their format was adopted anyway.

Two years into the UK scheme, it was examined by the House of Commons Select Committee on Public Accounts. Labour MP Gerry Steinberg described the scheme as a "mockery" and an "outrageous waste of [public] money". BP was one of a number of UK companies which had lobbied so successfully for a generous emissions allowance that it massively over-complied in the first year of the scheme, leaving the company free to profit from the sale of its surplus allowances. The fact that emissions were already limited by the government's Climate Change agreements led Edward Leigh, the Conservative chair of the Public Accounts Committee, to observe that the scheme seemed to be "paying these companies 111£ million for keeping emissions down to levels they had already achieved before they joined". Leigh also observed that "half the point of this was to try and encourage Europe to do a similar scheme.

The committee's enquiry revealed that the scheme's success was not in reducing greenhouse gas emissions but in turning the atmosphere into "a commodity market like any other" and that far from being a side effect, this had been the intention of the scheme.

(Corporate European Observatory and PLATFORM, 2009, pp. 4-5)

In the circumstances, it is not surprising that "caps" have got a bad name. If a solution for the problem of corporate lobby power in the political process could be found, a cap would be the simplest and most direct approach.

The starting point for understanding how a cap should work are the following easily available conversion figures. They show the carbon content of different fuels when burned, reduced to a common measure. Thus, 1 kg CO_2 = 1 Carbon Unit (Note the Global Warming Potential of non-CO_2 warming gases like methane are measured in units called "Carbon dioxide equivalents" which are noted with an "e" after CO_2, as in "CO_2e"). As examples natural gas = 0.18404 carbon units per kWh or industrial coal = 0.31304 carbon units per kWh (a tonne of industrial coal = 2339.1 carbon units)

(Carbon Trust, 2013)

(Matthews, 2012) For each physical quantity of a particular kind of fuel, or for each quantity of energy, it can readily be calculated how much CO_2 will be emitted when that quantity is burned. If the political will could be found, it is therefore entirely possible to construct a policy administration that could control how much carbon can be allowed to be burned in any time period.

You could do it like this. All fossil fuel sales would be banned unless first authorised by a permit. The number of permits, which would be denominated in carbon units, would be limited and reduced rapidly year on year.

In order to acquire some of the limited numbers of permits, the fossil fuel sellers would have to obtain them. As is obvious, the permits would be very expensive to buy if the cap were tight enough. The fossil fuel sellers would pass on the permit cost to their customers so that the price of fossil fuels would rise, perhaps very considerably. The prices of goods made with large amounts of fossil fuels would also rise. This would not be at all popular and would particularly hit people with a carbon intensive lifestyle, which, as we have seen already, is largely the very rich. However, poor people would be hit too. That is why it would be necessary that the large amount of money raised when permits are sold, should be recycled back to the population on a per capita or some other equitable basis. It might also be necessary to do more to help the high carbon poor in countries like the USA but that is a detail that I will not go into here.

This will achieve what Kevin Anderson wants to see, that is, a scheme that cuts the carbon intensive lifestyle of the rich most, while making a very large number of poor people better off, at least in the early stages of the process. The reason that they will be better off is that if the revenue from carbon permit sales is recycled back to the public on a per capita basis, then everyone, rich or poor, will get exactly the same amount of the revenue from permit sales. However, the poor tend to have a less carbon intensive lifestyle. Although prices for their lifestyle will rise, they will still get more from their share of the carbon permit revenues than they will pay extra in rising prices.

"The 1%", however, will be paying a huge amount more because, directly and indirectly, their energy intensive lifestyle accounts for 50% of all carbon emissions and carbon will have become very expensive. Despite this, they will only be getting back the same share from the carbon permit revenues as everyone else.

In the book *Sharing for Survival*, Laurence Matthews illustrates this graphically with a very simple example for an imaginary country consisting of only 10 people with CO_2 emissions as shown (in units of tonnes of CO_2). The total of all emissions is 15 tonnes and so the average is 1.5 tonnes. (Matthews, Cap and Share in pictures, 2012, p. 52)

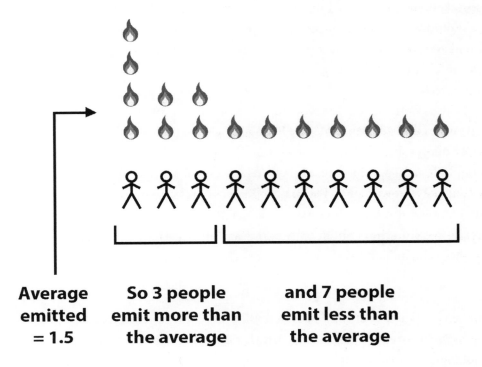

Average emitted = 1.5　　**So 3 people emit more than the average**　　**and 7 people emit less than the average**

(Matthews L. 2012) Graphic reproduced with permission

Laurence Matthews comments:

> A majority would be in favour of maintaining a tight cap, since they gain financially. This is a force to counterbalance the vested interests who would push for a cap to be relaxed or abandoned, and this counterbalance gives a certain political robustness to C&S in the face of shocks and political events.

If such a scheme was adopted in 2020, the number of carbon units permitted would need to be reduced by at least 10% per annum to have an outside chance of the planet staying under 2 degrees C. A reduction of available energy of this magnitude, if at all possible, would need to drive a massive reduction of production, chiefly, the production of things that enter into carbon intensive lifestyle of rich people in the manner explained above.

A policy like this would lead to a very dramatic process of "degrowth" because production is dependent on energy. With fossil energy availability radically reduced by a cap that really bites, the amount of production in the economy would be driven downwards. An upstream cap imposed on sellers of coal, oil and gas can cover ALL fossil fuels entering the economy and would be simple to impose, at least in administrative terms. Most countries already impose duties on fossil fuel sales so there are procedures already in place monitoring the input of fossil fuels into different economies.

Obviously, administrative simplicity is only a part of the problem of setting and operating a cap. Driving a contraction of the economy would be immensely unpopular, unless accompanied by multiple other policies and social changes to enable billions of people to achieve dramatic changes in their lifestyles. These changes should be, above all, concentrated on the rich and would have to be made anyway because of depleting fossil energy and materials resources. They are described in greater length in the final chapter and in this chapter are "parked" for now.

Needless to say, this is nothing like the working of the policy architecture designed in Europe by BP, its corporate allies and government. The European Union policy was designed, consciously or unconsciously, to deflect direct controls away from the fossil fuel industry onto its customers. It is riddled with loopholes and special clauses that make it easy for large businesses to game the system and generally to make it unworkable. Because of business pressure so many permits have been issued that there is no real restraint on emissions in practice. Rather than having a direct control over what fossil fuels are allowed into the economy, the policy architecture has been focused upon the users and uses of fossil fuels at the demand end. In the jargon, the policy is imposed "downstream" rather than "upstream".

As is obvious, the number of users and uses of fossil fuels "downstream" is much greater than the number of suppliers "upstream". Something that this diagram, again devised by Laurence Matthews, is intended to illustrate:

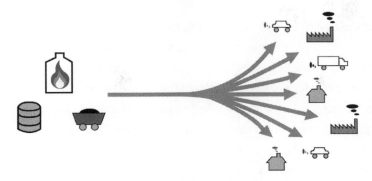

(Matthews L. 2012) Graphic reproduced with permission

It would have made sense to control emissions by capping the amount of fossil fuels going into the system at the source of initial supply. This is called capping the emissions "upstream". The fossil fuel suppliers would have to have emissions permits (indicated by the yellow rectangles) to cover the emissions caused by the fossil fuels they bring into the system.

This is illustrated in this diagram:

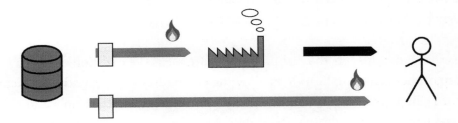

(Matthews L. 2012) Graphic reproduced with permission)

What happened instead in Europe was that the **ETS** was imposed downstream on large fossil fuel users. These are companies running power stations, cement works, steel mills and the like. This covers 45% of the EU's CO2 emissions.

Individuals are not covered in this scheme but could be **through "personal carbon trading" (PCA)** – based on "personal carbon accounts". The problem is that this would be administratively complex. Everyone would have to have their own personal carbon account, presumably by using a carbon card rather like a debit or credit card.

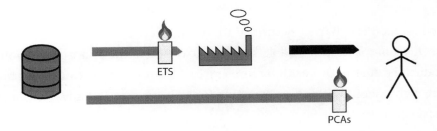

(Matthews L. 2012) Graphic reproduced with permission.

397

In the early stages of the European ETS, most permits to emit were initially distributed to the main emitters for free. This meant that, to the extent that the permits had any market value, it was the companies that captured their value. The mechanism and reasoning worked like this: companies that have to surrender their permits because they have been emitting CO_2 reason that, because the surrendered permits have a market value, surrendering them means the loss of this market value to the company. Thus, as far as the company is concerned, this loss when their permits are surrendered is one of their costs of operation. So, even though they were given the permits in the first place, they pass on this "cost" to their customers in increased prices.

Because it was designed by pushers of fossil fuels, the European Union established a system runs on a "pay the polluter" principle. The idea is supposed to be that, over time, more of the permits will be auctioned by states which will capture the revenue raised. However, there has been some dragging of feet on this and governments are reluctant to implement this system in favour of their fossil fuel corporations. Poland has even wanted to use revenues arising from ETS permits to subsidise new coal fired power stations. (Though been taken to court over this by an environmental NGO, ClientEarth).

The Earth's Atmosphere as a Common Pool Resource that ought to be managed as a global commons

What is at stake as regards who gets the carbon permit revenue is the question of who owns the right to use the earth's atmosphere. The implication of allowing companies to capture the market value of the permits is that the right to use the earth's atmosphere belongs to them. The implication of auctioning and revenues going to governments is that the right belongs to states. The idea that the Earth's atmosphere might "belong" to all of us – and that all of us have a responsibility for it – does not appear to have ever occurred to economists, corporate lobbyists, officials or politicians. Nevertheless, there have been more astute commentators who have grasped what is going on. It's another enclosure process. For example, at the time the ETS was being designed, two authors associated with a German environmental think tank, the Wuppertal Institute commented:

> Parcelling out shares of the global atmospheric commons to be exchanged among trading partners appears to be strikingly similar to the enclosure of the communal forests in 18th century Europe. Just as the enclosures put in place both property rights and forest protection, denying access to the common people, the assignment of emissions permits ensures protection by granting property rights, eliminating unregulated use by any player involved. (Ott & Sachs, 2000)

In the USA too, economist Peter Barnes described the atmosphere as a common pool resource and wrote a book titled *Who Owns the Sky?*. In his book, he argues that use of the atmosphere should be managed by a trust with a fiduciary duty to protect it by limiting its use and that the carbon revenue arising from the renting of these rights should be paid to everyone (in a US scheme) equally. (This is called "cap and dividend"). (Barnes, Who Owns the Sky? , 2003)

Policy is not made on a level playing field and the ETS, with all its weaknesses, is what we have ended up with. It has been complemented within the framework of the Kyoto Protocol with a scheme called the "Clean Development Mechanism".

The Clean Development Mechanism

The "Clean Development Mechanism" is particularly interesting for the way that it throws light on policy mechanisms which are supposed to work by "incentivising" change. As already explained, neoclassical economists assume that one can manipulate means-ends relationships in order to make environmentally benign behaviour pay in money terms. What is supposed to happen is that good environmental/climate ends are achieved by means of incentive schemes which make them financially worthwhile. What the experience of the CDM shows, however, and very clearly, is that what are incentivised are not changes in environmental behaviour but ways of "gaming policies" to cynically make as much money from them as possible.

The **clean development mechanism** (CDM) was supposed to be about supporting "clean" projects in "developing" countries so that they can claim carbon credits for "certified emission reductions" (CERs) which can be sold into the permit schemes operating in "developed countries". In practice, this has mainly meant into the European Union's Emission Trading System.

The idea was to encourage "developing" country projects in renewable energy, energy efficiency and fuel switching which would not have otherwise taken place. What was supposed to happen was that "emissions reductions" in "developing" countries would entitle projects to credits. The number of credits were to be calculated by *comparing actual emissions by the project concerned to a baseline of what would have otherwise have happened if the project had made no efforts to reduce its emissions.*

But how are projects supposed to establish "what would otherwise have happened"? This way of setting up the policy has been a recipe for fraud and for gaming. Many participants have created an inflated base line by increasing actual or stated emissions in the short term before the CDM project was established. Or they set up "projects" in order to close them down. The scams have been particularly profitable in projects that appear to "abate" the production of hydroflurocarbons which are very powerful greenhouse gases as well as gases which destroy the earth's ozone layer. Given the magnitude of the profits generated from CDM credits, it was profitable to build whole new facilities involving hydroflurocarbons just for the value of destroying the by-product. (SourceWatchWiki, 2009) The recognition that this is a problem finally led to a revision of the CDM crediting rules for the issuance of CERs, which were made more stringent in 2011:

> Yet it is still not stringent enough and still threatens to undermine the goals of the Montreal Protocol and the protection of the Ozone layer. The revised rules also do not apply until projects have to renew their crediting period. This means from 2012 until the end of the first crediting periods (seven years after a project started), well over 24... (Industrial Gases (HFC-23 & N2O),

2012) As of 1 June 2013, the CDM had issued 505,125 CERs, or 38% of all CERs issued, to 23 HFC-23 destruction projects (Wikipedia, Clean Development Mechanism, 2013)

Another scam has involved dams. Barbara Haye calculated that more than a third of all hydro-projects recognized as a CDM-project "were already completed at the time of registration and almost all were already under construction" (Haya, 2007). Several years later, despite intensive lobbying by NGOs the need for reform was recognised but governments were again dragging their feet, with many controversial and environmentally damaging hydroprojects still in the pipeline. (Yan, 2012)

The CDM shows clearly what is wrong with current climate policy. It has been infested by crooks. This statement is not meant as rhetorical overstatement for effect – but literally.

Chapter 47

The Climate Crisis, Land Use and Land based emissions

Land use and land use change are also major contributors to greenhouse gas emissions. There are climate threats from emissions that arise as a result of corporate forestry and large scale agribusiness. A technology like biochar, which could be used to sequester carbon in soils, is not likely to be helpful if applied by giant corporations – only if developed by small local actors.

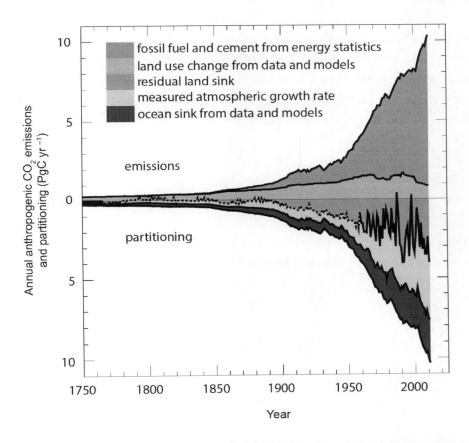

Source: Annual Anthropogenic CO2 emissions and their partitioning among the atmosphere, land and ocean. (IPCC. WG1. AR5: 487) http://www.climatechange2013.org/report/reports-graphic/ch6-graphics/

While fossil fuel use is certainly the main source of increasing greenhouse gases in the atmosphere it is not the only one. Land can either be a source of emissions or a sink, taking CO2 out of the atmosphere. It depends on how it is used. The diagram, taken from the 5th Assessment Report the International Panel on Climate change shows some of the processes and magnitudes and includes the oceans too. Carbon can be taken up by the oceans which become more acidic, but at least as a result, the carbon does not stay in the atmosphere as CO2. A part is reabsorbed in land sinks like peat bogs and biomass. The rest remains in the atmosphere.

There is a huge amount of carbon embedded and embodied in all forms of plant life and in soils too. When the plants and biomass grow, they take CO2 out of the atmosphere during the process of photosynthesis. However, if plant material (wood) is burned then the carbon goes back into the atmosphere as CO2, which is a serious concern when deforestation takes place. If there are changes in land use, for example, when land is cleared for agriculture, much carbon in soils is exposed and it oxidises. Peat bogs are also accumulations of carbon from moss. If they remain wet, they can absorb carbon from the atmosphere. If they dry out, they oxidise and add CO2.

That's not all. Agricultural practices have other significant greenhouse implications. Ruminant animals (cattle) make methane (CH4) in their guts and when they belch put significant quantities into the atmosphere. Paddy fields also give off methane which is a powerful greenhouse gas. Nitrogenous fertilisers lead to emissions of nitrous oxide (N2O), another powerful greenhouse gas. On the other hand, it seems that organic farming accumulates carbon in soils and plants. Preventing climate change is therefore more complicated than controlling fossil fuel combustion. We need a radical reduction in emissions from deforestation, land use and land use changes PLUS, if possible, measures to enhance carbon sinks. Unfortunately, a strategy that radically reduces the use of fossil fuels could have the unintended effect of increasing the consumption of wood as a fuel, speeding deforestation and carbon emissions from this source.

The diagrams below show the role of the other greenhouse gases. "Radiative forcing" expresses the contribution to the greenhouse effect in watts per square metre of the earth's surface. CH4 is methane and N2O, methane and nitrous oxide, are the main non-CO2 greenhouse gases but there are others. (The other ones – halocarbons, chlorofluorocarbons and hydrochlorofluorocarbons and hydrofluorocarbons - are more visible on the lower scale which is logarithmic.)

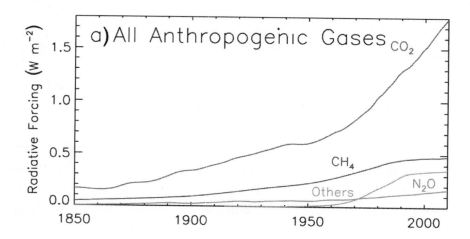

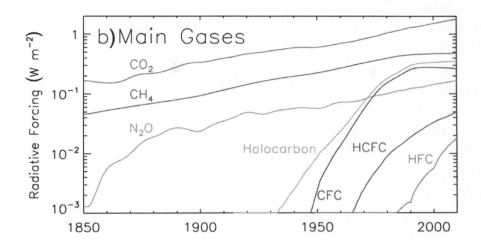

(IPCC. WG1. AR5: 679) Myhre, G., D. Shindell, F.-M. Bréon, W. Collins, J. Fuglestvedt, J. Huang, D. Koch, J.-F. Lamarque, D. Lee, B. Mendoza, T. Nakajima, A. Robock, G. Stephens, T. Takemura and H. Zhang, 2013

http://www.climatechange2013.org/report/reports-graphic/ch8-graphics/

Black soot is another problem. It is typically the result of inefficient open fire cooking when biomass is used as a fuel. The black soot changes the albedo of the surfaces it lands on and absorbs heat.

Land use and land use change – the climate threat from corporate forestry and agriculture

However you look at it, agriculture and land use is either a place to positively mitigate the climate crisis, or, if the wrong approaches are used, it is a place where the climate crisis will be made a lot worse. However, blanket solutions are not easy to find in agriculture and land use. This is because both problems and solutions are almost always context specific. There is an unavoidable on-the-ground complexity and context specificity in agriculture. To give one example, due to their methane emissions, cattle are often claimed to increase global warming. However, proper cattle management can help reclaim degraded land and thus, carbon sequestration by biomass accumulation.

Under current circumstances in which global corporations are making a bid to control global agriculture, there is no room for complacency. Careful and sensitive policy controls adapted to each place are difficult, perhaps impossible to administer. The big players seek to control the policy making process and turn it to their advantage and, in the process, a lot of futile or downright destructive approaches have been proposed. Biofuels have already been examined and shown to be a "granfalloon" – doing nothing to protect the climate but doing a lot to suit the agendas of the most powerful players in the climate policy arena.

There is also the proposal that has been developed at the United Nations Climate Negotiations called "Reduction of Emissions from Deforestation and Degradation" (popularly called the REDD). The plans and proposals would enable polluters in "developed countries" to buy carbon credits from projects in "developing" countries calculated from the difference between projected deforestation rates and the rate of actually occurring deforestation.

As mentioned above, the idea of a "baseline" which has been used to scam the Clean Development Mechanism. Critics have pointed out that one of the easiest ways for governments "to prove" they are lowering the rate of carbon emissions projected for a particular forest is to visibly stop local people making use of their customary resources – in forests protected by those same people for generations. At the same time, the rate of degeneration of the forests (the "baseline") can be exaggerated, so that money can be earned when there is a big difference between the inflated baseline and the reality. The policy as it stands encourages "gaming". In Guyana, the baseline projection assumed 0.45% deforestation pa though realistic estimates were 0.02% pa. Guyana could thus, increase deforestation 20 fold and still get REDD money. (Kenrick, The Climate and the Commons, 2012, p. 36)

Crucial to a safe climate is the ability to develop carbon sinks that will reduce atmospheric carbon into the land, into soils and forests. But can carbon sinks can be encouraged and enhanced without the policy process becoming a vehicle for more scams for corporate crooks and money junkies? A lot will hang on the answer. As already explained, a safe level of CO_2 in the atmosphere is certainly less than 350ppm and yet, at the time of writing, it is already 395ppm. Many climate scientists are pinning their hopes on the potential of land sinks and, in particular, on reforestation. For example, a study by James Hansen and others, quoted earlier, claims:

> ... it is not impossible to return CO_2 to 350 ppm this century. Reforestation and increase of soil carbon can help draw down atmospheric CO_2. Fossil fuels account for ~80% of the CO_2 increase from preindustrial 275 ppm to 395 ppm in 2013, with deforestation accounting for the other 20%. Net deforestation to date is estimated to be 100 GtC (gigatons of carbon) with ±50% uncertainty.

> Complete restoration of deforested areas is unrealistic, yet 100 GtC carbon drawdown is conceivable because: (1) the human-enhanced atmospheric CO_2 level increases carbon uptake by some vegetation and soils, (2) improved agricultural practices can convert agriculture from a CO_2 source into a CO_2 sink, (3) biomass-burning power plants with CO_2 capture and storage can contribute to CO_2 drawdown. (Hansen, Kharecha, Sato, Masson-Delmotte, Ackerman, & et, 2013)

Reversing the trend to deforestation by 2030 and then getting the trend to work in the other direction is seen by the Hansen and his fellow authors as being key to taking carbon out of the atmosphere and storing 100GtC in biomass and soils between 2031 and 2080. Forest and soil storage is seen as being possible through a variety of land use strategies: minimum tillage with organic agriculture in small holder rain fed agriculture reducing expansion of agriculture into forests; developing bioenergy from residues, wastes and dedicated crops that do not compete with food crops; reducing the use of animal products as livestock consumes more than half of all crops. (Hansen, Kharecha, Sato, Masson-Delmotte, Ackerman, & et, 2013, pp. 16-17)

On the other hand, these kind of strategies worry critics. They worry at the seeming impossibility of policy makers to frame programmes which are not taken up by large corporations and then developed in a way that negates their original intent - while expropriating people in the remaining land commons, mainly in the global south, who have been protecting the soils and the forests all along.

A major theme of this book is the way that big business processes of enclosure radically simplify eco-systems while destructively creating mono-cultures. In the case of forests, this has involved the creation of tree plantations with a limited number of species. These are not at all the same as natural forests with the much wider variety of species (with all of their human uses for the forest people adapted to living in them). Forests and tree plantations are very different and there is now much evidence that tree plantations don't help sequester carbon in the same way that a natural forest does.

Reviewing no less than 86 studies that have taken place over two decades, researchers have concluded that tree plantations have failed to function as carbon sinks as was originally intended. They do accumulate carbon in the trees themselves but the land conversion, in setting them up, typically leads to a massive loss of soil carbon. The rate of uptake of methane in soils falls too and there is a loss of stored C as ecological system degradation takes place. (Liao, Luo, Fang, & Li, 2010)

The central issue in this controversy is the question of scale. For example, critics of bio-fuels will usually agree that on a small scale bio-fuels can make sense. It is when they are scaled up that they become destructive.

Biochar – saviour or problem... or both depending...

This scale question also applies to a product called bio-char. With bio-char too there is fierce controversy. When plants grow by the photosynthetic process they take carbon out of the atmosphere and embody it in their cellular structures. This is a draw-down of carbon which reduces the amount of CO_2 in the atmosphere but, of course, when plants die, they are oxidised, burn or decompose in various ways and the CO_2 goes back into the atmosphere as the next stage of a "terrestrial carbon cycle".

Bio-char sequestration is held by many to be a way of slowing this process to a significant degree. Biomass that would otherwise rot or be burned is "charred" instead. It is "cooked", or pyrolised, in the absence of oxygen so that the biomass gives off flammable oils and gases which can be used separately and/or themselves be burned to produce the heat to keep the charring process going. The absence of oxygen in the chamber in which the biomass is "cooked" means that the carbon in the plant is not combusted and is left at the end of the process. What is left is not simple carbon but carbon with a form that matches the cellular and structural characteristics of the original plant. It is labyrinthine in form and has a massive internal surface area.

If the char is then put in soil it has been shown in many cases to improve soil fertility because it improves the water retention properties of the soil. Further, the structure of the char can function as an ideal habitat for beneficial soil microbes. Added to that, there are good reasons to believe that the char in the soil will stay there in a stable form for a very long time and is thus, a means of artificially sequestering carbon what has been drawn down from the earth's atmosphere. (Bruges, 2009)

These are the reasons that the creation of bio-char, and its sequestration in soils, has been suggested as a particularly promising approach to carbon sequestration. However, there are fierce debates about it with proponents and opponents taking very different points of view.

The critics of biochar argue that biochar is another granfalloon and that, taken up by large corporations, the promotion of biochar will do more harm than good. There is a danger of it being developed on a totally inappropriate scale by corporate agri-business who would sell the idea to officials and politicians. No doubt, using the economists notion of "economies of scale" to promote tree plantations planted in order to be pyrolised. Yet, as we have already seen, such plantations destroy soil carbon and are destructive in their own right. (Biofuelswatch, 2009)

When the policy actors are global corporations, biochar would probably be destructive. If the main actors implementing a biochar strategy are small communities and small farmers using genuine waste that would otherwise oxidise, it could be helpful.

The question is, as so often, how to break the power of the corporations?

PART EIGHT
Political Economy

Chapter 48

Co-opted States – The economics of politics

Most economics textbooks include a little homily about the difference between facts and value. Economics is supposed to describe the world as it is, rather than as economists think it should be. This homily is deconstructed. Power asymmetries in the political process mean that there is no clear separation between politics and economics and there never has been. Powerful economic actors have always had a predominant influence in the political institutions. In current conditions - of crisis at the limits to economic growth – dystopian politics are on the rise.

According to John Kenneth Galbraith:

> Economic instruction in the United States is about a hundred years old. In its first half century economists were subject to censorship by outsiders. Businessmen and their political and ideological acolytes kept watch on departments of economics and reacted promptly to heresy, the latter being anything that seemed to threaten the sanctity of property, profits, a proper tariff policy and a balanced budget, or that suggested sympathy for unions, public ownership, public regulation or, in any organised way, for the poor. (Galbraith, 2001, p. 135)

One of the central points for economics has always been to guide how government intervenes in the economy – principally adopting the viewpoint of the moneyed elite. However, if you read most of the textbooks you would not get this impression. To quote Galbraith again:

> Nothing more reliably characterises great social truth, economic truth in particular, than its tendency to be agreeable to the significant economic interest. What economists believe and teach is rarely hostile to the institutions that reflect the dominant economic power. Not to notice this takes effort, although many succeed. (Galbraith, 2001, p. 180)

The fact-value homily

Economics was originally conceived as "political economy" and has always been political. Despite this, many textbooks start with a little homily which draws on the difference between statements of fact and statements of values. This is the difference between the world as it is and the world as we would like it to be. According to many textbook writers, economics is a scientific study of how the world is and care should be taken not to contaminate the analytical truth with bias based on what we would like to see.

This formulation is naive. Any description of the world "as it is" always involves a choice. A choice of what to privilege as the focus of analysis in the first place, choices about how to frame the analysis, as well as choices about what evidence to look for and to consider allowable and relevant.

In this book, I have tried to describe and to theorise the world "as it is" as I see it. That means always relating economic ideas to the times in which they were thought and written down. There is no such thing as a theory of economics that is valid for all time and all economics needs to be the economics relevant to, and reflective of, a particular time in history. This includes how one sees the times that one is moving through and how they could evolve into the future.

This also explains why I have nothing in this book about supply and demand curves, or about how optimal allocation occurs in perfectly competitive markets, because this is so obviously theological drivel when the main allocation decisions in society are driven by the strategies of very large multinational corporations working closely together with officials and politicians. It is why I have such a lot about ecological limits and climate change. Economic textbooks claim to describe the world as it is but that is actually the last thing that they do. They have endless discussions, based on entirely hypothetical constructs that remind very much of the medieval theologians discussing how many angels could get onto the end of a pin.

If this book ever does get published and actually read by any of these theologians for money, they will no doubt attack it for being extremist. Yet it is a self-evident truth, a maxim in my world, that no observer can separate themselves from society and observe it from a neutral position. When economics is presented by textbook writers as unbiased description it shows just how much they lack self-awareness and political nous.

Bias

Of course, bias in analysis is something to try to be aware of. However, readers can better allow for bias if they are clear where the writer is coming from, because the writer is explicit and clear about their values. Sadly, generation upon generation of students have gone through the academic sausage factory, had their critical faculties slaughtered, and reproduced the same ideas in their essays, exams and dissertations. Academic and professional economists in the mainstream help construct the "consensus trance" as described in previous chapters. A view of the world in which economists are disinterested technicians describing the policy options for "the economy" which are decided by the politicians through the democratic process.

The fairy tale for the children is that we live in a democracy, and the state is there to look after the interests of everyone equally. After all, in a democracy every adult has a vote to keep the state focused on "the common good".

Yet since the state raises and disposes of enormous resources, and has the power to determine the conditions in which business and money makers operate, it's obvious that money makers take enormous efforts to influence it in their favour, and always have done. In order to ground economic theory in reality, we need to analyse who gets to have most influence in the politics that affect income distribution, resource allocation and matters pertaining to economic activity.

A moment's thought is all that is required to take in the obvious fact that, just because all adults have one vote, it does not follow that all adults have equal political-economic influence. Influence over the political process takes place on a very non-level playing field – or, to use the jargon of economics, the ability to influence the political process is asymmetric.

The power asymmetry of the political process

This can be summarised very briefly by saying that powerful corporate players are able to mostly get what they want while ordinary people are pretty much powerless. The corporate aristocracy is well resourced; well connected; well informed (as regards things that matter to their own agendas); well represented in the political lobby, in the courts, in negotiations; in the mass media which manufactures consent for their agendas. Their plans are well hidden in tax havens and secrecy jurisdictions and, when they need to be, they are well protected by security companies, mercenaries and friends in high places, including in the security and armed forces.

Particularly powerful are those business players in what I earlier described as the "hub dependencies" of an interconnected society – like the financial institutions, the energy sector and the mass media. They have always had close and direct connections into government, including often enough, into the security forces and the military. As is obvious, all these advantages makes it possible for the corporate elite to stitch up their own agendas and to co-opt whatever government gets elected. What is called "democracy" is a hollow charade.

This way of seeing things is nothing like saying that there is some conspiracy to control things - as if "the big people" all get together in one room and decide everything that happens. Yet the most powerful people in the world do have forums where they come together from time to time to share their ideas. They do so in order to create a kind of collective orientation for each other, and, at the same time, to further develop their "well connectedness" which is an important dimension of their power. The World Economic Forum or the Bilderberg Conference have these functions.

In a recent article about plans to develop shale gas in the UK, Paul Mobbs describes how the system works, not as a conspiracy but as business. His article includes a diagram of the connections between business and government that explains who is behind the push for fracked shale gas.

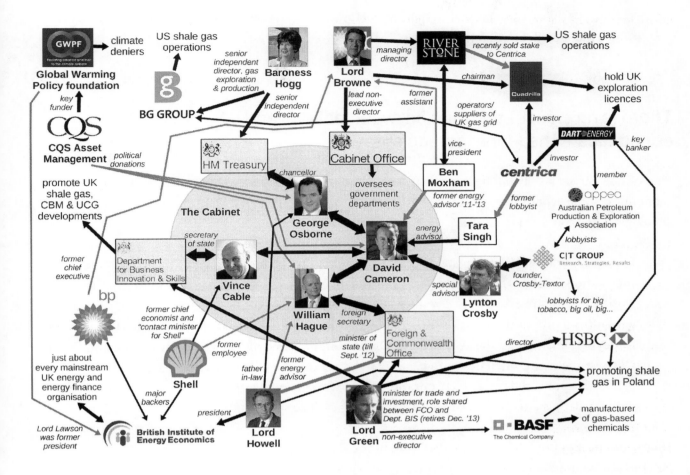

Reproduced with permission from Paul Mobbs

Mobbs comments:

There is a huge back-story to the diagram above. It's not a "plan", or a "conspiracy" - it's just business. If my local council is doing something dodgy then I'll get together with various other greenie friends and, mustering the resources of media and local political influence, I'll do something about it... *Do you think the world is any different for the leaders of the business world?* – it's just that when they play politics they're drawing on a wholly different set of people, who've been to a more elite and select bunch of schools and universities, and worked in certain corporate entities, that marks them out as (in terms the economic interests involved) "one of us"...

... Of course, just because people "conspire" together doesn't mean that they're "out to get you". Complex human societies have created hierarchies as a means to manage complexity – although that doesn't always work out well when the top of that system tries to oppose inevitable changes to society over time. There is, however, one distinguishing feature that determines whether public offices are being used for good or ill. If the actions carried out are done "for the common good" of those who these people work on behalf of, then clearly – irrespective of who they are or their pedigree – there is some merit to their role. However, in the case of unconventional gas, there's a whole lot of evidence that that isn't so..."

(Mobbs, 2013)

There is no clear separation between politics and economics – the Monetocracy system

Plan or conspiracy it may not be, but clearly there is no obvious separation between politics and economics. Some economists get this, others prefer to ignore it. Herman Daly and Joshua Farley's book "Ecological Economics" is very clear.

> Large corporations routinely help politicians set not only domestic rules of the game but also international rules. The trade adviser to President Nixon was vice president of Cargill, the world's largest grain exporter. President Reagan relied on a Cargill employee to draft the US agricultural proposal for GATT. President Clinton appointed Monsanto CEO Robert Shapiro as trade representative to the World Trade Organisation, President George W Bush relied on Enron CEO Kenneth Lay when designing energy policies. The WTO meetings in Seattle in 1999 were primarily sponsored by large corporations. Can we be sure that this advice and assistance come with no strings attached? (Daly & Farley, Ecological Economics, 2004, p. 330)

The economic and political are thus, two sides of the same system. It does not make sense to see them as separate. In their Schumacher Briefing, on "Gaian Democracy" Roy Madron and John Jopling describe this system as that of a "Global Monetocracy" which shares 6 components.

"First and foremost for a system to operate as a system it must have a shared purpose and, in the current situation, that shared purpose is money growth to maintain the debt money system."

The other components of the system are:

> Shared operational theories (like neo-liberal economics, the manufacture of consent and command and control management systems);

> An elite consensus of aggressive individualism, prominence for economic ideas about consumerism and the market, problem solving through techno-innovation, the centrality of private property ;

> The creation of an elite cadre of political leaders schooled in these ideas by free market foundations and philanthropists who ideologically groom young up and coming leaders with scholarships and fellowships;

A close partnership between government and business, with business in the leading role in a variety of government and joint management systems and,

Finally, a battery of interacting operational policies and instruments like interest rates, trade policies, tax systems, property and corporate law, public relations, scapegoats and bogey men to justify arms, surveillance and security activities, control of the mass media etc...

(Madron & Jopling, 2003, pp. 67-97)

Once one has seen the way "the system" works from the outside, one is left with the serious question of, what kind of politics could ever bring about fundamental change in the face of this interlocking network of elements? Is fundamental change, which would mean the take-over of the state by political movements dedicated to radically different purposes, actually be possible when things are so stitched up?

When the dominant system tries to oppose inevitable change – dystopian politics on the rise

I don't know and the answer will be discovered in the future. The experience so far appears to suggest a number of features which occur when, to use the words of Mobbs, "the top of the system tries to oppose inevitable changes to society over time".

Six processes are becoming visible.

Firstly, rather than address root problems at the systemic level, "policy makers" will oscillate between periods of austerity and periods in which bubbles are inflated in the asset markets.

The austerity will no doubt have an economic aim, to reduce state expenditure on social welfare, health, education and the like in order to focus remaining wealth streams on the banking and corporate elite. At the same time, the attack on the poor will have a second function - creating scapegoats to deflect the anger of the general population away from the elite towards vulnerable people instead - migrants, disabled and sick people. The message in much of the mass media is already that these people are "scroungers" who are exploiting taxpayers. The impression is given that they are the root cause of general problems.

The problem with austerity of course is that it does nothing to relieve depressed general economic conditions to get growth going again – which is what the system wants.

Secondly, attempts will be made to deal with problems in ways that create new problems. As the "limits to growth" theorists pointed out, the "limits to growth" emerge in "layers". Solving one problem by technological means leads to another problem emerging soon afterwards. One can see this with "fracking" and the other forms of "extreme energy". Energy resources are likely to be extracted under conditions of increasing cost to communities and the environment – with community resistance being responded to, in turn, by fracturing the democratic process. There is a danger here of an evolution towards forms of autocracy and conflict that would be deeply destructive to "well-being". In Britain, the current government has rigged the planning process to make it almost impossible for the relevant regulatory authorities to refuse permission for shale gas development. At the same time, the regulatory authorities do not have sufficient resources to monitor the developers closely. (Stevenson, 2013) In its "Infrastructure Bill" the government intends to make it easy for corporate lobbyists to get whatever they want with "Green tape" (i.e. protection of the environment and communities) being removed.

Thirdly, there are always ways of making money – in current conditions money addicts will find the most profitable opportunities by making "bads" rather than "goods". (Or illth rather than wealth). When a society is in crisis, there is money to be made providing security services, in mercenary businesses, making weapons and in military logistics, in running prisons and "corrective institutions", not to mention abundant contracts for public relations agencies and other institutions who work hard to massage appearances. As conflicts increase, such "economic sectors" will no doubt do very well and will foster close relationships with officials and politicians as some of their main clients.

This trend ties in with the imposition of austerity with its sub-agenda of making scapegoats of the poor and welfare recipients. We have seen that the elite are driven by extrinsic values in which money and power plays a major role. We have seen too that, given their motivations and value systems, the elite are not happy people. The roman philosopher, Seneca, argued that riches foster bad tempers because rich people expect things to go their way. When they don't, they become frustrated and angry. Perhaps that part explains a tendency to sociopathic behaviour, again mentioned earlier. The limits to growth are likely to be a future of frustration, petulance and fury which we can expect to see reflected in paranoid policies administered by increasingly vindictive institutions.

Fourthly, as the elite becomes more detached, violent and manipulative it will inevitably become more paranoid and, as we already know, there has been the development of mass surveillance by tapping into mass communications, using algorithms to identify emerging forms of dissent and ultimately being prepared to snuff them out with technological means. No doubt, the state will enrol many people, including cohorts of loyal bullies, to promote their agendas. If these functionaries are prepared to do and believe what they are told, and serve merely as instruments in the machines of power, they will be looked after and given opportunities to kick other people around.

Fifthly, while using the state for their own purposes, the elite has already largely withdrawn from making a contribution to the upkeep of public and government functions. As one American millionairess, the late Leona Helmsley, put it "Only the little people pay taxes". It is not surprising that states have huge deficits. The rich don't make any contribution in taxes and then, when money needs to be borrowed, governments pay more in interest payments to rich people in the finance sector. Instead of paying taxes the business elite move their incomes and wealth to offshore tax havens and secrecy jurisdictions so as to avoid taxation, regulation and public knowledge of what they are up to.

Six, nation states will progressively lose their power to unaccountable international institutions serving the multinationals. These institutions and legal processes are and will make government regulations to protect the environment and labour rights illegal under free trade and other rules. Such for example are the deeply threatening and autocratic implications of the Transatlantic Trade and Investment Partnership of 2013 which will grant big business the right to sue governments which try to defend their citizens. (Monbiot, This transatlantic trade deal is a full-frontal assault on democracy, 2013)

Chapter 49

Degrowth – Economics for the lifeboats

The chapter draws together themes for an alternative narrative for the future of society many of which have already been explored through the book. The chief focus is on household and local level community arrangements managed through distributed and federated arrangements that are democratic. Linked themes like what to do about land and human resources; the need for debt cancellation, money and tax reform are explained. If sufficient change can be brought about it will also be necessary to drive decarbonisation with an upstream cap on carbon emissions

The future thus, described is a projection of existing trends and appears very dystopian. If "Degrowth" occurs within existing political and institutional frameworks then it seems clear what will happen. We already have examples. Between 2009 and 2013 the Gross Domestic Product of Greece fell by more than 25%. Domestic consumption contracted dramatically. Thousands of small and medium size became insolvent. By January 2013 the unemployment rate was 27.1% and among young people it was 59.1%. The cost of heating oil rose by 35% so that a lot more wood was used for heating with a corresponding big increase in air pollution. Between 2009 and 2011 homelessness increased by 25% and the suicide rate by 75%. There was a massive growth of the fascist right party – Golden Dawn. (Markantonatou, 2014)

A system which has a growth focus in an era of limits is bound to become embroiled in dysfunctional activity and crises. Unfortunately those people able to counter-pose a view that clarifies what is going on, that resists futile and fruitless approaches, are likely to be perceived as a threat. The shale gas example shows how the governing system can become extreme and autocratic.

On the other hands various movements have emerged to counter-pose positive community responses to this gloomy picture of what might be ahead. Many groups have evolved alternative visions and narratives for the future. There are differences but many overlap and are largely compatible so that, in the coming times, they are good possibilities that they will cohere into a common, although differentiated, global movement.

The economy of the future is described by these different groups with different words in different languages and they do not always exactly translate into an identical idea. However, the words, like "Degrowth", "Decroissance" (French) or "Postwachstum" (German) share an idea of contraction of the economy in order to stay within ecological limits while at the same time including the idea that there will be a need for community and political solutions to the problems that we already know will emerge – the unemployment, the energy shortages, the hunger and the homelessness. Since 2008 there have been 4 global "degrowth conferences" each larger than the previous one – in 2008 in Paris, 2010 in Barcelona,

2012 in Venice and, most recently, in September 2014 in Leipzig in Germany. The alternative vision and philosophies for society that has emerged from this process is drawing on a variety of sources. This includes a lively dialogue between the theorists of degrowth in the countries of the global north with activists and strategists against poverty and environmental degradation in the south. For example, ideas like "buen vivir" from the indigenous people of the Andes have become sources of inspiration that are widely accepted. (Konzeptwerk Neue Oekonomie, 2014)

The Spectrum of Degrowth Perspectives

This does not mean that absolutely all "post growth" or "degrowth" thinkers share the same values and understandings of what needs to be done. There is a spectrum that spans from political right across to the left and includes feminist economic thinkers. Matthias Schmeltzer, an economic and political historian at the University of Geneva, and one of the organisers of the September 2014 Leipzig Degrowth Conference, describes 5 different schools of thought to be found among Degrowth thinkers in the German speaking world.

One of the trends is politically and socially conservative. The thinkers in this group acknowledges that growth is coming up against natural and social limits and diagnose the problem as citizens and states living beyond their means – driven by consumption, the expenditures of the welfare state, debt, greed and decadence. For these thinkers, contraction is unavoidable and will need to be brought about by a change in personal values in the form of more personal responsibility, a strengthening of the patriarchal family to take on more responsibilities, self-denial and a reduction in what they see as the burden being carried by the welfare state.

Over and against this is a feminist economic perspective. It has not been explicitly developed as a contribution to the degrowth debate but has become an important source of inspiration. For the feminist thinkers the growth economy exploits and impoverishes the "subsistence activities" of the household, the societies of the global south and nature. This endangers future reproduction – in favour of growing production. The future of humanity and nature presupposes and requires reproduction yet the capital accumulation process, the separation of paid and unpaid work, has come to devalue the reproductive activities mostly carried out by women. The solution to this is a process of de-commercialisation, re-developing commons based shared activities and resources and the development of non-hierarchical local structures. It is a perspective and strategy that matches well the redevelopment of local cultivation and food sources, the redevelopment of the local economy and particularly non monetised activities.

Other approaches to degrowth include social reformist; sufficiency orientated; and anti-capitalist approaches.

What Schmeltzer characterises as the Social Reformist School diagnoses the problems as arising in because politics is fixated on growth - driven by economic sectors, institutions and structures that have become dependent on it. Actually it would be better to describe some of the people in this group, not as advocates of "Degrowth" but as proponents of "A-Growth". This term is intended to mean a style of politics that is indifference to growth, a kind of "Growth Atheism" since GDP per capita is in any case a useless measure of social welfare. (van den Bergh, 2011)

Politicians and actors from civil society must bring about the end of the growth dogma and disentangle economic and institutional structures (like the social security system) from growth in the direction of sustainable kind of liberalism. It will be achieved by ecological taxation, policies to promote sufficiency, civic insurance systems, sustainable consumption and the development of alternative welfare indicators.

The Sufficiency School of Degrowth goes further. For the Sufficiency School it is impossible to adequately decouple resource use from growth. One consequence is that that overconsumption in the global north is taking place at the cost of the global south from which a large proportion of the material resources are extracted. The problem of growth and resource use is driven by the need to have a rising income in order pay interest on loans. It is further attributable to the volume of resources needed to sustain long distance large scale production chains. This Sufficiency School thus, not only proposes a sufficiency rather than a consumerist approach in life, it also argues for the need to re-develop more local and small scale forms of self-production. People must become "pro-sumers" – i.e. producers of what they themselves consume. To make this possible there is a need for land and financial reform, reform of work time and the extension of subsistence and regional economies.

The sufficiency approach has many similarities to that of the "Transition Movement" – an international network of groups that has come together to try to prepare local communities with information and practical projects for a future of "energy descent". The movement tends to avoid explicit political engagement and favours communities making their own initiatives like community gardens without waiting for politicians to wake up to the gravity of the crisis. (Transition Network. 2013)

Finally, there is the Degrowth of Capitalism Critics. Their argument is that capitalist growth causes multiple crises and that the "imperial lifestyle" in the global north is at the cost of the global south (for example the climate change impacts). According to the critics of capitalism, the drivers of growth are to be found in the property and power relationships including the processes of privatisation. The necessary counter politics involves the promotion of the commons, the promotion of the solidarity economy, climate justice and more democracy in economy and state.

Rather than advocating a top-down centralised form of socialist planned economy, people with this perspective tend to promote networked bottom-upwards forms of development. They see a place for exemplary projects at the same time as advocating political and trade union strategies for more economic democracy, state regulation and guided investment, reduction in working time, proposals for a basic citizen's income on the one hand, and maximum income limits on the other. (Schmeltzer, 2014)

In summary, new styles and understandings of politics and economics are emerging. There is variety and difference but, over a wide spectrum, the differences are best thought of as a healthy diversity. The diversity between the left and the greens can give rise to complementary relationships rather than being sources of deep division and antagonism.

Shaping New Utopias – or making the best in a difficult and highly uncertain time?

For all of that, it seems to me that an important issue hangs over this movement. How much are we in the business of designing and shaping the future, using the current crisis to re-envisage new kinds of "concrete Utopias" – and how much are we in the business of preparing to cope with a very difficult and chaotic time where involuntary degrowth happens anyway, opening up a Pandora's Box of problems so that we need practical and political tools to get through them. Are we in the business of advocating a voluntary process of degrowth by design, or are we developing the ideas for surviving an involuntary and very challenging process that will happen anyway – and containing quite a few unpleasant surprises?

There is, as yet, too much that is unknown and that we cannot know. The current world economic situation is above all characterised by "strong uncertainty". A highly complex society can disintegrate in many different ways that are unpredictable. I can, for example, write a book to attempt to describe a host of problems only to witness a type of disintegration not so far described in this book at all, for example, brought about by an unstoppable Ebola epidemic which paralyses physical and financial infrastructures and global trade. Or perhaps we will witness chaos brought about by political turmoil and war caused by the miscalculations of politicians in a horrific future that is completely unexpected. That happened before – in 1914. I can advocate an open source society based on knowledge commons only to witness a disintegration of the internet because of a shortage of essential materials. Alternatively, see the internet make possible a host of marvellous products for countries in the global south and then witness this internet using so much carbon energy that it helps tip humanity into runaway climate change.

Just as hottest months are *after* mid-summer because warmth accumulates and there is a lag, so, perhaps, techno-optimism is at its height when decline has already started. At a time like this it is possible to see the problems ahead, but they are still seen in the rosy glow, with a bright confidence that they can be fixed. It is even possible to imagine that these problems are a new opportunity to re-launch the utopian visions whose earlier versions failed.

Yet we should always take into account that our visions of the future are bound to be flawed by the limitations of what we know. All that we know, even if we go to university and think we know a great deal, is very limited indeed and the world in a short time will seem very different from what we expected it to be. The greatest challenge for all political and economic visionaries is that the world will inevitably evolve differently from what we expect, because of processes and issues that we could not know about in advance. This is true even though we are obliged to try to anticipate the problems of the future in order, if possible, to forestall them, and, if not, to cope and do as best we can with them.

Themes for an alternative narrative of the future of society

Despite the limitations of our knowledge, it is still helpful to promote constructive responses for anticipated problems and to weave these responses into an alternative narrative for society as a whole. It

419

is helpful to share with others a common story of a desirable future describing a bigger process in which many local projects fit. The story needs to be about more than the sum of many small parts, many small local level initiatives. People are more likely to be inspired to work for something where they can see it as part of a bigger picture, rather than embarking on a solitary struggle at a local level on their own.

In this respect it is possible to envisage a process of degrowth which starts as something to which people and groups are compelled to respond to help communities to survive. However if these responses are successful and networked, then the pioneers might accumulate political influence and power which they use to drive the policy more directly. Situations can change. A process that starts off largely involuntarily might end up steered more directly.

There are a number of big picture narratives at this time, and what follows is intended as a way of bringing them together. Degrowth is only one. Others speak and write of "the great transition", the solidarity economy, the co-operative movement and the commons. Several of these big picture ideas have been explored at various points in this book and there is a need to bring them together to describe a more meaningful economics as part of a different possible story for humanity. The fact that these narratives are slightly different reflects the fact that they were started in different places in different times by different people. It is inevitable that there will be differences, and indeed these differences are usually necessary because relevant movements must be adapted to different local conditions. What is important is that the values and ethical starting points are broadly the same – with the key ideas that economy is for people in inclusive communities, that justice, participation and protection of eco-systems is key, that there is a preparedness to enter into dialogues and learn from each other.

The first theme for a new big narrative is the re-definition of what prosperity and a good life means. This can draw upon visions and ideas from the global south like "buen vivir" or living to the full. There is a need to revive the idea that a good life is not about "having", it is not about buying more possessions. It is about flourishing as a human being – personal growth rather than growth of possessions and economic growth. This rests on the critique of affluenza and draws on the literature about extrinsic and intrinsic motivations. Economics in its present form, in its approach to means and ends, in its assumption of the need for incentivization, assumes extrinsic values. Yet people lead more authentic lives if they follow intrinsic motivations, if they do things for their own sake, if they can follow their beliefs and ideals. This mind set corresponds to a bio-centric rather than ego-centric world view. It leads towards the re-discovery and reconnection to the world as lived and experienced by indigenous and tribal peoples.

A second theme is that of "lifeboat projects". If, for example, people find they have lost their job and are flung out of their ordinary routines by the evolution of the crisis, they need places, networks and projects which enable them to re-stabilise their lives in a different way. There is the need for community level projects and activities for people to get involved where they can engage with what seems to them to matter most of all. Instead of being bullied into looking for paid work that does not exist. To a large degree, these networks of activities have to be neighbourhood based.

A community level movement is already emerging in response to the prospect of "energy descent" and economic crisis and it already shows what some of the typical institutions will be. There are community gardens which, when grown larger, can become community supported agriculture. There are repair workshops and centres for practical handicraft. These too, can expand with an agenda for developing a neighbourhood infrastructure to minimise the need to "consume".

Every city, town and village already shares kinds of infrastructure – public transport, libraries, and leisure services. The task at hand is to extend these shared facilities as much as possible so that people can have access to resources without needing goods as personal possessions.

The **Haus der eigenen Arbeit** in Munich has, over a number of years, become a model. There is now a network of similar workshops in different towns and cities in Germany. Workshops for wood, metal, paper/bookbinding, jewellery, textiles, upholstery, ceramics, art crafts, glass and blacksmith upgrade the facilities of local neighbourhoods. (HEi. 2014)

The principle here is that of 'convivial technology' described earlier. The technology is "low tech" or "intermediate" but appropriate in the sense of enabling ordinary people to be producers and product developers. Ideally, community workshops, micro-factories and/or "Fab Labs" will make possible "pro-sumption" arrangements with open source design in "Do It Together" production, repair and maintenance where people help each other. Hopefully, these arrangements will go a long way to reduce the need for mass production based on long distance supply chains, radically reducing the need for new resources. (Fab Foundation, 2014)

As in Italy, we can also try to ensure that there are a variety of co-operative arrangements to organise and support elderly and vulnerable people.

The aim here is to develop what has been called a "solidarity economy" - places where people can come together and help each other, learn from each other and develop ideas and projects together. The aim is to develop connections between people, the encouragement of creativity for its own sake and for the pleasure of doing things together.

A third feature of a new society is a different allocation of time. Not everyone will want to, or be able to, but research has shown that many people wish to trade income for more free time – 19% of the US population of working age and 23% of the Australian voluntarily decided to take less income to have more time in a 5 year period (Hamilton, Growth Fetish, 2004, pp. 206-207) As the crisis evolves, more people should and will want to do this. In addition, as the "baby boomers" reach retirement age and join the "young elderly" many of them will still be fit. They will be well enough to make a significant contribution to their communities and will get a lot out of doing so.

A different allocation of time and a more neighbourhood-based lifestyle can be facilitated too by more co-housing and arrangements for sharing. Earlier in the book, it was shown how such arrangements can save space, energy and unpaid domestic chores by sharing, as well as reducing the need for devices and a great deal of consumption. They will also increase sociability and thus, increase social cohesion which will be important in difficult times.

A fourth theme is the need to create a different *"life style package"* to that of the supermarket economy where the skills needed in the ecological economy are made available. It means trying to create a 'seed bed' for creative and interesting projects so that people are less centred on stressful employed work in order to earn money to buy their satisfactions in the shops. Instead, they would have access to places where they can pursue their different values and priorities enjoying creative opportunities and convivial social contact for its own sake – rather than because they have been "incentivised" to do so.

A fifth theme is the need for a different management approach to the corporate style of top down command and control. While all these community activities need to be well co-ordinated and networked, it does not need they need to be managed through a hierarchy. Because they engage people in a largely voluntary capacity, community organisations cannot expect to operate in an authoritarian way. If they are not being paid to be involved, why would voluntary participants consent to being bossed around? There is an evident need for alternatives to the top-down paternalistic we-know-what's-best-for-you command and control way of managing things.

So how will it be possible to make sure that the different community gardens, energy projects, tool libraries, workshop sharing arrangements evolve into a coherent whole? We will need some forms of overall co-ordination where shared purposes make it appropriate. The ideas of the management theorist Stafford Beer have much to tell us. These have already been described briefly in the chapter on entrepreneurship.

The basic principle is to minimise outside interference in each organisation - while at the same time facilitating co-ordination where joint involvement in a wider process makes it appropriate. These forms of co-ordination would be of these types, only to be activated where the bigger picture makes it appropriate: (a) conflict resolution procedures, (b) steps to achieve synergies, (c) developing a common strategic view of what is happening in shared environments and, (d) activities that clarify and develop shared value systems and purposes.

The diagram sums up the vision graphically and is 'recursive' in form. Recursive means nested similar to the way that Russian dolls are nested i.e. with similar arrangements inside wider arrangements. Thus, each 'operational unit', - a person, a work team, a whole project, a federation of projects activates a wider system for the conflict resolution, synergy, strategic and share policy co-ordination functions agreed and as needed – while at the same time taking the maximum decisions for their own operation autonomously. Graphically

A VIABLE SYSTEMS MODEL OF THE GREEN ECONOMY

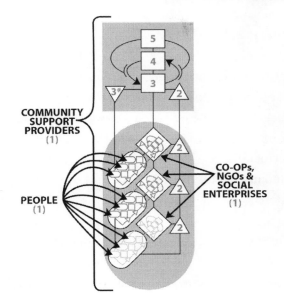

KEY TO NUMBERS:

1: OPERATIONAL UNITS
(Which are themselves Viable Systems)

2: STABILITY SYSTEMS
(Which resolve conflicts between operational units)

3: OPTIMISATION SYSTEM
(Which generate synergy between Operational Units & allocate resources)

3*. A SUB-SYSTEM of 3
(Which is responsible for audits & surveys)

4: STRATEGIC SYSTEM
(Which monitor the operational environment & plan for the future)

5: GENERAL POLICY SYSTEM
(Which defines the overall ethos, purpose and principles)

COMMUNITY SUPPORT PROVIDERS (1)

PEOPLE (1)

CO-OPs, NGOs & SOCIAL ENTERPRISES (1)

(Alexander, et al., 2013) Graphic by Oliver Sylvester-Bradley with permission *http://defactodesign.com*

The knitting together of community level organisations in a solidarity economy for basic provisioning will therefore seek community control in a decentralised and semi-autonomous way – while at the same time exercising collective control where appropriate. It will hopefully make possible the re-development of community co-ordination over local land areas, and a re-creation of the commons as a form of social and economic organisation, eventually evolving deliberative management of land, watersheds and energy systems on behalf of communities. One dynamic that is likely to force communities to move in this direction is their need to protect their living environments from depredations threatened by corporate agendas like fracking.

Federating the change agents

That will obviously be a long road. It has already been suggested that there will be many political problems in the process which will have to be worked upon. In earlier chapters, we saw that for co-operatives and community organisations to make headway, they need to federate and develop the networks for infrastructural support i.e. sources of local cost and interest free finance, insurance, shared marketing, training, research collaborations, legal and professional help, co-operative universities and colleges.

In the words of Michael Lewis and Pat Conaty, it is vital to "federate the change agents" in order to develop some political power. They compare the task to earlier visions for social and economic change like those of the so called 'guild socialists', Arthur Penty, R H Tawney and GDH Cole. In the early 20th century, these different authors argued for adapting and bringing up to date the ideas of the medieval guilds:

The overall idea of guild socialism was to democratize and functionally decentralise economic management within a federated model of collaboration and coordination between various forms of public, private and co-operative ownership. The guild motto was not for profit, not for charity, but for service. (Conaty & Lewis, 2012, p. 219)

In our own time, at the beginning of the 21st century, a network of networks that has pioneered ways for federated social economy actors to influence and co-create state policy is the *Chantier de l'economie sociale*. This emerged out a period of crisis in Quebec from the mid-1990s onwards. A variety of projects and businesses in the social enterprise sectors work together to intervene in the political process. These organisations, in housing, training, child and perinatal care, sheltered workshops, community radio, community television and recycling are connected into technical assistance and support networks, including research services, finance and promotion.

The *Chantier* (which literally means 'construction site) is described like this by one of its protagonists:

Brings together solidarity economy enterprises – both cooperatives and non-profits, social movements, including the union movement, the women's movement and others, and local development organizations with the mission to promote and develop the solidarity economy. We work in partnership with similar networks across the world, including the Brazilian Forum on the Solidarity Economy, with whom we have developed a strong and constructive partnership over the past years.... In our relationship to the state and political power, we are innovating not only in our demands and proposals, but in the very process of constructing economic policy. Researchers speak of the need for a process of co-construction of public policy, in which civil society is an active participant in defining and implementing policies in favour of the solidarity economy. (Neamtan, 2010)

Without powerful and intelligent federated organisation, the emergence of a local community economy may be supported by states in some aspects but in a way that is double edged and compromising. Governments will like the way that community self-help enables them to cut social, health and community expenditure. It will enable them to conserve resources for really important things – like their security apparatus and their prison building programmes.

A community economy at the local level is not a panacea, it is not an instant solution. It is better thought of as the set of tasks and problems to be worked upon that seem in current circumstances to be the most likely to be fruitful. There will still be dilemmas. It will be difficult for many people to drop out of the old economy and join a movement for community renewal when they are crushed by their debts which tie them to the existing system.

Land and Natural Resources

Access to land and "natural resources" will be a further problem. We have already seen that, influenced by mainstream economics, policies are being designed to "hardwire nature into financial markets". As "natural capital" becomes scarce, they become more valuable on international markets. They become objects of speculation and are being purchased by players in the financial markets. This is the very opposite of what is needed – which is that natural assets... more properly described as ecological systems, the inter-being of the planetary life force – needs to be put under the stewardship of ecologically aware communities.

Policies for land are central. As so often it is helpful to draw upon ideas from earlier epochs and bring them up to date. Finding ways to undo the effects of land enclosure has been a constant theme of radicals for generations – going back to the ideas of Thomas Spence in the 18th century who wanted land to be managed by parish trusts to whom rentals would have gone, in order to be used for public purposes. I have also mentioned the way that Gandhi's ideas led to a land gift movement that inspired the idea of community land trusts in the USA.

Community land trusts focus on the development of residential areas, but there are also powerful movements emerging among the world's poor farmers about land, cultivation and food production. They are developing their own ideas on an inter-continental scale and are challenging multi-national capital's plans for agriculture. Absolutely central is the organisation, La Via Campesina. It is the largest social movement in human history, involving 500 million families involved through 148 organisations in 69 countries. Members include peasants, landless people, rural workers, family farmers, artisans, fisher folk, indigenous peoples, rural women and youth. Through deliberative, consensus based and democratic processes *La Via Campesina* has evolved its own programme for "food sovereignty" which is aggressively counter-posed to the neo-liberal agenda for agriculture. (La Via Campesina)

The organisational power of La Via Campesina shows that it is possible to network on a vast scale. It provides a model of what can be done. There is a need to evolve organisations with ambitious programmes for the crisis to relieve ordinary people of their debt burdens, to pursue financial sector reform, taxation reform, ways to return control of land to communities, programmes to drive energy transformation and the degrowth process.

As most of these issues have been explored elsewhere in this book, I will not repeat the earlier material here – except to emphasise the connection between these issues and the building of local level projects.

Debt cancellation, money and taxation reform

Getting most people out of debt is a crucial part of any political programme. Without debt relief a great many people will have no chance to "start again" and thus, will be constrained in their participation in a community ecological transformation. Debt relief also requires monetary reform so that a post growth economy is not in a permanent deflationary state.

Site value taxation is equally vital. Re-developing localities and making them nice and efficient places to live is a strategy with a flaw in it under a regime of private land ownership. Nice places to live are places where land rentals and land prices are high. Private landowners can reap where a community has sown.

The appropriate response is for the land value created by a community to be taxed and for that money to be returned to the community to pay the expenses of community improvement.

A further point is that land value cannot be hidden in a tax haven. You cannot hide land. Site Value Taxes would not only remove the incentive for speculative bubbles that destabilise the financial system, it would stabilise the political system too - by removing the incentive for corrupt political involvement in land speculation.

Driving decarbonisation with an upstream cap – cap and share

Finally, and this would be the greatest challenge of all to achieve, we need to drive the process of degrowth very hard in a radically egalitarian way. This is the reason to promote a policy like cap and share (or cap and dividend) by rapidly reducing the amount of fossil fuels that can enter the economy, and hence the amount of carbon that can enter the economy. Doing this, will drive degrowth through shrinking the amount of carbon energy that can enter the economy in the first place.

The policy of cap and share was described in chapter.... Because we have a global emergency, the sale of fossil fuels needs to be banned without a permit. The number of permits allowed each year, denominated in carbon, need to be reduced in line with climate scientific advice. That means at least 6% per annum reductions on a global scale.

Just as a growing economy has always depended on a rising supply of energy, so the degrowth process can be driven by reducing the carbon energy allowed into the economy. When this is done in an equalitarian fashion, it will impose the biggest adjustments in lifestyle on the rich.

At this time (late 2013), no network of community groups have sufficient power to impose such a programme but as the crisis evolves we can hope and work to try bring about this change.

There is no question - it will be easier advocated and described than done. The research of Kahneman shows that people are loss averse and what we are describing here is a process of solving the problems of the world largely by concentrating the coming losses on the most powerful people on the planet. Time will tell if this is impossible, but it is worth remembering that there are not very many of these people and the alternative is a global catastrophe of unimaginable proportions...

... which is one possible ending to this chapter. Another ending goes as follows...

For me one of the most wearisome features of our culture is its need to be optimistic. For example, it is customary to conclude a book like this with an upbeat ending. As we have seen, "optimism bias" is integral to the way that the people running corporations and the state like to present things.

They all do it: the five year plan is about to be achieved; our troops are holding the line; we have the best regulations in the world... the superlatives always prove that our betters know what they are doing;

are succeeding in their policies; are selling the best of all possible products. It is so wearisome because, once you see it for what it is, there is no room in this narrative of elite success for the everyday troubles and failures that beset ordinary people. There is no room for vulnerability. There is no room for being human, authentic and truthful – and in this cultural atmosphere there is a social psychological cost.

That's why I think that just to be able to theorise about things as they actually are is a relief, a release from a burden. I couldn't give a monetary value to that, of course, but I think it is worth it.

As a friend of mine put it: "if freedom be an icy wind, then let it fucking blow".

Vaclav Havel on Hope

Hope is a state of mind, not of the world. Hope, in this deep and powerful sense, is not the same as joy that things are going well, or willingness to invest in enterprises that are obviously heading for success, but rather an ability to work for something because it is good.

Isn't it the moment of most profound doubt that gives birth to new certainties Perhaps hopelessness is the very soil that nourishes human hope perhaps one could never find sense in life without first experiencing its absurdity...

Human beings are compelled to live within a lie, but they can be compelled to do so only because they are in fact capable of living in this way. Therefore not only does the system alienate humanity, but at the same time, alienated humanity supports this system as its own involuntary master plan, as a degenerate image of its own degeneration, as a record of people's own failure as individuals.

Hope is not the conviction that something will turn out well but the certainty that something makes sense, regardless of how it turns out.

Chapter 50

But what if it's too late?

Without sufficient action a time may come when we have to admit that it is too late to prevent runaway climate change and/or that other forms of collapse has become inevitable, indeed that we are in the middle of a collapse. Then what?

"Those who witness extreme social collapse at first hand seldom describe any deep revelation about the truths of human existence. What they do mention, if asked, is their surprise at how easy it is to die.

"The pattern of ordinary life, in which so much stays the same from one day to the next, disguises the fragility of its fabric. How many of our activities are made possible by the impression of stability that pattern gives? So long as it repeats, or varies steadily enough, we are able to plan for tomorrow as if all the things we rely on and don't think about too carefully will still be there. When the pattern is broken, by civil war or natural disaster or the smaller-scale tragedies that tear at its fabric, many of those activities become impossible or meaningless, while simply meeting needs we once took for granted may occupy much of our lives.

"What war correspondents and relief workers report is not only the fragility of the fabric, but the speed with which it can unravel..............."

*From the **Dark Mountain Manifesto** by Paul Kingsnorth and Dougald Hine*

For over a quarter of a century there have been repeated discourses about what humanity must do in the light of the environmental crisis, about what we must do for sustainability, and increasingly about how little time we have left to act.

But at what point does one have to say, in order to stay in touch with reality – "it *is* now too late"? At what point do we accept that human society has acted but too little and too late and therefore the consequences that were predicted will now happen and are inevitable. We are led by the institutions of rich and powerful people whose plans have been successful for them while others picked up the losses, people who have not yet been found out, who have not yet learned the bitter lesson that things do go wrong. While they have talked about sustainability and the precautionary principle they have not taken decisions on that basis. As we have seen the power of fossil fuels over 200 years, of which they have been the leading beneficiaries has biased them (and some of 'us' too) to an optimism that is fatally hubristic.

At some point the consequences must arrive and we will pass the globally significant tipping points. But when? There are those who think that it is already time to say that it is too late – like for example Denis Meadows, one of the authors of the Limits to Growth study of 1972.

"In 1972 there were two possible options provided for going forward — overshoot or sustainable development. Despite myriad conferences and commissions on sustainable development since then, the world opted for overshoot. The two-legged hairless apes did what they always have done. They dominated and subdued Earth. Faced with unequivocal evidence of an approaching existential threat, they equivocated and then attempted to muddle through.

"Global civilization will only be the first of many casualties of the climate the Mother Nature now has coming our way at a rate of change exceeding any comparable shift in the past 3 million years, save perhaps the meteors or super volcanoes that scattered our ancestors into barely enough breeding pairs to be able to revive. This change will be longer lived and more profound than many of those phenomena. We have fundamentally altered the nitrogen, carbon and potassium cycles of the planet. It may never go back to an ecosystem in which bipedal mammals with bicameral brains were possible or not for millions of years". (quoted in Bates, A. 2014)

Most other people are reluctance to declare that it is too late and I suppose that this is not only because of our unwillingness to acknowledge that we are at the gates of this unpleasant new era in which a lot of people go to earlier graves. There are other reasons too. Perhaps if we declare, still prematurely, that it is too late we may provide the last and final justification to prevent the desperate action happening, at one minute to midnight, that could just forestall the approaching catastrophe.

In this chapter therefore I am not going to argue that it is too late – only to argue that it is probably too late - and therefore to consider what we will have to do if and when we are forced to acknowledge that we have no future other than an unstoppable slide into catastrophe.

In times like that ordinary people like you and me would, or will, have to work very hard. It will be back breaking labour without the powered devices of fossil fuel civilisation, performing tasks that we previously took for granted, doing things which are dirty, dangerous and unpleasant, like collecting and burying those who have died shortly before us.

In a collection of essays about Degrowth that was recently published Alevgül Sorman comments: "In a future scarce in energy we will have to work more, not less". (Sorman, A.H. 2014)

There are philosophical systems that will help us more during these times. Other people have been there before us – and they were not preference utilitarians. For the Stoic philosophers you started the day with a technique called the 'premeditation of evil'. You recognise that extreme misfortune happens and think through what your unpleasant day might be like so that you are able to accept the worst that the world throws at you, so that you stay in touch with the real world and respond to it as it really is – rather than lose touch with reality.

This is what Seneca wrote:

"The wise will start each day with the thought, 'Fortune gives us nothing which we can really own.' Nothing, whether public or private, is stable; the destinies of men, no less than those of cities, are in a whirl. Whatever structure has been reared by a long sequence of years, at the cost of great toil and through the great kindness of the gods, is scattered and dispersed in a single day. No, he who has said 'a day' has granted too long a postponement to swift misfortune; an hour, an instant of time, suffices for the overthrow of empires. How often have cities in Asia, how often in Achaia, been laid low by a single shock of earthquake? How many towns in Syria, how many in Macedonia, have been swallowed up? How often has this kind of devastation laid Cyprus in ruins? We live in the middle of things which have all been destined to die. Mortal have you been born, to mortals you have given birth. Reckon on everything, expect everything." Seneca's

(Seneca quoted in the Immoderate Stoic blog 2014)

Could this be a philosophy with which to live in a world where 4 degree to 6 degrees centigrade above the pre-industrial has become inevitable because of out of control methane emissions, a world where there is a rapid decline in cheap easily available fossil energy sources which might power the high tech devices that naive techno optimists thought could save us?

What otherwise would people live these circumstances? One thing would be certain – there would be a lot of dying. Life would once again become nasty, brutish and short for most people.

Yet people would still have to live in that time. By this I mean that there would or will be a gap between the realisation of the catastrophe that had befallen us and the actual time of our deaths. (Unless the American and European ruling elites manage to trigger a nuclear war with Russia in which case our exit might be very fast). There would still be decisions and arrangements to be made – not the least for those who were still young people or children. Between a terminal diagnosis and a death there is time that still has to be lived. Can we say anything useful about this period of time?

First of all there would be a lot of emotional work to be done. There would still be a lot of denial with some people and rage felt by others – of younger people for older people who knew or should have known and who did not do enough or nothing at all. There would be hatred against those who continued to promote fossil fuel production and deliberately attempted to mislead or head off the truth about climate change. It will be important in a situation like this for proper judicial processes to be organised in order to prevent a degeneration into the chaos of civil war and revenge killings.

Secondly people will have to think long and hard whether they still want to have children and, if they do not, how they are going to live out their last days – that is, if they do survive into old age. If they do have children how are they going to bring them up? How are they to explain the world that these children live in? What skills should these children have?

At least some people have begun to think about what a historical period like this would be like and come up with the concept of the *Planetary Hospice*. (Baker C. 2014) One thing that we can say about the Planetary Hospice is that it would be a set of arrangements for people to help each other get through the ordeal of life until they die, as best they can. It would not primarily be an economic arrangement although it would have to be connected to the hard work that everyone would have to do, it would be primarily be about mutual emotional support and the collective search for meaning in a time of this kind of character. As Carolyn Baker explains it:

"Many people who have spent time in hospices report that it has been the most meaningful of their lives. It provided a sacred space in which to reflect deeply on their lives: to evaluate relationships that were enriching; to make amends and restitution with respect to relationships that were difficult and painful; to provide service to others in their hospice environment; and to prepare mindfully and reverently for death.

"On a much bigger scale, this is what is needed as a response to climate change. The 'great dying' cannot be practiced in isolation. Never before have human beings required loving community to the extent that they do now."

Sometimes there might be other consolations. Thus it is said that when a power cut struck southern California in the 1990s, Los Angeles residents were alarmed about strange clouds in the sky. In fact they were seeing the Milky Way for the first time in their lives, previously hidden by light pollution. At the time that I am writing this electric lights displays of stars are being put all over my city as part of the Christmas consumer orgy. They add to the light pollution and it impossible to see the real stars.

It might be a consolation of such times that people would be able to see the stars and perhaps for the first time get a better measure of the importance of humanity when seen in the very long run - as a huge drama to be sure but also as a small transient event considered against the vastness of the cosmic process.

"... pessimism's critics have often assumed that it must issue in some kind of depression or resignation. But this assumption says more about the critics than about their targets. Who is it, exactly, that cannot bear a story without a happy ending? Pessimists themselves have often been anything but resigned. Indeed, they have taken it as their task to find a way to live with the conclusions they have arrived at, and to live well, sometimes even joyfully. If this cannot be true for all of us, it is not the pessimists who are to blame, but the problems that they grapple with." (Dienstag, 2006 p x)

Bibliography

(n.d.). Retrieved from Society for the Deceleration of Time: http://www.zeitverein.com/english/framesets_e/fs_zeitverein_e.html

Börsenturbulenzen: Aktienhändler riskieren mehr als Psychopathen. (25th. September 2011). Abgerufen am 27th. December 2013 von Spiegel Online Wirtschaft: http://www.spiegel.de/wirtschaft/unternehmen/boersenturbulenzen-aktienhaendler-riskieren-mehr-als-psychopathen-a-788232.html

(2013). Retrieved January 2nd, 2014, from Verbund Offener Werkstaetten (Association of Open Workshops): http://www.offene-werkstaetten.org/

Abrams, L. (2014, February 27). *Former oil exec calls Exxon CEO out on his hypocritical anti-fracking lawsuit.* Retrieved April 19, 2014, from Salon: http://www.salon.com/2014/02/27/former_oil_exec_calls_exxon_ceo_out_on_his_hypocritical_anti_fracking_lawsuit/

Adams, Tim 2011 "Who Owns Britains Green and Pleasant Land?" The Guardian 7th August 2011

AMEC Environment and Infrastructure UK Ltd. (2013, December). *Department of Energy and Climate Change.* Retrieved April 19th, 2014, from Strategic Environmental Assessment for Further Onshore Oil and Gas Licensing: https://www.gov.uk/government/uploads/system/uploads/attachment_data/file/273997/DECC_SEA_Environmental_Report.pdf

AchbarandAbbott (Director). (2004). *The Corporation* [Motion Picture].

Addison, P. (1975). *The Road to 1945.* London: Cape.

AEA. (2012). *Support to the identification of potential risks for the environment and human health arising from hydrocarbons operations involving hydraulic fracturing in Europe.* European Commission DG Environment.

Ahmed, N. (2013, May 13th). *Earth Insight.* Retrieved December 27th, 2013, from The Guardian: http://www.theguardian.com/environment/earth-insight/2013/may/13/1

Allen et al. *Measurements of methane emissions at natural gas production sites in the United States* PNAS downloadable from http://www.pnas.org/lookup/suppl/doi:10.1073/pnas.1304880110/-/DCSupplemental

Alexander, G., Peake, S., Espinosa, A., Walker, J., Giordano, F. R., Salfield, T., et al. (2013). *The Open Co-op Business Plan.* Retrieved January 4th, 2014, from The Open Co-op: http://open.coop/tiki-index.php?page=The+Open+co-op+business+plan#The_Open_Co_op_Business_Plan

Anderson, K. (2013, December 10-11th). *Rationale and Framing for Radical Emissions Reduction Conference.* Retrieved January 3rd, 2014, from Tyndall Centre for Climate Change Rsearch: http://vimeo.com/album/2648454/video/81836152

Anderson, K., & Bows, A. (2010, November 29th). Beyond "dangerous" climate change: emission scenarios for a new world. *Philosophical Transactions of the Royal Society A.*

Anderson, P. J. (2009). *The Secret Life of Real Estate and Banking.* London: Shepheard-Walwyn.

Aristotle. (350 BC). *Politics.* Retrieved December 28th, 2013, from The Internet Classics Archive: http://classics.mit.edu/Aristotle/politics.1.one.html

Backhouse, R. E. (2002). *The Penguin History of Economics.* London: Penguin.

Baer, P., & Spash, C. L. (2008, May). *Cost Benefit Analysis of Climate Change: Stern Revisited.* Retrieved January 3rd, 2014, from CSIRO Working Papers: http://www.csiro.au/files/files/pkec.pdf

Bajo, C. S., & Roelants, B. (2011). *Capital and the debt Trap. Learning from Co-operatives in the Global Crisis.* Houndmills Basingstoke: Palgrave Macmillan.

Baker, Carolyn 2014 "Welcome to the Planetary Hospice" in Open Democracy 17th June 2014 at https://www.opendemocracy.net/transformation/carolyn-baker/welcome-to-planetary-hospice

Bamberger, M., & Oswald, R. E. (2012). The Impacts of Gas Drilling on Human and Animal Health. *New Solutions Vol 22 (1).*

Banerjee, N. (2102, April 21st). Pennsylvania law on fracking chemicals worries doctors. *Los Angeles Times.*

Barlow, Darren Ross; Le, Cam Van; Barker, James Marshall (2009) *Patent for Perforating Gun Assembly and Method for Controlling Wellbore Pressure Regimes During Perforation* Patent Search and Patent Law Directory. Patent.com http://patents.com/us-20110000669.html

Barlow, M. (2012). Water as a Commons: Only Fundamental Change Can Save Us. In S. Helfrich, D. Bollier, & (eds.) (Eds.), *The Wealth of the Commons* (pp. 161-165). Amherst MA: Levellers Press.

Barnes, P. (2006). *Capitalism 3.0.* San Francisco: Berrett-Koehler.

Barnes, P. (2003). *Who Owns the Sky?.* Island Press.

Barnosky, A. D. (2012). Approaching a State Shift in Earth's Biosphere. *Nature Vol 486,.*

Barras, B. (2004). Life Projects: Development our Way. In M. Blaser, H. A. Feit, & M. Glenn, *In the Way of Development* (p. 47). London: Zed Books.

Bates, Albert 2014 in A Gathering of Silverbacks at http://www.resilience.org/stories/2014-06-03/a-gathering-of-silverbacks-age-of-limits-2014

Bawden, T. (2013, October 1st). "Climate change? People get very emotional about the subject. It's not all bad": Owen Paterson accused of being irresponsible after he plays down the dangers of global warming. *The Independent.*

BC Oil and Gas Commission. (2013). *What Chemicals are Used.* Retrieved from Frac Focus Chemical Disclosure Registry: http://fracfocus.ca/chemical-use/what-chemicals-are-used

Beer, S. (1973). *Designing Freedom.* Retrieved January 2nd, 2014, from Scribd Digital Library: http://www.scribd.com/doc/959241/Designing-Freedom-Beer

Bell, G. (2004). *The Permaculture Way.* Permanent Publications.

Bernays, E. (1928). *Propoganda.* Retrieved December 29th, 2013, from History is a Weapon: http://www.historyisaweapon.com/defcon1/bernprop.html

Biofuelswatch. (2009). *Declaration on Biochar.* Retrieved January 2014, from Biofuels Watch: http://bio-fuel-watch.blogspot.co.uk/2009/04/biofuelwatch-declaration-biochar-big.html

Birkin, F., & Polesie, T. (2013). The Relevance of epistemic analysis to sustainability economics and the capability approach. *Ecological Economics.*

Black, W. K. (2010, May 13). *Neoclassical Economic Theories, Methodology and Praxis Optimize Criminogenic Environments and Produce Recurrent, Intensifying Crises.* Retrieved January 2nd, 2014, from Social Science Research Network: https://papers.ssrn.com/sol3/papers.cfm?abstract_id=1607124

Black, W. K. (2005). *The Best way to rob a bank is to own one. How corporate executives and politicians looted the S&L industry.* Austin: University iof Texas Press.

Black, W. K. (2005). When Fragile Becomes Friable: Endemic Control Fraud as a cause of Stagnation and Collapse. *IDEAS Workshop: Financial Crime and Fragiliity under Financial Globalisation.* New Dehli: http://www.networkideas.org/feathm/may2006/William_K_Black.pdf.

Bollier, David (2013) *Rebuilding Ecuador's economy with open source principles* at Open Source.com November 2013 *http://opensource.com/government/13/11/flok-society-ecuador-economy*

Boscolo, L., & Bertrando, P. (1993). *The Times of the Times. A New Perspective in Systemic Therapy and Consultation.* W W Norton.

Bradford, H. (2012, April 27th). *These Ten Companies control enormous number of consumer brands.* Retrieved December 29th, 2013, from Huffington Post: http://www.huffingtonpost.com/2012/04/27/consumer-brands-owned-ten-companies-graphic_n_1458812.html

Brown, Lester R. (2011) *World on the Edge: How to Prevent Environmental and Economic Collapse.* Earth Policy Institute, Washington, available for download at http://www.earth-policy.org/books/wote/wote

Brown, M. T. (2010). *Civilising the Economy.* Cambridge: Cambridge University Press.

Bruges, J. (2009). *The Biochar debate. Schumacher Briefing 16.* Totnes, Devon: Green Books/Schumacher Society.

Burton, E., Friedman, J., & Upadhye, R. (n.d.). *Environmental Issues in Underground Coal Gasification (with Hoe Creek Example).* Retrieved April 22nd, 2014, from US Department of Energy: http://fossil.energy.gov/international/Publications/ucg_1106_llnl_burton.pdf

Caddie, M. (2012, July 31st). *Subsidies and Spinners.* Retrieved April 23rd, 2014, from Action Hope and Ideas: http://manu.org.nz/2012/07/31/subsidies-spinners/

Camus, Albert *The Plague*, Penguin Classics, 2013 (First published in French 1947) p 30-31

Carbon TrackerInitiative and Grantham Research Institute. (2013). *Unburnable carbon 2013: Wasted capital and stranded assets.* Retrieved April 21st, 2014, from Carbon Tracker: http://www.carbontracker.org/wastedcapital

Carbon Trust. (2013). *Conversion Factors 2013 Update - based on Defra/DECC figures.* Retrieved January 3rd, 2014, from The Carbon Trust: http://www.carbontrust.com/media/18223/ctl153_conversion_factors.pdf

CarbonTracker. (2013). *Unburnable Carbon 2013: Wasted Capital and Stranded Assets.* Retrieved January 2nd, 2014, from Carbon Tracker Initiative: http://www.carbontracker.org/wastedcapital#

Castoriadis C 1987 *"The Imaginary Institution of Society"*, Polity Press, Cambridge

Chambers, R. (1983). *Rural Development. Putting the First Last.* London: Routledge.

Chang, H.-J. (2002, September 4th). *Kicking Away the Ladder.* Retrieved December 29th, 2013, from Post Autistic Economics Review: http://www.paecon.net/PAEtexts/Chang1.htm

Chen, J., Al-Wadei, M. H., Kennedy, R. C., & Terry, P. D. (2014). Hydraulic Fracturing: Paving the Way for a Sustainable Future? *Journal of Environmental and Public Health 2014*.

Chomsky, N. (2013, June 4th). How to Destroy the Future. *The Guardian*.

Clark, A. (2008, January 5th). Their Emotions are Fried. *The Guardian*.

Coal Seam Fires. (2014). Retrieved April 25th, 2014, from Wikipedia: http://en.wikipedia.org/wiki/Coal_seam_fire

Conaty, P., & Lewis, M. (2012). *The Resilience Imperative. Co-operative Transitions to a Steady State Economy*. Gabriola IslandBC: New Society Publishers.

Connor, S. (2013, November). Gaps in data on Arctic temperatures account for the "pause" in global warming. *The Independent*.

Conoco-Phillips Canada Resources Corporation. (March 2013). Retrieved from http://www.mvlwb.ca/Boards/slwb/Registry/2013/S13A-001%20-%20Conoco%20Phillips%20Canada/S13A-001%20-%20Appendix%209%20-%20Hydraulic%20Fracturing%20-%20Mar%2025_13.pdf

Convergence Alimentaire (2012) *http://www.convergencealimentaire.info/map.jpg*

Corporate European Observatory and PLATFORM. (2009). *Putting the Fox in Charge of the Henhouse: How BP's Emissions Trading Scheme was sold to the EU*.

Costanza, R. (2006, October 19th). Letter: Nature: ecosystems without commodifying them. *Nature*.

Costanza, R. (1997). The Value of the World's Eco-system services and natural capital. *Nature*.

Crampton, C. (2012, July 4th). Welfare Reform Suicides Must not be Overlooked. *New Statesman*.

Cutillas, S. Llistar, D and Trarafa, G 2014 *"Debt Audit"* in "Degrowth. A Vocabulary for a New Era" D'Alisa G. Demaria F and Kallis G eds. London, Routledge Publishers.

D'Alisa G. & Cattaneo C. Household work and energy consumption: a degrowth perspective. Catalonia's case study , *Journal of Cleaner Production*, 2011, pp71-79

D'Alisa G and Kallis G 2015 "Post Normal Science" in "Degrowth. A Vocabulary for a New Era" edited by D'Alisa G, Demaria F and Kallis G , Routledge 2015

Daly, H. E., & CobbJr, J. B. (1994). *For the Common Good*. Beacon Press.

Daly, H. E. (1999) Uneconomic Growth in Theory and Practice. Feasta Review Number 1. http://www.feasta.org/documents/feastareview/daly.htm

Daly, H. E., & Farley, J. (2004). *Ecological Economics.* WashingtonDC: Island Press.

Davey, B. (2001). BA (Hons) in life. *Clinical Psychology No.7* , 36-38.

Davey, B. (2001, May). *Pathologies and Policies of Time.* Retrieved January 1st, 2014, from Barrons Gold Market Index: http://www.bgmi.us/web/bdavey/Pathologies.htm

Davey, B. (2008, April 18-19th). *The Degrowth Economy and Lifestyles.* Retrieved January 1st, 2014, from Conference on Economic Degrowth for Ecological Sustainability and Social Equity: http://events.it-sudparis.eu/degrowthconference/en/themes/6Panel%20on%20macrosocioeconomics/Change%20of%20economic%20institutions%20Oslo/Davey%20B%20Degrowth%20Paris%20april%202008%20paper.pdf

Davey, B. (2001). *University of the North Pole. Life.* Retrieved December 29th, 2013, from Strategy for Losers: http://www.bgmi.us/web/bdavey/Life.htm

Davey, B. (2007). What Future? *Journal of Critical Psychology, Counselling and Psychotherapy Vol 7.*

Davies, J., Shorrocks, A., & Sandstrom, S. (2008, February). *The World Distribution of Household Wealth.* Retrieved December 30th, 2013, from UNU-WIDER: http://www.wider.unu.edu/publications/working-papers/discussion-papers/2008/en_GB/dp2008-03/_files/78918010772127840/default/dp2008-03.pdf

Davies, R.J., et al., (2014). Oil and gas wells and their integrity: Implications for shale and unconventional resource exploitation, *Marine and Petroleum Geology,* http://dx.doi.org/10.1016/j.marpetgeo.2014.03.00

Davis, M. (2002). *Late Victorian Holocausts.* London: Verso.

Decanio, S. J. (n.d.). *Economics Is Not the Right Language for Addressing Climate Change.* Retrieved from Economics for Equity and the Environment Network: http://www.e3network.org/briefs/DeCanio_Economics_not_the_Right_Language.pdf

Defoe, Daniel (2013) *Journal of the Plague Year 1722* Project Gutenberg EBook #376

Deriu, M 2014 (a) *"Autonomy"* in "Degrowth. A Vocabulary for a New Era" D'Alisa G. Demaria F and Kallis G eds. London, Routledge Publishers.

Deriu M, 2014 (b) *"Conviviality"* in "Degrowth. A Vocabulary for a New Era" D'Alisa G. Demaria F and Kallis G eds. London, Routledge Publishers.

Dusseault, M., Gray, M. N., & Nawrocki, P. A. (2000). Why Oilwells Leak: Cement Behaviour and Long-Term Consequences. *SPE International Oil and Gas Conference*. Beijing: Society of Petroleum Engineers.

Diary of a Somebody. (2013). Retrieved from Financial Times How to Spend It Supplement: http://howtospendit.ft.com/

Dickinson (Ed), H. T. (1982). *The Political Works of Thomas Spence*. Retrieved December 31st, 2013, from Digital Text International: http://www.ditext.com/spence/dickinson.html

Dienstag, Joshua Foa,(2006) "Pessimism. Philosophy. Ethics. Spirit." Princeton University Press.

Die Bank Raeuber. (2008, March 22nd). *Der Spiegel*.

Douthwaite, R. (2011, July). *Deficit Easing - An alternative to severe austerity programmes in the eurozone*. Retrieved January 3rd, 2014, from Feasta: http://www.feasta.org/wp-content/uploads/2011/07/Deficit_easing_RD.pdf

Drinking Water Inspectorate. (2014, January 21st). *Severn Trent Water Ltd Plead Guilty to Supplyig Water Unfit for Human Consumption*. Retrieved April 25th, 2014, from Drinking Water Inspectorate: http://dwi.defra.gov.uk/press-media/press-releases/20140121-svt-pros.pdf

Ehlig-Economides, C., & Economides, M. J. (2010). *Sequestering carbon dioxide in a closed underground volume*. Retrieved January 2nd, 2014, from Journal of Petroleum Science and Engineering 70: http://twodoctors.org/manual/economides.pdf

Elliot, T. R., & Celia, M. A. (2012, February 21st). *Potential Restrictions for CO2 Sequestration Sites Due to Shale and Tight Gas Production*. Retrieved January 2nd, 2014, from Environmental Science and Technology: http://pubs.acs.org/doi/abs/10.1021/es2040015

EnglishHeritage. (n.d.). *English Heritage Disability History*. Retrieved December 28th, 2013, from Disability in Tudor Institutions: http://www.english-heritage.org.uk/discover/people-and-places/disability-history/1485-1660/hospitals-and-almshouses/

Fairlie, S. (2009, Summer). *A Short History of Enclosure in Britain*. Retrieved December 31st, 2013, from The Land Magazine: http://www.thelandmagazine.org.uk/articles/short-history-enclosure-britain

Fatheuer, T. (2011). *Buen Vivir*. Berlin: Heinrich Boell Stiftung.

Fischedick, M., Esken, A., Luhmann, H.-J., Schuewer, D., & Supersberger, N. (2007). *Geologische CO2-Speicherung als klimapolitische Handlungsoption : Technologien, Konzepte, Perspektiven*. Retrieved from Wuppertal Institute: http://epub.wupperinst.org/frontdoor/index/index/docId/2618

Fitch, C., Chaplin, R., Trend, C., & Collard, S. (2007). Debt and Mental Health: the role of psychiatrists. *Advances in Psychiatric Treatment* , 194-202.

Fleming, D. (2004). *The Lean Economy. A Vision of Civility for a World in Trouble.* Retrieved December 31st, 2013, from Feasta Website: http://feasta.org/documents/review2/fleming.htm

Floro, M. S., Grown, C., & Elson, D. (2011). Time Use, Unpaid Work, Poverty and Public Policy. *Feminist Economics Vol 17 (4).*

Fox, J. (Director). (2013). *Gaslands 2* [Motion Picture].

Fracking -The Great Debate. (2013, August 23rd). Retrieved from Private Eye: http://www.private-eye.co.uk/sections.php?section_link=in_the_back&issue=1347

Franck, G. (1998). *Ökonomie der Aufmerksamkeit. Ein Entwurf.* Carl Hanser.

Fraser, I. (2011, January 16th). *Moore: FSA Lacks Competence to Investigate Bank Failures.* Retrieved January 2nd, 2014, from ianfraser.org: http://www.ianfraser.org/moore-fsa-lacks-competence-to-investigate-bank-failures/

"Fred". (2012, July 29th). *Fracking report ex President is Cuadrilla Chairman.* Retrieved April 23rd, 2014, from Frack Off: http://frack-off.org.uk/fracking-report-ex-president-is-cuadrilla-ceo/

Freedman, J., & Edwards, D. (1988). Time Pressure, task performance and enjoyment. In J. McGarth, *The Social Psychology of Time* (pp. 113-133). Newbury Park California: New Perspectives.

From Mud to Cement. Building Gas Wells. (2003, Autumn). Retrieved from Oilfield Review: http://www.slb.com/~/media/Files/resources/oilfield_review/ors03/aut03/p62_76.pdf

Gaffney, M. (1994). *The Corruption of Economics.* Retrieved December 31st, 2013, from Economic Realities: http://homepage.ntlworld.com/janusg/coe/!index.htm

Galbraith, J. K. (2001). *The Essential Galbraith.* New York: Houghton Mifflin.

Gallagher, P. (1995, May 25th). *How Britain's Free Trade Policies Starved Millions During Irelands Potato Famine.* Retrieved December 29th, 2013, from The American Almanac: http://american_almanac.tripod.com/potato.htm

Gambino Lauren, 2014, Airline Cabin Crews Strike over Ebola Fears at LaGuardia Airport, *http://www.theguardian.com/world/2014/oct/09/airline-cabin-cleaners-strike-over-ebola-fears-at-laguardia-airport* Retrieved 20/10/2014

Gammage, B. (2011). *The Biggest Estate on Earth. How Aborigines made Australia.* Sydney: Allen and Unwin.

GCEC. 2014a. *Better Growth Better Climate: The New Climate Economy Report; The Synthesis Report.* edited by Felipe Calderon et al. Washington, D.C.: The Global Commission on the Economy and Climate.

GCEC. 2014b. *Finance.* In Felipe Calderon et al (eds) *Better Growth Better Climate* GCEC Washington

Gee, D., Vaz, S. G., & al., e. (2002, January 9th). *Late lessons from early warnings: the precautionary principle 1896-2000.* Retrieved April 23rd, 2014, from European Environment Agency: http://www.eea.europa.eu/publications/environmental_issue_report_2001_22

Georgescu-Roegen. (1993). The Entropy Law and the Economic Problem. In H. E. Daly, K. N. Townsend, & (eds.), *Valuing the Earth. Economics, Ecology, Ethics* (pp. 75-88). CambridgeMass: MIT Press.

Giampietro, M., Mayumi, K., & Sorman, A. (2013). *Energy Analysis for a Sustainable Future.* London: Routledge.

Giampietro, M., Mayumi, K., & Sorman, A. (2011). *The Metabolic Pattern of Societies: Where Economists Fall Short.* London: Routledge.

Gibson, C. (2012, October 22nd). *Koch Brothers Produce Counterfeit Climate Report to deceive Congress.* Retrieved January 3rd, 2014, from Desmogblog: http://www.desmogblog.com/2012/10/22/koch-brothers-produce-counterfeit-climate-report-deceive-congress

Global Warming and Climate Change Myths. (2014). Retrieved January 3rd, 2014, from Skeptical Science. Getting Skeptical about Global warming Skepticism: http://www.skepticalscience.com/argument.php

Global Warming Skeptic Organisations. (2013, August 16th). Retrieved January 3rd, 2014, from Union of Concerned Scientists: http://www.ucsusa.org/global_warming/solutions/fight-misinformation/global-warming-skeptic.html

Goldenberg, S. (2013, August 5th). Two children given lifelong ban on talking about fracking. *The Guuardian*

Gorrell, C. (2001 update 2009). Wall Street Warriors. *Psychology Today.*

Griessler, M. (1995). *China. Alles unter dem Himmel.* Sigmaringen: Thorbecke Verlag.

Grossman, D. (2013). Retrieved December 30th, 2013, from Killology Research Group: http://killology.com/

Gruver, M. (2011, September 3rd). *Wyomings Natural Gas Boom comes with Smog attached*. Retrieved April 20th, 2014, from Environment on NBCNews.com: http://www.nbcnews.com/id/41971686/ns/us_news-environment/

Gudynas, Eduardo 2014. "Buen Vivir" in "Degrowth. A Vocabulary for a New Era" D'Alisa G, Demaria F, and Kallis G eds. London Routledge

Gunderson, Lance H. and Holling C S (2002) *Panarchy. Understanding Transformations in Human and Natural Systems*. Washington: Island Press

Gunther, F. (2003). Sustainability through Local Self Sufficiency. In R. Douthwaite(Ed), *Before the Wells Run Dry*. Dublin: Feasta Books

Hall, C.A.S., R. Powers and W. Schoenberg.(2008). Peak oil, EROI, investments and the economy in an uncertain future. Pp. 113-136 in Pimentel, David. (ed). *Renewable Energy Systems: Environmental and Energetic Issues*. Elsevier London

Hall, C. A. (2012, November 8th). *Peak Oil Postponed? Lecture to Global Challenge Stockholm*. Retrieved January 1st, 2014, from You Tube: https://www.youtube.com/watch?v=YwdwUStzxww

Hall, C. A. (2012, March 30th). *Peak Oil, declining EROI and the new economic realities*. Retrieved January 1st, 2014, from The All party Parliamentary Group on Peak Oil and Gas: http://www.slideshare.net/APPGOPO/energy-return-on-energy-investment

Hamilton, C. (2004). *Growth Fetish*. London: Pluto Press.

Hamilton, C. (2010). *Requiem for a Species*. London: Earthscan.

Hamilton, James D (2009) "Causes and Consequences of the Oil Shock of 2007-08" Brookings Institution at www.brookings.edu/~/media/files/programs/es/bpea/2009_spring_bpea_papers/2009a_bpea_hamilton.pdf

Hansen, J., Kharecha, P., Sato, M., Masson-Delmotte, V., Ackerman, F., & et, a. (2013, December 3rd). ssessing ""Dangerous Climate Change"": Required Reduction of Carbon Emissions to Protect Young People Future Generations and Nature.. *PloS ONE(8) 12: e81648*.

Hardin, G. (1993). The tragedy of the commons. In H. E. Daly, & K. N. Townsend, *Valuing the Earth - Economy, Ecology, Ethics* (pp. 131-132). CambridgeMass: The MIT Press.

Harries-Jones, P. (2004). The "Risk Society": Tradition, Ecological Order and Time-Space. In M. Blaser, H. A. Feit, & G. McCrae, *In the way of Development* (pp. 279-298). London: Zed Press.

Harrison (ed), M. (1998). *The Economics of World War Two*. Cambridge: Cambridge University Press.

Harrison, F. (2005). *Boom Bust. House prices, Banking and the depression of 2010*. London: Shepheard-Walwyn.

Hartman, T. (2010). *Unequal Protection. How Corporations became "People" - And how you can fight back*. Ssan Francisco: Berrett-Koehler Publishers.

Hawken, P. (2007). *Blessed Unrest*. New York: Penguin.

Haya, B. (2007). *Failed Mechanism..* International Rivers.

HEi. (2014). *Was ist der HEi*. Retrieved January 2nd, 2014, from HEi - Haus der Eigenenarbeit: http://www.hei-muenchen.de/

Heidegger, M. (1950). *The Question Concerning Technology*. Retrieved January 2nd, 2014, from http://72.52.202.216/~fenderse/Technology.html

Henry, J. S., Christensen, J., & Mathiason, N. (2012, July 22nd). *Revealed: global super rich have at leasst $21 trillion hidden in secret tax havens*. Retrieved January 2nd, 2014, from Tax Justice Network: http://www.taxjustice.net/cms/upload/pdf/The_Price_of_Offshore_Revisited_Presser_120722.pdf

Hill, M. (2013). Regulating the Frackers: Just How Robust is the Legislative Framework. *The Greens Shale Gas Conference*.

Hirshberg, M. C. (2010, November 1s). *Why So Many Entrepreneurs Get Divorced*. Retrieved January 2nd, 2014, from Inc.: http://www.inc.com/magazine/20101101/why-so-many-entrepreneurs-get-divorced.html

HMTreasury. (2013, April 21st). *HMT Green Book: supplementary guidance*. Retrieved January 2nd, 2014, from GOV.UK: https://www.gov.uk/government/publications/green-book-supplementary-guidance-optimism-bias

Hochschild, A. R. (2012). *The Managed Heart. Commercialisation of Human Feeling*. Berkeley: University of California Press.

Holland, A. (2002). Are Choices Tradeoffs? In D. W. Bromley, & J. Paavola, *Economics, Ethics and Environmental Policy* (pp. 17-34). Oxford: Blackwell.

Holling C S *Spruce-Fir Forests and Insect Outbreaks* in Gunderson Lance H and Holling C S (2002) *Panarchy*. Washington: Island Press

House, K. Z. (2010, March 29th). *Is underground coal gasification a sensible option?* Retrieved April 25th, 2014, from Bulletin of the Atomic Scientists: http://thebulletin.org/underground-coal-gasification-sensible-option

Howarth, R. W., Santoro, R., & Ingraffea, A. (2011). Methane and the greenhouse-gas footprint of natural gas from shale formations. *Climate Change* , 679-690.

Howie, J. (2013, September 2013). *What Do Graduates Do 2013? Social Science Overview.* Retrieved December 27th, 2013, from Higher Education Careers Services Unit: http://www.hecsu.ac.uk/assets/assets/documents/Wdgd_social_science_2013.pdf

Howarth, R. W., Santoro, R., & Ingraffea, A. R. (2011, March 13th). *Methane and the greenhouse-gas footprint of natural gas from shale formation.* Retrieved April 20th, 2014, from Climatic Change: http://www.eeb.cornell.edu/howarth/Howarth%20et%20al%20%202011.pdf

Hughes, J. D. (2013, February). *Graphs.* Retrieved January 2nd, 2014, from Shale Gas Bubble - Post Carbon Institute: http://shalebubble.org/graphs/

Hunt, K. (2008, January 24th). *Market Culture "at root of rogue trading".* Retrieved January 2nd, 2014, from BBC Business: http://news.bbc.co.uk/1/hi/business/7207563.stm

Hunter, J. Peacock P. Wightman, A. Foxley M. n.d. *Towards a Comprehensive Land Reform Agenda for Scotland – Briefing Paper for the House of Commons Scottish Affairs Committee* http://www.parliament. uk/documents/commons-committees/scottish-affairs/432-Land-Reform-Paper.pdf

Ingraffea, A. R. (2013, January). *Fluid Migration Mechanisms Due to Faulty Well Design and/or Construction: An Overview and Recent Experiences in the Pennsylvania Marcellus Fluid Migration Mechanisms Due to Faulty Well Design and/or Construction.* Retrieved April 20th, 2014, from PSE Physicians and Scientists for Healthy Energy: http://www.psehealthyenergy.org/site/view/1057

Insley, J. (2012, June 23rd). *Worry for Homeowners who face the threat of fracking.* Retrieved April 21st, 2014, from The Observer: http://www.theguardian.com/money/2012/jun/23/fracking-undermine-value-home

Illich, I. (1973). *Energy and Equity.* Retrieved January 1st, 2014, from Clever Cycles: http://clevercycles.com/energy_and_equity/index.html#spestu

Industrial Gases (HFC-23 & N2O). (2012, May 30th). Retrieved January 3rd, 2014, from Carbon Market Watch: http://carbonmarketwatch.org/industrial-gases-hfc-23-n2o/

IPCC. WG1. Assessment Report 5 (2013) *Climate Change. The Physical Basis. Summary for Policy Makers.* http://www.climatechange2013.org/images/report/WG1AR5_Chapter06_FINAL.pdf

IPCC.WG3.Final Draft AR5 Presentation 2014
http://mitigation2014.org/communication/presentations-events/WG3_AR5_Master.pptx

IWPR. (2012, May 2nd). Uzbecks fear Angren Revival. *Online Asian Times*

Jackson, M. (Director). (2014). *The Truth About the Dash for Gas* [Motion Picture].

Jackson, T. (2009). *Prosperity Without Growth*. London: Sustainable Development Commission.

Jacobs, M. (1990). The Price of the Future. *New Internationalist*.

Jacobs, M. (1990, January 5th). The Price of the Future. *New Internationalist*.

James, O. (2007). *Affluenza*. London: Vermillion.

James, O. (2010, November 26th). David Cameron should measure mental health, not happiness. *The Guardian*.

James, O. (2010, November 26th). *David Cameron should measure mental health, not happiness*. Retrieved December 29th, 2013, from The Guardian: http://www.theguardian.com/commentisfree/2010/nov/26/david-cameron-happiness-mental-health

Johanisova, N. (2005). *Living in the Cracks*. Feasta Books.

Johnsson-Stenman, O. (2002). What should we do with inconsistent, non welfaristic, and undeveloped preferences. In D. W. Bromley, & J. Paavola, *Economics, Ethics, and Environmental Policy* (pp. 103-119). Oxford: Blackwell.

Kahneman, D. (2011). *Thinking, Fast and Slow*. London: Penguin.

Kallis Giorgos 2014. "Social Limits of Growth" in *"Degrowth. A Vocabulary for a New Era"* edited by D'Alisa G. Demaria F and Kallis G. London Routledge

Kant, I., & (Tr.)Ellington, J. W. (1993). *Grounding for the Metaphysics of Morals*. Hackett Publishing.

Kassotis, C. D., Tilitt, D., Davis, J. W., Hormann, A. M., & Nagel, S. C. (2013, December 16th). Estrogen and Androgen Receptor Activities of Hydraulic Fracturing Chemicals and Surface and Ground Water in a Drilling-Dense Region. *Endocrinology*.

Kasten, H. (2001). *Wie die Zeit Vergeht*. Damstadt: Primus Verlag.

Kay, J. (2010). *Obliquity*. London: Profile Books.

Keen, S. (2011). *Debunking Economics. The Naked Emperor Dethroned?* London, New York: Zed Books.

Kelly, M. (2012). *Owning our Future. The Emerging Ownership Revolution.* San Francisco: Berrett-Koehler.

Kenrick, J. (2012). The Climate and the Commons. In B. Davey(ed), *Sharing for Survival.* Dublin: Feasta Books.

Kenrick, J. (2011). Unthinking Eurocentrism. *Anthropological Notebooks 17 (2)* , 11-36.

Khor, M. (1995). *A WorldWide Fight against BioPiracy and Patents on Life.* Retrieved December 28th, 2013, from Third World Network: http://www.twnside.org.sg/title/pat-ch.htm

Kingsnorth , Paul 2012. *"High house prices? Inequality? I blame the Normans"* The Guardian 17th December 2012

Klein, N. (2000). *No Logo.* London: Flamingo.

Knight, D. (2013, November 29th). Personal Communication.

Kopits, Steven (2014) "Global Oil Market Forecasting: Main Approaches and Key Drivers" Columbia University, SIPA, Center on Global Energy Policy, http://energypolicy.columbia.edu/events-calendar/global-oil-market-forecasting-main-approaches-key-drivers

Korowicz, D. (2012, June). *Trade-Off. Financial System - Supply Chain Cross Contagion: a study in global systemic collapse.* Retrieved January 2nd, 2014, from Feasta: http://www.feasta.org/wp-content/uploads/2012/06/Trade-Off1.pdf

Kreitzman, L. (1999). *The 24 Hour Society.* Profile Books.

La Via Campesina. (n.d.). Retrieved January 4th, 2014, from La Via Campesina. The International Peasants Voice: http://viacampesina.org/en/

LaoTzu. (n.d.). *Tao Te Ching Translations Chapter 1.* Retrieved December 2013, 2013, from Tao Te Ching: http://duhtao.com/translations.html

Latouche, Serge, (2014) "Decolonisation of Imaginary" in *"Degrowth. A Vocabulary for a New Era"* Edited by Giacomo D'Alisa, Federico Demaria and Giorgos Kallis, London, Routledge.

Lasn, K. (2012). *Meme Wars: The Creative Destruction of Neoclassical Economics.* London: Penguin.

Law, Adam; Hays, Jake; Shonkoff, Seth B; Finkel, Madelon L, 2014. *Public Health England draft report on Shale Gas Extraction*, Mistaking Best Practices for Actual Practices, British Medical Journal. 26th[th] April 2014, Volume 348 p.8 http://www.bmj.com/content/348/bmj.g2728

Layard, R. (2006). *Happiness. Lessons from a New Science.* London: Penguin.

Le Quere, C. (2010, November 29th). *Human Peturbation of the Global Carbon Budget.* Retrieved January 4th, 2014, from Global Carbon Project: http://bfw.ac.at/400/smilex/GlobalCarbonBudget_2009.pdf

Levine, R. (2001). *Eine Landkarte Der Zeit.* Munich: Piper.

Lewandowsky, S., Gignac, G. E., & Oberauer, K. (2013, October 2nd). The Role of Conspiracist Ideation and Worldviews in Predicting Rejection of Science. *PLOS ONE.*

Liao, C., Luo, Y., Fang, C., & Li, B. (2010). *Ecosystem Carbon Stock Influenced by Plantation Practice.* Retrieved from PLoS ONE 5(5) e10867: http://www.plosone.org/article/info%3Adoi%2F10.1371%2Fjournal.pone.0010867

Linebaugh, P. (2013). Enclosures from the bottom up. In D. Bollier, & S. Helfrich, *The Wealth of the Commons.* Amherst MA: Levellers Press.

Little, M. G., & Jackson, R. B. (2010, October 26th). *Potential Impacts of Leakage from Deep CO2 Geosequestration on Overlying Freshwater Aquifers.* Retrieved January 2nd, 2014, from Environmental Science and Technology: http://pubs.acs.org/doi/abs/10.1021/es102235w

Lohan, T. (2014, January 10th). *The Four Big Dangers of Fracking.* Retrieved April 20th, 2014, from Resilience: http://www.resilience.org/stories/2014-01-10/the-4-big-dangers-of-fracking

Lubin, G. (2011, July 21st). *Citi's Top Economist Says the water Market will soon eclipse oil.* Retrieved December 31st, 2013, from Business Insider: http://www.businessinsider.com/willem-buiter-water-2011-7

Luck. (2012). Ethical Considerations in On-Ground Applications of the Eco-System services concept. *Bioscience Vol 62.*

Lyons, R. (2012). Residential Site Value Tax in Ireland. In E. O'siochru, *The Fair Tax.* Shepheard-Walwyn

Macalister, T. (2009, November 9). *Key oil figures were distorted by US pressure, says whistleblower.* Retrieved January 1st, 2014, from The Guardian: http://www.theguardian.com/environment/2009/nov/09/peak-oil-international-energy-agency

Madron, R., & Jopling, J. (2003). *Gaian Democracies Schumacher Briefing 9.* Green Books/Schumacher Society.

Mankiw, N. G. (2008, March 16th). Beyond the Noise on Free Trade. *New York Times*.

Martinez-Alier, J. (2002). *The Environmentalism of the Poor*. Cheltenham UK: Edward Elgar.

Maslow, A. (2013). Retrieved December 28th, 2013, from Maslow's Hierarchy of Needs: http://www.maslowshierarchyofneeds.net/category/hierarchy-of-needs/

Matthews, L. (2012). Cap and Share in pictures. In B. Davey(ed.), *Sharing for Survival*. Dublin: Feasta Books.

Mauer, R., & Tinsley, A. M. (2010, May 10th). BP has long history of legal ethical violations. *St Louis Post Dispach*.

McCarron, G. (2013, May 5th). *Symptomatology of a gas field – Independent Research Report*. Retrieved April 25th, 2014, from Bridging the Divide: http://btdinc.org/2013/05/05/symptomatology-of-a-gas-field-independent-research-report/

(2004). Traditional Ecological Knowledge and Sustainable Development. In M. Blaser, H. A. Feit, & G. McCrae, *In the way of development* (pp. 72-91). London: Zed Press.

McNally, D. (1988). *Political Economy and the Rise of Capitalism: A Reinterpretation*. Berkely: University of California Press.

Meadows, D. H., Meadows, D. I., Randers, J., & BehrensIII, W. W. (1972). *The Limits to Growth*. New York: Universe Books.

Meadows, D., Randers, J., & Meadows, D. (2005). *Limits to Growth, The 30 Year Update*. London: Earthscan.

Mearns, Euan, (2003) *The Changing Face of UK Electricity*, Energy Matter, Retrieved 29th April 2014 , from http://euanmearns.com/the-changing-face-of-uk-electricity-supply/

Myhre, G., D. Shindell, F.-M. Bréon, W. Collins, J. Fuglestvedt, J. Huang, D. Koch, J.-F. Lamarque, D. Lee, B. Mendoza, T. Nakajima, A. Robock, G. Stephens, T. Takemura and H. Zhang, 2013 Anthropogenic and Natural Radiative Forcing. In: *Climate Change 2013: The Physical Science Basis. Contribution of Working Group I to the Fifth Assessment Report of the Intergovernmental Panel on Climate Change* [Stocker, T.F., D. Qin, G.-K. Plattner, M. Tignor, S.K. Allen, J. Boschung, A. Nauels, Y. Xia, V. Bex and P.M. Midgley (eds.)]. Cambridge University Press, Cambridge, United Kingdom and New York, NY, USA, pp. 659–740, doi:10.1017/ CBO9781107415324.018.

Migchels, A. (2012). *JAK Bank*. Retrieved January 3rd, 2014, from P2P Foundation: http://p2pfoundation.net/JAK_Bank

MisesWiki. (2013, March 14th). *Richard_Cantillon*. Retrieved January 2nd, 2013, from Ludwig von Mises Institute: http://wiki.mises.org/wiki/Richard_Cantillon

Mobbs, P. (2013, July 25th). *"Behind every picture lies a story" – statistical reality versus PR-hype within the political project of unconventional gas in Britain*. Retrieved January 4th, 2014, from Mobbseys Musing: http://www.fraw.org.uk/mei/musings/2013/20130725-behind_every_picture_lies_a_story.html

Mobbs, P. (2014) (a). A response to DECC's public consultation on the 14th Onshore Gas and Oil Licencing Strategic Environmental Assessment. UK: Mobbs Environmental Investigations.

Mobbs, P. (2014) (b) A critical Review of the Public Health England Report "Review of the Potential Health Impacts of Exposures to Chemical and Radioactive Pollutants as a result of Shale Gas Extraction"

Monbiot, G. (2013, May 6th). Enough Already. *The Guardian*.

Monbiot, G. (2011, November 7th). *The 1% are the best destroyers of wealth the world has eveer seen*. Retrieved December 27th, 2013, from The Guardian: http://www.theguardian.com/commentisfree/2011/nov/07/one-per-cent-wealth-destroyers

Monbiot, G. (2013, November 4th). This transatlantic trade deal is a full-frontal assault on democracy. *The Guardian*.

Moriarty, Patrick and Honnery, Damon. (2012). *What is the Global Potential for Renewable Energy?* Renewable and Sustainable Energies Reviews, 16, 244-252.

Mudd, G. M. (2009, April). *The Sustainability of Mining in Australia*. Retrieved January 1st, 2014, from Monash University Department of Civil Engineering: http://users.monash.edu.au/~gmudd/sustymining.html

Mueller, J. D. (2006). *The Economics of Loving your Neighbour*. Retrieved December 28th, 2013, from Ethics and Public Policy Centre: http://www.eppc.org/publications/the-economics-of-loving-your-neighbor/

Murray, C. (Director). (2011). *RBS Inside the Bank that ran out of money* [Motion Picture].

Napoleoni, L. (2008). *Rogue Economics. Capitalism's New Reality*. New York: Seven Stories Press.

Neamtan, N. (2010). Ten Years After: Challenge and Proposals for another possible world. *World Social Forum*. Chantier de L"Economie Sociale.

Nelson, L. H. (2001). *The Rise of Feudalism*. Retrieved December 28th, 2013, from Lectures in Medieval History on WWW Virtual Library: http://www.vlib.us/medieval/lectures/feudalism.html

Nelson, R. H. (2001). *Economics as Religion*. University Park, Pennsylvania: Pennsylvania State University Press.

Nietzsche, F. (2009, January). *On the Genealogy of Morals. Second Essay*. Retrieved December 29th, 2013, from http://records.viu.ca/~johnstoi/nietzsche/genealogy2.htm

Norgaard, R. B. (2009). The environmental case for a collective assessment of economism. In R. P. Holt, S. Pressman, & C. L. Spash, *Post Keynesian and Ecological Economics* (p. 80). London: Edward Elgar.

O'Neill, J. (2007). *Markets, Deliberation and Environment*. London: Routledge.

O'Neill, R. (2013, December). *HSE looks less, counts less and couldn't care less*. Retrieved April 24th, 2014, from Hazards Magazine: http://www.hazards.org/votetodie/watchdogma.htm

Oreskes, N., & Conway, E. M. (2010). *Merchants of Doubt*. New York: Bloomsbury Press.

Osborne, S. G. (2011). *Methan Contamination of Drinking Water Accompanying Gas-Well Drilling and Hydraulic Fracturing*. Retrieved April 20th, 2014, from Proceedings of the National Academy of Science: http://www.pnas.org/cgi/doe/10.1073/pnas.1100682108

Oreskes, N., & Conway, E. M. (2010). *Merchants of Doubt*. New York: Bloomsbury.

Orrell, D., & VanLoon, B. (2011). *Introducing Economics. A Graphical Guide*. London: Icon Books.

Osbourne, J. (2012). A Planner's Perspective. In E. O'siochru(ed), *The Fair Tax*. Shepheard-Walwyn.

Oskin, B. (2014, 07). Wastewater Injection Triggered Earthquake Cascade. *Live Science*.

Ostrom, E. (1990). *Governing the Commons. The Evolution of Institutions for Collective Action*. Cambridge: Cambridge University Press.

Ostrom, E., & Gardner, R. (1993). Coping with Assymetries in the Commons. Self Governing Irrigation Systems can Work. *Journal of Economic Perspectives* , 93-112.

Ott, H. E., & Sachs, W. (2000). Ethical Aspects of Emissions Trading. *World Council of Churches*. Wuppertal Institut für Klima, Umwelt, Energie.

Parnell, J. (2013, February 28th). *UK Coal Use up by 35.2% in 2012*. Retrieved January 2nd, 2014, from RTCC Responding to Climate Change: http://www.rtcc.org/2013/02/28/uk-coal-use-up-32-5-in-2012/#sthash.4BTlLJ0k.dpuf

Peduzzi, P., & Harding, R. (2012). *Gas Fracking: Can we Safely Squeeze the Rocks?* Geneva: UNEP Global Environmental Alert Service.

Pettifor, A. (2006). *The Coming First World Debt Crisis.* Basingstoke: Palgrave Macmillan.

Pfohl, S. (1994). *Images of Deviance and Social Control.* New York: McGraw-Hill.

Picchio A. 2014 "Feminist Economics" in "Degrowth. A Vocabulary for a New Era" edited by D'Alisa G, Demaria F. and Kallis G London Routledge.

Picketty, Thomas (2014). *Capital in the Twenty First Century.* Cambridge Mass. Harvard University Press,

PIRC. (2011). *The Common Cause Handbook.* PIRC.

PositiveMoneyCampaign. (2013). *Our Proposals-Positive Money Campaign.* Retrieved January 3rd, 2014, from Positive Money campaign: http://www.positivemoney.org/our-proposals/

Powell, J. L. (2012, November 15th). *Why Climate Deniers have no scientific credibility - in one pie chart.* Retrieved January 3rd, 2014, from Desmogblog: http://desmogblog.com/2012/11/15/why-climate-deniers-have-no-credibility-science-one-pie-chart

Prior, T., Giurco, D., Mudd, G., Mason, L., Behrisch, J. (2012) *Resource depletion, peak minerals and the implications for sustainable resource,* in *Global Environmental Change.* Volume 22, issue 3, p.577-587.

Protess, Ben, *Wall Street continues to spend Big on Lobbying,* New York Times, August 1st 2011, http://dealbook.nytimes.com/2011/08/01/wall-street-continues-to-spend-big-on-lobbying/?_php=true&_type=blogs&_r=0

Public Health England. (2013, October). *Shale gas health review by Public Health England.* Retrieved April 25th, 2013, from Gov.UK: https://www.gov.uk/government/news/shale-gas-health-review-by-public-health-england

Ramose, Mogobe B. 2014 *"Ubuntu"* in D'Alisa G.; Demaria F. And Kallis G. "Degrowth. A Vocabulary for a New Era" Routledge, London, pp212-213

Rasmussen, D. (2013, July 23). Non-Indigenous Culture: Implications of a Historical Anomaly. *Resilience.*

Readfearn, G. (2013, October 2nd). Climate sceptics more likely to be conspiracy theorists and free market advocates, study claims. *The Guardian.*

Reiermann, Christian and Seith, Anne (16th June 2014), *Perlentaucher in der Flut*, Der Spiegel 25/2014, print issue, pp 68-70

Reuters. (2013, March 12th). *Japan's Methane Hydrate Gas Extraction Is First In The World.* Retrieved January 3rd, 2014, from Huff Post Green: http://www.huffingtonpost.com/2013/03/12/japan-methane-hydrate_n_2857733.html

Ricardo, D. (1819). *On the Principles of Political Economy and Taxation.* London.

Rivers CM, Lofgren ET, Marathe M, Eubank S, Lewis BL. Modeling the Impact of Interventions on an Epidemic of Ebola in Sierra Leone and Liberia. PLOS Currents Outbreaks. 2014 Oct 16. Edition 1. doi:

Rogers, D. (2013). *Shale and Wall Street - Report for Energy Policy Forum.* Retrieved January 2nd, 2014, from Shale Bubble: http://shalebubble.org/wp-content/uploads/2013/02/SWS-report-FINAL.pdf

Romm, J. (2013, November 25th). *Bridge Out: Bombshell Study Finds Methane Emissions From Natural Gas Production Far Higher Than EPA Estimates.* Retrieved January 2nd, 2014, from Think Progress: http://thinkprogress.org/climate/2013/11/25/2988801/study-methane-emissions-natural-gas-production/#

Rothwell, H. (. (1975). The Charter of the Forests. In *English Historical Documents Vol. 3* (pp. 337 - 340). London: Eyre and Spottiswoode.

Rowling, T. (2010, October 10th). Gas Toxins Found in Kingaroy Cattle. *Queensland Country Life.*

Ryan-Collins, J., Greenham, T., Werner, R., & Jackson, A. (2011). *Where does Money Come From? A Guide to the UK Monetary and Banking System.* London: New Economics Foundation.

Sahlins, M. (1972). *Stone Age Economics.* Chicago: Aldine.Atherton Inc.

Saka, G. (2011, April 30th). *The Decision Lab. Why Does Studying Economics Hurt Ethical Inclinations.* Retrieved December 27th, 2013, from Psychology Today: http://www.psychologytoday.com/blog/the-decision-lab/201104/why-does-studying-economics-hurt-ethical-inclinations

Sanderson E. W. et al. (2002)The Human Footprint and the Last of the Wild. *Bio-Science* (52) 891-904

Santarius, Tilman (2014) Umweltfreudlich mehr verbrauchen, *Le Monde Diplomatique/Kolleg Postwachstumsgesellschaften* Atlas der Globalisierung Der Postwachstum Atlas p14

Saunders, S., & Munro, D. (2000). THE CONSTRUCTION AND VALIDATION OF A CONSUMER ORIENTATION QUESTIONNAIRE (SCOI) DESIGNED TO MEASURE FROMM's (1955)

"MARKETING CHARACTER" IN AUSTRALIA. *Social Behaviour and Personality. An International Journal Vol.28.No.3* , 219-240.

Schroyer, T. (2009). *Beyond Western Economics.* AbingdnOxon: Routledge.

Schumpeter, J. (1987). *Capitalism, Socialism and Democracy.* London: Unwin.

(2014). *Shale gas and Water.* Chartered Institution of Water and Environmental Management.

Seneca - quoted in
http://blogs.exeter.ac.uk/stoicismtoday/2014/08/23/how-to-meet-the-morning-by-matt-van-natta/)

Shaxon, N. (2011). *Treasure Islands. Tax Havens and the Men who stole the World.* London: Bodley Head.

Shonkoff, Seth B. *"Gas Industry Study: New EDF and Industry Study is not representative of US Natural Gas Development"*, Physicians, Scientists and Engineers for Healthy Energy, September 2013, http://www.psehealthyenergy.org/data/Allen_PNAS_Study_2013_9_16_final.pdf

Skrebowski, C. (2011, September 16th). *A Brief Economic Explanation of Peak Oil.* Retrieved January 1st, 2014, from The Oil Depletion Analysis Centre Newsletter: http://www.odac-info.org/newsletter/2011/09/16

Smil, V. (2007). The Unprecedented Shift in Japan's Population: Numbers, Age, and Prospects. *The Asia-Pacific Journal:Japan Focus.*

Smith, A. (1759). *The Theory of Moral Sentiments.* Retrieved December 30th, 2013, from Wikisource: https://en.wikisource.org/wiki/The_Theory_of_Moral_Sentiments

Smith, A. (1776). The Wealth of Nations. *British Enclassica Philosophy Masterworks CD.* Magic Mouse Multimedia Production.

Smith, P. B., & Max-Neef, M. (2011). *Economics Unmasked.* Totnes: Green Books.

Smith, Y. (2010). *Econned.* New York: Palgrave Macmillan.

Sᐢᐧorman, A. H. 2014 "Societal Metabolism" in D'Alisa G, Demaria F and Kallis G. eds. *"Degrowth A Vocabulary for a New Era"* London Routledge

SourceWatchWiki. (2009). *Clean Development Mechanism and HFC-23 destruction.* Retrieved January 3rd, 2014, from Centre for Media and Democracy: Source Watch: http://www.sourcewatch.org/index.php/Clean_Development_Mechanism_and_HFC-23_destruction

Spash, C. L. (2002). Empirical Signs of Ethical Concern in Valuation of the Environment. In D. W. Bromley, & J. Paavola, *Economics, Ethics, and Environmental Policy* (pp. 205-221). Oxford: Blackwell.

Spash, C. L. (2011). Terrible Economics, Ecosystems and Banking. *Environmental Values 20* , 141-145.

Spash, C. L. (2008, January/Februrary). The Economics of Avoiding Action on Climate Change. *Adbusters.*

Spash, Clive L 2014 *Better Growth, Helping the Paris COP-out? Fallacies and Omissions of the New Climate Economy Report* SRE Discussion Paper 2014/04 Institute for the Environment and Regional Development. Vienna University of Economics and Business *http://www-sre.wu.ac.at/sre-disc/sre-disc-2014_04.pdf*

Sraffa, P. (1926). The laws of return under competitive conditions. *Economic Journal Vol 36.*

Stacey, R. (2007, June). *The Stacey Matrix.* Retrieved January 1st, 2014, from GP Training Net: http://www.gp-training.net/training/communication_skills/consultation/equipoise/complexity/stacey.htm

Stacey, R. (2012) T*he Tools and Techniques of Leadership and Management: Meeting the challenge of complexity,* London: Routledge

Stern, N. (2006). *The Economics of Climate Change: The Stern Review.* Cabinet Office - HM Treasury. Cambridge: Cambridge University Press.

Stevenson, A. (2013, November 11th). *Analysis: An Uncertain Future for Britain's Fracking watchdog.* Retrieved April 25th, 2014, from Politics.Co.UK: http://www.politics.co.uk/comment-analysis/2013/11/11/analysis-an-uncertain-future-for-britain-s-fracking-watchdog

Storr, A. (1994). *Solitude.* London: HarperCollins.

Suro, R. (1992, May 3rd). *Abandoned Oil and Gas Wells become Pollution Portals.* Retrieved January 2nd, 2014, from New York Times: http://www.nytimes.com/1992/05/03/us/abandoned-oil-and-gas-wells-become-pollution-portals.html?src=pmLink

Sustainability Support. (2010, August 2010). DERM Rejects Cougars Environmental Evaluation of UCG Plant. *Sustainability Support.*

Sutanto, T. N. (2012, October 31st). *Merchantilism in the Early American Colonies.* Retrieved December 28th, 2013, from façon de penser de l"apprenant: http://nuariza.wordpress.com/2012/10/31/merchantilism-in-the-early-american-colonies/

Swayne, M. (2012, February 9th). *Integrated weed management best response to herbicide resistance.* Retrieved December 31st, 2013, from Penn State News: http://news.psu.edu/story/151839/2012/02/09/integrated-weed-management-best-response-herbicide-resistance

Sweeney, Colm et al. *(2013,) Methane Emissions estimates for airborn measurements over a western United States gas field,* Geophysical Research Letters, 2013, Vol 40, Issue 16

Tainter, J. A. (1988). *The Collapse of Complex Societies.* CambridgeUK: Cambridge University Press.

Tait, D. R., Santos, I. R., & Maher, D. T. (2013, 12). *Atmospheric Radon, CO2 and CH4 Dynamics in an Australian Coal Seam Gas Field.* Retrieved December 20th, 2014, from SAO/NASA ADS Physics Abstract Service: http://adsabs.harvard.edu/abs/2013AGUFM.A53H..06T

Tait, D. R., Santos, I. R., Maher, D. T., Cyrnonak, T. J., & Davis, R. J. (2013). Enrichment of Radon and Carbon Dioxide in the Open Atmosphere of an Australian Coal Seam Gas Field. *Environmental Science and Technology* , 3099-3104.

Tart, C. T. (1994). *Living the Mindful Life.* Shambala.

Taylor, K., & Lambert, J. (2013, November 29th). *Response to Public Health England's "Review of the potential public health impacts of exposures to chemical and radioactive pollutants as a result of shale gas extraction.* Retrieved April 25th, 2014, from KeithTaylorMEP.org: http://www.keithtaylormep.org.uk/wp-content/uploads/Keith-Taylor-MEP-and-Jean-Lambert-MEP-Response_PHE-fracking-report_29112013.pdf

TaxJusticeNetwork. (2013, November 7th). *Financial Secrecy Index 2013.* Retrieved January 2nd, 2014, from Tax Justice Network: http://www.financialsecrecyindex.com/introduction/fsi-2013-results

The State of Queensland, Department of Employment, Economic Development and Innovation. (2010). *Investigation Report: Leakage Testing of Coal Seam Gas Wells in the Tara "Rural Residential Estates" Facility.* Government of Queensland.

The Unconventional Hydrocarbon Resources of Britains Onshore Basins. (2010, December). Retrieved April 23rd, 2014, from Department of Energy and Climate Change, UK Government: https://www.gov.uk/government/uploads/system/uploads/attachment_data/file/66171/promote-uk-cbm.pdf

Thematic Guide to Integrated Assessment Modeling of Climate Change [online]. (1995). Retrieved January 3rd, 2014, from Center for International Earth Science Information Network (CIESIN).: http://sedac.ciesin.columbia.edu/mva/iamcc.tg/RKP95/node11.html

Thompson, L. (2012, November 15th). *World-first research finds methane is "higher in CSG areas"*. Retrieved April 20th, 2014, from Daily Examineer: http://www.dailyexaminer.com.au/news/methane-higher-in-csg-areas/1622910/

Thornton, M. (2010, May 5th). *Biography of Richard Cantillon (1680-1734)*. Retrieved January 2nd, 2014, from Ludwig von Mises Institute: https://mises.org/page/1472/Biography-of-Richard-Cantillon-16801734

Tobin, J. (1998). *Neoclassical Theory in America: J B Clark and Fisher*. Retrieved December 31st, 2013, from Cowles Foundation for Research in Economics at Yale University: http://cowles.econ.yale.edu/P/cd/d07b/d0776.pdf

Tomori, O (2014) What can Nigeria's Ebola Experience Teach the World?" The Guardian 7th October 2014

TransportforLondon. (2004, July 7th). *Press Release: Jubilee line raises land value by estimated £2.8billion*. Retrieved December 31st, 2013, from Transport for London: http://www.labourland.org/downloads/articles/jle-land-value-press-release.pdf

Turner, G. M. (2012). On the Cusp of Collapse. Updated Comparison of the Limits of Growth with historical data. *GAIA 21/2* , 116-124.

Tverberg, G. (2012, July). *An Energy/GDP Forecast to 2050*. Retrieved 2014 January, 26th, from Our Finite World: 3rd

UNEP. (2013). Retrieved January 1st, 2014, from The Economics of Ecosystems and Biodiversity: http://www.teebweb.org/

UNEP-GEAS. Global Environment Alert Service. (2012, November). *Gas Fracking Can we Safely Squeeze the Rocks*. Retrieved January 2nd, 2014, from United Nations Environment Programme Global Environment Alert Service: http://www.grid.unep.ch/products/3_Reports/GEAS_Nov2012_Fracking.pdf

UK National Archives. http://www.nationalarchives.gov.uk/pathways/blackhistory/africa_caribbean/docs/trade_routes.htm

University of Colorado, D. (2012, March 19). *"Air emissions near fracking sites may pose health risk, study shows; sites contain hydrocarbons including benzene."*. Retrieved April 20th, 2014, from Science Daily: http://www.sciencedaily.com/releases/2012/03/120319095008.htm

US EPA. (2007, October 10th). *BP to Pay Largest Criminal Fine Ever for Air Violations*. Retrieved April 23rd, 2014, from United States Environment Protection Agency/News Releases/2007 Newsroom:

http://yosemite.epa.gov/opa/admpress.nsf/eebfaebc1afd883d85257355005afd19/ca0637fa729266968525737f0060bc4b!OpenDocument

Van Harmelen, Toon; Bakker, Joost; de Bries, Bert; van Vuuren, Detlef; den Elson, Michel; Mayerhofer, Petra. (2002) *Long term reductions in cost of controlling regional air pollution in Europe due to climate policy.* Environmental Science and Policy, August 2002

Vanek, J. (1995). Co-operative Economics. (A. Perkins, Interviewer) New Renaissance Magazine.

Veblen, T. (1909). The Limitations of Marginal Utility. *Journal of Political Economy Vol.17,* http://socserv.mcmaster.ca/econ/ugcm/3ll3/veblen/margutil.txt.

Veblen, T. (1899). *The Theory of the Leisure Class.* Retrieved December 28th, 2013, from Project Gutenberg: http://www.gutenberg.org/files/833/833-h/833-h.htm

Vetter, Andrea (2014). Die bessere Technik fuer morgen. Atlas of Globalisation Le Monde Diplomatique German version. p23

Walker, B., & Salt, D. (2006). *Resilience Thinking.* Washington: Island Press.

Walker, J. (2006). *An introduction to the VSM as a diagnostic and design tool for co-operatives and federations.* Retrieved January 2nd, 2014, from Eclectic Systems. Research Analysis and Design: http://www.esrad.org.uk/resources/vsmg_2.2/pdf/vsmg_2_2.pdf

WaronWant. (2013). *Sweatshops and Plantations.* Retrieved December 28th, 2013, from War on Want: http://www.waronwant.org/overseas-work/sweatshops-and-plantations

Warner, N. R., Jackson, R. B., Darrah, T. H., Osborn, S. G., Down, A., Zhao, K., et al. (2102, May 10th). *Geochemical evidence for possible natural migration of Marcellus Formation brine to shallow aquifers in Pennsylvania.* Retrieved April 25th, 2014, from Proceedings of the National Academy of science: http://www.pnas.org/content/early/2012/07/03/1121181109.abstract

Webb, A. (1878). *Sir William Petty.* Retrieved December 31st, 2013, from Library Ireland - A Compendium of Irish Biography: http://www.libraryireland.com/biography/SirWilliamPetty.php

Weber, A. (2013). *Enlivenment. Towards a fundamental shift in the concepts of nature, culture and politics.* Berlin: Heinrich Boell Foundation.

Weber, A. (2012). The Economy of Wastefulness. In D. a. Bollier, *The Wealth of the Commons. A World Beyond Market and State* (p. 7). Amherst, Mass.: Levellers Press.

Weiss, D. H. (2011, August 8th). *H-Judaic Discussion Log Online.* Retrieved December 27th, 2013, from Humanities and Social Sciences Net Online: http://h-net.msu.edu/cgi-bin/logbrowse.pl?trx=vx&list=H-Judaic&month=1108&msg=RizwZWCgeA8woVU9mNOEYQ

What is the Finance Innovation Lab. (2012). Retrieved from The Finance Innovation Lab: http://thefinancelab.org/about

What is Wrong With Economics. (2009, October). Retrieved December 31st, 2013, from OoCities.org: http://www.oocities.org/capitolhill/1931/secC1.html

Wigley, T. M. (2011). Coal to gas: the influence of methane leakage. *Climate Change* , 608-611.

Wikipedia. (2013). *Clean Development Mechanism.* Retrieved January 3rd, 2014, from Wikipedia: https://en.wikipedia.org/wiki/Clean_Development_Mechanism#Industrial_gas_projects

Wikipedia. (2013, December). *Frederich List.* Retrieved December 29th, 2013, from Wikipedia - the Free Encyclopedia: http://en.wikipedia.org/wiki/Friedrich_List

Wikipedia. (n.d.). *Friederick List.* Retrieved December 29th, 2013, from Wikipedia: http://en.wikipedia.org/wiki/Friedrich_List#cite_note-10

Wikipedia. (2013, December). *Potemkin Village.* Retrieved December 29th, 2013, from Wikipedia: https://en.wikipedia.org/wiki/Potemkin_village

Wilhelm(Tr), R., & Baynes (Tr), C. F. (1984). *I Ching.* London: Penguin Arkana.

Wilkinson, R., & Pickett, K. (2010). *The Spirit Level.* London: Penguin.

Williams, J., Stubbs, T., & Milligan, A. (2012). *An analysis of coal seam gas production and natural resource management in Australia a report prepared by John Williams Scientific Services Pty Ltd.* Canberra: Australian Council of Environmental Deans and Directors.

Wily, L. A. (2011). The Law is to blame. Taking a Hard Look at the Vulnerable Status of Customary Land Rights in Africa. *Development and Change Vol 42 (3).*

Wily, L. A. (2011). *The Tragedy of Public Lands. The Fate of the Commons under global commercial pressure.* International Land Coalition.

Witte, M. H., Crown, P., Bernas, M., & Witte, C. L. (2008). The Curriculum on Medical and other Ignorance. In B. Vitek(ed), & W. Jackson(ed), *The Virtues of Ignorance* (pp. 251-272). Lexington: University of Kentucky Press.

Wittfogel, K. A. (1957). *Oriental Despotism. A Comparative Study of Total Power.* New Haven: Yale University Press.

Wkipedia. (2013, August). *Kaldor-Hicks Efficiency.* Retrieved December 29th, 2013, from Wkipedia: https://en.wikipedia.org/wiki/Kaldor%E2%80%93Hicks_efficiency

WorkingGroup1. (2013). *IPCC Process.* Retrieved January 3rd, 2014, from Inter-governmental Panel on Climate Change: http://www.climatechange2013.org/ipcc-process/

Xenophon, & Dakyns(Tr), H. H. (2013, January). *The Economist.* Retrieved December 31st, 2013, from Project Gutenberg: http://www.gutenberg.org/files/1173/1173-h/1173-h.htm

Yan, K. (2012, February 2nd). *The Global CDM Hydro Hall of Shame.* Retrieved January 3rd, 2014, from International Rivers: http://www.internationalrivers.org/blogs/246/the-global-cdm-hydro-hall-of-shame

Young, R., Cowe, A., Nunan, C., Harvey, J., & Mason, L. (1999, October). *The Use and Misuse of Antibiotics in UK Agriculture.* Retrieved December 31st, 2013, from Soil Association: http://www.soilassociation.org/LinkClick.aspx?fileticket=RcHBJXC1Mxc%3d&tabid=1715

Index